WE CAN DO IT

A Community Takes on the Challenge of School Desegregation

MICHAEL T. GENGLER

ROSETTABOOKS NEW YORK

Thank you for purchasing this book. The author will donate the bulk of his profits to The Education Foundation of Alachua County, Inc.

We Can Do It:
A Community Takes on the Challenge of School Desegregation

For information, please contact RosettaBooks at production@rosettabooks.com, or by mail at 125 Park Ave., 25th Floor, New York, NY 10017.

First edition published 2018 by RosettaBooks

Cover Image Credits: Clockwise from top left: (1) W.E. Burghardt Du Bois, 4 J. Negro Education 328 (1935), courtesy of Journal of Negro Education; (2) Sermon, May 19, 1963, The Rev. Earle Page, courtesy of Ann Page; (3) Alexander v. Holmes Cty. Bd. of Education, 396 U.S. 1218, 1222 (1969); (4) Respondent's Petition for Rehearing with Motion to Expedite Hearing, Wright v. Bd. of Pub. Instruction, No. 972 (U.S. Jan. 22, 1970); (5), (6), (7) and (8), Gainesville Sun; (9) Daniel J. Meador, "The Constitution and Assignment of Pupils to Public Schools," 45 Va. L. Rev. 517, 525 (1959), courtesy of Virginia Law Review.

Appendix Image Credits: William S. Talbot Jr., Bernice Dukes, Charles Chestnut III, Ann Page, Bruce Tomlinson, Jessie Heard, Richard Niblack, John King, John Neller, Dan Boyd, Cora Roberson, Peggy Finley. Image of Rev. Thomas A. Wright courtesy of Mount Carmel Baptist Church, Gainesville, FL. Image of William Enneking courtesy of University of Florida. Image of Clif Cormier courtesy of Leslie Samler. Lincoln High School protest image is from the Gainesville Sun. Images of Brenda Wims, GHS Cheerleaders, and Chordettes are courtesy of the Matheson History Museum.

Library of Congress Control Number: 2017962735
ISBN-13 (print): 978-1-9481-2214-6
ISBN-13 (epub): 978-1-9481-2217-7

www.RosettaBooks.com
Jacket and interior design by Christian Fuenfhausen
and Girl Friday Productions
Printed in the United States of America

To the people of Alachua County

CONTENTS

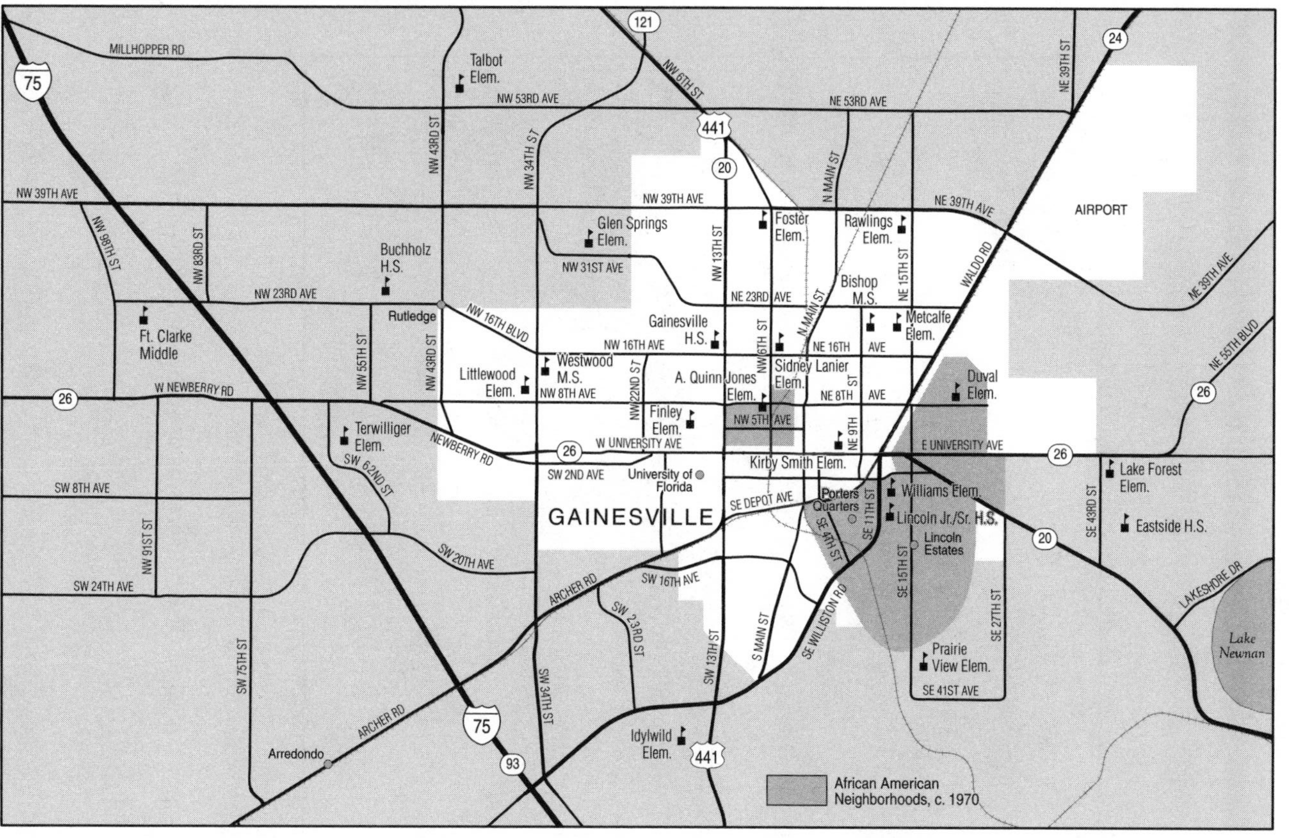

Gainesville, Florida with School Sites, 1965–1973

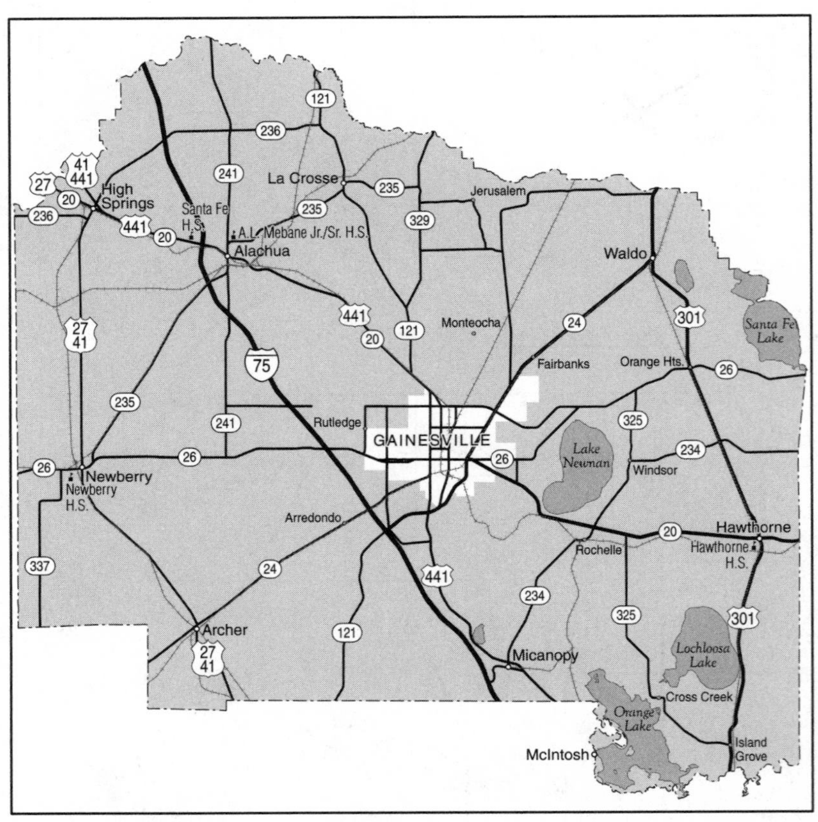

Alachua County, Florida with School Sites, 1965–1973

PREFACE

The People

We leave pieces of our hearts in many places. This is a story about Alachua County, Florida, where I grew up more than fifty years ago.

I graduated from Gainesville High School in 1962. Two years later, black plaintiffs represented by the NAACP Legal Defense and Educational Fund Inc. sued to desegregate the Alachua County schools. In response, well-intentioned white and black leaders in Alachua County together would end legal segregation, but not without unintended consequences.

Desegregation is thought of as something that was done *to* the South, as a second Reconstruction. It was that, but the history of the African American plaintiffs and their lawyers, the court decisions, federal enforcement efforts, and at times violent resistance leaves out what is arguably the most important part of the story. A law professor has commented, "The civil rights warriors knew how to knock doors down, but they had no way of preparing the beneficiaries for what awaited them on the other side."[1] Here we tell the story of the way school administrators, teachers, parents, and students of both races worked together to create desegregated public schools.

People trying to make desegregation work on the ground were guided, or not, by the courts. For necessary context, here we also tell the story of court rulings *after Brown v. Board of Education of Topeka*. Contrary to many narratives, in 1954, when *Brown* was decided, school administrators and black teachers and students had reason to believe that the South's dual system of white and black schools would remain in place. Early interpretations of *Brown* allowed the black schools to continue as long as any student could choose to go to a white school. Later, in 1968 and 1969, the NAACP Legal Defense and Educational Fund persuaded the Supreme Court that black students would not receive equal educational opportunity unless the

South's identifiable separate white and black schools were combined into single, unitary school systems. There would be neither white schools nor black schools, just schools.[2] In Alachua County, the school board decided in 1968 to replace historically black Lincoln Junior/Senior High School with a new campus intended to serve an integrated student body. That step, and its aftermath, exposed a division in the county's black community between those who wanted the black schools to be continued and made equal to the white schools and those who accepted the consequences of the unitary system.

Many African Americans in Alachua County remain unreconciled to the loss of the black schools. Continuing to test today's unitary school system against the former black schools, they inform the debate over the future direction for public schools. They also compel us to ask the question, "Did desegregation help or hurt the black community?" Some thoughtful responses are included in the afterword.

In Alachua County, at the time of desegregation, the public schools held marquee status. Problems with the public schools were high-stakes issues. The county's economic interests, including the University of Florida, its medical school, and large and small businesses, needed excellent public schools to recruit faculty members and employees. To those interests, desegregation was one more threat to the county's public schools that would have to be overcome. The connection between those interests and the schools was reinforced by the top-level community leaders who ran for, and were elected to, the school board. In the 1960s, until outbreaks of violence in 1970, there was no thought given to private schools or any other alternative for educating the county's children. Flight to another school district was not an option; the surrounding counties were mostly rural and poor. Alachua County therefore presents a best-case scenario for studying desegregation: there would not be opposition to deflect school leaders from their chosen course of compliance with the law.

Alachua County is also a good place for studying the course of school desegregation because of the daily coverage by the *Gainesville Sun* newspaper and its education editor at the time, the late Clif Cormier. The *Sun* also published diverse opinions of citizens of both races in the *Sun*'s Letters to the Editor. It is hard to imagine any other county with a more complete contemporaneous record of these events.

The most important lesson to be learned from Alachua County's history in these times of polarization is that members of both races came together to resolve issue after issue while desegregating their schools. The end of de jure school segregation was the most significant social change in the South since Reconstruction. Under the pressure imposed by the courts, the actors came to recognize needs and priorities not just of their own races but of Alachua County. They had to show both determination and compromise. Alachua County was spared not only white resistance but also the seemingly endless and divisive litigation by black plaintiffs that continued into the 1980s in places such as Dallas, Mobile, and Nashville, which thwarted school administrators' efforts to move to some version of unitary school systems. However imperfect the result, and whatever hard feelings remained, Alachua County's schools continued to serve the overwhelming majority of the county's white and black students. That experience is consistent with much of the South, which for decades after school desegregation was the most integrated region of the United States.[3]

Second, pedagogically, desegregation eventually required more than just putting white and black students together in the same schools. The courts and educators initially assumed the opposite. During the *Brown* arguments, responding to questions from Supreme Court Justice Felix Frankfurter about the supposed complexity of desegregation, Thurgood Marshall replied,

> But that is why, it seems to me, that the real basic issue as I said in the beginning, is what we want from this Court is the striking down of race.
>
> Now, whatever other plan they want to work out, the question is made about the educational level of children. That has been an educational detail since we have had public schools.
>
> They give tests to grade children so what do we think is the solution? Simple. Put the dumb colored children in with the dumb white children, and put the smart colored children with the smart white children – that is no problem.[4]

Florida's white and black schools presented the same basic courses and imposed the same graduation requirements. During the years of freedom-of-choice desegregation, 1965 through 1969, black students who elected to enter the white schools met the same expectations as whites. But when the Supreme Court ordered Alachua County to fully desegregate student bodies and faculties in February 1970, the schools had to make major changes in curriculum, extracurricular activities, music programs, and so on. The secondary schools also had to respond to episodic but serious outbreaks of on-campus violence.

Third, even as desegregation gained momentum, the historically segregated Southern universities and colleges of education failed to identify and address the changes that would have to be made if public schools were to survive for the benefit of both races (although individual professors would provide whatever help they could to their former students). As one teacher has put it, there was no manual. The people would have to work the problems out on their own, school by school, classroom by classroom, day by day. When problems arose, either from whites or blacks, the administrators, teachers, parents, and students, unprepared, would have to step up and show as much generosity of spirit and courage as was needed to overcome them. On the front lines of these changes were the teachers. Overarching all the other lessons to be learned from this story, in my opinion, is the thinness of their resources and the strength of their dedication to public education.

Fourth, it was Southerners, white and black, who had to dismantle the South's segregated schools and rebuild the systems to serve both races together. It may seem counterintuitive that the presumed beneficiaries and victims of segregation would succeed at that task. But aspects of the Southern race situation favored their efforts.

Most importantly, whites and blacks in the South were no strangers to one another. The reader will find here story after story of black and white familiarity across the racial divide, before desegregation.

During segregation, white and black Southerners had evolved separate cultures, but there were areas of overlap. In most situations, members of both races had a simple desire to be fair and respectful to others. Perhaps as a legacy of the South's hard times, Southerners of both races placed a high value on education and encouraged everyone to do so.

Many Southern whites and blacks are persons of faith. During desegregation, encouraged by many (but not all) of their clergy, they drew on that faith and its teachings. They strove to do unto others as they would want others to do unto them. They believed that they were their brothers' keepers. The Reverend Dr. Martin Luther King Jr.'s last speech, in Memphis just before his assassination, speaks of the Good Samaritan. Whether or not individuals were aware of this speech, they would have heard the story in Sunday school and from the pulpit. In those difficult times, faith helped to unite, not divide.

Fifth, during the desegregation years, top-level white community leaders filled positions on the school board. The statewide teacher strike in early 1968 led to the organization of Citizens for Public Schools by University of Florida faculty and local business leaders to examine the long-term needs of Alachua County public schools. That group and the chamber of commerce led the effort to pass a large school bond issue in 1968. Academic and business leaders were in place as public school advocates when desegregation and busing threatened those schools in 1970. Their advocacy reflected the broad consensus at that time of support for the public schools. The career educators who led the school system also sought and received access to white leadership groups and local government. The school board and the superintendent had both the courage and connections to push Gainesville's government and business interests on segregated housing and employment policies. Their efforts contributed to Gainesville's enactment of a fair housing ordinance in 1972 and modernization of building codes.

Sixth, the relative success of freedom-of-choice desegregation in Gainesville disrupted its formerly close-knit African American community. Despite *Brown*, Southern school districts legally continued under court decisions and Department of Health, Education, and Welfare rules to operate their separate black schools during the freedom-of-choice years. By September 1969, 39 percent of the county's black students were attending formerly white schools. In Gainesville, about one-third of African American students in grades 10–12 attended the previously white Gainesville High School (for most, that choice was made by their parents). The remaining two-thirds remained at Lincoln High School. The black students attending GHS were often middle class, children of college-educated parents. The students who remained at Lincoln were often poor and children of parents who had not attended college. Many Lincoln students resented those who had abandoned the black school. Lincoln's students emptied its classrooms in November 1969 for an unsuccessful eleven-day strike to oppose its closing and their imminent assignment to white schools. Many of those students arrived in their new schools in February 1970 unwilling (unlike the freedom-of-choice blacks) to submit to the white schools' academic and disciplinary rules.

On the one hand, contemporaneous data shows just how far behind segregation had left the county's black high school students. Senior placement test scores were disaggregated by race at Gainesville High for the 1970–71 school year. The minimum score for admission to a four-year state university was 300. In that year, the proportions of Gainesville High seniors who scored 300 or higher on the test were 54 percent of whites, 17 percent of blacks who had entered GHS from white schools under freedom of choice, and only 3 percent of blacks who entered GHS from Lincoln in 1970, when Lincoln closed. A similar disparity existed among students who scored between 0 and 199: 23 percent of the white seniors, 61 percent of black students who came to GHS from white schools under freedom of choice, and 88 percent of the Lincoln transfer students. Desegregated education started from this beginning point.

On the other hand, Lincoln High School was a repository of community spirit, history, and culture. Lincoln High had prominent alumni. As we will see in the afterword, some African Americans believe that even in its last years, Lincoln nurtured a higher proportion of black achievers than did the white schools.

Ironically, the NAACP Legal Defense and Educational Fund sought, and the Supreme Court ordered, midyear elimination of the South's separate black schools in 1970 because, in Justice Black's words, the court found that "Negro students in these school districts are being denied equal protection of the laws, and in my view they are entitled to have their constitutional rights vindicated now without postponement for any reason."[5] Vindication for the Lincoln class of 1970 would be diplomas from Gainesville High School, not Lincoln. But at the 1970 commencement, the graduating Lincoln transfer students by their choice proudly displayed red and white tassels on their caps and received Lincoln High School diplomas.

Seventh, most relevant to today's public schools, evolved techniques of black teachers to engage their students were mostly lost. When unitary systems were decreed, the usual method of compliance was moving blacks out of supposedly inferior black schools into white schools. In Florida, virtually every black high school was closed or repurposed. The white school was the model for desegregated public education. If the courts and the Department of Health, Education, and Welfare foresaw the consequences to black communities of the loss of their schools, they did little to deal with those consequences. Even when black school plants were preserved, black students and teachers in Florida became minorities (at least initially) in the formerly black schools. Simultaneously, the number of African Americans entering the teaching profession declined precipitously.

Alachua County

Alachua County is located in the northern part of the Florida peninsula, just a bit closer to the Gulf of Mexico than it is to the Atlantic coast. As the crow flies, it's about fifty miles from the Georgia state line. Prior to the Civil War, the county and the surrounding area produced long-staple Sea Island cotton, as well as cattle and timber products. In the early twentieth century, the University of Florida moved to Gainesville, the county seat. By the 1960s, tobacco, watermelon, and feed crops such as corn and hay had replaced cotton in the local agriculture. Cattle and timber products continued to be prominent. The University of Florida had grown to about fourteen thousand students. The University president, J. Wayne Reitz, earned $17,000, and the Gators' football coach, Ray Graves, earned $17,500. The new UF College of Medicine and J. Hillis Miller Health Center had just opened. The University admitted only white students. The population of Gainesville was around fifty thousand.

The University's presence made Alachua County and Gainesville different from other Southern communities of a similar size. University administrators and faculty would play a role in local desegregation. Their children attended the public schools. But despite the University's presence, Alachua County and Gainesville were more similar to the rest of the South than they were different. Through Alachua County's experience we can observe much about the Southern response to desegregation.

Among the questions we will answer are: Why were Florida schools segregated? Why were those schools desegregated? That answer is not as obvious as the reader might assume. How did the school leaders get community buy-in to desegregation? Why was Lincoln High School closed? Why did the courts uphold that closing? Why were Alachua County's remaining black schools desegregated in the middle of a school year? What pedagogic innovations helped the schools to get through desegregation? How did the students support change (or not)? How were black administrators and faculty brought into the desegregated schools? What leadership qualities succeeded in desegregated schools? (In the 1969–70 and 1970–71 school years, Gainesville High lost two much-loved white principals; a thirty-year-old Dan Boyd would take over in 1971 and lead GHS for the next twenty-five years.) In the afterword, as noted, surviving black teachers and administrators will discuss whether they believe desegregation helped or hurt their community.

The End of the Innocence

For anyone not there, the innocence and grace of Gainesville, Florida, around 1960 is beyond imagining. It was not that anyone reveled in segregation. The white community served by Gainesville High School was economically and socially diverse and extended into the county's rural areas, too. But school proceeded down a well-worn path. Student aptitude, or lack thereof, presented teachers with familiar patterns that could be managed. Teen social life and sports teams flourished. Behind the screen of segregation, prejudices did not show.

In other neighborhoods, along Fifth Avenue, in Porters Quarters, in Lincoln Estates, there was also innocence and grace but of a different flavor. Black teachers earned the respect and love of their students not just by meeting their educational needs but also by attending to their students' special personal circumstances. The black churches gave sustenance to the spirit and as much help as they could to the poor. The Red Terriers of Lincoln High School, led on to glory by their incomparable marching band, played football under the Saturday night lights at Citizens Field, the same field used by the all-white Purple Hurricanes of Gainesville High School. Lincoln High's annual commencement was a celebration of community pride. "Lift Every Voice and Sing" rang out, in addition to the school's alma mater. The Dignitettes sponsored a debutante ball for young black women. Many small black-owned businesses enjoyed the patronage of the black community. Segregation united the black community; desegregation would begin to divide it.

In the same schools for the first time in the county's history, both races had to learn hard lessons in reality.

The county at first struggled to achieve county-wide racial balance. By 2003, both blacks and whites had enough of busing (which mostly took black students to white schools), and the Alachua County system returned to zoned neighborhood schools. Notwithstanding this change, a significant majority of the county's black students now attend schools that approximately reflect the school system's racial makeup. Magnet programs help bring white students into some racially isolated east-side schools, although not all magnets are themselves reflective of the system's racial balance.

The social science underlying *Brown* implied that racial balancing would lead to equal educational opportunity. But long after de jure segregation was eliminated, and despite years of experience under No Child Left Behind and other standards-based reforms, a diminished but persistent learning gap remains between black and white students. A Supreme Court plurality would declare in 2007 that even when de facto segregation exists, as a general rule it is unconstitutionally discriminatory to assign students to K–12 schools on the basis of race.[6]

In one of the many ironies of this story, Alachua County's schools (like those in many other districts across the country) must once again take on the challenge of providing equal educational opportunities to students in racially isolated environments. The commitment of past black and white educators to equal educational opportunities should, I hope, inspire the county's (and the nation's) response. The generation that ended de jure segregation still has lessons to teach us, if we take time to learn from them.

CHAPTER 1
TINY TALBOT, JOHN DUKES

William S. Talbot

William S. Talbot (more familiarly known by his nickname, "Tiny"[1]) was Alachua County's superintendent of public instruction from 1965 until 1972. On his watch occurred a statewide teacher strike and local enrollment growth that could be met only with a $12.8 million bond issue for new schools. Talbot also had to do the superintendent's regular job of running a school system of over twenty thousand students and one thousand teachers.

But Talbot's overriding challenge and achievement was first token and later complete desegregation of Alachua County's public schools. Talbot had to bring off desegregation before a tough crowd made up of traditional Southern whites, a proud but fracturing African American community, and the academic establishment of the University of Florida.

No son of privilege, Talbot understood education from the inside out, as a practitioner if not as an academic. He also understood that public education has to benefit all children, not just an academic elite.

Like many Southern leaders of the period, Tiny kept his personal views on integration to himself. Tiny's son William S. Talbot Jr., known as Butch (who had a career as an oral surgeon), recalls that growing up, the issue was simply not discussed at home. Avoidance of the topic was typical among white families at the time. In an interview with the *Gainesville Sun* in 1972, after he had left the superintendent position, Tiny said that he entered that office as a segregationist. By the end of his term, he was speaking to downtown clubs to encourage dispersal of public housing in Gainesville as a way to achieve integration of the schools without busing.[2]

Clif Cormier, who was education editor for the *Gainesville Sun* during Tiny's years as superintendent, recalls that he never heard Tiny say one bad word about the racial situation despite intense conflicts with black leaders. Talbot loved to fish on the lakes near Gainesville. One of his favorite fishing buddies was Charlie Roberson, the husband of the black teacher and administrator Cora Roberson. The families lived close to one another, although on opposite sides of the invisible racial boundaries of Gainesville's residential areas. Fishing was one of the few recreational activities that could be enjoyed together by members of both races in the 1960s South.

Talbot continued to serve in the Alachua County school system after leaving the superintendency in 1972. He began suffering from Alzheimer's disease even before he retired in 1980, and he died of that disease in 1986 at age sixty-seven. No biographical or autobiographical sources on Talbot exist, but a sense of his early years can be gained from his family, friends, public records, and a few other sources.

John Dukes Jr.

John Dukes Jr., then head of the math department at historically black Lincoln High School, was chosen by Tiny Talbot in July 1966 to take over as principal of Lincoln Junior/Senior High School. Dukes and Talbot both worked through the desegregation years in Alachua County. In November 1969, they would find themselves together, using a police car bullhorn to attempt to quiet most of the student body of Lincoln and many parents, who were protesting the closing of the school as the county moved to a unitary school system.

Dukes became the first principal of the new, integrated Eastside Junior/Senior High School, which opened initially on another school's campus in February 1970, but then on its own brand-new campus in September 1970. Dukes moved to the county school staff as deputy superintendent of student services in December 1975. In that position he frequently worked with black students and their parents throughout the system on problem situations. He retired from that position in 1984, after forty years in the Alachua County schools. We are fortunate to have Dukes's story in his own words, in addition to remembrances of him by others.[3]

Beginnings
Tiny Talbot

Talbot's origins were typical of many Floridians of his generation. A brief look at those origins shows how one Southern school superintendent came of age and found his way into education.

On both his father's and mother's sides, Tiny came from Southern families traceable back to colonial times.[4] His mother's family came to west Florida from Georgia, and his father's came from Alabama. Members of both families served honorably in the Confederate army during the Civil War. Some died in battle. Tiny was related through his grandmother, Mary Angers Yon, to Everett Yon, an outstanding University of Florida athlete, decorated veteran of World War I, and athletic director at the University. US Senator Charles O. Andrews, who represented Florida from 1936 to 1946, was Tiny's uncle.

Tiny was born June 26, 1918, in Altha, Calhoun County, Florida. His father, William Shafto Talbot, was born in Andalusia, Alabama, in 1892. He married Tiny's mom, Flossie Moore Talbot, on May 15, 1915. Flossie was then nineteen.

Tiny's father, known as Will, was a businessman in Ponce de Leon, Holmes County, Florida. According to the family, Will owned a grocery and general store in Ponce de Leon. A local history has Will serving as vice president of the Ponce de Leon Chamber of Commerce in 1922. Will purchased a logging business in Ponce de Leon for $6,000 in 1925. The business consisted of a warehouse and repair shop and five one-ton trucks and trailers. The logs were made into crossties for the railroads.

Flossie, Tiny's mom, was born and raised on a farm in Walton County, Florida, not far from Ponce de Leon. At the time of Will Talbot's death, the family besides Tiny included an older sister, Edna, and a younger brother, Jim.

Flossie's family owned 440 acres of farmland and slash pine in the area. This holding was started when Flossie's father, Augustus "Gus" Moore purchased 160 acres in 1890. An unknown family member wrote a short description of Flossie's early life. According to this description, the Moore family lived in a small log cabin. There were no fence laws. Gus raised cows on open range. In the winter, when grass was scarce, he would drive the cows to the farm and feed them enough hay to keep them alive through the winter. On cold nights he would often build a fire around a pine stump so the cows could keep warm. Gus also raised produce that he sold in nearby towns. He rented the slash pine to turpentine producers.

Education was important to the Moores. Gus built a one-room school on his property that was known as Moore's School. As Flossie and her sisters grew up, because the school in nearby Westville (Holmes County) was considered better than the school in Ponce de Leon, Gus rented a house for the girls in Westville so they could attend school there. During the school year, Gus would take the girls to Westville on Sunday night by mule and wagon and pick them up on Friday afternoon. Westville was about seven miles from the family farm. The family owned a piano. Gus's wife, Joanna, hired an itinerant musician to teach Flossie and the other girls to play.

School records in Holmes County show that as a girl of eighteen, Flossie began teaching school in that county and continued for two years, 1914 and 1915. She married Will Talbot after the 1915 school year.

Gus died in 1924. Before his death, he would often come to Ponce de Leon to visit Flossie and to bring her produce. His wife, Joanna, died in 1959.

Tiny's father died in 1926 at age thirty-four, when Tiny was eight. Will's obituary in the Holmes County *Advertiser* relates that he was injured when the horse he was riding stopped suddenly, throwing him against his saddle horn. Will Talbot died a few days later at a hospital in Dothan, Alabama. According to the obituary, Will was "well and favorably known throughout this section."

After Will Talbot's death, Flossie married a local physician, Marion W. Eldridge, MD. Family members describe it as a marriage of necessity if not love. The couple cared for Flossie's three children and Dr. Eldridge's seven children by his first marriage. They lived in Ponce de Leon, where Dr. Eldridge was then practicing. Flossie's second marriage ended in 1932.

A stepbrother from that marriage, one of Dr. Eldridge's sons, Miles Eldridge of Blountstown, recalls that Tiny as a boy was smart and into everything, but that Tiny had no interest in helping with farm chores. He took a dislike to Dr. Eldridge and would be defiant toward him.

After Flossie's divorce from Dr. Eldridge, she continued to live in Ponce de Leon in the home that Will Talbot had built for the family. Her home there, like most others at that time, initially lacked running water and indoor plumbing. Flossie had to support herself and her children. She worked as a switchboard operator for Southeast Telephone Company until her retirement.

Tiny Talbot attended Ponce de Leon High School from 1931 until the last term of his senior year in 1935. He transferred to Jackson County High School in Marianna for his last term in 1935, graduating in that year.

Despite the hard times, Tiny found his way into normal high school activities. He played on the boys' basketball team (the school did not have a football team). The Holmes County *Advertiser* Tatler column frequently mentions Tiny as an honor roll student and a participant in plays, Glee

Club, and cheerleading. In one play, sponsored by the athletic association, Tiny played the title role in *He Was a Gay Señorita*. He had learned piano at his mother's insistence and taught himself guitar. He later said that with some other classmates, he was always making up songs, especially for hayrides. The Tatler duly reported Tiny's romance with Lynette Mayo (honored as most valuable player on the girls' basketball team).

John Dukes Jr.

John Dukes Jr. was born December 18, 1926, in Branford, Suwannee County, Florida. He began life with even fewer advantages than Tiny Talbot.

> Dukes says his motivation came from his father, but, he said, he was "almost ashamed to say why."
>
> "It was the things my father had to do and he was paid poorly or not at all for them. It was the way he looked when he came home, too, that made me want to do something better," Dukes said.[5]

According to Dukes, his father had many skills with his hands, including automobile mechanics and construction work, but he could barely read his name. Dukes's father traveled while working the livestock market, and as a boy Dukes would sometimes travel with him. His mother had an eighth-grade education. "They were just loving parents with no formal education to speak of, but they had common sense, and we were a happy family." Dukes had three sisters and a brother.

For seven of his eight years in school at Branford, Dukes earned money by sweeping out the local bank before it opened in the morning. Dukes also had a paper route. He finished eighth grade in Branford.

> The school I attended had two people in my class. . . . The school I attended there had two rooms. In one room you had all the kids through fourth grade, and in another room you had all the kids from fifth through eighth. Having only two people in my class, when we graduated from the eighth grade gives you an indication that we were underenrolled. Even with the total number of kids, it was a very small school. This was an entirely black school at that particular time and we had many chores to perform. We were not too far from the Suwannee River and around the Suwannee River there are a lot of swamps. We have quite a bit of dead wood in that area. One of our main tasks, especially during the winter,

was to go down in that area, pick up that dead wood, cut up those dead trees, and bring them back so we could have heat in those classrooms.

***

The drop-out rate was very high. In most rural areas I think you will find the interest or the desire to go to college and to high school is usually very low. I have had persons that told me as a little boy, that I would never make it, that I would never do anything, that I would be just like the rest of them. In that day it meant staying around Branford, being in and out of the so called juke joints. There was a place there called the Big House. The Big House was really the place where people gathered on the weekends and they had all kinds of activities that were not the best for kids. There were a lot of fights and a lot of murders that took place there.

***

I can recall my very first principal. His name was W.S. Lawes. He was a very intelligent person and very concerned about kids, but he believed in beating things into you. Now when I say beating, I do not speak literally. He would tell you that he would beat the blood out of you, if it took that to get you to do what you needed to do. The one thing that I remember about Mr. Lawes, not only would he beat you, you notice I did not use the word whip, he would beat you to get you to do what you were supposed to do. But he would also be at your parents house, in most instances by the time you got home in the afternoon, telling them what you had done. There were no telephones to call with these kinds of messages, but he would go in person and tell them. "Yes, I beat Johnny today, because he did not do such and such a thing."

***

In the small place where I was born, once you completed the eighth grade, your education was over. There was no place for you to go unless you decided to leave and go somewhere else.[6] My dad came home one Thursday, and I will never forget, he said, "Pack up everything you got, your rags." That is just about what they were – "You are going to Gainesville, and

> you are going to high school." I came to Gainesville in 1941. He took me to a lady's house by the name of Miss Catherine Cobbs, a lady whom I had never met, did not know prior to my coming to Gainesville. Somehow he had made arrangements, because she took me right in and started treating me as if I were her own. Believe it or not, I did not even have money enough to pay Miss Cobbs, for the board. I think my dad paid for two or three weeks in advance, and then it was not long before I started washing dishes at a place here called Sandwich Park. Soon I became a short order cook in the same establishment and was able to meet my obligations while I was going to school. My dad brought me over, got me started, and from then on, I took care of my own financial responsibilities.

Sandwich Park was a hangout for University of Florida students. Dukes would report for work at 4:00 p.m. and would not get off until 1:20 a.m.

At Lincoln High, Dukes played tackle for the football Terriers, under Coach T. B. McPherson.

> I was a tackle, and I remember when we played Alachua very vividly. T.B. said, "Dukes, you are country, you are cornfed, you are strong and you are fast. I do not want you to do but one thing. I want you to stay on number eleven. Do you know who number eleven is?" I said, "No." He said, "Number eleven is the quarterback. Even if he gets the ball, I want you to make him feel that he does not want it any more." So that night I just looked for number eleven, nobody else but number eleven. And I want you to know, we won that game. Going away and after the game he said, "Dukes, I told you to stay on number eleven. There were times when it looked like he was running away from the ball, rather than trying to get it." I am not bragging, but I had the reputation of being the strongest guy on the team.

McPherson was Dukes's coach, guidance teacher, and history teacher.

> The one thing T.B. did, among many of course, was to have us all believe that we were somebody important. Even as early as the 1950s, when it was most difficult to get a kid to feel that he was important, T.B. was doing that. I had another teacher by the name of Miss Bessie Louise White. She was the wife of Reverend D.E. White, who was the mortician

> in this area for many years. Mrs. White called all of us Mr. and Miss in spite of our youth. Somehow, I feel this made us believe that we had to measure up to something. Miss White gave us many lectures, which I adopted as part of my technique during my teaching career, because there are times when the kids can learn more if you just put that book aside and talk about some of the things they want to talk about. I really attribute the success of my teaching to that particular technique. I went to Daphne Duval Williams for math, and she inspired me to become a mathematician because I always marveled at the various things that were going on in math. . . . A. Quinn Jones, Sr., the principal, took a personal interest in me. I do not know why, but he did. . . . He made such an impression on me.

Leaving Home
Tiny Talbot

Tiny's journey to a college degree was roundabout. A paper in his own hand shows "June 7, 1935. Graduate Jackson County Hi. June 8, 1935. Leave Altha, Fla. for Andalusia [Alabama] & take up residence with J. V. Talbot, working for C. C. Talbot." Butch Talbot relates that C. C. Talbot, a relative, operated a restaurant near a factory in Andalusia.

Tiny left Andalusia to enroll at the University of Florida in Gainesville in August 1936. At the same time, he joined the Orange Grove String Band, a country band of some local renown that played at roadhouses and on WRUF, the University of Florida radio station. By June 1937, Tiny was also working in the University cafeteria, first as a busboy and later as a pancake cook. He met his future wife there, who was also working in the cafeteria. The lovely Reba Elizabeth Pickett came from a family no more prosperous than Tiny's, and a troubled home life. Reba was just shy of her sixteenth birthday when they married on June 1, 1938. She was an excellent cook of Southern favorites. Butch remembers longingly Christmas and Thanksgiving dinners at home. Reba's skills showed on her husband's waistline. Their marriage had its troubles, but it endured.

Along the way, Tiny campaigned for his uncle, US Senator Charles O. Andrews, in northwest Florida. Tiny attributed his interest and talent in politics to that early experience. Andrews, who was born in Ponce de Leon, began his career as a school teacher but later became a lawyer and worked his way up through various state political offices to his eventual election to the US Senate.

Tiny received a two-year associate degree from the University of Florida in 1938. Butch, their first child, was born in February 1940. Tiny managed to go to college more or less full-time only during the winter terms of 1937, 1938, 1941, and 1942. From start to finish Tiny took six years to earn his bachelor's degree from the University of Florida, graduating in May 1942. Tiny could best be described as a C student. He took a number of education courses, particularly in his last term. Given Tiny's need to support his family, demonstrating academic achievement could not be a priority.[7]

After graduation, Tiny worked as a bookkeeper for Langston and Hubbard Construction and then as a welder at St. Johns Shipyard. He entered the Army Air Corps in January 1944, serving as a gunnery instructor in bomber aircraft (although according to Butch he entered as an "entertainment specialist"). One reason Tiny became a gunnery instructor was because he could read. He was able to read the manual and pass on what he learned. He was discharged in March 1946 as a private first class.[8]

John Dukes Jr.

Dukes graduated from Lincoln in 1945 and was immediately drafted into the army. The army was still segregated when Dukes served. Everyone in his company was black, including the NCOs. But the officers were all white, except that in one instance the company was served by a black chaplain.

> I was discharged in 1949, and at that time integration was not even thought about in the military. I will not say it was not thought of, maybe I should retract that. It was thought about but not executed.

***

> It was understood. You see after having attended an all black school, after having lived in an all black society where black football teams played black football teams, all of our experiences were black. At this time very few people questioned it. I know once we said we would like to have played games of high school football under T.B. McPherson when we were so good, but I think we had ulterior motives. I think we wanted to vent the hostilities we had, because we always felt we were getting the leftovers, the hand-me-downs. There were many instances where we got equipment which was used and we

> got textbooks which were used and old. I think we wanted to vent our hostilities more so than to compete for the title so we could say we were the better team. I think this carried over, but I often think about that, and I find it rather amazing that most of us who lived in an era such as that can be as objective as some of us are, in a day like . . .
>
> ***
>
> During the military, I was one of thirteen persons of a total of around 450 men, who had a high school diploma. Thirteen out of 450 men in an outfit that had high school diplomas. So, I taught courses to those persons while in service. We taught those courses under what we called USAFI, United States Armed Forces Institute. We taught several persons how to read and how to do simple math as best we could with the limited knowledge we had. Some of those persons could not even read a newspaper, and even though we had not been taught any formal technique, we actually taught many of them how to utilize those particular things in the service.

In the army, Dukes initially served in a body-recovery unit (as did many black soldiers) in varied locations in the South Pacific, including Guam, Tinian, Saipan, Hawaii, Iwo Jima, and Hiroshima. But thanks to a chaplain, Dukes became a chaplain's assistant in that body-recovery unit and eventually a librarian and manager of an army movie theater. He also taught classes on Saturday mornings.

After his discharge from the army as a sergeant, Dukes initially had some difficulties adjusting to civilian life. He felt isolated, and at times thought about reenlisting. But despite being drafted, Dukes did not lose sight of his goal of going to college.

> . . . Having been exposed to Mrs. White, T.B. McPherson, A. Quinn Jones, Daphne Williams, and several others like that, I knew from the outset that I would not be satisfied until I got a college degree. There was another principal in Branford called Professor [Lawes]. You may know that during that day everybody was a professor. If you graduated from any school, did not even have a bachelor's degree, but if you started teaching, you were a professor. W.L. Lawes encouraged me, knew from the outset that I was going to try my best to do something else other than what several said we

were. . . . But those persons instilled within me, a desire to do something else other than hang around Branford and fight and throw bricks in barrooms.

***

[Being in the military] did not break my chain of thought of going to college at all because I did not have the finances. I saw the military as a means by which I could get through a college, a university, with some degree of ease, because I knew that the G.I. Bill was there to assist veterans through their training. Within one year of being drafted into the service, my dad died, and I had three sisters, Ella Mae, Edith and Juanita, and one brother, Richard, who is a policeman today in the city of Gainesville, who looked up to me as their father from then on. Staying in the service the additional two and a half years helped me to provide income for my mother and my kids.

Dukes enrolled at Florida A&M College in Tallahassee. To help support his siblings, he also worked as a cook at the Mayflower Hotel afternoons and evenings. He began a premed course with intentions of being a dentist but soon realized that with the additional burden of helping his family, he would not be able to afford the additional years of study. At that point he decided to be a math teacher.

Dukes also met and married his wife, Bernice, while at Florida A&M. Bernice's father taught painting and furniture finishing at Florida A&M, and her mother ran a neighborhood grocery store. John's fraternity had chosen Bernice as its queen, to ride on its float in the homecoming parade. Bernice initially had her doubts about John, but Bernice's parents liked him. John and Bernice married when she was nineteen. John: "Bernice was Miss Everything on campus. I am not bragging but she was a very pretty girl. She still is a very pretty girl. She would have been Miss FAMU, but I thought I would make her Mrs. Dukes first." They would have four children. Bernice eventually graduated from Florida A&M in 1957 and later received her master's degree from the University of Florida. She taught for many years in the Alachua County schools and was the first black teacher assigned to teach at Stephen Foster Elementary School.

John left Florida A&M with a master's degree in 1954 and returned that year to Lincoln High School to teach.

I had already accepted the position of dean of men at Arkansas A&M College. I was offered an assistant principal's job with no experience in Perry, Florida, I also had an opportunity to work in Suwannee County, in Live Oak. This was the county where I was born and twenty-five miles from where I attended school. Later Professor Jones asked me if I would come to Gainesville, and to me this was one of the greatest offers of all. I chose to come to Gainesville, and I have been here ever since.

Moving Up the Ranks
Tiny Talbot

The virtues of athletics, as well as their faults, have been broadcast throughout this land until in many places, people have acquired the idea that success in athletics depends entirely upon the number of games won by the squad. Failure is thought of in terms of games with scores unfavorable to the team.

As long as this condition prevails, and coaches are hired to produce winning teams alone, athletics will continue to be severely criticized and will not fulfill their two missions.

Educators have long recognized that a great deal of good may be accomplished by rightly directed play. A great deal is being done at present to make this phase of education worthy of its place in the school.

Athletics have a far bigger mission to perform than to bring in money or satiate those who wish for victory. Many times in our mad scramble for success we lose sight of the greatest objectives of athletics, which is character building. Where this great objective is tenaciously adhered to great things may be accomplished. Not only are the actual players gaining the higher values of character that athletics can give, but every loyal follower is a participant in a spiritual if not physical way.

Character traits may be desirable or undesirable, depending greatly on the influences that control the participation. Assuming that the influences are of the right kind, many desirable traits such as concentration, honesty, tenacity, generosity, loyalty, cooperation, obedience, manliness, sacrifice, humility, and self-expression may be brought out.

W.S. Talbot
Holmes County *Advertiser*
October 5, 1934, p. 4

As his first job upon his release from the military, Tiny was hired to supervise a Gainesville playground for the city recreation department in the summer of 1946. He was hired as a coach at Gainesville High School starting in the fall of 1946, a job he continued to hold through spring 1951. He worked for Bernays "Buster" Bishop, the head football coach, as an assistant football coach, but was the head coach for the other three boys' sports then offered. In the summers, Tiny continued to work for the city recreation department and coached the Gainesville American Legion baseball team.

The school system didn't have much money for sports. For baseball and basketball, Tiny drove the bus to away games, and Buster drove the bus to football games. The late Charles Denny III remembered that in 1949, the high school didn't have money to buy baseball uniforms, so the team wore American Legion uniforms. That team had been sponsored by the local tung oil processor and had "Tung Nuts" on the jerseys. In its hand-me-down uniforms, the GHS team was endlessly taunted by opponents.

As a coach, Tiny was a strict disciplinarian. Charles Denny recalled, "He would put your ass off the bus if you made trouble," but maybe Tiny bluffed a bit. Zero Mazo once succeeded in stopping Tiny from putting a player off the bus late one night in a desolate area in North Florida. Denny continued, "Once Neil Malphurs was arrested for shooting ducks at the Duck Pond. Tiny would not let him play."

O. W. Davis says that Tiny, as a coach, was an excellent organizer. He believed in repetition of basic skills. As catcher for the baseball team, O. W. says Tiny would make him throw to second base one hundred times in a drill. For basketball, he would have the players shoot foul shots and run plays over and over. Buster Bishop, who threw his foul shots underhanded, would occasionally challenge the basketball team to see who could make the most shots in a row. Buster usually won.

Tiny's 1934 article was unknown to his students as far as we know. But as a coach he walked the walk. Players remember that when coaching, Tiny never lost his composure. O. W. Davis recalls that Buster Bishop (who had something of a Napoleonic bearing) had a felt hat. "We were playing football at Ocala and it was raining. The end zone was under water. Buster wanted the game stopped but the referees would not stop the game. Buster took off his hat and threw it and kicked it. Buster was thrown out of the game and arrested, and Tiny had to take over as coach." There are no reports of tantrums involving Tiny. His only visible reaction to stress was chain-smoking. Concentrating on the game, Tiny would sometimes have two lit cigarettes, one in each hand. Butch Talbot recalls that Buster and his girlfriend used to come to Tiny's house to relax and play bridge with Tiny and Reba after football games, win or lose.

Writing as a senior at Ponce de Leon High School in 1934, Tiny defined character through the experience of the athlete. That model would carry him through the challenges of his superintendency. And he loved to appear on radio broadcasts of Gainesville High football games.

The career path from coach to principal in Southern school systems is well-known. Tiny's leadership qualities earned him appointment as assistant principal and dean of boys at Gainesville High School in September 1951. He was appointed principal at Sidney Lanier Elementary School in 1953, principal of Buchholz Junior High in 1955, and principal of Gainesville High in 1958. Tiny was loyal to his teachers. At commencement, he could recognize and call every student by name (although he kept the list in his suit pocket just in case). He later said that he learned students' names by attending English classes, because everybody had to take English.

Tiny continued his education as events permitted between 1946 and 1950, when he received his master of education degree. Despite his economic struggles during those years, he compiled a record of As and Bs in his graduate courses. He continued his graduate studies, completing eighteen more credits between 1951 and 1960, but did not complete his EdD degree.

For extra income, Tiny began working for Lester Hodge, whose family farmed in western Alachua County. Hodge, who later was a long-serving member of the Alachua County school board, hired Tiny to pack watermelons in rail cars for the Hodge farming operation. Tiny would work at that job in the spring and then work packing beans for shipment at McIntosh. He continued to work his side jobs loading watermelons and packing beans into the mid-1950s. Butch recalls that during the packing season, his dad would leave home at 6:00 a.m. and return at midnight.

Tiny and Reba had a second son, Randall, in 1950. Randall immediately charmed everyone, a trait perhaps inherited from his dad. Randall died in 1954 of a form of leukemia, now very treatable. Reba was devastated. Despite the family's need for an additional breadwinner, Reba did not go back to work until about 1958. She worked successfully as a teller at the First National Bank for several years.

There is little evidence of what motivated Tiny to be an educator. Butch notes that Tiny's mom started as a teacher, and may have encouraged him. Butch also tells the story of a mother who, driving by Tiny's house and seeing him working in the yard, stopped to thank him for straightening out her son. Tiny told Butch that such stories kept Tiny going when times got hard. A mentor was F. W. "Fritz" Buchholz, Florida's first Rhodes Scholar, who was an early football coach and long-serving principal at Gainesville High. Buchholz retired as principal in 1951.

Tiny, who loved to fish, would collect old fishing rods from friends. He would invite an underprivileged boy or two to go fishing with him on local lakes. Tiny was able to fish at lake cabins owned by Velma Bonacker, the sister of State Senator William Shands, and by Dorothy Phipps, a popular high school math teacher. After the fishing was over, the boys got to keep the fish and the rods and reels. Tiny later bought Mrs. Phipps's cabin on Long Pond, near Melrose.

By the early 1960s, Tiny had held high-visibility positions in the schools for over fifteen years. The children of many of his students were now moving through the school system. Store clerks, farmers, mechanics, businessmen, University professors, policemen, and local government officials—in short, all of white Gainesville—knew and loved Tiny.

John Dukes Jr.

John Dukes began teaching at Lincoln High in August 1954. Dukes states that the black schools were under a white supervisor named Edmunds, who because of his power over the black schools inspired fear among students and teachers. Dukes had an early encounter with Edmunds. After being warned that Edmunds was standing outside his classroom door, according to Dukes, "I said I did not have to put up with Mr. Edmunds. I guess I was a little ahead of my time in that respect because I was not afraid. I remember Mr. Edmunds finally saying he wanted to meet me. When he did, we sat with the principal and [Edmunds] said, 'This is the man. I heard him teach the other day, and I want him to head up the National Honor Society [for the black schools] in this county.'"

John Dukes became head of the math department at Lincoln High School. In Albert White's history of Lincoln High School, Dukes is mentioned frequently by his former students as a teacher who meant much to them, both in school and in later life. He also was recognized as a leader.

A. Quinn Jones was the main reason Dukes returned to Gainesville to teach, although Dukes loved Gainesville and most of his relatives were nearby. Dukes remained close to Jones, who died at 104 in 1997. Dukes on Jones in 1985:

> Professor Jones is an unusual type person. I have never met a man like him in my life. He had some habits which provided an opportunity for us to mimic and make fun of him. I was one of those persons who took advantage of those situations. I remember one day in a faculty meeting Prof had

> some difficulties getting teachers to keep the register. I had no problem with the register because I was a math teacher and it dealt with numbers that we had to keep up about the kids' attendance. Anyway, Prof had gone to the blackboard, and he had his crayons in his hand. He said we would have to do the registers right. He had a lisp, and he was saying that he was going to tally, and if the registers were not tallying, the teachers would have to keep them. The telephone rang, and the secretary came to get Prof out of the faculty meeting. Tom Collins will verify this because he was sitting right there when all of this happened. So I jumped up as soon as Prof left to go get his telephone call, and I went to the board and I said, "You all ain't doing nothing, you are going to work on the registers and they are going to tally. I mean, they are going to tally. They are going to tally. Do you hear what I say? They are going to tally." I am there saying all of this but before I finished Prof returned to the faculty meeting in this room and was standing in the door. Powers was making some kind of motion, and I thought he was telling me to keep going, but he was trying to warn me that Prof was behind me. Anyway I carried on about thirty seconds or so, and I turned around and saw Prof in the door. You know it was a long way from that blackboard to the place where I sat. Prof did not even sit. He did not even come in the room. He said, "Mr. Dukes," and I went to him and we walked down the hall. Prof would walk with you all the way down the halls of Lincoln and never say a word. He walked with me from the south end, almost sixty feet from that south door of Lincoln,[9] to within 15 feet of the north door of Lincoln, which was a distance I guess of about 150 feet. Then he looked at me and said, "Mr. Dukes." I was thinking that I was going to [be] fired. He said, "That blackboard that you asked me about. I got that blackboard for you." I said, "Thank you, Mr. Jones." We went back to the classroom and he has never said anything to me to this day about my mimicking him or making fun of him. I was a floating teacher. A floating teacher does not have a classroom. Therefore, I had asked him to give me a blackboard on the stage, because my classroom at that time was on the main part of the stage . . .[10]

Mildred Wanninger was an excellent, if formidable, math teacher at Gainesville High. This author's classmates recall an incident one day when, exasperated with a student in an accelerated math class, she hurled an eraser at him. She would not tolerate replies from students that did not include "Yes, ma'am." Dukes on Mrs. Wanninger:

> By this time the situation was beginning to loosen up a little bit, and Mildred wanted a group of the heads of the math departments. We developed a very close relationship, and right now Mildred and I are still very close even though she is retired. She was much older than I, but we developed a very close relationship. Mildred was a very efficient math teacher, and we worked very closely in reorganizing the math curriculum in the county. The year I was elected president of the group Mildred gave me strong support. You just could not ask for any more or any stronger support than I got from Mildred and others. I think this enhanced the relationship between blacks and whites. We no longer had a black math group and a white math group.

Dukes dates these events to the early 1960s.

Dukes was Tiny Talbot's choice to be principal of Lincoln High School in July 1966.[11] By then, Talbot had been superintendent of public instruction for a year and a half. Before making his choice, Talbot went to Lincoln High School to speak with teachers, parents, and students. Otha W. Nealy, the principal being replaced, was "a product of the old school 'do what the man said do,'" according to Lincoln's football coach, Jessie Heard. During a visit to Lincoln, Talbot spoke to Heard and the athletic director, T. B. McPherson. Talbot told them he was considering a prominent black principal from South Florida for Lincoln. Heard and McPherson told Talbot, "We got a man right here, Mr. Talbot. We said, well, because Dukes was qualified, we didn't need to go outside."[12] Another Lincoln teacher who recommended Dukes to Talbot was Mae Islar, who later became a principal of integrated high schools in Gainesville. And so Talbot interviewed Dukes and hired him.

According to Dukes, Talbot was the first superintendent to go to the Lincoln campus and to consult directly with members of the community. Talbot told Dukes that Dukes was the person they wanted to be principal. Another reason Talbot wanted Dukes to take the principalship was the way Dukes had stood up to a faction in the black community that had been critical of black teachers. Duke recalls what Talbot said to him, "'I want you to know that I admire what you did. That took guts, and that is what I think we need, somebody with guts, who will stand up. I want you really to consider it.' When I left after those two or three little conferences, I went back and told him that I would take the position. Tiny stood up and hugged me so hard it was not even funny. We became very close, as close as professional people, I think, could become after that."

John Dukes III, the principal's son, says,

> I know he had a moment of misgiving only out of respect for Mr. Nealy. But when it came to the job itself and being prepared to step into the job and do the job, he never had any doubt about that. He felt that that was where he belonged in terms of guiding a school along its path. So, as things move forward and I'm sure, again, I can't speak for the opposite side of this, but if I look at Tiny and some of the other administrators knowing that they are going to be faced with the choices of finding people to help implement on the opposite side of the line this thing which all of us are now going to have to find a way to endure if not embrace.

And so, although full integration of the Alachua County schools was still some years in the future, the schools had a white leader and a black leader who were working as a team. In the history of Alachua County, that was one first of many firsts that would follow.

CHAPTER 2
PROLOGUE: GAINESVILLE IN THE SIXTIES

But we must, as Christians, be first of all concerned with what happens here, where we have immediate responsibility. The place we live, this field we toil, is the place of our first responsibility as Southerners – whether we are Southerners by birth or by choice.

There is no doubt in my mind that desegregation will bring many difficulties and even disasters.

But I also see the injustice and the suffering of God's black children who are my brothers in Christ. I believe that their desire to walk as upright men, to be accepted as persons of equal worth and capacity, their desire to be judged as individuals, is a God-given desire.

The Reverend Earle Page, rector, Holy Trinity Episcopal Church, Rogation Sunday, May 19, 1963

***

In 1956 a group of elderly, leading Negroes came to my office to discuss the Supreme Court ruling on Segregation. We talked it over for about two hours and agreed on certain basic conduct for the good harmony of the two races. We have had the best race relations in Gainesville of any southern city until you [Cowles Communications, new owners of the *Sun*] arrived. The elderly, sensible Negro businessmen, and leaders, thought and acted with judgment, until your arrival and your venom stirred up the young, adventurous Negro youth.

Attorney Sigsbee L. Scrugg, June 13, 1963

***

> Negroes have had some of the lowest living conditions possible. In order to prepare the Negro for integration this environment must be eliminated. Of 60 miles of unpaved streets in Gainesville, most are found in Negro sections. Sewage lines have been neglected. Enforcement of sanitary and building codes is needed. Many houses from which 40 to 50 dollars a month rent is collected are without inside lavatory facilities and Negro children and women have to use outdoor facilities.
>
> Charles Chestnut III, June 28, 1963

***

> Alachua County with Gainesville as the hub of expanding educational institutions in Florida enjoys a position that is unique in its ability to provide education in great quantity and quality. If the degree of poverty is a direct function of education there appears to be little reason why poverty cannot be all but eradicated from the community by using our existing and potential resources.
>
> Employment Opportunities Council of Gainesville and Alachua County, November, 1969

During school desegregation, the leaders of Alachua County's public schools often pointed out that the schools served the entire diverse county population. The debate went back and forth: Should the schools be responsible for modifying behavior of pupils who only reflected community values, for better or worse, or should the community and city and county governments act to correct problems perceived as causing the schools' difficulties? Desegregation, intended to bring the races together, had that effect, but it also exposed deep, long-standing divides in the community that could not be bridged just by putting everyone together in the same schools.

Public facility desegregation preceded school desegregation. After only minor prodding by young moderate black demonstrators, the community's response gave hope that further desegregation could be managed. In contrast, by the late 1960s, just before full school desegregation, rock throwing, vandalism, and arson in and near black neighborhoods showed that some proportion of disaffected black youths were abandoning nonviolence. Before turning to school desegregation, then, it is important to have a sense of what was happening outside the schools.

African Americans had always been welcome in Gainesville stores (although for many years they were not allowed to try on clothing).

Restaurants, motels, and movie theaters mostly remained segregated. But even in the early 1960s, some white businessmen refused to follow local custom. Marvin Gresham was a pharmacist and in 1953 began operating Gresham Drug, just down University Avenue from Woolworth's. The drug store had a fountain. Gresham came from a poor family in Bunnell. His daughter, Brenda Gresham Rainsberger, says that anyone, regardless of race, had always been welcome to sit at the fountain and be served.[1] In 1970, as student body secretary at Gainesville High School, she would play a role when the county closed its black high schools and moved most of their remaining students to GHS.

The Alachua County government voluntarily dropped segregation in its facilities "long before" the major desegregation campaign in 1963.[2] The University of Florida's medical center and school, which had recently opened, quietly eliminated its segregated areas, apparently without outside pressure. The community hospital, Alachua General, held out until fall 1964 against efforts to desegregate its inpatient areas.[3]

The Reverend Earle Page, recently called to be rector of Holy Trinity Episcopal Church, made desegregation the subject of his sermon on Rogation Sunday, May 19, 1963:

> My concern at this point is not what happens in the nation, or what happens in another part of the country. Since I was born and bred in the south, I am very much aware that people in other parts of the country have often tried to escape their own problems by criticizing the south. A great deal can be said about all of this.
>
> But we must, as Christians, be first of all concerned with what happens here, where we have immediate responsibility. The place we live, this field we toil, is the place of our first responsibility as Southerners – whether we are Southerners by birth or by choice.

Page told his parishioners what they already knew—that the South was going to be desegregated, whether or not the people opposed it. Then he said,

> Now there is a later stage, in which the leadership of the movement is passing away from figures like Martin Luther King. A growing and significant number of colored people are rejecting what they call passive leadership. If they are met with violence, they are becoming more willing to retaliate in kind. The explosive consequences of this change in attitude

> must be taken seriously. It does not change the moral issues involved, but it does heighten their urgency.
>
> ***
>
> There is no doubt in my mind that desegregation will bring many difficulties and even disasters.
>
> But I also see the injustice and the suffering of God's black children who are my brothers in Christ. I believe that their desire to walk as upright men, to be accepted as persons of equal worth and capacity, their desire to be judged as individuals, is a God-given desire.[4]

Page was a native of Florence, South Carolina. He would soon find himself in the midst of the civil rights struggles in Gainesville as a member of the city's first biracial committee, as chair of its Human Relations Advisory Board, and eventually, as an ombudsman at Gainesville High School, trying to bring some measure of peace after violence there in 1970.

The campaign against Gainesville's remaining segregated businesses began in the summer of 1963. Charles Chestnut III and other young African Americans led this effort. Chestnut was twenty-three years old, a college graduate and funeral director. He would eventually be chair of the public schools' first biracial committee. He was elected the first black member of the Alachua County school board, on which he served from 1976 to 1992. He then was elected to the Alachua County Commission from 1992 to 2000. His family owns the Chestnut Funeral Home, which was founded by his grandfather in 1921.[5] The Chestnut family had long contributed to the city's black community.

Blacks of school age were accepted into Chestnut's group and participated in demonstrations. Chestnut at one point was summonsed to court for contributing to the delinquency of minors. The state field director for the National Association for the Advancement of Colored People, Bob Saunders, learned of the Gainesville situation and obtained Attorney Earl Jones of Jacksonville to represent Chestnut. The charges were dismissed. Jones would later serve as local counsel for the NAACP Legal Defense Fund in the lawsuit to desegregate Alachua County schools. Saunders also used his authority to create an NAACP Youth Council in Gainesville. That action gave the group official standing to take positions that the adult chapter probably would not have taken on its own. During one demonstration, Chestnut was accosted by an older white friend of the family, who asked Chestnut, "Does Charlie [Chestnut's grandfather] know what you're doing?" Joel Buchanan recalls on a different occasion that he and some other young blacks were arrested at the Humpty Dumpty restaurant.

When Chestnut, Buchanan, and the others were brought before Judge McDonald, the judge told Chestnut that he was disappointed in Chestnut's behavior, that Chestnut's grandfather had been such a fine gentleman. The elder Chestnut had a different set of priorities. Charles III: "My granddaddy never said one thing to me about the movement other than one thing. And he asked me a question. He said . . . you doing all this, what you going to do about jobs?"[6]

Following a confrontation on June 2, 1963, between black demonstrators and whites at a downtown movie theater,[7] the Gainesville City Commission, led by the young Mayor-Commissioner Byron Winn, responded by establishing the Bi-racial Committee. There were no blacks on the elected five-member city commission.[8] Mayor Winn himself owned and managed two popular restaurants, the Winnjammer and the Primrose. He took a strong public stand in favor of peaceful desegregation. "Our city has the choice of peaceful integration or violent integration. My leadership will be directed toward peaceful integration." The Alachua County Commission and the chamber of commerce pledged their support for the desegregation effort.[9]

They were soon joined by the Gainesville Ministerial Association. That body also agreed to integrate its own membership of clergy.

> We believe that the churches of our community, as institutions and through their individual members, must demonstrate God's equal concern for all men. We call Christians of all denominations to renew prayer that the spirit of our Lord Jesus Christ may guide our actions and form our attitudes in the decisions which face us.[10]

Winn reached out to "scores of restaurant owners and operators, motel men, theater owners and various civic leaders," including the White Citizens Council. As a result of those communications, many businesses agreed to desegregate. By June 7, Winn and the president of the local NAACP chapter, the Reverend A. F. Alexander, announced an indefinite suspension of demonstrations to allow time for integration to be negotiated voluntarily.[11]

Not everyone in the white community fell in line behind Mayor Winn. The prominent attorney Sigsbee Lee Scruggs opposed desegregation. Scruggs came to Gainesville from Jefferson County, Florida, in 1917; the only two paved roads in Gainesville then extended just a couple of blocks. He was named Sigsbee after the captain of the battleship *Maine* and Lee for the Confederate general.[12] As a young lawyer Scruggs had helped defend Marjorie Kinnan Rawlings in the libel case brought by Rawlings's friend Miss Zelma Cason over her characterization in Rawlings's book, *Cross Creek*. During World War II, Scruggs was a bomber pilot.[13]

Scruggs was as colorful as he was outspoken. He would get down on his knees before juries, with tears streaming down his face. He was rumored to keep an onion in a pocket of his suit. Before air-conditioning was common, during closing arguments, he would go to his face to wipe off the sweat, with perhaps a bit of onion on his fingers to assist the weeping. Despite Scruggs's outspoken views on segregation, his law firm served perhaps more black clients at that time than any other local firm. Many white lawyers did not accept black clients at all. Blacks were served through a separate waiting room, but according to a former law partner of Scruggs, they received the same services as whites, at lower rates.[14]

Scruggs blamed the changes that were occurring in Gainesville on Cowles Communications, which had recently purchased the *Gainesville Sun* from its local owners, the Pepper family. Scruggs gave himself credit for keeping Gainesville segregated after *Brown v. Board of Education*:

> In 1956 a group of elderly, leading Negroes came to my office to discuss the Supreme Court ruling on Segregation. We talked it over for about two hours and agreed on certain basic conduct for the good harmony of the two races. We have had the best race relations in Gainesville of any southern city until you [Cowles Communications] arrived. The elderly, sensible Negro businessmen, and leaders, thought and acted with judgment, until your arrival and your venom stirred up the young, adventurous Negro youth.
>
> ***
>
> Every shot, every cutting, every conflict, every insult, every firing of labor, the bad news of the disruption of our good relations, can largely be laid at your door, caused by your desire to use three million dollars to force your view-point on this community. Not by a desire to do good, but evil. Not by a desire to work, as between the races, for better understanding, but a burning, crusading desire to cause disruption, so that the force and power of a government in the hands of northern Democrats will be compelled to join you in further disrupting a community.
>
> People of differing beliefs should never be forced to integrate. Many Baptists believe in close communion. Even in this holy sacrament they should not be forced by law to accept a Methodist, Presbyterian or any other faith or belief.

> Beliefs are part of the human mind and thus a part of its faith and soul and should not be trespassed upon even by persons with a bitter, agonizing hatred of the South and its ways, and especially if reinforced by three million dollars.[15]

Scruggs owned the Humpty Dumpty restaurant. He held out, ordering his staff to continue refusing service to black patrons there.[16]

Medgar Evers had been shot and killed in Mississippi on June 12, the day before Scruggs's letter was published.

Amid the controversy, the *Sun* had cautionary words for the black community:

> A second problem is knottier. It concerns the cultural lag between the major strata of Negro and white societies. Involved is education, sanitation, moral standards and public conduct. The lag originated in yesterday's lamentable history, but it faces us today in stark reality.
>
> Most whites do not like exhibitionists, boors, filth or vulgarity. They avoid it among whites; they can be expected to reject it violently from blacks. Negroes are faced with the pressing problem of adjusting to a brand-new world. It can be likened to skipping 50 years into the future. A few Negroes are prepared. Most are not. If the contemporary majestic global Negro movement founders, it will be on the shoal of cultural lag.[17]

In a speech at the University of Florida in late June 1963, Chestnut highlighted two main problems:

> The biggest problem is gaining acceptance by whites. We must change the idea many whites have of the Negro. The opposition of the segregationist is intense to this.

The second problem was "preparing the Negro for integration." Chestnut continued:

> Negroes have had some of the lowest living conditions possible. In order to prepare the Negro for integration this environment must be eliminated.
>
> Of 60 miles of unpaved streets in Gainesville, most are found in Negro sections. Sewage lines have been neglected. Enforcement of sanitary and building codes is needed.

> Many houses from which 40 to 50 dollars a month rent is collected are without inside lavatory facilities and Negro children and women have to use outdoor facilities.[18]

Chestnut's statement was echoed at the same event by Mayor Winn: "It must be remembered that there is more to integration than civil rights and law. Washington, D.C., integrated too rapidly. The result was a surge of Negroes not ready for integration, a retreat of whites and a high crime rate. I don't wish this to happen in Gainesville. I want our integration to leave us a healthy and thriving city."[19]

Chestnut had to delicately bridge the gap between younger African Americans who wanted desegregation sped up and the white leadership that wanted time to persuade the more traditional businessmen of the need to move forward together. If some businessmen refused to desegregate, those who did would face potential isolation if white customers favored businesses that continued to enforce segregation. The *Gainesville Sun* observed: "All questions of time and deadlines for accomplishing integration are skirted by Chestnut. 'We have no deadlines. We want things now, but they have to be done in studied steps. We definitely don't want to push things unduly fast.'" Chestnut and the Youth Council ran a tight ship. "We would never think of inflicting someone who was unclean or ill-mannered on anyone," Chestnut told the *Sun*.

The *Sun* article went on, "Instead of mere 'integration,' [Chestnut] desires 'acceptance.'" Chestnut continued, "That's something you can't force on anybody. You have to more or less let a person realize on his own that the Negro deserves what he wants and is willing to work for it." Chestnut at this time rejected legal action to achieve integration. "We could force our way into places legally, but we'd really be unwanted then." Although Chestnut was strong in his advocacy for the black community, for such things as sewers and for impartial law enforcement, he saw violence as harmful to Gainesville's longer-term interest in attracting business and jobs.[20]

With blacks seeking entry to public accommodations around the state, the Ku Klux Klan saw an opportunity. On a night in September 1963, before twenty-eight persons were to be tried in connection with civil rights demonstrations in Ocala, the Klan scheduled a rally and cross burning in Marion County. Harold Rummel and a photographer from the *Sun* covered the rally. Rummel estimated attendance at five hundred. A Klan spokesman at the meeting said the Klan was organizing a series of public meetings and encouraging press coverage because the NAACP was meeting in public.

The first speaker said he was the Reverend Gail Price, pastor of the Central Baptist Church in Sanford. "The nation has been on a toboggan slide to hell—niggerism and communism—since the election of Pres. F. D.

Roosevelt in the 1930s." Rev. Price blamed television for "brain washing" the people. He said that he continued to preach segregation from his pulpit despite unsuccessful challenges.

The cross burning followed Price's speech. About fifty robed Klansmen joined hands and circled the twenty-five-foot cross while it burned. The emcee said that the cross burning had been postponed because some Klan members had been "on patrol" in the black section of Ocala.

Next, the Reverend W. D. O'Pry, who said he was a Baptist minister from Lake City, gave the main speech. Among his remarks: "Niggerism and Communism go together." Referring to the "Love thy neighbor as thyself" passage from the Bible, O'Pry said, "Don't tell me you have to love these niggers like your neighbors. I love my dog but I don't sleep with him." O'Pry informed his audience that Communists were behind the civil rights movement. "Then he added that the Jewish people are behind Communism. 'Both Stalin's and Khrushchev's wives were kikes.'"[21]

The Sixteenth Street Baptist Church in Birmingham was bombed on September 16, 1963. Four black girls, ages eleven to fourteen, were killed, and twenty-two other persons were injured. All but one of the church's stained glass windows were blown out. The Klan was eventually connected to that bombing.

Northern Florida would not follow the Klan. Rummel covered a rally at Lake Butler in December 1963 that was attended by only forty people. Some in attendance blamed the press coverage for the low attendance.[22] The passage of the federal Civil Rights Act in July 1964 occasioned some additional Klan rallies in the area,[23] but the Klan would not be a public force here (St. Augustine excepted) in the years ahead.

The federal Civil Rights Act, which took effect July 2, 1964, resulted in desegregation of most of the remaining segregated public accommodations in Gainesville.[24] At the state level, Democratic Governor Farris Bryant made a forthright, unambiguous stand in favor of compliance in a speech in his hometown of Ocala.[25]

Black voter registration in Alachua County doubled between 1956 and 1964. Blacks in 1964 made up 26 percent of the county's population and 19 percent of registered voters; whites with 74 percent of the population held 81 percent of voter registration.[26] But approximately 57 percent of Alachua County's blacks lived below the poverty level of $3,000 annual income.[27]

By January 1965, Neil Butler, who would become Gainesville's first black city commissioner (and later mayor-commissioner) and a leader during school desegregation, would commend the white community for achieving integration of public accommodations:

> I know how difficult it must be for some people who have been reared in a certain tradition to watch that tradition as it

> is abolished. For this reason, I have great respect for the man who can admit his wrongs and try to correct them.
>
> With God's help very soon perhaps we can all be proud to say we're Southerners and we are solving our problems. With the enthusiasm with which I condemn the evils of segregation, I also praise the men who dared stand up and try to correct these evils. Perhaps before long we will even feel at ease in all places.[28]

During the coming years, both the Gainesville and Alachua County governments would attempt to address African American grievances, which included the need for public and rent-assisted housing, employment opportunities, better public services in black neighborhoods, street paving, and alleged disproportionate police and court actions against blacks. Community-service organizations, both black and white, worked to resolve these issues.

In the spring of 1967, one writer would declare that the "militant" civil rights movement (by which he meant freedom rides, sit-in demonstrations, voter registration drives, and the other nonviolent movements) had "collapsed."[29]

But then came the riots of the summer of 1967, which erupted in urban ghettos in many cities across the United States, including Atlanta, Hartford, Dayton, Newark, West Palm Beach, Tampa, and most violently in Detroit. Gainesville was spared, but a new black militancy gained impetus nationally.

By late 1967, in Gainesville, some issues were being driven by leaders who identified with the national black power movement. Some of these leaders were from the University of Florida or from outside Alachua County. Black leaders who described themselves as "militant" would not on their own achieve any significant outcomes in Gainesville, but they brought a different rhetoric and different tactics to local issues.

In December 1967, a group of black and white protesters, led by Irwin "Jack" Dawkins, alleged at a city commission meeting that a black female inmate at the city jail had been solicited for sex by a police officer. At the time, the jail did not employ female matrons. Dawkins alleged that the city police department was "Klan infested." The mayor-commissioner, Walter E. Murphree, MD, asked the city manager to investigate and to report back to the commission.[30] But before the city commission could complete its review, a grand jury was convened to review the matter.[31]

On December 19, the day after the grand jury convened, a publication called *Black Voices* was distributed by Dawkins and a fellow protester, Carol Thomas, a white, in the hallway outside the grand jury room and outside the courthouse. The broadside accused the grand jury and the police department of being racist and Klan infested, and called the grand jury "fixed." The state attorney was referred to as a "negro-hating hunkie." Any black members of the grand jury would be "Uncle Toms." Five of the eighteen grand jury members were African American, and thirteen were white.[32]

Judge James C. Adkins Jr. found that Dawkins and Thomas had committed criminal contempt of court and sentenced Dawkins to six months in jail and Thomas to four months. Dawkins and Thomas were taken to jail immediately.[33] The next day, Adkins denied bond to both prisoners.[34] The grand jury did not return an indictment of the police accused of sexually abusing the female prisoner.

Counsel affiliated with the American Civil Liberties Union took up the cause of Dawkins and Thomas. State appellate courts affirmed Judge Adkins's actions, but the federal courts intervened, ordering Dawkins and Thomas freed on February 5, 1968, on $1,000 bond each.[35] The Fifth Circuit Court of Appeals eventually found the December handbill to be protected speech under the First Amendment.[36]

There the matter might have ended. But while Dawkins and Thomas were still in jail, a new issue of *Black Voices* stated on January 5, 1968, that until bail was granted to Dawkins and Thomas, all white businesses in the black community "are hereby closed down." During the first week of January 1968, arson attacks on five such businesses were reported.[37] Then the homes of Judge Adkins and Assistant State Attorney Mack Futch were firebombed.[38] The firebombing of Judge Adkins's home did only $300 in damage, and no one was home at the time, but publicity of the incident helped his 1968 campaign for election to the Florida Supreme Court. A conservative Democrat, he would serve as a justice from 1969 through 1987, and as chief justice from 1974 through 1976.[39]

Vandalism in Gainesville had become a serious enough problem that in January 1966 city police began strict enforcement of the city's curfew law for persons under the age of eighteen. The two judges with authority over these crimes issued stern warnings to juveniles and their parents.[40] But a new wave of property crimes that dated from January 1968 would continue in Gainesville right through the final desegregation of county schools in 1970.

Martin Luther King Jr. was assassinated in Memphis on Thursday, April 4, 1968. Rioting spread in black areas around the country. In Gainesville, the Reverend Thomas A. Wright, president of the local NAACP chapter, issued a statement that urged both greater attention to black grievances and continued nonviolent action.[41]

The cause of Jack Dawkins then became mixed up with reaction to the King assassination. Dawkins was back in jail after being arrested in connection with arson of a store in a black neighborhood. On the afternoon of Saturday, April 6, a group of about seventy-five demonstrators marched from Mount Olive Baptist Church, located in a black neighborhood northwest of downtown, to the county jail to demand the release of Jack Dawkins.[42] The leaders of the Saturday night march were from the Southern Christian Leadership Conference, the University of Florida's Afro-American Student Association, and a new organization called the Florida Black Front. Speakers at the church said that King's assassination had "killed nonviolence and just about killed integration." "Everytime a policeman raises his nightstick from now on he's gonna die." "We're gonna make this town wake up or there ain't gonna be no town here in two weeks." At the jail, one of the leaders said that they were there to get Dawkins out. The group left the jail, according to the press, only after the leaders promised that "next time" they would really get Dawkins out. That evening, three of the march leaders were arrested for inciting to riot. Groups of blacks drove around town; others gathered near the police station, on the edge of a black neighborhood. Sheriff Joe Crevasse asked Governor Claude Kirk to send in a sixty-man riot-control squad, and some nearby National Guard troops were placed on alert.[43]

Jack Dawkins went missing before his arson trial, which had been moved to Ocala.[44] He remained at large, and the trial was never held.

The following day, Sunday, April 7, an interracial group of local clergymen organized a march and memorial service at the Alachua County courthouse for Dr. King. The service was attended by an estimated one thousand people, including Gainesville's mayor and Ralph Turlington, a Gainesville representative in the state legislature who then served as Speaker of the House. The march and rally were peaceful. Then Marshall Jones, a University of Florida professor, urged a sit-in at University Avenue and Main Street to protest the grand jury's excusing of the charges of police sexual abuse of black women. His speech was not part of the planned ceremony. He called the community "racist." Only a very small number joined the sit-in, and twenty-one were arrested while the rest of the crowd watched quietly.[45]

Sunday evening black neighborhoods experienced a four-hour outburst of violence, including firebombing, rock and bottle throwing, and some shots being fired. National Guardsmen entered the city to assist police and the riot squad that had deployed on Saturday night. By 1:00 a.m., the area was reported quiet. A total of 366 guard and law-enforcement personnel were used. The guard was deactivated at 8:00 a.m.[46] This outbreak was the only time when National Guard troops were used to stop violence in Gainesville.

White and black leaders in Gainesville continued to work on the same set of issues that had been identified before Dr. King's assassination. Republican Governor Claude Kirk, who took office in 1967, launched "Operation Concern" in Gainesville, a program of his Division of Economic

Opportunity to attack poverty. Kirk, for the cameras, captained a bulldozer in a black neighborhood on June 20, 1968, to destroy a shack. He explained, "This is not a publicity gimmick." The Rev. Wright, speaking at a lunch for the governor, said that the city was not reaching young persons from age fourteen to twenty. He said that more sports programs would help and expressed skepticism that young blacks would go to street dances the police department was planning at its new neighborhood police facilities. The governor countered, "There has to be something more meaningful than play, something meaningful like jobs."[47]

As the clock wound down toward complete integration of Alachua County's schools in February 1970, incidents of rock throwing, vandalism, and arson continued, generally believed to be caused by young black males. During 1968, there had been twenty-eight arson cases, but in the first four months of 1969, Gainesville police recorded thirty-seven arson cases.[48] At the same time crime rates in Gainesville were soaring. The overall crime rate in Gainesville increased 54.7 percent in 1968 over 1967, the largest increase of any city in Florida. Robberies rose 120 percent in 1968 over 1967. The *Sun* suggested in 1968 that the city needed a new police chief.[49] One of the most unfortunate incidents of vandalism was the 1969 destruction of the recreation equipment at a three-year-old boys club in a black neighborhood.[50] The city paid $1,800 in 1969 just to repair windows on its mosquito fogger trucks that were shattered by rocks thrown in black neighborhoods. These slow-moving, noisy trucks made perfect targets for rock throwers.[51]

The schools had not been immune from the disorders that were affecting Gainesville's black community. Superintendent Talbot stated that overcrowding was a major cause of the problems in the schools. He said that after Gainesville High went on double sessions in September 1968, vandalism and disciplinary problems dropped considerably. During the 1968–69 school year, about 21 percent of black students attended white schools under the county's freedom-of-choice desegregation plan. Nevertheless, in the spring of 1969, a few incidents of black-on-white violence in the schools produced both headlines and concern. A black student threw an open knife and hit a white teacher at Lincoln High School (she was not injured). A white student at Howard Bishop Junior High was stabbed by a black student after the white student threw spitballs at the black student. A white Westwood Junior High student was hospitalized in critical condition after a black girl stabbed him near the school. Superintendent Talbot stated that in his fifteen years in the county school system, he had not heard of a single school stabbing. The students responsible for these incidents were expelled, but there was no sense that the violence problem had been solved. Talbot sought to send more assistant principals to the schools in part to keep better control of student violence.[52]

That many of the rock throwers in Gainesville's black neighborhoods were still in school, and mostly in the black schools, would have been obvious. It would also have been obvious that those students would be going to school with whites by the 1970–71 school year, when, under the county's desegregation plan, there would be no more all-black secondary schools. In fact, complete integration of the schools would be ordered in February 1970 at the midpoint of the coming school year. Whether anything should or could have been done earlier, the schools were already out of time to prepare for major changes they knew were going to happen.

Drugs were another problem that the schools would have to deal with at the same time as they were desegregating. Drug use, accompanied by rebelliousness toward adults, mostly by white students at that time, would impact school discipline, as we will see in later chapters.

This history would not be complete without mentioning that Gainesville, and its schools, hosted several future rock stars, from the late 1960s into the early 1970s. Tom Petty graduated, a year late, from Gainesville High in 1968. One of Petty's English teachers was Shelton Boyles, whom we will meet later. Boyles, frustrated, took Tom aside to tell him that "he could get this stuff." Tom replied, "I'm going to play music, I don't need this stuff." Boyles, not giving up: "You're going to need this stuff for your day job."[53] Others who passed through included Bernie Leadon and Don Felder, later of the Eagles, Stephen Stills, Benmont Tench III, and Marty Jourard of the Motels. Starting in garage bands, some were also members of GHS music groups, but they soon were taking paid gigs at local bars. Some band members, wearing their hair long and clothes from the counterculture, faced the same hostility as blacks from a segment of the white population.[54] The bands played to white audiences; the local music scene went on without involvement in desegregation.

The black and white communities in Gainesville had identified housing, municipal services, and jobs as the most significant issues (apart from education) that had to be addressed to bring the black community into the economic and social mainstream. By the end of the decade, how had Gainesville done?

Confirming Charles Chestnut's point on housing, 35.4 percent of all Alachua County dwelling units in 1960 were "dilapidated or deteriorated and contained no plumbing facilities."[55] From 1966 to 1969, in Gainesville, 200 substandard housing units were razed and 1,000 units rehabilitated to meet minimum code requirements. By 1969, the number of substandard dwellings in Gainesville had been reduced to 1,650 out of 20,000, or to 8 percent. But it was not possible to determine the proportion of substandard dwellings in the county outside Gainesville.[56] In addition, many new single-family homes were built by private contractors during the 1960s on the margins of existing east-side black neighborhoods, increasing middle-class black home ownership. Housing was perhaps the easiest issue to deal with, given the availability of federal financial assistance during those years.

Gainesville's effort to obtain federal funds to construct new low-income housing began in 1966. An earlier move in the late 1950s to establish an authority in Gainesville for low-income housing had failed to gain support.[57] By December 1968, 742 units of public and rent-assisted housing were funded or under construction. Of these units, 100 were in a high-rise building reserved for elderly residents. The remaining 642 units were in five developments, or projects, located in or near east-side black areas.[58] The reinforcement of segregated housing patterns during the 1960s would have consequences for school desegregation, as we will see.

There were no definitive press reports measuring progress in paving streets and extending sewers into the black slum areas of Gainesville, but the issue faded from view.

The actual impact of the many efforts specifically directed at job creation can't be measured, but black leaders applied strong pressure to city and county governments to hire more blacks. At first, in 1967, the answer was that more blacks were not being hired because the city was not finding more qualified blacks to hire. A spokesman for the county said the county commission did not control many county jobs and "considerable county money is spent on welfare and other programs." Black reaction to the city's employment steps came after the disturbances that followed the assassination of Martin Luther King Jr. Black leaders renewed their plea for more white-collar jobs in city and county government, and for an emergency job pool to employ persons willing to work.[59]

The city and county commissions established a joint Employment Opportunities Council in January 1968 to review all facets of employment issues and to seek solutions.[60] The council was chaired, successively, by Attorney Joe C. Willcox, then president of the chamber of commerce, and Joseph W. Fordyce, the president of Santa Fe Junior College. Its other members included Stephen C. O'Connell, then president of the University of Florida, and nine top-level leaders from the county's banking, retail, construction, medical, and agricultural areas. The only African American on the council was C. W. Banks, MD.

As the council proceeded with its study, government and private employers came forward with more definite proposals. The University of Florida and the Veterans Administration hospital pointed out that they generally had unfilled positions and encouraged more blacks to apply.[61] Governor Kirk's Operation Concern brought part-time summer jobs in 1968 for 100 poor young people. Those jobs were with federal, state, and local governments and were funded by a federal grant.[62] A similar program in 1969 employed 150 young persons.[63] In 1969, the council identified and contacted 850 employers who might be willing to offer summer jobs to young people living below the poverty level. Of those employers, only 371 replied; 146 summer jobs were listed.[64]

The Employment Opportunities Council released its report in November, 1969. In its workforce survey, the council's interview teams obtained information from 3,452 persons sixteen and older living in areas where the poor were concentrated. The council's goal had been to contact 100 percent of persons in these areas; it succeeded in obtaining interviews with about one-third of potential subjects. The sample obtained was 90–95 percent African American; the council noted that whites living below the poverty line were not concentrated geographically and could not easily be located.[65]

The council reported that in Alachua County about six thousand families, representing 29.3 percent of the population, had heads of household who earned less than $1.75 per hour or a corresponding weekly wage level set by the Social Security Administration as the poverty income level.[66] Ninety-four percent of counties in the United States in 1966 had lower incidences of poverty than Alachua County. The county's relative position had improved by three percentage points since 1960.[67] Ten percent of households in Alachua County were headed by persons age twenty or under, and all 10 percent were receiving incomes below the poverty level.[68]

The council found that employment at some level was generally available in the county to persons who were willing to work and that only 1.5 percent of the county's population (six hundred out of a workforce of forty-one thousand) that would normally be considered in the workforce were unemployed.[69] Employers complained that many younger workers were leaving the county for places with higher wages, causing employers to lower standards for open positions. Moving on to the more troubling issue, the council asked, "Why then do we have poverty? . . . Solving the problem of poverty is not simply a matter of hiring the unemployed, as jobs are available for all."[70]

With respect to the hiring of blacks, the report stated that most local employers

> . . . were exceedingly aware of their responsibilities to overcome this factor of racial discrimination by attempting to hire Negroes, in many cases for the first time, in other than unskilled and semi-skilled positions. The problem, as many of the employers observed, is to find <u>qualified</u> Negro workers and workers who are motivated to give a day's work for a day's pay and stay on the job. These were the principal complaints about hiring Negroes, but they applied also to

> whites who are of the same economic class. The environmental factors which produced poorly qualified and poorly motivated workers can be considered the root causes of poverty in this county. Practically all the causes of poverty stem from the early environment in which the child is reared. Training, education, motivation and ambition, attitude and health are all affected.[71]

For its time, the council report tried with some courage to address the hard issues facing Alachua County as it worked to deal with both disaffected black youth and school desegregation. The council report only looked forward; there was no attempt to look back. But the report is a mirror in which we can see the legacy of segregation.

The council report recommended short-term training and jobs programs for the chronically unemployed, day care to allow parents to work, and new industry for Gainesville. Health issues identified by interview subjects were estimated to limit employment of approximately 1,700 members of the county workforce. But the bulk of the commission's recommendations focused on the need for better-educated job applicants. The report emphasized early childhood education to prepare children to succeed in school (the federally funded Head Start program in 1968 reached only 450 children in Alachua County) and vocational training for persons "not motivated or intellectually equipped for college."[72]

There was not going to be a quick fix for poverty and, by implication, for black disaffection. The council had to find a solution, but that solution had to be one that had a chance of support in the community:

> Alachua County with Gainesville as the hub of expanding educational institutions in Florida enjoys a position that is unique in its ability to provide education in great quantity and quality. If the degree of poverty is a direct function of education there appears to be little reason why poverty cannot be all but eradicated from the community by using our existing and potential resources.[73]

The council hoped that its report would be used by other agencies such as the Community Action Agency and the Florida State Employment Service to formulate more specific programs.[74] Those agencies adopted no large-scale programs to address the council's recommendations. And so, as the decade ended and county schools became fully integrated, poverty was one more social problem that the community laid at the steps of its schools.

CHAPTER 3
FLORIDA'S SEGREGATED PAST

> The sure guarantee of the peace and security of each race is the clear, distinct, unconditional recognition by our Government, National and State, of every right that inheres in civil freedom, and of the equality before law of all citizens of the United States without regard to race. State enactments, regulating the enjoyment of civil rights, upon the basis of race, and cunningly devised to defeat legitimate results of the war, under the pretence of recognizing equality of rights, can have no other result than to keep alive a conflict of races, the continuance of which must do harm to all concerned.
>
> *Plessy v. Ferguson*, 163 U.S. 537, 560–61 (1896) (Harlan, J., dissenting)[1]

School desegregation in the 1960s in Florida, as in other Southern states, did not come about because Florida's white citizens woke up one morning and decided to welcome blacks into their schools. It was one thing to integrate a restaurant, where diners might occasionally spend an hour or two. Children and young people attended school five days a week, sat together in class at close quarters, played sports, and made social contacts. White teachers had never taught black students, and black teachers had never taught white students. Black and white students had never sat in the same classrooms, played on the same teams, or belonged to the same clubs. That the same conditions existed in many other parts of the country, whether de jure or de facto, only reinforces the significance of the Southern experience. To understand the task faced by Florida's school leaders in the 1960s, we also need to understand the development of school segregation in Florida and Florida's reaction to *Brown*.

Unlike New Orleans, which also had extensive ties to the Caribbean, Florida would emerge from its colonial period under Spain without an established free black and mixed-race population. Such a population grew up under Spain, under the relatively flexible Spanish slavery regimen and its sanctuary policy for escaped slaves that was confirmed by a royal decree in 1693. However, when Florida passed to England in 1763, most of the free black population left with the Spanish settlers for Cuba; others fled to the Seminoles. Spain regained Florida in 1783 but did not have strong control. Under American pressure, led by Secretary of State Thomas Jefferson, Spain ended its policy of sanctuary for runaway slaves in 1790. But slaves continued to escape across the border, and Spain proved unable to enforce its new policy. When the United States took over Florida in 1821 under the Adams-Onis Treaty, most of the free blacks again departed with the Spanish colonists.[2]

Florida remained a frontier area well into the nineteenth century. Florida's first census under the United States, in 1830, recorded a population of only thirty-five thousand. The Spanish legal system's treatment of slaves and free blacks did not persist. The new territorial government quickly enacted laws similar to those in effect elsewhere in the South that enforced the British and American system of chattel slavery, and denied many civil rights to free blacks. Florida did not become a state until March 3, 1845. Florida's advocates argued in Congress for its admission to maintain the balance of free and slave states that would otherwise have been altered by the admission of Iowa as a free state.[3]

The area surrounding Gainesville was ideal for raising long-staple Sea Island cotton, which became a dominant crop, tended by slaves. The 1860 census for Alachua County shows a white population of 3,757 and a black population of 4,465 (slaves, except for 8 "free colored"). Alachua County would have a black majority through the 1910 census. See table 1 below:

Table 1. White and Black Population of Alachua County, 1850–2010 (From US Census Documents)

Year	White population	Percent	Black population	Percent	Other races	Percent
1850	1,617	64%	907*	36%	n/a	
1860	3,757	46%	4,465**	54%	n/a	
1870	4,935	28%	12,393	72%	n/a	
1880	6,446	39%	10,016	61%	n/a	
1890	9,673	42%	13,260	58%	n/a	
1900	13,279	41%	18,965	59%	n/a	
1910	15,112	44%	19,092	56%	n/a	
1920	17,144	54%	14,473	46%	n/a	

Year	White population	Percent	Black population	Percent	Other races	Percent
1930	19,068	55%	15,313	45%	n/a	
1940	22,723	59%	15,984	41%	n/a	
1950	40,475	71%	16,586	29%	n/a	
1960	55,814	74%	19,490	26%	n/a	
1970	82,665	79%	21,563	21%	536	0.5%
1980	119,344	79%	28,880	19%	3,100	2%
1990	140,787	77%	34,427	19%	6,382	4%
2000	160,128	73%	42,062	19%	15,227	7%
2010	172,156	70%	50,282	20%	24,898	10%

**Slave; includes one "free colored."*
***Slave, includes eight "free colored."*

School segregation in the Southern and border states came about by default. The earliest schools for the freed slaves educated blacks exclusively; later, state public school systems incorporated these schools as separate schools for blacks. During Congressional Reconstruction, neither the federal nor state governments set up any explicit legal impediments to segregated schools. The major Reconstruction civil rights enactments, including the Fourteenth Amendment to the US Constitution, the Civil Rights Acts of 1866[4] and 1875,[5] and the Reconstruction Act of 1867,[6] did not touch on education. Congress deleted a provision requiring equal access of both races to schools from Massachusetts Senator Charles Sumner's bill that became the Civil Rights Act of 1875.[7] Civil rights could be granted by the stroke of a pen; schools would cost money. Also, education had traditionally been a state function. The federal government left education of the former slaves, to the extent it was part of Reconstruction at all, to the chronically underfunded and temporary Freedmen's Bureau. Missionary societies and other voluntary groups from the North also tried to fill the need of the newly freed slaves for education.[8] This history would again become relevant when *Brown v. Board of Education* reached the Supreme Court in 1953; in the midst of considering *Brown*, the Supreme Court justices ordered the parties to research whether Congress, which submitted the Fourteenth Amendment, and the state legislatures and conventions that ratified it, understood that it would abolish segregation in public schools.[9]

Before the end of the Civil War, Florida allowed no organized schools for blacks.[10] Under the compulsion of Congressional Reconstruction, Florida adopted a new constitution in 1868. That constitution granted full civil rights to all citizens without regard to race.[11] The Florida legislature in 1869 acted under the 1868 constitution to establish a uniform system of public schools.[12] Although white members of the legislature attempted to include a compulsory segregation clause,[13] as enacted the law did not contain any provision either authorizing or forbidding segregation of the races in the schools. Alachua County (together with every other county in Florida) chose from the beginning to operate segregated schools under this law.[14]

In 1872, Florida enacted a comprehensive civil rights statute that forbade racial discrimination in the schools, although private schools established exclusively for white or colored citizens, and maintained by voluntary contributions, were excepted from the law's nondiscrimination requirement.[15] The law forbade racial discrimination in public accommodations and in selection of jurors. This law also provided "that every discrimination against any citizen on account of color by the use of the word, 'white' or any other term in any law, statute, ordinance, or regulation, is hereby repealed and annulled."[16] The Florida law was probably patterned on the civil rights bill introduced by Senator Sumner, which eventually became the Civil Rights Act of 1875. Jerrell Shofner states that the law had little impact on Florida's already segregated society.[17]

With the disputed election of Republican Rutherford B. Hayes as president in 1876, Reconstruction came to an end across the South.

Florida adopted a new constitution in 1885. That constitution required that "white and colored children shall not be taught in the same school, but impartial provision shall be made for both."[18] Other laws supplemented constitutionally mandated school segregation. A major revision of the Florida public education law in 1955 continued the requirement for separate white and black schools (which was still in any event required by the Florida constitution).[19] The various statutes requiring racial segregation in Florida's public schools were finally repealed in 1965.[20] The constitutional requirement remained in effect until adoption of the 1968 constitution.

The question must be asked, Why did schools come to be segregated by law in Florida and throughout the South and in many border states? The white community in the South simply would not tolerate whites attending school with blacks. An incident that occurred in Jacksonville in 1864, then under federal occupation, provides an example. A school teacher from the North, Esther Hawks, had opened a school there. At first, many white children attended with the children of freedmen, but after six weeks all but one had dropped out. "The last mother to take her child out told Mrs. Hawks that she would be glad to have her offspring in school, but the neighbors 'make so much fuss' that she had to give in."[21]

The majority opinion in *Plessy v. Ferguson* itself was grounded in social attitudes:

> So far then, as a conflict with the Fourteenth Amendment is concerned, the case reduces itself to the question whether the statute of Louisiana [requiring separate accommodations on railroads] is a reasonable regulation, and with respect to this there must necessarily be a large discretion on the part of the legislature. In determining the question of reasonableness it is at liberty to act with reference to the established usages, customs and traditions of the people, and with a view to the promotion of their comfort, and the preservation of the public peace and order. Gauged by this standard, we cannot say that a law which authorizes or even requires the separation of the two races in public conveyances is unreasonable, or more obnoxious to the Fourteenth Amendment than the acts of Congress requiring separate schools for colored children in the District of Columbia, the constitutionality of which does not seem to have been questioned, or the corresponding acts of state legislatures.[22]

With respect to school segregation, white fear of miscegenation was never far from the surface.[23]

The social attitudes that gave rise to school segregation in the South created an opening for those who ultimately used Jim Crow laws to deny black populations the same educational opportunities as white children and to oppress blacks economically.[24] School segregation in the South became an established way of life. Generations of citizens, teachers, and school administrators passed through segregated schools. Segregation ground on, unimpeded by legislatures or courts that could have made other choices but did not.

Despite the barriers posed by legally mandated segregation, there were African American leaders in Florida who actively opposed segregation even during the Jim Crow years. Paul Ortiz has documented the early protests, primarily over economic issues, of black fraternal organizations, churches, and labor unions, as well as community boycotts of white businesses. Those efforts served as models for later more widespread organized resistance to segregation.[25]

During the 1940s, the NAACP Legal Defense and Educational Fund obtained a series of court decisions that required admission of blacks to previously segregated public university graduate-school programs.[26] When Florida in 1947 enacted the Minimum Foundation Program for increasing state funding of education, those funds were made available without discriminating between black and white schools. The stated reason for the Minimum Foundation Program was to attract business to Florida. But Florida leaders were aware of the higher education desegregation suits by the Defense Fund and hoped the increased funding would help them to prove that the state's black schools were equal to the white schools.[27]

The NAACP Legal Defense Fund's direct challenge to segregated public schools in four states (the cases that eventually went to the Supreme Court as *Brown*) caused the Florida legislature in 1953 to approve a two-year, $100 million plan for new schools for both races. The Florida superintendent of public instruction, Thomas D. Bailey, acknowledged that one purpose of this spending plan was to forestall legal challenges to segregated schools in Florida. He argued that consolidation of the many small schools serving black students would allow "emphasis on vocational courses, which, really, are more important to the Negroes than to the Whites."

> We believe that the great majority of Negroes in Florida do not desire non-segregation and will continue to have faith in the leadership which is providing impartial facilities for both races as rapidly as possible in a comparatively young state whose chief problem has been an adequate source of revenue for all purposes. We do not believe that the solution will come by edict from any source but by working together toward the accomplishment of an objective which we have mutually and freely pledged ourselves.[28]

Dr. Robert Gore, then president of Florida A&M College, opined in 1952 that the majority of black educators believed enough progress was being made to forestall a court fight for desegregation in Florida.[29]

Dr. John McGuire, executive secretary of the white Florida Baptist Convention, said in 1953 that an antisegregation ruling was expected from the Supreme Court. McGuire predicted that Florida would follow some other Southern states in abolishing its public school systems, leaving education of both races to the churches and private schools. McGuire said that Florida's 311,000 Baptists would be among the first church groups to set up a private school system if segregation were to be ended.[30]

When the Supreme Court decided *Brown v. Board of Education* in 1954, Florida leaders scrambled to denounce the decision. Democrat D. R. "Billy" Matthews, the US congressman who represented the mostly rural district that included Alachua County, called the decision "as terrible a thing as World War I, World War II or the emergence of communism."[31] In 1956, all but one of Florida's US representatives and senators signed the "Southern Manifesto," which pledged its signers to use "all lawful means" to reverse *Brown* and "to prevent the use of force in its implementation."[32]

The Florida House of Representatives in 1955 memorialized Congress to enact legislation or propose constitutional amendments to allow school segregation to continue. Although the memorial stated that it was not intended to deprive blacks of equal education, nevertheless it spoke as shrilly as possible about the dire consequences of desegregation: "civil strife, riot, breaches of the peace and all the human misery heartache and physical suffering attendant thereto . . ." The memorial asserted that Florida had provided equal schools for whites and blacks, "thus lending legal force to the time honored custom and native inclination of the people of Florida, both negro and white, to maintain and preserve a segregated public school system . . ."[33]

Florida had a gubernatorial election in 1956 that matched incumbent Democratic Governor LeRoy Collins against three opponents, two of whom were outspoken segregationists.[34] Although in 1956 Collins opposed the "noise and confusion" in some other states, he publicly supported continued segregation. A recent biographer states the obvious: that had Collins spoken out against segregation in 1956, he would have caused the election of his far-right segregationist opponent, Sumter Lowry.[35] Lowry didn't just play the race card; he brandished it: "I've got one platform: Segregation, it's a four by four, it's a mile long, and there's room for every cracker in the state of Florida to get on right now."[36] By taking a more moderate stand, Collins was successful in receiving support from Florida's business community, which feared the disruptions that were occurring elsewhere in the South because of *Brown.*

After his election, Collins, in his January 1957 inaugural address, emphasized that Floridians would have to obey decisions of the Supreme Court as the law of the land.[37] Moderation was a hard course to steer; Collins was equally subject to charges that he failed to defend segregation and that he was a hypocrite. An example: "The Governor doesn't sit on the fence, he runs on it."[38]

The Florida legislature continued to vent its anger over *Brown*, approving three separate resolutions on the subject. Under Florida law, Collins as governor was not obligated to take a position on those resolutions, but he was allowed to do so. The resolutions placed him in a difficult position. Collins signed a 1956 concurrent resolution that denounced *Brown* and some other Supreme Court cases and urged adoption of a federal constitutional amendment to define states' rights.[39] But Collins balked at the legislature's 1957 resolution asserting that *Brown* and other states' rights decisions of the Supreme Court were null and void. He handwrote the following message on the interposition resolution before he sent it on to be filed with the secretary of state:

> This concurrent resolution of 'Interposition' crosses the Governors desk as a matter of routine. I have no authority to veto it. I take this means however to advise the student of government, who may examine this document in the archives

> of the state in the years to come that the Governor of Florida expressed open and vigorous opposition thereto. I feel that the U. S. Supreme Court has improperly usurped powers reserved to the states under the constitution. I have joined in protesting such and in seeking legal means of avoidance. But if this resolution declaring the decisions of the court to be 'null and void' is to be taken seriously, it is anarchy and rebellion against the nation which must remain 'indivisible under God' if it is to survive. Not only will I not condone 'interposition' as so many have sought me to do, I decry it as an evil thing, whipped up by the demagogues and carried on the hot and erratic winds of passion, prejudice, and hysteria. If history judges me right this day, I want it known that I did my best to avert this blot. If I am judged wrong, then here in my own handwriting and over my signature is the proof of guilt to support my conviction. LeRoy Collins[40]

Collins withheld his signature, without comment, from another 1957 resolution that requested a federal constitutional convention to make the US Senate the final judicial authority in states' rights cases, with power to overrule the Supreme Court.[41]

The Florida legislature enacted a pupil-assignment law in 1955. Pupil-assignment laws were an initial Southern oppositional response to the Supreme Court decision in *Brown v. Board of Education of Topeka*. Under the pupil-assignment laws, a student seeking to attend a school other than that to which he was assigned had to pass a race-neutral but burdensome and humiliating application process. The not-so-hidden agenda was to freeze in place the current assignment of pupils to separate black and white schools.

Governor Collins signed the state's first pupil-assignment law in 1955 and subsequent amendments in 1956 and 1959.[42] Governor Collins also signed a 1957 law, responding to the Little Rock crisis, that would have automatically closed any school if any federal authority directed National Guard or other military forces to that school to prevent acts of violence.[43] But he vetoed a law passed by the legislature in 1957 that would have set up private schools.[44]

Despite the legislature's memorials and resolutions, no further legislation was enacted in Florida to oppose desegregation, in part because of Collins's efforts. He appointed a special committee to advise him on legislative responses to *Brown*. In its report of July 16, 1956, that committee gave as its first objective "to maintain the public school system of the State of Florida."[45] The report recommended strengthening the state's pupil-assignment law and granting the governor emergency powers to suppress disorders, but stopped short of recommending any actions that would constitute outright defiance of *Brown*. Blowing off steam, the report then fulminated at some length against *Brown* and some other recent US Supreme Court decisions. "The socialistic, communistic, un-American writings, associations and activities of the 'modern authority' cited by [the Supreme Court in *Brown*] have been so often detailed that they will not be recited here."[46] This committee was chaired by retired Florida Appeals Court Judge L. L. Fabisinski. Judge Rivers Buford, who would later serve as counsel to Governor Claude Kirk, was vice-chair.

Florida's pupil-assignment law, similar to those enacted in North Carolina and Alabama, required county school boards to establish procedures, not explicitly based on race, to control which children attended which schools.[47] The law provided a mandatory, detailed standard by which school boards were to determine pupil assignments:

> In the preparation and conduct of such tests and in classifying the pupils for assignment to the schools which they will attend, the board shall take into account such sociological, psychological and like intangible social scientific factors as will prevent, as nearly as practicable, any condition of socio-economic class consciousness among pupils attending any given school in order that each pupil may be afforded an opportunity for a normal adjustment to his environment and receive the highest standard of instruction within his ability to understand and assimilate. In designating the school to which pupils may be assigned there shall be taken into consideration the request or consent of the parent or guardian or the person standing in loco parentis toward the pupil, the available facilities and teaching capacity of the several schools within the county, the effect of the admission of new students upon established academic programs, the effect of admission of new pupils on the academic progress of the other pupils enrolled in a particular school, the suitability of established curriculum to the students enrolled or to be enrolled in a given school, the adequacy of a pupil's academic preparation for admission to a particular school, the scholastic aptitude, intelligence, mental energy or ability of the pupil applying for admission and the psychological, moral, ethical and cultural background and qualifications of the pupil applying for admission as compared with other pupils previously assigned to the school in which admission is sought.[48]

Pupils were permitted to apply for enrollment in any school in the county where they resided, but school boards were required to hold hearings on such applications. An application could be approved only if the school board found that enrollment of the pupil was in the pupil's best interest, would not interfere with the proper administration of the school or with the proper instruction of the pupils there enrolled, and would not endanger the health or safety of the children there enrolled.[49]

Early in the battle to end segregated schools, civil rights lawyers challenged the constitutionality of the North Carolina pupil-assignment law. The Fourth Circuit Court of Appeals in 1956 held the law was not unconstitutional on its face, meaning that plaintiffs would have to show that the law had been applied in a discriminatory manner in individual cases.[50] The US District Court for the Northern District of Alabama held in 1958 that the Alabama pupil-assignment law was not unconstitutional on its face. The US Supreme Court affirmed.[51]

Following his reelection as governor in 1956, Collins appointed an Advisory Commission on Race Relations in 1957 to study the desegregation issue further. Judge Fabisinski also chaired this commission, which now included only four members. Rivers Buford was not among them. Doak S. Campbell, then recently retired as president of Florida State University, was a member. The commission reported to Collins in March 1959. The 1959 commission report (which was released toward the end of Collins's full term as governor) plainly stated the case for compliance with *Brown*.

> We have discussed and studied this subject for the last two years. It is not at all difficult to state the problems of desegregation but it is very difficult to attempt to resolve those problems.
>
> We have tried to avoid "wishful thinking," for the matter cannot be resolved by mere wishing, but must be faced realistically. We have also tried to approach the problems dispassionately, for the very reason that the problems are charged with emotion. And we have attempted to deal with the subject constructively, for too much is at stake to risk the destruction of institutions essential to the welfare and progress of our state.[52]

The 1959 report took note of developments that had occurred since 1956. Both state and federal courts had ruled that Florida universities could not exclude applicants to graduate programs on the basis of race. Central High School in Little Rock had been desegregated by court order and with the intervention of federal troops. Commonwealth and federal courts had struck down the legislative underpinnings of Virginia's "massive resistance" program. In Arkansas and Virginia, the closing of schools to prevent desegregation had been ruled unconstitutional.

By contrast, both North Carolina and Florida, relying on their pupil-assignment laws, had begun the desegregation process, and the courts had allowed the pupil-assignment laws to be used by the affected school boards. The commission took comfort from a holding by a US District Court that the Florida pupil-assignment law gave black plaintiffs in Dade County an adequate remedy to enforce their right under *Brown* to be admitted to public schools without regard to race.[53] North Carolina and Florida schools had remained open. The commission concluded that Florida should continue to apply its pupil-assignment law in good faith, even when doing so would result in the admission of black students to white schools. The commission recommended against any additional legislation on desegregation. "Under the decisions of state and federal courts, there is no legislation which can accomplish – what is so apparently the hope and desire of many – the maintenance of complete segregation by race in a free public school system."[54]

Compliance with *Brown*, in this view, meant that only those black students who could meet standards set by individual school boards would be admitted to the white schools. The Supreme Court in *Brown II* held that there would be "a transition to a racially nondiscriminatory school system." But exactly what those words meant remained to be worked out. There was not the slightest hint that Florida's leaders foresaw that the Supreme Court in 1968 would order an end to dual-race school systems, in part relying on that holding in *Brown II*.

The Fifth Circuit Court of Appeals reversed the Dade County District Court decision on November 24, 1959. The court found that the school board had not adequately informed students that they had a right to enroll in schools previously attended solely by either race. "Indeed, there is nothing in either the Pupil Assignment Law or the [school board's] Implementing Resolution clearly inconsistent with a continuing policy of compulsory racial segregation."[55] And so began the struggle in Florida to eliminate the barriers that continued to keep blacks in all-black schools.

In reaction to *Brown*, Governor LeRoy Collins and the Florida legislature publicly opposed school desegregation. Governor Collins and his advisers showed as much courage as the times would allow in turning Florida away from outright defiance at a critical inflection point.[56] But following the initial "noise and confusion," state governments throughout the South had very little to do with school desegregation as it moved forward on the ground. In Alachua County, as elsewhere, the task of desegregating the schools would fall to the school superintendent, school board, principals, teachers, students, and parents.

CHAPTER 4
WHY WERE PUBLIC SCHOOLS DESEGREGATED?

> This vicious situation, it seems to me, represents the very heart of the evils in education against which our campaign should be directed. It would be a great mistake to fritter away our limited funds in sporadic attempts to force the making of equal divisions of school funds in the few instances in which such attempts might be expected to succeed. At the most, we could eliminate a very minor part of the discrimination during the year that our suits are commenced. We should not be establishing any new principles, nor bringing any sort of pressure to bear which can reasonably be expected to retain the slightest force beyond that exerted by the specific judgment or order that we might obtain. And we should be leaving wholly untouched the very essence of the existing evils.
>
> Attorney Nathan Margold, reporting to the NAACP on strategies to end de jure segregation, c. 1930

Why was the South's separate system of black public schools abolished? We think we know the answer, but for the African American leaders who eventually succeeded in eliminating those schools, a different outcome was a considered possibility.

An unintended consequence of segregation, especially in the South, was that the segregated black communities through their own efforts and often with their own funds built a separate public education system. Segregation was a dam to keep blacks in their place, but it channeled black resources and creativity into husbanding the separate black schools.

Black public schools in the segregated South played an overwhelmingly important role. However inferior to the white schools, and however ignored and underfunded by white school boards, those schools gave not only education but identity to the South's black communities.[1] The schools were perhaps an even more fundamental source of strength to black communities than the black churches.

Generations of black children were formed by that system, taught by black teachers, coached by black coaches, and led by black principals. No less than their white compatriots, African Americans gave credit to their schools for the success they achieved in later life.

In defiance of efforts after Emancipation by some whites and blacks to limit black education to vocational studies, many Southern black secondary schools and colleges taught academic subjects along with other more practical programs.[2] By the 1930s, the historically black colleges were turning out black physicians, lawyers, businessmen, teachers, nurses, ministers, and other professionals who built and served the black communities of the 1950s and 1960s.

Historically black colleges and universities continued even after integration. For a time, the federal courts required the Department of Health, Education, and Welfare to make special provisions for historically black state colleges in desegregation plans under the Civil Rights Act of 1964.

> The process of desegregation must not place a greater burden on Black institutions or Black students' opportunity to receive a quality higher education. The desegregation process should take into account the unequal status of the Black colleges and the real danger that desegregation will diminish higher education opportunities for blacks.[3]

In the afterword, we will return to the experience of the historically black colleges and universities in the years since Southern public schools were desegregated.

Before deciding to go to court for integrated unitary school systems, African American leaders carefully considered the alternative of retaining but equalizing the South's black schools. The analysis that led them to demand integration is especially pertinent today, sixty years after *Brown v. Board of Education*, when many thoughtful persons believe that desegregation, by itself, failed to level the educational playing field for blacks.

The National Association for the Advancement of Colored People was founded on Lincoln's birthday, in 1909, through the merger of the black intellectual Niagara Movement of W. E. B. Du Bois with a group of white New Yorkers, initially to combat lynching.[4] It came to be the predominant organization representing black interests in the court cases to end postgraduate, college, and public school segregation.

The NAACP's campaign to end elementary and secondary school segregation has its roots in a study by the American Fund for Public Service (also referred to as the Garland Fund). This fund was a charity founded in

1922 by Charles Garland, a young white graduate of Harvard Law School and heir to a substantial bequest from his Boston family. The fund supported organizations that sought social change across a wide political spectrum.

Around 1930, the directors of that fund, through their Committee on Negro Work, found that in South Carolina, more than ten times as much was expended for the education of white children as for African American children; that in Florida, Georgia, Mississippi, and Alabama, more than five times as much; and in North Carolina, Virginia, Texas, Oklahoma, and Maryland, more than twice as much. The Committee on Negro Work found that the seven worst states measured by the disparity in expenditures for black schools were South Carolina, Georgia, Mississippi, Louisiana, Florida, Alabama, and Arkansas.[5] Manifestly, separate education was not equal.

The Garland Fund in 1930 granted the NAACP funds for a legal analysis aimed at the most promising ways to challenge segregation in the courts. A white lawyer from New York, Nathan Margold, was selected to research and write that analysis.[6] His report dealt first with public school segregation, but also with residential segregation and segregation of common carriers, and to a much lesser extent with exclusions from voting and jury service.[7]

But how exactly were segregated schools to be attacked? The legality of such schools had been upheld by state courts in Massachusetts and New York, among other states, and had been assumed by the Supreme Court in *Plessy v. Ferguson*.[8] Margold concluded on the basis of cases decided prior to 1930 that separate schools and other facilities did not, in and of themselves, violate the Fourteenth Amendment.[9] But Margold also found that black children forced to attend segregated schools that did not provide resources equal to those of the white schools were denied equal protection of the laws under the Fourteenth Amendment.[10]

The American Fund's Committee on Negro Work had recommended bringing taxpayer suits in what it found to be the seven worst states to compel those states to provide equal expenditures for white and black schools.[11] Nathan Margold's major task was to analyze the potential effectiveness of the proposed taxpayer suits. He concluded, based on a review of individual state laws, that those laws did not provide an effective statewide remedy. In this opinion, he was proven correct, for as we know, lawsuits to end segregation in the South had to be brought against individual county school boards.[12] But actions against county school boards to force the allocation of equal resources to the separate black schools faced another problem. Margold found that such actions, although likely to succeed on constitutional grounds, would fail in their purpose, because of the inherent difficulty in measuring and enforcing compliance. Margold's legal analysis states:

> Viewing each state as a whole, it is safe to assume, subject to later verification, that only a very small part of the prevailing discrimination occurs in violation of state law and can be remedied thereunder. For the most part, we have a situation in which each of the seven states requires segregation of the white and colored races in its schools under conditions which enable its officers to provide accommodations for the colored schools, grossly inferior to those provided in the white schools. Coupled with this, we have the consistent, long continued practice of those officers to take ample advantage of the opportunity which the state law affords them and the complete absence of any way of stopping this practice through resort to any remedy provided by state law. We have, in a word, segregation irremediably coupled with discrimination.
>
> This vicious situation, it seems to me, represents the very heart of the evils in education against which our campaign should be directed. It would be a great mistake to fritter away our limited funds in sporadic attempts to force the making of equal divisions of school funds in the few instances in which such attempts might be expected to succeed. At the most, we could eliminate a very minor part of the discrimination during the year that our suits are commenced. We should not be establishing any new principles, nor bringing any sort of pressure to bear which can reasonably be expected to retain the slightest force beyond that exerted by the specific judgment or order that we might obtain. And we should be leaving wholly untouched the very essence of the existing evils.
>
> On the other hand, if we boldly challenge the constitutionality of segregation if and when accompanied irremediably by discrimination, one can strike directly at the most prolific sources of discrimination. We can transform into an authoritative adjudication the principle of law, now only theoretically inferable from Yick Wo v. Hopkins,[13] that segregation coupled with discrimination resulting from the administrative action permitted but not required by state statute, is just as much a denial of equal protection of the laws as is segregation coupled with discrimination required by express statutory enactment. And the threat of using this

> adjudication as a means of destroying segregation itself, would always exert a real and powerful force at least to compel enormous improvement in the Negro schools through voluntary official action.[14]

Margold's legal insight was that the wide discretion permitted by state laws in the allocation of funds between white and black schools, and used as a shield behind which local officials could practice discrimination, could be turned into a sword ultimately to overturn the entire system of separate white and black schools. Although *Brown v. Board of Education* did not rest on Margold's legal ground of unconstitutionally broad discretion, it did rest on the irremediability of the discrimination resulting from legally segregated schools.

The Margold Report began rather than ended the debate within the African American leadership over the best way to attack discrimination in education. Another milestone in this debate is the 1935 yearbook of the *Journal of Negro Education*, published by the Howard University School of Education. That publication brought together thirteen African American leaders of diverse opinions to discuss "The Courts and the Negro Separate School." Among them were the pioneering black sociologist E. Franklin Frazier; Ralph Bunche, later a Nobel Peace Prize winner and United Nations undersecretary general; Alain Locke, the longtime head of the Philosophy department at Howard University, who received his bachelor and doctorate degrees from Harvard and was the first black Rhodes Scholar; W. E. B. Du Bois, the first black to receive a PhD from Harvard and an early member of the NAACP leadership and editor of its publication, *The Crisis*; Horace Mann Bond, later the first black president of Lincoln University and father of Julian Bond; and Charles H. Thompson, the founder and editor of the *Journal of Negro Education* and a longtime dean at Howard University. The participants debated whether separate black schools should continue, and under what circumstances, and whether court action should or should not be undertaken to end racially segregated schools.

The yearbook took as given that prior court decisions had already ruled separate but unequal schools for African Americans were unconstitutional.[15] But still open was whether blacks should seek equalization of the separate black schools, or admission of black students to white schools.

The psychological argument against separate black schools was advanced by Howard Hale Long, who became a prominent black psychologist. Although Long did not have the benefit of later research relied upon in *Brown*, his articulation of the negative psychological impacts of segregation presages those studies.[16]

Representing the opposite position was W. E. B. Du Bois. Commentators have often ignored that Du Bois shared the integrationist ideal for education of the other contributors to the 1935 yearbook. Du Bois differed from them in his view that separate black schools were still needed for a transitional period, until race relations could evolve to a point that black children would be educated with white children in a mutually accepting environment.

Du Bois noted that there were then four million African Americans of school age in the United States, of whom two million were in school, and of these, four-fifths were taught by forty-eight thousand African American teachers in separate schools. He stated that fewer than five hundred thousand were in mixed schools in the North, where they were taught almost exclusively by white teachers. He also stated that there were seventy-nine black universities and colleges with one thousand black teachers, plus a number of private black secondary schools.[17]

> The question which I am discussing is this: Are these separate schools and institutions needed? And the answer, to my mind, is perfectly clear. They are needed just so far as they are necessary for the proper education of the Negro race. The proper education of any people includes the sympathetic touch between teacher and pupil; knowledge on the part of the teacher, not simply of the individual taught, but of his surroundings and background, and the history of his class and group; such contact between pupils, and between teacher and pupil, on the basis of perfect social equality, as will increase this sympathy and knowledge; facilities for education in equipment and housing, and the promotion of such extra-curricular activities as will tend to induct the child into life.[18]

Du Bois said that he would welcome a time when such an education could be obtained by blacks in integrated institutions.

> Much as I would like this, and hard as I have striven and shall strive to help realize it, I am no fool; and I know that race prejudice in the United States today is such that most Negroes cannot receive a proper education in white institutions. If the public schools of Atlanta, Nashville, New Orleans and Jacksonville were thrown open to all races tomorrow, the education that colored children would get in them would be worse than pitiable. It would not be education. And in the same way, there are many public school systems in the North where Negroes are admitted and tolerated, but they are not educated; they are crucified.

***

> But the futile attempt to compel even by law a group to do what it is determined not to do, is a silly waste of time, money and temper.[19]

Du Bois was equally unsparing of his peers. He stated that blacks unrealistically disparaged their own black schools and teachers. He attributed that disparagement, first, to a metaphysical unwillingness to accept segregation even as a temporary and opportunistic option, and second, to an ingrained black opinion that blacks on their own are unable to maintain schools that are equal to those maintained by whites.[20] He urged that blacks turn their pride, resources, and energy to building black educational institutions that would equal white institutions.[21]

> It is difficult to think of anything more important for the development of a people than proper training for their children; and yet I have seen wise and loving parents take infinite pains to force their little children into schools where the white children, white teachers and white parents despised and resented the dark child, made mock of it, neglected it, bullied it, and literally rendered its life a living hell. Such parents want their child to "fight" this thing out,—but dear God, at what a cost! Sometimes, to be sure, that child triumphs and teaches the school community a lesson; but even in such cases, the cost may be high, and the child's whole life turned into an effort to win cheap applause at the expense of healthy individuality. In other cases, the result of the experiment may be the complete ruin of character, gift, and ability and ingrained hatred of schools and men. For the kind of battle thus indicated, most children are under no circumstances suited. It is the refinement of cruelty to require it of them. Therefore, in evaluating the advantage and disadvantage of accepting race hatred as a brutal but real fact, or of using a little child as a battering ram upon which its nastiness can be thrust, we must give greater value and greater emphasis to the rights of the child's own soul.[22]

Contrast Du Bois's defense of separate black schools with the testimony of white psychologist Henry Garrett of Columbia University, who testified on behalf of the school board of Prince Edward County in 1952 in one of the companion cases to *Brown v. Board of Education*. Garrett was a native of Virginia and had received his early schooling there. Garrett is here being cross-examined by Robert L. Carter, who was one of the trial lawyers for the NAACP.

> Q. Do you consider, Dr. Garrett, that racial segregation, as presently practiced in the United States, and in Virginia, is a social situation which is adverse to the individual?
>
> A. It is a large question. In general, wherever a person is cut off from the main body of a society or group, if he is put in a position that stigmatizes him and makes him feel inferior, I would say yes, it is detrimental and deleterious to him.
>
> Q. . . . Do you know of any situation involving racial segregation of Negroes . . . where this stigmatism has not been put on the separation?
>
> A. I think, in the high schools of Virginia, if the Negro child had equal facilities, his own teachers, his own friends, and a good feeling, he would be more likely to develop pride in himself as a Negro, which I think we would all like to see him do – to develop his own potentialities, his sense of duty, his sense of art, his sense of histrionics . . . The Negroes might develop their schools up to the level where they would not [want to] mix, themselves; and I would like to see it happen. They would develop their sense of dramatic art, and music, which they seem to have a talent for – [and] athletics, and they would say, "We prefer to remain as a Negro group."[23]

Black arguments for separate black schools created an intellectual slippery slope. Du Bois saw black institutions as the best solution, at least for those times, for black achievement, because those institutions would encourage a sense of historical black identity and, he hoped, solidarity. But opponents of integration (who certainly would not have wished for Du Bois's separate black social movement) could apply the same reasoning to support segregation laws. Du Bois's 1935 yearbook article was cited, entirely out of context, as black authority supporting segregation by Prince Edward County's Supreme Court brief in one of the companion cases to *Brown*.[24] That, despite Du Bois's concluding point:

> I know that this article will forthwith be interpreted by certain illiterate "nitwits" as a plea for segregated Negro schools and colleges. It is not. It is simply calling a spade a spade. It is

> saying in plain English: that a separate Negro school, where children are treated like human beings, trained by teachers of their own race, who know what it means to be black in the year of salvation 1935, is infinitely better than making our boys and girls doormats to be spit and trampled upon and lied to by ignorant social climbers, whose sole claim to superiority is ability to kick "niggers" when they are down. I say, too, that certain studies and discipline necessary to Negroes can seldom be found in white schools.[25]

In the 1935 yearbook debate, support for achieving integration through court action was provided by Alain Locke and Charles H. Thompson, among others.

Locke argued that black defenders of separate black schools were advocating for short-term interests, such as continued careers for black teachers and administrators. He saw segregation in the South as a historical anomaly that arose because the separate private and missionary schools for blacks during Reconstruction were taken over as part of the public education system as that system developed. But although black schools became public, there was no corresponding commitment on the part of the Southern authorities to support those schools as public institutions.[26] Locke's argument for integration, like that of Margold, was based on practicalities:

> It may be argued that this principle [of equitable sharing of public funds] concedes "equal but separate accommodations." It does not and cannot,—for in the first place few if any communities can afford the additional expense of entirely equal accommodations, and it would require as much and the same kind of effort at the removal of the social bias of the community and the reform of its conscience to secure general admission of the principle of common equity as to secure the abolition of the dual system. Up to a certain point, communities will pay a price for prejudice, but not such an exhorbitant price as complete equality requires.[27]

But Locke also came down squarely in favor of the benefits of integration for both whites and blacks:

> . . . the student [in an integrated environment] is better conditioned to the eventual stress which he must undergo in the adult community and the white or non-Negro student will have the additional educative exposure and experience with Negro associates under more advantageous circumstances

> than the casual associations out of school life. Much of the arguments *pro* and *con* on this side of the issue assume absolute or minimal non-contact of whites and Negroes as children and as adults. This is contrary to fact,—there is considerable and often intimate association, especially in Southern communities. Only it is unfavorable and takes place under educationally disadvantageous conditions to both groups. The school is the logical and perhaps the only effective instrument for the corrective treatment of this situation. It is immediately tolerable to children, though unfortunately not to their parents under the prevailing traditions.

Locke believed that the addition of some social education to school programs would satisfactorily ease the transition to integrated schools.[28] And he was in favor of acting now:

> It is purely academic to argue the well-known relationship between law and public opinion or the written and unwritten law as an extenuation of a temporizing policy on this issue. Nothing is more contrary to fact than the rather widespread policy and program of gradualism.[29]

Thompson pointed out that in the South, control and administration of the separate black schools were almost exclusively in the hands of whites and that blacks had no meaningful voice through elected office or otherwise to challenge inequities.[30] The courts therefore were the only place in which relief could possibly be obtained. The question, then, was whether seeking relief in the courts would have greater advantages or disadvantages. Thompson concluded that based on white reactions to prior legal challenges to unequal segregated schools, blacks should not fear that white resistance would either be violent or obstructive.[31] He also argued that blacks have the best schools in the states in which the most lawsuits had been brought.[32] He urged that court decisions could lead public opinion.[33]

Although Thompson conceded the constitutionality of separate schools provided they were equal,[34] he believed that separate schools could not provide equal education. He gave three reasons: First, "to *segregate* is to *stigmatize*." Second, separate schools are uneconomical. "Those who argue that the separate school with equal facilities is superior to the mixed school with prejudice should know that the separate school, or separate anything, with equal facilities is a fiction." Third, the separate school "results in the *mis*-education of both races. . . . the Negro develops an almost ineradicable inferiority complex and evolves a set of Jim Crow standards and values; the white child develops an unwarranted sense of superiority – if not an actual contempt for or indifference toward the Negro. And both races develop a misunderstanding of each other that necessitates all of the expensive and ineffective race-relations machinery that we have in this country at the present time."[35]

In 1935, blacks were still being lynched, if less frequently than during the 1920s and prior decades. The Depression continued. Jim Crow laws were pervasive in the South. If not legally mandated in the North, racial separation was the norm. Through that clouded atmosphere, the 1935 yearbook offers a glimpse of these black intellectuals' shining hope, of their faith in their country and their fellow man, that inspired the quest for school desegregation. Their dream was the same as Martin Luther King Jr.'s in his 1963 speech at the Washington Monument. Whether their faith and hope were justified is still a question to be debated.

After winning some cases that required black graduate or professional students to be admitted to white institutions,[36] the NAACP under the legal leadership of Thurgood Marshall turned its attention to segregated public schools. By the time the five cases ultimately decided by the Supreme Court in *Brown* went to trial, Marshall had obtained a resolution of a black leadership conference at Howard University in June 1950 that pleadings in all future education cases would be aimed at obtaining education on a nonsegregated basis and no relief other than that would be acceptable.[37] But participants in the desegregation effort differ as to the extent of grassroots support for that decision. Richard Kluger refers to a statement by William Hastie, a former dean of Howard Law School and federal appellate judge:

> A lot of the black communities around the country had the bit between their teeth by then. They were just fed up with what we called "doghouse education," and it was clear that the segregation fight was going to be pushed at the secondary- and elementary-school level, NAACP or not. It would have been futile to try damming the tide of human emotion that had been let loose.[38]

The late Robert L. Carter was a leading attorney for the NAACP and the Legal Defense Fund from 1944 through 1968. Carter disagreed with Mark Tushnet's conclusion in 1987 that the NAACP's decision to attack segregation was motivated by a perceived desire of the organization's rapidly growing membership.[39] Carter (then serving as a US District Court judge) stated in 1988,

> I believe the Association could have held back on its all-out attack on [school] segregation without adverse organizational effect. While the national staff was committed to

> an attack on segregation per se, there was no compelling demand from the local units that such an attack be launched. Local units would have been satisfied at the time if the organization had opted for litigation merely to upgrade the black schools. Indeed, black teachers and principals were very wary about the attack on segregation, and with good reason. Our success cost a number of them their jobs [citation omitted], even if they benefited in the long run.
>
> . . . The black community was divided on the issue. Some felt very strongly that a direct attack on segregation would be irresponsible behavior because of the possibility of failure, while others were convinced that such an attack was the only prudent course. I believe that the majority sentiment in the black community was a desire to secure for blacks all of the educational nurturing available to whites. If ending school desegregation was the way to that objective, fine; if, on the other hand, securing equal facilities was the way, that too was fine.[40]

Carter believed that the presentation of W. E. B. DuBois at the 1950 conference was among the most influential in gaining support for ending school desegregation. DuBois, according to Carter, did not take a direct position on the issue, but emphasized the economic exploitation of blacks and that "blacks had to become knowledgeable about the ways and means of such exploitation in order to free themselves from bondage."[41]

The arguments in the 1935 yearbook had been resolved, at least for the time.

The five cases decided in *Brown* were chosen as test cases by the NAACP Legal Defense Fund[42] largely on the basis of local conditions and black community support. The five cases originated in Clarendon County, South Carolina; Topeka, Kansas; Claymont and Hockessin, Delaware; and Prince Edward County, Virginia. Richard Kluger opens his history of school desegregation with the story of the black plaintiffs and local retaliation against them in the South Carolina case.[43] The NAACP used a variety of expert witnesses to illustrate the social and psychological damage of segregated schools. Its opponents fought back with experts of their own. The federal district courts in South Carolina, Kansas, and Virginia and the Delaware chancery court all refused to hold that segregation was per se unconstitutional.[44]

But the NAACP's strategy to end segregated schools prevailed at the Supreme Court. This book is about the long, hard, and divisive process of implementing *Brown* in one Southern county. To understand that process, it is necessary to understand as best we can what *Brown* did and did not decide.

The Equal Protection Clause of the Fourteenth Amendment to the US Constitution, on which *Brown* is based, is a fairly simple statement that no state may act in a way that discriminates against any person on the basis of race:

> (1) . . . No State shall make or enforce any law which shall . . . deny to any person within its jurisdiction the equal protection of the laws.[45]

The Supreme Court reviewed the historical background of the amendment (discussed in chapter 3, supra) and failed to find conclusive evidence that it should or should not be applied to segregated schools. We can speculate that a court subscribing to today's originalist theory of legal analysis, using the same evidence, might well have decided to uphold de jure segregation. Cutting this knot, the *Brown* court then found:

> In approaching this problem, we cannot turn the clock back to 1868 when the Amendment was adopted, or even to 1896 when *Plessy v. Ferguson* was written. We must consider public education in the light of its full development and its present place in American life throughout the Nation. Only in this way can it be determined if segregation in public schools deprives these plaintiffs of equal protection of the laws.
>
> Today, education is perhaps the most important function of state and local governments. Compulsory school attendance laws and the great expenditures for education both demonstrate our recognition of the importance of education to our democratic society. It is required in the performance of our most basic public responsibilities, even service in the armed forces. It is the very foundation of good citizenship. Today it is a principal instrument in awakening the child to cultural values, in preparing him for later professional training, and in helping him to adjust normally to his environment. In these days it is doubtful that any child may reasonably be expected to succeed in life if he is denied the opportunity of an education. Such an opportunity, where the state has undertaken to provide it, is a right which must be made available to all on equal terms.[46]

In *Brown* the court held, "Separate educational facilities are inherently unequal."[47] Twenty-four years after the Margold Report, the court used more recent sociological evidence, much of which had been introduced by the NAACP Legal Defense Fund in the lower-court cases, to hold that the unconstitutional irremediability results from "a feeling of inferiority that may affect [children's] hearts and minds in a way unlikely ever to be undone."[48] Funding disparities had been recognized as unconstitutional by some of the lower-court decisions reviewed by the Supreme Court in *Brown*, but the Supreme Court preempted the argument that equal allocation of tangible assets between white and black schools could ever make de jure separate schools constitutional.[49] By this ruling, the court spared both plaintiffs and school boards from the endless, inconclusive litigation feared by Margold over equality of separate schools.

The path to the Supreme Court decision in *Brown* was blazed by the African American lawyers of the NAACP Legal Defense Fund. They had at their disposal only the meager funds that could be raised by that organization's own efforts and the donated services of other legal experts (some of whom were white). The cases were first argued before the US Supreme Court on December 9, 1952, and reargued a year later on December 8, 1953. When the Supreme Court ordered that *Brown* be reargued, the NAACP Legal Defense Fund was out of money and had to make an emergency appeal for another $15,000.[50] When the five cases were reargued to the Supreme Court, the United States solicitor general at last intervened and filed a brief in support of desegregation but was not allowed to present oral argument. A number of other organizations filed amicus curiae briefs supporting desegregation. But there was no federal Civil Rights Act, no Office of Education to enforce federal desegregation standards, and no government support of any kind at the trial stage.[51] Thurgood Marshall's teams traveled and worked under hostile conditions, gave courage to fearful black plaintiffs who often faced retaliation by white opponents, and sought support from often-divided black communities. African Americans won the victory in *Brown*.

One year after its first decision in *Brown I*, the Supreme Court considered enforcement of that decision. It was in that *Brown II* opinion that the phrase "all deliberate speed" appears. *Brown II* held that the goal of enforcement was "to effectuate a transition to a racially nondiscriminatory school system."[52]

To enforce desegregation, the Supreme Court turned to the US District Courts (in 1955, before the passage of the Civil Rights Act of 1964, there was no other alternative). The Supreme Court hoped that local school boards would take the initiative, but that court understood that having raised the issue to one of constitutional principle, only the federal court system could judge whether school boards had complied.[53]

In 1955, the Supreme Court in *Brown II* did not define what would constitute a "racially nondiscriminatory school system." *Brown* did not resolve whether historically black public schools would or could continue side by side with the newly integrated schools. That vacuum was soon filled. After the US Supreme Court decisions in *Brown*, each of the five companion cases decided by the Supreme Court were remanded to the respective courts from which they originated with instructions to implement the Supreme Court decisions. *Briggs v. Elliott* was remanded to the US District Court for South Carolina. That court, taking up the Supreme Court's invitation to consider local conditions, in 1955 interpreted *Brown* to have only a limited impact on de jure dual-race school systems:

> [The Supreme Court] has not decided that the federal courts are to take over or regulate the public schools of the states. It has not decided that the states must mix persons of different races in the schools or must require them to attend schools or must deprive them of the right of choosing the schools they attend. What [the Supreme Court] has decided, and all that it has decided, is that a state may not deny to any person on account of race the right to attend any school that it maintains. This, under the decision of the Supreme Court, the state may not do directly or indirectly; but if the schools which it maintains are open to children of all races, no violation of the Constitution is involved even though the children of different races voluntarily attend different schools, as they attend different churches. Nothing in the Constitution or in the decision of the Supreme Court [in *Brown*] takes away from the people freedom to choose the schools they attend. The Constitution, in other words, does not require integration. It merely forbids discrimination. It does not forbid such segregation as occurs as a result of voluntary action. It merely forbids the use of governmental power to *enforce* segregation. The Fourteenth Amendment is a limitation upon the exercise of power by the state or state agencies, not a limitation upon the freedom of individuals.[54]

All the Equal Protection Clause required school districts to do, under this interpretation, was to end any actions that *denied* equal protection of the law. School districts were not required to act affirmatively under the Equal Protection Clause to secure equal rights for citizens. Professor Daniel

J. Meador of the University of Virginia Law School concluded optimistically that "no general realignment of pupils in a formerly segregated school system is legally necessitated by *Brown*, and furthermore . . . permitting of racially separate schools is consistent with the Constitution, so long as no official compulsion is present" [footnote omitted].[55] This interpretation of *Brown* provided a legal justification for freedom-of-choice desegregation plans. The federal Fifth Circuit Court of Appeals, which then included Florida, quickly adhered to this opinion. Other federal circuits that covered Southern states also relied on it.[56]

The Civil Rights Act of 1964, and the issuance of desegregation guidelines by the Department of Health, Education, and Welfare under that law, would solidify, at least for a time, the legal basis for freedom-of-choice desegregation. The real crisis for Alachua County and other Southern school districts would not come until the courts, again principally at the insistence of the NAACP Legal Defense Fund, came to question whether freedom of choice satisfied *Brown*'s mandate for racially nondiscriminatory school systems.

CHAPTER 5
ALACHUA COUNTY'S FIRST STEPS TO SCHOOL DESEGREGATION

> One of the "musts" in our educational program is to get your Negro schools comparable to the white system if we are to preserve segregation.
>
> Howard Bishop, Alachua County school superintendent, 1951

> Wright believes the school board was leaning toward desegregation but would never have taken the step voluntarily. Politically and socially, it wasn't going to be easy. The suit removed the burden.
>
> "They were waiting for us to make the move," said Wright. "I really believe they were relieved once we filed suit."
>
> The Reverend Thomas A. Wright, in the *Gainesville Sun*, January 25, 1970

> Each person in our schools and our community must share in the responsibility for seeing that a smooth and orderly transition takes place. This does not mean that each person must be in favor of desegregation; it means that each person will accept responsibility for meeting the situation in such a manner that the children do not suffer either educationally or emotionally.
>
> William S. Talbot
> May 24, 1965

The Alachua County school board in the early 1950s was still committed to segregation. By that time, population growth had produced overcrowding in many of the county's schools, and especially at Gainesville and Lincoln

High Schools. The county began to plan for construction of a new white high school. But School Superintendent Howard Bishop reminded citizens in 1951, "One of the 'musts' in our educational program is to get your Negro schools comparable to the white system if we are to preserve segregation." R. L. Johns, a University of Florida professor who would later critique the school board's 1968 construction plans, said in the same year, "If you do not build a new Negro high school along with the white school, then the Negroes can sue and get in the white school."[1]

A 1953 bond issue (probably associated with the Florida legislature's $100 million plan for new school construction) enabled the construction of four new high schools in Alachua County. Two white high schools were built: Gainesville High, which moved from a building that had been constructed in 1923, and Santa Fe Junior/Senior High, which replaced smaller schools in the northwest part of the county (the Santa Fe River, named for the Spanish colonial mission of Santa Fe de Toluca, forms the northern boundary of Alachua County). The new Lincoln High School (to enroll grades 7–12), constructed in a newer black neighborhood on the southeast side of Gainesville, replaced the old Lincoln High building that had also been constructed in 1923. A. L. Mebane Junior/Senior High consolidated black secondary school facilities in the northwest county. The new GHS opened in the 1955–56 school year, and the three other schools opened in 1956–57.[2] Under *Brown*, continuing to maintain a dual school system, by itself, as yet raised no constitutional issues. That the school board built the new black high schools at least in part to keep blacks from wanting to go to the white schools did not infringe any rights that were then enforceable even after *Brown*.

The Alachua County school board's first direct response to *Brown* was its implementation of the Florida pupil-assignment law. Beginning in 1956, the school board adopted pupil-assignment resolutions.[3] The initial resolution froze in place the existing segregated school system and provided that any changes in pupil assignments would have to comply with the pupil-assignment law. According to school board attorney Winston Arnow,[4] the resolution text followed similar resolutions used in North Carolina.[5] The *Gainesville Sun* stated that Alachua County schools would at least for the time being remain segregated, until any pupil transfers could be processed under the resolution.[6] In December 1960, probably in response to recent Fifth Circuit decisions,[7] a revised resolution[8] was adopted on the advice of Attorney Arnow.

The 1960 school board resolution required the board to assign every student to a school for each school year. The student and his or her parent were to be notified of the school assignment by the board. A parent desiring assignment of his or her child to a different school had to file a written application with the school board within seven days of the registration date for such school, or such other period specified by the school board. Applicants could be required by the board to take tests to document their suitability for enrollment at the school that they wished to attend. The board was to evaluate applications using the factors provided in Section 2 of the pupil-assignment law,[9] which were recited in the resolution. The board had to set attendance zones for each school. This resolution remained in effect for subsequent years.

In the early part of 1962, as editor of the *Hurricane Herald* at Gainesville High School, I found myself in the principal's office. The principal was William S. Talbot.

In search of stories about something besides our beloved Purple Hurricanes, and perhaps a Florida Scholastic Press Association award, we had taken a survey of the student body. This survey was not just a sample. One question went something like, "Are you in favor of integrating the schools?" Eight years after the decision in *Brown v. Board of Education*, no African Americans yet attended school with whites in Alachua County. No one had thought to stop us from asking the question, and we did not have the sense not to ask. The answer came back, as best I recall, 62 percent "no."

No one had to tell me that I was not going to publish this answer. But the faculty adviser, Peg Westmoreland, and I decided that Mr. Talbot should know of the result. I made an appointment to see him. I gave him the news. He said, gesturing to his shoulders, "Mike, my shoulders are big and broad. I can handle whatever comes. But I'm just not ready."

Neither of us could know then that Talbot would, as superintendent, preside over the desegregation of Alachua County's schools beginning in 1965. Talbot's candid answer is the answer that any school administrator would have given, off the record, to that question. Virtually no one, in the South and in other places such as Boston and Chicago, was ready for the changes that were still to take place under *Brown*. But despite his misgivings, Talbot in 1962 gave assurance that he would be equal to the challenge when it finally came.

Alachua County in 1963 held a referendum under a state constitutional amendment to decide whether its school superintendent would continue to be elected or would be appointed by the school board.[10] Some feared that the current superintendent, E. D. Manning Jr., would be appointed by the school board to serve indefinitely if the referendum passed. Talbot was then still principal of Gainesville High. One week before the referendum, Talbot publicly voiced his opposition to appointing the superintendent.[11] Shortly thereafter, he privately offered his resignation as GHS principal to the school board.[12] The appointment referendum failed,[13] but as a result the field was open for electing a new superintendent. After the referendum, Talbot's resignation letter became public, but its contents were probably no secret. In that letter, he stated that he planned to seek the superintendency, whether it was elected or appointed.[14]

Talbot formally announced his candidacy on January 9, 1964.[15] Publicly, Talbot said in 1972 that he believed county teachers did not favor Manning, under whom, he alleged, teacher salaries had increased only $400 in eight years. So Talbot ran to increase teacher pay but then found out as superintendent that there were no funds available for teacher raises.[16] Talbot's son Butch (without direct evidence from his father) believes that Talbot decided to run for superintendent mainly because Talbot genuinely believed that he had the fortitude and intelligence to perform the job better than any other foreseeable candidate.[17] The late Tommy Tomlinson, who later would serve Talbot as deputy superintendent, said Talbot decided to run because Talbot had serious reservations about Manning's capability.[18]

Talbot was opposed by Harry Evans, a former educator with a doctorate in education. Talbot won election on May 5, 1964, by a margin of 11,139 to 4,030 for Evans. Talbot carried all precincts, black and white, except for three small rural precincts.[19] He would not take office until January 1965.

The Gainesville High faculty loved Talbot. At one of his last meetings with the faculty, he was given some good rolls of toilet paper. The presenters told Tiny that when he became superintendent, they wanted better toilet paper in the school's bathrooms. Sometime after Tiny was sworn in, a new shipment of toilet paper arrived at the school. It was purple.[20]

As elected superintendent, Talbot (as did his predecessors) made sure that graduates of local high schools would receive favorable consideration when, as college graduates, they applied for teaching jobs.[21] That practice, which was followed in both the white and black schools, meant that generations of students could follow in the footsteps of their former teachers. Traditions and skills were passed from generation to generation. Teacher alumni of Alachua County schools knew the families of their students. Despite that practice, by the 1960s only a small minority of Alachua County teachers were alumni of county high schools.

Many teachers contributed to superintendent election campaigns, but in those days the amounts were small. Superintendent elections allowed teachers a voice in the schools that they would not have had if the same resources had been spread among the five elected school board members. Even during the years when the county elected its superintendent, though, teachers and administrators sometimes became actively involved in school board campaigns.[22]

Talbot was not rule-bound, especially when the welfare of students or alumni was at stake. Tomlinson:

> Lots of kids left the system to go into the service, lacking maybe a half year or two or three credits to graduate. When

> they returned, and needed jobs, some would come to us [Tomlinson and Talbot] about their high school records. We would go over the records, and if they had been close to graduating we would speak to the principal and if he agreed we would issue them diplomas. Many officers in the Gainesville police department got their diplomas this way.[23]

During the campaign for election as superintendent, Talbot said that GHS was prepared to accept a black student for the 1963–64 school year, but that she withdrew her application.[24] There is no evidence suggesting that any attempt had been made previously to desegregate the Alachua County public schools.[25]

But it was soon clear that African Americans would press for desegregation in the 1964–65 school year. In the spring of 1964, according to the school board, the parents of fifteen black students requested transfers to what were then exclusively white schools by filing preference cards.[26] Those applications, together with all fifty-nine other transfer requests, were denied by the school board, apparently on April 29, 1964.[27] Under the school board's procedures, the parents of all students whose preferences were denied could take the next step by requesting assignment in accordance with their previously expressed preferences. Of the fifteen black students whose preference cards requested transfers to white schools, eleven took the next step and asked for assignments from the school board.[28] The school board initially denied all of those applications, apparently on June 9, 1964.[29]

Ironically, just at the time the school board was digging in its heels, integration surfaced as an issue in the campaigns to fill two of the five school board seats and to elect a new superintendent. At the end of April 1964, three of the four candidates for the two open school board seats and both candidates for superintendent (Tiny Talbot and Harry Evans) pledged to plan for the orderly, peaceful integration of schools.[30] The positions of all of these candidates were consistent with those of other community leaders, as we saw in chapter 2. Almost ten years had passed since the "noise and confusion" of 1955 and 1956. Even if they were not calling for immediate desegregation, none of the local white leaders wanted the confrontations that they knew would follow resistance.

By applying for assignments to white schools, the black parents attempted to comply with the Florida pupil-assignment law and the school board's pupil-assignment resolution without filing a court case.[31] In a 1970 interview, the Reverend Thomas A. Wright Sr., who was president of the local NAACP chapter, said that black leaders approached the school board to ask for voluntary integration before filing suit. He added that his group tried to obtain assistance from the city's biracial committee. That committee responded, according to Wright, that it only represented the city of Gainesville but the school board was a county-wide organization.

> Wright believes the school board was leaning toward desegregation but would never have taken the step voluntarily. Politically and socially, it wasn't going to be easy. The suit removed the burden.
>
> "They were waiting for us to make the move," said Wright. "I really believe they were relieved once we filed suit."[32]

In a recent interview, Wright confirmed that the school board would not move voluntarily: "They had us to understand that this was out of the question."[33]

The superintendent at the time, E. D. Manning Jr., and Tommy Tomlinson, who under Superintendent Talbot was the county staff member most closely involved with desegregation, disagreed when interviewed in 1970. They believed it unlikely that the NAACP lawsuit accelerated action to desegregate the schools.[34]

By July 1964, the black parents were not going to wait any longer for the school board to act. Fourteen students, eleven of whom were black and three of whom were white, through their parents filed a class action on July 2, 1964, in federal district court for an injunction forbidding the Alachua County school board and Superintendent Manning to operate a "compulsory biracial school system."[35] The action also asked the court to order the school board, within a period of time to be determined by the court, to present a plan for the reorganization of the county's school system into a "unitary nonracial system."[36] This distinction is important; in 1964 it was clear from *Brown* that a compulsory biracial school system was illegal, but the courts had not yet determined whether the South's dual-race school systems would have to be merged into single systems serving both races. When the courts eventually took the second step, the South would finally have to confront the fundamental educational issues posed by desegregation. The students were represented by lawyers from the NAACP Legal Defense and Educational Fund Inc., Constance Baker Motley[37] and the late Jack Greenberg, and by local counsel Earl M. Johnson of Jacksonville, Florida.

The school board and Superintendent Manning had lost whatever opportunity they may have had to avoid court supervision of the Alachua County schools. Although we will never know, they may have preferred passing the integration buck to the court, as suggested by the Rev. Wright. The federal lawsuit would remain active for fourteen years.

The Reverend Wright was forty-two years old and married, with four children, one of whom was in college, when he moved with his family from St. Augustine to Gainesville in August 1962. His wife, Affie Mae Clayton Wright, was a teacher in the Alachua County schools. He had been active in the civil rights movement in St. Augustine, where he had been pastor of Saint Mary's Baptist Church. He came under pressure in St. Augustine because of his activism and decided to leave his church there. Rev. Wright moved to Gainesville after obtaining an appointment as pastor of Mount Carmel Baptist Church, which was then located on NW Fifth Avenue in one of the city's historically black neighborhoods.[38]

Rev. Wright by his own account initially wanted to avoid the kind of conflict in which he had been involved in St. Augustine.[39] He states that he was warned by his brother that Gainesville was one of the headquarters for the Ku Klux Klan in Florida (Gainesville had been a center of Klan activity in the 1920s; at one point the mayor and police chief were acknowledged Klan members).[40] But Rev. Wright's reputation as a community leader had followed him to Gainesville. Soon after his arrival, he was asked to serve as president of the local NAACP chapter. He initially agreed to do so for six months but served in that position for seventeen years.[41] He led the effort to file the lawsuit against the school board, and his daughter, LaVon Wright, was one of the named plaintiffs in the suit.

Subsequent to the filing of the federal court case, the school board voted on July 9, 1964, to assign three black students to Gainesville High School commencing in September 1964 but denied the transfer application of one student.[42] Those three students, LaVon Wright, Joel Buchanan, and Sandra Williams, became the first black students to attend white schools in the Alachua County system.[43] By October 1964, the school board reported that it had granted the assignment applications of the remaining seven black students who the board said had sought to attend white schools.[44]

The Alachua County desegregation case was initially filed in Pensacola, but it was assigned to the court's Gainesville division and to District Judge G. Harrold Carswell, who was then sitting at Gainesville.[45] Despite allowing all but one of the black applicants to attend white schools in the 1964–65 school year, the school board immediately opposed the federal lawsuit, contending that it was not operating a segregated school system.[46] Attorney Arnow argued that since 1956, when the board adopted its initial resolution under the state pupil-placement law, the system was no longer segregated.[47] In 1964, that argument was inconsistent with established law in the Fifth Circuit. The Court of Appeals for the Fifth Circuit had ruled in 1959 that Florida school boards could not claim to have satisfied constitutional desegregation obligations solely because of Florida's pupil-assignment law.[48] But the Supreme Court had not ruled on that issue.

Attorney Arnow also adopted a legal argument current at the time among opponents of integration that the Fourteenth Amendment to the US Constitution was itself unconstitutional because it had not been properly adopted. Attorney Arnow focused on the amendment's proposal by only thirty-three members of the US Senate, of a total of seventy-two, there being thirty-six states at the time of the amendment's proposal on June 8, 1866.[49] It would be tempting to accuse Attorney Arnow and the board of taking an extreme, or even frivolous, position in defense of segregation. However, this argument was also being made by the State of Florida in *McLaughlin v. Florida*, then pending before the US Supreme Court. As a lawyer with ethical obligations to represent his client diligently, he could hardly have omitted the argument. Although the State of Florida argued the issue,[50] the Supreme Court ignored the point in finding against the State.[51] This and other similar challenges to the Fourteenth Amendment failed.[52] So emotional was the reaction to *Brown* that Southern supporters of segregation were even moved to revisit alleged illegalities of Reconstruction.

Curiously, at the same time that the school board argued that black students were free to choose to attend white schools, the board also stated that it almost never granted any requests by students (white or black) to attend schools other than the ones to which they had initially been assigned.[53]

After receiving the initial pleadings, the federal court took no further action on *Wright v. Board* until April 1965. By then, under new Superintendent Talbot, the school system had obtained Department of Health, Education, and Welfare approval of a desegregation plan under Title VI of the Civil Rights Act of 1964. Such a plan was needed if the schools were to continue receiving federal funds.[54]

The Alachua County plan was announced March 2, 1965, following two months of study.[55] The school board, in introducing the plan, noted that in 1963 the population of Alachua County was estimated to be 86,300, comprised of 56,173 white and 30,127 black citizens. The public schools served 13,534 white students and 6,396 black students with 563 white and 263 black teachers.

The plan described portions of the school system's programs that had already been integrated, such as the Manpower Program, vocational education, adult education, salary schedules for all personnel, four schools (including GHS, Buchholz Junior High, Stephen Foster Elementary School, and P. K. Yonge), staff meetings and training programs, and the school camp ("integration" as used in the plan included even token integration). The plan stated, "To some sections of the country the above seems a slow-moving integration program. Our community feels that we have made great strides in moving toward an integrated school program. All of our efforts have been made without incident or adverse publicity."[56] The plan recited that during the two months of study, meetings had been held among the superintendent, the school board and its administrative staff, and the public, as well as with county, state, and federal officials. Continued community meetings and in-service programs for school staff were to take place according to the plan prior to the commencement of classes in the fall of 1965.

The new plan did not change the basic premise that black students wishing to attend formerly white schools had to declare their desire to do so. The new plan differed from the 1960 board resolution under the pupil-assignment law by requiring student preferences to be honored except in exceptional circumstances, and by more explicit written advice to students and their parents of their right to school choice. Omitted from communications was language that had previously reserved the board's right under the pupil-assignment law to consider "attendance area, transportation facilities, uniform testing, available facilities, scholastic aptitude, and other factors, except race."[57]

A key provision in the plan stated that students requiring transportation would normally ride the buses that regularly served the school they attended (although the board could require students to ride other buses).[58] The board thus bound itself to provide transportation to black students who desired to attend white schools.

Although the plan itself made no reference to attendance zones for individual schools, board officials testified that the dual zones formerly in effect for white and black schools in Alachua County had been abolished effective for the 1965–66 school year.[59]

Apparently concerned that transfer floodgates might be opened by the new plan, the school board required that when a student requested assignment to another school, the principal of the receiving school had to confirm that the receiving school had not reached its capacity prior to the student's transfer.[60] However, under the plan, in the event of insufficient space in any school, pupils were to be assigned on the basis of proximity to that school.[61] Presumably to make more space in the Gainesville schools, out-of-county residents were excluded from all Gainesville schools but were allowed to enroll in county schools outside of Gainesville.[62]

With respect to staff, the Alachua County plan stated that it would continue to be the policy of the board to employ and assign teachers on the basis of their qualifications, but that no changes would be made in teaching assignments except as necessary to fill vacancies. The plan stated that a personnel study would be initiated immediately by the board and superintendent.[63] Following this study, the school board voted that individual school principals would be permitted to hire new teachers without regard to race, color, or national origin.[64] That change satisfied the first of two requirements of the HEW 1965 General Statement for staff, published by the Department of Health, Education, and Welfare in April 1965, that race could not be used as a basis for the initial assignment of staff who served pupils.[65] There is no record of any steps taken at that time by the board to satisfy the second HEW requirement, that steps be taken toward elimination of segregation of teaching personnel and staff resulting from prior segregation.[66]

Superintendent Talbot was to take the lead in publicizing the plan and explaining it to the community. The central school administrative staff and school principals and teachers were also enlisted in this effort.[67]

Attorney Arnow on March 17, 1965, filed the school board's Title VI plan with the federal district court in a supplemental answer.

District Judge Carswell held a hearing on the plan on April 6, 1965. Attorney Earl M. Johnson, representing the plaintiffs, objected to the plan on several grounds. As reported in the press, Attorney Johnson made clear that the NAACP Legal Defense Fund sought a fully unitary school system, not side-by-side white and black schools. Johnson contended that the school board's freedom-of-choice plan "is pregnant with the opportunity for economic reprisal."[68] Judge Carswell responded (without explicit reference to *Briggs v. Elliott*) that the law did not require school integration, merely an end to compulsory segregation. He stated that the Alachua County plan went as far as any of which he was aware in cases in the US Fifth Circuit Court of Appeals. In response to Attorney Johnson's objection that the plan did not require desegregation of faculties, Judge Carswell responded that he would adhere to decisions in prior school suits, which did not yet require desegregation of faculties.[69]

In his April 7 decree, Judge Carswell found that the plaintiffs had not established that the Alachua County public schools had been segregated by compulsion, but found that prior to September 1964, there had been de facto segregation. He found that the plaintiffs were entitled to a decree placing the Alachua County schools under court supervision. He found that the school board's Title VI plan complied with all requirements of law. Judge Carswell therefore approved the school board's Title VI plan as the court-ordered plan for operation of the Alachua County public schools. He denied the plaintiffs' requested injunction related to integration and stated that consideration would be reserved "pending demonstration of good faith compliance" by the school board with the plan as ordered.[70]

Under HEW policy, school districts that were under court orders to desegregate would continue to be eligible for federal funds as long as they complied with those court orders.[71] Judge Carswell's decree therefore satisfied the obligation of the Alachua County school board to comply with Title VI of the Civil Rights Act. Judge Carswell rather than HEW would have the final say as to the adequacy of the school board's future compliance with the Civil Rights Act. HEW nevertheless would play a strong role through its regulations in defining compliance for all Southern school districts, including those that would continue under court supervision.

The attorneys for the black plaintiffs in the Alachua County case quickly moved to supplement the record and to amend the decree. They argued that the record "clearly shows the pattern, policy and practice of racial segregation complained of by plaintiffs and the court's failure to find 'that there has been compulsory segregation in the public schools' ignores this record."[72] The plaintiffs did not press this matter until December 1966, and the court took no further action in this case until April 1967.

Not until May 1968, in other litigation, would the Supreme Court end use of choice-based plans to satisfy constitutional standards when racially separate school systems persisted in spite of such plans.[73] The Alachua County litigation would play out simultaneously with similar litigation throughout the South. Freedom-of-choice plans to end segregation of schools were the preferred response in virtually all Southern school districts. Such plans would continue to be expressly permitted by the Department of Health, Education, and Welfare in its published rules and policies.[74] The NAACP Legal Defense Fund would eventually succeed in its arguments that free choice only resulted in the preservation of illegal dual-race school systems. But local school officials, who feared the disruptions that even token integration might cause, could not be expected to go beyond what their attorneys advised and what district court judges approved.

Superintendent Talbot reported in a memorandum dated May 24, 1965, after completion of the assignment process for the 1965–66 school year, that all 329 black students who had requested assignment to white schools under freedom-of-choice had been assigned to white schools. Those 329 black students were approximately 5 percent of the 6,600 black students expected to enroll in the system for 1965–66 and represented every grade level.[75] The superintendent also reported that his office would be a resource for the staff and teachers in preparing for these changes. A remedial reading program had been adopted, and the school system was now participating in the Head Start program. Twenty-four key Alachua County personnel were to attend Equal Educational Opportunities Institutes on Desegregation at the University of Florida. The system also applied for a federal grant to provide in-service training for teachers and other personnel to deal with problems related to desegregation.[76] Talbot concluded:

> Each person in our schools and our community must share in the responsibility for seeing that a smooth and orderly transition takes place. This does not mean that each person must be in favor of desegregation; it means that each person will accept responsibility for meeting the situation in such a

> manner that the children do not suffer either educationally or emotionally.

The county's desegregation plan was approved by the Department of Health, Education, and Welfare on June 9, 1965, with assistance from Congressman D. R. "Billy" Matthews.[77] At the first school board meeting of 1966, the board voted to commend school board attorney Winston Arnow for his work in the past year.[78]

Three years after my meeting as a GHS student with Talbot, he was now on point for the county's school-desegregation effort. Under his guidance, the school system had moved from resistance to compliance with the law, as found by the US District Court. In an assessment of race relations in Gainesville in November 1965, the *Gainesville Sun* reported, "The school integration picture, which has never been a source of serious criticism, is rosy, according to Talbot."[79]

Even more nonchalant, the school board in May 1966 rejected Talbot's proposal to allow Alachua County teachers and principals to participate in a desegregation institute at the University of Florida.[80] Under a federal grant, $24,000 would have been allocated to support attendance by Alachua County school personnel.[81]

The April 1965 HEW General Statement, together with the NAACP Legal Defense Fund's motion protesting the 1965 district court decree, served notice that the 1965 decree in *Wright v. Board* was only a first step toward a goal that so far remained undefined either by the courts or by HEW. Despite authorizing freedom-of-choice plans, the HEW 1965 General Statement provided,

> The responsibility to eliminate segregation rests with the school authorities and is not satisfied by rules and practices which shift the burden of removing discrimination to the class or classes of persons discriminated against.[82]

Although Alachua County had already met the General Statement's goal of some desegregation in all grades by the 1967–68 school year,[83] the relatively small number of black students in white schools (13 percent in 1966–67)[84] would become an issue for the 1967–68 school year.

And population growth and school plant deterioration were creating even more urgent problems for the schools that Talbot would have to deal with, at the same time as he continued to oversee desegregation.

CHAPTER 6
DESEGREGATION UNDER FREEDOM OF CHOICE

So we were put in, I guess, as test cases of what integration could be, I guess, and it wasn't something that we volunteered for. I'm sure that my dad had a well thought out vision of putting us in and preparing us for what was to come, because he certainly knew or had wind of, especially in talking to Tiny and others about what was going on in the system, as to what was going to come at some point anyway. So I guess his feeling was that "we put them here now, and perhaps at the moment that the fullness of integration happens, however it happens, whether it's completely voluntary or embraced by the system, or whether or not the system is brought into this kicking and screaming." We would already be there, and thus perhaps better able to navigate through whatever it was that was the result of decision making of those beyond the school laws.

John Dukes III, on attending J. J. Finley Elementary School in the fifth grade in 1966

I always thought that that was wrong. I felt if you were good enough to teach us, you should be good enough to teach your own kids. Okay. And so most of us that were contemporaries during that time really felt that that was unfair to us as children.

Donnie Batie, MD, who chose to remain at Lincoln High until it closed in 1970

From the 1965–66 school year through the first half of the 1969–70 school year, the Alachua County public schools operated under freedom-of-choice desegregation plans. The US District Court approved each of those plans, but the NAACP Legal Defense Fund continued to object, as it did in its other pending cases across the South. The Fund (and eventually the US Office of Education) argued that only the complete elimination of dual-race school systems would provide black children with the "racially nondiscriminatory school system" constitutionally required by *Brown II.*

That argument now placed the South's black schools in the crosshairs of the movement for equal educational opportunity, inside and outside the federal government. If all students, regardless of race, were to be assigned to a single school system, the necessary consequence would be the end of the exclusively black schools, either through desegregation or closure. As we observe the reaction of Alachua County's African American community, we need to remember that NAACP and government leaders perceived the black students in those schools to be victims, not beneficiaries.

Freedom of choice remains important, not as "token" desegregation but because it set expectations in both the white and black communities for the way a unitary school system might operate. The development of the legal attack on freedom of choice and its impact on Alachua County will be traced in later chapters. But, on the ground, how did freedom of choice operate during the years it was in effect? How did the students and teachers react and adapt?

The potential problems Alachua County would face, and recommended responses, were outlined by a biracial district Steering Committee Related to Desegregation in September 1965. On the one hand, there was fear that black students would not measure up to academic standards in the white schools. "Negro educator is caught in the middle because parents will blame students' lack of progress on past teachers. All teachers must understand this so the correct action can be taken when talking to parents." And, "Child now enrolled must stay even though he is being used by parents or other groups." On the other hand, black students were expected to meet the same standards as white students: "Grades should be fair and if teacher or principal feel child should be put back or fail, take proper action. Communicate with parents first. This has proven to work best."[1]

Alachua County cannot be faulted for placing barriers in the way of African American students who chose to attend the white schools. Many black students in those schools were highly motivated and succeeded academically. Many joined varsity sports teams, student government, and, to a lesser extent, other extracurricular activities. Shelton Boyles, a white English teacher at Gainesville High School who would later be elected to the school board, concludes that the blacks who attended the white schools under freedom of choice smoothed the way for the end of the county's dual school system.[2] But the perceived success of freedom of choice masked a set of issues that would not emerge until the closing or desegregation of the county's separate black schools in 1970. Subsequently, we will consider the reasons that the progress made under freedom of choice failed to prepare the county for full desegregation.

During freedom of choice in Alachua County, many members of the African American community continued their support of the two historically black high schools, hoping (without any basis in the continuing court proceedings) that those schools would be given equal resources rather than being closed. Table 2 (see appendix) shows the numbers of black students who transferred to historically white schools during freedom of choice, as reported to the US District Court by the Alachua County school board. In summary, from 12 blacks enrolled in white schools in 1964–65, the first year of desegregation in Alachua County, 2,603 black students, or 39 percent[3] of black students in the county, had elected to attend historically white schools in 1969–70, the last year of freedom of choice. In Gainesville, the percentages were higher, with 54 percent of black students in grades K–6 attending white schools, 29 percent of black students in grades 7–9, and 32 percent of black students in grades 10–12. Some of the increase at the elementary school level in Gainesville is attributed to the unitary zoning plan for Gainesville elementary schools proposed by the school board and approved by the US District Court for the 1969–70 school year.[4] To encourage additional desegregation, the plan provided that students at schools in which the student's race was in the majority could transfer to a school in which the student's race was in the minority.[5]

The impending closure of Lincoln and Mebane High Schools had been public since December 15, 1967. The black community did not begin to protest those closures until February 1969. It is possible that the school board's decision to close the two black schools may have contributed to declining enrollment.

Although black students and their parents did not abandon the historically black schools, ever-increasing numbers of black students were attending white schools. Had the county not changed over to a unitary system in February 1970, the continued exodus from the historically black secondary schools would have imperiled their continued viability. Freedom-of-choice desegregation also affected Lincoln's football team and band as some of the outstanding players and band members chose to attend Gainesville High.[6]

Table 3. Lincoln and Mebane Enrollment, 1965–1969[7]

School, grades	Sept. 1965	Sept. 1967	Sept. 1968	Sept. 1969
Lincoln, 7–12	1,584	1,499	1,510	1,271
Lincoln, 10–12		545	597	569
Mebane, 7–12		667	600	576
Mebane, 10–12		308	270	251

The first black students who attended white schools endured resentment and isolation, both at the white schools and within their own communities. Joel Buchanan, one of the first three black students to attend Gainesville High School in September 1964 before Alachua County's freedom-of-choice plan was adopted, was required to take tests by the school board under Florida's Pupil Placement Law. He entered as a junior. "All I used to hear as a child was, the white children do not do these things, the white kids are this and the white kids are that and you heard all these fantastic things about white folks, oh, they were just perfect. Now they were going to have a black boy go to the school. I became a man without a world, or a boy without a world. The blacks at Lincoln High School did not care for me because I was leaving their school, going to a white institution, and of course, the whites did not want me."[8]

When it became known that the three black students would be attending GHS, Lincoln's Assistant Principal Daphne Duval Williams called them to her house for counseling about the risks that they would face. Buchanan recalled Williams' caution:

> I could be killed. I would be hurt. My life would be an open book. I was definitely going to fail. The pictures I had seen on television of the kids in Alabama going to school with the governor standing there saying, "We won't let you in," with the state trooper cars. I remember looking at the television when the President of the United States decided, or said, "We're going to send the troops in to see if those boys and girls get into that school." That same thing could happen here. I was leaving friends that I had been in school with from first grade; all of a sudden, I would not be with them any more. I would be the only black boy in the large school and Gainesville High was larger than Lincoln High School.[9]

In retrospect, Buchanan's account of that session portrays a dedicated, lifetime black school educator trying to come to terms with desegregation, as much as she wanted to assure herself that the three students' consents were truly informed. After Lincoln closed in 1969, Duval Williams would be assigned as an assistant principal at formerly white Howard Bishop Junior High. She retired in 1971.[10] Duval Williams had started teaching at Lincoln in 1928 and held many key positions there, in addition to teaching math. In a 1972 interview, she said the blacks clamored for integration at first, then they were so hurt by what was happening that they turned against it.[11]

The first three African American students to attend GHS did not ride the bus but were driven to school every day by the Reverend Thomas A.

Wright. Wright states that the FBI kept in close touch with him during that year.[12] Buchanan says that along the route they drove to school, there were police cars at different points. He also believes that there was a detective from the police department on campus. The three students at first entered their classes after the start of class and left before classes ended, avoiding the hallways during the change of classes between periods. On his first day of class, when Buchanan entered the cafeteria for lunch, the room went totally silent. When the three black students sat down at a table to eat, the white students got up and left. But then some teachers invited the three black students to eat with the teachers.[13]

During freedom of choice, in the later years, the desegregation of faculties would begin. Some black teachers would be asked to teach in the white schools. But there was no question that black students and teachers who transferred to white schools under freedom of choice were obliged to meet the expectations of the white schools. Curricula were not changed. Extracurricular activities were not modified, although black students were not excluded. Some black students ran successfully for student officer positions. Under Jim Niblack, the head football coach, black football players soon were making strong contributions to Gainesville High's successful teams during the freedom-of-choice years.

Black students who entered the white schools under freedom of choice had varying experiences. Many would gravitate to Lincoln High School for social activities. Others, including Joel Buchanan, would eventually find their way to a more comfortable accommodation to the white schools.

> I would get notes dropped in my chair, or dropped by from students saying, "I'm glad you're here. I want to be your friend, but I can't because of my friends." Or, "I'm praying for you." It would relax a little bit, and finally it began to smoothly come together. Some teachers discussed it in class, but some did not. I think I had very excellent teachers that year. I recalled four teachers discussing our presence there. Barbara Gallant [World Cultures and Contemporary Issues], Mrs. Winifred [Grand] [English], Joe Lowe [Social Studies], Mrs. Ash [biology], those are the only four I can recall. They tried to make it better.

***

> Another of my teachers was Mrs. Philpott [Art]. One day it was nasty in her class and she got her Bible out and read the Bible to the students. She had a few tears in her eyes about the way things were, and reprimanded a student for his very

> vulgar words to me. After that, things became much better. In other words, we had the support of the teachers. I remember doing a paper in a class and getting a "B" on it, and there was a note that questioned if I should have that "B." I remember going to the Alachua County school board meeting one evening to discuss our role at the school and the work we had performed there. It was with Superintendent William S. Talbot. He knew what I made on the test the day before.
>
> ***
>
> The teacher questioned if I should get a "B" on that paper because I was black. There were teachers there that taught us because they had to, but did not care to. But then we also had some teachers who wanted to be the first; or, they selected the very best teachers for the first time because the city of Gainesville and the Alachua County school board were determined that they were going to have a very good outcome. And they did – there were no problems.

Buchanan faced some harassment. But Buchanan's second year at GHS was "much better." Buchanan would graduate from GHS with "above a C average."[14] He would become one of the first black students at the University of Florida, where as a student he served as social secretary for Stephen C. O'Connell, the University president, and his wife.[15]

Meanwhile, in the black schools, a system that had existed since Reconstruction was under challenge. Buchanan recalls the reaction of some black teachers. "The black teachers wanted to know what it was like at the white schools, because they had heard how great it was. They wanted to, and I remember good, sharing things back to them, but when we would say things about Lincoln – it was like we were criticizing things at Lincoln – where we were not criticizing Lincoln High School, we were just discussing the differences."[16]

Adult leaders in the black community were the driving force encouraging more black students to enroll in the white schools. Cynthia Cook, who transferred to Gainesville High from Lincoln as a tenth grader in 1967, recalls that she did not want to go. Cook's mother was a teacher. Her family belonged to Mount Carmel Baptist Church, the Reverend Thomas A. Wright's congregation. She says that her parents were influenced by experiences the Rev. Wright shared with the congregation about his children, Philoron and LaVon, in the white schools. Frank Coleman, whose father was a juvenile court counselor and whose mother was also a teacher, remembers that groups of parents would get together to discuss desegregation. The

Rev. Wright was involved in those discussions. "Here is what [Dr. Martin Luther] King wants, let's go with it and see if it works because it was all we had. There was no conversation. The parents knew the issues and believed they had properly prepared us."[17] "We looked up one day, and we were told this is what you're going to do. And I can remember some positive things about the conversation about going to [Howard Bishop Junior High] and about how we were going to have a better opportunity."[18] Coleman's parents sent him to Bishop when he was in the ninth grade, in the 1966–67 school year.

John Dukes III and his sister Carmen believe they were the first blacks to attend J. J. Finley Elementary School. They entered Finley in September 1966, when John was in the fifth grade and Carmen was in the fourth grade. Their parents had decided for them that they would attend white schools because they wanted their children to have better opportunities through the resources of the white schools.[19]

> So we were put in, I guess, as test cases of what integration could be, I guess, and it wasn't something that we volunteered for. I'm sure that my dad had a well thought out vision of putting us in and preparing us for what was to come, because he certainly knew or had wind of, especially in talking to Tiny and others about what was going on in the system, as to what was going to come at some point anyway. So I guess his feeling was that "we put them here now, and perhaps at the moment that the fullness of integration happens, however it happens, whether it's completely voluntary or embraced by the system, or whether or not the system is brought into this kicking and screaming." We would already be there, and thus perhaps better able to navigate through whatever it was that was the result of decision making of those beyond the school laws.[20]

John and Carmen recall that the teachers at Finley were not welcoming. Both state that teachers often would not call on them; John says that his teacher then said on his report card that John needed to pay better attention and participate more in class. Carmen remembers:

> The only kids that were open to me in my class were like one girl that was from Mexico and then a guy that was from Japan. So it just wasn't a positive experience for me at all, because I went from a school where I was at the top of the class, really active in everything, and outspoken, into really

> just, really, you know, it had me to lose my self-esteem and my self-confidence.
>
> And then a lot of the kids that lived in the neighborhood of the black school that I went to, they kind of had a problem with me because they felt like I thought I was better than them because I went to another school. So I lost friendship. So it was just a whirlwind of things, and it just wasn't a good experience for me.[21]

John:

> Educators typically believe in other educators. I think that even during that time, that was true, because there was no way [John Dukes Jr.] and my mother could envision a teacher of students differentiating another student from others when that student was behaviorally good, intellectually on a par with all you had in your classroom, if not above, but yet would not acknowledge you or give you the same type of opportunity and respect as the other students were given in the classroom.[22]

John says it was easier for him as a boy. Boys would tend to sort things out by fighting, and the treatment he received from teachers only brought out his competitive nature in his classwork.[23] Later, at Westwood Junior High, John began playing football. Sports also provided an outlet for black male students.

When John finished at Finley in June 1968, he hoped to go to Lincoln. His father was Lincoln's principal. "That was where I was questioning, 'cause I was like, 'Why can't I go to Lincoln?' And he told me. He said, 'Look, the plan right now appears that when integration moves in full force that they will probably close Lincoln. It doesn't make sense for me to send you there, knowing that what's going to happen is that very shortly after they're going to close, and you'll be put off to another school.'"[24]

Melvin Flournoy was transferred to a white elementary school in Gainesville when two small segregated schools in Micanopy were closed by the school board. He entered the white schools in the fifth grade, also in the 1966–67 school year. Although that choice was made for him, he came up through the white school system from the fifth grade on during the freedom-of-choice years. Flournoy says that both the white and black students from Micanopy were behind their Gainesville classmates. Flournoy gives his teacher, Frances Lastinger, credit for saving his academic career. "She upset me almost every day because she took away my recess. She even took away my PE time. She took those times away from me so she could tutor me during her planning periods and breaks. . . . She either liked me or recognized some potential in me because she did a lot of focused tutoring for me and gave me Cs and Ds. She was tough and I love her to death. The next year I got to be a safety patrol." Flournoy's family could not afford to send him on the safety patrol trip to Washington, DC, but the school found a sponsor for him and he went on the trip. Flournoy became a star football player for Gainesville High and the University of Florida. He would have a career as a coach, teacher, and administrator in schools in Alachua County and elsewhere in Florida.[25]

Alvin Butler also became a star football player at GHS and the University of Florida. He is now coprincipal of a large psychological counseling service in Florida, the ITM Group. Butler was attending A. Quinn Jones Elementary School in the fifth grade when black community representatives identified him, around 1964, as a possible member of the first group of black students to enter white schools. Unlike most of the other members of that group, Butler's family was not middle class. His parents had not gone to college, and both worked as cooks, his mother at A. Quinn Jones Elementary School and his father at a University of Florida fraternity. But for Butler to join that group of black students, he would have had to skip a grade, and his mother did not want him to do so. Butler later entered the old Buchholz Junior High in the seventh grade, in the 1965–66 school year, one year before the school was closed.[26]

At the junior high level, in the early years of freedom of choice, there were teachers who failed to provide support. Frank Coleman remembers that in the eighth grade, he and the other black student in his algebra class made Fs the first semester. The teacher would not call on them or answer their questions. Later, she told the principal that Coleman and the other black student were not prepared. They were put back into a general math class for the second semester, but in that class the teacher was able to tell that both students had good math backgrounds. They had A averages on the tests in that class. Coleman also remembers an English teacher at Bishop who would frequently use the word *Nigras*. But Coleman says his teachers at Gainesville High were encouraging.[27]

Black students who attended the white schools under freedom of choice were exposed to racial taunting by white students, but they learned not to react. Janice Cambridge and Alvin Butler both remember hostile students and some less than welcoming teachers at Buchholz. The confrontational atmosphere at Buchholz in Butler's seventh-grade year distracted him from his usual enthusiasm for academics. He believes that the white students had not been with black students previously. "They'd stand at the end of the hall and call you names and stuff. Or I remember going to chorus one time and some guy behind me singing racial words into the song." When Butler reached Howard Bishop for the eighth grade, he began playing in the band.

"You're playing next to another person with an instrument. You've got to work together." Through band, Butler was able to bond with other students in ways that were not happening just through the classroom experience.[28] Cambridge also found a better atmosphere at Bishop.[29]

As the son of a juvenile court counselor, Frank Coleman entered Howard Bishop and Gainesville High knowing that he would have to be on his best behavior, regardless of any racial confrontations. He tried to stay away from trouble.[30] Looking back, Coleman says that some of the racism he encountered at GHS hurt to the core. He needed, and relied on, black adults for support. He had his father, he had an uncle who coached football at Ocala Howard, the black high school in Marion County, and he knew Coach Hightower at Lincoln. Their advice was, don't let it bother you, do the best you can and keep moving. Coleman says kids today don't have that foundation. Like Coleman, Cynthia Cook relied on her parents for help to withstand incidents of racism.[31]

Cook remembers that classes at GHS were harder for her than they had been at Lincoln. She retook Algebra I, but had a B average for the class. She received her first ever C in Spanish, from Lucille Fain, but she remembers Fain as sweet and someone who went out of her way to help black students.[32]

Lincoln High closed in Flournoy's eighth-grade year at Westwood. At first, Flournoy remembers, "kids were getting along pretty well because we had gone to school together for a while at Idylwild and Westwood. We had become friends and learned a lot about each other. But the moment the older kids started having their problems at GHS, all of a sudden, we forgot about our friendships and all hell broke out even at Westwood for a brief moment. I remember there were a group of us going around, separating people and stopping the craziness. I mean, because you're talking about people that yesterday were friends. And because their brothers were fighting up at Gainesville High School, we have to be mad at each other at Westwood." Flournoy had been in the white schools for three and a half years. "It's pretty hard to hate and dislike people you know. I was involved in the student government, the Junior Honor Society, and in a lot of stuff at school. So I got to know people like James Crawford, Kim Charles Simpson and Kathy Smerdon, and a lot of really good people of all races, genders, and socioeconomic backgrounds." Flournoy also gives credit to his parents, who never taught their children racial hatred.[33] His father and mother both served on Westwood's initial biracial committee, appointed in fall 1970.[34]

Coleman would also find his way into student government. He served in the GHS senate in all three years he attended GHS. Coleman's dad worked with local representative and Speaker of the House Ralph Turlington to bring Coleman to the Florida House of Representatives as a page when Coleman was a sophomore.[35]

Peggy Finley and Sandra Sharron, who taught English at GHS during freedom of choice, recalled black students who performed outstandingly at academics and were active and accepted in extracurricular activities such as cheerleading. Judy Joiner, who taught German and history, remembers that her best German student was an African American girl who entered GHS under freedom of choice and won a prize at a state convention.[36] Sharron felt honored one year to have all of the tenth-grade black girls in one of her English classes. She does not recall an incident in her classroom that was ever racial in overtone. Although Sharron does not know why the black girls had been placed in her class, the school may have been making an effort to combat the isolation that blacks experienced when they were scattered among white students in their other classes.[37]

To the very end of the freedom-of-choice years, three-fifths of all black students, and two-thirds of black senior high students, would choose to stay in Alachua County's black schools. That choice was consistent with choices being made by black students throughout the South. The US Civil Rights Commission reported in February 1966 that only small numbers of African American students were attending school with whites.[38] Prophetically, the commission viewed the historical, strong identification of black communities with their own schools as a barrier to further desegregation. The commission gave as an example an interview with the school superintendent in Lexington, Kentucky, who stated that there was "strong attachment to the Negro high school by the Negro community even though the Negro high school has known inadequacies." The superintendent cited the school's athletic, academic, and extracurricular achievements as "tending to increase the Negro student's identification with his school."[39] The commission noted fear of black educators of losing their jobs. And

> One Mississippi Negro principal interviewed by a Commission investigator reasoned that Negro youngsters should be realistic about their employment opportunities, and that Negro high schools that emphasize trades are more suitable than white high schools. He also stated that because of economic and cultural deprivation, many Negro children enter school much less prepared for education than white children. Until this gap is repaired, he thought, dual schools would be advantageous. The attitudes of such educators are relevant because they frequently are among the most respected members of the Negro community and their opinions influence the choices made by Negro parents and children.[40]

The commission also found that freedom of choice, by placing the burden of desegregation on African Americans, left black students, and parents, subject to fear, harassment, and intimidation.[41] In its findings, the commission stated that the slow pace of desegregation "is in large measure attributable to the manner in which free choice plans – the principal method of desegregation adopted by school districts in the South – have operated."[42]

There was much variation in the quality of Southern black schools from district to district. By all accounts, Lincoln High School had strong academic programs and turned out many, many successful alumni. That history will be discussed further in chapter 9. Here, we are concerned with the perceptions and decisions of individual students and families who chose the black schools during freedom of choice.

Donnie Batie remained at Lincoln until it closed, graduating from Gainesville High in 1971. Batie went on to the University of Florida and was one of the first African Americans to graduate from its medical school. Batie's family was poor. He had three brothers and two sisters. His father was a laborer who also raised chickens. The family would process as many as thirty-seven thousand fryers every three months. After hurting his back at his laborer's job, Batie's father had to give up that job as well as farming, but he became a janitor at the University of Florida. The family also cleaned married student housing at the University and did yard work. Batie's mother worked as a maid for a University professor. When Batie was chosen for the National Honor Society at Lincoln, Principal Dukes took the group to Morrison's Cafeteria for dinner. Batie says it was his first time in a restaurant. Apart from some of his father's coworkers, Batie had little contact with whites. In the black schools, Batie excelled in math, but he had trouble in English. Neither his teachers nor any members of his family ever encouraged him to try the white schools under freedom of choice.[43]

Brenda Wims was one of five children born to Mr. and Mrs. Willie Wims Sr. Because of the family's poverty, Brenda's mother was forced to raise her five children as a single parent. At that time, if the children's father remained in the household, their mother would have been disqualified for public assistance. When Brenda graduated from Duval Elementary School in June 1965, her mother tried to borrow money from anyone who would help to buy Brenda the white dress she would have to wear to the ceremony. When the money could not be found, Brenda told her mother she didn't want to graduate, that she didn't want to put on the white dress. While her mother napped, Brenda watched the graduation ceremony through her bedroom window.

Wims's sixth-grade teacher at Duval was Janie Norton, the wife of Cornelius Norton, a prominent black educator in Gainesville. Wims gives Janie Norton credit for nurturing her, despite Wims's poverty and her weight problem. After entering Lincoln High in the seventh grade, Wims worked to be a smart kid. "And in order for them to get the answers from me, they couldn't say I was fat, or they couldn't pick at me. They always had to say good things." She became involved in student government. Wims never considered leaving Lincoln for Gainesville High under freedom of choice. She says that her family did not have transportation, and she wanted to help her family by caring for younger siblings at home. "And you wouldn't have a way to get to Gainesville High School, and you wouldn't have anyone over there to look out for you. Because at Lincoln High School, if you didn't have lunch money, you didn't have to do anything but go to the front office. Mr. Dukes would make sure that you get a meal, and we at my house we never even considered it, never considered it." Bus transportation was provided to black students who attended GHS under freedom of choice. Although Wims knew about the transportation, she chose to stay at Lincoln. Wims was elected secretary of the Lincoln student body for the 1969–70 school year, just in time to play a major role in the events that ended freedom of choice. Wims was the first of her family to graduate from high school. She achieved her ambition of college and graduate degrees and recently retired as director of professional development for the Duval County school system.[44]

Gertrude E. Jones had two daughters, Angela, born in 1957, and Princess, born in 1959. During the troubles that arose in 1970 after Lincoln was closed, Jones would write a letter to the *Sun* urging her community to accept desegregation. She obtained admission for Angela and Princess to the University's P. K. Yonge school. Despite their mother's support of desegregation, the girls did not want to go to P. K. Yonge. "My husband thought the kids should make up their own mind to go where they wanted to go. He said they'll be happier, and they'll make better grades." Jones says the girls also wanted to remain with their friends. Jones says that the girls' teachers in the black schools were good. Both eventually graduated from Eastside High School.[45]

Alvin Butler says, "There still was, I want to think, some concern for the academic difference between the two schools. So people who maybe felt that they couldn't do the academics, a lot stayed at Lincoln, and that was a real thing that was happening, didn't really talk about a lot, but it certainly was happening." That difference, whatever the cause, would have consequences when Lincoln closed and all of its remaining students were transferred to formerly white schools. Butler is quick to add that he opposed Lincoln's closing, especially because of its history, and even left his GHS classes to join a Lincoln protest march. "You know, it meant that there wouldn't be another option. It was just going to be one choice. So I liked the idea of having a choice at that point."[46]

Frank Ford stayed at Lincoln until he was transferred to Gainesville High when Lincoln closed. He denies knowledge of freedom of choice, although during the years in question, Ford apparently lived independently, apart from his parents, who would have received the school board notices. He remembers that when he and the remaining Lincoln students were transferred to Gainesville High in February 1970, some regarded the blacks who were already there under freedom of choice as disloyal. "Any black kid that was already at GHS when we got there, we didn't like that."[47]

Batie was aware that children of John Dukes Jr. and other black school personnel were attending the white schools. "I always thought that that was wrong. I felt if you were good enough to teach us, you should be good enough to teach your own kids. Okay. And so most of us that were contemporaries during that time really felt that that was unfair to us as children."[48] Despite their resentment toward blacks who had volunteered to attend white schools under freedom of choice, both Ford and Batie would work to encourage cooperation by the former Lincoln students after Lincoln closed.

Wayne Mosley, who would in 1969 lead the protests against the closing of Lincoln High School, says that he was comfortable where he was; he liked the teachers and liked his fellow students.

> I liked everything about Lincoln and that community, you know, from the time I was born, from shooting marbles, until I left to go into the service. Southeast Gainesville and Northeast Gainesville, Southwest Gainesville was all I knew. And I didn't see no reason why I had to go to Gainesville High to be any better. I felt like I was just as great or better than they were even at the time of the closing of our schools. I was on different committees, and at my senior year, eleventh grade year, we outshined GHS all the time. But because of being black, we didn't get the recognition.[49]

Reconciliation would come. Mosley says that for reunions, his Lincoln class of 1970 incorporated black classmates who were already at GHS under freedom of choice. "Because it wasn't their fault they went to GHS as we saw it. We felt like it was the decision made by their parent. Because a lot of the students that went [to GHS under freedom of choice], their parents were teaching at Lincoln. So it wasn't the fact that they didn't have an opportunity to go to Lincoln. Their parents made a decision to let them go to GHS. So we couldn't fault the parent nor them. You good enough to teach us, why you ain't teaching your own? You didn't question adults back there then. We didn't care until they tried to take away our school."[50]

CHAPTER 7
THE JUDGES' TURN I

Beginning of the End of Freedom of Choice

When the United States Supreme Court in 1954 decided Brown v. Board of Education the members of the High School Class of 1966 had not entered the first grade. *Brown I* held that separate schools for Negro children were "inherently unequal." Negro children, said the Court, have the "personal and present right" to equal educational opportunities with white children in a racially nondiscriminatory public school system. For all but a handful of Negro members of the Class of 1966 this right has been "of such stuff as dreams are made on."

Circuit Judge John Minor Wisdom
United States v. Jefferson County Board of Education
372 F.2d 836, 848
December 29, 1966

The fact that Negro children may not choose to leave their associates, friends, or members of their families to attend a school where those associations are eliminated does not mean that freedom of choice does not work or is not effective.... There must be a mixing of the races according to the majority philosophy [expressed in the Fifth Circuit opinion in *Jefferson County*] even if such mixing can only be achieved under the lash of compulsion.

Circuit Judge Walter Pettus Gewin, dissenting
United States v. Jefferson County Board of Education
380 F.2d 385, 404
June 27, 1967

The central problem after *Brown v. Board of Education* was defining the extent to which formerly de jure segregated school systems would have to change.

If Southern school systems granted African American children the right to attend white schools, why would any other steps be necessary to satisfy the constitutional test of *Brown*? Virtually every Southern school system, including Alachua County, eventually took such steps.[1] Why could those school systems not continue to maintain their formerly all-black schools for those students who did not exercise their right to transfer to the white schools?

The courts and the federal government answered, there should be no black schools, no white schools, just schools. That solution to the question unresolved by *Brown* would have much greater impact (whether for good or ill) on African Americans than it would on whites, as we will observe. This chapter tells the story of the way the courts and HEW came to conclude that the former dual systems should be replaced by single unitary systems. If by a different route, the courts came to the same conclusion as Nathan Margold had in 1930.

By 1966, an overwhelming majority of Southern school districts relied on freedom of choice to comply with *Brown* and the Civil Rights Act of 1964.[2] The Department of Health, Education, and Welfare reported that as of January 1966, 98 percent of school districts in the seventeen-state border and Southern regions had been certified to receive federal funds under the Civil Rights Act.[3] The US Civil Rights Commission concluded in 1966 that freedom of choice to that point had generally been upheld by the courts as a lawful method for complying with *Brown*, although some freedom-of-choice plans had been questioned in their implementation.[4]

The NAACP Legal Defense Fund had never accepted freedom of choice as the end point of the struggle for equal educational opportunity.[5] White school boards now drew up a second line of defense around freedom of choice. The Department of Health, Education, and Welfare, along with the Justice Department, still under President Johnson, had to choose sides. The courts would have to rule.

By 1965, ten years after *Brown*, it had become obvious that under freedom of choice there had not been any significant movement of black students into formerly all-white schools. The Southern Education Reporting Service presented statistics showing that as of December 1965, less than 1 percent of black students were enrolled in formerly all-white schools in Alabama and Louisiana.[6] The numbers were only slightly greater for Florida, at 9.76 percent.[7] For Alachua County, as we have seen, the percentage for the 1965–66 school year was about 5 percent.[8]

In February 1966, the US Commission on Civil Rights released a survey of school desegregation.[9] Relying on the Southern Education Reporting

Service statistics and other surveys, the commission agreed that desegregation efforts to date had resulted in "very low" numbers of black students attending schools with whites. The commission concluded that freedom of choice was inherently limited as a means to achieving desegregation.[10]

By early 1966, the NAACP Legal Defense Fund had focused its efforts on defeating freedom of choice as an acceptable minimum desegregation program.[11] In Florida, the NAACP field secretary at a press conference in January 1966 charged that freedom of choice "is a plan to extend racially segregated schools." The NAACP investigative effort in Florida apparently sought to find counties that had denied blacks the right to transfer to white schools, and to ask HEW to deny federal funds to those districts. The NAACP stated that it had found discriminatory practices in Indian River, Bay, Martin, and Levy Counties, among others.[12]

Notwithstanding this conflict, freedom of choice was preserved by the Department of Health, Education, and Welfare in its revised guidelines of March 1966, under Title VI of the Civil Rights Act of 1964.[13] But the new guidelines for the first time treated dual school systems themselves as a form of unlawful discrimination. HEW declared, "It is the responsibility of a school system to adopt and implement a desegregation plan which will eliminate the dual system and all other forms of discrimination as expeditiously as possible."[14]

School districts relying on freedom of choice had to take other actions to desegregate if freedom of choice by itself was not resulting in sufficient progress.[15]

The clarity of the mandate in the HEW March 1966 Revised Statement was still not matched by certainty of mechanics and timing. However, the new guidelines did include more examples of actions that would move systems further toward that mandate. For the first time, in addition to freedom of choice and unitary attendance areas as acceptable methods of compliance, HEW recommended closing of schools originally established for one race, particularly when they were small and inadequate. HEW also encouraged pairing of predominantly black and white schools so that some grades would attend one school and other grades would attend the other school.[16]

Instead of merely reserving his right to test the performance of freedom-of-choice plans, the commissioner of Education[17] stated that he would scrutinize with special care the operation of voluntary freedom-of-choice plans. The commissioner adopted qualitative measures, such as community support for the plan and the efforts of the school system to eliminate identifiability of schools on the basis of race by virtue of composition of staff or other factors, and quantitative goals for transfers of black students out of segregated schools.[18]

The HEW March 1966 Revised Statement was issued during the Fifth Circuit review of the *Jefferson County* cases. The Fifth Circuit on its own motion brought the guidelines into the case by requesting the parties to brief some legal points related to the guidelines.[19] Although the Fifth Circuit had previously said that it regarded the guidelines as a minimum standard for desegregation plans,[20] *Jefferson County* was the first desegregation case heard in the Fifth Circuit in which the legality of the guidelines was squarely argued.

The Fifth Circuit released its opinion in *United States v. Jefferson County School Board*[21] on December 29, 1966. This decision, although not reviewed by the US Supreme Court, is in this author's opinion the single most important decision in all of the post-*Brown* cases on school desegregation.[22] Eleven years after *Brown,* the quest for equal educational opportunity had come to a turning point. For *Brown* to make a difference for the vast majority of Southern blacks who still attended separate black schools, the court would have to find a way to overcome the developed law of freedom of choice.[23]

The majority opinion in *Jefferson County* was written by Judge John Minor Wisdom for the three-judge panel. Judge Homer Thornberry joined Judge Wisdom to form the majority. Judge William Harold Cox of the US District Court for the Southern District of Mississippi, sitting by designation, dissented.

Judge Wisdom came by his appointment to the Fifth Circuit through his work for Dwight Eisenhower as a member of a Louisiana delegation to the 1953 Republican convention. He succeeded in seating his delegation, which supported Eisenhower, over another delegation that was loyal to Sen. Robert Taft. Eisenhower in 1954 appointed Wisdom to the President's Commission on Anti-Discrimination in Government Contracts. Eisenhower appointed Wisdom to the Fifth Circuit Court of Appeals in 1957. Judge Wisdom came from a traditional, privileged New Orleans background.[24] His father had been a pallbearer for Robert E. Lee.

Judge Thornberry was elected to replace Lyndon Johnson in the US House of Representatives in 1948 when Johnson was elected to the Senate. He was appointed to the US District Court for the Western District of Texas by President Kennedy in 1963, and by President Johnson to the Fifth Circuit Court of Appeals in 1965. Although by origin a politician rather than a practicing lawyer or judge, Thornberry followed the same set of principles on civil rights as his mentor, Lyndon Johnson.[25]

Judge Cox was nominated by President John F. Kennedy at the request of Mississippi Senator James O. Eastland to be a district court judge in 1961. Senator Eastland was at that time chair of the Senate Judiciary Committee. Judge Cox was Senator Eastland's roommate at the University of Mississippi. As a judge, Cox was known for making derogatory remarks about African Americans, once referring to blacks seeking to register to vote as chimpanzees. That remark prompted an unsuccessful impeachment attempt. As the trial judge in the 1964 murders of civil rights workers Michael Schwerner, Andrew Goodman, and James Chaney, Cox was overruled by the Supreme Court when he threw out the indictments of most of the defendants. Later, referring to criticism that his sentences were too lenient, he said, "They killed one nigger, one Jew and a white man. I gave them all what I thought they deserved."[26]

For lawyers of my generation, Southerners of conscience like Judge Wisdom and Judge Thornberry defined justice. Even if we never tried a civil rights case, their example showed us the steadfastness to basic principles, whether or not those principles were shared by our peers, that should be universally applied to legal problems.

Jefferson County is important not only for what it decided, but also for what it left undecided. *Jefferson County* established that school districts that were formerly segregated de jure must take affirmative steps to end dual-race school systems. *Jefferson County* found that the HEW March 1966 Revised Statement was within the power of HEW to promulgate under the Civil Rights Act of 1964. The opinion is also important because despite struggling mightily, the Fifth Circuit was either unwilling or unable to articulate a workable standard by which desegregation plans could be judged effective or ineffective.[27] It may be argued that the failure of the Fifth Circuit in 1967 to formulate such a standard in *Jefferson County* (and the corresponding failure of the Department of Health, Education, and Welfare) led directly to the 1969 orders of the US Supreme Court, granted on appeals by the NAACP Legal Defense Fund, that abruptly and finally ended separate black schools (and freedom of choice). Those 1969 orders would have a profound effect in Alachua County, as we will see, and throughout the South.

Judge Wisdom, quoting from Shakespeare's *The Tempest*, stated the issue as follows:

> When the United States Supreme Court in 1954 decided *Brown v. Board of Education* the members of the High School Class of 1966 had not entered the first grade. *Brown I* held that separate schools for Negro children were "inherently unequal." Negro children, said the Court, have the "personal and present right" to equal educational opportunities with white children in a racially nondiscriminatory public school system. For all but a handful of Negro members of the Class of 1966 this right has been "of such stuff as dreams are made on."[28]

Before proceeding to the arguments of the defendant school boards, Judge Wisdom agreed that the Civil Rights Commission and Southern

Education Reporting Service studies cited by the NAACP Legal Defense Fund demonstrated the ineffectiveness of efforts to date to achieve meaningful desegregation.[29] Going straight to the Fourteenth Amendment and *Brown*, Judge Wisdom held, "*The only school desegregation plan that meets constitutional standards is one that works.*"[30]

Prior to the Civil Rights Act of 1964, the courts alone had the task of defining what equal protection of the laws meant in the public school context. Judge Wisdom acknowledged the difficulties that court mandates under *Brown* posed in the day-to-day administration of Southern school systems:

> We approach decision-making here with humility. Many intelligent men of good will who have dedicated their lives to public education are deeply concerned for fear that a doctrinaire approach to desegregating schools may lower educational standards or even destroy public schools in some areas. These educators and school administrators, especially in communities where total segregation has been the way of life from cradle to coffin, may fail to understand all of the legal implications of *Brown*, but they understand the grim realities of the problems that complicate their task.[31]

As examples of these problems, Judge Wisdom cited flight of parents to suburbs, the increase in private schools that promoted resegregation, the unwillingness of some white teachers to continue teaching in integrated schools, the preference of some black children to remain in formerly all-black schools, and the achievement gap between white and black children.[32] In this connection, without yielding the field to Congress,[33] Judge Wisdom welcomed the Civil Rights Act and the HEW guidelines as "belated but invaluable helps in arriving at a neutral, principled decision consistent with the dimensions of the problem, traditional judicial functions, and the United States Constitution."[34] But it was judges who had to make that decision. "We grasp the nettle."[35]

What the Civil Rights Act added, according to Judge Wisdom, was not just authority of the federal government to grant funds to school districts to assist with desegregation and to withhold funds from noncomplying school districts, but also the authority of the attorney general to sue in the name of the United States to desegregate a school system, and to intervene in private actions to desegregate school systems when a case is of general public importance.[36] All of those provisions resulted from the congressional intent that "*formerly de jure segregated public school systems based on dual attendance zones must shift to unitary, non-racial systems – with or without federal funds.*"[37]

The Civil Rights Act's grant of authority to the Department of Health, Education, and Welfare to establish standards for desegregation plans, and to withhold funds from noncomplying school districts, was within the authority of Congress under established principles of constitutional law.[38] "Local loyalties compelled school officials and elected officials to make a public record of their unwillingness to act. But even school authorities willing to act have moved slowly because of uncertainty as to the scope of their duty to act affirmatively."[39] In addition to upholding the HEW March 1966 Revised Statement as a valid exercise of authority by the department under the Civil Rights Act, the court held that in determining the adequacy of desegregation plans, the courts were obliged to give great weight to the Revised Statement.[40] The court hoped that the guidelines would bring increased uniformity in the administration of desegregation cases:

> What Cicero said of an earlier Athens and an earlier Rome is equally applicable today: In Georgia, for example, there should not be one law for Athens and another law for Rome.[41]

The defendant school boards contended that because the HEW guidelines required school boards to take affirmative action to end segregation, the guidelines were contrary to the Civil Rights Act of 1964 and the constitutional underpinning of *Brown* and the Equal Protection Clause.[42] If the school boards had won this argument, passive freedom-of-choice plans would have been allowed to persist indefinitely. Judge Wisdom rejected that argument and its basis, the dictum in *Briggs v. Elliott* discussed previously.[43] The Fifth Circuit held the dictum could not be used to defeat the obligation of school districts under the Equal Protection Clause and *Brown* to provide all students, not just those choosing to attend white schools, with the benefits of a unitary school system.[44]

The Fifth Circuit also rejected the school boards' claim that in order to require systems to take affirmative action to end segregation, the plaintiffs would have to show harm to particular students resulting from a dual system. The court held that when a state has imposed de jure segregation, equal protection of the laws is denied not only because of the harm described in *Brown* but also because a classification based on race is itself invidious under the Equal Protection Clause.[45] "Relief to the class requires school boards to desegregate the school from which a transferee comes as well as the school to which he goes."[46] The Civil Rights Commission and Southern Education Reporting Service studies cited by the NAACP Legal Defense Fund were relied upon by the Fifth Circuit at numerous points in its findings that desegregation results did not conform to the constitutional mandate.[47] The court also relied on *Brown II*, which discussed the relief to be granted to the plaintiffs in *Brown I*, as envisaging the remedy of a unitary integrated school system.[48]

Finally, the court rejected the school boards' argument that HEW and the courts could not take race into account affirmatively in establishing standards for desegregation:

> The Constitution is both color blind and color conscious. To avoid conflict with the equal protection clause, a classification that denies a benefit, causes harm, or imposes a burden must not be based on race. In that sense, the Constitution is color blind. But the Constitution is color conscious to prevent discrimination from being perpetuated and to undo the effects of past discrimination.[49]

The court concluded that freedom-of-choice plans without the new requirements of HEW had little prospect of undoing past discrimination or of coming close to the goal of equal educational opportunities. The court also found that freedom of choice as then administered promoted resegregation. In a much-quoted statement, the Fifth Circuit held,

> The only relief approaching adequacy is the conversion of the still-functioning dual system to a unitary, non-racial system – lock, stock and barrel.[50]

The school boards also attacked the HEW March 1966 Revised Statement as violating three provisions in the Civil Rights Act that had been added by late amendments. One of those amendments attempted to bar HEW from ordering assignment of students to public schools in order to overcome racial imbalance.[51] The second provision forbade HEW and the courts from relying on the Civil Rights Act to order busing to achieve racial balance.[52] On the basis of legislative history, the Fifth Circuit thrust aside these arguments as applying only to school systems that were segregated de facto and not de jure.[53] Therefore, HEW could properly in the case of former de jure systems take the actions complained of. The court also stated that Congress could not take away the courts' Article III authority to exercise their equitable powers in upholding the constitution.[54]

The third provision applied to faculties and school personnel:

> Nothing contained in this title [Title VI] shall be construed to authorize action under this title by any department or agency with respect to any employment practice of any employer, employment agency or labor organization except

> where a primary objective of the Federal financial assistance is to provide employment.[55]

The school boards argued that HEW was forbidden by this provision to require desegregation of faculties and school personnel. But the court found HEW's authority over faculty desegregation to be consistent with the overall purpose of the Civil Rights Act, which was to end segregation of schools, "for one of the keys to desegregation is integration of faculty."[56]

In a significant limitation of the reach of the Civil Rights Act, the court's holding in *Jefferson County* was restricted to de jure and not de facto segregation.[57] The increasingly explicit legal requirements that applied to school systems formerly segregated by law would not be carried over (even under the Civil Rights Act) to systems in which segregation was the result only of residential patterns, as existed outside the South. That limitation of the opinion is attributed by legal scholar Frank Read to Judge Wisdom's need to preserve a majority when the case was later considered en banc.[58]

The court finally turned to the principal purpose of its opinion, which was to establish, through its equitable powers to enforce the Equal Protection Clause of the Fourteenth Amendment, minimum requirements for desegregation plans in the Fifth Circuit (and by implication, for Alachua County's plan). Those standards closely paralleled the HEW March 1966 Revised Statement.[59] The court in addition required any systems with still-segregated grades to include in their plans a statement that children in such grades had an absolute right to transfer to white schools.[60]

With respect to integration of faculty, both the HEW guidelines and the courts relied on statements of principles rather than fixed goals.

The HEW March 1966 Revised Statement required that new hires be made without regard to race. Dismissals and promotions were to be without discrimination. If a teacher was displaced because of desegregation, no vacancy was allowed to be filled unless the system could show that no such displaced teacher was qualified to fill the vacancy. A downsizing required the qualifications of all faculty members to be reviewed. Staff desegregation for the 1966–67 school year was to make significant progress.[61]

The court was less specific. The court did not defend existing black faculty:

> As evidenced by numerous records, [faculty segregation] has resulted in inferior Negro teaching and in inferior education of Negroes as a class. Everyone agrees, on principle, that the selection and assignment of teachers on merit should not be sacrificed just for the sake of integrating faculties; teaching is an art. Yet until school authorities recognize and carry out

> their affirmative duty to integrate faculties as well as facilities, there is not the slightest possibility of their ever establishing an operative non-discriminatory school system.[62]

The court ordered that school systems cease racial discrimination in the hiring of new faculty members and "take affirmative programmatic steps to correct existing defects of past racial assignment. If these two requirements are prescribed, the district court should be able to add specifics to meet the particular situation the case presents."[63]

The court required schools to be equalized, but did not shield black schools from being closed.[64] The provisions of the *Jefferson County* model decree related to the black schools will be further considered in chapter 8 in connection with decisions made in Alachua County.

Jefferson County was reconsidered by all twelve judges of the Fifth Circuit. The majority opinion, delivered per curiam and published March 29, 1967, adopted Judge Wisdom's original opinion with some minor clarifications. This en banc opinion restated the court's holding that school boards in the Fifth Circuit have "the affirmative duty under the Fourteenth Amendment to bring about an integrated, unitary school system in which there are no Negro schools and no white schools – just schools."[65] To the extent that nine prior Fifth Circuit opinions could be read to conflict with that holding (many had discussed *Briggs v. Elliott*), they were expressly overruled.[66] Before *Jefferson County*, the Fifth Circuit had committed itself so strongly to the legality of freedom of choice that the court believed it could not change direction without overruling itself.

Upon the en banc reconsideration, Fifth Circuit Judges Gewin and Griffin Bell filed separate dissents, with which each concurred. Fifth Circuit Judge Godbold dissented in a separate opinion, and Judge Coleman concurred in the result in a separate opinion that criticized the majority. These dissents offer a glimpse of the path eventually not taken with regard to desegregation of de jure school districts. At the time *Jefferson County* was decided, it was by no means clear which side of the freedom-of-choice issue would eventually prevail in the Supreme Court, or even whether that court would step in to resolve the intra- and intercircuit conflicts.[67]

Taken together, the main point of the dissenting judges was that *Brown* did not require school boards to eliminate dual school systems as long as free choice operated freely.[68] Borrowing in his turn from the Greeks, Judge Gewin stated that the majority opinion (which overruled Fifth Circuit opinions that rested on *Briggs v. Elliott*) was spawned like Athena from the brow of Zeus, without any substantial legal ancestry.[69] Judge Griffin Bell (later attorney general under President Jimmy Carter) was even more caustic in his classical analogy, comparing the vagueness of the majority opinion to the obscurantism of the Roman Emperor Caligula, whose laws were said to be posted only in narrow places and in fine print.[70]

After asserting that true freedom of choice would result in eventual elimination of dual school systems, Judge Gewin stated,

> The fact that Negro children may not choose to leave their associates, friends, or members of their families to attend a school where those associations are eliminated does not mean that freedom of choice does not work or is not effective.... There must be a mixing of the races according to the majority philosophy [expressed in the Fifth Circuit opinion in *Jefferson County*] even if such mixing can only be achieved under the lash of compulsion.[71]

Judge Gewin continued,

> It is not our function to condemn the children or the school authorities because the free choices actually made do not comport with our notions of what the choices should have been. When our concepts as to proportions and percentages are imposed on school systems, notwithstanding free choices actually made, we have destroyed freedom and liberty by judicial fiat; and even worse, we have done so in the name of that very liberty and freedom we so avidly claim to espouse and embrace.[72]

Judge Griffin Bell agreed with the majority that *Brown* required eventual abolition of dual school systems. But he contended that a unitary system could be achieved through attendance zones drawn without regard to race, but with regard to neighborhood schools, as approved by the Fourth Circuit in the Charlotte desegregation case. Freedom of choice could then be exercised by any student who found himself in a minority-majority school.[73]

In *Wright v. Board*, the US District Court responded on April 3, 1967, to the plaintiffs' motion for further relief based on *Jefferson County*. Judge Carswell issued an oral order on April 3 that in effect required Alachua County to redo its freedom-of-choice process for the 1967–68 school year.[74] Attorney Arnow and a school administration official, speaking to the press, minimized the changes that would be necessary to the county's freedom-of-choice plan. The county moved quickly and began distribution of revised registration forms by April 17.[75]

The district court approved a written decree prepared by school board attorney Arnow on April 25, 1967, that incorporated the judge's oral order.[76] The decree did not, in accordance with the model decree in *Jefferson County*, enjoin the Alachua County school board from "discriminating on the basis of race or color in the operation of the school system."[77] The decree did adopt a condensed version of the statement of principle from *Jefferson County*:

> It is ORDERED, ADJUDGED and DECREED that the Defendants, as set out more particularly in the body of the decree, shall take affirmative action to disestablish all school segregation and to eliminate the effects of the dual school system . . .[78]

The decree in *Wright v. Board* closely followed the Fifth Circuit's form of decree from *Jefferson County* with respect to pupil assignment, school equalization, new construction, desegregation of faculty and staff, and reports to the court.[79]

After all of the controversy before the Fifth Circuit, the Alachua County desegregation plan as ordered by Judge Carswell remained principally dependent on freedom of choice. School equalization provisions, as we have seen, were added, but closing of historically black schools was required if they could not quickly be equalized. Provisions for integrating faculty and staff were added, but they, too, were statements of principle. Reporting requirements with respect to both student and faculty assignments were added.

In December 1966, reacting to the three-judge panel's decision in *Jefferson County*, Talbot had reinforced the message that the county would comply with court orders. Perhaps not understanding the implications of *Jefferson County*, Talbot believed that the county's freedom-of-choice plan was effective and would continue to satisfy legal standards.

> Desegregation is no longer an issue here and we have fully accepted the laws of our three branches of government in toto. We are abiding by every requirement of our court order and no one is standing in the way of pupils or teachers, telling them which school to attend. I don't even think in terms of integration or segregation and I say let's get off the subject and get down to the business of educating our children.[80]

Talbot had earlier praised freedom of choice as "the closest thing to real democracy that we have in our school system."[81] *Jefferson County*, quite in spite of the strong language of Judge Wisdom, allowed freedom of choice to last for two more school years. As Alachua County moved on to address its need for more schools to reduce overcrowding, that delay would both help and hurt the school system.

CHAPTER 8
TOWARD A UNITARY SYSTEM

School Board Responds to Financial and Accreditation Pressures

If I disagree with those people, I can vote them out of office, I don't have to take it out on the children. I have no right to do that. Rather, it is my duty to shoulder my share of the burden.

Sigsbee L. Scruggs, advocating for school bond issue, September 26, 1966

We make this recommendation [to support the proposed 1966 school bond issue] wholeheartedly in the hope that there is a new change in heart and mind of the community, and an end to separate and unequal facilities, and that there will be realization that a poorly trained child, whether Negro or white, weakens a country and a community.

NAACP Executive Committee, Gainesville Chapter, October 1, 1966

We have been able to hold our own with other medical schools with our salaries. But, all things being equal, a professor who has a choice to make is not likely to take a job in a place where the public school system is in trouble.

Emmanuel Suter, MD, dean of University of Florida College of Medicine, October 1, 1967

> Race is not a factor in these recommendations [for Alachua County school construction]. It would be impossible to work up a plan based on freedom of choice.
>
> Dr. Charles E. Chick, Head of Surveys, Florida Department of Education, December 16, 1967

Despite Alachua County's continuation of its freedom-of-choice plan following *Jefferson County*, population growth and economic considerations, not court action, would propel Alachua County to a unitary school system. By 1966, many new classrooms were needed. To utilize old and new classroom space efficiently, the school system had to decide which white and black schools would continue and which would be closed or repurposed. The fate of the county's two black high schools would be decided as the county planned for a $12.8 million bond issue, which county freeholders eventually approved in May 1968.

Alachua County did not experience the explosive population growth of some other Sunbelt areas during the 1950s and 1960s. The county's population grew at impressive rates, however. From 1950 to 1960, the county grew from 57,061 to 75,304, an increase of 32 percent, and from 1960 to 1970, the increase was from 75,304 to 104,228, or 38 percent. From 1950 to 1970, the black proportion of the county's population fell from 29 percent to 21 percent, approximately the proportion that has continued to the current time.[1]

As we have seen, four new high schools for white and black students were constructed in Gainesville in the mid-1950s. These schools and other expansions were financed in part by state capital funds and by a 1953 county bond issue that voters approved overwhelmingly.[2]

By the 1964–65 school year, many of these schools were overcrowded. The plaintiffs in the federal desegregation lawsuit obtained capacity and enrollment figures for each Alachua County public school. Average class sizes had been kept to the low thirties in elementary schools and to midtwenties in the high schools (both white and black). But the table below shows the cumulative numbers of students and percentage over capacity for the white and black schools located in Gainesville.[3]

Table 4. Overcapacity of Alachua County Schools, School Year 1964–65

School type	No. enrolled	Capacity	No. over	Percent over
White K–6	6,057	5,330	727	13.6%
White 7–9	2,049	1,780	269	15.1%
White 10–12	1,893	1,750	143	8.2%
Black K–6	2,290	1,980	310	15.7%

School type	No. enrolled	Capacity	No. over	Percent over
Black 7–12	1,526	1,425	101	7.1%

During the 1964–65 school year, there were under construction some additional classrooms and facilities, and others were planned, all at existing schools. Some significant construction was under way or planned at black schools.[4] No new schools were planned, the school board chair commenting that although new schools were needed, there were no funds available.[5] Jasper Joiner, a school board member, explained in the spring of 1966 that Alachua County system enrollment had increased by an average of 1,004 students per year over the six years since a 1960 state survey of county school facilities, a rate that theoretically required the addition of thirty-three classrooms per year.[6] Enrollment in the 1965–66 school year of 20,517 was up by 1,094 students over the 1964–65 total.[7]

The Alachua County schools faced problems besides overcrowding. Superintendent Talbot told the University City Kiwanis Club in October 1965 that although Alachua County ranked in the top seventeen Florida counties in the ability to pay for the necessities of life, it ranked fifty-eighth (of sixty-seven) in school funding. Salaries for long-serving teachers ranked twenty-fifth in the state, but the county's starting salary of $4,100 was close to the bottom ranking. White teachers in the junior ranks could easily be recruited from student wives at the University of Florida, according to Talbot, but the system had much difficulty recruiting black teachers at that salary level. The low salaries for junior teachers created too much turnover. Talbot said that the Alachua County schools averaged three to five books per student in its school libraries, but by 1966 that number would have to increase to ten per student for the schools to remain accredited.[8]

The overcrowding, in addition to causing educational issues, complicated the county's efforts to move to a more integrated school system. Because the county's white population by now was increasing faster than its black population, a significant exodus from historically black public schools to the white schools would compound the overcrowding at the white schools.[9]

Superintendent Talbot and the school board had been seeking state approval of a junior college to be operated by the school board. The junior college, to be named Santa Fe Junior College, was approved for initial operation in the fall of 1966.[10] The junior college was funded primarily by the State of Florida. In addition, the superintendent and board were seeking to add more vocational programs to the existing offerings. Serving the needs of students who did not plan to go on to four-year colleges was a continuing priority of Superintendent Talbot. Population growth and lack of funds also hampered the county's ability to make improvements in these areas.

School funding in Florida in the 1960s was still under the Minimum Foundation Program, which became effective in 1947. That program was Florida's first attempt to equalize spending for schools based in part on a county's financial resources to support its schools. The Minimum Foundation Program substantially increased state funding for public schools, and for the first time made no distinction in allocating state funds to counties on the basis of black or white enrollment.[11] Originally intended to supply the counties with approximately 75 percent of funding needs, the state proportion had declined to 48 percent by 1967, with the counties paying 39 percent and the federal government (a source not contemplated in 1947) paying 13 percent.[12]

Under the Minimum Foundation Program, Florida counties were required to maintain a minimum local funding level of ten mills but could, by a vote of county freeholders, levy additional funds to support their schools. Alachua County adopted levy increases in the 1960s, but those increases required referenda every two years and were controversial. In 1965, Superintendent Talbot, supported by four of the five school board members, sought an additional four-mill levy for the next two years.[13] The voters in November 1965 approved only three mills, which was estimated to yield $1.5 million over two years.[14]

The Minimum Foundation Program was abandoned in the early 1970s in favor of the new Florida Education Finance Program, which again significantly increased state financial assistance to county school boards.[15] Those reforms came too late to make any difference to Alachua County's management of enrollment growth, low teacher salaries, and desegregation.

The school board had no choice but to go to the voters for approval of a bond issue for new elementary and secondary school facilities. In January 1966, the school board appointed a blue-ribbon citizen's committee to study the county's school needs and to make detailed recommendations to the board. Lester Hodge, who recently retired from the school board but had served on the board for twelve years, chaired the committee. Hodge pointed out that the most recent full plant survey by the state Department of Education, conducted in 1965, failed to take into account integration, which started in 1964.[16]

At the same time, the school board asked the Florida Department of Education to update its school plant survey for Alachua County. Dr. Charles E. Chick, the head of school surveys for the Florida Department of Education, oversaw the survey update. Dr. Chick's survey team released its report in January 1966. Dr. Chick found that to meet the anticipated enrollment of 23,362 students by 1971, the county would need to raise $13,527,590 through a school bond issue.[17]

This January 1966 update noted, "Because of desegregation, county school board policies affecting attendance areas served by various schools within the county have been changed."[18] According to this survey, no new construction was recommended at either of the county's two black secondary schools, Lincoln Junior/Senior High School and A. L. Mebane Junior/Senior High School. Apparently contemplating that some black students would choose to attend formerly all-white secondary schools, the plan stated that future excess enrollments at the black secondary schools would go to the white schools.[19]

The report classified Lincoln High School grades 7–12 in Capital Outlay Class C-2, which was defined as a "school center which is satisfactory in all major respects; generally, adequate site, satisfactory building or buildings, enrollment projected to below the maximum desirable for the type of school." Lincoln was to continue as a junior/senior high school. A. L. Mebane, the other historically black high school in the county, was classified for grades 10–12 in Capital Outlay Class C-5 (the lowest), defined as "school center is unsatisfactory in one or more major respects . . . Pupils should be transferred and/or school closed as soon as adequate new facilities are constructed elsewhere to house pupils."[20]

When this survey update was being prepared, in late 1965 and early 1966, it would not have been apparent either to the state survey teams or to the Alachua County school board that the NAACP Legal Defense Fund and the courts would soon require the South to end its dual school systems. The 1965–66 school year was the first year during which Southern districts were subject to the April 1965 HEW General Statement under the Civil Rights Act of 1964, and that guidance relied on freedom of choice. Leaving Lincoln in place as a school that would serve a black student body was consistent with existing law.

Predictions that Southern counties would not be able to afford separate dual school systems were coming true in Alachua County. Construction plans initially recommended by the school board would have converted historically black A. L. Mebane High School to an elementary school and sent all of its junior and senior high school students to the nearby white Santa Fe Junior/Senior High School. All-black elementary schools in Waldo, Micanopy, and Newberry were to be closed.[21] According to Talbot, those elementary schools had a combined enrollment of four hundred and would not meet accreditation standards.[22] The junior high grades at the black Douglass Elementary School in High Springs were also to be transferred to Santa Fe Junior/Senior High, and junior high grades at three other black elementary schools in Archer, Hawthorne, and Waldo were similarly affected. Those elementary schools were unable to offer separately taught departmental courses such as English or science to their seventh- and eighth-grade students.[23] New junior/senior high schools for both black and white students were to be constructed at Hawthorne and Newberry. Black junior and senior high school students from those areas would no longer be bused to Lincoln in Gainesville.[24]

Black opposition to the elimination of black secondary schools, which would become the most difficult aspect of Alachua County's desegregation, first surfaced when the elimination of Mebane Junior/Senior High was announced. A petition signed by 259 black citizens from the area served by Mebane protested its elimination as a junior/senior high school. Members of the white community of that area also opposed sending the Mebane students to Santa Fe. The white and black communities in the Hawthorne and Newberry areas seemed to accept that their new junior/senior high schools would be fully integrated.[25]

Chester Shell, the black educator for whom Shell Elementary School in Hawthorne is named, pleaded with the school board to continue the Head Start program at that school instead of moving it to the white school in that town. He said, "Shell used to have the best school in Alachua County, but now it's dwindling to nothing."[26]

The elimination of the upper grades at Douglass in High Springs was protested by an elderly black former teacher:

> She didn't give her name but board chairman Dale Smith knew her and called her "Miss Katherine."
>
> Miss Katherine said she had been a school teacher. She told of the Depression days when Negroes scrimped up all the money they could get out of their own pockets to match up with money from President Roosevelt's administration to build their school with.
>
> Then she told a joke on herself. It went like this:
>
> One day this little rascal was not behaving in my class, and I told him "You come here now and I am going to give you a spanking."
>
> He looked at me and said, "Don't you know there's a law now that says teachers can't whip pupils?"
>
> I thought for a while, and then, grabbing my switch, I said to him, "Yes, that's right, there is such a law, but the time ain't come here yet for the law to make any difference."
>
> When the laughter died down, Miss Katherine added, "There may be a law about not having seventh and eighth grades in elementary schools, but the time hasn't come here that it makes any difference."[27]

The school board's blue-ribbon committee in April 1966 recommended a bond issue of $11.8 million for a five-year school construction plan, with an additional $2.5 million in state capital funds to be obtained between 1966 and 1971.[28] The committee projected enrollment growth from the current 20,782 to 26,103 by 1970.[29] The committee scrapped consolidating the junior and senior grades at Mebane with Santa Fe and instead recommended spending $254,000 to refurbish Mebane, retaining it as a junior/senior high school.[30] Taxes on a $12,000 home would have increased by about $20 initially, but with anticipated growth in the tax base, in the later years of the twenty-year bond issue, the additional burden was estimated at about $10 annually.[31] A standing-room-only crowd of more than nine hundred strongly supported the bond issue at a public hearing held by the school board in May 1966.[32] The board approved the bond issue on June 9, 1966,[33] but that approval only set the stage for an up or down vote by county property owners.

Talbot, members of the school board, business leaders, and the press worked to persuade voters to approve the bond issue. Three of the five county school board members were to be elected that year, and all eleven of the candidates supported the bond issue, although a few had qualifications.[34] After approving the bond issue, the school board appointed a new committee, headed by State Representative Ralph Turlington and businessman Walter "Sonny" Lee, to mobilize voters in the referendum.[35] Turlington assumed the speakership of the Florida House of Representatives in 1967. White leaders, businesses, and groups threw themselves into supporting the bond issue. In addition to overcrowding, loss of accreditation was threatened at a number of county secondary schools. The committee succeeded in gaining the public support of a multitude of civic organizations and businesses. Sigsbee Scruggs, who had been Talbot's ally in the referendum to keep the superintendent's office elective, appealed to voters to separate any dissatisfaction with school policies from the need for financial support: "If I disagree with those people, I can vote them out of office, I don't have to take it out on the children. I have no right to do that. Rather, it is my duty to shoulder my share of the burden."[36]

With the referendum just days away, the Executive Committee of the NAACP chapter urged black voters to support the bond issue (in spite of the planned closure of Mebane and the absence of major improvements at Lincoln). In a letter to the *Sun*, the NAACP first pointed out that black schools in the county were unequal, that black teachers were being harassed, that their relatively low National Teacher Exam test scores were being used to create insecurity, and that there was only one black employee in the school system's central administration. But the letter concluded,

> We make this recommendation [to support the bond issue] wholeheartedly in the hope that there is a new change in heart and mind of the community, and an end to separate and unequal facilities, and that there will be realization that a poorly trained child, whether Negro or white, weakens a country and a community.[37]

Freeholders narrowly defeated the bond issue in the election held October 4, 1966. With 8,560 of 8,714 qualified freeholders voting, 4,232 voted for the bond issue and 4,328 voted against.[38] The bond issue lost heavily in outlying precincts and failed to gain sufficient support in Gainesville. Gainesville precincts with large proportions of black voters split the vote about equally between "for" and "against."[39]

Gainesville was stunned. Alachua County was believed to be the first county in Florida to defeat a school bond issue in the previous ten years, but it was joined by Polk County in the same time frame. Key local businesses such as Sperry and General Electric, and the University of Florida—all dependent on good schools to recruit employees and faculty—were fearful of the future.[40]

The postmortem analysis attributed the bond issue's failure to opposition in the county's rural areas. But an Alachua resident pointed out that of the "against" votes, 1,453 had come from rural precincts and 2,728 from Gainesville.[41]

No opponent of the bond issue publicly gave desegregation as a reason for opposition. Nor were there any private "segregation academies" in the county at this time that would have competed for funds with the public schools.

Perhaps in reaction to the bond issue's defeat, construction supervisor Walter Ebling, who had strongly supported the bond issue, overwhelmingly defeated W. T. Bryant in the Democratic primary runoff for school board.[42] Bryant had given only qualified support for the bond issue and was known to be an opponent of increased taxes for the schools. He wanted to force the state legislature to adopt tax reforms.[43] Ebling won the general election in November 1966, against a Republican opponent. He would serve on the school board through the difficult years ahead.

Superintendent Talbot, from the front lines of the enrollment crisis, wasted no time in pressing the school board in March 1967 to lay the groundwork for another bond issue election in November 1967, the earliest time at which such an election could be held under state law. Talbot said that his staff had been in contact with community groups, and the staff believed that the community would be receptive to another bond election. He also stated that it was now clear that the legislature was not going to bail out counties with any emergency funding. But the school board was not ready for a new committee or for a bond issue referendum in 1967.[44]

Claude Kirk, Florida's first Republican governor since Reconstruction, took office in January 1967. Kirk proposed significant cuts to state funding of public schools in April 1967, as part of his "no new taxes" budget. That message drew swift and angry responses from the Florida Education Association and others, including Talbot and Alachua County teacher representatives. Kirk's hard line on school spending began his confrontation with Florida teachers, which would eventually spiral into a statewide teacher strike in 1968.[45] But Kirk's program, and his subsequent fight with the Florida legislature, was more evidence that county school boards could not expect increased state funding for construction.[46]

Amid the threats and counterthreats related to teacher pay, Citizens for Public Schools was organized by some white Gainesville community leaders in October 1967. It was nonpartisan, and its purpose was to examine long-term needs of the Alachua County schools.[47] Part of the motivation came from the University of Florida. W. Jape Taylor, MD, a cardiologist at the University medical center, served as cochair of Citizens for Public Schools. The *Sun* reported that the strongest impetus at the University was coming from deans who were responsible for faculty recruiting. Emmanuel Suter, MD, the dean of the College of Medicine, said that professors tend to ask about the quality of the public schools before they ask about their salary. "We have been able to hold our own with other medical schools with our salaries. But, all things being equal, a professor who has a choice to make is not likely to take a job in a place where the public school system is in trouble." School PTA groups also seemed more active as the 1967–68 school year began.[48]

The Gainesville Area Chamber of Commerce, "always an advocate of good schools but seldom very active about it," also established a supporting committee. The chamber's new president, Attorney Joe C. Willcox, in his installation speech in October told the chamber,

> In the long run, no chamber of commerce can exceed in quality the community it seeks to serve, and unfortunately, our community is on the brink of diminished quality because of critical needs in public school education. . . . We cannot successfully compete for desirable industry when we must give the obvious answer to the initial inquiry, "Do you have top quality schools?" Our existing businesses and institutions, including our great university, are handicapped in attracting qualified people because of their reluctance to bring their families into an atmosphere of inadequacy in the public schools system.[49]

This time an A-team of top-level spokesmen from GE, Sperry, and the J. Hillis Miller Health Center at the University of Florida were out front. As a first step, Citizens for Public Schools, together with other organizations, manned a get-out-the-vote effort in support of the optional four-mill levy proposed by the school board for 1968 and 1969.[50] Public response to these efforts was initially very lukewarm, with only three hundred of twenty-five thousand invitees appearing at the first chamber-sponsored forum.[51] But freeholders approved the four-mill levy in November 1967.[52] Talbot thanked several community groups, including Gainesville Women for Equal Rights, a local civil rights organization, as well as teachers and school staff, for their successful efforts to secure the four-mill levy.[53] Following the vote, the chamber of commerce asked the school board to approve a bond issue by the beginning of 1968.[54]

Two days after the successful millage election, the school board appointed another blue-ribbon committee to study school funding. Osee Fagan, a former state representative, was appointed on behalf of the Greater Gainesville Chamber of Commerce, Bob Sanders on behalf of Citizens for Public Schools, and Mrs. John Major on behalf of the League of Women Voters.[55] Joe C. Willcox, the chamber of commerce president, would also play a leading role in advocating for the bond issue.

Southern Association of Colleges and Schools accreditation results for Alachua County's high schools were announced in November 1967. Gainesville High was placed on probation, mostly due to overcrowding. Newberry High School lost accreditation due to "very inadequate facilities." A. L. Mebane High went on probation due to inadequate facilities, teachers teaching out of field, and the auditorium being used simultaneously for music, physical education classes, and study hall. The white Santa Fe High and black Lincoln High were both placed on the "warned" list. The comments for Lincoln cited overloaded teachers, general overcrowding of facilities, and the need for a special reading program at the junior high level.[56]

The school board in December 1967 obtained a second revision to the February 1965 state-facilities survey. Both black high schools, Lincoln and Mebane, were now classified in Capital Outlay Class C-5 (the lowest) for grades 10–12,[57] according to which the facilities should be closed for those grades and students transferred elsewhere.[58] The December 1967 survey provided that all students in grades 10–12 at Lincoln High should be transferred to a new senior high school to be constructed in southeast Gainesville in the vicinity of the white Lake Forest Elementary School, or to other white high schools in the county.[59]

In addition to assessing the suitability of current school plants, a major purpose of the survey was to match new construction to anticipated enrollment growth. The survey found a developing imbalance in enrollment growth among the county's senior high schools. Enrollment in grades 10 through 12 at Lincoln and Mebane in recent years was stagnant or declining, according to the survey. In comparison, since the 1961–62 school year, enrollment at the county's four historically white high schools had increased dramatically, except at the then-rural Santa Fe High School.[60] Those changes were occurring at least in part because increasing numbers of black students were choosing to attend white schools under freedom of choice.

The 1967 state survey assumed complete school integration, not freedom of choice. By December 1967, *Jefferson County* had been decided by the Fifth Circuit, and the NAACP Legal Defense Fund's opposition to freedom of choice was affecting all pending school-desegregation cases. Chick said that the survey team's recommendations were based on students' proximity to schools. "'Race is not a factor in these recommendations,' he said. 'It would be impossible to work up a plan based on freedom of choice.'"[61] Whatever the cause, there was a critical need for more space to house senior high school students in Gainesville. The 1967 updated survey followed the 1966 update in providing for a new high school in west Gainesville. There was no room for more students at the Lincoln campus, and the plant, according to the survey, in its current configuration was not suitable for future use as a senior high school. It was on that basis that the survey urged construction of a new senior high school approximately two miles east of the Lincoln campus.

Outside Gainesville, the survey did not support the new high schools in Newberry and Hawthorne that had been proposed by the school board in 1966. The report instead favored busing high school students from those towns to new schools to be located on the outskirts of Gainesville.[62] New high schools in Newberry and Hawthorne had been criticized by University of Florida Education Professor R. L. Johns (the same Professor Johns who had encouraged the school board to build new black high schools in 1951 to preserve segregation). Johns urged that any new high schools be built in or near Gainesville, where there were more students in need of new classrooms, and higher-quality education could be provided in larger secondary schools.[63]

The survey's results, including the proposed elimination of the county's two black senior high schools, were detailed in the *Sun* on December 15, 1967.[64]

The 1967 state plant survey update only began the school board's planning process for new construction and bond financing. The school board's chair, Jasper Joiner, in January 1968 gathered an informal group of principals and parents to discuss options for the 1968–69 school year. The school board recognized that funds from any future bond issue would not be available for the next school year, at least. The consensus plan was to concentrate on relieving the secondary school overcrowding at Gainesville High School by placing that school on double sessions. It was already on staggered sessions. By removing grade 9 from Gainesville's two white junior high schools and placing those students at GHS, more room could be made at the two white junior high schools.[65]

A proposal to place Mebane's senior high school pupils at white Santa Fe High School to relieve overcrowding at Mebane was also discussed. Many black senior high students were reportedly being bused from High Springs past Santa Fe High to Mebane. Although this plan did not involve transferring junior high school students, as did a 1967 plan, it still was opposed by Santa Fe's principal, L. B. Lindsey. He said that any Mebane student who wished to attend Santa Fe could do so under freedom of choice, and no one should be forced to attend a school unless he asked to do so. He also said that Santa Fe was oriented to a four-year college-preparatory program, but Mebane focused more on a vocational curriculum.[66] According to Mebane Principal Oliver Jones, the black students from the area preferred to remain at Mebane, with only nineteen choosing to attend Santa Fe.[67]

Meanwhile, the school board moved forward to purchase sites for the two new high schools proposed in the 1967 state plant survey update. Two forty-acre parcels were approved for purchase on February 8, 1968.[68] Those parcels became the sites for the future Eastside High School and for Buchholz High School in the northwest part of Gainesville. As recommended in the 1967 state survey, the Eastside High site was near the white Lake Forest Elementary School, but also just east of the east-side black neighborhoods, and about two miles east of Lincoln. Under housing patterns at that time, the new east-side secondary school would serve a zone with a substantial white majority. Talbot said that he hoped construction of those two schools could begin during the current school year or in the 1968–69 school year. The *Sun* again reported that the new high school on the east side would replace grades 10–12 at Lincoln High if the school board were to follow the state recommendations.[69]

The school board, on the basis of the 1967 state survey update, was implementing its version of a unitary school system for the county, in which there would be no remaining separate black and white schools. To achieve a unitary system at the secondary school level, the school board eliminated both of the county's historically black senior high schools. That decision was seen in 1969 by many in Gainesville's African American community as striking at its heart. There would be an eleven-day strike by Lincoln students, and charges of racism against the school board. The courts would eventually uphold the school board's decision. But at the time that these plans were made, was the school board acting consistently with court and federal agency policies on desegregation?

Geography defined the possibilities for integrating the Gainesville schools. The urban area was much wider east to west than it was north to south. And recent changes had reinforced Gainesville's segregated housing patterns, making desegregation more difficult. The completion of highway I-75 in the mid-1960s to the west of Gainesville stimulated commercial and white residential development in that direction. Construction of lower-cost tract homes in white areas on Gainesville's northeast side, which boomed into the 1950s and 1960s, virtually came to a halt. Meanwhile, black neighborhoods had spread to the east and southeast. Newly constructed public housing was also built mostly in the east-side black neighborhoods.

The Office of Education had in December 1966 published revised guidelines under Title VI of the Civil Rights Act of 1964 to apply to desegregation plans for the 1967–68 school year. Those rules urged more rapid progress toward desegregation but did not attempt to mandate continued use of historically black school buildings, even when those buildings may have been adequate or capable of being made equal to white facilities. They repeated language from the HEW March 1966 Revised Statement regarding the discontinuance of small, inadequate black schools.[70]

The 1967–68 Revised Statement also carried forward language from the HEW March 1966 Revised Statement, which stated that in measuring the effectiveness of freedom-of-choice plans, "the single most substantial indication . . . is the extent to which Negro or other minority group students have in fact transferred from segregated schools."[71]

The Fifth Circuit Court of Appeals in *Jefferson County* had in March 1967 adopted a form of decree that in essence left to the school boards the decision to equalize or close formerly all-black schools. On that point, the Fifth Circuit's model decree was in basic accord with the NAACP Legal Defense Fund's proposed decree filed in *Wright v. Board* on September 26, 1966.[72] The *Jefferson County* decree included a heading, "Inferior Schools." On the one hand, "in schools heretofore maintained for Negro students, the defendants shall take prompt steps necessary to provide physical facilities, equipment, courses of instruction, and instructional materials of quality equal to that provided in schools previously maintained for white students. Conditions of overcrowding, as determined by pupil-teacher ratios and pupil-classroom ratios shall, to the extent feasible, be distributed evenly between schools formerly maintained for Negro students and those formerly maintained for white students." On the other hand, the decree stated, "If for any reason it is not feasible to improve sufficiently any school formerly maintained for Negro students, where such improvement would otherwise be required by this paragraph, such school shall be closed as soon as possible, and students enrolled in the school shall be reassigned on the basis of freedom of choice." With respect to new construction, the decree provided that school boards, "to the extent consistent with the proper operation of the school system as a whole, shall locate any new school and substantially expand any existing schools with the objective of eradicating the vestiges of the dual system."[73] The April 1967 post–*Jefferson County* court order then applicable to Alachua County echoed the Fifth Circuit's language: "The defendants, to the extent consistent with the proper operation of the school system as a whole, shall locate any new school and substantially expand any existing schools with the objective of eradicating the vestiges of the dual system."[74]

As late as January 1969, State Superintendent of Public Instruction Floyd Christian, in a visit to an Alachua County school board meeting, commented that it was obvious that many black schools in Florida would have to close down because school boards would not integrate them. "Negro pupils will have to be shifted to white schools. It will not necessarily be wasteful to close Negro schools because they can be used for other purposes, such as vocational schools."[75]

The school board's plan to eliminate Lincoln and Mebane as academic senior high schools, and to assign their students to existing or planned schools that also served white students, was consistent with then-current administrative and court guidance, and with the stated position of the NAACP Legal Defense Fund in its proposed decree in *Jefferson County*. Had the school board instead proposed to make major improvements to Lincoln, the school board might have been subject to a charge that such construction would unlawfully perpetuate the dual school system. As an example, the Norfolk school board, after negotiating with the local black community, proposed to build a new Booker T. Washington High School close to its predecessor in a black neighborhood. The NAACP Legal Defense Fund sued the school board, alleging that the site of the new school would perpetuate dual schools. Eventually, following a negotiated settlement, the replacement school was built near the original school and close to historically black Norfolk State University.[76] The Office of Education and the NAACP Legal Defense Fund at that time were focused on moving more black students out of black schools, not on preserving those schools as desegregated facilities.

Separately from the desegregation issue, the school board faced a local political reality in choosing between the Lincoln campus and a new high school to serve Gainesville's east side. Both the 1965 and 1967 state surveys recommended a new high school on Gainesville's more affluent, white, and rapidly growing west side. Gainesville's east side then held a substantial but less affluent white population. During segregation, there was no perceptible difference in the schools that served whites on the east and west sides. But now the west side would receive a brand-new junior/senior high school. Had the school board chosen to send the east-side white students to an upgraded Lincoln, both the east-side white community and, potentially, members of the black community would have pointed to the special treatment being given the west side. Only by providing a new high school on the east side could the school board assure both white and black east-side residents that they would, in fact, receive equal treatment with the west side. Both new schools would eventually be constructed according to the same plans.

To shield the former black schools from arbitrary closings, a new legal doctrine under the Equal Protection Clause would have to be developed by civil rights attorneys and the courts. According to that doctrine, the burden of desegregation, including busing, could not disproportionately impact either race. By the time that doctrine had been developed, it was too late for most of the South's closed black schools, including Alachua County's two historically black high schools. Just how deeply the black community in Alachua County would feel the impact of those closings is a major topic to be examined later.

Amid the continuing search for solutions to overcrowded schools, more than half of Alachua County's teachers on February 19, 1968, joined the statewide teacher strike called by the Florida Education Association. Various feints and delays had pushed the strike into early 1968. Teachers later expressed regret that they did not walk out during the high school football season.[77] A special session of the legislature called as a last-ditch effort to avoid a strike had passed a funding package that was unacceptable to the teachers and to Governor Kirk.[78] A key provision opposed by teachers eliminated the option of county freeholders, by referendum, to exceed the ten-mill mandatory county property tax contribution to the Minimum Foundation Program.[79]

The strike placed Superintendent Talbot and his assistant, Tommy Tomlinson, in a difficult position. Both viewed themselves as teacher advocates, but the school board made clear that it wanted the schools kept open during the strike.[80] Replacing more than half of the system's teachers proved impossible, however. Substitute teachers of any background were recruited, including junior college graduates and housewives with even less formal education.[81] Public resentment of the unqualified substitutes would dog the school board. Both the Greater Gainesville Chamber of Commerce and Citizens for Better Schools, who were leading the efforts for the proposed bond issue, came out early against using unqualified substitute teachers.[82] The League of Women Voters, more supportive of the striking teachers, sought closure of all county schools unless they could be staffed by "permanent, well qualified and fully certified teachers."[83]

During the strike, the Greater Gainesville Chamber of Commerce kept up its campaign to educate voters about the need for a bond issue.[84] The chamber urged citizens to visit the schools during classes as part of that campaign. But the classroom-visit program, originally intended to generate support for the proposed bond issue, was suspended by the school board. More parents were visiting the schools during the strike, and some regular teachers were also visiting to investigate the quality of substitutes.[85] A leader of the bond issue campaign agreed that citizen visits to classrooms during the strike could be disruptive.[86] For all practical purposes, community efforts for a bond issue for new schools took a backseat during the teacher strike.

Despite threatening to veto the legislative compromise passed at the legislature's 1968 special session, Governor Kirk allowed that package to become law on March 7. That package provided some new taxes for education, over Kirk's objections, but its financial provisions failed to satisfy the Florida Education Association, and the law also failed to grant teachers collective bargaining rights. The state board of education issued a face-saving proposal to end the strike, which would have allowed teachers to return to work without retaliation, and which contained some financial concessions. Professor R. L. Johns told Alachua County teachers that the FEA had won a tremendous victory in achieving the compromise financial package. He said, "It won't do you any good to stay out now. Go back. You need to be brave, but a dead soldier can't do any more fighting."[87] On the basis of the state school board proposal, the Florida Education Association called off the walkout.[88] Predictably, other states took advantage of the strike to recruit Florida teachers and graduating students to positions outside Florida.[89]

In Alachua County there would be as happy an ending as circumstances permitted: there would be no retaliation against teachers who had gone out on strike. Superintendent Talbot determined that the striking teachers' resignations had not been properly submitted to the school board, and all of the teachers were reinstated without adverse action.[90] Some teachers discharged for striking in other counties were given jobs in Alachua County.[91] Significant teacher pay raises were later approved by the school board, ranging from $800 a year (15.7 percent) for starting teachers to $1,872 (17.3 percent) for teachers with a PhD.[92]

Frances Lunsford, an Alachua County teacher who in 1968 was a district director of the Florida Education Association, said in 1973, "The walkout teachers found a camaraderie with others they had never associated with. Later, this helped us a great deal with integration." The local FEA chapter included both black and white teachers in its strike meetings.[93] About equal proportions of black and white secondary school teachers had walked out.[94]

With the strike over, a consensus emerged that a school bond referendum should be scheduled for May 28, 1968, the day of the spring primary runoff election. Osee Fagan, addressing the school board in March 1968 said, "An awareness that schools are our responsibility exists now that never before prevailed in Alachua County. . . . We should ask for this bond issue before apathy sets in."[95]

The school board on April 4, 1968, set May 28 for the bond referendum. At the same meeting, the board approved the 1968–69 plan for operating the county's secondary schools. As anticipated, Gainesville High School was placed on double sessions with eleventh and twelfth grades attending in the morning and tenth grade in the afternoon. But ninth-grade students were retained at the junior high schools rather than being moved to Gainesville High as had been originally proposed. The junior highs would operate on single sessions. At other schools, double sessions were to be used as necessary with the lowest grade to be broken out for the afternoon session.[96] The historically black A. L. Mebane Junior/Senior High School was subsequently placed on double sessions.[97]

It remained for the school board to finalize the school construction plan that the bond issue would support. By law, state funds could be used only for construction of schools approved in state surveys. But the school board could approve construction not sanctioned by a state survey if only county funds were used to fund the construction. The school board approved the final construction plans related to the bond issue on April 11, 1968. That plan required $12,770,000 to be borrowed, and $4,627,193 from other sources, for a total of $17,397,193.

The construction plan closely followed the 1967 state survey update, except that new high schools were again added for Hawthorne and Newberry, and a middle school was proposed for High Springs.[98] Keeping high schools open in the smaller outlying towns avoided emotional reactions from voters. In 1956, when high schools in High Springs and Alachua were closed and consolidated into the new Santa Fe High School, movements arose in High Springs and Newberry to secede from Alachua County to join neighboring Gilchrist County. Newberry had refused to join in the Santa Fe consolidation.[99] Jasper Joiner, the school board chair, explained that the Hawthorne and Newberry schools would answer needs for community schools in those areas. He said the schools would have at least one hundred students in each grade, which was the minimum number of students recommended by the state for effective and economical high school programs.[100] Hawthorne High School had lost accreditation in 1966, and Newberry in 1967. For the first time in the county, all of the new schools would be constructed with air-conditioning.[101]

Also, the school board approved $130,000 for new vocational education facilities at Lincoln and $228,200 for vocational and special-education facilities and a remodeled science lab at Mebane.[102] Those schools would still cease to be academic senior high schools after the construction program was complete. Chair Joiner commented that there was not sufficient interest in vocational training in the county to support a special area vocational center.[103]

In summary, four new junior/senior high schools, in the east and northwest sections of Gainesville and in Hawthorne and Newberry, were to be constructed, together with six new elementary schools, four in Gainesville and one each in High Springs and Alachua. Improvements were to be made at virtually all other schools. The bond resolution permitted the board to reallocate funds based on changed needs as the project progressed.[104]

The legislature in its 1968 special session had removed counties' authority to levy more than ten mills for schools. That action worked in favor of the bond issue, because the county's optional three-mill levy approved in 1967 would have to be rolled back. It was estimated that the $12.7 million bond issue could be financed for an annual cost to taxpayers of about three mills, so that there would technically be no increase in taxes.[105]

The new junior college, which had commenced operations in September 1966, would, in accordance with unrelated state law changes, transition from school board jurisdiction to a separate board of trustees under state supervision.[106]

The county had to elect a superintendent of schools and two school board members in 1968. The May 7 primary election campaign overlapped with the bond issue campaign and focused voter attention on the schools.

Willard Williams and Jasper Joiner, both of whom had served as school board chairs, did not seek reelection. Williams decided to seek election to the county commission, and Joiner had suffered from health problems. Both open school board seats were contested in the Democratic primary, and by Republican candidates in the general election in November.

John Perdue, then principal of Howard Bishop Junior High, ran against Talbot for superintendent in the Democratic primary. Both superintendent candidates said they would support a vote to change the superintendent position from elected to appointed. Talbot, who had vigorously argued in favor of electing the superintendent in 1963, was asked at a candidates' forum for the reason he changed his position. Talbot responded that he had supported the elected superintendent in the 1963 vote to prevent the possible appointment of E. D. Manning Jr., the incumbent superintendent. He said he was willing to resign anytime the voters wanted an appointive superintendent. "I am willing to call for a referendum any time after May 7 and if the voters approve the appointive position I am ready to resign."[107]

Professor Robert Cade, MD, a Republican candidate for school board and the inventor of Gatorade, criticized the county's freedom-of-choice desegregation plan: "The free choice plan may be fine but I don't think they (Negroes) really have a choice here. I find it hard to believe Negroes in my neighborhood are sending their children on long bus rides clear across town of their own volition. I am in favor of integrated neighborhood schools." Talbot countered that the plan was working, and the proof was that for the last two years there had been no visits of organized protesters to his office.[108] The other school board candidates did not express their views on desegregation in the press. This exchange marked the only occasion that desegregation surfaced publicly as a disputed issue in county school elections during the period prior to 1970.

Talbot easily defeated Perdue with 60 percent of the total vote. Democrats Benford Samuels, DDS, and Professor William F. Enneking, MD, were the victorious school board candidates. They would each serve on the board through the difficult years ahead. Both men emphasized Gainesville's need for public schools of the highest quality, and the electorate had responded to that message.

Samuels was born in Oxford, Mississippi, and graduated from the University of Mississippi. He received his DDS from Emory University and came to Gainesville after serving in the navy. Samuels had taken a leadership role in the campaign to pass the 1968 school bond issue. He served terms as president of the Rotary Club, Boys Club, and United Way. For his service as a school board member from 1969 to 1976, and chair in 1972 and 1976, he was chosen Public Servant of the Year by the League of Women Voters in 1977. He was on the advisory committee that helped establish the University of Florida's dental school.[109]

In sharp contrast, Enneking was from Madison, Wisconsin. His daughter, Kayser Enneking, MD, says that he first wanted to be a football coach. Enneking went on to graduate from the University of Wisconsin at Madison and, after a stint in the navy during World War II, from the University of Wisconsin medical school. He did additional active duty in the navy during the Korean War, with two years at a forward MASH hospital. His first professional appointment was at the University of Mississippi medical school in Jackson in 1956. He was recruited by the University of Florida College of Medicine in 1960 as its first orthopedic surgeon, and became a leader in the profession.

Kayser Enneking believes that her father became aware of racial issues in the South during his years in Jackson, and was inspired to take a lifelong interest in civil rights. He also had seven school-age children. She says that he saw school integration proceeding in Alachua County and a need for strong leadership on the school board. She believes "Pop" decided to run for school board on his own, and that he was not pressed to run by the University.[110] Tomlinson, who worked closely with Enneking, believed Enneking ran to advocate for an appointed superintendent. That position, of course, implied that Talbot should be replaced. However, according to Tomlinson, Talbot and Enneking formed a good working relationship as Enneking became more familiar with Talbot and local issues.[111] Despite Talbot's offer to resign, the appointed superintendent would not appear on the ballot until November 1970; Talbot would serve until the eventual appointment of a successor in January 1972.

During his time on the school board, in spite of his professional commitments, Enneking would play a leading role. Tomlinson remembers, during some crisis, that cars would speed though the school board's parking lot at night, screeching their wheels. At one point, during the night, shots were fired into the school board offices; visitors are still shown the bullet holes. To keep everyone safe, Enneking decided to hold an after-hours meeting at his house. Enneking's petite wife, Margaret, opened the door and invited Tomlinson in. She then joined the group, filled her pipe with one hand, and propped her feet on the coffee table. Although Margaret remained behind the scenes on school matters, she was not a silent partner to her husband.[112]

The bond issue was overwhelmingly approved by the voters on May 28, 1968. Of the 11,557 qualified freeholders, 10,243 voted, and of those, 7,585 (74 percent) voted in favor of the bond issue and 2,658 voted against. The bond issue was supported in Gainesville and the county's rural areas.[113] Public support came from key business leaders and from the *Sun* newspaper. The Alachua County Parent Teacher Association led a grassroots campaign to communicate with individual voters.[114] The chamber of commerce Classroom '68 campaign, which spearheaded these efforts, made the difference. Talbot said, "We educators tried to pass the bond issue the last time. . . . This time the people themselves got behind it."[115]

The day before the Alachua County bond election, the US Supreme Court decided *Green v. County School Board of New Kent County*. That decision resolved the freedom-of-choice issue left hanging in *Jefferson County*. In response to an NAACP Legal Defense Fund lawsuit, the Supreme Court unanimously held that *Brown* requires school boards to end dual school systems, not just to allow black students the right to attend white schools. ". . . The fact that in 1965 the Board opened the doors of the former 'white' school to Negro children and of the 'Negro' school to white children merely begins, not ends, our inquiry whether the Board has taken steps adequate to abolish its dual, segregated system."[116] The court held that school boards have a constitutional obligation to adopt other affirmative means of ending dual school systems when freedom-of-choice desegregation plans fail to produce that result.[117] "Rather than further the dismantling of the dual system, the [freedom of choice] plan has operated simply to burden children and their parents with a responsibility which *Brown II* placed squarely on the School Board." Echoing the Fifth Circuit in *Jefferson County*, the Supreme Court held that school boards must "fashion steps which promise realistically to convert promptly to a system without a 'white' school and a 'Negro' school, but just schools."[118]

The chamber of commerce, the PTA, the school board, the teachers and students on double sessions, and the black students who to this point had chosen to remain at Lincoln and Mebane could not know that, in response to an NAACP Legal Defense Fund appeal, the Supreme Court in January 1970 would order the county to end freedom of choice and implement a unitary system while that system was still under construction.

CHAPTER 9
LINCOLN HIGH SCHOOL

We Wanted Them to Make It Equal

Dear Lincoln High, We love Thee,
Thy name will ever be,
A song of praise immortal
We pledge our loyalty.

Girded with light and knowledge
You brighten up the way
Through strife, defeat and victory
Honor to Thee we pay.

Hail Alma Mater, Hail Thee
Majestic red and white
None greater can transcend Thee
Our love shines pure and bright.

We bow in adoration
And honor to you bring
We shall your name through years defend
In praise to Thee we sing.[1]

The Alachua County school board resolved in early 1968, consistently with the 1967 update to the state survey of county school facilities, that the county's two black senior high schools would not become part of the county's unitary system. When the NAACP Legal Defense Fund eventually challenged that decision in March 1970, both the US District Court and the Fifth Circuit Court of Appeals would uphold the school board's decision.[2]

But a large segment of Gainesville's African American community did not accept that result, and for many, even after more than forty years, the loss of Lincoln High School remains an open wound.

To understand why, we need to examine Lincoln's history, its role in the black community, and the ways the black schools kept many students engaged in the educational process. We also need to understand that once the courts decided that the last vestiges of dual school systems and freedom of choice were depriving black students of their constitutional right under *Brown* to equal education, Lincoln could not have continued to play its historical role for the black community. And, to understand why the integration of African American students into Alachua County's white secondary schools flared into violence, we also need to understand the state in which segregation had left the young people who chose to the bitter end to remain in the black schools.

The black public schools in Alachua County grew from the first schools for freed slaves established just after the Civil War through the encouragement and protection of the Freedmen's Bureau. In Gainesville, the first school for blacks was formed by Catherine Bent, who arrived there in 1865. Miss Bent was a white teacher from Newburyport, Massachusetts, who was supported financially by the National Freedman's Relief Association of New York. That organization had been formed by the American Missionary Association and the Congregational Church. She was joined in Gainesville in 1866 by Harriet Barnes of Norwich, Connecticut. Other white teachers arrived from the North around the same time to teach in Gainesville and other areas in Alachua County.

> Throughout the South freedmen and their children greeted schooling with near universal enthusiasm. The Gainesville youth were no exception, for according to their teachers, "never were children more eager to learn, or more rapid in their improvement." The teachers faced one major obstacle, however, in the "assaults" on the schoolroom by white boys. These hurled missiles "in some cases aiming deliberately at the teachers, and sometimes hitting them." The ladies found these young whites especially belligerent, reporting, "nothing would please them as much, as to have a battle with our children and kill some of them."[3]

An African American board of trustees in 1867 purchased a site for a permanent school building that became the Union Academy. Members of the black community built the school according to plans from the Freedmen's Bureau.[4] The odds were daunting. At the end of the 1860s, Union Academy and other schools for blacks enrolled only 345 of the estimated 10,000 blacks in the county's total population.[5] But from Union

Academy's earliest days, it was the beginning point for the achievements of Gainesville's black citizens.

By 1870, Union Academy began receiving some financial support from the Alachua County Board of Public Instruction, which had been organized in 1869 under the Constitution of 1868 and the school law of 1869. By 1873, black teachers had taken over from the white teachers who came south immediately after the Civil War.[6]

Normal schools for training white teachers were established by the state as early as 1880, but state-supported training for black teachers was limited to courses of one to two months. During the mid-1880s, Union Academy trained teachers under these provisions.[7] It was not until 1887 under the Constitution of 1885 that the state established a normal school for blacks.[8] Union Academy continued to train teachers in state-supported summer sessions and county-funded special institutes for persons preparing for the teacher exam.[9]

The wood Union Academy building, part of which was fifty-five years old, was replaced in 1923 by a new brick building that was named Lincoln High School, financed in part by an Alachua County school board bond issue and in part by a grant from the Rosenwald Fund, which assisted construction of many black schools in the South. Lincoln High School later added eleventh and twelfth grades, graduating its first senior class in June 1925.[10] Lincoln was accredited by the state as a high school in 1926, only the second black high school to achieve that status in Florida.[11] This school was located in Gainesville's older black neighborhood, just northwest of downtown. The 1923 building later became the A. Quinn Jones Elementary School, and later the A. Quinn Jones Center. It remains in use by the school district.

Union Academy and its successor, Lincoln High, were led by Principal A. Quinn Jones from 1921 until his retirement in 1957. "Prof" Jones graduated first in his class from Florida A&M College in 1915 and earned a master's degree from the Hampton Institute in 1935. Jones also taught high school classes and classes that helped local black teachers gain state certification.[12] Jones was one of many exceptional black educators who went beyond the minimum effort that might have satisfied local school boards. His efforts and those of his teachers made the achievements of Lincoln High alumni possible.

The years after the Civil War, and continuing into the twentieth century, were hard in the South. Per capita income in the South in 1880 was one-third of per capita income in the North. In the ten years between 1870 and 1880, the gap between the South's agricultural and industrial output and that of the North grew larger.[13] By the 1920s, Alachua County was still mostly rural and poor. The county's 1925 population was 32,584, and Gainesville counted 8,466 citizens.[14] Of the county's population age ten and over, 2.2 percent of the whites and 28 percent of the blacks were illiterate.[15]

In 1925, the school board did not have sufficient funds to keep the schools open. Lincoln was ordered closed at the end of six months. Prof Jones led the successful effort by the Lincoln community to raise enough money not only to acquire such things as library books and lab supplies to achieve state accreditation, but also to pay the teachers for the remainder of the full eight-month term.[16] During three school years, from 1929 to 1931, the school board reduced the school year to four months and charged tuition of six dollars per month for elementary students and ten dollars per month for junior and senior high students.[17] Jones required his teachers to collect the tuition from Lincoln students. Jones also led other fundraising efforts, such as school concerts, dinners, and the sale of sandwiches, that succeeded in keeping Lincoln open for the full eight-month term during those three years.[18]

The private contributions continued; the black community raised $1,400 to $1,500 in 1946 to start the school's band, and obtained donated instruments.[19] As late as fall 1965, the Lincoln band boosters were raising $6,800 to replace the eleven-year-old uniforms of the school's marching band.[20]

With the proceeds of a 1953 bond issue, four new high schools were constructed by Alachua County, two of which were white and two of which were black. The new Lincoln High School opened for the 1956–57 school year, together with the new A. L. Mebane High School in Alachua. The school's faculty was encouraged to help plan the new building. Committees that grew out of the school's self-evaluation for state accreditation in the 1952–53 school year worked on planning the new school during the 1953–54 school year.[21] As an example, Andrew Mickle, newly hired as the school's tailoring instructor, helped plan the tailoring lab.[22]

The new Lincoln High was located in the newer black neighborhood on Gainesville's far east side. The school's relocation there encouraged African Americans to move to that more suburban neighborhood, which had room to grow to the east and south.[23] The 1923 building stood in an older black neighborhood west of downtown that was surrounded by traditionally white areas and could not in those times expand in any direction. The development of black neighborhoods to the east would be a complicating factor in desegregation.

Lincoln and Mebane opened two years after *Brown I*, and a year after *Brown II*. When those schools were built, the continued operation for blacks of the historically black public schools had not been declared unconstitutional. That step did not come until 1968 in *Green*.

By providing new, much improved high schools in 1956 for the county's black community, the school board succeeded, as it hoped, to bind the black community even more strongly to its separate schools.[24] Lincoln High continued to be in the forefront of black high schools in Florida.

In 1964, Lincoln was one of the first black high schools in the state to be accepted for full accreditation by the Southern Association of Colleges and Schools, meeting the same standards as white high schools. Prior to 1964, the Southern Association had placed all black schools in a separate category of "approved," which was not equivalent to full accreditation.[25]

Albert White is the most determined advocate of Lincoln High. White graduated from Lincoln High School in 1962 and later became executive director of the Greater Gainesville Chamber of Commerce and an executive at the municipal electric utility. At Lincoln, he was an honor student, vice president of the student council, quarterback for the football team, and a member of several other sports teams. He has written a history of Lincoln High that describes its people—the teachers, principals and coaches, and many individual students and their later achievements. The members of each graduating class from 1925 through 1970 are listed by name. The connection to Lincoln of black business leaders, teachers, doctors, lawyers, and some professional athletes is celebrated. As much as a history of Lincoln High School, it is a history of the black community in Gainesville, since the Gainesville black community of those days could not avoid passing through Lincoln High.[26]

Teaching in the black schools, despite pay that until the 1940s in Florida was below that of white teachers,[27] provided one of the few opportunities for blacks to enter the middle class. Teaching also allowed blacks to remain in their home communities, rather than leaving for the North or for Southern cities that provided more economic opportunities and more open societies. Black teachers often held leadership positions in their communities. Being a black teacher was not only a position of honor and respect, but also one that carried specific responsibilities to black communities and their children.

Black schools shared the same goals as the white schools, but as the black schools separately evolved, black educators developed special ways of dealing with the needs of their students. Teachers were expected to take an active interest in their young charges' personal welfare in addition to their academic progress, or lack thereof. As members of a closely knit and bounded community, teachers knew not just their students but their students' families. They would visit their charges at home when necessary.[28] They might attend the same church on Sunday. Many public school teachers also taught Sunday school, which provided another opportunity for them to work on students' reading and other skills.[29] All of these activities took place close to the students' homes, not miles away in a white neighborhood. Charles Chestnut III and others recall that despite the absence of many telephones when they were growing up, if a young person had done something wrong at school, his parents would know about it even before he got home in the afternoon.[30] Black educators were supported by a network of black colleges, black education associations, and black education journals.[31]

Brown notwithstanding, no one ever informed the teachers and students at Lincoln that they should not, or could not, set high goals for students' future achievements. Many Lincoln students went on to Bethune-Cookman College, Florida A&M University, and other universities and colleges, and on to their own successful careers.

Lincoln was more than a place where African American young persons showed up for class. Charles Chestnut, the grandfather of Charles Chestnut III, founded and coached the school's first football team beginning in 1923.[32] Lincoln's football teams enjoyed wide support and much success on the field, even winning the black high school national championship in 1939.[33] The school's mascot, the Terrier, was a symbol of "intelligence, strength, speed and fearlessness," and the school colors of red and white symbolized, respectively, hardiness and courage and purity and innocence.[34]

Lincoln provided opportunities for its students to join clubs, to participate in student government, to be cheerleaders, band members, and majorettes, to act in plays, to sing in the chorus,[35] and, for those who had not dropped out (a persistent problem), to walk down the aisle at graduation in view of their families and receive their diplomas. The Rev. Wright, who sued successfully to desegregate Alachua County's schools, recalled that commencement at Lincoln High School was the highlight of the year for Gainesville's black community. In Wright's opinion, nothing has replaced it.[36] The ceremony from Lincoln's earliest years opened with James Weldon Johnson's "Lift Every Voice and Sing."[37] Everyone came in their best clothes and enjoyed a couple of hours of celebration, affirming the community's pride of race.

Principals at white schools did not, and were not expected to, join in playground games with their students. As former athletes, black high school principals did. John Dukes Jr., Lincoln High's principal when it closed, would often join students in games of touch football.[38] Dukes at Lincoln convened what he called the Gents Club, at which he taught social skills, such as tying a necktie, to boys who would never learn those skills at home.[39] Playing football for Coach Jessie Heard included lessons in representing the school's brand to the world outside the school. No less so than in the white schools, Lincoln's winning football teams helped to inspire school pride. When asked what kept students at Lincoln during freedom of choice, Coach Heard answered, "The Big Red, and the teachers. . . . So that was the glue, I think, that held Lincoln together, because there was just so much pride there."[40]

Gainesville's geography and demographics allowed Lincoln to serve the city's entire black student population from grades 7 to 12. Students and teachers were together under a single administration, in the same building, for the most important six years of their education. Lincoln students came together from diverse backgrounds, from the educated middle class to desperately poor single-parent families. Friendships were formed and bonds arose between teachers and coaches and their students. From their teachers, students learned not just English and math, but also, in a supportive setting, life skills they would need as adults. Not just in the white schools was there a prelapsarian state of grace.

Geography and demographics also meant that if there was to be a unitary school system in Alachua County, the Lincoln school community would have to be broken up. The school board had made the choice in early 1968, before the 1968 bond issue, before *Green*, that instead of one white and one black high school, there would be three high schools in Gainesville, all of which would house both white students and some portion of the black students formerly housed at Lincoln. Similarly, there would be four schools that would absorb the lower grades at Lincoln. The faculties and student bodies at those schools would reflect the area's broader demographics.

In every one of those schools, because of the racial balancing that was generally required when school systems converted from dual operation to unitary operation, black teachers and black students would find themselves in the minority. Gainesville's west side was predominantly white. Gainesville High was able to take in the large African American community west of downtown, which was closer to GHS than it was to Lincoln. The new west-side school would have to rely on busing of blacks. The planners assumed the new east-side school would serve what was then a large, if less prosperous, east-side white population, together with some part of the east-side black community. If the school board had chosen to improve the Lincoln campus instead of closing it, Lincoln would have been subject to the same racial balancing requirements as the other two high schools.

It was at just this point that there emerged a disconnect between many in the black community and those controlling *Wright v. Board*. The late Rev. Wright, the president of the local NAACP chapter and father of one of the named plaintiffs, plainly states that at some point during the case, he and other local black leaders agreed that their attorneys should pursue total integration:

> And we talked a long time. And then [the NAACP Legal Defense Fund lawyer] said to me, Reverend Wright, we want Alachua County to go all out. We don't want talking. I said, Attorney, let me tell you what. Just those three [the first three black students to attend Gainesville High] have caused so much trouble. And he said I'm going to argue for total integration at the building downtown and you need to

> be there at the beginning of my argument. And I was there at the beginning. And everybody who needed to decide that we would go for total integration met for two days and they said we are going to do.[41]

The timing of those consultations is less clear, however. At the hearing in *Wright v. Board* on April 5, 1965, local counsel for the NAACP Legal Defense Fund advocated against freedom of choice and for a fully unitary school system.[42] In September 1966, the NAACP Legal Defense Fund filed its written objection to Alachua County's continuation of its dual school system, in the form of its draft decree in *Jefferson County*.[43] At the time of his 2012 interview, Wright was ninety-two. He died two years later, in 2014. Those with whom he may have consulted are probably no longer living. His autobiography and an earlier interview barely mention the school-desegregation case.[44] In 2012, Wright was not sure of the name of the lawyer who consulted with the black leaders.

Charles Chestnut III has a different recollection. He believes that the NAACP Youth Council from the start wanted Lincoln kept open but made equal, but that the older African American leadership, including the Rev. Wright, believed that complete desegregation was a more important objective than saving Lincoln.[45]

> And our basic position at that particular point in time, in terms of the youth council, was that no matter what was going on, if you're going to put a million dollars into GHS, equally give that amount to Lincoln High School.
>
> And so that was the basic thing. Because we were pretty pleased in terms of the education that we were getting from our teachers there. They all had had degrees. They all had certificates. So, hey, what's the basic difference between, you know? They were all licensed by the state, all accredited by the state and all that kind of stuff, so what's the basic difference? And then when Reverend Wright came in and got to be president of the adult chapter, you know, that we kind of worked with him a little bit. And I think he was aware at that time of what our position basically was.
>
> Tiny Talbot knew what our position was. And so as a result of that, [the Rev. Wright] initially filed a suit and used his daughter as the main [plaintiff] in the suit. And so we automatically joined with him in that particular action. We weren't going to fight with him and argue with him and saying, well, you don't have to do this. . . . And we'd always felt that the answer to our demands in terms of equally funding

> the schools, that the answer [of the school board] to that was close [Lincoln High School].[46]

Despite the NAACP Legal Defense Fund's consistent position in *Wright v. Board* that Alachua County's dual school system had to be terminated, many black teachers continued to remain at Lincoln High because they were waiting for the school board to bring Lincoln up to the same quality as the county's white high schools. It was also reported that black teachers who volunteered to teach in white schools "were ostracized in some quarters."[47] According to Dr. John Rawls, a teacher and administrator in the Alachua County schools before and after desegregation, some believed that those black teachers were putting the black schools down.[48] The late Andrew Mickle was a beloved teacher of tailoring both before and after integration, as well as being Lincoln's swimming and tennis coach. Mickle told an interviewer in 1972 that many teachers saw integration as good but that just as many were against it. According to Mickle, black teachers who believed their pay was equal to the white teachers favored integration.[49] As we saw in chapter 6, many students who remained loyal to the black schools looked askance at the students who had gone to white schools under freedom of choice. Interviewed in 1972, Mabel Dorsey, who graduated from Lincoln and taught there from 1944 to 1968, said that by the time Lincoln closed, there were two factions in Gainesville's African American community, with one group being very supportive of Lincoln and the other not so much.[50]

Bettye Jennings, who agreed when asked by Talbot to be one of the first black teachers to teach in the county's white schools, states, "We were not asking for integration, we were asking for equality."[51] Her husband, Ed Jennings Sr., who served on the Gainesville City Commission and for a term as mayor, frames the issue more starkly:

> But, see, the black man didn't get what he asked for. He asked for equality. He got integration. Because the white man said the only way I can give you equality is to integrate you. And I'm more concerned about how you are going to mix with my people than I am you getting equal education. So equality was put on the back burner and it will come out occasionally, but the main thing was, how can we integrate you? And it should not have been. It should have been, how can we give you equal treatment? And equal quality. And that's not what they did.[52]

Donnie Batie, MD, and Brenda Wims both believe that Lincoln should have been kept open as a senior high school and made equal to GHS. Batie makes the point that the Lincoln campus was on Waldo Road, a major highway. Because of Lincoln's location, Batie believes that whites would not have objected as much to attending Lincoln as they might have to attending black schools more isolated in black residential neighborhoods. Wims: "What was in our minds, just bring us the things they have over [at GHS]. Make it equal on our side of town. But Mr. Talbot was saying we don't have money to do that. But we do have money to take and bus you over there, because there are seats available for you over there."[53]

Charles Chestnut III in 1969 supported keeping Lincoln open and bringing in some white students, but he is candid in admitting that he and others did not foresee that had Lincoln been retained, Lincoln would (at least as the court would have ordered) have had a white-majority student body and faculty:

> Q. . . . But what I'm saying is, hypothetically, let's assume the school board decides okay, we're going to leave Lincoln where it is. And we're going to bus the white people into Lincoln, which is what I understand some of the people wanted to do. So at that point Lincoln becomes 70/30. So how would that have helped? That's a tough question.
>
> A. Yeah. Because we did, I know at that point, I didn't particularly see it that way, I guess, because knowing that that possibility wasn't going to happen anyway. Because Tiny had said that white people are not going to send their children on the east side of town, you know. So that never got into being to play with that. The powers that be were controlling everything anyway, so, hey—you know, that wasn't going to happen. We didn't see and, you know, I didn't, this much younger generation, at that point, did not, did not see that as being the thing.
>
> We knew and felt that we would still, as I said—our initial thing was equal funding. That was it. It all, and all of this other stuff, led into it. And then that Supreme Court decision and everything and with that forced busing, that, that's when we began to say, oh boy, did the wrong thing. Did the wrong thing. . . .[54]

The loyalty of a significant portion of Gainesville's black community to Lincoln High School was not, as the US Civil Rights Commission had generally opined, just another barrier to overcome on the way to the promised land of integration.[55] That loyalty was not to segregation as such, but it was as much a product of segregation as historic white attachment to separate white schools. During the five school years that Alachua County operated under freedom of choice, 1965–66 through 1969–70, the majority of African American students and teachers at the secondary level would not choose to transfer to the white schools. Apparently freedom of choice had not only eased white fears of greater black presence in white schools, but also played to expectations in the black community that the black schools would continue their historic role for the foreseeable future.

When faced with the closing of Lincoln High School, its remaining students, who were even less ready for desegregation than their future white classmates, did not understand or care about constitutional principles. For them, going at last to the white schools was not "such stuff as dreams are made on." Their disillusionment was shared by many of their elders. What they understood was that they were losing their school. They were not going to give up their school without a fight.

Despite desegregation's attractiveness as a simple solution, it was not a simple task. Thurgood Marshall once said during his tenure with the NAACP Legal Defense Fund, "The easy part of this job is fighting the white folks."[56] The Legal Defense Fund position was ". . . only integration will make certain that black children receive the same education as white children."[57] Alachua County was not the only community where many African Americans wanted improvements to the schools that served them more than they wanted integration. The same conflict arose in Boston, with much the same result.[58] The late Derrick Bell, then a lawyer for the NAACP Legal Defense Fund, was asked in 1961 by blacks in Leake County, Mississippi, to sue to reopen a black school that had been closed. "I recall informing the group that both LDF and NAACP had abandoned efforts to make separate schools equal, but if they wished to desegregate the whole school system, we could probably provide legal assistance. . . . Following my detailed exposition of what their rights were, it was hardly surprising that the black parents did not reject them. To put it kindly, they had not been exposed to an adversary discussion of the subject."[59]

In Alachua County we must deal with two conflicting narratives: on one hand, courageous black plaintiffs and lawyers and courageous school leaders and teachers overcoming the formidable obstacles to the legally mandated unitary school system, and on the other, equally courageous black teachers and students believing that process would only cause them harm. But our purpose is to review history, not just narrative.

In light of all the facts, there were reasons that the white school, however imperfect, became the model for educating members of both races. Despite the Supreme Court's Olympian pronouncement in *Green* that there should be no white schools, no black schools, just schools, at the time of desegregation in the South, there were only white schools and black schools. In 1954, or even later, it would have been a useful exercise to assess both white and black schools and to attempt a synthesis of the best features of each, for the benefit of both races. But no one ever thought of that. By 1970, there was no time left for a redesign. In the afterword, we will reexamine the features of black schools that still merit close attention almost fifty years after the end of the South's dual school systems.

There are contemporary sources from which we can derive an objective sense of the educational circumstances of Alachua County's black students as they faced desegregation. One source is a 1972 evaluation of Lincoln High by a history of education class at the University of Florida College of Education. Dr. Arthur O. White taught the class. Members of the class reviewed the available records of the school, including course lists and report cards. Some newspaper clippings were collected. Students interviewed a number of former Lincoln teachers and alumni. The full study was never published, and its work exists only in informal notes.[60] The interview portion of the study used a questionnaire, but interviewers and interviewees seldom hewed to the formal interview structure of the questionnaire. One paper refers to an interview committee report, which, if it ever existed as a separate document, is not in the file.

This study provides only snapshots, not a comprehensive picture. The study focuses on Lincoln's academic performance and gives little attention to the school's role as a catalyst for black advancement. And even those snapshots, coming from a variety of teachers and former students at the school, show deeply conflicting opinions of the school's performance. But some history is better than none at all.

First, there is no question that right up to its closing, Lincoln High School lacked the resources of Alachua County's white schools. That fact magnifies, and does not detract from, the achievements of Lincoln's teachers and alumni. Students used obsolete hand-me-down textbooks, and science labs and equipment scarcely served their purpose.[61] The *Sun*, which had the archives to back it up, in a December 1969 editorial reminded its readers that Charles Chestnut III in 1963 had referred to the "inadequate" education he received at a black high school, and that Neil Butler "firmly seconded" Chestnut.[62] Despite many positive comments by former Lincoln students about their teachers, some former Lincoln students who entered white schools noted that some Lincoln teachers were less competent.[63] Brenda Wims (a career educator herself), says of Lincoln, "Our vision, of course, was different from theirs, because when we have a vision, then you have to have people with the skills to implement the vision. And the teachers we had were teachers that had been there quite a while."[64] Batie notes that at Lincoln, there were not a lot of students who were academically inclined or who might have considered college; that student population was difficult for the Lincoln teachers.[65] Alvin Butler, who entered the white schools under freedom of choice in the seventh grade, says that some of his friends who remained at Lincoln were not pushed as hard by their teachers as he was at Gainesville High.[66]

Florida in 1963 began to require a score of at least 500 on the National Teachers Examination for permanent certification to teach in its public schools, and to receive salary increases. In 1965, just over 50 of the 253 African American teachers in the Alachua County system had scores of 500 or more on the test. By contrast, almost all of the county's 563 white teachers had achieved that minimum score. But a majority of Alachua County's black teachers were on continuing contracts, a status that exempted them from taking the NTE as a condition of employment.[67]

Second, it should come as no surprise that black students as a group were less well prepared academically than their white counterparts. And within that group, blacks who were choosing under freedom of choice to attend white schools were a stronger group of students than those who remained in the black schools. Anecdotally, many of the students who transferred to white schools under freedom of choice were sons and daughters of black teachers, ministers, and other black professionals.[68] The disparity between the two groups of black students would affect the schools' ability to cope with the two-thirds of black students who would be forced into white secondary schools when freedom of choice ended in 1970.

Senior placement test scores at Gainesville High in the 1970–71 school year were disaggregated by George Thomas, a GHS guidance counselor, to show scores for white students, for black students who entered GHS under freedom of choice from previously white junior highs, and for Lincoln students who entered GHS directly in February 1970. Fifty-four percent of the white students scored above 300, the minimum score for acceptance into a four-year state university; 17 percent of the blacks who entered GHS from white schools scored above 300, and only 3 percent of the Lincoln transfers scored above 300. Whether or not the test disadvantaged otherwise qualified blacks, the Lincoln students were less prepared for the test than the other group of black students. A similar disparity existed among students who scored between 0 and 199: 23 percent of the white seniors, 61 percent of the black students who entered from white junior highs, and 88 percent of the Lincoln transfer students.[69] The top senior placement test scores at Lincoln High School declined over the period of freedom of choice. The top score in each year was consistently in the high 400s (495 was a perfect score, achieved by a Lincoln student in 1960) from 1956 through 1962, but generally ranged in the 300s in 1963 and thereafter.[70]

A common caveat to standardized test results is that the tests are culturally biased in favor of white middle-class test subjects. The Coleman Report in 1966 had this response: "They are culture bound. What they measure are the skills which are among the most important in our society for getting a good job and moving up to a better one and for full participation in an increasingly technical world."[71]

The county determined in 1965 from reading tests given over the past three years to sixth graders that students in most of the black schools were reading one to three years below grade level. At that time Talbot estimated that it would take as long as ten years to bring all pupils up to the average statewide score of 250 on the senior placement test. In 1965, the county began obtaining federal funds under the Elementary and Secondary Education Act, P.L. 89–10, for special reading programs.[72] Talbot could not have foreseen then that the county's black schools would eventually have to be integrated or closed. When integration came in 1970, the reading deficits of a large proportion of black students in grades 7–12 would become a major challenge for the white and black teachers in the fully integrated white secondary schools.

During the protests over Lincoln's closing in November 1969, the *Sun* pointed out that only a handful of Lincoln graduates were going on to college, compared with a much larger proportion from the county's white schools. But the *Sun* also acknowledged that the senior placement test was viewed by some as skewed in favor of white middle-class students, and that Lincoln's students came from black elementary schools that themselves were not performing at the level of the white schools.[73] Isaac Jones is a 1962 Lincoln graduate who later received a PhD in counseling technology from the University of Maryland and served as director of federal programs at Santa Fe College in Gainesville. He commented that Lincoln High students took the senior placement test "cold turkey," whereas at Gainesville High students were proctored.[74]

The 1972 College of Education study found that in 1961, 24 Lincoln graduates went on to four-year colleges, and 5 entered junior colleges.[75] Lincoln graduated 105 seniors in 1961.[76] In their 1972 interviews, both Neil Butler, who graduated in 1947, and Andrew Mickle, who taught at Lincoln from 1955 through its closing, placed the college attendance rate of Lincoln graduates at about 30 percent of the typical graduating class. Lincoln unquestionably performed strongly when compared with other black schools, but its record for college placements was not comparable to that of Gainesville High.

In 1955, arguing against immediate desegregation in *Brown II*, the State of Florida had called attention to statewide statistics that showed disparities between white and black achievement. The state provided 1,050 scholarships of $400 for each year for college students desiring to enter the teaching profession. Those scholarships were allocated to each county in proportion to that county's population by race. The average score of 740 white applicants in 1954 was 340, and that of the 488 black applicants was

237. In 1953, the 664 white applicants scored an average of 342, and the 503 black applicants, 237. The brief argued that black teachers were needed, and removing the proportional allocation of these scholarships by race would deny these scholarships to black college students.[77] The brief also called attention to the general black-white disparity in senior placement test scores. In 1953, for example (the most recent year used), only 9.4 percent of black seniors scored above the fiftieth percentile score for white students.[78]

A separate problem that would affect black students' experience in white schools was dropping out. The 1972 Records Committee paper includes a random survey of dropout files from 1951 to 1967. The median grade for withdrawing was the ninth grade. The predominant reason for males dropping out was to work, and for females, either pregnancy or to work. Of the 155 dropouts during the 1962–63 school year, a Lincoln High guidance department file showed that 55 students left due to lack of interest, 23 left to work, 22 left either due to delinquency or truancy, and 28 moved away from the county. Oliver Jones, a son of A. Quinn Jones and in 1972 assistant principal at Shell Middle School in Hawthorne, estimated that 60 percent of students in seventh grade completed twelfth grade and graduated.[79] Mabel Dorsey, who taught home economics and physical education at Lincoln, believed that in 1970, out of 250 students who started in the first grade, 100 would graduate.[80]

Course offerings at Lincoln High School failed to match those available at Gainesville High at the time of desegregation. Individual student files showing courses taken and activities were available only randomly before 1950. The Records Committee concluded that the course offerings in the 1930s and early 1940s were exclusively academic, although girls took as many as four years of home economics. A course in carpentry was offered in 1945, but because of the incompleteness of the records, it is impossible to say whether such courses were offered earlier.

On its new, larger campus, from 1956 the school continued to offer typical high school academic courses and greatly expanded its vocational offerings.[81] Individual student files show the availability of math courses through trigonometry and science courses including biology, chemistry, and physics, but the only foreign language course that was available during those years appears to be Spanish.[82] One student teacher who interned at Lincoln in the spring term of 1969 stated, "Academically speaking in my subject field, the mathematics program was fairly limited compared to the white schools. Alg. I, Alg. II, and Geometry were offered. There were about 2 or 3 classes of each. There were no Alg. III or Trig. classes, let alone calculus."[83] Taking courses not available at Lincoln may have given added impetus to freedom-of-choice transfers to white schools.

Third, discipline, more than inadequate academic preparation, would create much difficulty when the last students from the black schools came to the white schools in 1970. And discipline, or lack thereof, at Lincoln High School, is the topic about which African Americans are most in disagreement.

Most Lincoln faculty members for whom there are completed questionnaires in the 1972 College of Education study rated discipline at Lincoln as "strict but necessary" on a scale that ranged from "too strict" to "lenient." Mabel Dorsey made the best case for discipline at Lincoln. She stated that the Lincoln faculty would not allow the "disruptive, irresponsible behavior that is now going on in the high schools."[84]

Corporal punishment was still used in the 1960s in both the black and white schools in Alachua County. But corporal punishment was much more a part of the educational experience in the black schools. Oliver Jones, Prof Jones's son, confirms that Prof had no discipline problems in his classes "because he was quite a disciplinarian. If you just got out of order and didn't pay attention or what have you, you knew you'd get a spanking."[85] Prof Jones himself acknowledged that he employed corporal punishment in the schools.[86] Dr. John C. Rawls tells that he summoned a father repeatedly to discuss his son's conduct. According to Rawls, the last time the father appeared, he told Rawls, "I'm tired of this. You do anything to him that you want, all I ask is that you leave breath in his body." Rawls adds, "He didn't say how much." Rawls had no further problems with that student.[87] Charles Chestnut III recalls one teacher who would tell his students, "I will appeal to your brain, and if that doesn't work, I will appeal to your hide." But girls would be struck on their hands with a ruler.[88] Frank Ford, who was in grade 11 when Lincoln closed, remembers a teacher who would use an automobile fan belt on her students "if you didn't understand nouns, pronouns, verbs, adjectives, and stuff like that . . . you know, that was just, that was the culture at that time. But that wasn't just in English at Lincoln, that was in all the classes. . . . So you had to learn, you know, to keep from getting that paddling."[89]

Some sense of the state of discipline at Lincoln High School can be gained from comments by intern teachers who taught at Lincoln in spring 1969. These comments were found in Lincoln's records during the 1972 College of Education study.

> A. The white teachers I worked under or observed had a terrible time with discipline as they couldn't hit the students and that was how the students were accustomed to being disciplined. They desperatly [*sic*] needed training in working with blacks. They were teaching there because they needed the jobs and not because they wanted to.

***

> B. I feel that the University of Florida should have given the interns they sent out to Lincoln special training. We were prepared to intern at a typical middle class white school and not the situation we were put in.

***

> F. There appeared to me to be a high rate of absences. You could count on at least 3 or 4 absences every day. Many students missed because they had to stay home and babysit when their parents had errands to do. If it rained somewhere between ¼ to ⅓ of the students missed school.

***

> L. For the most part I found the students I worked with basically good kids and quite likable. This was in the classes that had good discipline. In the classes where there was no discipline it was impossible to teach let alone get to know them.[90]

By the 1968–69 school year, sixteen of eighty-three teachers in grades 7–12 at Lincoln were white.[91]

Donnie Batie has mixed views of the white teachers at Lincoln. He recalls that a white male teacher in seventh grade earned the respect of his students. But the Lincoln students could sense when white teachers did not respect them. "Once you got to know the teacher, you pretty much knew where they stood. Either they felt comfortable around blacks, they would respect us, or they did not feel comfortable around us, and they would fear us. I felt that some females were so naïve in the way they approached us . . ." Batie uses the term *dumb blonde* not lightly, but as an image some teachers conveyed. "And school is to be enjoyed, okay? And although you were the teacher, we wanted to see you as a person, okay? We really desired to see you other than standing in front of us telling us what to do. And so some of the teachers would be able to become comfortable around blacks, and others would not. And you know, as with kids, we're teenagers, okay? You have to understand teenagers. So teenagers is going to push the envelope anyway, and if you allow them to push it and get you uncomfortable, then they got you, and they're going to do, they would basically eventually take over your class."[92]

Sam Taylor Jr., a 1964 Lincoln graduate,[93] was interviewed at his office at the University of Florida on July 12, 1972. He was a doctoral student in political science, having received his undergraduate and master's degrees from the University of Florida. At the time of his interview, he was president of the University of Florida student body, the first black to hold that position. His interview report:

> Sam's opinion is that the teachers lacked a philosophy with which to relate to students, therefore expectations of students was very low. No incentive was given and no inspiration for bettering onsself was evident. He experienced a feeling of "wonder" at the time wasted in class. The teachers role in general was viewed as that of policemen and keeping the "lid on" i.e. keeping the blacks in "place" in the social structure. White values were impressed on the students by the teachers and held up as ideals; however, when Sam and a friend asked twice to arrange a visit to Gainesville High School they were dismissed simply by the principal saying it couldn't be done.[94]
>
> Administrators were considered very poor but were believed to be chosen by the school board for that very reason. New Lincoln had a shell of a building that looked, from the outside, very nice. However, the inside had no books, for example, the biology text in the early 1960's was a 1948 book of which there were not enough copies for even one class (40 to 50 students), let alone an entire grade. No supplies were available, for example, the chemistry teacher, in order to teach something in chemistry, personally went to the University to ask for a few chemicals. It was implied that going to the school board would have been hopeless. Equipment was nonexistant, for example, the biology class saw a microscope once, and that was from the distance of the room.
>
> In spite of all this some excellent teaching was taking place. The better teachers were usually Bethune-Cookman graduates, for example, Sam's english teacher. She insisted that the school work be done, was therefore interesting and got Sam "turned on" to English. Also, it was a smaller than usual class. His chemistry teacher was also considered excellent.
>
> Sam is one of the excellent musicians who emerged from the Lincoln band (without benefit of private lessons of which thought was never given). He recalls a good band in the mid

and late 1950's but by the time he graduated it was not good. However, the pride and loyalty of the community and school for their band was never waving. The same pride and loyalty held true for the football team. Under the coaching of T.B. McPherson they had a 10 year winning streak, but the team like the band, was going downhill in the 1960's.

Lincoln was one of two black high schools in the county and students from surrounding areas were bussed in for high school. There was no incentive even to go to high school or get the diploma because a black high school graduate could only get the same job that his drop-out classmate did two years earlier.

At one point in Sam's high school career (grades 7–12) the school came up for re-evaluation. It was described as the biggest "farce". Students and teachers were alerted and primed for the week the evaluation team was going to be there, books appeared in the classrooms, students stayed in the classroom in their seats, raised their hand were issued hall passes, dressed their best and behaved while teachers taught for four days. As soon as the team left the building Friday afternoon, things were immediately back to the normal chaos.

Sam attended Lincoln for the seventh through twelfth grades, was an honor student, salutatorian of his graduating class, President of the band and the senior class. He continued his education at the University of Florida earning a Bachelor and Masters degree in Political Science and is now a doctoral student in Political Science. His many activities on the U.F. campus include past Vice President of the student body and current President of the student body. He is the first black to hold either of these positions.

His home environment played an important role in his successes to this point. His mothers position of teacher gave advantage of prestige as well as additional income. The fact that his grandmother lived with the family gave the advantage of "mother" in the home.[95]

The questionnaire accompanying Taylor's interview shows that he believed the average class size at Lincoln at that time was forty to fifty students. It also notes that in Taylor's opinion, discipline in the classroom was only "occasionally enforced by a few teachers."

Fourth, through their black principals and teachers, Lincoln High and the other black schools enjoyed a measure of autonomy. School leaders such as Prof Jones and John Dukes Jr. were free to advocate for the black schools from within the system. It is a myth, though, that this autonomy (at least in Alachua County) resulted in anything resembling freedom of expression. Through various means the white school board and administration kept the black schools in their place.

In the 1940s, when John Dukes Jr. was a student, a black school board employee named Harold Jones (nicknamed "Rat," and apparently not related to A. Quinn Jones), as "supervisor" of the black schools, was relied upon by the white school administration to keep the black principals and teachers in line. He apparently had an office in an outbuilding at the rear of the old Lincoln High building. It is related that Harold Jones did all the hiring and firing within the black schools and that he personally passed out paychecks to the black staff.[96]

Not allowed to attend principals' meetings with the school superintendent in an official capacity, A. Quinn Jones would sit just outside the meeting room at a door to hear the proceedings.[97] John Dukes, a great supporter of Jones, said, ". . . in Professor Jones' era it was the submissive kind of attitude that you had to have in order to be successful."[98] But despite whatever Jones had to endure, Prof Jones "was always his own man and not afraid of the system," according to a former Lincoln High teacher.[99]

Dukes on Harold "Rat" Jones:

> And Harold operated the school system as if he were a white man with a white man's characteristics. But he was a black man. That is he tried to create fear in the hearts of teachers. . . . And he had all the black principals in the county jumping. They were afraid of him, they were just afraid of him. For example, they tell me that on many occasions if Harold decided to go fishing and had picked up the checks of teachers, they waited for Harold to come back. They were supposed to be paid on the sixteenth. If Harold decided to go fishing, they would have to wait until he got through fishing [or] something, before he decided to give them their checks. Also, he had teachers cleaning his house. Yes, cleaning his house, and I mean cleaning, washing windows, scrubbing floors and all these kinds of things. That was one of the conditions of staying. If you did not do them, you would be gone.

When Dukes was in his first year of teaching at Lincoln, Harold Jones's wife, Angie, asked Dukes to do something. Dukes told her that he would not do it. "And I want you to know it was not long, just a day or two, that Harold told me, 'You did not do what my wife asked you to do, and I will get you, if it is the last thing I do.'" Harold Jones's wife died not long after that incident. Dukes was asked to go to the funeral. "I said no, I am not going. You may call me a lot of things, but I am not hypocritical. I know how he felt about me, and I know how I felt about him. . . . She was a live rascal when she was living and as far as I am concerned the only thing she is now is a dead rascal." Soon after, according to Dukes, he was warned by the wife of A. Quinn Jones that Harold Jones was telling Prof Jones that Dukes was after Prof Jones's job. Prof Jones's wife assured Dukes that she and Prof Jones did not believe those accusations. When A. Quinn Jones retired in 1957 as Lincoln's principal, he was succeeded by Otha W. Nealy.

Dukes further relates that after Talbot became superintendent, Harold Jones "decided that Tiny had to go." When Harold Jones learned that Dukes was under consideration by Talbot to become principal of Lincoln, succeeding Nealy, Harold Jones tried to block the appointment. Dukes says that Talbot told Dukes, "I know what you are talking about. Harold came in here and he tried his best to do everything he could to get me to turn thumbs down on you. 'You were not this, and you could not do this, and you could not do that.' But you are my choice and you do not have to answer to Harold. You do not have to answer to but one person and that is Tiny Talbot." Dukes became Lincoln's principal on July 1, 1966.[100] Jones did not continue to have the authority he enjoyed under prior administrations.[101]

The demise of "Rat" Jones was a major victory for black faculty, but it did not remove the unspoken limits on their activities. According to Joel Buchanan, during the period of desegregation, most black teachers and their children were not active in the NAACP, because the teachers feared for their jobs.[102] One well-respected history teacher at Lincoln, Tom Coward, found that in his obsolete textbooks, Washington, Jefferson, and Jackson were discussed, but not any historic African American leaders. Coward had been teaching at Lincoln since 1952. Reviewing his lesson plan dealing with the role of pressure groups in 1967, Coward decided to augment the textbook discussion of labor unions with a discussion of the NAACP, CORE, and SNCC.[103] A white supervisor visited his class and told Superintendent Talbot. Coward was removed from the classroom "so I wouldn't be a part of getting students to riot." That breach of decorum was not fatal, however. He was appointed dean at Lincoln, serving in that position from 1967 through the school's closing in 1969. Coward's career as an administrator in the school system continued until 1983. He was elected to the Alachua County Commission, serving from 1974 to 1992, with three terms as chair.[104]

John Dukes III states that his father was not in favor of Lincoln's closing.

> He loved his staff. He loved the environment. He loved the kids and he loved the opportunities that that collective of teachers and staff had to create what had always been created

> at Lincoln. Creating something out of little or nothing. That was a challenge. It was something he bought into. It's why he came here and stayed here instead of going somewhere else, because he had opportunities that one, would have paid more, two, would have probably put us in much better cities than here at that time. And yet he decided that, because he found his way here, that he could make a difference here, and that is what he was going to do whatever he had to do to make that come true. So, taking that attitude and transferring it into the changes that were coming. If there is such a thing as being the person that was probably among the ideal choices to try to guide from way over here to somewhere towards the center, because you weren't going to be allowed to cross the line, but if you can just find a way to navigate and get here and while you're doing that also take care of some of those who were going to be professional in this place.
>
> Because that was another concern. What's going to happen to my teachers? What's going to happen to my administrators, my coaches? You know, all of these people, because I'm going to go to a new school, I know that. But what happens to everybody else, because everybody's not going to be able to go from here to there with me? The system was not going to even allow for that. So for him, he had to embrace that that particular thing was going to occur. I don't know the conversations that I'm sure he had with some of those persons, knowing that change was going to happen and that when it did occur, there was going to be this dispersion. There were going to be some who were going to move up, there were some who were going to move laterally, but it was just a matter of how to best work given the lot that we know we have. This is our hand. What's going to be our best play?

Despite the passionate opposition in the African American community to Lincoln's closing, and whatever their personal misgivings, it would fall to Alachua County's black educators to dismantle the old black schools. In integrated schools, they would be expected to teach white students and to bring the black students at least to a peaceful acceptance of the new regime. Even more so than their white counterparts, Alachua County's black educators would face unprecedented challenges for which they had not been prepared.

Were Dukes and the other educators who did their best to carry out school board policies regarded as sellouts by their community? Speaking of John Dukes, Bernice Dukes and John Dukes III agree that the respect

Dukes enjoyed in the black community insulated him from black accusations of disloyalty. John Dukes III says there were probably some in the black community who believed Dukes had sold out, but they would never have made that accusation to his face.[105]

John Dukes Jr., as Lincoln's principal from 1966 until its closing in 1969, is not a disinterested witness. Dukes became the first principal of Eastside Junior/Senior High when it opened, initially on the Howard Bishop campus, in February 1970, and continued as its principal until December 1975. At that time he joined the county school administrative staff as deputy superintendent for student services.[106]

But it is fitting to allow Dukes to have the last word on Lincoln High. In his 1985 interview with Joel Buchanan, Dukes reflected on his experience at Lincoln. He took issue with the notion that the education at Lincoln was inferior:

> B: Now this is a question that I should not ask, but I have to ask it. They say that black institutions did not prepare persons for society, and that many times a black institution was inadequately supplied and the persons leaving there were not able to get the very best.
>
> D: I take issue with that because some of it may or may not be true. I would say that you have failure in any and every university or college. You also have persons who are not going to be successful even if you sent them to Yale, and I know you have many who are not successful at the University of Florida. All of them are not, in my opinion, the slowest learners in the world either, but sometimes there is something else that encourages a person to do this or that. I have had students in my classroom, especially in algebra and calculus in particular, who when they came in would have [an] attitude that would turn anyone off, including themselves. But somewhere along the way, those persons became relatively successful with either a readjustment or their personalities, or some other experience that [they] had. I had a student one time, a student had been labeled dumb. I tried everything that I thought of to make this kid more successful. One day we were playing touch football, he was playing opposite me, and I told him what he could not do. I told him he could not move me out of my position, unless I wanted him to, and waited for that effect. I played with my kids. We played softball together, we played football together. I would go to the playground and play games with them. This boy

would try his level best to do that. One night I thought that might work in the classroom, but I did not say a thing to him. I do not mind calling his name, because he would tell you today that this happened. Vernon Hayes. He is related to the Hayeses over there in west Gainesville. I said, "You cannot get math. In the first place, you do not have what it takes, you are easily led by somebody else, you quit things you cannot do. Why do you not find something else to do, you cannot do it." And I want you to know, his mother told me later on that he came home and said, "I am going to show him." Now I am not saying that this will work in any case, but I discovered that he did not want anybody to tell him that he could not do something. Then when I thought about it, that is how I got to school, because I had persons who would tell me as a thirteen or fourteen year old boy around Branford, that I would never amount to anything, that I would be just like all the rest of the boys around there. I told myself that I do not have to be like them, I am going to be like me. Even today I have my own philosophy. I will be like I want to be, not like you want me to be, and not like you tell me to be. I believe I can be anything I want to be. I do not care what you think. I do not care whether you think I can or cannot. I think I can be anything I want to be and I think this is the way I motivated the Hayes fellow. I told him that he could not do math. So, consequently, I do not feel that I received an inferior education. I feel that I am as good a math teacher as they have in this country. I know I was as good as any and better than most. I was as good as any and better than most. I knew that because I could tell by the way my kids responded. I can tell by the fewer discipline problems that I had in teaching the kids. I knew I was good.

***

All of my training was at a black university. By comparison, I have had courses at the University of Florida, many courses out there, and I see [no] significant difference in what I was taught out there or the way it was taught at Florida A&M. It all depends on the student and the instructor in the classroom. If you have a student who wants to learn, and a teacher that wants to teach, it makes no difference where the institution is, in my opinion.[107]

CHAPTER 10
THE JUDGES' TURN II

The Supreme Court Orders Alachua County to End Its Dual School System in February 1970

In no uncertain terms I have been told by both sides that I let them down. There are some who think I should have maintained the status quo; there are others who are mad because I didn't go far enough.

William S. Talbot, March 3, 1969

[Alachua County] is another Florida school district where impressive progress has been made under a freedom of choice plan. The plan has been implemented by zoning in the elementary schools of Gainesville (the principal city in the system) for the current year. The results to date and the building plan in progress should facilitate the conversion to a unitary system.

United States Circuit Court of Appeals
Fifth Circuit (en banc, per curiam)
Singleton v. Jackson Municipal Separate School District (including *Wright v. Board of Public Instruction of Alachua County*)
December 1, 1969

> Insofar as the Court of Appeals authorized deferral of student desegregation beyond February 1, 1970, that court misconstrued our holding in *Alexander v. Holmes County Board of Education* . . .
>
> United States Supreme Court, per curiam
> *Carter v. West Feliciana Parish School Board*
> (including *Wright v. Board of Public Instruction of Alachua County*)
> January 14, 1970

As we saw at the end of chapter 7, Judge Carswell issued a revised order in April 1967 that imposed some additional conditions on Alachua County but left essentially intact the county's freedom-of-choice plan for desegregation. But the Supreme Court in May 1968 in *Green* had found that freedom-of-choice plans standing alone were unconstitutional. Under Alachua County's plan, steadily increasing numbers of black students were attending formerly all-white schools, but by the 1968–69 school year, as reported in October 1968 to the court in *Wright v. Board*, 78 percent of the county's black students remained in historically black schools.[1]

Faculty assignments across racial lines proceeded more slowly. For 1967–68, the county reported 39.5 white teachers were teaching in black schools and 6.4 black teachers were teaching in white schools (the fractional amounts relate to part-time assignments).[2] By the 1968–69 school year, 49 white teachers taught in black schools and 17 black teachers taught in white schools. Of the white teachers in black schools, 29 were divided among grades 7–12 at Lincoln and Mebane. Sixteen of 83 teachers in grades 7–12 at Lincoln were white, but only 1 teacher out of 112 at Gainesville High was African American.[3] All teacher assignments across racial lines had been voluntary.[4] Alachua County's difficulties in recruiting teachers would be substantiated in a study of the system by Dr. J. B. White and the Florida Education Research and Development Council. That study was authorized at Talbot's request by the school board in January 1969.[5]

The NAACP Legal Defense Fund quickly followed the school board's October 1968 report with a motion for further relief based on *Green v. County School Board of New Kent County, Virginia*. The Defense Fund alleged that there was less than 7 percent integration in the Alachua County schools (taking into account both black students in white schools and white students in black schools, divided by the total number of white and black students). The motion asked the court to restrain the county from assigning students for the 1969–70 school year on the basis of freedom of choice without first demonstrating to the court that other methods, such as unitary nonracial zones or pairing, would not produce greater desegregation.

The motion asked for a survey and plan to be submitted by the school board no later than November 15, 1968.[6]

Attorney Winston Arnow, who had served as school board attorney since 1948, had resigned at the end of December 1967 to accept appointment by President Johnson as a judge in the US District Court for the Northern District of Florida. Harry Duncan, a law partner of Arnow, replaced him as school board attorney.[7]

Judge Arnow sat with Judge Carswell on January 22, 1969, at the pretrial conference on the NAACP Legal Defense Fund motion.[8] Apparently Judge Arnow did so to emphasize to Arnow's former client, the school board, that the board needed to move quickly and convincingly to end the county's dual school system. According to Talbot, "I believe they implied that either we come up with an acceptable plan or they will do it for us."[9]

Judge Carswell's January 23 order gave the county until March 21, 1969, to file a plan with the court that would eliminate the county's dual school system in accordance with *Green v. County School Board of New Kent County*. Objections to the plan were to be filed by April 1, 1969, with an evidentiary hearing on the plan to be held, if needed, April 10, 1969.[10]

In response to the January order, the school board suspended the $130,000 project to add vocational facilities at Lincoln High School, and put together two plans for ending the dual school system, one of which would become effective in September 1969 and the other in September 1970. The board anticipated that all of the new schools intended to relieve overcrowding would be ready by September 1970. Talbot said to the press that the county could be ready to end the dual system by September 1969 only by extensive busing of students.[11] Under both plans, because of the planned construction of the new east-side high school, Lincoln High School was to be closed.[12]

In order to preserve sufficient time for school assignments for the 1969–70 school year, Judge Carswell on February 14, 1969, moved up the deadline for submission of the county's integration plan from March 21 to February 27, and set March 4 as the date for a nonevidentiary hearing on the plan.

The school board, assisted by the Florida School Desegregation Consulting Center (a contractor of HEW's Office of Education), raced to meet the new deadline. Superintendent Talbot summarized the plan for the press for an article that appeared on February 26.[13] The school board held a public meeting on the plan on February 26, 1969, and approved the plan at a board meeting that night.[14]

The school board's plan was filed with the federal district court on February 28, 1969.[15] It was accompanied by extensive exhibits showing demographic data. Although the plan acknowledged the currently effective legal standards under *Green*, it was a plea for mercy in view of Alachua County's difficulties with overcrowding and its bonded construction plan that would permit "practically complete, if not complete, integration with the school year beginning in September, 1970."[16] The bulk of the changes to eliminate the county's dual system were to occur in September 1970. The two new Gainesville junior/senior high schools would initially open in September 1970, only with grades 7–10, and would add eleventh and twelfth grades in future years, because "it is not considered good practice to open a new school with a graduating class, because of time needed for parental clubs planning for activity programs in sports, music and other activities; and it would involve transferring students from an accredited school to one which may take three years to become accredited."[17]

Lincoln Junior/Senior High would close at the end of the 1969–70 school year. All students in grades 11 and 12 at Lincoln in September 1970 would be assigned to Gainesville High School to complete their high school years. They would remain together, if at a different location, and would not find themselves opening either of the two new high schools.[18] The Florida School Desegregation Consulting Center noted Lincoln's elimination as an academic high school without comment in its report and pointed out the likely use of the campus for vocational and other programs.[19]

The plan was complex and heavily dependent upon new schools either under construction or planned under the bond issue. For example, in the northwest county (High Springs and Alachua), a new middle school (grades 5–8) was to be constructed in High Springs, and a new elementary school was to be constructed in Alachua. With that construction completed, the formerly black Douglass Elementary School in High Springs would be closed, the all-black A. L. Mebane K–12 campus at Alachua would become an integrated middle school, and grades 9–12 from Mebane would move to Santa Fe High School, midway between High Springs and Alachua, which would also receive improvements. The construction would not be complete in time for the upcoming 1969–70 school year.[20] Mebane had lost senior high school accreditation in November 1968.[21]

Faced with overcrowding and constrained financial resources, the school board could not afford to abandon its formerly all-black schools. Of the eight formerly all-black schools, three were to be repurposed as integrated schools, two (A. Quinn Jones Elementary and Lincoln Junior/Senior High School, both in Gainesville) were to become centers for specific remedial or vocational programs, and one (Douglass Elementary in High Springs) was to be eliminated. Duval and Williams Elementary Schools, both located in black Gainesville neighborhoods with students able to walk to school, would remain open despite the likelihood that they would continue to be predominantly black under the new plan. To address that issue, the plan allowed black elementary students to transfer to a white school in their zone, but not to another black school ("majority to minority transfer"). The white elementary school in Archer was to be closed, with its students transferred to the formerly all-black elementary campus in Archer, which was to be improved.[22]

Faculty integration would also have proceeded in stages with a ratio of approximately four white teachers to one black teacher in all schools by the 1970–71 school year.[23]

Commenting on Duval and Williams, Talbot earlier had asked, "Should you take a student out of Duval, who would rather go there, and bus him to a white school so you can make room for a white pupil who does not want to go to the Negro school? . . . I say no. The U.S. Civil Rights Act does not say you must bus pupils around just to achieve racial balance."[24] Alachua County had desegregated under court order. But to this point it would be fair to say that the white school board and administration had been supportive of the court-approved desegregation plans. They had moved promptly to execute those plans. School board candidates had uniformly expressed approval of peaceful desegregation of the county's schools. Now, pushed to go beyond freedom of choice, Talbot and the school board began to resist more changes to achieve desegregation. Referring to deliberate speed, Talbot had privately said to Tommy Tomlinson, "I'm running as fast as I can."[25]

The end of freedom of choice would also bring into the open the continuing loyalty of many African Americans to the black schools.[26] As we saw in the preceding chapter, significant numbers of Alachua County's African Americans still did not foresee that the result of a unitary school system, as envisioned by the NAACP Legal Defense Fund and the courts, would be racial balancing in all schools. For better or worse, whether Lincoln stayed open or not, black students and teachers would become minorities in every school.

Lincoln's elimination as an academic junior/senior high school should have come as no surprise. That step had been recommended by the state Department of Public Instruction facility survey update in December 1967. Lincoln's future elimination had been reported in the press in December 1967, December 1968, and January 1969.[27] Lincoln was on "warned" status, one step from loss of accreditation.[28] But black citizens first voiced organized, public opposition to Lincoln's closing at the February 26, 1969, school board meetings. They also objected to the conversion of A. Quinn Jones Elementary School to a center for federally funded remedial reading programs.

Charles Chestnut III had been a leader in the 1963 desegregation of Gainesville's theaters and restaurants. He would have a leadership role in the troubles that were now brewing over desegregation. Chestnut accused the school board of closing Lincoln because it feared white students would not go there. "Why not zone in some whites in Lincoln and leave it as it is . . . What you are saying is that in order to get integration you have to move all the black people to white schools." The Reverend Lloyd Haisley, pastor of the AME Bethel Church, expressed the concern that integration would be used to discriminate against black principals and teachers. "The Negroes in our community want Lincoln as an academic high school with a Negro principal . . . Negro children need some leaders they can look up to. . . . We don't mind losing our identity but we do hate to lose our jobs."[29]

At the formal school board meeting the same night, the Rev. Wright protested that closing Lincoln as an academic institution would eliminate it as a social and cultural center. "I'd like to see total desegregation but we may continue to have separate communities for some time. . . . From a social point of view it would be better to maintain an academic center at Lincoln."[30]

The press report of the meeting states that after hearing from Wright,

> . . . the board appeared to be willing to change its plans and make the East Side School a vocational school, leaving Lincoln as it is.
>
> However, Talbot pointed out that Lincoln's future had been determined by the bond issue and to change plans now would be a costly process.[31]

Shortly after the school board approved the plan, Superintendent Talbot commented, "In no uncertain terms I have been told by both sides that I let them down. There are some who think I should have maintained the status quo; there are others who are mad because I didn't go far enough." He continued, "Some who called me think . . . we can do without the federal money and we should tell HEW we don't want it. . . . But we are dealing with Judge Carswell and he's given us an order to desegregate. There is no choice."[32] Talbot later answered concerns about the possible loss of jobs by black teachers and principals: "I'm not sure these arguments are concerned with what's best for the children. The education of our children is our primary concern." Talbot had been characterized as "unflappable" in a *Sun* profile in October 1968 even when his recommendations drew dissent.[33] Now beginning to show some frustration, he added, ". . . this appears to be open season on superintendents with no bag limits."[34]

Responding to black criticism that no white students were being zoned to Lincoln or other schools in black neighborhoods, Talbot forthrightly answered that zoning white students into black neighborhoods would create the risk of white flight. "'It's strictly conjecture on my part as to whether those whites will stay,' Talbot said. 'The only thing we have to go by is what happened elsewhere. Generally, the whites do move away if forced to attend Negro schools.'"[35]

The school board and Talbot, having only nine months earlier avoided disaster for the public schools by winning the bond election, now faced a new threat to the schools' survival. It was by no means clear or inevitable that the separate communities in Gainesville would continue to support the public school system that had been so laboriously built over many years within the county's limited economic base.

The Rev. Wright tried to reconcile desegregation with keeping Lincoln open as a center for the black community:

> EDITOR, Sun: The N.A.A.C.P. is definitely in favor of total integration of the schools in Alachua County. This should have been done years ago. We have been moving too slow in this respect.
>
> Due to some strange circumstances that confront the black community, there ought to be at least one first class high school located in the black community. We should not have to strip the community of all academic high schools in order to maintain total integration. In any community with as many black people in it as Gainesville, there is a need for a high school in the black community that can deal with the fears, frustrations and limitations of black children that have developed over the past. Some black children with good desires and potential have trouble adjusting to white dominated integrated schools and would never be able to finish high school in such environment. There are white children that would face the same problem.
>
> We are going to have two communities in Gainesville for some time. And since this is the case, from a social point of view, there is a need for an academic high school in the black community, that can serve as a sounding board for the community. Blacks need access to a school center that can be used for programs and lectures dealing with problems peculiar to black people. Blacks need to do this in a way without feeling that they are being tolerated in a predominantly white integrated school.
>
> In any community where one-quarter of the school population is black,[36] there is a need for a school that will serve all the children that have interests in extra-curricular activities such as football, basketball, and band and the choir. At this time there is some doubt as to whether white-dominated

high schools would be willing to absorb all these children. An academic high school in a black community provides a great deal of social outlet for black people which for several reasons they do not feel free to share at other schools.

Even if Lincoln High is 50 per cent white and 50 per cent black, with an academic program, the school could still be an educational center for the black community and could also be used somewhat as a laboratory, dealing with both groups.

The N.A.A.C.P.
Gainesville
Thomas A. Wright, pres.[37]

The closing of Lincoln High School became the single most important issue to Gainesville's African American community during the many years in which the schools were undergoing desegregation. That community's response to Lincoln's closing will be examined subsequently. But the NAACP Legal Defense Fund, which represented the Alachua County plaintiffs, chose consciously or not to hold its fire on that issue in 1969 and to focus entirely on aspects of the county's plan that appeared to evade or delay implementation of a complete unitary school system. It was not until *March 1970*, after Lincoln had been closed, that Defense Fund lawyers objected to its elimination as an academic high school and Lincoln would finally have its day in court.[38]

Judge Carswell proceeded as scheduled with a nonevidentiary hearing on the school board plan on March 4, 1969. The NAACP Legal Defense Fund had previously asked for a full evidentiary hearing at which witnesses could be called and a written record could be set up for appeal.[39] School board attorney Harry Duncan read the plan. Judge Carswell praised it as ". . . the most fortuitous plan I have ever seen. . . . I think this plan could be a historical milestone."[40]

At that hearing, Earl M. Johnson of Jacksonville, the NAACP Legal Defense Fund's local counsel, orally argued that A. Quinn Jones Elementary School and Lincoln and Mebane High Schools should be retained as regular academic schools.[41] Johnson argued that the plan required too much busing of black students and that busing continued to make segregation possible.[42] To the press at Gainesville, the Rev. Wright stated that the NAACP would contest the closing of Lincoln High as an academic high school, together with the closing of Douglass Elementary School in High Springs and the conversion of A. Quinn Jones to a remedial reading center.[43]

The written objections of the Defense Fund, filed March 19, 1969, did not include any of those issues. Nevertheless, Attorney Johnson stated to the press that such an objection had been made.[44] The subsequent court history of the 1969 Alachua County litigation before both the district court and the Fifth Circuit is devoid, prior to March 1970, of any mention of the closing of black schools. To be brought before those courts in the current round of litigation, those issues had to be raised formally in the Defense Fund's March 19 written objections.

Judge Carswell, following the March 4 hearing, denied the NAACP Legal Defense Fund's motion for a full evidentiary hearing on the plan. He stated, "There are simply no more relevant facts to be obtained. Every request for information and data by either party has been buttressed by an order of the court and has been complied with." Judge Carswell said that any suggestions from scholars or experts could be made part of the briefs and would be fully considered. The case record does not show any Defense Fund allegation that the school board failed to provide any information requested by the Defense Fund. Judge Carswell:

> In the final analysis, however, the posture of this litigation for this year simply calls for a judicial decision which must be made by the Court upon facts now thoroughly and fully developed.
>
> Moreover, there is a time factor involved here. This school system is operating under a Jefferson-type decree which went into effect September [actually, April] 1967. Further protracted delays could only lead to waste of public funds for educational purposes in the necessary planning for the opening of the schools in September, 1969, together with attendant utter confusion for thousands of school children, faculty, and those charged with the administration of the public schools.[45]

During the Senate review in early 1970 of Carswell's qualifications for appointment to the Supreme Court (he had been nominated by President Nixon), it came out that Carswell had one of the highest rates of reversal in appealed cases among district court judges in the Fifth Circuit. Carswell, then sitting on the Fifth Circuit bench, solicited endorsements of his Supreme Court appointment from his fellow Fifth Circuit judges. John Minor Wisdom and Elbert Tuttle were among those who refused to endorse him. When those refusals became public, they seriously damaged Carswell's confirmation, which was defeated in the Senate. In a 1979 interview, Judge Wisdom commented, "He was the type of judge who would try to dispose of cases on motion rather than sit through a trial. He had an inordinate number of cases which he decided either on summary judgment or on motion to dismiss. I just thought he was a lightweight."[46]

Carswell's refusal of an evidentiary hearing at this point in the Alachua County litigation may have been a reflection of his desire to avoid trials, or it may have been motivated by a desire to move the case forward quickly, given the need for the county to have a desegregation plan in place for the 1969–70 school year. Carswell was not the only district court judge disinclined to hear evidence on desegregation plans.[47] Carswell's review of the county's plan and the NAACP Legal Defense Fund objections in 1969 would be his last substantive involvement in the case. He was appointed to the Fifth Circuit Court of Appeals on May 12, 1969.

The NAACP Legal Defense Fund objections to the Alachua County plan, filed March 19, 1969, were signed by William L. Robinson, at that time a staff lawyer with the Fund's New York office. Robinson first came to the NAACP Legal Defense Fund as a law student at Columbia Law School through the Law Students Civil Right Research Council. He joined the staff of the Defense Fund in 1967. He later served as associate general counsel for the Equal Employment Opportunity Commission, and then as executive director of the Lawyers Committee for Civil Rights Under Law. He was founding dean of the District of Columbia Law School, where he continues as Olie W. Rauh Professor of Law.[48]

The Defense Fund disagreed that the school board's inability to complete its new schools by September 1969 was legal justification for any further delay in moving to a unitary system under *Green*. The Defense Fund also argued that it was possible for the school board to end its dual system for the 1969–70 school year. Its more particular objections included the plan's failure to explain the method of assigning students to the proposed compensatory or vocational education centers to be housed at the Jones Elementary and Lincoln High School buildings, and the plan's zoning that would cause Duval and Williams Elementary Schools to remain exclusively black.[49]

The school board, in responding to the Defense Fund's filing of March 19, 1969, argued that the Defense Fund misinterpreted or ignored evidence that the Defense Fund had itself requested. The school board stated that the plan as proposed for the 1969–70 school year would result in an increase in African American students attending previously all-white schools from 1,512 to about 3,700. The board admitted the likelihood that there would be a black majority at the new A. Quinn Jones reading center, but argued that federal P.L. 89–10 guidelines for such programs favored consolidating such programs to provide better quality services. The board explained in greater detail the inefficiency and confusion of moving toward a unitary system in the 1969–70 year and then reassembling students, faculty, and resources upon completion of the new schools in 1970–71. In its plea for more time to complete its unitary system, the school board emphasized statements in *Green* that required systems to end dual systems at the earliest practicable date and in another Fifth Circuit case that spoke to the feasibility of plans. The school board concluded that the Defense Fund objections were without merit.[50]

Judge Carswell approved the school board's plan for the years 1969–70, 1970–71, and 1971–72 on April 3, 1969.

> The Court finds that the freedom of choice plan under which this system has operated since September 1967 has worked effectively in all but a very few instances. It is apparent that the freedom of choice plan has not worked effectively, or rather not at all, in three elementary schools, i.e., Duval, Williams and A. Quinn Jones. The Court concludes that the establishment of arbitrary zone lines at this point, however, would definitely result in substantially less integration in the system than is now the case and even more importantly, this Board, through its plan filed February 28, 1969, has effectively come forward with concrete proposals which will eliminate the last vestiges of segregation throughout the entire system. The Court notes with particular emphasis that the county system is being divided into four broad zones and that as soon as buildings are complete, all now funded and some under construction, the plan will be fully effective and operative, and no later than 1971.[51]

The NAACP Legal Defense Fund appealed Judge Carswell's decision to the Fifth Circuit Court of Appeals on May 2, 1969.[52]

Enrollment figures reported to the court in September 1969 for the 1969–70 school year showed that 2,730 African American students, or 39.3 percent of all black students, had enrolled in historically white schools.[53] The school board had also made progress in faculty integration. Sixty-six white teachers were teaching in historically black schools and 64 black teachers were teaching in historically white schools, with an additional four black teachers on the county instructional staff. There were 1,057 teachers, of whom 810 were white and 247 were black.[54]

There would be no further material changes to the county's plan,[55] and no changes to reported enrollment and faculty numbers, before the US Court of Appeals decided the NAACP Legal Defense Fund's appeal of Judge Carswell's April 3, 1969, approval of the school board's desegregation plan.

The NAACP Legal Defense Fund substituted Attorney Drew S. Days III for William L. Robinson in *Wright v. Board* on October 6, 1969.[56] Drew Days, the grandfather of the attorney, had taught at Union Academy and was the first president of the Lincoln High PTA in the 1920s.[57] Drew S. Days

III graduated from Yale Law School in 1966. He served in the Peace Corps in Honduras for two years and then joined the NAACP Legal Defense Fund as a staff attorney in 1969, where he served for eight years. He served as assistant attorney general for civil rights in the Carter administration, after which he joined the faculty of Yale Law School. From 1993 to 1996, Days was solicitor general in the Clinton administration. He is Alfred L. Rankin Professor Emeritus of Law at Yale Law School. At Yale Law School, he founded and directed the Orville H. Schell Jr. Center for Human Rights.[58] Attorney Days, along with other more senior Defense Fund lawyers, would continue on the Alachua County case through the remaining period covered by this work.

By the time Alachua County was preparing its revised desegregation plan in early 1969, the broader desegregation picture had changed. In March 1968, the Johnson administration's HEW Office for Civil Rights had issued new desegregation guidance under Title VI of the Civil Rights Act of 1964. The new guidance required unitary school systems by the 1968–69 school year, or at the latest by the 1969–70 school year.[59] The Supreme Court issued its *Green* decision on May 27, 1968. The court held that there had to be "meaningful assurance of prompt and effective disestablishment of a dual school system." The court also held that any revised desegregation plan had "realistically to work and work *now*." However, the court did not refer to the March 1968 HEW guidance, and remanded the *Green* case to the district court without setting a deadline for New Kent County, Virginia, to implement a unitary school system.[60]

Then, in the 1968 presidential election, the Democrats lost badly. Nixon ran on a Southern strategy, catering to Southern opposition to more school desegregation. Hubert Humphrey polled only 42.7 percent of the popular vote, with Nixon taking 43.4 percent and George Wallace taking 13.7 percent. More to the point for school desegregation, of the eleven states of the former Confederacy, Democrats carried only Texas. George Wallace carried Louisiana, Mississippi, Alabama, and Georgia. President Johnson had commented on signing the Civil Rights Act of 1964 that it would cost his party the South. He was proved correct.

Nixon wasted little time in putting distance between his team and Johnson's. On November 26, 1968, his aide Patrick Buchanan told the press that Nixon disagreed with the Supreme Court's *Green* decision on freedom of choice.[61] The new Nixon administration quickly found itself under pressure from Southern senators and representatives to allow school districts more time to complete their desegregation plans. A period of indecision ensued.[62]

On the Supreme Court, Earl Warren had been replaced on June 23, 1969, by Warren Burger as chief justice. Abe Fortas had resigned from the court on May 14, 1969, because of ethics problems that had also contributed to the failure of his appointment as chief justice to replace Earl Warren. His seat had not been filled. President Nixon in August 1969 nominated Judge Clement Haynsworth of the Fourth Circuit Court of Appeals in Richmond to succeed Fortas, but Haynsworth's nomination was rejected by the Senate in December 1969. Judge G. Harrold Carswell was nominated by Nixon on January 19, 1970, but that nomination also was rejected by the Senate on April 8, 1970. That seat eventually went to Harry Blackmun, but not until June 9, 1970.

Meanwhile, the NAACP Legal Defense Fund was attacking dual school systems under *Green* throughout the South.[63] The Defense Fund's perceived need for swift closure came just at the time when Alachua County needed until September 1970 to complete its already-committed unitary school system.

Alexander v. Holmes County Board of Education was the first case under *Green* to reach the Supreme Court from the Fifth Circuit.[64] That case was the result of NAACP Legal Defense Fund motions for further relief seeking an end to freedom-of-choice plans for the 1968–69 school year. The District Court for the Southern District of Mississippi had approved continued use of many school district freedom-of-choice plans. The NAACP Legal Defense Fund and the US Department of Justice appealed those decisions to the Fifth Circuit.[65] By the time those cases reached the Fifth Circuit, it was too late for the Fifth Circuit to make a decision that would affect the 1968–69 school year.

The United States and the NAACP Legal Defense Fund agreed that the Fifth Circuit should decide those cases summarily so that its decision would affect the 1969–70 school year.[66] In response, the Fifth Circuit on July 3, 1969, ordered the school districts to end dual systems by the start of the 1969–70 school year. To bring about this result, HEW was to work with the school boards to prepare desegregation plans for implementation at the beginning of the 1969–70 school year.[67]

By coincidence, on the same day, July 3, 1969, the Nixon administration issued a somewhat confusing statement that offered to extend the deadline for compliance with the HEW March 1968 desegregation guidelines until the 1969–70 school year, with some flexibility allowed for special circumstances, such as serious shortages of facilities. The statement also suggested that the Department of Justice would take a more flexible approach in cases subject to court order.[68] Although the NAACP Legal Defense Fund was already committed to ending freedom of choice by the start of the 1969–70 school year, this joint HEW/DOJ statement may have reinforced the Defense Fund's sense of urgency.

In *Alexander*, under heavy pressure from Southern senators and representatives, including Mississippi's John Stennis,[69] the Nixon administration reversed course and weighed in on the side of the school districts. In

Green, under President Johnson, the United States as amicus curiae had argued with the NAACP Legal Defense Fund against freedom of choice.[70] Now, the Department of Justice, by motion filed with the Fifth Circuit on August 21, 1969, supported by the Department of Health, Education, and Welfare, argued that the Fifth Circuit's orders to end dual systems in these cases by September 1969 should be delayed because time was too short and administrative problems too difficult for implementation of the new desegregation plans by September 1969. The Fifth Circuit then remanded the cases to the district court to hear evidence on that issue. The district court found as a matter of fact that the time was too short. The Fifth Circuit on August 28, 1969, upheld the district court ruling and postponed the date for submission of new desegregation plans for the thirty Mississippi school districts to December 1, 1969. That Fifth Circuit decision stayed its July 3, 1969, ruling that these districts had to implement their new desegregation plans by the beginning of the 1969–70 school year.[71]

The NAACP Legal Defense Fund once again found itself standing alone.

Justice Black, receiving the application of the NAACP Legal Defense Fund to vacate the Fifth Circuit stay, expressed his frustration in his ruling of September 5, 1969, in *Alexander*:

> These cases [*Green*, *Brown* and *Griffin v. School Board*, 377 U.S. 218 (1964)], along with others, are the foundation of my belief that there is no longer the slightest excuse, reason, or justification for further postponement for the time when every public school system in the United States will be a unitary one, receiving and teaching students without discrimination on the basis of their race or color. In my opinion the phrase "with all deliberate speed" should no longer have any relevancy whatsoever in enforcing the rights of Negro students. The Fifth Circuit found that the Negro students in these school districts are being denied equal protection of the laws, and in my view they are entitled to have their constitutional rights vindicated now without postponement for any reason.[72]

He nevertheless was obliged to defer consideration of the issue to the full Supreme Court.

As a practical matter, the Fifth Circuit stay of August 28, 1969, remained in effect as school began for the 1969–70 school year. Across the South, and in Alachua County, schools opened under their existing desegregation plans, which for the most part relied on freedom of choice. Nevertheless, school boards could not know when complete desegregation would be ordered. The full Supreme Court took up the *Alexander* case on an expedited basis in October 1969.

Although abandoned by the United States, the NAACP Legal Defense Fund was joined for this pivotal case by the Lawyers Committee for Civil Rights Under Law[73] and the National Education Association as amici curiae in urging reversal of the Fifth Circuit stay. The school boards and the United States argued that the stay be affirmed.

The Supreme Court repulsed the Nixon administration's change of course. The court's unanimous two-page per curiam opinion, delivered October 29, 1969, held:

> The question presented is one of paramount importance, involving as it does the denial of fundamental rights to many thousands of school children, who are presently attending Mississippi schools under segregated conditions contrary to applicable decisions of this Court. Against this background the Court of Appeals should have denied all motions for additional time because continued operation of segregated schools under a standard of allowing "all deliberate speed" for desegregation is no longer constitutionally permissible. Under explicit holdings of this Court the obligation of every school district is to terminate dual school systems at once and to operate now and hereafter only unitary schools.[74]

The Fifth Circuit on November 7, 1969, remanded the cases to the Southern District of Mississippi, directing that faculties and student bodies be merged into unitary systems by December 31, 1969.[75] The NAACP Legal Defense Fund, having won in *Alexander*, pressed forward with another round of motions across the South demanding immediate integration.[76]

The Fifth Circuit consolidated the NAACP Legal Defense Fund's appeal of Judge Carswell's April 3, 1969, order in *Wright v. Board* with similar appeals from each of the states in the Fifth Circuit, which at that time included Alabama, Florida, Georgia, Louisiana, Mississippi, and Texas. Fifteen individual school districts were before the court in this case. Prior to the Supreme Court's decision of October 29, 1969, in *Alexander v. Holmes County*, the Fifth Circuit had decided to consider these cases en banc. There were at that time fifteen judges on the Fifth Circuit bench, all of whom sat on the case, although some judges did not participate in one or more of the proceedings on individual school districts.

The consolidated cases that included *Wright v. Board* were argued to the Fifth Circuit during the week of November 17, 1969, after the Supreme Court's decision in *Alexander*. The Fifth Circuit required the Justice Department to file a memorandum of law stating its position on each of the fifteen cases in view of *Alexander*.[77] Both the Department of Justice and the NAACP Legal Defense Fund now agreed, partly on the basis of *Alexander*, that the Alachua County plan previously approved by Judge Carswell on April 3, 1969, failed to move swiftly enough to a unitary school system.[78]

Tiny Talbot, Tommy Tomlinson, and Harry Duncan, the school board lawyer, traveled to Houston for the en banc argument of Alachua County's case. We might suppose that all Southern school boards engaged ruthless, highly paid, sophisticated lawyers to fight desegregation at every turn. Tommy Tomlinson:

> When our case came up, Judge Carswell left because he had been assigned to our case as trial judge. Harry Duncan was not the most organized person. The courtroom was bigger than a basketball court and the lectern for counsel was way out in the middle. When Harry got up there to argue, he fumbled around and dropped some papers and couldn't find something. He looked at Tiny and me. He looked desperate. I thought I knew what he wanted and I took it out to him. Judge Wisdom called out, "Young fella, do you have a law degree?" I said no sir. I was scared. Judge Wisdom said, "You just practiced before the Fifth Circuit Court of Appeals." The other judges laughed, so I guess what I did was okay.[79]

Superintendent Talbot, returning to Gainesville after the arguments, acknowledged the possibility that the Alachua County schools would have to be fully integrated during the 1969–70 school year. Reflecting a common view among Southern school administrators, Talbot said, "Everybody can tell you what [a unitary school system] isn't, but no one knows what it is."[80]

But on December 1, 1969, the Fifth Circuit in its unanimous en banc, per curiam decision refused to follow the timetable ordered by the Supreme Court in *Alexander*.[81] The Fifth Circuit, in *Singleton v. Jackson Municipal Separate School District*, acknowledged that the Supreme Court's decision in *Alexander* required that school districts "begin immediately to operate as unitary school systems." Conversion to a unitary system required "the merger of faculty and staff, students, transportation, services, athletic and other extra-curricular school activities." "The new modus operandi is to require immediate operation as unitary systems. Suggested modification of unitary plans are not to delay implementation." "The focus of the mechanics question is on the immediacy requirement laid down in Alexander v. Holmes County."[82]

Singleton, the case involving Alachua County, included school districts in all six states of the Fifth Circuit, not just the Southern District of

Mississippi, as had *Alexander*. In this case, the Fifth Circuit was not willing to order complete faculty and student body integration during the 1969–70 school year. A factor was the absence of plans implementing *Alexander* in any of the school districts.

> It will be difficult to arrange the merger of student bodies into unitary systems prior to the fall 1970 term in the absence of merger plans. The court has concluded that two-step plans are to be implemented. One step must be accomplished not later than February 1, 1970 and it will include all steps necessary to convert to a unitary system save the merger of student bodies into unitary systems. The student body merger will constitute the second step and must be accomplished not later than the beginning of the fall term 1970.

In a footnote, the court added,

> Many faculty and staff members will be transferred under step one. It will be necessary for final grades to be entered and for other records to be completed, prior to the transfers, by the transferring faculty members and administrators for the partial school year involved. The interim period prior to February 1, 1970 is allowed for this purpose.
>
> The interim period prior to the start of the fall 1970 school term is allowed for arranging the student transfers. Many students must transfer. Buildings will be put to new use. In some instances it may be necessary to transfer equipment, supplies or libraries. School bus routes must be reconstituted. The period allowed is at least adequate for the orderly accomplishment of the task.[83]

The Fifth Circuit ordered that plans for the merger of student bodies into unitary systems be filed no later than January 6, 1970, with February 1, 1970, set as the deadline for district court action to approve final plans for the start of the 1970–71 school year. The court recommended the appointment of biracial advisory committees in school districts in which there was no black school board member. The court gave specific guidance for plans at both steps one and two of its proposed procedures. Such plans were to permit any student to transfer from a school in which his race was in the majority to a school in which his race was in the minority.[84]

The court then commented on some of the specific issues faced by the individual school districts before the court. With respect to Alachua County:

> This is another Florida school district where impressive progress has been made under a freedom of choice plan. The plan has been implemented by zoning in the elementary schools of Gainesville (the principal city in the system) for the current year. The results to date and the building plan in progress should facilitate the conversion to a unitary system.[85]

The Fifth Circuit decision in *Singleton* did not satisfy the NAACP Legal Defense Fund, which on December 10, 1969, sought a temporary restraining order and other relief from Justice Hugo Black as circuit justice in cases involving three of the school districts in Louisiana. The Defense Fund sought full student body integration on February 1, 1970.

This case came to the Supreme Court as *Carter v. West Feliciana Parish School Board*. Justice Black this time did not defer to the full Supreme Court. On December 13, 1969, as interim relief pending full-court consideration, he ordered the school districts to integrate their student bodies by February 1, 1970, and to take no steps that would be inconsistent with or prejudice or delay student body integration beyond February 1, 1970.[86]

The United States, in a terse four-page memorandum, supported consideration of the cases by the full Supreme Court but (contrary to the Justice Department's position before the Fifth Circuit) urged the Supreme Court to affirm the Fifth Circuit's December 1 opinion that postponed student body integration to September 1970. Seeking a compromise, the United States suggested that if the Supreme Court made September 1970 a uniform deadline for all Southern school districts to achieve unitary systems, the United States would bring suits to enforce that deadline against noncomplying school districts or states. The memorandum acknowledged that its proposed solution "will sacrifice the rights of some school children for the remainder of this school year."[87]

The full Supreme Court on January 14, 1970, reversed the Fifth Circuit. "Insofar as the Court of Appeals authorized deferral of student desegregation beyond February 1, 1970, that court misconstrued our holding in *Alexander v. Holmes County Board of Education* . . ." The opinion of the eight-justice court was issued per curiam, but not unanimously.[88]

Justice Harlan, joined by Justice White, supported the court's order but stated that in his view additional clarification and guidance should be provided to the lower courts in implementing unitary systems. Those courts should then issue orders under *Alexander* requiring immediate integration. Justice Harlan also recommended a further round of plan review (not to delay implementation) for any school district to prove, if it could, the unworkability of the plan ordered to be implemented. He suggested that a period of eight weeks would be reasonable from a finding of non-compliance with *Green* to full operation of the plan finally approved.[89] Four justices, Black, Douglas, Brennan, and Marshall, expressed disagreement with Justice Harlan's statement as retreating from the court's views in *Alexander v. Holmes County Board of Education.*[90] Chief Justice Burger (who had replaced Earl Warren in June 1969) and Justice Stewart stated in a memorandum,

> We would not peremptorily reverse the judgments of the Court of Appeals for the Fifth Circuit. That court, sitting en banc and acting unanimously after our decision in *Alexander v. Holmes County Board of Education, ante* p.19, has required the respondents to effect desegregation in their schools by February 1, 1970, save for the student bodies, which are to be wholly desegregated during the current year, no later than September. In light of the measures the Court of Appeals has directed the respondent school districts to undertake, with total desegregation required for the upcoming school year, we are not prepared summarily to set aside its judgments. That court is far more familiar than we with the various situations of these several school districts, some large, some small, some rural, and some metropolitan, and has exhibited responsibility and fidelity to the objectives of our holdings in school desegregation cases. To say peremptorily that the Court of Appeals erred in its application of the *Alexander* decision to these cases, and to direct summary reversal without argument and without opportunity for exploration of the varying problems of individual school districts, seems unsound to us.[91]

The Supreme Court's January 14, 1970, decision ended the litigation for the Fifth Circuit and for Alachua County. From Justice Black's interim decision on December 13, 1969, thirty-five days remained to the February 1, 1970, deadline for unitary school systems, and from the full court's January 14, 1970, decision, seventeen days remained.

The Fifth Circuit had to issue new instructions to the district courts. The Fifth Circuit did so on January 21, 1970, to all fifteen districts in *Singleton*, including Alachua County. The court's one-paragraph en banc decision simply declared that the Supreme Court's order requiring desegregation of student bodies on February 1, 1970, was made the order of the Fifth Circuit.[92]

Had the Alachua County case reached the decision stage a year later, Alachua County might have benefited from the policy that the Nixon administration, after more deliberations, adopted in the spring of 1970. That policy clearly required school districts to abandon their dual school systems, but created state biracial councils to work out a more flexible, local approach to implementing unitary systems. Ultimately, that policy greatly assisted the conclusion of the desegregation effort begun with *Brown* and earned Nixon praise even from his critics.[93] The Nixon administration and Congress also provided funds to school districts to assist with the impacts of desegregation, beginning in 1970 under existing laws and eventually under the Emergency School Aid Act of 1972 and its extensions.[94] Congress also continued to fund programs under the Elementary and Secondary Education Act, despite a series of antibusing amendments (which could not bind the courts).[95]

In the entire 1969 court review process, the impossibility in the current school year, because of unfinished school buildings, to implement Alachua County's complete unitary school system would not register with the NAACP Legal Defense Fund, the Justice Department, or with the Supreme Court. Now not just the Alachua County school system but the county's entire white and black communities would be put to the test.

CHAPTER 11
LAST ROUNDUP FOR THE FIGHTING RED TERRIERS

In all my 42 years, I was never so saddened as I was earlier in the evening when an elected member of the school board said, "we can't name the new school Lincoln High because all the whites will move out." Such statements make it hard for me to defend Gainesville against charges of racism.

Neil Butler, November 29, 1969

It is now a day and age when education is of the utmost importance not only to the black man, but every man. We no longer ask or beg for better educational facilities and equal opportunities, we as blacks demand them. We demand the best for our children also. In this community and surrounding area Lincoln High School is the only and largest predominantly black high school, it would only be unrealistic and unjustifiable to phase this institution out. The white man has short-changed the black man so long that when this wrongdoing is about to be brought into the open he uses such tactics as phasing out black institutions. The day has arrived when people have become aware that the whites have cheated the blacks in this community of top educational facilities.

Wayne T. McClellan, December 6, 1969

In order for all of us to live happy, productive lives we are going to have to communicate with each other. We can either fight each other for the rest of our lives or we can learn to live in harmony and to assist each other to attain the goals that we each seek.

> We cannot educate our children to live a life that can never be again. Our children must learn this feeling of understanding and cooperation. The board believes that the best way to develop this mutual trust and understanding is to develop a good unitary school system.
>
> Alachua County school board, December 11, 1969

In the midst of uncertainty over whether Alachua County would have to implement a unitary school system during the 1969–70 school year, the frustration of the African American community boiled over into an eleven-day student strike at Lincoln High School to protest its closing as an academic high school.

But as the school year opened, all was calm. In August, Superintendent Talbot, now past freedom-of-choice desegregation, the 1968 teachers' strike, and the 1968 bond issue, said it looked like the 1969–70 school year would be the best year since he became superintendent in 1965.[1] The county's building program had produced three new elementary schools and additions to others that would allow all elementary schools to operate with a seat for every pupil on a single shift. Both predominantly white junior high schools in Gainesville, and Gainesville High, would remain on double sessions, as would all-black A. L. Mebane Junior/Senior High at Alachua. But the building program was expected to finish in time for student body integration in September 1970, including the two new junior/senior high schools on Gainesville's east and west sides. The most serious issue appeared to be parental unhappiness with the school board's decision to extend the minimum distance for bus transportation of students from 1.5 miles to 2 miles from schools.[2]

All Alachua County teachers met in August at the First Baptist Church in Gainesville to hear from a guest speaker on communicating with students. The location was chosen for its air-conditioning, which then was not available in any comparably sized school facility. The Reverend Fred Laughon, pastor, welcomed the teachers and gave the invocation. After the guest speaker, Superintendent Talbot asked teachers to prepare for a unitary school system. He said the sociological aspects might be challenging but asked them to have a spirit of compassion and understanding. "Our aims, hopes and prayers are for you to teach 30 individuals per class this year – and plan for 1970–71 – to foster a school system where every individual is taught as an individual and graded, petted, loved and spanked for his individual ability and not his color."[3]

Schools opened on schedule and without major incident. At Gainesville High School, which continued on double sessions with an enrollment of 2,600, the entering sophomore class was enthusiastic at orientation. Principal Joe Hudson was introduced as "Number One Principal of the Number One School in the State." The school's basketball team had won the state championship the year before. Its football team, led by senior black quarterback Eddie McAshan, had gone 9–0–1.[4] McAshan had been signed by Georgia Tech. Only much later was it revealed that in 1966 and 1967, because of death threats, the FBI had provided protection for McAshan and Jim Niblack, the football coach.[5] Black athletes were believed to have greatly assisted racial peace. "Eddie did more to unify the student body than anyone else," according to a GHS dean.

Some blacks were being accepted into service clubs, sponsored by such groups as Kiwanis and Rotary. For the first time, two black male students were elected student body officers. Despite recent legislation forbidding school boards from banning the playing of "Dixie,"[6] the GHS band had quietly dropped the traditional halftime rouser in the prior school year.[7]

The school board reported to the court that as of September 1969, 269 black students in grades 10–12 had enrolled at Gainesville High, while 569 black students in those grades remained at Lincoln High School. One-third of the 342 tenth-grade black students attended Gainesville High, while 28 percent of the 219 blacks in grade 12 were enrolled at GHS.[8] In July, the school board had reported only 214 black students would be enrolled at Gainesville High in the 1969–70 school year.[9]

Across town, Lincoln High School prepared for its final year. The graduating class in June 1969 had been told by its speaker, the Reverend Rudolph Matthews, that the days of all-black schools were numbered.

> Matthews said that the white man is confused about what to do with the Negro schools.
>
> "I have had boards of education come to me with this problem and I say to them, 'You have created this monster, now you've got to live with it. . .you knew all the time that separate but equal was a lie.'"
>
> He said he does not want to see the Negro race go separate ways in America.
>
> "I want you to be a proud part of America. When we study history it is not black history we want to learn, not white history, and not red history, but just history with all the contributions the black man has made in this country."[10]

John Dukes Jr., the Lincoln principal, had to listen as Matthews continued:

> [Matthews] noted that when Negro schools are phased out Negro principals are the first to lose their jobs. "This," he said, "was planned ahead by the whites.

> "They out-thought us. They put unqualified men in those jobs. I said a long time ago we wouldn't always be competing with ourselves. We're competing with the world now and the world will not accept mediocrity."[11]

Dukes at this point did not know what his future would be in the Alachua County system.

There was no *Gainesville Sun* article about the first day of school at Lincoln in September 1969. But Jessie Heard, the football coach, called the fall 1969 season "the Last Roundup." Although he had an outstanding record as coach of the Fighting Red Terriers, he was not assured of a coaching job after the 1969 season.[12]

Black dissatisfaction with the anticipated closing of Lincoln High School, first voiced publicly in February 1969, continued to simmer. Russell Henry argued to the school board on September 11 that there had been no reasonable explanation for converting Lincoln High School from an academic high school to a vocational center. He alleged that all committee meetings on the subject had been nothing but arguments. The school board chair, H. Dale Smith, asked Henry to select five "knowledgeable citizens" and to arrange a meeting with Superintendent Talbot.[13] That meeting, which included two school board members, failed to produce agreement.[14]

Russell Henry and Charles Chestnut III asked the school board to give the Lincoln name to the new high school to be built on the east side of Gainesville. But the board voted on November 20, 1969, to name the new high school "Lakewood" after the neighborhood in which it was to be located. Dr. William Enneking was the sole board member who favored naming the new school Lincoln. Benford Samuels, who voted with the majority for the Lakewood name, told the meeting that white residents in the area of the new school would identify a school named Lincoln as a black school and would move to other neighborhoods to avoid sending their children to the new high school.[15] His position (if not the justification) was consistent with Justice Brennan's in *Green*: there should not be white schools or black schools, just schools.[16] In 1972, after leaving the superintendent's job, Talbot would express his own regret that the school board had not "taken the bull by the horns" and named the new school Lincoln.[17]

Charles Chestnut III said, "We've never won an argument with this board before and we don't expect to. It's a racist board responding only to the white political structure. . . . The reason they don't want that school named Lincoln is because white people won't want to send their children there. We're tired of talking. It doesn't do any good. But wait till trouble starts and they'll come running to us wanting to talk. . . . The white people have been having their way all this time, what's wrong with sending white students to Lincoln?" Chestnut also objected to the use of the Lincoln campus for compensatory education and vocational programs. He said those actions would perpetuate Lincoln as an all-black school.[18] Gainesville's first recent black city commissioner, Neil Butler, later said, "In all my 42 years, I was never so saddened as I was earlier in the evening when an elected member of the school board said, 'we can't name the new school Lincoln High because all the whites will move out.' Such statements make it hard for me to defend Gainesville against charges of racism."[19]

Other circumstances were adding fuel to the fire. Thieves stole the street clothing of the Lincoln High School football team during the game against Lincoln Park High School at Citizens Field on November 8. The student council sponsored a dance after the game, and the players' lockers held their dress clothes for the dance. Coach Heard and the *Sun* appealed for contributions to make good the players' losses.[20]

Heard credited football with changing his life. "No telling where I would be without football . . . I would probably have been driving a pulpwood truck back in Alabama." He played as a running back in high school. Shug Jordan, the head football coach at Auburn, saw Heard play while attending a black high school championship game. Jordan sent Heard to Jake Gaither at Florida A&M. After college, before being injured, Heard played for a short time for the Los Angeles (later San Diego) Chargers.[21] At a recent meeting, Heard showed this author some of his many community awards.[22] One is a small, simple plaque: "I am my brother's keeper." Given to Heard by a religious group, it expresses his bond with his players and students.

As head football coach at Lincoln High, Heard curated a tradition. He dressed one hundred players at a school with a male student body in grades 9–12 of no more than four hundred. The team received financial support from the black community. The Red Terriers traveled by air-conditioned motor coach to away games, with players in red blazers and dark slacks. Before home games, the team assembled by itself for a meal and mental preparation at locations such as Austin Cary Forest.[23] Heard watched over every player, not just to make sure he played his best but as a father figure.

Discipline on sports teams enhanced discipline in school. Wayne Mosley was a starting linebacker for the Terriers in fall 1969:

> Oh, man. Now those was the coaches. They didn't take what these coaches do today. They was your coach 24/7. If they caught you up around the Tipping Inn or anywhere with a beer in your hand or a cigarette, you paid for it Monday morning when you got back to school. . . . And they know most of the time, that's where we was going to be at. So they would catch us there, and then you were on the Dog Track Monday afternoon. And the Dog Track, nobody wanted to

> be on it. If you played any kind of sports at Lincoln, you knew about the Dog Track. The Dog Track was an oblong path, seven utility poles long, on which guilty players ran laps until the coaches decided they had learned their lesson.[24]

Many of Coach Heard's players came from single-parent homes. He designated one home game every year as Mothers' Night. The mother of every senior player came on the field to be introduced with her son and given flowers.

Responding to changing times, Heard enrolled Lincoln in the Florida High School Activities Association, which oversaw athletic competition in the formerly all-white schools. Lincoln began to play football with some historically white schools.

Heard also initiated the short-lived "Jamborees," season-opening exhibitions at which local football teams, white and black, played each other for a quarter. Heard says Jim Niblack, the very successful head coach at Gainesville High, initially refused to play ("Get out there and beat me and scald me in a quarter, and I've got to live it down, blah, blah, blah"). So did Bill Caton, the coach at Ocala High School, and the coach at Palatka ("We don't play against black boys").[25]

Then Coach Heard invited a reporter from the *Sun* to his house to listen in on an extension phone while Heard polled some coaches at neighboring high schools. Again, Niblack and the Palatka coach turned Heard down. Heard asked Niblack if he would play Lincoln if Heard could find one other team to play Lincoln. Finally, Bill Caton at Ocala agreed to play Lincoln in the Jamboree. Coach Heard went back to Niblack: "Coach, I got me one now. Now you play me." So Niblack, still grumbling according to Heard, agreed that GHS would play in the Jamboree.[26]

Coach Heard:

> [The Red Terriers] lined up on the field, under the goalpost. I had about seventy-five dressed out. Niblack had a million dressed out. And my kids started making noise under the goalpost, pounding the ground and getting ready. And they looked at us, and the boys said, "Come on!" And some guy hollered, one of them drunks on the sideline, on the fence, hollered, "I've been waiting for this for forty years!"[27]

As it turned out, the 1968 Jamboree was fun, peaceful, and perhaps a small step toward racial reconciliation. Six thousand fans filled Citizens Field. In the quarter that GHS and Lincoln played, GHS prevailed by a score of 7–6. The GHS quarterback was Eddie McAshan. The Terriers beat Ocala, GHS's archrival, 6–0.[28]

Finally, the day came for the team's last football practice before its 1969 season-ending game. The *Sun* reported, "After 48 years, thousands of athletes and almost 500 football games, Lincoln's Red Terriers end it all tonight when they host the Vikings of Jacksonville Raines at 8 o'clock on Citizens Field." Heard had already been assured by Superintendent Talbot that he would be a head coach at one of the two new Gainesville high schools. Talbot gave him this assurance partly because Heard had "kept his nose clean."[29] John Dukes, too, already knew that he was going to be principal of one of the new high schools.[30]

For the last time at Lincoln, Heard followed his season's end ritual. Heard shook the hands of all of his players. Some members of the trumpet section of the Lincoln band came in uniform to the football practice to blow taps, part of Heard's tribute to seniors playing their last game.[31] This time it was taps for the school, too. On Saturday night, November 22, the Red Terriers beat Raines, 27–7, closing out an 8–1-1 season.[32]

On Monday night, black students, parents, and community leaders met at Lincoln High School. A protest over Lincoln's closing had been in the planning stages for some time. Heard relates that it was delayed until it became certain that the Red Terriers would not move on to the state football playoffs.[33] Bernice Dukes recalls that there was a meeting at the family home with the student leaders before the boycott. "There was one in particular who was a leader, and he was very, very angry, very rebellious, and he wanted to do a lot of things that would've caused more problems. And [John Dukes Jr.] was able to talk him down and get him to see that was not the right approach. That would be like throwing oil on the fire."[34]

At the meeting at Lincoln High, Wayne Mosley, who was student body president in addition to being a linebacker for the Red Terriers, says he told one of the adult participants, "'I'm not going to leave Lincoln. I leave here dead before I go to GHS because they want to close it because I'm black.' She said, well, tell them that. And that's what started the march. I went on stage, and told the student body the next morning if they want to close our school, then we'll close it ourselves."[35]

On Tuesday, November 25, students began a boycott of Lincoln High School. Only 45 of Lincoln's 1,145 students from grades 7 to 12 reported to class.[36] A march originating at the school made its way to the courthouse, to the Santa Fe Junior College building on West University Avenue, from there to the University of Florida, and then to the school board headquarters on East University Avenue. Members of the football team kept the marchers in the street, away from pedestrians and store windows. Some members of the group, by then estimated to be two thousand, occupied the school board office and said they would not leave until Superintendent Talbot returned. He had been attending a conference in Tampa. Mosley led the march.[37]

Tommy Tomlinson, Talbot's assistant, said at the school board office, "They just marched in. I haven't even heard their demands. They're just a wild group with nothing specific in mind but making noise." Chestnut said that he did not advocate the boycott, "But I do support the students 100 per cent in whatever they decide to do . . . Any school named Lincoln would appease the students, I think, because there would be black identity and a continuation of tradition. The white community would not stand for the passing of GHS."[38]

Talbot later said that his secretary called him in Tampa. Death threats had been made against Talbot. A sheriff's deputy met him outside of Tampa and escorted him back to Gainesville.[39] When Talbot returned around 3:00 p.m., he and school board member Enneking met outside the school board offices with the protesters. Using a loudspeaker on a police car, Captain Courtenay Roberts tried to act as moderator, taking questions and attempting to allow Talbot and Enneking to answer. LHS Principal John Dukes and student leaders "managed to keep the crowd orderly but not quiet." One young person shouted, "We want our black school or we won't go to any school at all."[40] Talbot later said of the experience, "Never face a mob and try to explain things when emotions are that high. You must talk only to the leaders, not with 1,200 screaming people."[41]

The *Sun* was quick to take the side of the school board. In an editorial the same day as the boycott began, the *Sun* asked rhetorically, "The full thrust of Negro legal and moral endeavor for the past 20 years has been to share-and-share alike with whites. What's wrong with sharing a nice new school with whites? . . . Abe Lincoln is our favorite president, but his name was over-used in labeling Negro schools in the South and has become associated with second-rate education. Who needs it?" The *Sun* then suggested that the "whiteness" of Gainesville High might be eliminated by renaming that school (an idea that would gain some traction later among black students).[42]

The closing of formerly all-black schools was a common response to desegregation, and black protest was a not uncommon reaction. For example, HEW's Office of Civil Rights in late 1968 refused to reverse the closing of a black junior high in nearby Dixie County.[43] A field representative from the Office of Civil Rights told Dixie County parents that HEW would approve any plan that provided for the elimination of a dual school system. The initial school board plan that continued the black school and the board's later plan that closed it were both satisfactory to the Office of Civil Rights.[44]

In the spring of 1969, in Florida alone, organized protests against the closing of black schools were reported in Apopka, Ocala, West Palm Beach, Deland, Daytona Beach, and Sarasota, and it is unlikely that this list is complete.[45] In Fort Myers, two schools that were formerly named for black poet Paul Dunbar were not closed but renamed and used as integrated schools. The Lee County NAACP charged the school board with saying, in effect, that a school named for a black man is not fit to be attended by white students. The school superintendent ordered the names temporarily restored and agreed to review the issue. White boycotts in Hillsborough and Manatee Counties, however, suggested that white students would not attend formerly all-black schools if they were in the minority in such schools.[46] The subsequent legal battles over the closing of black schools, including Gainesville's Lincoln, will be examined in chapter 15.

The Rev. Wright later recalled that Lincoln's former principal, Otha W. Nealy, visited Wright at his church after the Lincoln strike had been going on for two or three days, to urge Wright to get the children out of the streets. Wright says he replied, "They haven't been out there long enough yet." Nealy asked Wright if he would go see Talbot. Wright says he answered, "Well, maybe I'll go after four or five more days."[47] Wright would be one of the group of black leaders who reached a preliminary agreement with Talbot that Talbot announced on December 5.

A state official said that it was up to local authorities to invoke truancy laws to force parents to return their children to school. Those laws applied to children between the ages of six and sixteen.[48]

The Florida field director for the NAACP, Marvin Davies, explained, "We're not boycotting because we want segregated schools, but because we want to make sure integration works once the schools are integrated." He said blacks wanted to continue to have schools located in their communities so black students were not disadvantaged by travel to distant white schools. That idea underlay the emerging legal doctrine of "disproportionate burden," which would be acknowledged by the courts but would not result in many victories for its African American advocates.[49] Davies said that blacks also did not want to see tax money wasted on what they considered to be unnecessary new schools. "Of course, there is a stigma attached to black schools now. Well, that stigma was put on the schools by the city fathers and school boards who founded them." Davies added, "The dropout rate of black kids in newly integrated schools is really high, and it's high because white teachers don't take the time to understand the special problems of the black kids or just ignore the kids entirely." Nevertheless, Davies favored school integration as the starting place for teaching whites and blacks to live together and for blacks to gain a decent chance for economic independence.[50]

On the second day of the strike (as the Lincoln High group preferred that it be called), about 1,200 students stayed out of class and marched the same route, out to the University of Florida campus and back to the school board headquarters on East University Avenue. They sang spirit songs and the Lincoln High alma mater. When they reached the school board headquarters, Talbot and Enneking attempted to explain the reasons for closing Lincoln High as an academic center, responding to questions by students and parents. They were shouted down. After cheers of "Mighty, mighty, we'll show whitey," the group left. On the grounds of the school board headquarters were paper, cans, and bottles. Enneking said, "I don't think they understand the long-range implications of what we are trying to do and obviously they are in no mood to listen."[51]

Many black students at Gainesville High supported their friends at Lincoln during the strike. Cynthia Cook recalls that one day, some Lincoln students entered Barbara Gallant's class to urge black GHS students to join the Lincoln march. The response, according to Cook, was instantaneous. "Let's go," said Bernadette Rivers. Cook, Rivers, and some of their friends left the class (over Gallant's objection) to march with the Lincoln protesters.[52]

As the strike continued, the Lincoln students gained support from black students at the University of Florida. The Black Student Union offered some advice on strategy to the Lincoln group. A leader of Students for a Democratic Society at the University and a minister employed at Santa Fe Junior College spoke in support of the demonstrations.[53] However, according to Mosley, the demonstrations remained a spontaneous movement by the Lincoln community.[54]

Brenda Wims, who was secretary of Lincoln's student body, was chosen to be the students' spokesperson. She appeared on Charles Chestnut III's weekly television program, *Color Us Black*, and met with Superintendent Talbot and the school board. Adult community leaders would make sure that Wims had transportation to scheduled meetings. Wims recounts one day when Talbot told her, "Young lady, you are really a good spokesperson. But it ain't going to do anything for you here."

> And I said to him, I don't see why not. And he says, I'll tell you why. You want to know why? I said, yes sir. He said, because your mama and daddy don't pay the most taxes and we going to shut that school down. . . . And I said it's still not fair. Well, he said, fair or not, that's what's going to have to happen. So after then, [the adult community leaders] come, I said, I'm not going back, because he told me that they're going to close the school, and there's nothing I can say or do. [Talbot said] but you are going to be somebody someday. You keep that up. But you going to have to go over there now. You might as well go back and tell them. You all just need to go over there in this, go in on and do this. I was just so hurt. Mr. Dukes said, well, Brenda, you've done everything that you can do, and we're proud of you. But I was so disappointed.[55]

Although they might offer advice behind the scenes, black faculty could not openly support the protest.[56] According to Wims, John Dukes worked with the student leaders of the strike, providing advice on what to do and how to do it. She says that Dukes and other adult leaders also paid for food for the striking students from Elmer "Pop" Henry's restaurant in Porters Quarters.[57] Elmer Henry's son, Scherwin Henry, was then a senior at Lincoln. Scherwin would later be elected to the Gainesville City Commission.

The strike continued. Talbot said that when the new east-side school opened, the Lakewood name would be reviewed by registered students, faculty, and parents, who could recommend a new name.[58] But that concession did not stop the strike.

During the Lincoln strike, a black journalism student from the University of Florida had many conversations with black citizens at Sharpe's Barbershop. That shop was located at the corner of N.W. 7th Street and N.W. 5th Avenue, in the center of a black neighborhood. The *Sun* article:

> The conversation is not controversial yet.
>
> All that is needed to start them, however, is the question: "I'm doing a story on the Lincoln High School boycott. Can I ask you all a few questions?"
>
> "What'll you want to know about it? I'll tell you," the speaker is called Nat. He is a wino, around 40 years old.
>
> Nat's face is a comic mask of bitterness partially hiding the hatred he has for the society which crowded him into overpriced, rat infested ghetto housing, gave him a menial job that couldn't pay for the luxuries which an affluent society constantly flaunts in his face, and forced him into inferior public schools that no white neighborhood would tolerate.
>
> "They wanted integration. They passed a bond issue for it, didn't they?" Nat asked. "So they got it. I don't think it's right to close down Lincoln. They should integrate it.
>
> "That's been a good school for years. I went there. I finished there. "I've got nieces and they want to finish there. They don't want to be mixed up with white folks."
>
> "Ah, hush, nigger," said a voice from the rear, "you don't know what you talking about."
>
> The voice belonged to a Mr. Johnson, a black maintenance worker at the University of Florida. Johnson opposed Nat's stand on Lincoln.
>
> "It (Lincoln) ain't no good. It should have been wiped off the map long ago.

"It's no good, the niggers out there ain't no good. If it was any good, then all the teachers out there wouldn't send their kids to white schools.

"You see," Johnson said, "when a thing is rotten all the way down there ain't nothing you can do with it. They ought to done closed it down."

The conflict of opinion between Nat the wino and Johnson reflects the internal division within Gainesville's black community on the Lincoln High boycott.

Many older blacks share Johnson's opinion on Lincoln High School. They say Lincoln offers their children an education inferior to the education offered whites at Gainesville High School. For this group of blacks, the day Lincoln closes will be a day of celebration.

There is a group of blacks younger than Johnson's group but older than the striking Lincoln High School students, who oppose the boycott.

This group fought the "good" fights of the civil rights movement in Gainesville – desegregation of movies, lunch counters and, most important, desegregation of schools.

Cleveland Sharpe is a member of this group.

"I don't know what they're after," Sharpe said of the boycotting students.

"Some say they want the school to remain academic. Others say they want the new school named Lincoln. Personally I'm not in favor of either one.

"That's what we picketed for a long time ago, desegregation of schools, and now they don't want it."

Sharpe says he has talked to many black students who transferred from Lincoln to GHS and who now would not consider returning to Lincoln.

"When they first integrated GHS the black students who went there wanted to get back to Lincoln quick," Sharpe said.

"They didn't have any background that prepared them to compete with the white students.

"Those that stuck it out now like GHS better than Lincoln. They don't want to go back. They don't care what happens to Lincoln," he said.

By this time, Nat the wino is in a rage. No one is siding with him. No one seems to want to save Lincoln.

Frustrated, angry and more than slightly drunk he lashes out at the middle-class blacks – a black teacher and a black truancy officer – who have up to this point remained silent.

"Ask them," Nat said pointing to the pair, "Ask them about Lincoln."

The black teacher gets up and walks out of the shop. The truancy officer is still silent.

"Ask him what he thinks about Lincoln," Nat the wino said. "He won't say nothing because he works for the school board.

"He's got his son in a white school, GHS, and he won't say nothing about Lincoln. Ask him. Ask him what he thinks about it."

Except for a few cutting jokes aimed at Nat, the truancy officer has remained silent on the Lincoln issue.

Many middle class blacks like the truancy officer and the teacher that walked out say they are against irregular and potentially unlawful acts like the Lincoln boycott.

They are more bitterly opposed to these things than any white person can ever be.

Theirs is the voice of reason that white people want to hear. But it is not necessarily the authentic voice of the ghetto.

That voice is far more angry and impatient. It can heave a molotov cocktail into a store window, a rock into a police car, or passively boycott a high school.

The true voice of Gainesville's black ghetto is the voice of its young. And Nat the wino comes closer to articulating that voice than the silent truancy officer or the intelligent Cleve Sharpe.

Nat is starting to leave now, raving some biblical quote.

"The Bible told them," he said, pointing to his opponents, "To honor thy father and mother and good white folks."

Many blacks were against the boycott from the start. Others, who were originally for the boycott, have now changed their position.

Oscar Gilbert owns a repair shop on NW 5th Avenue in the heart of Gainesville's worst black ghetto.[59]

Gilbert was against the Lincoln High walkout from its inception.

"When Thurgood Marshall (former NAACP lawyer now U.S. Supreme Court justice) was fighting to break down segregation he found separate schools was one of the main causes of segregation, Gilbert said.

Gilbert said black children who attend separate schools feel inferior to white children, and white children feel superior to the black children who cannot attend their school.

"We wanted integration. The local school board saw that the only way this could be done was to close our colored schools and build new schools.

Why?

"Because we would always go to the white schools more than they would come to ours," Gilbert said.

"They're (the school board) doing it the only peaceful way they can," he added.

Not only is Gilbert against the Lincoln boycott, he is an ardent supporter of Alachua County School Superintendent W.S. Talbot.

"Talbot is doing a better job of integrating the schools than the president of the University of Florida," Gilbert said.

"He has tried to integrate the schools and the University of Florida is still the most segregated institution in Gainesville," he said.

Gilbert was skeptical about the amount of community support behind the Lincoln boycott.

"It's not from the heart," Gilbert said. "If it was from the heart, then every teacher at Lincoln would not have their kids in white schools."

Gilbert represents the conservative viewpoint within the black community. There are others not so conservative who are against Lincoln remaining the type of academic school it is now.

"I'd like to see Lincoln as an academic school in the existing plant," said a black teacher, now teaching at a predominantly white school.

"It's senseless to abandon it, a waste of the taxpayers money," he said.

"It would be more logical to update its facilities than abandon it.

"And since the court has ruled that faculty-student ratios must be 3:1 (75% white and 25% black) the population of blacks and whites in South East Gainesville comprises enough people to populate both schools.

While the black teacher supports keeping Lincoln as an academic school, he is against the type of education currently being taught at Lincoln.

"I'm not in favor of keeping Lincoln all black," he said. "I am in favor of integrating it and keeping it as an academic center.

"You find different environment at white schools. Kids are getting pushed more. They receive more encouragement and financing from home."

The teachers said the boycott, because it stimulated parent-student cooperation, may bring about needed changes at Lincoln.

Rev. T.A. Wright is head of Gainesville's NAACP, the group that originally started the desegregation proceedings back in 1964.

Wright originally supported the student boycott and was in favor of keeping Lincoln as an academic school because of its cultural significance.

"It served as a social center for the black community," Wright said.

"Commencement at Lincoln was the highlight of the year. This was the crowning event of the black community.

"At commencement we got to push in terms of educational values, black community values. Black speakers would tell us where we needed to go, what had been done, and what still needed to be done," Wright said.

For these reasons, Wright said he originally supported the boycott. But now, after talking to parents and students, he has changed his position.

The reasons Wright gave for this change are: inadequate facilities at Lincoln and the poor performance of its graduates.

"Students told me themselves that there were only 5 teachers out of 60, that they would actually rate as dedicated teachers," Wright said.

"What I think we need to do now is push for every consideration we can get at the Eastside high school.

"And push to make sure every teacher at Lincoln gets every consideration they can get if Lincoln is phased out," Wright said.

"Out of this I hope we can find a good candidate to run for the school board," he said. "We need an elected officer to represent the black community."[60]

Thanksgiving evening, the Lincoln protesters elected the Reverend L. A. Haisley and Mrs. Odessa W. McClendon as their spokespersons to discuss the walkout with the school board. Summarizing a slightly revised set of issues, a parent said, "We want our black principal, our black band leader and a high school in the black community. The whites can come to us."[61]

The school board voted to hold an emergency meeting with the representatives of the Lincoln protesters on Monday, December 1. The meeting was watched by plainclothes sheriff's deputies but remained orderly. Before the meeting formally opened, school board chair Dale Smith said that he had invited County Judge John Connell to explain the legal consequences of the protests. As permitted at the time, the elected Judge Connell was not a lawyer. His jurisdiction included juvenile court matters. Connell told the parents that their children could be sent to correctional institutions if they continued to stay out of school and that parents were subject to prosecution for contributing to their delinquency. He said the school board could petition his court to take action against the students. During Connell's speech, a black participant asked, "Are we in a juvenile court hearing or a hearing of the school board?" Connell replied, "When I get through speaking, friend, you'll be in a school board meeting." At another point, Russell Henry, who had been active in the Lincoln protest, raised his hand to ask Connell a question.

> "Who are you and what are you?" Connell questioned.
> "Is that important?" Henry shot back.
> "Yes."
> "Forget it," Henry said.

After about fifteen minutes, Chair Smith asked Connell to end his remarks.

The blacks accused the school system of failing to bring black schools up to the same level as white schools. According to the official minutes, it was alleged that the historically black schools could not get books and materials as ordered.[62] There were also accusations that the white schools discriminated against blacks in extracurricular activities. The GHS choral director was accused of maintaining two singing groups, one white and one black. A mother said her daughters had sought to join the white group and were told that "their personality and conduct didn't fit in." Talbot and school board members denied the allegations that black schools were not kept up to the standards of white schools.

To the list of demands for a black principal, a black football coach, and a black band leader were added better facilities and maintenance, better bus service, and a lunch room menu prepared by a black lunchroom supervisor.

A representative of the League of Women Voters, Sue Legg, addressed the meeting but took no position on the central issue of maintaining Lincoln as an academic high school. She said the league opposed the use of the Lincoln campus for compensatory education for middle school students. She said that the formerly all-black A. Quinn Jones Elementary School was being used for a similar program for elementary students and that it had enrolled only 24 white students out of a total enrollment of 296. "We feel schools of this type perpetuate economic and racial segregation of a group of children in our county."[63]

The minutes of the December 1 school board meeting also reflect a discussion of the race of members of facility survey teams for the past four years. "Chairman Smith stated that this matter should be closed until the county's desegregation plan is acted upon by the Court and then he will ask that five or six leaders sit down with board members and the Superintendent to discuss the situation further."[64]

The only result of the meeting was a 4–1 vote by the school board, on the recommendation of Enneking, to reconsider the naming of the new east-side junior/senior high school.[65]

On the same day, December 1, the Fifth Circuit Court of Appeals released the *Singleton* decision, which allowed Alachua County and the other school districts until September 1970 to integrate their student bodies in unitary school systems. Had the NAACP Legal Defense Fund allowed that decision to stand, Lincoln would have remained open through the end of the 1969–70 school year.

On Thursday, December 4, juvenile court officers showed up at Lincoln High School to begin obtaining the names of students who might be charged with truancy and parents who might be charged with contributing to delinquency of a minor. Talbot did not comment, since he was reported to be meeting with black community leaders, but he had previously stated he would not take any action on truancies, leaving that step to the school board.[66] Connell disclaimed that his actions had been requested either by Talbot or by the school board.[67]

Talbot told the press on Friday, December 5, that he and black community leaders had reached agreement on seven points, which were disseminated to the Lincoln students.[68] But meetings with those leaders continued over the weekend.[69] Parents of the striking students began collecting funds for legal defense costs in case truancy prosecutions were initiated.[70]

The *Sun* ran letters to the editor about the crisis on Saturday, December 6. These letters speak of long-held frustration finally released, a frustration focused on the impending loss of Lincoln High School but flowing from deeper sources. In their own voices:

WE WON'T BE CHEATED AGAIN

EDITOR, Sun: In a community where blacks are a 13 per cent minority or less, it seems rather strange that he has little or no say-so concerning his child's education. Not only as a taxpayer is he denied these rights but as a citizen also. It is no more than just, that we as a black minority should have our say in the building and planning of our school's power structure. Even though we are a minority we will no longer step aside or take the back row, we want to be recognized.

It is now a day and age when education is of the utmost importance not only to the black man, but every man. We no longer ask or beg for better educational facilities and equal opportunities, we as blacks demand them. We demand the best for our children also. In this community and surrounding area Lincoln High School is the only and largest predominantly black high school, it would only be unrealistic and unjustifiable to phase this institution out. The white man has short-changed the black man so long that when this wrongdoing is about to be brought into the open he uses such tactics as phasing out black institutions. The day has arrived when people have become aware that the whites have cheated the blacks in this community of top educational facilities.

Instead of making Lincoln High School a quality institution that is second to none, which it is capable of being, they would rather phase it out, all seemingly to deface the black man of a proud heritage. We as blacks have suffered enough setbacks in our long history, it is time that we are equal not only in educational knowledge, but as men. We as blacks in this community are proud of the heritage, tradition, and educational institution that we have established at Lincoln High School. Let us not only be recognized as blacks in this community but as Lincolnians also.

WAYNE T. McCLELLAN

WE DEMAND

EDITOR, Sun: Welfare recipients are at the crossroads of starvation and hell as an American citizen in the state of Florida, which is one of the most prosperous states in the union. The welfare recipients are either old, disabled or children. Although our leaders and representatives sing a song, "Help these poor children, we are going to do all we can," now it seems that our so-called helpers has mounted us on a "razorback jackass," down $16 million worth of new beautiful roads or highways.[71] We have been tossed, driven and humiliated. We have been hungry so long that malnutrition has possessed our body and our children's bodies. We do not have the energy to sit on this "razorback jackass," neither does this poor beast have a mind to carry us, because he has to care.

Well, it all boils down to this skill in job training and guaranteed jobs for us after we finished our skill training.

In case someone is wondering why we are not saying education. Well I tell you, to poor people and for poor people, education means high school diplomas and so many years in college.

So that is ancient history for poor people to grasp because it only means a word used by our great society to justify the grateful for their token father and mother handouts. We would rather be trained in skilled, meaningful professions and guaranteed jobs after we have been trained. Then we would not have to accept handouts and would be well on the way to supporting our family properly and not have to worry where or when we can afford the next meal and how we are going to clothe our children or pay the rent.

Oh yes, in the past few years we have been mulling in an integration stew in our school system called freedom of choice. However, the choice has always been the decision of the School Board, without the participation of the students and staff that the decision effects.

It seems to me since the school board has enough money to build two new schools, one of them should be a vocational school instead of taking Lincoln High to serve the purpose. Surely if black schools are closed they would have to attend white schools; then the white students can be put in black

> schools because the blacks are more acceptable to humanity than some of the whites. It seems to be a matter of alienating the black students from the mainstreams of society. To the students of Lincoln High, my sincere sympathy.
>
> It seems all our lawmakers are mentally disturbed or mighty stupid. They have been mulling in an integration stew as I have already said. I also sympathize with the school-board, poor old Pharaoh, but I am in sincere sympathy with the depressed Israelites at Lincoln High School. Of course, who knows kids, Moses might be on his way to help you out of Egypt land, so keep the faith baby.
>
> SAVANAH WILLIAMS[72]

Wayne Mosley says that he and Alex Henry at some point during the controversy boarded the Seaboard train at Waldo for Washington, DC, to carry their protest to HEW. According to Mosley, a HEW official advised them that it was not the position of HEW that Lincoln should be closed.[73] That meeting may have influenced the Florida School Desegregation Consulting Center, a HEW contractor, to recommend in January 1970 that the new east-side junior/senior high school be named Lincoln and that it carry on as many of the traditions of Lincoln as possible. But that report would also concur with the school board's decision to replace Lincoln with a new campus at the east-side site.[74] Because the Alachua County schools were subject to continuing court orders, HEW could act in the district court proceedings only through the Justice Department.[75] The Justice Department did not appear in *Wright v. Board* at the district court, which eventually would have to deal with this issue.

Judge Connell announced on Monday, December 8, with the strike continuing, that he would begin issuing summonses to parents of Lincoln High students who remained out of school. Connell was also reported to have discouraged the Gainesville police department from issuing parade permits to the protesters. The protesters did not march on December 8, but met near the school. The city's Human Relations Advisory Board appointed the Reverend Clarence D. Weaver Jr. to work with Lincoln students to try to end the strike.[76]

Judge Connell's office served forty-eight summonses on Lincoln High parents on December 8. His office estimated that five hundred to six hundred of the striking students were between the ages of six and sixteen, all of whom were expected to receive summonses. From today's distance, the reactions of the students and parents could easily be predicted.

Isaac Caffey, an assistant principal at Lincoln, received truancy papers. His fifteen-year-old son, Marion, had participated in the nine days of the strike. Caffey told the *Sun*, "I don't think Connell's effort to break the strike will succeed; it (hearings) will aggravate the situation more than anything else."

> Caffey said he had not been pressured by the school board to put his son back into attendance at LHS.
>
> "My job and what my boy does are two different things. I don't think his actions will jeopardize me with the school board," Caffey said.

Caffey was later appointed an assistant principal at Gainesville High.

The *Sun* reported that LHS sophomore Ida Dixon "was jubilant on receiving her summons": "This don't mean a thing. If we have to go to jail we all will. We'll stay out of school until we get what we want – Lincoln High School." A mother, Mrs. Flora Mae Cleveland, said, "I will be glad to go. Anything I think is right, I'll go to hell for."

On that Monday morning, 150 students of 1,200 attended class at Lincoln, the highest total since the strike began.[77]

Commenting the same day, the *Sun* saw the unspoken issue in the protests as "the legal 'mix' of 70 percent white and 30 percent black and the feared inundation of black culture." "Twelve years ago in Arkansas, the bigot opposed integration with invective and threats. Today in Gainesville, he is joined by the black." The *Sun* again defended the ideal of integration and the school board's unitary school plan as one "which state authorities and the federal courts are convinced will achieve meaningful integration." The *Sun* called the cause of saving Lincoln "spurious."[78]

Judge Connell went ahead with his version of a solution, the hearings on his summonses to the Lincoln High parents and students. Four lawyers, led by Richard Wilson, represented the defendants.

The *Sun*:

> It was discovered that the petitions were improperly executed and the summonses issued by Connell stated the students were delinquents, rather than truants.
>
> Connell then called for his seal and proceeded to amend, sign and stamp the petition on the spot. Wilson objected, saying the law required a 24-hour period between the time a petition is signed and served as a summons. Connell overruled the objection.

> At one point Wilson complained, "This is worse than Judge Hoffman's court in Chicago."[79]
>
> Connell replied, "That is your opinion and you're welcome to it."
>
> Summoned as prosecution witnesses in the case were: D.H. Land, supervisor of attendance records for the school board; Chief Juvenile Counselor Jack Gamble, LHS Principal John Dukes; and Assistant Principal Isaac Caffey.
>
> Caffey refused to answer on the grounds that it might tend to incriminate him. He invoked the Fifth Amendment on the advice of counsel Herbert Schwartz.
>
> Motions to have the judge disqualify himself on the basis of statements he made to the school board and the press concerning the case, motions to transfer proceedings to a court of record, motions to supply copies of a petition of facts concerning individual cases to the defense, and motions to redraw petitions and summonses, all were denied by Connell.
>
> It prompted Wilson to say it was "the most flagrant violation of constitutional rights" he had ever encountered.
>
> "The very guts of the rules established for justice in this country have been kicked aside," Wilson added.
>
> The judge cut Wilson off, saying he didn't have time to listen to a speech.
>
> Several times Judge Connell tried to question the parents, and Wilson shouted that they did not have to answer on the grounds that it might incriminate them.
>
> Despite objections of counsel that they had conflicts in other courts for hearings Thursday, the judge said a full day of hearings had been scheduled and he would proceed with them.[80]

As a result of the first day's proceedings, one case against a fifteen-year-old protester was dismissed.[81]

It was not until December 11 that Talbot and board attorney Harry Duncan briefed school principals and the press on changes that would have to be made by February 1, 1970, because of the Fifth Circuit's ruling in *Singleton*. The Fifth Circuit's opinion did not require any changes to the plans to open the new east-side high school as an academic center and to use the Lincoln plant for compensatory and vocational education.[82]

The following day, December 12, the eleven-day Lincoln strike ended with students returning to class. The school board approved a seven-point resolution on December 11 that, according to the *Sun*, was worked out by community leaders of both races and the school board (the principal negotiators for the board were members Ebling, Enneking, and Samuels). The agreement left intact the elimination of Lincoln High School as an academic high school. Among the groups that pressed the school board to end the crisis was the Greater Gainesville Chamber of Commerce, which had played a strong role in gaining approval of the 1968 bond issue. Black parents and students voted to ratify the agreement at Bartley Temple Church that evening. Alex Henry, a black parent who helped bring about the agreement, said, "Both the parents and kids were pretty well satisfied. . . . The black people believe that they can be heard from now on and kept informed by the whites. . . . We think we have been heard and will not be overlooked from now on."[83]

Judge Connell was required to drop all truancy cases. He agreed to do so as to all students who returned to class. An attorney for the students said that students would have been back in school on December 8 had it not been for Connell's actions.[84]

The school board's resolution made significant changes to the agreement reached by Superintendent Talbot on December 5. The full text of the December 11 resolution:

We are now living in an integrated world. No matter how anyone feels about integration, this is a fact of life. The black person will have to compete with the white person in areas where the white person excels and the white person will have to compete with the black person in areas where the black person excels.

In order for all of us to live happy, productive lives we are going to have to communicate with each other. We can either fight each other for the rest of our lives or we can learn to live in harmony and to assist each other to attain the goals that we each seek.

We cannot educate our children to live a life that can never be again. Our children must learn this feeling of understanding and cooperation. The board believes that the best way to develop this mutual trust and understanding is to develop a good unitary school system.

The board realizes that it has made mistakes in the past. The mistakes that have been made were not deliberate attempts to mislead anyone, but were evidence of the fact that we did not adequately understand the feelings of the entire community. It is obvious that while the board was attempting to offer the best possible education to everyone in the county, the move to convert Lincoln into a technical school was interpreted by the black community as more evidence that the white community does not deal fairly with the black community. As a result there is not as much faith and trust between the two areas as would be desirable.

The Lincoln boycott has been successful because it has opened new avenues of communication between the school administration and school board and the black community. The board intends to keep these lines of communication open and expand them.

The board believes that this will help prevent future problems of lack of communication and understanding.

The board would encourage the present student and parents committee involved in the Lincoln boycott to appoint a member whose responsibility would be to attend every school board meeting, the way other interested organizations do, and report back to that organization on the transactions of the board and to offer help and advice.

The board believes that this will help prevent future problems of lack of communication and understanding.

Members of the board have met with groups of interested white parents in east Gainesville and they have expressed a sincere desire to cooperate with black parents to develop a school of which they can all be proud. The board believes that this expression of cooperation will be most helpful in developing the necessary trust and faith among the parents in all areas of our county.

1. The administrative positions in the secondary schools in the Alachua County school system are available on the basis of merit. We are interested in finding the best people available for these positions regardless of race. This is particularly desirable because of our fast approaching unitary school system.

2. The staff of Lincoln High School will be reassigned in the county to comparable positions by the Superintendent with the approval of the school board. Mr. Dukes, presently principal of Lincoln High School, will be assigned to the principalship of a secondary school in the City of Gainesville.

3. Participants in all phases of extra-curricular student activities will be selected on the basis of merit.

4. In regard to the Eastside High School:

> As soon as the principal is selected, a committee will be formed to work with him. This committee will be made up of students and their parents who will attend the school. The committee will be formed of 5 whites (3 parents and 2 students) and 5 blacks (3 parents and 2 students). This committee, with the principal as the non-voting chairman, will set up guidelines and procedures to select school colors, a name, symbols, songs, etc. The committee will establish a method of resolving tie votes internally.
>
> The committee's recommendations will be forwarded by the principal to the Superintendent, who will then forward them to the board with his recommendations for the board's decision. The committee will also express their preference for head coach, band director and choral director.
>
> 5. The black community will furnish a representative approved by the Superintendent to his building committee, policy committee, transportation committee, and insurance committee, and to other committees formed at the request of the board.
>
> 6. A committee will be formed by the Superintendent composed equally of blacks and whites responsible for recommendation to the Superintendent on all non-academic matters pertaining to integration. As requested by parents, school principals will form similar committees for their schools.
>
> 7. The board will meet with three representatives of the black community to discuss with them and their lawyer the feasibility of joining with them in an appeal to the federal court in regard to retaining Lincoln High School as an academic school. The board in no way binds itself to support this appeal nor does the black community relinquish further appeal should the board vote against such a common appeal.[85]

Board members Smith and Simmons were recorded as voting against the resolution because they could not support point 4, related to Eastside High School.[86] To the press, they said that the point tied the hands of the school principal.[87]

To Talbot's December 5 list,[88] through further negotiations, the school board added the points about black membership on the superintendent's administrative committees, biracial committees at the superintendent's office and at individual schools, and the possible appeal to the federal court to retain Lincoln as an academic high school. This compromise gave the black community increased involvement at many levels of the school system, through which they could have access to information earlier in the planning process and the ability to express their views as issues arose. The Bi-racial Committee to advise the superintendent about integration issues would be required by court order in August 1970 in *Wright v. Board*.[89] The biracial committees at each school would provide much valuable service in the days to come.

The school board eliminated Talbot's agreement to preserve Lincoln student records, trophies, class pictures, and other mementos at Lincoln, and his agreement for intramural sports competition among senior high students based on grade level. The records and memorabilia of Lincoln High School would subsequently be lost through vandalism or neglect. That loss continues to grieve Gainesville's African American community.

Nondiscrimination in extracurricular activities had been required by court order since April 1967.[90] Inclusion of that point in negotiations suggests that blacks believed the schools were not honoring the court order.

Black and white parents and students were given an equal voice in choosing the name, mascot, and school colors of the new east-side high school. The Eastside committee recommended that the new school be named Eastside, that its mascot would be the Rams, and its colors orange and green. The school songs were to be selected by the music department at the new school. Those recommendations were approved by the school board.[91]

The school board did not take court action to reverse the closing of Lincoln High School as an academic high school. Lincoln's closing had been incorporated in the county's court-approved desegregation plan on April 3, 1969.[92] In little over a month, Lincoln High would be permanently closed as a collateral result of the NAACP Legal Defense Fund's appeal to the US Supreme Court of the December 1, 1969, Fifth Circuit decision in *Singleton*.[93] Lincoln students would find themselves starting the spring term in formerly white schools.

CHAPTER 12
THE FRUITBASKET SOLUTION

Enneking pointed out that pupils of both races will be the losers in a fruitbasket turnover Feb. 1.

"Do we sacrifice education for the sake of a deadline?" Enneking asked.

"As one who had an inferior education I am not inclined to worry about that," Johnson replied.

School board member William Enneking, MD, and NAACP Legal Defense Fund lawyer Earl M. Johnson, December 20, 1969

"I feel certain the black community would not join you in appealing for the sake of delaying," Neil Butler told Enneking. Said the Rev. Wright, "We have been in contact with our attorneys and we are in full accord with him that, the quicker the better, no delay."

Neil Butler and the Reverend Thomas A. Wright to William Enneking, MD, December 22, 1969

We're not here to threaten you, to intimidate anyone. But it is not right to make wholesale changes in the middle of the year that are not in the best interest and for which you are not ready. We're not going to put up with it.

Ralph Cellon, white parent, December 30, 1969

We have an order from the federal district court to get up a plan and I will not be held in contempt by that court.

William S. Talbot, January 20, 1970

> If unification is viewed as an exciting situation to liven up a dull part of the school year . . . if it is seen as a way to meet 600 additional individuals . . . if it is seen as an educational experience in itself, 1969–70 could be considered the most valuable year in the history of Gainesville High School. It is up to us – students from both Lincoln High School and Gainesville High School – to make unification work. We can do it.
>
> Roberta Berner, Gainesville High editor, February 1, 1970

In affected districts across the South, and in Alachua County, the midyear 1970 desegregation was called the "fruitbasket turnover." The senior high schools were most significantly affected, because both black high schools were closed in midyear and their students assigned to previously integrated but predominantly white high schools. The Gainesville white secondary schools were already severely overcrowded pending the opening of the new east- and west-side junior/senior high schools financed by the 1968 bond issue. But many outlying elementary schools also experienced disruption.

"Fruitbasket" meant that everyone was suddenly thrown together, not according to anyone's plan for transition to a unitary system. That event occurred, as we have seen, because the NAACP Legal Defense Fund, after failing to obtain orders for unitary systems by September 1969, pressed for and eventually obtained a US Supreme Court order requiring student body integration by February 1970.

Following the fruitbasket turnover, Alachua County would see some violent racial confrontations at predominantly white schools, diminished attention to studies, and attempts by the school administration and school board to find solutions that would, for a time, fail to satisfy either the white or black communities. White flight to private schools and away from east-side neighborhoods gained an impetus that might not have existed in more favorable circumstances. It is not remarkable that the schools experienced unrest and indiscipline, but it is praiseworthy that Alachua County's public schools survived and eventually found entirely new ways to educate their diverse student population.

The school board desegregation plan approved by Judge Carswell on April 3, 1969, governed the Alachua County schools as the 1969–70 school year began. That plan for the first time added compulsory zoning at the elementary schools in Gainesville and caused greater integration of the teaching staff across the county. White discontent began to surface. Principals began to receive requests from parents to change zones, which if granted would have violated the April 3 plan. Some white parents characterized as influential sought transfer of their children out of classes taught by black teachers. "'These are not rednecks,' one principal said. 'Maybe we need to re-identify rednecks,' another principal interjected. 'The people we have been referring to as rednecks have caused the least amount of trouble.'" There were reports that some parents had given false addresses to obtain seats for their children in schools with a greater preponderance of white students. Unusually high purchasing activity was reported for city real estate far from black neighborhoods.[1] And white students zoned into historically black Duval and Williams Elementary Schools, where they formed small minorities, silently began to stop showing up for class.[2]

During the fall term the county still faced the possibility that the Fifth Circuit would follow *Alexander* and order student body integration by January 1. Without yielding the point that a January 1 deadline was infeasible, Superintendent Talbot sought to reassure the public that the school system could meet that deadline if forced to do so by the court. "If it comes to pass I believe I could sit down with the principals in one afternoon and come up with a unitary system. Some education would be lost in the process but it wouldn't be chaotic. We have too many good pro's in the system for that to happen." Integration of the faculty at Gainesville High School at the required ratio of one black teacher to four white teachers[3] would not be possible, however, until Lincoln High School ceased to be an academic center. According to Talbot, it was not possible in the market to recruit additional black high school teachers. He pointed out again that the county system would be operating on a full unitary basis starting in September 1970 with the completion of more new schools.[4]

In the midst of the Lincoln High School strike, the Fifth Circuit Court of Appeals issued the *Singleton* decision on December 1, which required integration of faculties and student activities by February 1, 1970, but allowed the fifteen school districts, including Alachua County, to delay student body integration until September 1, 1970. By requiring faculty integration by February 1, the opinion accelerated the exchange of teachers so that in all schools there would be one black teacher to every four white teachers. To achieve these ratios, approximately forty-six elementary school teachers and fifty high school teachers would have to be transferred at midyear.[5]

Talbot's next step in moving forward was to request the Alachua County Education Association, the local teachers' organization, to recommend criteria for the transfer of teachers between white and black schools.[6]

The ink was barely dry on the December 11 agreement ending the Lincoln High School strike when the NAACP Legal Defense Fund on December 13, 1969, filed its motion in the US Supreme Court for an injunction requiring Alachua County and seven other school districts in *Singleton* to continue to plan for total desegregation by February 1:[7]

> The delay of desegregation until 1970 which the Court of Appeals approved in the Alexander case, and which this court disapproved, was sought to be justified by reference to

> administrative difficulties to be caused by immediate desegregation. Petitioners understand the Alexander decision to mean that such justifications may no longer be accepted as a basis for delay, and that where the courts have adjudicated that an unconstitutional dual system exists, the remedy must be "at once . . . now." We understand the Alexander rule to tolerate no delays for the solution of administrative obstacles to desegregation. We believe that the strict application of the Alexander rule is fully justified and fully equitable in view of the passage of more than 15 years since [*Brown*] declared segregation unconstitutional and in view of the public officials' resistance to desegregation which has characterized those districts which remain segregated in 1969.[8]

The NAACP Legal Defense Fund argued that unless immediate integration of student bodies occurred,

> thousands of Negro children in the cases at bar have at stake a continued denial of their constitutional rights. Many of these youngsters will have read or been told that this Court ruled on October 29, 1969, [in *Alexander*] that the law requires desegregation at once. These children must surely be lead [*sic*] to believe that a legal system that promises rights at once, and translates "at once" for Negroes' rights to mean ten months later, deals with them a cruel and special cynicism and hypocrisy.[9]

The Defense Fund also argued that unless the Supreme Court took immediate action, the Department of Health, Education, and Welfare would experience administrative difficulties in preparing desegregation plans that could be implemented in February, and that there would be confusion in the Fifth Circuit as to exactly what was required by *Alexander*.[10]

The civil rights warrior's blood still runs hot in William L. Robinson, a Defense Fund lawyer who for a time handled the Alachua County case. When asked in June 2017 whether he and the other Defense Fund lawyers ever discussed postponing full desegregation in the *Alexander* and *Carter* cases to the beginning of the following school year, September 1970, Robinson replied, "We had been trying for years, if not decades, to get segregation eliminated. Postponing to the next school year never entered our mind. It was never raised. No thought was given."[11]

There was no time for any of the school districts to oppose the Legal Defense Fund's motion for a preliminary injunction. In addition to the per curiam opinion issued by Justice Black on December 13, 1969, in *Carter v.*

West Feliciana Parish School Board,[12] Justice Black issued a similar order related to Alachua County's case on December 15, 1969.[13] Those orders required the school districts to take necessary steps to integrate their student bodies no later than February 1, 1970. The full Supreme Court would have to rule on the NAACP Legal Defense Fund's certiorari petition, but Justice Black was unwilling to postpone further actions by any of the school boards in *Singleton* pending full-court review. Justice Black ordered the NAACP Legal Defense Fund to file its petition for certiorari by December 19, 1969, and for the defendant school boards to file their responses by January 2, 1970.

US District Court Judge Charles R. Scott had on December 11 set a hearing for December 19 in *Wright v. Board* to implement the Fifth Circuit's December 1 decision in *Singleton*. But with Justice Black's orders of December 13 and 15, the purpose of the hearing shifted to integrating not just faculty and student activities by February 1 but also integrating student bodies. This hearing is one of the few district court hearings in the Alachua County case for which a transcript was made.

Judge Scott reminded school board attorney Harry Duncan that Justice Black and the Fifth Circuit, implementing Justice Black's order, had vacated the portion of the prior Fifth Circuit opinion in *Singleton* that allowed the school boards to postpone student body integration to September 1970. Attorney Duncan objected that the desegregation plan previously approved on April 3, 1969, by Judge Carswell contemplated completion of construction that would not be ready by February 1, 1970. Judge Scott agreed that the school board "can't go out here and create a school building out of thin air that might be just a foundation now." But Judge Scott made clear that unfinished construction was not an excuse for further delay. He warned Attorney Duncan that the school board would have to do what it needed to do in good faith to comply with the Supreme Court's order.[14]

Judge Scott's written order, filed December 22, left no doubt as to his intent. "It is the opinion of this District Court, upon which the responsibility lies for the enforcement of the mandates of the federal appellate courts, that the aforementioned orders [by Justice Black and the Fifth Circuit] require the defendants to implement a unitary school system by February 1, 1970, unless and until orders to the contrary are issued from the Supreme Court of the United States or the United States Court of Appeals for the Fifth Circuit."[15]

Having failed to obtain relief from the court, the school board then turned to the NAACP Legal Defense Fund, asking it to back away from the February 1, 1970, deadline, at least for Alachua County. As the plaintiffs' representatives, the Defense Fund could agree to a postponement of student body integration until September 1970.

The *Sun* reported that at the federal courthouse in Gainesville after the December 19 hearing, Dr. Enneking asked Earl M. Johnson, the Defense Fund's local counsel, if Johnson would consider asking the court to allow such a delay "in the interest of education."

> Enneking pointed out that pupils of both races will be the losers in a fruitbasket turnover Feb. 1.
>
> "Do we sacrifice education for the sake of a deadline?" Enneking asked.
>
> "As one who had an inferior education I am not inclined to worry about that," Johnson replied.
>
> However, the NAACP attorney, who is also a member of the Jacksonville City Council, did say he is in favor of a proposal which would leave out graduating senior classes from any shuffle.
>
> Beyond that, Johnson said, neither he nor his clients will entertain any suggestion that the NAACP ask for a delay until Sept. 1.
>
> "Suppose your clients agree that they want an education first and are willing to wait until our buildings are finished for integration," Enneking pressed.
>
> "It would be very hard for me to acquiesce to such a delay," said Johnson. "I am not about to ask for a postponement of desegregation."[16]

Dr. Enneking made a second try at a school board meeting on December 22, 1969, to review desegregation plans. That meeting attracted an overflow audience of concerned parents and teachers to school board headquarters. Enneking asked whether black leaders would join with the school board in an appeal to the Supreme Court to delay further integration until the new secondary schools were ready. "'I feel certain the black community would not join you in appealing for the sake of delaying,' Neil Butler told Enneking. Said the Rev. Wright, 'We have been in contact with our attorneys and we are in full accord with him that, the quicker the better, no delay.'"[17]

There was no perceivable daylight between the NAACP Legal Defense Fund lawyers and senior black leaders in Gainesville. Although Enneking was negotiating for a joint appeal to the Supreme Court, a simple stipulation in US District Court between the Defense Fund and the school board to delay student body desegregation would have sufficed to stop the fruitbasket turnover. The Defense Fund may have feared that if a bargain were struck with Alachua County, all of the other hundreds of affected school districts across the South, even those resisting to the bitter end, would want the same concession.

Singleton would have required exchanges of teachers between Lincoln and GHS, and integration of sports teams and student activities on February 1 in any event, even if entire student bodies did not move. But the precise outlines of student activity integration were not clear, and the Fighting Red Terriers may well have been allowed to play out their remaining sports schedule in the absence of objections. Nevertheless, it could have appeared to black leaders that the resulting changes would so alter the Lincoln community that saving it for one more term no longer outweighed the benefits of moving immediately to a unitary system.

Would either side, while negotiating the December 11 agreement over the closure of Lincoln High School—still believing that student body integration would not be required until September 1970—have reached the compromise that they did on December 11? Would not both the white and black communities and the school board have had a common interest in avoiding the February fruitbasket turnover? These questions, in hindsight, may seem to have an obvious answer, but the parties on December 11 could not foresee either the Supreme Court's reaction to the Fifth Circuit decision in *Singleton* or the NAACP Legal Defense Fund's determination to achieve complete integration no later than February 1.

In the end, it was Gainesville's black leadership that refused to stop the fruitbasket turnover. The irony was not lost in the resulting turmoil. First, the students and parents of Lincoln High gave up the battle to save Lincoln High School in return for the school board's concessions just days before. Now, as a result of the black leaders' refusal to make any concessions in *Wright v. Board*, Lincoln students would lose the last half of their final school year at the Lincoln campus. The *Sun* characterized that position as "stiff backed and dramatic":

> It is a bit ironic, however, that the fire and brimstone rains so heavily on Alachua County – which peaceably integrated in [1964], which has 27 per cent of its pupils attending integrated schools, and which is hastily throwing up buildings for full integration in September.
>
> The February 1 deadline smacks of vengeance visited on whites for past sins. It smacks of a black moral victory in exchange for a disordered timetable, strained racial relations, chaotic school administration, and emotional uprooting of thousands of our children.

Although lamenting that integration had been delayed as long as it had been, the *Sun* now advocated taking legal action to postpone the school board's unitary September plan until September.[18]

Superintendent Talbot and his staff prepared three integration plans, two of which were the most likely to be approved by the school board. The plans were published in the *Sun*,[19] as had been requested by members of the public at the December 22 meeting.

Plan 1 would have moved only students who would be moved anyway in September, and only to new schools where they would remain in September. Integration at the secondary level in Gainesville would take place by pairing the three city junior highs (including the junior high portion of Lincoln) so that grades 7 and 8 would attend either Westwood or Bishop Junior Highs and all ninth graders would attend Lincoln. All students in grades 10 through 12 would remain in place. Talbot characterized this plan as one based on humanism rather than numbers and grades as the basic philosophy. Talbot pointed out that if students in grades 10, 11, and 12 were transferred, it would adversely affect academic programs in every school, state competitions in music and sports, and leadership courses in government. John Dukes, outside the public meetings, advocated strenuously that the district find a way for at least the Lincoln junior and senior classes to complete the current school year at Lincoln.[20]

The "September Plan" was a redesign of the unitary plan previously approved by Judge Carswell in April 1969 for implementation in September 1970. A subsequent court review of the plan would result in other changes, but for now the plan approved by Judge Carswell in April was intact except for timing. The school board now had to achieve student body integration by February 1970. The September Plan in concept simply brought forward to February what would otherwise have occurred in September under the plan already approved by the district court. The board also had to achieve the required ratios of African American and white faculty members at all schools. Tomlinson recalls assembling school principals in a boardroom to reassign the faculty. "There would be a principal going around offering to trade one white math teacher for a black English teacher."[21]

Under this plan, at the secondary school level, junior high students in grades 7, 8, and 9 who would attend the new east-side and west-side junior/senior high schools would start attending those schools in February but on the campuses of Bishop and Westwood, in separate afternoon sessions. Junior high students from Lincoln who would be zoned to Westwood or Bishop in September 1970 would attend the morning session at those schools with the current student bodies. A total of 700 students in grades 7–9 from Lincoln would find themselves at one of the four city junior high schools. At the senior high school level, all students in grades 10, 11, and 12 in the Gainesville High zone (including those from Lincoln) would attend GHS. Grades 11 and 12 would attend GHS in the morning and grade 10 would attend in the afternoon. Gainesville High would absorb a total of 580 students from Lincoln in grades 10–12. Under this plan, Lincoln would be closed for grades 7–12, and Mebane would also be closed as a senior high school.

To hear more public reaction to the plans, the school board met at Gainesville High on Monday, December 29. The meeting was attended by an estimated 1,300 persons, spilling into the aisles and floor of the auditorium. As reported by the press, speakers at the meeting agreed in opposing any plan that required midyear changes in student assignments. Dr. Enneking told the meeting that the school board was retaining counsel to ask the Supreme Court to grant the county a postponement of the September Plan to September.

Ralph Cellon, a county commissioner, spoke for a committee of one thousand Alachua–High Springs residents of both races. He received a standing ovation when he said, "We're not here to threaten you, to intimidate anyone. But it is not right to make wholesale changes in the middle of the year that are not in the best interest and for which you are not ready. We're not going to put up with it." Cellon would soon help to establish the private Rolling Green Academy in Alachua.

There was black opposition to the February 1 deadline. Cellon was supported by Catherine Taylor, a black resident of the northwest county area. Wayne Mosley, the Lincoln High senior who was one of the leaders of the Lincoln strike, said, "We're going to stay at Lincoln. If you can integrate other schools you can integrate Lincoln just as well. We're not going where you want to send us, we're going where we want to go."

Neil Butler, the black city commissioner who on December 22 had stood firm on the February 1 deadline, said, "I would ask that you do what is right, not what is popular, not what is politically expedient. Any decision will be unpopular with a major section of the community. Either way you go, you're going to be in the wrong. You need to have guts enough to do what is right."[22]

The school board did not immediately act to approve a specific integration plan for February 1. However, the board favored the September Plan, should it be necessary to integrate student bodies in February.[23] The board probably recognized that Talbot's Plan 1, which preserved the three senior high grades at Lincoln High School for the remainder of the school year, would not move the county to a unitary system under current court decisions. Enneking said that if student body integration were required on February 1, the board would seek permission from the Florida High School Activities Association to allow black students to fulfill athletic schedules in their old schools for the remainder of the year.[24]

The school board's resolve to continue fighting the fruitbasket turnover was only strengthened by the December 22 and December 29 school board meetings. Represented by Gainesville attorney Sam Dell, the school board filed on December 31, 1969, a brief opposing the granting of certiorari by the Supreme Court in *Wright v. Board*. That brief argued for a delay of student body integration to September 1970, because the schools needed for a unitary school system would not be ready until then. This brief accused the NAACP Legal Defense Fund of misleading the court both as to the extent of integration achieved in Alachua County by September 1969 and as to the length of time it would take the county to achieve complete integration. Dell argued that full student body integration would occur in September 1970, with the latter two years of the three-year April 3, 1969, plan needed only to clarify the status of new schools and grade placement in those years.

> In [*Alexander v. Holmes County Board of Education*, 396 U.S. 1218 (1969)], this court said it was against the background of denial of fundamental rights to thousands who are attending schools under segregated conditions, that the Circuit Court should have denied all motions for additional time. No such background exists in this case. It is against the background of uncompleted facilities already under construction and to avoid multiple transfers of students' records, libraries and teachers that an additional four months of schooltime is requested.
>
> ***
>
> These respondents do not believe that they are operating a dual school system. Admittedly some remnants of a previously operated dual system remain – but not by design. Operation of a school system with integrated administrative and teaching staffs, integrated buses, athletics and extra-curricular activities, and twenty-five out of thirty schools with integrated students and with buildings under construction to provide space for integrating the students of the five unintegrated schools as quickly as they can be used, and with the right of such students to in the meantime transfer from the school in which his race is in the majority to a school where his race is in the minority, does not seem to these respondents to be a dual school system in the sense condemned by decisions of this Court which it has felt warranted in drastically disrupting the school system to remedy the situation.[25]

Attorney John C. Satterfield of Jackson, Mississippi, was engaged on January 6 by the school board on Dr. Enneking's motion to work with

Attorney Duncan.[26] Satterfield was one of the South's preeminent lawyers in representing school boards resisting integration. He represented Mississippi Governor Ross Barnett in opposing the integration of the University of Mississippi. He represented many of the school boards involved in the 1969 litigation. A group representing Lincoln High later called Satterfield's engagement frivolous. "The further you delay the more troubles we will have," said Mrs. Odessa W. McClendon, the parent chair of the Committee for the Lincoln High School Crisis. Dr. Enneking explained that Satterfield was engaged because he was recommended by US Senator Spessard Holland and he was admitted to the bar of the Supreme Court, which Duncan was not. "We are not necessarily putting Alachua County in the image with the State of Mississippi as you suggested."[27]

In the midst of the uncertainty, the deacons of First Baptist Church held a prayer breakfast about the schools. In the church bulletin of January 8, the deacons urged that "parents will not fill their children with fear or hatred. Rather, they will teach their children the importance of cooperating with the authorities in education." And: "We consider this situation a challenge to accomplish a good thing that will help future generations to be citizens of good will towards all peoples."[28]

Three school board members stated on January 6 that they did not plan to run for reelection in 1970. They included Walter Ebling, the construction supervisor from Micanopy who had come on the board in 1967 to help support the 1968 bond issue, as well as Dale Smith[29] of High Springs and T. E. Simmons of Archer, both long-serving members and the only two remaining members of the board that was in place when Superintendent Talbot took office in 1965. Talbot reminded the press that he, too, would not be serving beyond the end of his current term in 1972.[30]

Just a day before the Supreme Court would rule, and too late to have any effect on the outcome, Florida's governor, Claude Kirk, entered the controversy. He filed a brief arguing against the February 1 deadline, which affected many counties besides Alachua, urging that increased costs might force the closing of some public schools.[31]

The full Supreme Court ruled on January 14 that the school boards would have to integrate student bodies by February 1. The court granted the NAACP Legal Defense Fund's petition for certiorari and reversed the Fifth Circuit's opinion in *Singleton*. The court did not hear oral arguments. The one-paragraph per curiam opinion contained no discussion.[32] By resolving the extent of integration required by February 1, the decision affected seventeen Florida counties (including Alachua), with 942,000 students, or two-thirds of all public school enrollment in the state.[33]

The Florida Education Association reacted by objecting to the lack of planning for integration. The association's executive secretary said, "It's a critical problem. Quite frankly, we've all been negligent in not doing more planning for this. . . . School boards, school administrators and teacher organizations have been negligent. We haven't done the job we should have done." The FEA had recently hired Walter Smith to work with a human relations team to help affected counties in their transition to fully integrated faculties and student bodies. Smith had previously worked with HEW on desegregation plans. The FEA team was intended to organize human relations committees and seminars for students, teachers, and parents. The FEA spokesman said, "I think parents are going to be the key to the whole issue. I think teachers and pupils are more ready to accept it than parents."[34]

The Florida NAACP field director, Marvin Davies, told the press after a conference of state NAACP board members and chapter presidents that the organization would file contempt actions against any school board that did not comply with the Supreme Court's ruling to integrate by February 1. He also said that the organization would oppose abandonment of any good school buildings, "whatever neighborhood they are in."[35]

With the February 1 deadline only twelve days away, the school board met on January 19 to consider adoption of a plan for complying with the court orders to operate a unitary system. The first item of business was the engagement of Attorney Satterfield. Now that the Supreme Court had ruled on January 14, implicitly refusing to be swayed by the arguments of the school board in opposing the NAACP petition, only the remedy of a possible rehearing remained. School board member T. E. Simmons personally had a forty-five-minute conversation with Satterfield:

> [Simmons] said Satterfield told him he (Satterfield) personally believes that two justices – Byron White and John M. Harlan[36] – have had a change of heart since siding with a 6–2 majority in Wednesday's Supreme Court decision that would expedite total integration here by four months.
>
> Chief Justice Warren E. Burger and Justice Potter Stewart cast the two dissenting votes in Wednesday's decision.
>
> Satterfield believes there's a chance the court would entertain a petition to reconsider its ruling.
>
> "Mr. Satterfield told me that in his opinion, Alachua County has by far the best desegregation record of any school district he has seen in the South," said Simmons.
>
> "He said he thinks if he could just get the court to read our record they'd decide, 'there's a chance to prove that we're not ramming anything down the throats of the people down there,'" Simmons added.
>
> The board then unanimously approved a motion to engage Attorney Satterfield to work with school board attorney Harry Duncan to apply for a rehearing at the Supreme

> Court and ask that further integration be deferred to September, 1970.[37]

The school board next considered whether to adopt a desegregation plan to comply with the Supreme Court's January 14 decision. Superintendent Talbot recommended adoption of the September Plan.

The Alachua County Classroom Teachers Association had previously polled the school faculties to learn their preference. A large majority of teachers had chosen the September Plan. A letter from the Human Relations Committee of the CTA was read into the record by Benford Samuels, which stated that the September Plan "affects more people equally and fairly, will cause fewer problems in human relations thus effecting a more favorable teaching-learning climate. The welfare of the children comes first and under this September Plan the education of the children will be foremost."[38]

But on this point, the board divided. Simmons opposed adopting any plan to comply with the court orders:

> "Satterfield said if you make a final decision saying what you intend to do in compliance then there's no need appealing. . . . If you're saying you're going to do it, then you've done it as far as that court is concerned."
>
> "We have an order from the federal district court to get up a plan and I will not be held in contempt by that court," Talbot replied.
>
> "What I do recommend is your acceptance of this plan, subject to our attorney's appeal to the Supreme Court and the Governor's (Claude Kirk) appeal," Talbot continued.
>
> After a discussion over wording of a motion, the board approved Talbot's "September Plan" by a 3–2 vote. [Ebling, Enneking and Samuels voting yes, Simmons and Smith voting no]
>
> At Simmons' insistence, Talbot's plan was accepted with the stipulation that it will be implemented only if the board remains under court orders by Jan. 30.
>
> ***
>
> Talbot appeared disappointed when the board stalled on his plan. He said it represented the hard work [of] his staff and principals, much of it done during the weekend.

> Simmons asked, "Supposing we approve this plan for Jan. 30 and the court comes along and approves our appeal for a delay, on Feb. 1, won't we be in a fine fix?"
>
> "I'm not going to dodge anything," Talbot answered. "I'm going to obey the law. I'm looking at the facts square in the face."[39]

Talbot as Alachua County's last elected school superintendent could stand up to the divided school board without fear of pressure, or worse, from the board. There can be little doubt that Talbot as much as any of the school board members wanted a delay of student body integration to September 1. But Talbot, unlike the board members, would have to open the schools in February whether or not Satterfield could persuade three more justices of the Supreme Court to change their votes. It is unlikely that Satterfield's advice dramatically changed the course of desegregation in Alachua County. Tommy Tomlinson confirms that there was little preparation for the February 1970 desegregation and that planning included only the county administration, principals, and teachers.[40]

The author, in informal discussions in Gainesville, has encountered a sort of urban legend that the county could have avoided the midyear desegregation by simply paying a fine. There is no evidence that local African American leaders, the NAACP Legal Defense Fund, or the district court would have tolerated such an outcome. On the other hand, if Talbot and the school board had chosen to disobey the court order, they would have forfeited the legitimacy of their actions. Many others, both white and black, would have been encouraged to defy the court in order to disrupt desegregation. Because they had the courage to choose compliance, Talbot and the school board were able to maintain their leadership role against whatever opposition might arise in the future.

Notwithstanding the school board vote on January 19, Talbot and his staff prepared a schedule (with no actions taking place before January 30) according to which full desegregation would move forward if the Supreme Court failed to approve a delay. Easter vacation would be moved up to Tuesday, January 27, though Friday, January 30, and a semester break was scheduled for February 2–5. All teachers would work on Monday, February 2, and teachers being transferred to new schools would attend orientation workshops on February 3, 4, and 5. The first full day of classes would be Friday, February 6.[41]

The December 11 agreement to close Lincoln High School as an academic high school appeared to come apart. The Lincoln High School Protest Committee demanded at the January 22 meeting of the school board that the Lincoln High School plant be converted to an integrated academic junior high school. Led by Alex Henry, who had been active in the earlier protest, the parents' committee argued that using the facility for compensatory education for middle school students and for vocational training would still result in an inferior, segregated school. The committee's letter charged that no whites would attend either the compensatory or vocational programs. "We want an education, not a vocation. . . . We haven't waited 15 years for a vocational school."[42] The school board abandoned the compensatory education program in the summer of 1970 because of fears that it would become all black.

During this period, John King, the student body president at Gainesville High, and Bill Hunt, another student government representative, decided to travel across town to Lincoln High School to speak to a meeting organized by Lincoln students to discuss the midyear desegregation. "And so here are two white boys walking into the middle of what was a very, very irritated, agitated crowd. We went there. I did, naively, to represent student government that we were welcoming, that we wanted to do what we could to help in the transition, and basically left the meeting . . . really having not attempted any engagement, we actually feared for our safety. And that set the tone for me as to what might occur as we transitioned into the [February] merger."[43]

At the January 22 meeting, the school board agreed to apply for a $255,000 federal grant for in-service training for teachers that would help make teachers aware of cultural differences between the races. Teachers would be taught not to identify some students as failures, but to allow them to proceed at their own pace. The program would train sixty teachers at a workshop in June, and all classroom teachers would attend some sessions in August as part of preplanning for school opening in September.[44] None of that training would help teachers deal with the fruitbasket turnover.

On Friday, January 23, in a prelude to a riot the following week at Lincoln High School, 150 to 200 black youths, roaming in groups of 8 to 10, threw concrete blocks, bricks, rocks, and bottles at cars on a highway near the Lincoln campus. There was one arrest. Members of a family from Plant City were injured, and there was other property damage. There had been an earlier basketball game at Lincoln, but police did not connect the violence to the game.[45]

The Rev. Wright warned in an interview published January 25 that he was not optimistic that the Lincoln High School student body would adjust at Gainesville High School. He was more optimistic that black students would have a better experience at the new Eastside Junior/Senior High in September. "I hope they can find a sense of belonging to the Eastside school. It won't be a Negro school but it isn't far from the black neighborhood."[46]

Governor Kirk, who to this point had confined himself to court filings at the Supreme Court, now turned defiant. Kirk, urging Southern voters to reject George Wallace's third-party campaign for president in December 1967, had distinguished himself by calling George Wallace a "flaming liberal." He had added that it would be "un-American" to vote for Wallace.[47] Wallace would later pay Kirk back in kind. In June 1970, political columnist Nick Thimmesch, visiting Wallace's home, saw a pet monkey in a cage. Thimmesch asked Wallace the monkey's name. "Claude Kirk," Wallace replied.[48] Kirk told the press on January 23, 1970, that he was planning to issue an executive order forbidding school boards from "forced busing," altering school calendars, or spending unbudgeted funds to comply with the Supreme Court's February 1 deadline.[49]

Kirk also escalated his feud with Democratic Education Commissioner Floyd Christian, who favored compliance with the Supreme Court orders. Kirk called Christian "as useless as hip pockets on a hog." That comment brought Christian to charge Kirk with grandstanding and credit grabbing. Christian, referring to state and local school officials, their attorneys and parents, said,

> . . . I am concerned that the governor's most recent actions to distort the record and impugn the good efforts of many men and women who have been working very hard to steer a sane and sensible course through these troublesome times. . . . These people have not been grandstanding or making political speeches. They have been working and toiling. And they have not been interested in the newspaper headlines or credits – only in the results.

Christian's office had also filed a brief with the Supreme Court on January 14 (the same day the full court overruled the Fifth Circuit in *Singleton*) to persuade the court that Florida could not afford to integrate in the middle of the school year.[50]

District court judges in cases involving Jacksonville and Orange County schools interpreted the recent Supreme Court decisions to permit some all-black schools and continued freedom of choice, adding to the confusion and encouraging at least one other county to pull back from cross busing (that change, involving Volusia County, was later reversed by the US District Court).[51] Dade County was permitted by a district court judge to delay pupil desegregation until September but was not permitted to continue any all-black schools.[52] Alachua County school board attorney Harry Duncan commented that the differing results across Florida resulted from different judges, different cases filed at different times, and the willingness of local NAACP lawyers to allow some plans to go forward without motions for further relief.[53] The forlorn hopes of Judge Wisdom, that the same laws would apply in Athens and Rome, and of the solicitor general, that the Supreme Court would set a uniform time schedule to move to unitary systems, would not be realized. As the February 1 deadline approached, confusion continued across the South.[54]

A crescendo of litigation had followed the Supreme Court's *Green* decision in May 1968. That litigation had defined what a unitary school system was not, but there was still little clarity around what a unitary system *was*. The Department of Health, Education, and Welfare had annually advanced its standards for satisfactory desegregation under Title VI of the Civil Rights Act of 1964 and had enforced those standards by withholding federal funds from noncompliant districts. But even under the HEW regulations, school boards that satisfied federal district court orders were deemed to be compliant, leading to a patchwork of jurisdictional authority across Florida and the South. Now, with the Nixon administration seeking to slow the change from freedom of choice to unitary school systems, the burden of defining the constitutional standard reverted again to the courts. And the composition of the Supreme Court had also changed, leading in *Carter* to the first separate opinions in a major Supreme Court desegregation case. The theme of those separate opinions was exactly the lack of court guidance around defining and implementing unitary school systems.

These circumstances perhaps help to explain the NAACP Legal Defense Fund's determination to press for full desegregation now, whatever that might mean, and the Supreme Court majority's determination to close off the endless litigation, whatever the breakage might be. School administrators had to pick up the pieces as best they could.

But the headlong rush to force student body integration at midyear, coupled with the perceived lack of a definition of *unitary system*, played into the hands of politicians such as Governor Kirk. A Florida pundit said at this point that Kirk had guaranteed his reelection as governor in 1970 by his actions.[55] The Supreme Court denied Kirk's petitions without comment on January 26.[56]

Attorney Satterfield filed the Alachua County school board's petition for rehearing with the Supreme Court on January 22.[57] Satterfield sought a delay for Alachua County because of the county's unique circumstances, caught as it was just short of completing its building program to provide a unitary system. His petition was more masterful than Attorney Dell's earlier brief opposing the NAACP Legal Defense Fund's certiorari petition, but it made essentially the same argument. Satterfield argued that the county was already operating a unitary system "to the extent of its physical and economic capacity." He said that allowing Alachua County to complete its desegregation plan on schedule in September 1970 was consistent with the Supreme Court's holdings in *Alexander* and *Carter* that desegregation take place at once.[58] The petition was designed to open just the narrowest crack for Alachua County without calling into question the Supreme Court's prior decisions. By arguing so narrowly, Satterfield hoped to persuade three more justices to side with Burger and Stewart and to carve out an exception for Alachua County. Satterfield backed up his contention that Alachua County was unique in its progress to a unitary system by referring to the records of 267 other school districts that had been before various courts in the states comprising the Fifth Circuit.[59] The Supreme Court denied the rehearing petition without opinion on January 26, 1970.[60]

The only remaining hope of avoiding the fruitbasket turnover was Governor Kirk's original action in the Supreme Court against the other forty-nine states and the secretary of Health, Education, and Welfare. In that case, Kirk asked the court to define "unitary" school systems and to apply the same desegregation standards in all the states. The Supreme Court dismissed that case without opinion on January 27.[61]

A violent outburst at Lincoln on Thursday, January 29, caused Lincoln High's final closing. Principal John Dukes ordered all students to leave the campus in midafternoon on Thursday and to report to the schools to which they had been transferred for Friday classes. The violence apparently started when "several nonstudents entered the school in the early afternoon and began tearing up lockers in the halls." About ninety windows were broken. Student leaders were unsuccessful in regaining control. Reports differed as to what started the rock throwing at police, but a tear gas canister was fired by police, and violence escalated. Police were not only subjected to thrown objects, but one officer was injured by being kicked in the back. Police responded with more tear gas. A group of about one hundred students fled to the nearby highway, where they threw rocks and bottles at passing cars, injuring some motorists. A Southern Bell employee, Guenter Sommer, was beaten by blacks after leaving his truck, which was rocked by blacks. Fearing the worst, authorities deployed forty-five city police officers, twenty sheriff's deputies, and twenty Florida Highway Patrol following the incident.[62]

Lincoln students later complained that the police aggravated the incident by firing tear gas. The investigative report spoke of a broken police car windshield, a charge by an estimated two hundred students toward the police, and "mobs run at us with great quantities of rocks and bricks." The report said that students were dispersed by a total of five tear gas devices.[63]

During this incident, a white reading teacher was injured when she was hit by a thrown broomstick outside her classroom. She fell, hitting her head and suffering a possible concussion. She said that the person who threw the broomstick appeared to be an adult, and that she did not recognize him as a Lincoln student.[64] The teacher resigned in March 1970.[65]

Neil Butler, the black city councilman, commented, "This is the kind of situation I've tried to avoid. . . . Once something like this gets started no leadership can stop it. It just burns itself out, one way or another."[66] Governor Kirk, who by chance was at a nearby community center to review progress on his antipoverty program, Operation Concern, did not visit the scene of the Lincoln High School confrontation.[67]

There also was a fight at Gainesville High School the following day, January 30, after which two students were expelled. During that incident, the *Sun* reported that a Lincoln High student ran through the GHS parking lot carrying an iron pipe. He walked to the gym, where he was recognized by police as the person who had assaulted another officer at Lincoln the previous day. He was arrested.[68]

The sports seasons ended for Lincoln and Mebane with the closings of those schools. Lincoln Principal John Dukes asked the Florida High School Activities Association to cancel Lincoln's remaining sports schedules after the violence on January 29. Mebane's principal elected not to request a waiver of rules that normally ended a school's participation in sports if the school closed. Since both schools closed without submitting a request for a waiver, their teams were no longer able to participate in sanctioned events.[69]

Governor Kirk, after failing to obtain a hearing on any of his petitions to the Supreme Court, on January 31 issued his executive order forbidding school officials in Volusia and Manatee Counties from taking some actions that would be necessary to comply with existing court orders. The two counties were forbidden to change their school calendars, to incur expenses above those previously budgeted, to reassign masses of pupils, to forcibly bus students for racial balance, or to close schools to implement forced pupil reassignment.[70]

The Florida Commissioner of Education, Floyd Christian, asked Attorney General Earl Faircloth, also a Democrat, whether Christian should advise school officials to obey the courts or the governor if the governor were to direct the school officials to disobey the courts. Faircloth, although not a party, filed his February 2 opinion with the district court in *Wright v. Board*:

> To obey or not obey the law as declared by "direct orders of federal courts" – that is the question which now must be answered. The answer is quite clear. We must all obey the law as declared by the direct orders of the federal judiciary. Those direct orders may not be agreeable to us, they may be loathsome to some, but they are of superior rank in our system of jurisprudence – under our government of laws. This principle is so well established that today most school children know it as well as all law students, lawyers and, surely, the Governor. And our own Florida Supreme Court has pronounced the principle with great clarity.

Faircloth referred to a prior incident in which, during the administration of Governor Farris Bryant, the federal court had ordered Florida to reapportion its legislature, contrary to the Florida constitution's apportionment scheme. Then:

> The principle was also written in blood at Appomattox a little over a century ago. And even though you and I, and the Governor, as well as the parents of school children in this state violently oppose bussing students to achieve integration, and even though we believe some of the orders are totally irresponsible, irrational and unrealistic, still we are bound to obey and not to defy. We are bound first by the law of our system of law and, second, because to teach defiance and rebellion as high public officials we present a sorry spectacle, a sordid and vulgar example before the youth of our nation.[71]

In Alachua County, as Superintendent Talbot had predicted in November, it was not that difficult to design a plan that would integrate student bodies in midyear, even without the completion of the new schools. The question remained whether that plan would work.

At a more detailed level, for example, at Gainesville High, the total enrollment would increase to 2,050 in the morning session for grades 11 and 12, and to 1,050 in the afternoon session for grade 10 as a result of adding the 580 students being transferred from Lincoln. A smaller number of students would be transferred from Mebane to GHS. The school would once again have to hold regular classes in the cafeteria, language lab, and teaching auditorium. Many Lincoln High transfer students would remain in their old classes for some subjects but would be distributed among other GHS students for other classes.[72] GHS gained nineteen additional teachers, all of whom were African American. GHS now had 132 teachers, of whom 23 were African American.[73] The school would not achieve the ratio of one black teacher for every four white teachers called for in the plan approved for September 1970 by Judge Carswell in April, 1969.[74]

Assistant principals, deans, and guidance counselors, who would play a key role in this round of desegregation, were overwhelmingly white throughout the system. At the secondary school level, just prior to February 1, there were only three black assistant principals compared to thirteen whites, one black dean compared to six whites, and three black guidance counselors to sixteen whites. All of the blacks in these positions were then serving in all-black schools.[75] The school board's February 9, 1970, report to the court pledged intense recruiting efforts to obtain more black teachers and guidance counselors. The school board also encouraged black teachers to enter the system's leadership growth plan, to develop a talent pool of future administrators.[76]

At Gainesville High School, the *Sun* reported that student leaders were preparing to accept the transferring Lincoln students "in all phases of the school's activities." The school newspaper, the *Hurricane Herald*, published a "unification edition" that was distributed at both GHS and Lincoln. According to the newspaper, the transferring students were to be welcomed in extracurricular activities, band, cheerleading, athletics, and student government. The GHS student government resolved that class officers of the two schools would continue to serve in their positions for the remainder of the year. Principal Hudson expressed optimism.[77] Under editor Roberta Berner, the school newspaper ran an editorial entitled "We Can Do It" asking students of both races to make integration work peacefully:

> While students' willingness to integrate Gainesville High School is widespread, much griping and some threatening has been done during the past few weeks about the February desegregation deadline.
>
> Realistically, for uninterrupted education and plan completion, unification should have been postponed until September. But, realistically, we need to face unification squarely now—sans griping and the non-solution of boycotting.
>
> On February 2, when some 3,200 of us return or newly come to GHS, understanding and level-headedness will be necessities. Unless we react coolly to integration, mere overcrowding can become a pressure-pot situation. Education could be set farther back than many people feel it will by mid-year desegregation.
>
> If unification is viewed as an exciting situation to liven up a dull part of the school year . . . if it is seen as a way to meet 600 additional individuals . . . if it is seen as an educational experience in itself, 1969–70 could be considered the most valuable year in the history of Gainesville High School.
>
> It is up to us – students from both Lincoln High School and Gainesville High School – to make unification work. We can do it.[78]

The September Plan as implemented in February required transfer of three hundred teachers and six thousand students. There were fears that teachers being transferred would not be prepared for their new assignments despite the administration's three-day orientation program. Bus routes had to be extensively reorganized in county areas outside of Gainesville. But on the eve of the first day of classes, school administrators hoped for the best.[79]

All around the South, school leaders waited. Willie Morris had attended the public schools in Yazoo City, Mississippi. In his book *Yazoo*, Morris eloquently describes the peaceful integration of the public schools there in January 1970. Yazoo City was one of the thirty Mississippi districts that were the subject of *Alexander*. Morris tells us that earlier, when a Mississippi county to the north integrated, Fannie Lou Hamer spoke to a group of black children: "You not just *frightened*, you scared to death, ain't you? *You scared to death*. But you jus' remember, they ain't gonna be savin' you. You gonna be savin' *them*."[80] Who would be saving whom by integration is a question that remains open to this day, and to which we will return.

February 6, the first day of Alachua County's September Plan in February, went smoothly. There were no network TV cameras or out-of-town press. Attendance was close to normal, especially at the secondary schools where trouble had been feared. The day before, Superintendent Talbot had his principals briefed by law-enforcement officers. "I would hate to see our schools disrupted by 3 or 4 per cent of the students or by non-students. I hope all of our principals have the intestinal fortitude to step in and get troublemakers out of school," Talbot told the *Sun*. Police were on the alert but were not called onto any campus. The formerly black Shell school in Hawthorne was now an integrated middle school. Elizabeth Greene, Shell's black principal, expressed her gratitude that some parents came to school the first day. "The parents are with us, and that is very important. The problems we thought we would have are rapidly diminishing."[81]

Assistant Superintendent Tommy Tomlinson reported at the end of the first full week of student body and faculty integration that all remained calm. "I certainly think we have pulled off the impossible in the small amount of time we had."[82] Officially, at least, it looked as though the better natures of everyone involved would triumph in the end over the fear and anger of the past year. For one week, Alachua County proved that outcome was possible.

CHAPTER 13
INTO THE FIRE

Blacks were just pushed into GHS without any "yes" or "no." Everything was done because the white man said so. When the Lincoln kids wanted things changed, the whites became scared.

Lincoln transfer student, Gainesville High, June 16, 1970

I've taken more crap from Negro students in one month than I have in years of teaching white students.

Teacher, March 15, 1970

We have a minority of blacks and whites who are literally beyond control. They are amenable to discipline up to a point, but upon the slightest provocation they become quite defiant. How to overcome this is a real problem. Either they deliberately provoke incidents or they merely react out of genuine feelings.

Joseph Hudson, Gainesville High principal, March 30, 1970

I am black. I was born, raised, married and became a mother right here in Gainesville, so you see I have all the reasons for wanting Gainesville to stay "The City Beautiful." I know the race situation is very morose now, but it's only because we have made it that way. Why is it we try to incriminate the other fellow? Aren't we all to blame? . . .

Segregation is obsolete. Rioting is superfluous. We can do without both of them. I want to say to my race, please, let's put our best foot forward.

Gertrude E. Jones, black parent, March 29, 1970

The most visible impact of the midyear desegregation, and the one that captured the attention of the press, was racial confrontation. Creation of unitary school systems, as envisioned by the Supreme Court in *Green*, presented many educational challenges to the schools. However, if the schools were to respond to those challenges, they would first have to solve the problem of interracial hostility that led in many districts to violence. Alachua County was not spared.

Bay County was the other Florida school district involved in *Carter*. There, just days after the February desegregation, a disagreement between a white boy and a black girl in a junior high cafeteria escalated into a "chair swinging" brawl. The authorities closed two schools temporarily. Seventeen students were arrested, and the school board expelled seven students, suspended four, and deferred action on two. The superintendent took a hard line. "We're going to have order in the schools regardless of what it takes. If it means expelling half the student body, this we'll do." There were to be discussion sessions among teachers and students when the schools reopened. Black assistant principals were to be hired for all four junior high schools and both high schools in Bay County.[1]

Manatee High School in Bradenton was temporarily closed because of racial violence that allegedly arose over the morning pledge of allegiance. The Manatee superintendent said the pledge grievance was "not negotiable. We will not require any student to recite the words to the pledge, but he must stand and show respect for the beliefs of the other students when it is said."[2]

Students boycotted four black high schools in Palm Beach County that were scheduled to become mostly white in September.[3] Armed guards were posted at the school administration headquarters in West Palm Beach after a confrontation between two hundred black students and the superintendent. A teacher there was wounded in the head. In Lee County, the school board suspended one hundred black students for ten days each for protesting an alleged nonobservance of black history week at a formerly all-black junior/senior high school. The superintendent declared, "I have no sympathy for the march and there will be no change in our social study program."[4] In Jacksonville, fifteen black students and seven white students were suspended for a hallway brawl at a junior high school.[5]

The NAACP's Florida field secretary, Marvin Davies, refused to accept black responsibility for the unrest. On February 14, he accused white school boards and superintendents of doing little to address racial issues prior to integration. ". . . When they [white leaders and black and white students] meet there's nothing but hostility. Then they come running to the NAACP and say, 'Hey, fellows, help us with this black community.'" Davies asserted that white school administrators should get the white and black student leaders together to solve problems. "It usually takes only a few minutes and everything will be okay."[6]

In Alachua County, some problems began to surface. In the two elementary schools in the small community of Archer, it was discovered in mid-February that classes remained segregated even though the buildings had been integrated. A black parent complained that no black teacher was teaching any white student. School board members Smith and Simmons, both from outside Gainesville, commented favorably on the practice. "The children are so happy, though," Smith said. Simmons, who was himself from Archer, said the practice was motivated by "education not integration. These children have been with their teachers for 100 days and we see no reason to shift them for the next 80." There also were reports that white parents had threatened to withdraw their children if classes were integrated. Smith, who had voted against implementing the September Plan, said that it was up to Superintendent Talbot, not the school board, to decide the best way to implement the integration court orders.[7]

Talbot quickly moved to desegregate the Archer schools. He sent Wendell Kilpatrick, the assistant superintendent of instruction, to Archer to review the situation on February 16. When Kilpatrick arrived, expecting to meet with principals and other school officials, he found "a crowd of 60 or 70 parents, nearly all of them white," who were there to protest any changes for the remainder of the school year. Board member Simmons also attended the meeting. Talbot required classrooms to be integrated. Classes were to be taught by teams of three teachers, two white and one black. Talbot did not object to temporary groupings of children on the basis of test scores for diagnostic purposes, but he would not accept permanent assignments on the basis of race for an entire school year. "At any rate, if there has to be groupings, I want them by individual subjects and not by color."[8]

Santa Fe High School, located between Alachua and High Springs, like many high schools in the South, had played sports under the "Rebels" nickname since its opening in 1956. Confederate flags and the playing of "Dixie" were part of every sports contest. By the start of the current school year, 83 of 784 students in grades 7–12 at the school were African American, attending under freedom of choice. Of those students, 46 were in the senior high grades 9–12.[9] As of February 6, the school absorbed an additional 280 black students. The northwest part of the county had a higher proportion of black citizens than Gainesville. Santa Fe, which now included only grades 9–12, became 43 percent black.[10]

Throughout the South, African American students did not want to be "Rebels." The black students at Santa Fe, who now made up a significant minority there, began to protest the school's nickname and Confederate symbols. On February 19, about half of the black students at the school peacefully protested by boycotting classes.[11] White Principal L. B. Lindsey appointed a sixteen-member biracial committee to recommend a solution. Lindsey was a native of the area and had been a principal at the school since it opened in 1956. The committee, composed of eight teachers and eight students, quickly recommended preserving the school colors, scarlet and gray, but dropping the Confederate symbols. The changes were supported by the athletic coaches and the band director. On February 20, the black students were back in class, but about two hundred white students boycotted, accompanied by thirty to forty parents. Principal Lindsey bought a temporary peace by expanding the committee to twenty and then twenty-four persons, adding eight parents.[12]

The nickname dispute brought racial tensions to the surface at Santa Fe. Confrontations began to occur. The school suspended seven students (six black) for "minor disturbances." A cross was burned on a white teacher's lawn, and five white youths were arrested. They were not disciplined by the school. A coach said, "I hate as much as anyone to give up the Rebel nickname. I have always impressed upon my players to take pride in the name 'Rebel' because a rebel never quits. But I don't think it is possible to keep the name and have harmony at the same time."

> Some white students understood how the Rebel symbols can be like waving the red flag to the blacks.
>
> "Suppose," said one youth, "that we were forced to go to Mebane and they had symbol there of a black fist. We wouldn't like that either."
>
> Teachers at Santa Fe are reluctant to discuss the matter. When they do it is in guarded words. It is apparent, however, that the school people feel the students could defuse the explosive situation if the parents kept their hands off.
>
> The point was made during the ill-conceived Sunday meeting. A Negro parent arose and said the kids should be allowed to handle the problem. A white man disagreed and there was a brief verbal exchange.
>
> Finally, the black man said, "you just proved my point. You see, you and I are adults and obviously we will never be able to agree."[13]

The *Sun*, which ran an editorial urging Santa Fe to drop its Confederate symbols, said a week later that it had been hit by complaints of "meddling, callousness, slander, intolerance, ill-faith, snobbishness, atheism and miscegenation."[14]

Principal Lindsey charged the twenty-four-member biracial committee to take up all grievances and racial problems that he referred to it. He said that he would not be a voting member or engage in committee deliberations. On the "Rebel" issue, he told the committee not to feel pressured by the community to make a hasty decision.[15] After taking time to reconsider the issue, the committee on March 12, 1970, voted 18–5, with one abstention, to eliminate the Rebel mascot and nickname.[16] In April, the students voted to replace the Rebels with another nickname, and selected Raiders as the new nickname.[17] The issue caused no further problems.

For the previous five school years, increasing numbers of African American students had been attending Alachua County's white schools. White and black students and teachers had adjusted to this change. As we observed previously, the white schools continued operating much as they had before.[18] There had been some interracial fighting. In the second school year of freedom of choice, 1965–66, dances at junior highs were ended, and dances were cut back at Gainesville High to seven, from almost every weekend formerly. Reasons other than integration were given officially.[19] One school leader said in 1967 that he wished he could end all school social events so that teachers would not have to break up fights. Going into the fruitbasket turnover, school officials recognized that absorbing the remaining black students into the white schools would present instructional challenges.[20] But school leaders did not expect a breakdown in discipline and did not develop ways ahead of time to cope with such a breakdown.

Nationally, racially motivated school violence had been a problem but not an overwhelming one. The House General Subcommittee on Education surveyed all twenty-nine thousand public and private high schools on racial violence during the 1969–70 school year. That survey was completed long before the *Alexander* round of desegregation in the South. Of the 15,066 principals who responded to the survey, 18 percent reported some form of student protest during the current school year, with racial issues causing about one-third of those protests. The major issues were dress codes and general disciplinary rules.[21]

The principals of all Alachua County schools were forming biracial committees, although the actual membership varied from school to school. The school board confirmed the authority of school principals to appoint such committees for their schools without school board review.[22]

Three weeks into the February desegregation, the school leadership was ready to declare at least an initial victory. Superintendent Talbot thanked the school board members, the staff, and the teachers for the fine manner in which the plans of the federal government were carried out with so little strife, due to their excellent leadership. Board member Dr. Samuels added the thanks of the school board to the twenty-two thousand students in Alachua County for making the plan successful. Superintendent Talbot is recorded as heartily concurring.[23]

But black resentment that boiled over in January over Lincoln's closing still simmered. The former Lincoln students arrived at Gainesville High both frightened and angry, according to one former GHS teacher. There was immediate tension.[24] At least some black students blamed whites for the fruitbasket turnover. At the end of the 1969–70 school year, a black student commented, "Blacks were just pushed into GHS without any 'yes' or 'no.' Everything was done because the white man said so. When the Lincoln kids wanted things changed, the whites became scared."[25] Although the events leading up to the midyear desegregation were well covered by the *Sun*, none of the former GHS students interviewed for this book understood at the time the reasons the midyear desegregation had been ordered by the Supreme Court.[26] From this distance, it is impossible to say whether explanations from the school administration would have eased the resulting hostility or made it worse.

Just as the schools appeared to be settling down to business, forces that did not want education to proceed began asserting themselves. On March 5, there were some unrelated racial incidents at Gainesville High that put the school on edge. A white student said that he was pulled into a restroom by two black students and then beaten by three other black students who were inside. A set of keys was stolen. Two black students were arrested and charged with strong-arm robbery. Another white student was beaten in the school's parking lot. Police Chief Joiner called the beatings "serious," but neither student was hospitalized.[27]

That night, vandals broke into the closed Lincoln High School building and broke an estimated six hundred windows. Police attributed that incident to small children.[28] The school board decided to have that area patrolled by a security guard.[29]

On March 11, a white GHS student was robbed at knifepoint in the school parking lot. A black student was arrested and charged with the crime. A black girl who shouted obscenities at a police officer at the Red Barn restaurant, near the GHS campus, was also arrested. Police had been called to the restaurant because of a fight in progress.[30]

Isaac Caffey, a black assistant principal at GHS who had been reassigned from Lincoln, said that the racial situation at GHS had been going reasonably smoothly until the March 5 strong-arm robberies.[31] But according to other sources, the entry of the Lincoln transfer students in February changed the school's racial atmosphere. "Overnight the climate changed from benign tolerance to mutual distrust, despite efforts by the student leaders of both GHS and Lincoln to promote a harmonious atmosphere." An official from the county school staff commented, "We put out the welcome mat for them and we got the raised fist in return."[32] A white former student recalls that there was constant fighting behind the teaching auditorium and the gym (although there was no fighting in class). "There was no one to handle the kids."[33] From February, among students and teachers, white and black, "There's going to be a riot" became a constant undertone at Gainesville High.[34] Ted Covey, a white student who graduated from GHS in 1971, remembers speaking to a Lincoln transfer student about the tension. This student told Covey that Lincoln's student leaders decided just before the fruitbasket turnover, "We're not going to do anything as a group unless the white kids start raising the Rebel flag. And if that happens, then we're going to act."[35]

Although they were now attending the white schools, the African American students were still being counseled in their community by the black teachers and other community leaders. According to Brenda Wims, John Dukes "always told us to keep your dignity and to respect the persons that are there. Don't cause a problem. If they close [Lincoln], then do the very best you can in that environment. He never, ever advocated us fighting or doing anything destructive."[36] Despite their own misgivings, according to Frank Coleman, the black teachers stayed positive and tried to make the students stay positive, "because they didn't want us to do anything crazy." Nor did Coleman hear anything negative from the white teachers about the way desegregation had been handled.[37]

Most of the reported injuries resulted from black-on-white violence. But white former students recall that there was ample harassment and provocation by some whites. A few white students took on the role of enforcers, initiating or continuing white violence against blacks. Anecdotal evidence suggests that violent incidents were more numerous than the press reported. Students riding school buses were frequent targets.[38] School bathrooms at GHS became no man's land. Bathroom violence might involve pulling off girls' earrings or worse. When asked later how she coped with that situation, a former white student leader said, "You didn't go."[39] The bathroom situation was one of many daily irritants to which students had to adjust. Stairs were places where shoving took place; students learned not to enter stairwells alone when changing classes. The school had an orchestra. Most students owned the instruments they played and carried their instruments between classes and back and forth to school.[40] During some racial disturbances, blacks would grab and break instruments.[41]

White Gainesville had never been exposed to school violence. Strong-arm robberies, knifings, and muggings were new dangers. Even a small number of such incidents by black perpetrators, occurring where there had been none before, caused an emotional and angry response by white parents.

Those incidents also caused an arms race among students. One student estimated that one out of three boys in his physical education class was carrying a knife. Black students reported incidents of gun carrying and shooting by whites.[42] A white former student confirms that he and some of his friends had loaded guns in their cars parked at the school.[43] John King, elected GHS student body president for the 1969–70 school year, recalls an incident in which a white student drove to the back of the GHS campus while brandishing a gun out the window of his car, which brought in police.[44]

For black students, the impact of the fruitbasket turnover was immediate and direct. It was not just something experienced during classroom changes. Suspensions and expulsions seemed to fall more frequently on black students, senior term paper deadlines became an issue, and there were disruptions of classes and of student government. The Rev. Wright saw even good black students becoming alienated by classroom teachers who were "intolerant in giving tests and grades." Superintendent Talbot pointed out that he knew of no complaints of classroom discrimination reported either to principals or to his office.[45]

The NAACP Legal Defense Fund persuaded the Supreme Court in *Alexander* and *Carter* to order midyear student body integration because "a legal system that promises rights at once, and translates 'at once' for Negroes' rights to mean ten months later, deals with them a cruel and special cynicism and hypocrisy."[46] But 1970 was not 1954. Many Lincoln transfer students were not about to react to their supposed deliverance with humility and gratitude.

Some clenched-fist black power symbols were painted at GHS. The symbols were sandblasted before students arrived on campus for classes. Some white students began wearing clothing with the Confederate flag sewn on; some blacks had Black Panther emblems on caps and vests.

A school board meeting on March 12, 1970, was attended by white parents who wanted the school board to take stronger actions against black-on-white assaults. Seven black students were expelled by the school board at the meeting. One of those students was arrested by sheriff's deputies and removed from the meeting as he was denying his involvement to the school board. Superintendent Talbot said that 95 percent of the problems were occurring in grades 7–12, and Gainesville High and Westwood and Eastside Junior Highs were the most seriously affected schools. He estimated that teachers were spending 30 percent of their time dealing with discipline issues. He added that he had assigned eleven teachers and six deans, "call 'em school policemen if you will." The school bus administrator said that offenses on buses had increased 75 percent in the past month. School board member Simmons suggested putting two adults on every school bus, to an "amen" at the March 12 school board meeting. Talbot said he and the principals were working on new disciplinary guidelines. A black community leader at the same meeting complained of white intimidation of black students and claimed that nobody listens.[47]

The schools were unprepared to deal not only with the violent incidents, but also with the impacts of those incidents. Clif Cormier, the *Sun*'s education editor, allowed himself a brief comment on the situation in an otherwise straight news story. Cormier, himself a former decorated Marine Corps officer who went ashore in the invasion of Iwo Jima, said,

> Being able to control his students and maintain discipline is as much a source of pride with a principal as with a Marine company commander and his troops. As a result only the more serious cases which find their way into the police records become public knowledge.

It was not possible to gauge the full extent of the violence because only incidents resulting in suspensions or worse were reported to the school board. Students being bullied were reluctant to report incidents for fear of more bullying. And rumors could be more damaging than the actual assaults. Superintendent Talbot during his tenure had no public affairs director to deal with the media. Talbot spoke directly to the press and maintained an unvarnished candor that today would seem ingenuous. But now he suggested that every school should have a person designated to communicate with the public as a way of controlling rumors.[48]

By mid-March, Gainesville High Principal Joseph Hudson wanted the county to explore having full-time plainclothes policemen in troubled schools. He added that because of hostility to uniformed policemen, having police in uniforms on his campus would be "self-defeating." Hudson said one alternative would be to use volunteer parents but said that "screening volunteers to eliminate extremists would pose serious problems." Talbot agreed that some security was needed at GHS, Eastside, and Santa Fe but added that they would have to patrol in pairs, one white and one black. He said the schools had no available funds to pay the $4.50 per hour that the guards would cost.[49]

> Investigations of robbery and beatings at GHS since the [February] merger with Lincoln point to a small cadre of incorrigible students who have transferred their modus operandi to the GHS campus.
>
> "We have a large number of good, cooperative students from Lincoln High," said Hudson. "But there is also a militant group who have dedicated themselves to disrupting any harmony we are able to build up.
>
> "The only thing I can do is identify them and remove them from school."

> White teachers complain of open hostility from black students.
>
> "I've taken more crap from Negro students in one month than I have in years of teaching white students," one teacher said.[50]

So far there were problems but no solutions.

Barbara Gallant, a GHS teacher who actively supported integration, wrote the *Sun* to give a different picture of education at the high school. She said that "over 99 per cent of the students, both black and white, have behaved in an exemplary manner. With pressures from extremists on both sides they have continued to attend school, write term papers, participate in sports and extracurricular activities, and carry on with the general business of living. . . . I would like to raise a rousing cheer to the way our students have maintained their 'cool.'" She reminded readers that adults had caused the current overcrowding by failing to pass the 1966 school bond issue. She said there had been numerous fights at the school before it went on double sessions two years earlier to ease the overcrowding. Gallant warned that overcrowding posed the danger that a fight could bring in more students, resulting in a "major explosion." She asked the community to thank the overworked deans, counselors, assistant principal, and principal for maintaining daily calm in a school built for sixteen hundred students but currently accommodating over three thousand. She also asked that credit be given to the vast majority of the newly absorbed students from Lincoln and Mebane for carrying on to the best of their ability and to the twenty-five hundred students who had been at GHS and were trying to make the situation work.[51]

Interviews with former teachers and students confirm a view closer to that of Mrs. Gallant than to that portrayed on a daily basis in the *Sun*. For most students, something like a normal learning experience was going on, however clouded the atmosphere had become. Teachers and most students would soldier on through the early years of full desegregation despite the outbreaks of violence. But in-school violence could not be allowed to become a permanent feature of the educational experience. If it was to be ended, or at least minimized, the unprepared school leaders, teachers, and students would have to find ways to deal with it.

Why did violence become a problem during desegregation? For the most part, during freedom of choice, black and white students had managed to go to school together peacefully. But we need to recognize that students in grades 10–12 range in age from fifteen to eighteen. Long before desegregation, there was fighting at GHS—behind the gym or off campus. An aside: at Gainesville High when this author attended, Duane Eddy's

1958 hit "Rebel Rouser" was banned from play at school dances because it started so many fights among white boys.

After desegregation, fighting continued ("white-white, white-black, black-black") as a small number of students worked out their differences. Although it seemed at the time that much fighting had racial overtones, in retrospect, to Mary Rockwood, a 1973 GHS graduate, it was a fighting culture, and "they're just fighting."[52] Under freedom of choice, even in the fifth grade, John Dukes III was working out his position at J. J. Finley by fighting.[53]

Desegregation offered another excuse for some male students to fight. Frank Coleman, a 1971 GHS graduate who attended Howard Bishop Junior High under freedom of choice, remembers:

> The ones who were idiots [at Howard Bishop] were idiots when we got ready to graduate [from GHS]. They didn't change. And they would make sure that they incited whatever they could start, whatever they wanted to start. Now what you'd find is they pretty much, once a week, came over initially, they would try and fight you. But most of us learned to just kind of back away and just ignore these guys. And some of the white guys who were a little more open in their thinking sort of sided with us. Frank, don't even pay any attention to [two named white students]. Just ignore these guys. You know they're crazy. But they didn't go anywhere, and they didn't change their way of thinking. We learned to respect each other to a certain extent. In other words, you stay out of my way, I stay out of yours.
>
> But see, what you have to understand is I know African American guys that are the same way. You see, in other words, they're hot under the collar, and they don't take a whole lot of mess either. We've always been in that situation where we've been sort of told, well, hell, you know, you can't go downtown doing this, and you can't go over here doing that. Okay? And as long as things were segregated, I guess we just did what we had to do.
>
> But when you let that group of guys, who were not going to be intimidated by anybody, work with another group of guys who are not going to be intimidated, of course, they found each other. Now what you may have heard and what the *Gainesville Sun* probably saw were the ones who talked the most and had the most to say, which wasn't, in my neighborhood, it was the empty wagons make the most noise. I always felt like that, and I always knew that.[54]

It would be most unjust to lay the blame for the school violence on black students generally. Not only were most black students keeping out of trouble, but many black students intervened courageously to protect whites. During disturbances, teachers were expected to keep their students in their classrooms. While some students were outside running down the hall, Peggy Finley, a petite English teacher, was confronted by a black female student who insisted on leaving class to use the restroom. Finley moved in front of the classroom door to prevent her from leaving. Immediately, a black male student jumped up and stood in front of Finley, ending the confrontation.[55] Frank Ford, a Lincoln transfer student who graduated from GHS in 1971, was not on student government or on an athletic team. But he could stand up physically to just about anyone. He says that in his classes, he and his friends would not tolerate abusive or violent behavior. "It's like, you develop a reputation. And it's like, don't bother with him. He'll hurt you. And whether you will or not, people perceive you to be one way, and they will pretty much stay in line. . . . Because if you stand back and do nothing, then a situation will get worse." Ford, now the owner of a roofing business, and Sandra Sharron, his English teacher, have remained friends since their days at GHS. "She had this Doris Day haircut and everything. And she was all bubbly and bright and everything. And she looked like a teacher. And she's just a nice person. And if I liked you, nothing was going to happen." Sharron: "I don't think you can, student or old person, you can't be around a group of people who like you and continue to create havoc. Somebody is going to intervene somewhere along the way. So I think that's what a lot of people have forgotten about GHS. We went through years, but all along the way, there were great things happening. Great friendships being forged."[56] But despite these efforts, multiplied many times over, the violence continued.

School board member Enneking laid some responsibility for parent discontent on the *Sun* and its education editor, Clif Cormier. Enneking also accused the *Sun* of giving too much attention to the bad things and not enough to the good. He said that if the *Sun* had covered a recent Eastside Junior High PTA meeting, the paper "would have seen how parents of both races are working together."[57]

Cormier, taking Enneking's hint, ran a story on Eastside. John Dukes, the former principal at Lincoln then serving as principal of Eastside in its temporary location on the Bishop campus, praised parents and students for their involvement in the new school. He agreed that disciplinary problems were worse than expected but did not see those problems as racial in nature. Without blaming the press specifically, he cautioned that people seemed to be too eager to report riots when they saw students congregating peacefully on the playground. In September, when its new campus was to open as a junior/senior high school, Eastside was expected to house a student body that would be 54 percent white and 46 percent black.[58]

The state attorney cleared a black GHS student of criminal charges in connection with the assaults and robberies. The school board had previously expelled that student. Following the dismissal of charges, this student made statements on a radio broadcast that caused Tommy Tomlinson, Superintendent Talbot's principal assistant, to fear racial issues if the student was not readmitted to GHS. Principal Joe Hudson agreed. The student was readmitted. Superintendent Talbot later defended the readmission as an appropriate administrative action not requiring school board approval.[59]

Gainesville High School was closed on Thursday morning, March 26, by violence involving an estimated three hundred to four hundred students (approximately two thousand eleventh and twelfth graders attended the morning session at GHS). The flash point showed just how combustible the mix had become. Some white students, angered at the black student's readmission, decided to protest. During first period, they began parading around the campus carrying a Confederate flag and singing "Dixie." The group was variously estimated to be between twenty and forty students. Black students who were interviewed for a later police report said that the white students were recruiting others to beat up black students who had been allowed to return to GHS. Black students in the area began banging on windows of classrooms to get black students to come out of class. The white students eventually raised the Confederate flag on the "victory pole" on the school mall.[60] That pole was traditionally used to hoist a red-and-black hurricane flag to celebrate school sports wins.

According to the *Sun*, Principal Joe Hudson and the head football coach, Jim Niblack, took the flag down and brought the flag raisers into the auditorium to listen to their alleged grievances. Some blacks followed them into the auditorium. When the meeting broke up, the blacks blocked the exits and fighting started. During the transition from first to second period, students from other areas of the school collected, and more fighting occurred. Hudson called city police when students refused orders to stop roaming the campus. Sheriff's deputies also responded. At 9:00 a.m. Captain Courtenay Roberts ordered the campus cleared.

Police then had to break up a large group of blacks across the street from the school. Eastside Junior High was also closed as a precaution.

This disturbance was not just pushing and shoving. Three male teachers were injured. Several students were taken to a hospital for treatment. A *Sun* reporter was kicked in the head when he and a sheriff's deputy attempted to aid a white student who was "being pummeled" by about twenty blacks.[61] Sheriff's Department Inspector Ron Stanley said, "I was right in the middle of the fighting (March 26) and every white student I saw was either running from a group of Negroes or on the ground being kicked by Negroes." He added that he did not see any weapons being used, unless chairs and pipes could be called weapons.[62]

Dean of Boys Tom Evans, a white, had severe facial injuries. He was isolated in the gymnasium and beaten by blacks. Just before that beating, while being chased by black students, Evans took shelter in the classroom of Elizabeth Mallonee, a young white English teacher. Mallonee had prevented her students from leaving her class to join the riot. She regrets that she did not persuade Evans to remain in her classroom. According to Mallonee, blacks targeted Evans because he was enforcing the school's conduct policies. "The black kids were angry, and they didn't behave the same as the white kids, and they still don't. But we have come to see that now."[63] Mack Hope, one of the white students who helped raise the Confederate flag that day, remembers Evans as "an equal opportunity guy. He was tough on everybody. He was what a dean was supposed to be."[64]

In the aftermath, the issue of security guards on campus was again raised. Hudson had told the *Sun* shortly before that the county should explore this option. At the time of the disturbance, Superintendent Talbot was in Tuskegee, Alabama, trying to recruit black teachers. His assistant, Tommy Tomlinson, said about the security guards, "This is not a decision for a small group to make. This is a community problem and a parent problem."[65]

Gainesville High was closed the following Friday and Monday for an abbreviated Easter break. But the violent outbreak only served to bring more grievances to the surface.

At a city commission meeting called to consider the GHS unrest, Neil Butler, the black city commissioner, showed his fellow commissioners an envelope that he said contained the names of witnesses to the raising of the Confederate flag. Butler said that just as there is no place in the community for anyone who physically abuses another, there is no place for anyone who mentally or psychologically abuses another. Butler also argued that there was a disparity in the number of blacks arrested compared to whites. He said that he was reviewing his position on the need for a police review board, which he had earlier opposed. He called for meetings among black and white parents, school board members, and law enforcement as soon as possible "in order that we who love this community can avoid future such incidents. Let us get together and propose some guidance and direction. If we have ever needed leadership we need it now, and may God help this community if we don't provide it now."[66]

Butler had said of the earlier Lincoln disturbances that once things like that start, leadership can't stop them; they just have to burn themselves out. Gainesville had experienced infrequent but significant racial violence in the past, but never inside schools. The previous racial violence had occurred around singular events, such as the Martin Luther King Jr.

assassination, and had started and stopped spontaneously. The school violence arose not from an isolated triggering event, but from circumstances that would have to continue indefinitely if Alachua County was to have public education. After the GHS disturbance, Butler now took the position that leaders would have to lead, whether or not they believed they had any chance of succeeding.

Butler's fellow city commissioner, G. M. Davis, a white, later said, "I'm just afraid that we as parents may have failed in that we didn't forewarn our children that the school is legally integrated and this is the way it is going to stay. It's up to us to do it."[67]

Mayor-Commissioner Walter E. Murphree, MD, urged everyone not to come to any conclusions about the causes of the disturbance. He said the purpose of the city commission meeting was to review law-enforcement needs. He said the proper place for a detailed discussion of the incident was the school board.[68]

Black students and parents met at Bartley Temple United Methodist Church on the night of March 26. They discussed a boycott but concluded "it wouldn't do any good," according to a teacher who attended the meeting. A spokesman for another group that wished at that time to remain anonymous said they had been in touch with the black community and had been concerned about constructive community action for some time. This group also wanted GHS reopened for a normal school day on the Tuesday after Easter. The group wanted to work behind the scenes to help open channels of communications between blacks, whites, and school personnel. Principal Hudson was to hold a meeting on the evening of March 27 with white and black community leaders.[69]

Police Captain Courtenay Roberts denied rumors that a student had been found in a restroom bleeding from knife wounds, that there had been an assault or robbery behind the GHS auditorium on Thursday night, and that police had suffered injuries more serious than bruises and gashes caused by fists and feet.[70]

The March 27 meeting included approximately seventy parents and Superintendent Talbot. Early in the meeting Talbot suggested that Gainesville police provide some protection at GHS, but the parents were not ready for that possible solution. City Attorney Osee Fagan had led the chamber of commerce effort to pass the 1968 school bond issue and was a parent of a GHS student. Fagan said, "I hate to admit that in Gainesville High School in 1970 we are considering monitors in the halls and policemen. Knowledge and understanding won't prevail in this type of situation." GHS had no parent-teacher association, and Fagan suggested that the recent violence could be a cause around which parents could unite. "I wonder if there aren't a lot of things we should begin to examine ourselves.

In fact, I wonder if the students themselves might not be better equipped to come up with a solution, since they know more about the problem." Neil Butler and Alex Henry, who now was the parent of a GHS student transferred from Lincoln, agreed with Fagan. Henry said, "If we just take it upon ourselves to tell our children that they must live together, there will be no need for a policeman or anything else. But it is going to take a concerted effort among all of us to do this." City Commissioner G. M. Davis agreed that a grievance committee should be formed so that students and parents could discuss their problems peaceably. He also opposed any law-enforcement presence on school grounds.

Principal Hudson, on whose watch the GHS events were unfolding, had a different view. "We have a minority of blacks and whites who are literally beyond control. They are amenable to discipline up to a point, but upon the slightest provocation they become quite defiant. How to overcome this is a real problem. Either they deliberately provoke incidents or they merely react out of genuine feelings."[71] Hudson later estimated this group to consist of thirty whites and seventy-five blacks.[72]

Before the end of the school year, Hudson would request reassignment. His successor, John Neller, the much-loved former GHS basketball coach, would last only a year himself as GHS principal.

Jim Temple, principal of Buchholz Junior High (which shared the campus of Westwood Junior High as a result of the February desegregation) was the chair of the superintendent's discipline committee. At the March 27 meeting Temple outlined the committee's proposal for restoring discipline. "But before the plan would work, parents and school officials alike 'must recognize that the vast majority of students are directing their talents' toward the good of society and are completely willing to work within a democratic system."

The plan was intended to address symptomatic behavior that could eventually lead to major breakdowns of discipline. Those symptoms included violent disorders, repeated absences, harassment of teachers, and repeated passive resistance.

The plan would have two basic objectives, according to Temple. First, it was intended to keep troublemaking students off the streets after being suspended. By keeping these students in school, the plan also was intended to reduce juvenile delinquency and the incidence of "non-student agitators" who congregated around secondary school campuses and contributed to disruptions. Second, it would allow disruptive students to continue their education in temporary social-adjustment classes taught by a teacher skilled in guidance counseling.

Talbot said that keeping track of who belonged on campus and who did not was "an impossible problem." Being able to distinguish students from nonstudents, according to Talbot, was "the big problem immediately facing us." Like so many of the problems now surfacing, controlling campus access had never been an issue in Alachua County. School campuses were unfenced. Classroom doors opened directly onto outside passageways. Anyone could walk onto the campus to disrupt classes or could even enter a classroom.[73]

Gertrude E. Jones, a black parent of two daughters who had chosen to remain at Lincoln until it closed, wrote to the *Sun*:

Fellow citizens of Gainesville, I know that I am only a small person when it comes to being heard, but I lay awake at 2 a.m. this morning, not being able to sleep because my heart is so heavy and saddened by the things that happened in our city. We have been for so long an ideal city and just the other day we won an award for being one of the most beautiful and cleanest cities in the United States. Is this another case of beauty being only "skin deep?"

I am black. I was born, raised, married and became a mother right here in Gainesville, so you see I have all the reasons for wanting Gainesville to stay "The City Beautiful." I know the race situation is very morose now, but it's only because we have made it that way. Why is it we try to incriminate the other fellow? Aren't we all to blame?

Just think about it for one second. When was the last time you, the head of the family, sat down and said; come, let's have a family prayer and give thanks to God for all the many wonderful things he has given us. He has blessed us with life, health and strength, which enabled us to have a nice comfortable home with plenty to eat. And three or four cars – yes, even the kids have to have their own car.

And mother, when was the last time you said "thanks" for being able to have healthy children? Is this something we take for granted? Yes, I know, because I'm the mother of two girls. They are both healthy, physically and mentally, but until you have worked with kids that are not, you can't really say how thankful you are. But you didn't raise them up to send to school only to wonder if they'll come back home safe or not.

I am sure some of us are saying we must have failed our kids somewhere along the years and I'm sure we did what we thought was right in bringing them up. But did we once stop to ask God for guidance in bringing up our children? They need God today as no generation ever needed Him before. They need faith as no other generation ever needed it before. And we must give it to them but we must have faith in ourselves. If we have taught our kids hate and bigotry at home, when they get to school there's no other way possible for them to act. If you say you don't want your child to sit with a black child in school, when he gets to school he's not going to sit with this child.

I'm sure we've heard the saying "black is beautiful." I have to agree that's true, but there's nothing more beautiful than black and white, especially when they are living together as sisters and brothers and seeing one another as human beings.

It's true that we have some people in both races who will never face reality, but I'm sure there are plenty of us who are tenacious enough to stand up and say no matter what, we are not going to let the sinister elements of our city tell us that we can't live together, because we know better.

Now to our kids, our future Americans? Is this what we have to look forward to, a school campus full of kids who have everything a person could ask for, nice homes, cars, money and yet still aren't satisfied to be able to go to school and try to get a good education so that one day you can hear your parents say with a smile "that's my son" or "that's my daughter?" Instead, you are not only beating up one another but your teachers also. Is it so hard to try and understand the other person's feelings? Deep down within, we are all made of the same thing. When you were fighting on the campus Thursday and a black face got cut or scratched, were you surprised to see that his blood was red also?

We have enough of our men fighting in Vietnam. They are fighting together for peace. Why can't we do the same? If we intend to have peace in the world, we must first have peace at home.

We are all proud of our flag, our American flag. Let's fly it proudly and if we feel the need for another one, let's paint it black and white and let it represent US together as one people fighting for peace.

There has been a prodigious amount of anger, hurt and bloodshed, but so far no death. Do we want it to come to that? Please, let's all try to look at our plight with a more vigilant eye and see what we can do to make our schools a place for education instead of a battleground.

As I said before, I am black. But one of my best friends is white. Shakespeare said, "There's nothing either good or bad, but thinking makes it so."

Let me stress again that most problems would be satisfactorily solved and most goals reached if we would do something about it now. Let's do it now. Do you want to live here in a segregated world only to go to Heaven and find out that it's integrated?

When you feel the need to incite a riot, instead, recite your prayers. Remember, black and white is beautiful.

Let's get together now or we'll all be quoting John Greenleaf Whittier's saying: "For all sad words of tongue or pen, the saddest are these: It might have been!"

Segregation is obsolete. Rioting is superfluous. We can do without both of them.

I want to say to my race, please, let's put our best foot forward.

MRS. GERTRUDE E. JONES[74]

After her letter was published, Jones received letters and phone calls from both blacks and whites. She says that some told her she didn't know what she was talking about, and others, many, were really nice. "You do what you think you should do and let it go," Jones says. She did not involve herself further in the desegregation controversy.[75] Jones was the first African American to become a manager at the local post office, rising eventually to assistant postmaster.[76]

A group of black and white parents and other concerned citizens met at Gainesville High on Sunday, March 29. Russell Ramsey, then a doctoral student at the University of Florida and a substitute teacher at GHS, had been teaching at GHS on March 26. When he learned of the meeting, he decided to attend out of a sense of community involvement. After he took the microphone during a particularly heated exchange and asked the group to quit yelling and focus on possible solutions, someone said, "Okay, you be chairman." At the meeting, according to Ramsey, some whites wanted a strong police presence at GHS, while blacks wanted more black teachers, deans, and assistant principals. "And then you had a few University idealists there who wanted to have freedom, whatever that was all about." No one was satisfied.[77] But Ramsey's significant involvement with Gainesville High and the Alachua County schools began with that meeting.

Ramsey, a graduate of West Point, was a former army major who had served in Vietnam. He had also been at Little Rock in 1957 as a member of the 101st Airborne Division when members of that unit safeguarded the integration of Central High School.[78] He would later head the system's Mountain Top School for students who failed to progress in on-campus isolation classes. Later, he would direct the vocational program at the former Lincoln High School, and a federally funded program for emotionally disturbed students.

Superintendent Talbot told a meeting of parents and students at GHS on Monday, March 30, that he favored having police "on hand." He acknowledged that the Gainesville City Commission, the city manager, and the city police chief disagreed with him. School board members Smith and Simmons were present. Ramsey also attended and said that a straw poll at the Sunday meeting showed a majority opposed police on campus. The debate at the March 30 meeting went back and forth. One white student said the fighting on the previous Thursday worsened after police arrived and that the police became targets. Some parents were fearful of more violence unless there was a police presence. GHS Dean of Boys Tom Evans was in the audience, with his nose bandaged and two black eyes. He listened but did not comment.

Hudson said there were rumors that some teachers would not return to the school on Tuesday. He said, "Our teachers are not trained in riot control and they don't feel they should have to be. They're educators."

The state attorney was continuing to investigate and was considering charges against the students who raised the Confederate flag and against the students who assaulted Dean Evans. Talbot said two students involved in the flag raising had been identified and that they would be suspended from school on Tuesday.[79]

At the city commission meeting Monday night, Superintendent Talbot formally asked for a visible police presence at GHS. He said that some teachers might not return to the school without police protection. No action was taken by the commission on Talbot's request, but the city manager assured Talbot and the audience that police would be available and could be on the GHS campus "in minutes." A white city commissioner explained that the city manager had administrative responsibility for the Gainesville police department. The commissioner said there had been tense situations in Gainesville before and that leaders of the black and white communities had risen to the occasion in the past to work out problems. The informal biracial committee that met with school officials on March 27 had previously voted 49–14 against stationing police on campus.[80]

The violence at GHS was especially hard on Talbot. Tomlinson:

> Well, it was kind of a personal insult because, I don't care where Tiny worked, that was still his school. And he always bled purple and white. It was kind of tough on him. And, you know, particularly with the injuries and stuff like that. And we thought about, we discussed in our emergency meeting about closing the school for a while. But then we thought, well, the logistics of that is tremendous. What will these kids do, you know? Hell, there's [3,200] of them roaming around, and it's better to try to keep them in one spot and corral them and work with them there. So we kept the law presence for several days. And, you know, it got better.[81]

Gainesville High opened peacefully on Tuesday, with a normal complement of teachers present. About thirty-five city policemen were stationed just a couple of blocks north of the campus at a shopping mall in case of trouble.[82] Talbot walked the halls with Charles Chestnut III and others.[83]

Hudson suspended four students, two white and two black, for ten days as a result of the March 26 disturbance. The two white students were identified as having raised the Confederate flag, thereby inciting the riot. The two black students were identified as having started the fighting.[84]

Tension spread to Newberry High School. Police were sent to the school at the request of Superintendent Talbot as a precaution on Tuesday, March 31, but were not needed. Principal Wyndell Everett said that there had been nightly painting of Confederate flags all over the school since the March 26 disturbance at GHS. Black students at Newberry refused to take the bait.[85]

On Tuesday, March 31, students at Howard Bishop Junior High were required to participate in a drug-awareness training session led by Alachua County sheriff's deputies. These programs were required by the school administration for Gainesville secondary schools. Some Bishop students disrupted the program by refusing to remain quiet during a film.[86]

Then on Thursday, April 2, violence closed Howard Bishop Junior High. A significant number of Lincoln Junior High students had been transferred to Howard Bishop, which is located on Gainesville's northeast side. Police were called to the campus to break up the disturbance. Several hundred students were involved. Several white students were observed to be injured, but it could not be determined whether any black students were injured. As a precaution, classes did not meet that afternoon for Eastside Junior High, which shared the Howard Bishop campus, but during the afternoon session. About 125 black students marched from Howard Bishop to a nearby highway intersection in a black neighborhood, where they began throwing rocks and bottles at police. They were chanting black power slogans.[87] According to a former white ninth grader from that year, despite its location on Gainesville's northeast side and some very entrenched racist attitudes, Bishop was less prone to violence than Gainesville's other secondary schools. After the April riot, however, he and some of his friends hid chains and rebar in nearby woods in case of future violence. But the campus quickly settled down.[88]

Westwood Junior High's turn came on Friday, April 3. The unconfirmed provocation was the display of a Confederate flag on a school bus, which was challenged by black students wearing black power armbands. A brawl there broke out at 7:00 a.m. Police were called, and the campus was cleared, with the last buses leaving at 11:00 a.m. According to Superintendent Talbot, who was losing patience, "They saw it happen at other schools and decided it had to happen here." He did not know the immediate cause but said that "asinine" demands of black students contributed. They had demanded a search of all school lockers for Confederate flags. Buchholz Junior High, which shared the Westwood campus, held classes in the afternoon session without incident. Buchholz Principal Jim Temple said that attendance that day at Buchholz was about 500 of the 750 students enrolled.[89]

At Eastside, which met in the afternoon on the Bishop campus, classes on April 3 went on as usual. But Principal Dukes had to order teachers to lock classroom doors while police cleared the campus of black students who would not either attend class or leave. More disorders at the school occurred later that afternoon.[90]

At Gainesville High, on April 3, a white student was mugged by blacks while walking across the street from the school and suffered a broken jaw and bruised back. There was no mention that the Confederate flag or black power symbols were involved.[91]

Early on the morning of Sunday, April 5, an unknown person fired a shotgun into the home of Superintendent Talbot. Neither he nor any members of his family were home at the time. Police said that the blast did about seventy-five dollars in damage.[92] It would not be the last time that Talbot would be the target of violence.

As midterm integration proceeded in Florida, schools across the state were tense. But in a number of counties what was then referred to as "cross busing" was angering white parents. In some counties, because of geography and demographics, desegregation could only be accomplished by busing some students out of their neighborhoods. One of those counties was Manatee, on the Gulf coast south of Tampa and St. Petersburg. On Monday, April 6, under a US District Court order, the county was to begin busing an additional 2,600 students and transfer 107 teachers to desegregate four remaining all-black schools. As part of the order, some children from predominantly white West Bradenton were to be bused to a school in Palmetto, in a black neighborhood about fifteen miles away. Furniture and equipment had already been moved in anticipation of the transfers. The US Supreme Court had on Friday turned down a petition for delay without comment. The county school board and superintendent had chosen to comply.

Governor Kirk, who had crawled out on a limb on the issue and could not easily climb down, swung into action. On Sunday, April 5, Kirk "suspended" the Manatee County school board and superintendent, and on Monday he showed up with the lieutenant governor to run the schools. Kirk told a press conference that he had not taken similar actions in other counties because they were "not involved in a vicious, horrible, illegal act of forced busing." He also said that it made no sense to implement an integration order forty-five days before the end of the school year. When the school board offices were deluged with calls from parents wondering where to send their children, they were told to send them to the schools that they had previously attended prior to the effective date of the court order.

The president of the Florida NAACP stated his belief that the organization could have Kirk jailed. Earl Faircloth, the Democratic attorney general, employed a locally appropriate metaphor, saying that Kirk had "opened a legal barrel of snakes."

The next day, Kirk made a speech to the state legislature, saying that he had taken over the Manatee schools to get the busing issue to the US Supreme Court. US District Judge Ben Krentzman after a hearing that afternoon found Kirk in contempt of court. On the strength of that order, the Manatee school superintendent, Dr. Jack Davidson, resumed control of the Manatee schools. Davidson said that if Kirk interfered again, Davidson would report Kirk's actions to Judge Krentzman as further evidence of contempt.[93]

But on Wednesday, April 8, two Kirk aides entered the school superintendent's office and locked themselves inside. They were accompanied by two other Kirk staff members, the county sheriff, and five deputies. US marshals attempted to serve arrest warrants from Judge Krentzman on all nine, but the Kirk aides who were holed up in the superintendent's office refused to come out. The other men refused to accompany the marshals. The marshals departed but told the press that they regarded all nine men as under arrest. After the marshals left, "about a dozen Florida Highway Patrol officers in riot gear" took up stations outside the superintendent's office. The building was picketed by about 150 black young people, who chanted black power slogans. A white onlooker said, "I say thank God for Claude Kirk, courageous Claude." She was a member of a local group opposed to busing that claimed one thousand members.[94]

After a brief absence from Bradenton while his wife gave birth to their son Erik, Kirk returned to the Manatee superintendent's office at 4:30

a.m. on April 10, backed by ninety state troopers and sheriff's deputies. "I was told by the governor's office that if the marshals try to enter the area and arrest anyone they will be fired on," said the US attorney. A Kirk aide denied that the threat was made. Kirk himself told a news conference that he "would meet force with force." Kirk told the press that his takeover of the Manatee schools would not end until Judge Krentzman's busing order was withdrawn and the Supreme Court agreed to schedule a hearing on the legality of forced busing. Meanwhile, the Justice Department's Civil Rights Division in Washington sent two of its lawyers and more federal marshals to Tampa. Attorney General Earl Faircloth weighed in, saying that it would be illegal for paychecks to be drawn to pay Manatee County school personnel while the school board and superintendent were being kept from performing their duties.[95]

Judge Krentzman held Kirk personally in contempt of court on Saturday, April 11, subject to a continuing fine of $10,000 per day, unless Kirk relinquished control of the Manatee County schools by Monday, April 13. Kirk in response claimed that Judge Krentzman had no jurisdiction over Kirk's actions. Also cited were the sheriff of Manatee County, who had supported the Kirk takeover, and others involved.[96]

In a face-saving move, the Department of Justice agreed to intervene in the pending Fifth Circuit appeal of Judge Krentzman's desegregation order and to seek referral of the plan by that court to the Department of Health, Education, and Welfare for more study. Kirk told the press that the Department of Justice had agreed to join Kirk in seeking modifications of the plan. Kirk also said that the Justice Department had agreed to consult with the state on future desegregation plans. As a result of this agreement, Kirk stepped down as Manatee superintendent on Sunday, April 12. Superintendent Davidson said that Judge Krentzman's desegregation order would be implemented on Tuesday, April 14.[97]

Alachua County was spared these theatrics. The process began to identify and correct the causes of the problems. As the investigations and bridge building went on, it became apparent that the violence was a symptom, not the disease. But would the symptom bring education to a halt before the disease could be identified and treated? Was this a disease that would ever respond to treatment?

CHAPTER 14
SEARCHING FOR ANSWERS

> Our public schools have been given the task of producing a desired social change, but we are ill equipped to do that. Social change is a community relations problem, not just an education problem. We now have an atmosphere of innuendo and mistrust. We've got to zero in on the trouble.
>
> Jim Temple, chair, principals' disciplinary committee, April 2, 1970

> But the situation has deteriorated to the point that something has to give. The kids who want an education are entitled to one.
>
> Joe Crevasse, Alachua County sheriff, agreeing to temporary police patrols at Gainesville High, April 6, 1970

> The teacher supervising the group learned some new words, but they got down to some serious talks. We found out things about ourselves that we didn't know before. We whites have habits that we don't realize we have, and for years the blacks have resented this.
>
> Tommy Tomlinson, April 17, 1970

Russell Ramsey came from a younger generation than Butler, Wright, Talbot, Hudson, and the school board members. As crisis meetings continued, Ramsey stated what is obvious to us today but was not then: that rapid social changes were sweeping by too fast for local assimilation.

Jim Temple, the chair of the principals' discipline committee, said, "Our public schools have been given the task of producing a desired social change, but we are ill equipped to do that. Social change is a community relations problem, not just an education problem. We now have an atmosphere of innuendo and mistrust. We've got to zero in on the trouble."[1]

Joe Hudson, who would resign as principal of GHS, commented after the end of the 1969–70 school year that schools are expected to solve problems that society at large refuses to face.[2]

Finally forced together by the midyear 1970 desegregation, Alachua County's white and black communities had no choice but to begin to deal openly with the issue of race. Unless they did so, they would never understand what was now going so terribly wrong in the two communities that had coexisted separately ever since the county was first settled—and peaceably for the most part during the recent years of civil rights protests.

Desegregation started with a simple concept: unless whites and blacks went to the same schools, blacks would not get an equal education. But the converse of that concept remained to be proven: that blacks would get an equal education if they went to the same schools as whites. The Supreme Court, and even more so the Fifth Circuit Court of Appeals, well understood that their decisions to enforce constitutional rights in the schools would have potentially disruptive social consequences. Having embraced the constitutional concept, the courts could only place their ultimate reliance on the people to make that concept real on the ground. In 1970, no more so than in 1954, no one could know the distance that would have to be traveled by each Southern county to regain educational equilibrium or what unimagined formula might enable it to do so.

Superintendent Talbot, who at that point had been an educator for twenty-five years and superintendent for six years, opined that Lincoln High School was run by the students and Gainesville High was run by the parents. According to the *Sun*'s Cormier, Talbot's statement implied that discipline at GHS prior to February 1970 had been stricter than at Lincoln.

Cormier contrasted that view with Ramsey's: "Generally, in black schools, discipline is a whip or chain hanging on the wall behind the principal or coach. Integrated into white schools, blacks easily get carried away with the atmosphere of freedom and indulgence."[3] Some Lincoln transfer students agreed that the relative absence of corporal punishment at GHS contributed to the initial discipline issues. Frank Ford: "They didn't do that at GHS. So at GHS, we had a lot of energy. It's like, whoo!" Wayne Mosley: "Once integration came about, you can't touch a child now. And I think it was the white one didn't want a black, like, having the right to touch and spank their kid, so they had to be evenly spreaded that you couldn't beat the black one neither."[4] Bettye Jennings was one of the system's first black teachers asked by Talbot to teach white students. After integration, according to Jennings, it was not possible for a black teacher to touch a white student ("See you in court").[5]

Corporal punishment was still permitted at GHS.[6] But as the events of March 26 demonstrated, paddling some students was not going to fix the hostility that was driving the violent behavior of many students.

At its meeting on April 2, 1970, the school board heard the completed recommendations of the principals' disciplinary committee from its chair, Jim Temple. The board voted to implement the recommendation for isolation classes immediately by stationing a temporary classroom building at the county juvenile detention home. The board originally intended the facility would be operated in conjunction with County Judge John Connell and juvenile court authorities.[7]

The discipline committee called for a staged approach to misconduct. Students guilty of serious antisocial behavior or criminal conduct (and their parents) would receive one warning. If there was a second incident, the student would be permanently expelled. Separate "social-adjustment classes" were to be established at each school for students who were involved in repeated conduct that disrupted the learning process of other students. If a student failed to respond favorably to the in-school social-adjustment classes, principals could suspend students to the central isolation class facility at the juvenile home. Students sent to that facility would not be reassigned to regular classes without the certification of the isolation class instructor and the receiving principal.

The committee also recommended that any misconduct serious enough to be called to the attention of the dean of students would result in a notice to the student, his or her parents, the guidance counselor, the principal, and the classroom teacher if the student had been referred by a teacher. The same parties would be notified of the action taken to correct the misconduct. The school administration would keep records of these actions and analyze them to determine the effectiveness of the program.[8]

On April 5, the school administration reacted to the violence by publishing new disciplinary rules for principals and teachers to follow. The display of the Confederate flag and black power symbols on clothing or elsewhere were banned (although negotiation with students on these symbols was permitted). Students were required to be in their classrooms during class time, and anyone not in a classroom was to be removed from the campus, by police if necessary. Hall passes were required for students on the campus between classes. Teachers were to lock classroom doors from inside upon intercom instructions and to keep their students in the classrooms until further orders. Students were asked to stay in groups of four or more when possible and not to become isolated. The time for changeover between double sessions was extended to keep students from both sessions from congregating during the changeover. Students who walked to school were to stay away from the areas where buses picked up students for the ride home.[9]

Superintendent Talbot continued to press his point that there should be a police presence on campus. Alachua County Sheriff Joe Crevasse agreed with Talbot, and together they persuaded the city to agree to a joint patrol to be manned by sheriff's deputies and city police. The patrols began on Tuesday, April 7. Two sheriff's deputies and two Gainesville city police officers were to be stationed at Gainesville High and the joint Westwood-Buchholz and Bishop-Eastside campuses. The police were to be present in parking lots and at bus unloading and loading areas, where troubles had frequently started. They would not patrol the school walkways. Crevasse said he had previously agreed with Police Chief Joiner that the students had to be given a chance to work out the problems themselves. "But the situation has deteriorated to the point that something has to give. The kids who want an education are entitled to one." Talbot hoped that the patrols could be discontinued in a week. But he said, "The main thing is that the kids getting off the buses early in the morning will have someone to look to for protection. They're pretty scared since all this trouble started."[10]

On April 6, following Governor Kirk's takeover of the Manatee County schools, Sheriff Crevasse told the Alachua County Commission that he had discussed the Gainesville school situation with the governor. Crevasse toughened his stance, saying that he was prepared to put armed guards in the classrooms, restrooms, parking lots, and anywhere else there was a need for protection. "If we have to live by the gun to keep our schools open, live by the gun we will."

Talbot said that schools would no longer be closed because of disturbances, but teachers would be charged with maintaining decorum in the classrooms. Students who did not go into their classrooms would be forced to leave the school.[11]

During the week of April 6, the junior high campuses were quiet. However, there were reports of disruption of GHS adult evening classes by "militant" students who had been excluded from day classes.[12] Superintendent Talbot said he had received complaints from adult students who wanted to withdraw because of harassment. He stationed a guard at GHS during night classes to deal with the problems. He said that students removed from day classes should have to come before the school board before being admitted to night classes.[13] At Newberry High School on the evening of Monday, April 6, a confrontation between groups of whites and blacks occurred, allegedly over the Confederate flag. Four white adults who refused to leave the area were arrested for unlawful assembly. One of the whites had a shotgun, and he was charged with possession of a firearm while engaged in a crime.[14]

At Talbot's request, Gainesville High School was closed to students Wednesday and Thursday, April 8 and 9, for teachers to get to know one another better and for "long range improvement of the climate of learning and teaching at GHS." The school board attributed the closing to the "local emergency" created by midyear court-ordered integration, and the ten days of dissent by students against the closing of Lincoln Junior/Senior High School.[15] Workshops on handling of racial problems were held. The teachers met in sixteen separate groups led by psychologists from the University of Florida. The session leader was the late psychologist Dr. William O. Matola. A week later, a report on the meetings was made to the school board and discussed at an otherwise unidentified "county task force on education problems." School officials wanted some good news. The report recommended that the encounter groups be continued, and they were.[16]

Barry Wolfe, PhD, then a graduate student at the University of Florida, was one of the psychologists who led the workshops. Wolfe, from Washington, DC, had graduated from Howard University as the top psychology student in his class. He also was the first white student to play varsity basketball there. Wolfe was interested in community mental health. "So there's a riot at Gainesville High School. And that set off alarm bells throughout the city. . . . We were told that all mental health personnel in the city were being called to action to help deal with the aftermath of the riot."

Wolfe and his fellow interns led discussions by mixed-race groups of teachers at GHS and later at other schools. Wolfe says that this was the era of the encounter group, and the techniques used came from National Training Labs sensitivity training. Wolfe admits that there was only informal evidence of the efficacy of this technique. But "we really believed in the efficacy of conversation. You know, let's talk this out. Let's really speak our minds, and maybe we can get past all of not only the hostility, but all of the implicit hostility." The interns had some training in encounter groups but none at all using this technique in racially charged situations. "It was trial by error. Trial by fire. I remember being petrified." The interns were only supposed to facilitate conversations. If the interns sensed that group members were not speaking their minds, they were supposed to do whatever they could to encourage them to do so.

Wolfe says that the teachers were reluctant to speak out, and when they did, initially, they started with generalizations. A white teacher was concerned that black teachers didn't work as hard and wanted special treatment. A black teacher responded, "We never show you our real face. We know white people. And we know how you think, and you really don't know us at all." The black teachers disagreed with the white teacher's characterization. Some black teachers believed the white teachers were favored. The white teachers said that too much time was spent disciplining black students. The black teachers objected that too much attention was given to black students' behavior because they were black, not because they were necessarily more disruptive. The major themes of desegregation were being played out in Wolfe's group. "My memory is that the issues got out, but they were not resolved. That's my general feeling about the groups, in general. That we could help them get out what each side thought of the other, but we either didn't have time, or they were not ready to move past that. So it was really like there was a little success, but certainly not what I was hoping for, and I think what other, most people were hoping for." Wolfe says that one teacher group did become quite explosive, which caused some people to question whether the program should continue. The teacher sessions, according to Wolfe, lasted for five or six sessions over a month or two.[17]

Judy Joiner, daughter-in-law of former school board member Jasper Joiner, joined the GHS faculty in September 1969 as a young German and history teacher. She agrees with Wolfe that the people who were leading the sessions didn't know how to do it properly. She believes that her group was led by a school guidance counselor. She found the interracial focus groups very awkward. The guidance counselor would ask leading questions, and "people would just kind of get upset." Much more valuable, according to Joiner, were unforced, informal discussions among teachers about the school's racial problems.[18]

The school board on April 9 ratified the disciplinary rules that had previously been announced on April 5. It passed a resolution commending Gainesville High's staff, teachers, students, parents, lunchroom workers, custodial workers, secretaries, aides, and others for efforts beyond the call of duty on March 26 and before, "to the point of endangering life and limb."[19] But it hesitated to take any further actions, despite hearing proposals from outside the school administration that were intended to prevent future outbreaks through improved communications.

The Reverend Fred Laughon of First Baptist Church spoke to his congregation through the church bulletin, "Good News," of April 9:

> So often it is said that our schools are undergoing so much racial tension and, in some cases, open conflict. "The sad thing is that no education is going on." But there is education. The most important subject that could be considered, "How People Live Together," is being taught in every classroom in our area. –This is therefore more important than arithmetic, Chaucer or an introduction to ancient History. We are all getting a revelation.[20]

David Horne was a young black instructor at Santa Fe Junior College. As a psychology student at the University of Florida, he had helped operate an Afro-American center supported by the Inter-Fraternity Council.[21] Horne asked the school board to appoint young black and white adults to act as ombudsmen at the troubled schools. According to Horne, they would act as a buffer between students and administrators. They would interact with students in hallways between classes and in lunchrooms. He had first made the proposal at a special meeting of the city commission on Saturday, April 4. Horne said that black youths in Alachua County grew up on the black side of a double standard and now they refused to accept the white orientation of the schools. He characterized the ombudsmen as young adults who would be trusted and respected by the students. The ombudsmen's activities would be "to prevent the motivation for mass rioting in the Alachua County schools." A motion by board chair Samuels to explore the proposal failed for lack of a second. Superintendent Talbot nevertheless said that he would discuss the proposal with his principals, and if they approved, he would attempt to find funds to pay for it.[22]

During the discussion of the ombudsman proposal, the following exchange took place between William Murray, former student body president at Lincoln and now co-president at GHS, and school board member Dale Smith:

> "You don't know how important this is," [Murray] said. "You can't really talk to the school administration, it's part of the establishment."
>
> The generation gap between Murray and the 65-year-old H. Dale Smith became apparent.
>
> "What's wrong with the establishment," Smith asked. "If you really want to communicate with administrators all you need is desire and trust."
>
> "You can't tell us how to feel," Murray answered politely.
>
> "We're trying to tell you how to act, not how to feel," Smith answered.

Murray had earlier objected to the inclusion of hippie headbands in the school board order banning offensive symbols. Talbot countered that some headbands were made of horsehide and some of those had been used as weapons during the March 26 disturbance.[23] The school board order was not amended.

By April 14, one week after the police had been stationed on the three troubled campuses, the police were removed to standby status at Talbot's request. There had been no major incidents during that week. Students had been meeting with police to discuss alternatives to assure student safety. The vice president of the GHS student body said that students agreed that police should be removed but kept on standby.[24]

Meetings continued. At Gainesville High, the newly reactivated parent-teacher association added students, becoming the Parent Teacher Student Association.[25] Robert M. Atkins, a white, said, "We are determined that parents will be involved in helping the school rather than in leaving our students and the administrators to fight the problems." About one hundred persons attended the group's organizational meeting on April 14. Atkins characterized the parents behind the organization as moderates, "not radical in either way." The committee formed during the crisis under

Russell Ramsey's leadership continued as the Action Group, an advisory committee to the PTSA.[26]

GHS Principal Joseph Hudson, Alex Henry (the interim GHS PTA president), one black and one white student representative from GHS, and a student from each of the two Gainesville junior high campuses spoke at an open forum on April 15. That meeting at the Gainesville city hall was sponsored by the Democratic Women's Club of Alachua County. After the March 26, 1970, riot, and the subsequent dialogue, white and black student leaders were optimistic that the troubles were over. William Murray said that the raising of the Confederate flag was "only the straw that broke the camel's back. . . . When we first came to GHS there was a clear separation in some classes. Whites were here and blacks were there. Our students were afraid to go to the administration so it built up." The student leaders predicted that the worst was over and there would be no more trouble.[27]

At the forum, David Horne's ombudsman proposal was favored by GHS Principal Hudson, but he said the GHS faculty was divided. "Some [teachers] oppose it very strongly." Hudson praised the April 8 and 9 workshops for teachers and said they were now much better prepared to deal with student problems. Hudson said that these discussions would continue during the school year and over the summer. Shirley Conroy, the Democratic Women's Club chair, said the current activities were "palliative" and that long-range programs were needed to work on deeper underlying causes of racial distrust.[28]

At Superintendent Talbot's request, the school board held a special meeting on April 16 to review the status of its initiatives to address the racial troubles. Dr. Boyd Ayers was among the psychologists retained by the school board. Dr. Ayers said that as a result of the double sessions and other factors, many teachers at Gainesville High simply did not know one another. He agreed with Tommy Tomlinson that much progress had been made as a result of the two-day stand-down on April 8 and 9. Ayers advocated deeper structural changes at GHS to eliminate racial differences. The changes that Ayers wanted to pursue, and the result, are discussed in chapter 20, "The Students."

Rumor control continued to be essential for stopping violence. Talbot told the board that each school now had designated staff rumor-control contacts to answer public inquiries. He said that one thousand copies of the contact roster would be distributed to the general public. The roster was also published in the *Sun*.

Talbot hoped to increase the number of teachers designated to attend a summer workshop at the University of Florida from 70 to 150 teachers. Those teachers would be expected to pass on what they learned when they returned to their schools in the fall.

Details for the isolation classes at the county juvenile shelter were announced. Those classes were ready to start in a temporary classroom on April 20, with staffing arrangements in place.

At the school board's special review session on April 16, blacks in the audience inquired about the future of students who had been expelled before the isolation classes were established. Nine students had been expelled by the school board during the troubles, and some seniors had already missed sixteen days of school, which meant that they could not graduate. Talbot said, "Tell them to come see me." He agreed to give consideration to waiving the sixteen-day rule.[29]

At the end of April, Talbot confirmed that Joe Hudson, Talbot's successor as principal at Gainesville High, had asked for another assignment within the school system. Hudson had previously served as Talbot's assistant principal when Talbot was GHS principal. Talbot said that Hudson had experienced severe pressure because of the racial situation at GHS, and denied that there was any dissatisfaction with Hudson's work.[30] Hudson was forty-six at the time of his request for reassignment. He was later reassigned as principal of Terwilliger Elementary School.

According to a more candid recent assessment, the late Hudson was a fine principal as long as nothing was going wrong, but (as events proved) he could not manage the problems stemming from the fruitbasket turnover.[31] Black students had experienced their principal's leadership through personal familiarity. Hudson (along with some other white educators) could not or would not establish that rapport. That failure should not be attributed to racism; Hudson had led from his desk before desegregation, and it may be inferred that he simply did not have the capacity or desire to change. Black resentment of the midyear desegregation in 1970 might have made it impossible for any GHS principal of either race to stabilize the school. But managing racial unrest was now part of the GHS principal's job, whether or not anyone could be found with the ability to do it.

The principal's position at GHS had to be filled for the coming school year. Parents of students at the still-unfinished Buchholz Junior/Senior High persuaded the school's principal, Jim Temple, to remain at that school. Temple had been mentioned as a possible successor to Hudson. Then, at the school board meeting on April 30, a petition from 109 Gainesville High teachers asked that John Neller, a former coach, assistant principal, and dean at GHS, be appointed to succeed Hudson. Teacher Barbara Gallant, who presented the petition, told the school board that a majority of GHS teachers believe Hudson "has been the greatest." She said that many of the problems at GHS were not the fault of the principal, but resulted from overcrowding and double sessions. The petition stressed Neller's past experience at the school, his work with the faculty, and the school's need for continuity.

At the same school board meeting, Talbot advised the school board that the principal at Santa Fe High, L. B. Lindsey, would probably also request reassignment. That school had to absorb most of the students in grades 10–12 from Mebane in February, and Talbot said that Lindsey also was weary of the pressures.[32]

Talbot also announced that a grant of $6,500 from the Department of Health, Education, and Welfare had been obtained through the Florida School Desegregation Consulting Center in Miami to fund David Horne's ombudsman proposal for Gainesville High through the end of the current school year. The school board this time did not vote on the proposal. At the board's April 9 meeting, the proposal had died for lack of a second to a motion to consider it. Talbot said that Principal Hudson, who had also favored the proposal, would be responsible for screening, hiring, and controlling the ombudsmen during the current school year.[33] Hudson would later credit the ombudsmen with helping to reduce racial tensions. He recommended that they be retained for the 1970–71 school year.[34]

Among the ombudsmen were Charles Chestnut III and the Reverend Earle Page from Holy Trinity Episcopal Church. In addition to his activity on the city Human Relations Advisory Board, Page had served as a mediator when the University of Florida campus erupted in racial unrest in the late 1960s. Page and his wife, Ann, invited students of both races to Holy Trinity for Sunday night discussions of controversial issues, often with guest speakers. The Rev. Wright said of Page, on Page's retirement in 1985, "The black community felt his church was a good sounding board and always open to discussion."[35]

Tommy Tomlinson, Superintendent Talbot's assistant, said in April that the toughest problem following the March 26 violence was getting the students to talk to one another again. The psychologists from the University of Florida and other local agencies also facilitated encounter groups with students. Tomlinson believed the most helpful session occurred when ten violent whites and ten violent blacks were put together in a discussion group supervised by a teacher. Tomlinson: "We did this for several days. The teacher supervising the group learned some new words, but they got down to some serious talks." Tomlinson said, "We found out things about ourselves that we didn't know before. We whites have habits that we don't realize we have, and for years the blacks have resented this."[36]

By the end of April, student and teacher-administrator discussion groups were functioning at Gainesville High under the leadership of Barry Wolfe and Paul Shagoury, both interns from the University of Florida. They told the *Sun* at the time that the starting point to minimizing violent outbreaks was clearing up notions that black and white races have of one another. Shagoury attributed the mistaken notions to lack of contact between the two races.

Eighteen student groups and twelve teacher-administrator groups were functioning. The student groups included ten to twelve students, equally divided by race and sex. Each group had a leader. Student groups were classified as "hot," meaning that they expressed the greatest sense of grievance or anger, or "cool," meaning that members were more cooperative. The psychologists sought to heat up the cooler groups as a way of making the experience more useful. The student groups and the teacher-administrator groups had come forward with thirty-nine recommendations for improving the situation at GHS. Shagoury emphasized that parents continued to be the link between each student and the community. A parent asked the obvious question: Why were there no parent groups? Shagoury replied that it would be more difficult to organize parent groups, but invited any interested parents to indicate their interest.[37] Apparently no parent groups were formed.

Speaking today about the student encounter groups, Barry Wolfe is no less skeptical about their long-term value than he is about the teacher groups. Wolfe says the main grievance voiced by black students was that white teachers were biased toward black students and disciplined black students more often than whites. Wolfe says the one good thing about the groups was that the psychologists succeeded in overcoming reluctance to discuss the hard issues. "But resolution, not so much. People left the groups with the same thoughts and feelings and attitudes with which they entered the group. . . . As far as I know, it didn't lead to any positive action. And of course, in retrospect we all should have had more training. We should have had some clear goals in mind. But the feeling I had was we were let loose on these unsuspecting teachers and students. And we tried to do the best we could, but I don't think we were prepared for anything that might have happened."[38]

The Ohio National Guard on May 4 shot and killed four students and wounded nine others at Kent State University in Ohio. The Kent State shootings resulted in a protest holiday at the University of Florida and similar closings at many universities and high schools across the country.[39]

On the evening of May 7, some black students at GHS met off campus and prepared a set of demands that they presented to Principal Hudson the following day. Those demands were unrelated to the Kent State situation or the Vietnam War. The press reported that an undetermined number of GHS students, both white and black, did not attend classes on Friday, May 8. Hudson said that the school would remain open. He said he believed the absenteeism was linked to the University of Florida protest holiday. Among the demands made by the black students were equal representation of both races in the GHS student body senate and house, changing the name of the school, and more black teachers and more extracurricular activities. Most of the grievances were already under consideration by the various student, parent, and teacher organizations. The black student group also protested the results of the recent student body elections.[40] But a different account emerged following a special school board meeting held the following Tuesday, May 12.

On Tuesday, May 12, it was reported that an estimated 35 percent of the GHS student body had walked out on May 8. The school remained open. The students who left the school included both white and black students. Principal Hudson was not available for comment, but Superintendent Talbot attributed the new protests to radicals who were trying to close the school for the rest of the year. He said, "GHS is not going to close today or for the rest of the year."[41]

In response, the school board called a special meeting on May 12 to hear from some GHS students and other interested citizens. The meeting was called (according to the minutes) to discuss rumors of a lack of discipline at the school. Principal Hudson did not attend. At the May 12 meeting, eight GHS students (among them Maggie Enneking, the daughter of school board member William Enneking, MD) reported in summary that "discipline has broken down at GHS and the present administration is unable to cope with the situation." They said that they hadn't learned anything during the months since the spring session began on February 6 and that classroom teachers were frightened and allowed rules to be broken at will.[42]

Cormier, the *Sun*'s education editor and the chief chronicler of all of these events, now pieced together a different picture of the events of the past few days than had previously been reported. According to Cormier's account, in the morning of Friday, May 8, there was a spontaneous protest meeting of students in the auditorium. That meeting was apparently linked to the Kent State protest day at the University of Florida. But when the meeting broke up, most students refused to return to their classrooms. When the tenth graders arrived at GHS for the afternoon session, they decided that if the eleventh- and twelfth-grade students from the morning session were not in class, the tenth graders should not have to attend class either. At some point there were more students milling around outside the classrooms than were in class, and classes were suspended.

According to Cormier, on Monday, May 11, black student leaders had asked Principal Hudson for permission to hold an assembly of only black students during class time. Permission was granted. The purpose of the assembly was to present Hudson with a list of demands, including a demand for a student union. When some white students attempted to enter the auditorium, they were prevented. The following day, Tuesday, May 12, a group of white students requested permission to hold their own meeting, also during class time. They were also granted permission to do so. But black students entered the white students' meeting and refused to leave, at which point the white students in the meeting walked out and left the campus. At one point the intercom reported that classes had been cancelled for the day, but they had not been. Classes continued with approximately three hundred students absent. There was no violence.

At the May 12 school board meeting, students and parents cited other incidents of failures by teachers or other school officials to follow through on complaints of a lack of student discipline. Some complained that there was more emphasis in the classrooms on sensitivity group training and discussions of race than on academic subjects. It was alleged that there was unrestricted smoking in the halls and profanity. The board also was told that teachers were reluctant to enforce disciplinary rules because they didn't believe they had the backing of the administration. One parent said teachers should be dismissed if they couldn't maintain discipline. "My child might as well not have gone to school this year. It's only been an experience of hate."

In response, Talbot reaffirmed that GHS would continue to observe a normal school year and schedule. At the May 12 meeting, on Talbot's recommendation, Neller was named to take over as principal of GHS effective July 1. In the meantime, Neller and Tommy Tomlinson from Talbot's staff would serve as associate principals. The school's entire staff of counselors was reassigned to patrol the school's halls and enforce discipline through the end of the school year. They were to be assisted by the coaches and assistant principals. The ombudsmen, recently appointed, and the deans would continue their activity.

Board member Dr. Enneking said that prior to the May 12 meeting, he was under the impression that the teachers were doing their jobs and all was well. He referred to a statement by Barbara Gallant, a teacher at GHS, who said that she was pleased with the amount of education taking place. Enneking agreed with Neller's appointment as principal but questioned the need for additional man power, stating, "We don't want martial law at GHS."[43]

GHS Assistant Principal Isaac Caffey, who came to GHS from a similar position at Lincoln High, later confirmed that there were unprecedented discipline problems at GHS. He said that unruly students were placing strains on teachers. "Teachers come to us in tears with these problems. They don't know what to do. Sometimes I feel like crying too . . . after 32 years." Teachers who had trouble dealing with students of their own race before integration now faced the additional difficulty of disciplining students of a different race. Caffey appealed to parents to help the schools with this problem.[44]

Shelton Boyles, then an English teacher at GHS, and Ramsey believe that the students and others who complained to the school board on May 12 were unfairly condemning of the GHS staff. Boyles agrees, however, that conditions at the school were not as they were being portrayed to the school board.[45] Russell Ramsey says that the media overplayed the violence and easily 95 percent of GHS students wanted no part in it.[46] Another former teacher, Isabelle Norton Whitfield, says that in her classes a normal learning experience was taking place. She says that she did not have racial troubles in her classes, either before or after the riot.[47]

Talbot also ordered that there would be no further general assemblies of students until the end of the current school year. It was time to get back to the nuts and bolts of education. About one month remained of the four-month spring term that had started on February 6 with the fruitbasket turnover.[48]

Two days later, at the school board's regular meeting on May 14, the board announced the replacement of L. B. Lindsey, the principal of Santa Fe High School (where the dispute over the Rebel nickname had occurred). Talbot had previously reported that Lindsey was also weary of the racial tensions that had emerged at Santa Fe since February 6. Talbot said that Lindsey and school board member H. Dale Smith of High Springs wanted the announcement made now. Lindsey was fifty-one at the time of his reassignment and had served as Santa Fe principal since the school opened in 1957. He was reassigned to the county staff.[49]

Federal funds were obtained for eighty Alachua County teachers and administrators to attend a summer workshop of a few weeks that would emphasize human relations, team teaching, and small-group instruction. Six Saturday follow-up sessions would later be held during the school year. The number of funded places was less than the 150 places Talbot had sought earlier, but now firm plans could be made for attendees.[50]

A symbolic but important effort to create a spirit of unity at Gainesville High was initiated by GHS head football coach Jim Niblack. After consulting with leaders in the black and white communities, he proposed to build a trophy room addition to the GHS gym that would display the athletic trophies and photos of hall of fame athletes from both Lincoln High and GHS. The project had the support of the GHS Boosters Club and a local contractor. Proceeds from the spring intrasquad football exhibition game would be contributed to the project.[51] That proposal was never implemented.

Not every school involved in the fruitbasket turnover was experiencing the same level of continuing tension as Gainesville High. Howard Bishop Junior High, to which many of the seventh through ninth graders from Lincoln were assigned, had also seen some violence in March. However, its faculty sent a resolution to the *Sun* in which the faculty voted to commend Principal Roy Tower. The accompanying letter from a Howard Bishop teacher praised Tower for his handling of that incident and its aftermath. Following the incident, Tower had invited community leaders to speak to students and had held discussions directly with the students. The letter said that Tower had gained the respect and trust of the students. Tower had encouraged teachers to discuss racial issues with their students, but had also maintained "an atmosphere conducive to learning." "With the aid of his fine supportive staff, Mr. Fred Hill, Mrs. Daphne Williams and Mr. Lamar Simmons, Mr. Tower has created a unique learning climate at Howard Bishop. He has united faculty, staff, students and parents."[52] Daphne Duval Williams had been a math teacher and later a dean and assistant principal at Lincoln Junior/Senior High, where she started teaching in 1928. She would retire in 1971.

By May 27, Talbot was able to confirm that calm had returned to Gainesville High. Talbot noted that some parents were unhappy because some teachers were not going to require final exams, but Talbot said teachers had that option when Talbot was principal, before desegregation. He said that beginning in September, Principal Neller would be assisted by two associate principals, one for the morning session and one for the afternoon session. Talbot said that having separate administrative staffs for the morning and afternoon sessions would ease the workload for the principal. He took blame for not providing Hudson with enough staff.[53]

At the May 28 school board meeting, the board continued to review the comprehensive report prepared by the Florida Education Research and Development Council on the educational programs of the county schools. Despite the turmoil, the board had given some attention to this report at most of its regular meetings throughout the spring. At this meeting, a member of Talbot's staff covered the report's findings on the system's teachers. The schools continued to suffer high teacher turnover, attributed to the hiring of wives of University of Florida students who would work for low starting salaries. Those teachers would then leave the system when their husbands completed their work at the University. Recognizing that the county had finite financial resources, the report recommended increasing starting teacher salaries to address this problem rather than freezing starting salaries and rewarding teachers who stayed in the system.[54]

Of the roughly one thousand teachers in the county, 30 percent were student wives, including 34 percent at the junior high level and 19 percent at the senior high school level. The county was experiencing annual turnover of 25 percent, compared to a national rate of 10 percent.[55]

The junior-senior prom was held in the GHS gym. Elizabeth Mallonee, the young English teacher, was junior class sponsor. The theme was "The Age of Aquarius." "And some students made beautiful black-light posters that would show up in black light each of the zodiac symbols. And I remember at midnight the DJs putting on 'The Age of Aquarius' and everybody just dancing and singing and having a great time."[56] Somehow, GHS still had enough high school magic that for one night—peace guided the planets and love ruled the stars. Student prom attendance was down. A large contingent of plainclothes police also was present, but there were no problems.

Mercifully, graduation day came at last for the 868 seniors in the Gainesville High class of 1970. At the student awards ceremony that preceded graduation, Principal Hudson received a plaque and a standing ovation from the audience of students and parents.[57]

In sorrow, loyalty, and pride, the black seniors who transferred to Gainesville High in February chose (and were allowed) to receive diplomas from the black high schools they attended for all but the last four months of their high school years. The graduation ceremony, in a stiflingly hot University of Florida gym, was peaceful. Of the 142 seniors who transferred to GHS from Lincoln, 133 chose to receive Lincoln diplomas. All 24 seniors from Mebane chose to receive Mebane diplomas. Those students wore mortarboard tassels and received diploma cases in the colors of their prior schools, red and white for Lincoln and green and white for Mebane.[58]

William L. Robinson, one of the civil rights warriors who fought all the way to the Supreme Court to win the right of the Lincoln and Mebane seniors to receive GHS diplomas, had no comment when told of the seniors' diploma choice.[59]

CHAPTER 15
THE JUDGES' TURN III

Lincoln High School's Day in Court

I think the majority of the representatives of the black community who have spoken to me about Lincoln object to its being closed as an academic center.

Alachua County school board chair Walter Ebling, testifying in *Wright v. Board*, April 20, 1970

Nevertheless, this Court would not lose sight of one of the purposes of a unitary school system, viz., to give the highest quality education to all students in the system. If Lincoln remained open with its inadequate facilities and space, those students there enrolled would not receive the same quality education as those students enrolled in the more modern academic facilities. Therefore, this Court concludes that the Lincoln facility was rightfully closed so that students could be enrolled elsewhere where facilities were improved.

US District Judge David Middlebrooks, Order, *Wright v. Board*, April 24, 1970

The record in this case does not sustain this charge [of discrimination] on a facility basis nor on any other basis. There were ample educational reasons to discontinue Lincoln as a high school and to transfer its students to Gainesville High where the student body, as of February 24, 1970, was 2,263 white and 779 Negro.

Judge Griffin Bell, US Circuit Court of Appeals, Fifth Circuit, *Wright v. Board* August 4, 1970

Whether Lincoln High School should have been replaced by the new Eastside High School is still much debated. To Lincoln's advocates (and the advocates of other historically black public schools) the cultural value of Lincoln to Gainesville's African American community outweighs all other considerations. And, as we saw in chapter 11, many blacks see the replacement of Lincoln as racially discriminatory.

For good or ill, the school board's decision to replace Lincoln with a new school under a new name would be judged by developed legal standards, as they stood in the late 1960s. We saw in chapters 6 and 7 that the NAACP Legal Defense Fund; the Health, Education, and Welfare Department; the Civil Rights Commission; and the courts understood desegregation to mean that blacks would go to school with whites. If schools were to be "just schools," neither black nor white, the cultural or community connection of any school to one race or the other was not relevant. In at least one case from this era, black community members (not represented by the NAACP Legal Defense Fund), perhaps echoing the 1935 views of Du Bois, argued the unconstitutionality of "the sociological harm done to the black children when they see every school steeped in black culture either downgraded or destroyed, while schools steeped in white culture flurish [*sic*] and prosper." The district court found educational reasons for closing the contested black schools. The court also stated, "We are commanded by the Appellate Courts to view schools as schools – neither white nor black. That a facility was designed, sited and built to accommodate children living in a black or white area cannot now lend to the bricks and mortar an aura of black or white cultural attractiveness."[1]

Possibly relevant, according to a just-developing legal doctrine, was the concept that neither race should be disproportionately burdened by desegregation. That doctrine could scarcely apply to Eastside; white students to the west of Waldo Road would have to travel farther to Eastside than blacks who lived east of Waldo Road. Even later de jure decisions requiring school boards to retain historically black schools rested on the absence of a factual, educational basis for closing them.[2]

It should not be surprising that when the NAACP Legal Defense Fund finally challenged Lincoln's closing in March 1970, the courts proved unsympathetic. Possibly the Defense Fund recognized the inevitability of a loss when it chose not to challenge Lincoln's closing earlier in *Wright v. Board*.

Despite many objections by African Americans, few closings of black high schools were contested in court. The bench trial over Lincoln's closing provides a window through which we can see the disconnect between the law and community values.

Wright v. Board was now being heard by District Court Judge David L. Middlebrooks. He was appointed to the vacancy created when Judge Carswell moved to the Fifth Circuit Court of Appeals on June 20, 1969. Judge Middlebrooks was nominated by President Nixon on October 6, 1969, and confirmed by the Senate on December 10, 1969. Judge Middlebrooks had been in private practice in Pensacola prior to his appointment, and he returned there after his resignation from the federal bench in 1974.

In its March 9, 1970, objections, the Defense Fund sought a court order reopening Lincoln High for the remainder of the 1969–70 school year.[3] As we have seen, the Defense Fund attorneys and senior black leaders in Gainesville had in December 1969 refused when asked by the school board to delay the February 1 integration of student bodies. Had they agreed to the school board's request, Lincoln would have continued to serve all classes as an academic junior and senior high school through the end of the 1969–70 school year. Now, just a month after the February end of Alachua County's dual system, the Defense Fund wanted to send the Lincoln transfer students at Gainesville High back to Lincoln for the remainder of the 1969–70 school year. Judge Middlebrooks would not have been aware of the December negotiations. But he ruled on March 27, 1970, that making any further revisions to school attendance in Alachua County during the 1969–70 school year would be too disruptive.[4]

In objecting to the elimination of Lincoln High as an academic high school, the NAACP Legal Defense Fund relied on two recent lower-court opinions in which the federal courts had overturned school board closings of formerly black schools.[5]

In one of those cases, which arose in Pittsburg, California, the district judge ruled in August 1969 against closing an otherwise adequate predominantly black elementary school and busing its students to three predominantly white elementary schools. "Where, however, the closing of an apparently suitable negro school and transfer of its pupils back and forth to white schools without similar arrangements for white pupils, is not absolutely or reasonably necessary under the particular circumstances, consideration must be given to the fairly obvious fact that such a plan places the burden of desegregation entirely upon one racial group." The court concluded under *Green* that the school board plan was not, at least at the current stage of the court proceedings, "a good faith, reasonably adequate implementation of the constitutional principles involved."[6]

The other case arose in Oxford, Mississippi. The school board proposed to close the Central High School building, which was serving as a black high school. The district court judge orally ruled in January 1970 without referring specifically to *Green*,

> I think justice in this case requires that this building be used and that it not be terminated. To terminate it, frankly, as

> this Court sees the present situation from this evidence here today, would be only for racial reasons. It would be for the reason that the white people are willing for the colored children to come to the white sections of town to go to white schools but the white people are not willing to let their children go to the colored section. I think that is the reason and we might as well tag it for what it is. But the building is there, it is too good a building, it can [be] made better, which I am sure this board will do. Thus, the court cannot, in good conscience, approve a plan that will permanently close this large plant and force a great number of children into split sessions at Oxford High School. That would adversely affect the upper six grades. The evidence here fails to convince me that it is the sound thing to do. The expert opinion of the board's consultant is that Plan A is superior from an administrative and logistical standpoint, as well for feasibility of building use, and this Court is further convinced that from the entire community's sharing the burden of converting to a unitary system it is the more advisable arrangement to order at this time.[7]

After deciding against any more student transfers during the current school year, Judge Middlebrooks on April 20, 1970, held an evidentiary hearing on the Defense Fund's remaining objections to the Alachua County desegregation plan.

School board attorney Harry Duncan appeared flustered. Duncan was no match for the Defense Fund's Drew S. Days III, the future solicitor general. The only evidence that Duncan offered on behalf of the closing of Lincoln as an academic high school was testimony by Walter Ebling, then chair of the school board, and Tommy Tomlinson, assistant superintendent and the staff member who had prepared the pupil counts and dot maps at each stage of Alachua County's desegregation. The desegregation plan prepared by the Florida School Desegregation Consulting Center in January 1970 for Alachua County to comply with the district court's December 19, 1969, order was also in the court file and apparently recognized by both sides as part of the record.[8]

Ebling testified that Lincoln was chosen by the school board as the site for a centralized vocational program and for a centralized program for middle school students in need of compensatory education. He explained that there were three other possible sites for these programs: Gainesville High and the new east-side and west-side junior/senior high schools then under construction. The two new schools were being built according to basically identical plans. Of the schools, Lincoln was the smallest, and although it had some laboratory rooms, it lacked complete science laboratory facilities that would be desirable for an academic high school. Lincoln, according to Ebling, also lacked the flexible classroom space that was being planned for the two new schools. Ebling added that bringing the Lincoln High labs up to the standards of the other schools would cost $120,000 for three new lab rooms. Duncan asked Ebling why those labs had not originally been installed at Lincoln in 1956, when they had been contemporaneously provided at the new Gainesville High. Ebling replied, "The demand for this type of classroom space did not exist. The students at Lincoln High School are not enrolling in the science classes or the classes that provide mathematical background leading to this type of instruction to the extent they need or have demand for this type of facility."[9]

Days cross-examined Ebling regarding Lincoln. He asked Ebling what the reaction had been of Gainesville's black community to the proposed use of Lincoln as a vocational facility. Without waiting for Duncan to object, Judge Middlebrooks asked Days how this testimony might be pertinent to the Defense Fund's objections to the school board plan.

> MR. DAYS:
>
> I am simply trying to establish that the Board was aware of an objection to the use of Lincoln from the black community.
>
> THE COURT:
>
> Well, did it have to do with an objection insofar as a unitary school system was concerned? If that is the point you are making, proceed. If it isn't, I think it is immaterial.
>
> We are all interested in what people in the communities feel, but unless it has something to do with a unitary school system or the establishment of one, I don't think it would be material.
>
> MR. DAYS:
>
> Well, I think it is material to the extent that although the black community might not speak in terms of unitary school systems, they were objecting to the closing of a very good black academic facility.
>
> THE COURT:
>
> Go ahead and proceed.
>
> . . .

THE WITNESS:

I think the majority of the representatives of the black community who have spoken to me about Lincoln object to its being closed as an academic center.[10]

Days continued his attack. Under cross-examination, Ebling admitted that the planning for both the centralized vocational facility at Lincoln, which would be operated for county high school and adult students by Santa Fe Junior College, and for the middle school compensatory education center were not very far along in April 1970.

Q. Will the children be required to go to the compensatory center at Lincoln, or is it going to be a voluntary basis?

A. It is my understanding it will be on a voluntary basis and the need will be identified and they will be encouraged to take advantage of it. I don't believe there is any plan for making it a requirement.

Q. Do you have any idea what the racial composition of the Lincoln middle school will be?

A. No, sir, I do not.

Q. Has the board made any attempt to determine what it might be?

A. No, sir, the Board hasn't.

Q. If it turned out that the population of Lincoln middle school were all black, will that effect [*sic*] the decision of the Board to maintain a compensatory education center at Lincoln?

A. I cannot answer the question. I can say it wouldn't effect [*sic*] my thinking. I cannot answer for the Board.

Q. Is it your understanding that children who are in a compensatory education program at A. Quin [*sic*] Jones [a historically black elementary school that was the site of a compensatory education program for elementary students, and at which white attendance had declined] will be sent to the Lincoln middle school once they reach a certain grade?

> A. Hopefully not. It is a possibility some of them might be. It would be hoped that those at A. Quin [*sic*] Jones would by that time not be in need of any special attention and would be in the normal classroom setup.[11]

Days's questions attempted to establish that the new Lincoln compensatory and vocational facility was no more than a return to freedom of choice and that blacks but not whites would choose to attend the proposed new facilities at Lincoln.

Judge Middlebrooks added his own questions after Ebling had been questioned by Duncan and Days. He established that the new but unfinished east-side junior/senior high was approximately two miles from the Lincoln campus. And he clarified that the centralized vocational programs at Lincoln were already in operation.[12]

Attorney Days called the final witness on Lincoln's elimination as an academic high school. That witness was Charles Chestnut III. He had participated in the meetings between the black community and school board representatives, including Superintendent Talbot, that ended the November student strike at Lincoln. Through Chestnut, Days introduced a one-page summary prepared by Talbot at that time that stated the reasons Lincoln was being eliminated as an academic high school. Chestnut further testified that at meetings at which school board members had been present, the board members had agreed with the reasons given by Talbot.[13]

In the written summary, Talbot stated that whites would not attend schools that were more than 40 percent black. He based that position on results in Washington, DC; Richmond; Detroit; Chicago; St. Louis; and other cities. Second, he said that the black neighborhood surrounding Lincoln had a high crime rate and that blacks would not assist police. He said whites would not go back into that neighborhood for evening school events and that they had stopped attending Lincoln High football games because of vandalism and rock-throwing incidents. Talbot said the system could not bus in white students to achieve racial balance,[14] that it was unconstitutional to have all-black schools, and that the new schools had been sited to achieve better racial balance. Talbot's summary does not say in so many words that whites would not attend Lincoln High at its existing location, but that fear can certainly be implied.

On one hand, even a well-founded fear of white flight, or of white unwillingness to send children to schools located in black neighborhoods, could not legally be used as the only reason for closing a black school.[15] Similarly, the Civil Rights Act's barring of federal officials and courts from using busing to achieve racial balance did not and could not restrict courts from ordering busing when it was constitutionally required in formerly de

Reasons Why Lincoln High School has been phased out:

1. In the Supreme Court ruling in Washington, D. C. of the People vs. Superintendent Hansen in this court case fifteen years ago, Superintendent Hanson explained to Congress and the other leaders of America that in any school situation where the Negro population became greater than 40%, the white population would migrate from this school community and leave the community Negro. Superintendent Hanson was instructed to integrate 50-50, fifteen years ago. Today, Washington is 95% black as he predicted. We do not find a record in any city in American where the population was greater than 40% Negro that they have integrated a school without the whites moving out. Such cases are: Richmond, Detroit, Chicago, Harlem, St. Louis, and others.

2. Crime rate in Negro community -
Negro is not assisting police, but in many cases, yelling - Brutality.
3. School will be isolated - can't get games now with Lake City, Starke, Santa Fe, P. K. Yonge.
4. Whites will not go back to school at night for activity program.
5. Cannot bus for racial balance.
6. Unconstitutional to have a black school.
7. One new school is abutting Negro property - second new school is in a sparsely developed community.
8. Whites have quit Lincoln High football games. (Broken windows in cars, tires slashed.)

EX. NO. I
Identification

\- 1 -

jure segregated districts.[16] Talbot's statement, however honest and well-intentioned, contained elements from which a court could have inferred bad faith reasons for closing Lincoln.

On the other hand, Talbot's written summary shows the extent to which the school board's commitment to achieving racial balance—and to the school system's survival—trumped any consideration of preserving Lincoln as an academic high school.

Days argued that the school board's programs for using the Lincoln High building were too indefinite. He also argued that the reasons given by Talbot (and, according to Chestnut, by the school board as well) "really involve criteria and considerations that are unconstitutional and have been rejected time and again by every court in this country from the Supreme Court on down. . ."[17]

Duncan might have called the court's attention to the 1967 state survey that had classified Lincoln High in Class C-5 as a senior high school, and the school board's decision to replace Lincoln with a new, integrated academic junior/senior high school located about two miles east of Lincoln and just outside the east-side black residential area.[18] Duncan might have reminded the court of the school board's obligation under the then-current HEW Title VI guidelines[19] and the court's April 25, 1967, order in *Wright v. Board* to site new schools at locations "with the objective of eradicating the vestiges of the dual system."[20] He might also have referred to the January 1970 report of the Florida School Desegregation Consulting Center, which concluded that the new Eastside Junior/Senior High School was located so that it met the criteria for school construction and site selection in *Singleton*. That report also found that that funds from the 1968 bond issue had been committed to construction of the Eastside school, and that "to develop Lincoln to a point where it would approach this new school as a suitable facility for academic training would require the expenditure of a large sum of money which is not included in the bond issue and which is not available from other sources at this time. Both facilities are not needed at this time for academic programs. An educational decision of which facility to use would have to result in selection of the new facility."[21] Duncan did not refer to any of this material.

Judge Middlebrooks told counsel at the end of the hearing:

> I will make this observation to you.
>
> It will be part of the order, any order that comes forth, and that is that the Fifth Circuit Court of Appeals was, in the opinion of this court, very wise in suggesting that in the Orange County case that more emphasis should be placed on site selection. It is going to be a part of the order of this court that in the future School Boards in the Northern District of Florida, specifically the Gainesville, Tallahassee and Marianna divisions, must use a form of site selection which will insure that there will not be any possibility of planned segregation.
>
> It is the opinion of this court that ultimately that the greatest single factor that we can use to eliminate any remaining indication of racial segregation in schools is to make sure in site selection that there is no hint of segregation.[22]

At this hearing, Days had to argue seemingly contradictory positions. To keep Lincoln open as an academic high school instead of allowing it to be replaced by Eastside, Days had to persuade the court that eliminating Lincoln High School unconstitutionally burdened the African Americans who lived in the Lincoln neighborhood. That argument implied that white students, equally sharing the burden of desegregation, would (or could be forced to) attend the academic programs at Lincoln. To defeat the siting of vocational and compensatory education programs at Lincoln and a compensatory education program at A. Quinn Jones, Days had to persuade the court that whites would not attend those programs at those locations. If whites would not attend the latter programs, why would they attend the academic program at Lincoln? As we saw from Judge Middlebrooks's interjection during Ebling's testimony, Days could not argue Lincoln's historical role in the black community, which was the reason the black community wanted to keep it.

Judge Middlebrooks denied the NAACP Legal Defense Fund's objections to the Alachua County plan, as implemented according to the school board's February 9, 1970, report. With respect to the Defense Fund's point that converting Lincoln High to a compensatory and vocational center unfairly burdened black students, Judge Middlebrooks first noted that the Defense Fund's objection did not go so much to the establishment of a unitary school system as to the good faith of the school board. The strength of the objection had to be considered by comparing the desirability of Lincoln High as a vocational center to its continued use as an academic high school. He found that there was a long-term need for vocational training and that the State of Florida had promoted vocational programs. He found that initially, the school board's decision to implement vocational training

> evidences no manifestations of bad faith but rather a good faith effort to promote existing state policy. To accomplish this purpose there had to be selection of a site to conduct classes and to provide training. The testimony given by defendants' witnesses revealed that because two new high schools were nearly completed and would be ready for occupancy in the year 1970–71, and because Lincoln did not have facilities necessary for the study of applied sciences and chemistry, Lincoln should be closed and its students transferred to other schools. However, its function as an educational facility was not negligible and for this reason the board felt Lincoln could be used as a vocational center and center for underachievers. Thus, rather than expend large sums for additions to Lincoln to bring it up to par with more modern academic facilities, the decision was made to close Lincoln as an academic center and to convert it to its present use.

Having heard and considered the extent of this testimony, this Court is of the opinion that the defendants did not possess a bad faith motive when the declaration was made to close Lincoln school. There is a sincere need for skilled craftsmen in today's economy and the school board, as an arm of the State of Florida, recognized this need. For this reason the school board has initiated a vocational program, though limited in scope at present, which will provide those students upon graduation from high school with a special skill so that they may be employed without the benefit of a college education.

As was stated in [*Green v. County School Board of New Kent County*], the role of the district court is to assess the effectiveness of the proposed unitary school system as a whole. Where the plan promises effective, meaningful desegregation and the establishment of a unitary system, this Court perhaps should not consider the wisdom of internal board action which indirectly affects the desirability of certain features of the plan.

Nevertheless, this Court would not lose sight of one of the purposes of a unitary school system, viz., to give the highest quality education to all students in the system. If Lincoln remained open with its inadequate facilities and space, those students there enrolled would not receive the same quality education as those students enrolled in the more modern academic facilities. Therefore, this Court concludes that the Lincoln facility was rightfully closed so that students could be enrolled elsewhere where facilities were improved.

Unlike the closing of a school involved in Quarles v. Oxford Municipal Separate School District, Civ. Action #WC6962-K, (N.D. Miss., Jan. 7, 1970) [cited by the NAACP Legal Defense Fund in its March 9 objections], this Court finds that the defendant school board here was motivated by nondiscriminatory considerations. Further, in Quarles, the closing of that academic facility was particularly repugnant to the Court because that existing facility was to be permanently shut down. But that is not the case here as Lincoln, having been closed as an academic facility, will be effectively utilized as a vocational center.

In short then, when one considers the totality of the evidence presented, it becomes clear that the defendant school board was not moved to act by discriminatory motives but

> rather by genuine intentions to promulgate a flexible, high quality educational system in Alachua County, Florida.[23]

The NAACP Legal Defense Fund appealed. On August 4, 1970, in an opinion by Judge Griffin Bell, the Fifth Circuit affirmed Judge Middlebrooks's decision on Lincoln, briefly stating, "The record in this case does not sustain this charge [of discrimination] on a facility basis nor on any other basis. There were ample educational reasons to discontinue Lincoln as a high school and to transfer its students to Gainesville High where the student body, as of February 24, 1970, was 2,263 white and 779 Negro."[24]

The court of appeals agreed with the Defense Fund that the historically black Duval and Williams Elementary Schools had to be paired with nearby white elementary schools to achieve racial balance. Students would be bused from their neighborhoods for specified grades so that each grade would combine students from Duval and Williams with students from previously white schools. The appeals court allowed the compensatory education programs at A. Quinn Jones and Lincoln to continue subject to district court supervision to assure that all children in need of such training, both white and black, were assigned on a mandatory rather than free-choice basis. The vocational program at Lincoln was allowed to continue for students who chose to attend.[25] The Defense Fund did not seek Supreme Court review of the Fifth Circuit decision.

The courts, responding to *Brown*, proved sufficiently courageous to follow *Brown*'s constitutional principle to its logical conclusion, that formerly de jure dual systems would have to convert to unitary systems. To realize that constitutional principle, the courts were willing to order the end of freedom of choice and the start of cross busing. That series of decisions reignited the controversy over desegregation and had significant political fallout. But the federal courts at every level, with only a few exceptions, balked at enforcing the disproportionate-burden doctrine in school desegregation cases. A limit to judicial intervention had been reached. It was one thing, in theory, for courts to say that the burdens of desegregation should be shared equally by both races. Achieving that goal on the ground, rightly or wrongly, worked against the goals of maximizing the chances for successful integration and preserving the public schools. As the era of de jure desegregation litigation came to a close, courts proved willing to approve plans that, like Alachua County's, established acceptable unitary systems while at the same time minimizing white flight (in other words, limiting the mandatory transfer of white students to predominantly black schools).[26] This choice was faced all over the South and in the North as well.[27]

The Lincoln example is representative of the fate of black high schools. Florida school boards discontinued all but a handful of historically black senior high schools as they ended de jure segregation.[28] Besides *Wright v.*

Board, there is only one other contemporaneous reported case arising in Florida in which the closing of black high schools was litigated. Broward County was ordered to continue operating historically black Dillard High School, as recommended by the Florida School Desegregation Consulting Center, but permitted to discontinue historically black Blanche Ely High School, which was found to have inferior facilities.[29] A different school was later named Blanche Ely High School and continues under that name.[30]

In a few large urban centers in Florida, some historically black high schools emerged from de jure desegregation with black cultural identity and pride intact. One example is Jacksonville's Raines, Lincoln's last football opponent. Opened in 1965 as a segregated black school, Raines was initially desegregated but is now virtually all African American. Raines emphasizes its heritage. Dade County's Miami Northwestern Senior High has operated continuously since 1955 on the same urban Miami site, serving the Liberty City neighborhood, but remains virtually all black despite magnet programs.

In Hillsborough County, two historically black inner-city high schools, Blake and Middleton, were converted to junior high schools in 1971 under the county's desegregation plan. As in the case of Gainesville, many in the Tampa inner-city communities served by Blake and Middleton were never reconciled to the loss of those schools.[31] As part of an updated desegregation plan agreed to by the NAACP Legal Defense Fund, the school board, and other parties, Hillsborough County opened a new school under the historically black Blake High School name in 1997 in a downtown location not far from the old Blake. Later, a new Middleton was opened in 2002 in the same east-side neighborhood as its namesake.[32] Turning aside opposition from the NAACP Legal Defense Fund, the Eleventh Circuit ordered Hillsborough County released from court supervision in 2001, finding that the school district had achieved unitary status.[33]

Hillsborough's experience with the new Blake and Middleton is pertinent to any school district with geographically isolated minority populations. One purpose of the new schools was to serve minority students in their own neighborhoods. However, the Hillsborough County school board is committed to diversity in education and was unwilling to construct new schools to serve only those minority students. Neither school's zone encompasses the entire minority neighborhood in which it is located, and both schools contain magnet programs intended to attract students from throughout the district.[34] Blake has a highly regarded performing arts magnet, and Middleton a STEM magnet program. According to Florida's school rating system, both schools initially were low performing. However, Blake achieved an A rating in 2010 and maintained a B rating until the advent of stricter standards in 2015–16. Middleton achieved a B rating in 2012 and has since received Cs.[35] Blake's ethnically diverse enrollment has remained fairly steady at over sixteen hundred. The Blake neighborhood now has a black and Hispanic population. At Middleton, magnet enrollment has also produced a diverse student body of almost sixteen hundred. The alumni associations of old Blake and Middleton have been active in supporting the new schools and helping their students.

In other areas, historically black high schools remained open but were transformed into desegregated schools. Orange County's Jones High School has continuously operated on its pre-integration site, but in a new building, and with extensive magnet programs. In Pinellas County, black community protests preserved historically black Gibbs High School for a time. When Pinellas County desegregated in 1971, under court-mandated racial balancing the enrollment at Gibbs became 91 percent white.[36] Eventually Gibbs was converted to a magnet high school specializing in the performing arts and business and technology. It is housed in a new facility completed in 2005.[37]

Escambia, Lee, and Leon Counties preserved the names of formerly black high schools at new facilities in different neighborhoods from their namesake schools. Escambia County's Booker T. Washington High School is a professional magnet school at a new campus. Lee County's Dunbar High at Fort Myers is now a STEM and International Baccalaureate magnet. Tallahassee's original Lincoln High School closed in 1970, but a new high school carrying that name opened in 1975.[38]

Judge Middlebrooks on his own motion on May 17, 1971, found that Alachua County's school system had achieved unitary status and dismissed *Wright v. Board*, "reserving in this Court the authority to consider future problems."[39] The NAACP Legal Defense Fund appealed the dismissal but did not contest Middlebrooks's finding of unitary status.[40] The Fifth Circuit then overruled the dismissal to preserve the school board's obligation to file periodic reports.[41] The school board's last report to the court was filed May 10, 1974. On his own motion, US District Judge William Stafford gave notice on June 15, 1977, that he intended to dismiss *Wright v. Board*.[42] Attorney Earl M. Johnson notified the court that some members of the class of plaintiffs believed that the school board was operating its school system in violation of the court's final desegregation order. He stated that they wanted to retain Attorney Stephan Mickle, but that Attorney Mickle needed more time to prepare pleadings.[43] No appearance or pleadings were filed by Attorney Mickle. Judge Stafford again gave notice on July 13, 1978, of his intention to dismiss the case. He received no response. By order dated August 14, 1978, Judge Stafford dismissed *Wright v. Board*.[44]

The end of *Wright v. Board* also ended the legal status of the Alachua County school system as a de jure segregated district. The system was now deemed to have placed its black students in the position they would have been in had there never been de jure segregation. From this point on, any actions by the school board that implicated racial issues would be subject to the much different and still developing constitutional standards applicable to claims of de facto discrimination.

Lincoln's building was initially used for a limited vocational program operated by Santa Fe Junior College. After the county prevailed in a dispute with the junior college over state designation and funding for a regional vocational center, the building functioned as the Lincoln Center for the Human and Mechanical Arts with Russell Ramsey as principal for the school years 1972–73 and 1973–74. That center offered an extensive program of vocational education to which students were bused from their parent schools. According to Ramsey, the center was discontinued when Santa Fe Junior College received funding for a program that offered selected high school students dual course credit at the high school and junior college level for advanced vocational education. Other vocational courses were transferred back to the county high schools.[45] The school board then made the building a middle school under the Lincoln name, which continues to this day.

The evolution of Lincoln's replacement, Eastside High School, will be considered in chapter 16 and in the afterword.

CHAPTER 16
REACTION, REBUILDING

Personally, I resent having to send my children to Williams School just to prove to everyone that my heart is in the right place. Whether my heart is pure or defiled integrationally is nobody's business but mine and God's and I prefer to let personal relationships with individuals remain the testing ground for my compassion toward my neighbor. To use Williams School as the symbol for acceptance or rejection of the black man is simplistic and erroneous. I am surprised at the prejudice, rumor, and hysteria which liberal persons allow themselves when discussing a Christian, Baptist school –prejudice and rumor which they would quickly squelch if talking about an integrated public school.

Sandra J. Davis, October 3, 1970

If you can tell me what I'm supposed to do, I'll listen. [Black parents are also unhappy with the court decision on Duval and Williams] but those parents are not in the NAACP. The NAACP doesn't speak for Gainesville. I have to call New York to find out what they [NAACP] want. . . . Personally, I don't have the guts to walk across that railroad track on Eighth Avenue and I don't see how we can expect our children to do that. I'm not a cheerleader nor am I anti-black one iota. But this is a case of five percent of the population telling 95% of the others what to do. . . . Not a single black student was ever denied the right to transfer to a white school when we had freedom of choice.

William S. Talbot, August 17, 1970

We were upset about the closing of Lincoln, and I guess we thought we could fight our way out. That didn't work,

> and now we're working to make Eastside the best school anywhere.
>
> We've learned to get along, and we all make a real effort to be equal. We are concerned with our school. We want it to be the best.
>
> Two Eastside students to *Gainesville Sun*, June 20, 1971

> With you, life is still warm. You are our tomorrow, our society. You are still very much a part of us, because we love you.
>
> Neil Butler, mayor-commissioner of Gainesville, address to Gainesville High School graduating class, June 15, 1971

An immediate consequence of the violence in the public schools was the founding of five new private schools in Alachua County. Neighboring counties were rural and had less developed public school systems. Only new private schools could serve parents who were unwilling to expose their children to what they feared would be more disorder and a decline in the quality of education.

The Martha Manson Academy was started in Gainesville in September 1969 as a for-profit elementary school. A predecessor had operated for younger children.[1] Among its first teachers was Myra Terwilliger, a former teacher and principal in the Alachua County system, for whom Terwilliger Elementary School is named. The school's founder explained that there was no policy to exclude blacks, but the school imposed a minimum IQ requirement of 100. The initial enrollment was approximately 65,[2] which had grown to 100 by spring 1971.[3] The school was eventually absorbed by Oak Hall Preparatory School as its elementary school department.

Rolling Green Academy began holding classes in Alachua in January 1970. Plans for that school moved forward in response to the Supreme Court's orders for midterm desegregation of student bodies in December 1969 and January 1970.[4] It initially opened with an enrollment of around 100 in kindergarten through eighth grade.[5] In spring 1971 it enrolled 250 students.[6] The school's enrollment dropped after racial tension diminished in the public schools, and the school failed financially in the early 1980s. It had a reputation as a "segregation academy."[7]

Brentwood School opened in 1971 on Gainesville's west side. It currently enrolls about 240 students in prekindergarten through fifth grade.

Heritage Christian School tried to start a junior high in the spring of 1970 following the racial unrest in the county's secondary schools. University Baptist Church operated the school, which already housed a preschool and elementary grades 1–3. In seeking students, that school emphasized discipline and nonsectarian Bible-based Christian teaching.[8]

Recruiters for the school angered Buchholz Principal Jim Temple by soliciting students and parents at the temporary Buchholz campus in June 1970. Temple, who also served as a Baptist minister in nearby Brooker, had preached a sermon on private schools the Sunday before the recruiting incident. He said, "If we affirm the teaching of the Bible, then we cannot confirm or condone any institution that builds walls around people and ministers to the need of a privileged and select group of pupils." The Reverend Carl George, pastor of University Baptist, fired back, "If the people knew about private education they wouldn't put up with the inefficiency of our public schools. It's atrocious." According to George, the main problem with public schools was that they first ask the student what he'd like to learn. "I say that's an abdication of moral leadership. You can't teach people with no calling for moral authority." George accused the public schools of coddling pupils like Little Lord Fauntleroys.[9]

Heritage Christian School's attempt to start a junior high did not succeed in 1970, but the school added three elementary grades for the fall 1970 term.[10] In March 1971 enrollment stood at 260, and the school planned to double in size by the following school year.[11] George later said that the education processes of 75 percent of the children in the public schools had been disrupted because of the midterm desegregation in the 1969–70 school year. He said that the survival of the public schools depended on restoring discipline. George admitted that his school currently enrolled no blacks, but said it had no policy against enrolling black students.[12] Heritage eventually also failed, but Gainesville continues to have a faith-based private school, Cornerstone Academy, which occupies the former Heritage buildings.

Oak Hall Preparatory School in June 1970 announced its opening for the 1970–71 school year in Gainesville. In its first year, Oak Hall would have grades 7–10 and would hold classes in the school building of Highlands Presbyterian Church. The school had 65 students in its first year of operation, but planned for 100 in 1971–72 and for a limit of 200.[13] The planning for Oak Hall had begun in February 1970 by a steering committee of medical doctors and other professionals with school-age children. The first headmaster was Myra Terwilliger's son, Bishop Blackwell. The school was to be nonsectarian and would admit students without regard to religion or race. "We felt that since Gainesville is an educational community and since so many parents are sending their children to private academies out of town and out of state, we should provide at least one such school in our own city," according to one of the founders. The school would offer a college-preparatory program. It would add a grade per year until the full grade 7–12 program was complete.[14] Oak Hall is fully accredited and continues to enroll approximately 800 students in grades pre-K through 12.[15]

As Gainesville grew, so did its Roman Catholic population. A small elementary school at St. Patrick's parish had been founded in 1959. By spring 1971, St. Patrick's enrolled 270 students, 10 of whom were black. The school, then open for twelve years, claimed that it had never discriminated against blacks.[16] The Catholic schools eventually came to include two elementary schools (grades pre-K–8) and a high school (grades 9–12). They included Roman Catholic religious teaching. However, that expansion, which depended on authorization from the Diocese of St. Augustine and local financial support, cannot be traced to the troubles in the public schools in 1970. The Roman Catholic schools in the state had been segregated by race, but the schools in each locality were desegregated at approximately the same time as the neighboring public schools.[17]

In later years, some other small private or faith-based schools were founded that continue in operation today. Much later, some charter schools would complement the existing public school system.

The new private schools were facts on the ground. Many other Southern counties were seeing significant changes in public school demographics as white parents reacted to desegregation by pulling their children out. Advocates of public education raised the alarm in Alachua County. Responding to those concerns, one parent wrote the *Sun*:

> Significantly, the words "Heritage" and "Christian" represent to me the educational goals of Heritage Christian School; and I believe that I'm giving my children something precious by sending them to HCS. Together, HCS and my husband and I can hope to transmit as much of our cultural and religious heritage to our children as possible. I know children who would thrive on such an education; and I'm thankful I live in a country in which I am free to choose this type of education. Those who don't want it are not forced to accept it. Amen.
>
> In choosing HCS we are, thus, automatically rejecting the drug culture which has pervaded the public schools in the form of its life-style: the long hair, the sloppy appearance, the lack of purpose, anarchy, and the drug-oriented music. For this is true that integration gave HCS its birth, but not its conception.
>
> Personally, I resent having to send my children to Williams School just to prove to everyone that my heart is in the right place. Whether my heart is pure or defiled integrationally is nobody's business but mine and God's and I prefer to let personal relationships with individuals remain the testing ground for my compassion toward my neighbor. To use Williams School as the symbol for acceptance

> or rejection of the black man is simplistic and erroneous. I am surprised at the prejudice, rumor, and hysteria which liberal persons allow themselves when discussing a Christian, Baptist school – prejudice and rumor which they would quickly squelch if talking about an integrated public school.
>
> So, I say, let us all quit worrying about the other fellow's school and concentrate on making the one we have chosen the best that it can be; and I predict every parent in Gainesville will be pleased with the education that his children receive in school this year. When was the last time you remember that so many parents showed so much interest in the education of their children? It will surely benefit all of our children if we just let it.
>
> SANDRA J. DAVIS[18]

The Florida House Education Committee held hearings on school issues around the state in early 1971, visiting Gainesville on January 21 and 22. One committee staff member put forth an idea that would much later become state policy, a voucher plan to allow the state to reimburse non-public schools. "The legislature ought to scare you people into action by trying out the voucher plan, because you guys have a lock on the market. A lot of valuable ideas are drowned in bureaucratic decadence." Dr. R. L. Johns of the University of Florida College of Education rebutted: "What you're saying is like telling us to take LSD because it's not as bad as heroin. It is evident that the voucher plan is not working where it has been tried and the only ones who want it are Southern segregationists and Northern Catholic schools."[19]

The Fifth Circuit Court of Appeals on August 4, 1970, had upheld the school board's decision to close Lincoln High School. However, the decision also ordered the school board to pair historically black Duval and Williams Elementary Schools with white schools to achieve a better racial balance. In addition, the court ordered the appointment of a Bi-racial Committee to "serve in an advisory capacity to the school board in the area of the promulgation and maintenance of zone lines, in pairing problems, and in school site location as well as in such other areas as may appear appropriate from time to time."[20] The school board promptly moved to appoint the Bi-racial Committee. The five white nominees were recommended by Talbot and the five black nominees by the NAACP.[21]

The Fifth Circuit's order to pair Duval and Williams with white schools brought Talbot to the end of his patience. On August 6, he commented that busing to achieve desegregation of Duval and Williams would inconvenience not only white students but also black students. He also pointed out that five years previously, the pupil ratio in the east Gainesville neighborhoods was two white pupils for each black pupil. In 1970, the ratio was 50/50. "I'm not a sociologist to say this is good or bad, but the east side of our city is turning black because that's where all the low cost housing projects have been built." The schools could not bring about desegregation within the traditional neighborhood school pattern as long as city neighborhoods became even more segregated.[22]

Now it was the turn of white parents to protest. White parents on Gainesville's east side greeted the Fifth Circuit decision with a pledge to boycott Duval and Williams if pairing with white schools were implemented. A standing-room-only crowd of four hundred parents (estimated to have two thousand school-age children) met in the "sticky hot" cafeteria at Howard Bishop Junior High on August 17, 1970. Advocates of the east-side boycott focused their discontent on the mostly white schools on the west side and argued that the assumed racial balance of 70 percent white to 30 percent black should be achieved by busing throughout Alachua County.

Talbot (who himself lived in a modest home on the east side) spoke to the protest meeting. "If you can tell me what I'm supposed to do, I'll listen." He told the white parents that black parents were also unhappy with the order, "But those parents are not in the NAACP. The NAACP doesn't speak for Gainesville. I have to call New York to find out what they (NAACP) want. . . . Personally, I don't have the guts to walk across that railroad track on Eighth Avenue and I don't see how we can expect our children to do that." His remarks were drawing loud cheers. "I'm not a cheerleader nor am I anti-black one iota. But this is a case of five percent of the population telling 95% of the others what to do. . . . Not a single black student was ever denied the right to transfer to a white school when we had freedom of choice." Talbot's reference to freedom of choice drew more cheers. A lawyer engaged by the protesting parents advised them to send their children to private schools.[23]

Before the school board could approve any new school assignment plan, the Bi-racial Committee would have to review it. The committee's first meeting was on August 20. Charles Chestnut III was elected chair. The committee was unable to agree on a specific plan for Duval and Williams. However, on the motion of the Reverend Thomas A. Wright, the committee's first action was to recommend unanimously to the school board "that the racial ratio 70/30 in county be made the ratio in all county schools – as nearly as possible before school year 1970–71." The committee recommended that zoning, busing, pairing, and clustering, together with the use of middle schools, should be used to achieve the county-wide racial balance.[24]

Despite an opening-day ratio on September 14, 1970, of 68 percent white to 32 percent black students across the county, A. L. Mebane Middle School, Alachua Elementary, Archer Elementary, and Eastside Junior/

Senior High opened with black majorities.[25] The Bi-racial Committee's August vote set the stage for years of racial balancing efforts, which would not end until a 2003 redistricting returned the county to neighborhood schools and significant resegregation. Racial balancing is discussed further in chapter 17 and the afterword.

With the opening of the 1970–71 school year just days away, the school board had to act on Duval and Williams. At its August 24 meeting, the school board approved a plan, proposed by school board member Enneking, according to which Duval and Williams would each become part of a separate cluster of three schools, two of which had been predominantly white. That cluster concept would result in an initial student population that according to board statistics would be 70 percent white and 30 percent black. Two schools in each cluster would house grades K–4 and the remaining school (Duval or Williams) would have grades 5 and 6. Instead of using three east-side schools as part of these clusters, as the Florida School Desegregation Consulting Center had recommended,[26] Duval under the Enneking plan was clustered with two east-side elementary schools, and Williams was clustered with two west-side schools. The plan affected a total of twenty-five hundred students and sixty teachers.

The Bi-racial Committee's position that schools should be balanced countywide to 70/30 ratios for 1970–71 was rejected by the board. That decision angered citizens from Archer and the High Springs/Alachua areas, who claimed that their local elementary schools had become 80 percent black. The school board agreed in principle to seek a 70/30 ratio across the county for the 1971–72 school year.[27] The next day, the Bi-racial Committee endorsed that decision.[28]

Under the board's plan for 1970–71, the more prosperous, better-educated west side was being asked to help solve the racial imbalance problem. When the school board's plan was announced, a group of west-side parents protested. They charged that fifth- and sixth-grade students at Williams would be exposed to drugs, because that campus adjoined the Lincoln vocational school site. Those parents threatened to start another private school. Talbot answered that Williams had been operating for fifty years and no drug problems had been reported there. Talbot added that he would seek federal funds to provide playground security through mother ombudsmen. Talbot stood up for the school board's plan: "If I went on the radio this afternoon and said what's been argued here, tomorrow I'd have parents from the other end of town saying the opposite."[29] Despite the protests, the school board did not modify the plan, which was filed with the court on August 26.[30]

The faculty at Williams now had to reassure the vocal west-side parents that their fifth and sixth graders would be safe and well taught. Hundreds of west-side parents turned out for a meeting of the Williams PTA on

September 2. They were welcomed by the Reverend William E. Ferguson. "We in this community stand ready to help you. Leave your fears and worries behind." The teachers were introduced by black Principal Cornelius Norton (a new elementary school on the west side was named for Norton in 1992). The fifth- and sixth-grade teachers from west-side Littlewood and Terwilliger Elementary Schools had moved to Williams as part of the desegregation plan, joining the teachers of those grades who had previously taught there. Members of the county staff and board member Enneking also spoke to the parents. Two-thirds of the 760 fifth- and sixth-grade students would be bused from the west side.[31]

To move the students to the six clustered schools would require thirty buses and cost $75,000, which was not in the county budget. At least one adult monitor would ride each bus and remain at the destination school during the day to assist as a paraprofessional.[32] The order for new buses would not be filled until February. In the meantime, both white and black parents protested the children's long walks to the pickup points. The parents laid at the feet of the school board the failure of the county and city to construct sidewalks on busy east-side roads that the school children had to walk. Talbot offered to renew the school board's request for sidewalks if the protesters would accompany him to city hall and the courthouse. "I'll help you all I can, but you'll have to make the same noise in front of those people as you made here."[33]

The school district obtained $30,000 in federal funds to hire paraprofessionals for the Duval and Williams busing program. Those funds were available to assist districts dealing with cross busing. The bus monitors worked well. A student journalist working for the *Sun* accompanied two white paraprofessionals on their ride from Metcalfe, an east-side elementary school, to Duval with a busload of fifth and sixth graders. Both were parents, one a nurse and one a teacher's aide. They had firm charge of their bus. Students sat in assigned seats, enabling quick attendance taking and identification of troublemakers. Before the busing started, all of the students at Metcalfe walked to school. Most had never ridden a school bus before. The paraprofessionals eased the transition. At Duval, the nurse ran the school clinic, and the teacher's aide worked with one of the school's teacher teams. The school had four teams of four teachers each, and one paraprofessional worked with each team. The sixth paraprofessional served music and physical education classes. At the end of the school day, the two paraprofessionals from the Metcalfe neighborhood rode the school bus home with their pupils. The black children who were bused from Duval and Williams to white schools had black paraprofessionals riding the buses and helping out at the white schools during the school day.[34]

Despite this support, fewer whites than expected showed up at the clustered schools. Opening attendance was down at Littlewood and

Terwilliger, the two west-side schools that had been clustered with historically black Williams Elementary.[35] By the midpoint of the school year, white attendance had also decreased at Stephen Foster and Metcalfe, the two white east-side schools paired with Duval.[36]

The clustering of formerly white schools with Duval and Williams worked better than expected. One of the white fifth graders bused to Duval in 1970 was Joel Achenbach. He went on to Princeton and a career as a science writer for the *Washington Post*. He wrote affectionately of his first year at Duval for the *Post* in 2007:

> It was, in retrospect, an ambitious social experiment. It was also clumsy, and at some level outrageous, reducing all of us to a single characteristic of white or black.
>
> Yes, I found it rather awkward going to Duval, but only because I found it rather awkward being alive, being 9 years old, being kind of brainy and very skinny and self-conscious about our family being poor (although probably not as poor as most of the kids who walked to Duval from the neighborhood). I was 57 pounds of insecurity.
>
> And those girl creatures: transfixing, terrifying.
>
> But racial tension? None. I'm not suggesting that we were ultra-enlightened, that we were little angels of egalitarianism. Just that race didn't matter as much as other things. My Mom's second marriage broke up: That mattered.[37]

Assistant Superintendent Tomlinson believed the Duval and Williams clusters were successful. First, they ended all-black schools deep in black neighborhoods. Second, more children benefited from the education that the clusters provided. The clusters also brought the affected communities together for the first time. "The schools have borne the brunt of integration so far. But we can't do it all. I think the community at large can learn a lot from the experience of their schools."[38]

Duval Principal M. L. Jackson, speaking in May 1971, was very positive about the past year at Duval. He was also one of the few black Alachua County school officials who openly praised desegregation at the time. Duval had settled at a ratio of 60 percent white to 40 percent black.

"Whites not accustomed to the black community were a little apprehensive. It turned out to be a fabrication. No truth that whites can't walk through the black community. The problem is adjusting to learning the other culture. As a teacher I see getting the two cultures together important for understanding each other." And: "'We've had a marvelous year. Parents and children adjusted to the change well. I wouldn't ask for any more cooperation. Most of the black teachers appear to me to be satisfied with integration. Some prefer it the other way.' Blacks, he says, asked for integration, but then 'decided they didn't want it as given.' He explains, 'Some demonstrative, not necessarily aggressive, groups would like separate schools in order to emphasize black culture more and enlarge blackness in the minds of people.'"

Jackson believed that recognition of black culture could be accomplished through a revised social studies curriculum for integrated classes. Under Jackson, Duval used audio-visual aids and guest speakers. Jackson, then sixty-five, retired at the end of the 1970–71 school year.[39]

Also in response to the Fifth Circuit's August 4 decision, the compensatory reading program at A. Quinn Jones school was terminated.[40] The black students in that program were reassigned by place of residence to the schools they would have attended. The school board was unwilling to assign students to the program on a mandatory basis to achieve desegregation, as the court of appeals had ordered.[41] The Rev. Wright argued unsuccessfully to the school board's Bi-racial Committee that the program should be continued in a newer building that could also house a similar program for gifted students, to achieve better racial balance.[42] The Bi-racial Committee agreed that the program as it existed should not be continued but was unable to agree on a definitive recommendation for continuing the program.[43]

This program's fate exemplifies the best intentions of school administrators colliding with the conflicting objectives of desegregation. The program at Jones was designed to bring together in one place students in need of better reading skills. In 1968–1969, the county had thirty-six hundred students in many locations being helped by a federal program for reading problems, established under the Elementary and Secondary Education Act, P.L. 89–10, enacted April 1, 1965. The program was limited to students from low-income families with reading deficits. It benefited poor, mostly black students. New federal guidelines adopted in 1969 required greater selectivity in bringing students into the program and more intense efforts with what would be a smaller number of students. Talbot estimated that the number of students in the county program would be cut in 1969–70 to two thousand students. John Dukes, then principal at Lincoln, said that the program had been "of tremendous help."[44]

The county had decided in July 1969 to use part of its P.L. 89–10 funds to install a special focused reading program for both white and black students at A. Quinn Jones. This program in some ways appeared to assist desegregation, because the mainstream students then at all-black Jones would be reassigned to other nearby white schools. The program was funded initially with $150,000 from the 89–10 grant. The student-adult ratio would be 15:1, through the use of specialists and aides in addition to teachers. The facility included a media production center, which would provide teacher-improvement materials, including videos of actual classroom instruction. The school board had also appropriated $12,000 specifically directed to a medical clinic at the Jones center. The health services were to include speech and hearing therapy, pediatric services, pediatric psychiatry, vision care, and emergency care and remediation. Immunization serum and medication for skin and intestinal parasites were to be provided to the clinic at no cost by the county health department.[45] Counselors were to recruit around three hundred pupils from the area around Sidney Lanier, Jones, Duval, and Williams Elementary Schools. Many of Gainesville's poorer students were concentrated in those schools, but three of the four schools were all black. The assistant superintendent for instruction said, "We are most emphatically trying to integrate [Jones] as much as possible." The program would be an "advanced Head Start," with free breakfasts and lunches for the children. Today Jones might be called a "magnet" school. From the beginning, the NAACP criticized the program as a scheme to keep black students in the "ghetto" school.[46]

White students eligible for the program chose not to attend at the Jones site. Judge Middlebrooks determined that the program's resulting all-black enrollment was not because of any action by the school board. He pointed out that during segregation, the quality of teaching in black schools had been inferior. The resulting lag in black students' learning was what created the need for unitary school systems.

> It seems that plaintiffs [represented by the NAACP Legal Defense Fund] have taken an inconsistent position when they would deny these underachievers an opportunity to improve their reading skills and be brought up to the normal learning level of children in their own age group. Certainly, there are underachievers in the negro community and they should have every benefit for improvement that is open to them. Thus, initially, the wisdom of this program is unassailable.[47]

Board member Enneking commented, "Race should not be a factor in compensatory education, even if it means an all-black school."[48] But at that time the failure of the program to attract white students spelled its end.

The school board, which had requested a rehearing by the Fifth Circuit of its August 4, 1970, decision on Duval, Williams, and the Jones and Lincoln centers, decided on August 26 to drop its efforts to obtain further review of that decision.[49] The Fifth Circuit denied the school board's request for a rehearing on September 3.[50] "I think we're talking about pie in the sky anyway. We've been beating our heads against a stone wall. I move that we close the case and be done with it," said board member Dale Smith.[51]

In the midst of these controversies, elections were under way for three seats on the school board. There were six candidates for the three seats. Five of the six candidates responded to questions from the League of Women Voters. When asked if they agreed with the school board's current system of desegregation, all five said no.[52] The elections resulted in the defeat of eight-year veteran board member T. E. Simmons of Archer by a narrow margin. Had he been reelected, he would have been the only board member from outside Gainesville. Simmons was replaced by Eugene Todd, a professor of education at the University of Florida and a vocal critic of the current school administration. E. D. Manning Jr., the former superintendent, defeated the Reverend William E. Ferguson, a black, by seventy-nine votes. Todd and Ferguson had been endorsed by the *Sun*. The remaining seat was claimed uncontested by Robert Howe, a businessman who had been chair of the chamber of commerce education committee and president of the Alachua County Council of Parent and Teacher Organizations.[53] In November, voters approved changing the selection of the superintendent from elected to appointed, 10,846 for and 7,000 against.[54] Democrat Reuben Askew defeated Claude Kirk for governor.

Assessing the midterm 1970 desegregation and its aftermath, everyone hoped that the lessons learned would bring peace to the secondary schools in the new school year. There had been violence in spring 1970, but there had also been much work by students, parents, and teachers on its underlying causes.

During the 1970–71 school year, Eastside and Buchholz Junior/Senior High Schools would move to their new campuses, constructed with funds from the 1968 bond issue. Both schools were air-conditioned, among the first air-conditioned schools in the county.[55]

At its opening on its new campus, Eastside included only grades 7–10. Principal John Dukes Jr. set himself a high bar. His unofficial motto at Lincoln High was "A school where teachers who want to teach can teach and students who want to learn can learn." Dukes carried that motto with him to Eastside. "And if we can't get the job done here then we deserve to be put on a boat and pushed out to shore."[56] Dukes was proud that Eastside was the only secondary school in the system that did not have a major disturbance during these years. According to John Dukes III, his son, Eastside avoided disturbances because of Dukes's plan, which included every employee at the school, from the coaches and assistant principals through the custodial staff.[57] A white student liked Eastside because there was a good school spirit, students could work individually, and Dukes laid down the rules so everyone knew what they were.[58]

Tiny Talbot had chosen Hebron Self to be one of the five white members of the initial Bi-racial Committee. The school board and the court approved that choice. Self's family became part of the Eastside community when the school opened. Hebron Self's father, a blacksmith and welder from Tennessee, in 1947 bought twenty acres of what was then rural land on Kincaid Road southeast of Gainesville, and Hebron grew up there. Hebe, as he was called, played basketball for Tiny Talbot when Tiny was Gainesville High's coach. Hebe would have graduated with the class of 1949, but he flunked a course and stopped attending school.

Hebe married his high school sweetheart, Hazel Tillis. Hazel's parents taught their children to be respectful of black people; the family lived near black neighbors and had friendly contact with them. Hazel remembers bringing her teachers violets or jasmine from her yard. Her father or an uncle drove the school bus serving that area. Hebe and Hazel met while singing in the junior choir at First Baptist Church. Hazel graduated from GHS in 1949. For the last time, at graduation, the girls wore formal gowns and carried a dozen roses; later classes would wear caps and gowns.

Like so many other GHS dropouts, after serving in the army for three years, Hebe in 1958 was granted his high school diploma by Talbot on the basis of army training courses that he had completed. Hebe became an attendance (truant) officer for the Alachua County Sheriff's Department and later for the school board. According to Hazel, Hebe's critical skill was his ability to express himself without making anybody mad. Hebe and Hazel lived on the Self family property and raised four children. As desegregation proceeded, many other white families moved to the west side, but they kept their property on Kincaid Road. The family still owns it.

In its early years, for some, Eastside High School was a model of what an integrated high school could be. Hebron Self was active in the parents' group at Eastside that selected the school colors, mascot, and other symbols. In 1973, Hebe and Hazel's daughter Donna would be in the first graduating class at Eastside. She was band president. Their other two younger children would follow in Donna's footsteps at Eastside. Today, Donna says she still bleeds orange and green, the Eastside colors. Dana Self, who graduated in 1978, played flute. Dana and Gertrude Jones's daughter Angela often practiced together at one another's homes. Dana recalls that at proms, both white and black bands performed, and there were no problems. By then, she says, Eastside classes were about half black and half white. Both Donna and Dana praise their teachers, some of whom began their careers at Lincoln. Hazel says her children never went anywhere without their black friends. Eastside held a fish fry every year as a fundraiser. Hebe and some friends would go to Suwannee, on the Gulf coast, to catch the mullet for the fish fry. John Dukes, the acknowledged master, cooked the hush puppies. Hazel concurs with those who say that under Dukes, Eastside had less trouble than Gainesville High or Buchholz.[59]

The new building for Buchholz Junior/Senior High opened in December 1970 on the northwest side, also with grades 7–10. This otherwise welcome event brought forth more parent protests. Because the county lacked enough buses to serve the new campus, given all of its other transportation commitments, Buchholz and Westwood Junior High would initially operate on a 7:00 a.m. to 1:00 p.m. schedule. The school board heard the protests but approved the new bell schedules for both schools.[60] Buchholz's white principal, Jim Temple, would continue at the new site, and Lincoln's former head football coach, Jessie Heard, became that school's head football coach.

John Dukes had become close to Jessie Heard while the two served at Lincoln and wanted Heard to be his coach at Eastside. Talbot insisted, however, that at each of the two new high schools, a white and a black would occupy what were the two most important positions. In addition to the obvious purpose of installing recognized leaders of both races, those assignments were intended to prevent any high school from attracting disproportionate numbers of black students, as Lincoln had in the past.[61] If Gainesville's black students gravitated to either of the new schools, the desired racial balance at those schools would be adversely affected. Eastside's head football coach would be Rabbit Smith, a graduate of Palatka High School who later played football for the University of Georgia and the Chicago Cardinals. At Georgia, his playing weight was 155 pounds. Before he came to Eastside, Rabbit was the running backs coach and chief recruiter for the University of Florida's football Gators. He was initially assisted by Kim Helton, who had volunteered at the school in its first semester of operation and then interned there just before his hiring. Both white coaches would play a role in maintaining discipline at the school.[62]

Meanwhile, Gainesville High continued to house grades 10–12. Grade 10 at GHS now included only students from the Gainesville High School zone as defined in the system's desegregation plan. Enrollment declined from thirty-two hundred to twenty-six hundred. But under that plan, to avoid transferring high school students twice, and to allow stability in sports and extracurricular programs, all black and white students from the Gainesville secondary school district in grades 11 and 12 remained at Gainesville High. This policy kept the Lincoln transfer students who were in grades 10 and 11 in February 1970 at GHS, now in grades 11 and 12. The school remained on double sessions. John Neller and a beefed-up staff took over at GHS.

The *Sun*'s Cormier characterized the small, forty-year-old Neller as someone who might lead the choir or teach English literature. But Neller, like seemingly all of the other male leaders, had played high school football. Neller joked that at P. K. Yonge, teammate Doug Dickey was his backup quarterback. Dickey had just taken over as head coach of the University of Florida's Gators. Neller had also served as GHS head basketball coach.[63]

Neller graduated from the University of Florida in 1953, served briefly in the air force, and then returned to the University for his master's degree. He recalls interviewing at Santa Fe High School for a teaching job, plus head basketball and assistant football coach. The principal, L. B. Lindsey, was unimpressed. Neller's professors pleaded his case with Lindsey behind the scenes. Neller got the job. He says Lindsey thought coaches needed to be six feet five to deal with his country boys. After Neller decided to leave Santa Fe for Gainesville High, one day Lindsey accosted Neller: "Come in here. Sit in this chair." Neller sat, expecting a dressing-down. Lindsey said, "I want you to come back and be principal of this school." Neller replied, "We've come a long way from when you wouldn't even let me see the gym!"[64] LaRue Boyd played basketball at GHS under Neller and later at Florida under the emotional Norm Sloan. Boyd said Neller was loved by his players for his ability to motivate by inspiring, not bullying. Neller had an inextinguishable knack for getting people on his side. His gentle but tenacious engagement with people would gain the school a much-improved experience in the 1970–71 school year.

Cormier wrote that the Lincoln transfer students in February 1970 found themselves in a college-oriented, high-achieving Gainesville High. "Except for the athletic teams, it was a tough company for Lincoln's blacks to crack, so tough they didn't even bother. In effect there were two schools on the NW 13th Street campus, one black, one white." Expectations for student self-control were also new to some transfer students.

Neller, stating his goals:

> We need to prepare our students for life skills. We shouldn't simply be teaching someone for a grade, but to improve his weaknesses. The society of GHS has changed. Today we have to consider the behavioral expectations of the students. If education has no meaning or purpose then it becomes irrelevant.

The dress code was relaxed. Photo ID cards were issued to students, the better to keep out nonstudents. Students were warned, "Those students, who by their actions, are not mature enough to continue as productive members will be denied the privilege of being members." During troubles, students would not be prevented physically from leaving their classrooms, but once outside they would be subject to arrest or expulsion. Still missing would be social activities such as pep rallies and dances (except for the traditional junior-senior prom and senior dance).

Instead of homeroom, each teacher would be assigned twenty students to befriend and counsel. The student senate would have an equal number of elected black and white members. The only black student body officer said that she did not think discussion groups begun in the prior year to unify the school would be needed. "They're too much trouble, and they're boring." The incoming student officers all hoped for more enforcement of school rules. "We lacked all kinds of enforcement last year. That's why everything got so lax."

Neller would have a staff of seven deans, three for each of the double sessions, with a head dean serving an overlapping shift. They would be "walking deans," patrolling between periods. There would be four assistant principals and a coordinator of student affairs. The ombudsmen continued their work. The *Sun*'s feature on GHS was bordered by a display ad for Oak Hall School.[65]

The *Sun*, cheering from the sidelines, enthused,

> . . . the main point is that the Alachua County school system is ridding itself of racial hangups and is melding together superior management, superior physical plants, and superior teachers to produce superior students prepared to meet life as it really is.
>
> We believe the next nine months will provide a profound and rewarding educational experience for Alachua County's 23,000 school students. This is because the School Board, Supt. Talbot and the 1,000 teachers have prepared well.[66]

Talbot personally recruited the late Wayne Floyd to be head dean under Principal Neller. Floyd had been a football coach at P. K. Yonge for a while, but at the time he was head football coach at Walker High School in Jasper, Alabama. The deal was made in Talbot's living room with Neller also present. Floyd saw the job at GHS as a step up, and he had a wife and two children. He accepted the job despite knowing it was a bad situation, but he says he knew he had good people to work with. Floyd remembers that Neller, like Talbot, had a smooth, easy way and never got excited. "I wanted to be like them when I grew up." According to Floyd, whenever there was trouble, Tomlinson and Talbot were right there. Talbot was at GHS so often that Floyd would ask Talbot to show his hall pass.

Floyd grew up on a farm near Dozier, Alabama. His father also had a general store in town. Black families lived and worked on the farm. "We were always fair and honest with them." Their children and Floyd were playmates. Floyd plowed a mule until he graduated from high school in 1951, "and I'm not sorry about it one bit. But I did want to get out from behind that mule." He won a football scholarship to Auburn but lost it when he was injured. He entered the military and eventually graduated from Troy State. Of desegregation, Floyd says, "It was something that had to be done. We had to do the best we could to get through it." He claims no special training for his dean's job.

> Being born and raised up in south Alabama, we had a lot of blacks up there, and yes, I've dealt with them all of my life. What you do and what you don't do, you just got to use your head, you had to do what you think is right and try to do the good thing. We didn't try to persecute any students, we just tried to take care of the problems. . . . My answer was dealing with students openly and letting them know where you stood, and they would let you know. And I dealt with a lot of black parents up there, and we would call them in if we were having a lot of problems with certain students, and they were always ready, willing to help. I had grandmothers in my office that had more, whoo, they were just super. They wanted to control the kids, too, and they did.

Floyd and his deans were first responders, covering the halls and bathrooms between classes and putting themselves in harm's way to break up disturbances. Floyd remembers that one morning some black students belonging to separate gangs started fighting when leaving the school buses. "Belt buckles, everything." All of the deans and some of the teachers circled around the fighters, keeping the disturbance contained. A couple of people from the county office came out, and someone called the police. The deans pulled out the students who started the fight and got them into the deans' offices. When the next morning buses arrived, all of the deans were at the bus stop, keeping order. GHS was not closed.[67]

As it turned out, actual system enrollment for the 1970–71 school year would be under 22,000. But because P. K. Yonge, the University laboratory school, no longer counted, its 1,000 students had to be subtracted. On that basis, the count approximated the projection made in the January 1966 update of the state facility survey for the county. That update had been prepared to test the need for the 1966 failed bond issue. In that survey, total enrollment for the 1970–71 year was projected to be 23,362. The survey had recommended that the system be designed for 24,603 students to allow for future growth.[68]

At this time, the Lincoln campus held some vocational courses offered by Santa Fe Junior College, but its future use was up in the air because of the dispute between the county school system and the junior college as to which organization would hold the state designation (and funding) for the area vocational center.

School board member Enneking wanted Lincoln to reopen under freedom of choice as a complete high school with football team, band, and both academic and vocational programs.[69] The school board never supported that plan. Enneking's proposal framed the issue, however: If the black community wanted the school board to keep the community's black high school, and if whites chose not to attend, what business was it of the courts to stop it? Under all of the precedent cases of the time, it was unconstitutional for the school board, which had previously maintained a de jure school system, to set up a school that everyone knew would become all black. Separate could never be equal. Long after *Brown*, the cause of optional public schools established to serve the needs of black students continues to be argued. Today, outside the context of de jure segregation, there do not appear to be constitutional barriers.[70]

Five more criminal prosecutions that lingered from the prior spring were dismissed by the state attorney.[71] The readmission of a GHS student after dismissal of charges against him had triggered the March 26 violence at GHS.

Neller quickly insisted that the judicial system hold violent students to account. Student Carl James assaulted two male teachers and a coach on September 30, 1970, in an incident that started when James, in a hall, was asked to produce a hall pass. The coach, Brady Greathouse, received a cut that required eight stitches. Neller took the teachers to the county judge's office, and they signed affidavits that led to James's arrest. Neller says he wanted to dispel any impression that the school was not going to prosecute assaults on teachers. James was expelled.[72] An Eastside student, who had been expelled in the prior year but allowed to return, was also expelled for refusing to leave a room and committing physical violence against a dean.[73] James pleaded guilty in January 1971 to the assault on Greathouse in return for the dropping of two other charges.[74]

GHS Principal Neller said that his school had not received the funds necessary to cope with the 1970 integration of the school. He added that the campus, which was still unfenced, was very hard to control. Solutions such as more vocational courses, on-campus isolation classes, individualized instruction for nonreaders and others with severe academic deficits, better teaching materials, and more time for teachers to prepare imaginative lessons were discussed but depended on additional funds.[75]

Neller acknowledges that the closing of Lincoln High the year before was traumatic for both the black and white communities. Neller is the most self-effacing of persons. But he says firmly that his year as GHS principal was "the crucial year to make sure it worked." He also firmly believes that he was the best person "for that job at that time in that situation." He had the support of the faculty. Like so many of Talbot's protégées, Neller had spent almost his entire career in the Alachua County system. He personally knew many in the community. Despite his exit after one year in the job, this author found no source that did not praise him. Neller confesses that when he took over, he had no precedent or master plan to move the school toward safe and effective learning. Some lessons he had learned from Talbot, one of which was not to make snap decisions. But as issues arose, Neller believed that it was his duty as principal to resolve them personally. Neller early on decided that he had to maintain cordial relations with each of the many factions at the school. He says that many whites "really blasted me for that."

Neller says that the second day he was principal, a white parent called Neller, threatening "to shoot me some blacks." Neller appreciated that this family was capable of acting on that threat. He asked them to let him look into the issue. When he had time, he went to their home and asked about the problem. It turned out that there was at least a possibility of Peeping Tom activity in the girls' gym classes. Neller took action to correct the problem. He later thanked the parent, first, for bringing the issue to his attention, and second, for not bringing his gun to GHS. Neller encouraged the parent to call Neller any time he had a problem.

The first week of class, there was a dispute among the cheerleaders.

> I had never been trained for a lot of this, either. . . . So, I had a meeting with them in the cafeteria. And I didn't know how deep the problem was, I didn't know exactly the extent of it, people hadn't told me. But it was interpersonal relationships. And oh my me, we were sitting there and I didn't know, what am I going to do? And I said, everybody look outside. What do you see? And there was silence. I said, well, let me help you. I see a metal post over here. And pretty soon, they said they saw all the other things, objects. I said, now look inside this cafeteria. What do you see? I said, you see human beings, people. I said, I'm not going to tell you how to act, or anything. But I can say this to you: you have got, for this school, you all have got to get along. That doesn't mean you don't dislike somebody, this or that, but as a group you all have got to have a good working relationship. And that's the last time I had to meet with them. They understood what I was saying, you know, that you don't have to be the best of friends with this one or that one or whatever it is, but as a group, because you all are in a position where people see you, and it affects the entire community . . .

Later, some black GHS students wanted to participate in a demonstration by University of Florida students that was to take place at the University during class time. Desegregating the University had been slow, and many black students, once there, were angry at their treatment. According to Neller, it would not have been possible to stop the GHS students from leaving school. But he says he had to force his deans to allow the students to leave their classes. Beforehand, Neller obtained the agreement of the students to leave campus in an orderly manner. When the time for the march came, they posted a student at each of the three wings of the school to make sure that the group remained peaceful. Neller says he was proud of the students for keeping their word.

On another occasion, some black students wanted to have a teach-in on the football practice field during class time. Neller refused, in keeping with policy that there would not be student-led assemblies during school time. Neller had been at the school since five that morning, and the discussion of this issue wasn't over until ten that night. As he was leaving his office, he encountered Cleve Kendall, the custodian. Kendall said, "Boss, I wanna let you know everyone's still for you." "And that just did a whole lot to help me, you know, because I was just adamant that we weren't going to do what they wanted to do."

Early one winter morning, while it was still dark, there was a disturbance in the library. Neller went to investigate. Bob Acosta, an assistant football coach, was coming up the walk with a black male. Acosta said, "Mr. Neller, you need to step to the side." "And I said, 'Why, Bob?' This guy had a glove on his hand. [Acosta] said, 'He's got a pistol in there.' So what Bob said to me was, 'You get behind me.' And I said, 'No, Bob, I'm not going to do that. We're going to walk together.'" The black male had entered the library in a dispute over a girl. He was not a student.

Mary Lewis, a 1948 graduate of Lincoln and a graduate of Florida A&M in physical education, was teaching PE at Santa Fe High School when Superintendent Talbot recommended her to be dean of girls at Gainesville High. L. B. Lindsey, no doubt annoyed at being manager of the farm team for GHS, told Lewis that if he had his way, she would not be leaving Santa Fe. Lewis, tall and athletic, had her classes under control. "I didn't send students to the office. For little things or for anything." She began at GHS in the fall of 1970, under Neller.

She describes her work at GHS:

> When you got to GHS, on the right side there was a podium and they would be talking, saying we're not going to do this, we're not going to take that. So the deans were trying to keep everyone inside, and they were going on about not being treated fairly. These were blacks. So I asked them, what is the problem? They said some of the teachers don't act right. I said what do you mean, they don't act right? They said they don't want us in their class. I said, now wait a minute, I can't go along with you on this. You say white teachers don't want you in their class. I have walked around here and every teacher I saw was teaching the class. Now it's up to you to

> receive what they're giving. Don't put it on the teacher, put it on yourself. Now I saw some of you blacks back in the back all together. And I said I see you all in the back and the whites are sitting in the front. And they said that's the way the teacher has us. And I said I don't believe the teacher told all of the whites to sit in the front and all of the blacks to sit in the back. I said I'll never believe that. They said you don't come in the classroom. And I said I don't have to come in the classroom. I see you through the window and you are sitting back there talking. I said the teacher is trying to teach the people who want to learn, who want to receive something, and you are saying she put you in the back. Ask her if you can sit up front or on the side and that will calm some of that down. They didn't expect that from me.
>
> And I had other blacks and I monitored their classes. I told them you don't have to sit in the back. I do not believe a teacher at Gainesville High School is going to tell you to sit in the back because you're black. I said I'm not accepting that. Next time a teacher tells you to sit in the back because you're black, come get me. Come get me and let me know. You want to sit in the back so you can talk. And you say she isn't teaching nothing. No, she can't teach you anything because you're making it difficult right there. You've got to focus on the teacher and not your friend.

Lewis would serve as a dean at GHS until 1988. In the 1970–71 school year, about half the deans were African American. Lewis singles out black athletes and the Black Student Union for helping to keep things under control. There was a Black Student Union at the University of Florida, upon which the GHS organization was probably modeled. It had assisted the Lincoln protesters in November 1969. Students or teachers would bring issues to the GHS Black Student Union. According to Lewis, "This was a group of students who tried to make sure everyone was being treated right, to keep the black guys together. They didn't do anything wrong. They weren't rabble-rousers."[76] GHS principals from those years agreed that the Black Student Union played a positive role.[77]

If Neller did not have enough to do, 1970–71 was the year for the Southern Association of Colleges and Schools to evaluate Gainesville High for continued accreditation. The SACS Visiting Committee included teachers and administrators from other Florida high schools, each assigned to examine a subject matter area within his or her expertise. Also included were some junior college and University faculty members. The committee was chaired by the dean of the University of Florida College of Education,

Dr. Bert Sharp. GHS faculty members and administrators were tasked to do a "self evaluation" before meeting with the Visiting Committee.

The Evaluation Report of the Visiting Committee, although speaking in education school jargon, nevertheless demonstrates that SACS was holding faculties accountable for adapting to desegregation.

> Because of the sociological changes which have been taking place in Gainesville in the past few years, this report is even more significant for the assistance it can provide in understanding the community.
>
> The question which inevitably arises upon review of data such as presented in this report is "What does this have to say regarding the educational programs appropriate for this student body?" Answers to this question are not intended to be found in this report, but evidence in this report should be the basis for decision making in curriculum and educational activities.[78]

SACS had specific review criteria to be followed. Nevertheless, the Visiting Committee conscientiously pursued the extent to which the programs at GHS were responding to the needs of the student body then present in the school. There would be no looking back, as far as the Visiting Committee was concerned. The committee's conclusions were generally favorable, but it called on the school to develop coordination between school and community agencies, to involve more parents and other groups in the community, and to discover the way both dropouts and graduates viewed the school.[79] Principal Neller could take comfort from the committee's statement, "A spirit of esprit de corps exists throughout Gainesville High, and an atmosphere conducive to experimentation exists and is encouraged."[80]

In January 1971, the three newly elected school board members took office, Robert Howe, E. D. Manning Jr. (the former superintendent), and Eugene Todd. They joined William Enneking, MD, and Benford Samuels, DDS. Samuels was elected chair, and Enneking vice-chair.

At its first business meeting of 1971, the board approved a cooperative program with the University of Florida's Institute for the Development of Human Resources to train twenty-eight classroom aides. The University had received $150,000 in federal funds to train mothers of low-income families in heavily integrated, low-income neighborhoods. Fourteen teachers would also be involved in the program. The one-year program would pay each trainee $2,300, plus $400 for each dependent. The school board would have to fund the program after its first year if the program were to continue. The previous board had rejected the program in December.[81] The board also voted to buy twenty additional buses at a cost of $7,800 per bus to provide improved transportation service for the 1971–72 school year. The board also agreed that in the 1971–72 school year, no classes would begin earlier than 8:00 a.m. nor end later than 4:00 p.m.

The effects of student health on learning had been a concern of board member Enneking. He had advocated medical and dental exams for Head Start pupils, with records to be kept. In spring 1971, the University of Florida Department of Community and Ambulatory Medicine sponsored medical and dental exams for all 480 students at Mebane Middle School in then-rural Alachua. The exams showed that 97 of the students had serious medical problems, from heart defects to skin diseases. Few had previously seen a doctor. There were 81 students with abnormal hearing and 140 with abnormal vision. A dentist identified 47 students with major abnormalities. Obesity, anemia, and worms were among the most frequently noted problems.

The county had no facilities to screen or examine children. The county public health department only took care of obviously ill or referred children. A public health nurse visited Mebane once a week. A Mebane counselor said many sick children received home remedies, such as a drop of turpentine for a toothache. To deal with the medical issues, students would have to be transported to health care facilities from the rural community. Richard A. Henry, MD, said that health care problems arose from lack of parent education, parent resentment, and much red tape in utilizing public health services and working with state agencies.

Student health was another problem the school board was expected to solve. The doctors and school personnel in the study hoped that similar programs could be funded and supported by the school board.[82] The county health department responded by committing to a preventive dental program for all fifth graders in the school system by May 1971.[83]

Merit pay for teachers was another new issue that the school board had to resolve. The board had earlier set aside $200,000 for a merit pay plan for teachers. New board members Howe and Todd, as well as holdovers Enneking and Samuels, had favored allocating the $200,000 on a differentiated basis. But at the school board meeting on January 26, the Alachua County Education Association opposed any plan that would distribute awards based on subjective evaluations. One teacher pleaded, "My goodness, after the way our schools have survived all these disruptions it seems you would be happy to give us a small bonus for our efforts along with your kind praises." Roy Tower, the ACEA president, said that 68 percent of members opposed merit pay.[84]

One teacher told Talbot privately that merit pay was loaded with the potential for racial strife among teachers. Many black teachers were admittedly less qualified than the teacher cadre as a whole. White teachers were expected to take most of the merit awards. Todd advocated in-service and other training programs to help disadvantaged teachers.[85]

Talbot continued to be in favor of merit pay, stating that the principals had worked out a plan based on the subjective judgment of the superintendent. Teacher Barbara Gallant objected to Talbot's idea, saying that each principal works for his own school, but teachers work together. Todd responded that teachers are willing to abide by principals' judgment on which teachers get tenure, so why could they not take a principal's judgment on merit pay?

New board members Howe, Manning, and Todd now agreed with Tower, as did Enneking, at least for the current school year. Enneking joined the new board members, saying, "I still believe merit pay would be best, but not if it means forcing it down the throats of the teachers." After rejecting any merit pay plan for the current year, the board voted to recognize the ACEA for future "professional negotiations," a euphemism for collective bargaining.[86] The county would not adopt merit pay for teachers.

An unexploded firebomb, thrown through a window, was waiting on Superintendent Talbot's office floor when he arrived at work on Monday morning, April 19. The prior Saturday night three stores in black neighborhoods were struck by firebombs. Then, early on the morning of Wednesday, April 21, a firebomb started a fire that severely damaged the A. Quinn Jones school building.[87] No arrests were ever made for any of these incidents.

Black student protests would occur at several schools in spring 1971. Spring would bring similar protests in subsequent years, but despite the unrest these protests did not blow up into full-scale riots like those in spring 1970. At GHS the ombudsmen continued to help. Like the deans, they were out in the halls at GHS, approaching students who were expressing anger and keeping up with issues as they arose.[88] At Buchholz, in March, black grievances triggered by the paddling of two seventh-grade students led to black student walkouts. The school was closed for two days.[89] At Santa Fe High School, interracial fighting that required police intervention broke out in April; about two hundred black and white students left the campus as their parents had instructed if there was violence. There was more fighting on June 8, but the school remained open throughout these incidents.[90]

The costs of desegregation were having a major impact on the school system's finances. The system began the 1970–71 school year with a $1,250,000 balance. Additional unforeseen expenses included busing at Duval and Williams and additional assistant principals in the schools, who helped maintain order and eased the increased workload of the teachers and principals. The schools would end the year with a balance of $100,000 to $300,000. All in, the system would have $1,522,000 less to spend in 1971–72 than it had in the prior school year. Talbot said the system had to cut twenty-seven assistant principals, but that step would save only $201,000.[91]

Faced with teacher protests, the school board later decided to retain the assistant principals, but possibly at their regular teacher salaries without an additional pay supplement. Board chair Samuels said, "I am personally concerned with the low teacher morale in this county, as low as I have ever seen it. There are reasons for the low morale which the board has no control over and there are others which it does. I'd like to see us finish the year with morale on the upswing."[92]

Air-conditioning was another concern. The schools operated during September and October, and April and May, four months when ambient temperatures were in the eighties and nineties. Only schools built since the 1968 bond issue were air-conditioned. The school board estimated that under its current utilities rate structure, the annual cost of electricity alone for a completely air-conditioned school system would be $1.2 million.[93]

The 1970–71 school year ended without a repeat of the violence of 1969–70. Discipline was still a problem, there were too many suspensions, and tension continued, if not at the flash point of the prior year. The number of expulsions for the year was twelve, eight from Eastside, three from Gainesville High, and one from Hawthorne.[94] But there was a sense that matters would get better in the future, not worse. Gainesville High's junior-senior prom was held at the University of Florida's Reitz Union. Instead of the eighteen policemen in attendance the preceding year, this year there was only one.[95]

Tommy Tomlinson, who had been on point for desegregation almost from the start, said that parents tend to equate change with confusion, and there had been many changes. "We are doing things differently than they did and people are naturally reluctant to change. All learning does not necessarily have to remain the same." Teachers and principals worked harder in the 1970–71 school year than they ever had before, according to Tomlinson. For many, concepts such as individualized learning, team teaching, and behavioral objectives were unfamiliar. Many educators took in-service training and courses at the University of Florida.[96]

A sampling of high school administrators and student leaders agreed that a change in student attitudes mattered most in the school year just ended. Among the student comments:

> From Gainesville High: "The students are just tired of the chaos. They decided to take their education more seriously, and as a result we have a much better situation." "Most of our teachers are really concerned about our education. The administration has shown great leadership this year, and everyone is trying hard to work together."

> From Eastside: "We were upset about the closing of Lincoln, and I guess we thought we could fight our way out. That didn't work, and now we're working to make Eastside the best school anywhere." "We've learned to get along, and we all make a real effort to be equal. We are concerned with our school. We want it to be the best."
>
> From Buchholz: "We must look at the problem from both sides. The students finally realized that the situation could get better, but violence would not help the process." "Violence can get you nowhere. It can only hurt the situation. I think most people realized that."[97]

Jim Temple, principal of Buchholz, summed up: "Last year, our most important concern was just the holding schools together, with any kind of glue we could find. We did not get the cooperation we needed from some members of the school board, but the faculty and student body took it upon themselves to make this year better. So far, it has worked. We are dealing with more than physical integration. We also have the problem of cultural and social integration. These problems are not completely solved. You can't solve 150 years worth of wrong in one year, but we have made great strides in addressing the problems." An assistant principal at Eastside credited the school's winning football team as "a tremendous cementing factor. . . . Until that time, the bond just wasn't there." At Gainesville High, changes that minimized student time out of the classrooms helped.[98]

By the end of the school year, GHS Principal Neller had solved many problems that would not trouble his successor. But Neller was exhausted and asked to be reassigned "for health reasons." The resignation was reported July 30, 1971. He had first requested Talbot to relieve him in May but had a change of heart. Neller was forty.[99] Talbot said Neller had done an outstanding job, but the work left him physically and mentally exhausted. "Maybe he tried to do too much. He was right on top of everything . . . never missed a meeting. Delegation of responsibilities is a very difficult area in a school of that kind."[100] Neller initially became the supervisor of the schools' student scheduling process, which led eventually to his position as chief of technology for the school system.[101]

The 927 graduates in the Gainesville High School class of 1971 received their diplomas at Florida Field on June 15. All wore the colors of Gainesville High. Neil Butler, the mayor-commissioner of Gainesville, was the speaker. He said that he was a product of the slums. He voiced his disappointment that to obtain desegregation in Alachua County blacks had to go to court. "That was a moral issue that should not have been placed on the courts. That established a dangerous precedent of society escaping moral responsibilities." He gave everyone a much-needed lesson in the reason we have schools in the first place. He told parents not to sell their offspring short. He told the graduates, "With you, life is still warm. You are our tomorrow, our society. You are still very much a part of us, because we love you."[102]

CHAPTER 17
RACIAL BALANCING

The Ideal Meets Reality

I wouldn't be here today had I been raised in an America which only educated its wealthy children.

Governor Reuben Askew, November 19, 1971

We have a community that continues to be unconcerned about the quality of life for all of its citizens. You are making the lowest income persons the most transported. Blacks continue to get the shaft.

City Commissioner Neil Butler, March 22, 1973

Those people are transients. We work and pay taxes. That school was built with our taxes. Why don't you bus their children to a black school.

Parent from Fairbanks at school board meeting, May 10, 1973

The Supreme Court decision in *Carter* and the 1970 fruitbasket turnover only began Alachua County's struggles with desegregation. As the first full school year under the county's unitary system ended in June 1971, the long-term prospects for Alachua County's historically inclusive (if segregated) public school system were unclear. There had been much progress, but peace was still only wished for. Many whites still wanted integration to work, but the midterm desegregation in 1970 and the disorder that followed left a wake of fear and doubt. They remained to be convinced that the school board could restore an educational environment as they had known it. African American students, educators, and parents found themselves uprooted from their traditional, sustaining schools and forced into white schools where many felt cast adrift, disliked, and unwelcome. It would have been hard in 1971 to find any Gainesville blacks who thought they were better off than they were in 1969.

Statewide, the large urban counties continued to experience racial unrest in their schools. The Florida PTA Congress adopted a resolution calling for an antibusing constitutional amendment at its convention in November 1971. But it also resolved to support compliance with court orders.

The new Florida Governor Reuben Askew brought a different message to the convention: "I wouldn't be here today had I been raised in an America which only educated its wealthy children." He expressed the fear of many that as "the businessman, the doctor, the lawyer, the accountant and even in a few instances the school board member and the public school teachers" withdrew their children from the public schools, they would stop supporting public school funding. Askew said if that trend continued, the quality of public education would decline "until only the very poor, both white and black are left . . . and the great American system of public education is reduced to a baby-sitting service run on federal welfare." He had the same plea as Superintendent Talbot and the Alachua County school board. Only broader community desegregation could end the busing that was fueling white opposition to school desegregation.[1]

Overshadowing all of the other issues in Alachua County was the racial imbalance that resulted, and in some areas accelerated, when the county first implemented its unitary system. The issues raised in the early public debates over racial balancing would continue to frame the conflicts in the county over desegregation that continue to this day.

The school board, in its report to the court on August 27, 1970, pledged for the 1971–72 school year to take "all feasible steps to accomplish as near as possible a county ratio in the system of the same proportion as the black and white students are throughout the county that attend the public schools."[2] This report had never been formally approved or rejected by the court, but it came to be regarded as legally binding by the school board.

The court orders then in effect for Alachua County stemmed from *Carter*. That decision and *Alexander* had only required the affected school districts to implement unitary school systems in the middle of the 1969–70 school year. Those decisions provided no parameters for constitutionally acceptable unitary school systems. The Supreme Court in April 1971 gave additional guidance regarding unitary systems in *Swann v. Charlotte-Mecklenburg Board of Education* and four companion cases.[3] *Swann* is remembered today for ordering large-scale busing to desegregate the Charlotte-Mecklenburg school district in North Carolina.[4] But that case also set a lower bar for unitary school plans than the Alachua County school board was using. *Swann* held that uniform, district-wide mathematical ratios were not constitutionally required.[5] The court stated that ratios could be used by school districts and could also be used by district courts as a starting point for analyzing the effectiveness of a unitary plan.[6] *Swann* also held that in a large, urban district converting to a unitary system, some all-black schools could remain as part of a unitary system, although in a previously de jure system there would be a presumption against schools that were significantly out of balance with the rest of the system.[7] Finally, the court stated that once a unitary system is established under a constitutional plan, desegregation plans do not thereafter have to be continually modified to account for changes in neighborhood racial composition.[8]

Justice Burger's opinion for the unanimous court in *Swann* reaffirmed the court's commitment to the principles of *Brown* but stated that in devising equitable enforcement remedies, trial and error necessarily played a role.

> We are concerned in these cases with the elimination of the discrimination inherent in the dual school systems, not with the myriad factors of human existence which can cause discrimination in a multitude of ways on racial, religious or ethnic grounds. The target of the cases from *Brown* to the present was the dual school system. The elimination of racial discrimination in public schools is a large task and one that should not be retarded by efforts to achieve broader purposes lying beyond the jurisdiction of school authorities. One vehicle can carry only a limited amount of baggage. It would not serve the important objectives of *Brown* to use school desegregation cases for purposes beyond their scope, although desegregation of schools ultimately will have impact on other forms of discrimination.[9]

Notwithstanding *Swann*, Talbot and the school board continued to believe, because of the board's August 27, 1970, report pledging "all feasible steps" to a uniform racial balance, that such a balance was legally required from year to year. Board member Enneking on June 24, 1971, argued instead that the board should assign additional teachers to improve the quality of education at schools that came to house higher percentages of black students.[10] Under *Swann*, even that step was not legally required, but Enneking believed that some action would be educationally desirable to deal with resegregation. Special programs to enhance the quality of education for black students had been ordered as a remedy for de jure segregation by the Fifth Circuit in *Jefferson County* in 1967[11] and were subsequently endorsed by the Supreme Court in 1977 in *Milliken v. Bradley*.[12]

Achieving the desired 70 percent white, 30 percent black racial balance in each school was perceived as a prerequisite for solving the other problems associated with desegregation, such as in-school violence, educational deficits, and white flight. Countywide racial balancing would answer complaints of both white and black parents that this or that neighborhood was being unfairly singled out to bear the burden of desegregation. If the board took the steps it could to head off resegregation, it might avoid renewed legal battles with the NAACP Legal Defense Fund. For whites, sending their children to school with blacks was as much an issue as ever. Interracial contact over the past two years had if anything decreased many whites' comfort level with integration. The board hoped that by adding white students to some schools, the whites already in those schools would stay. Second, by making sure that no school had a significantly higher ratio of whites to blacks than any other school, schools with high ratios of white students would not attract even more white parents seeking to remove their children from schools with high ratios of black students.

At first, local leaders broadly favored uniform racial balance in the schools. The white and black members of the Bi-racial Committee supported that goal sooner, not later. Gainesville Women for Equal Rights, a civil rights advocacy organization composed mostly of University spouses and African American teachers and some community activists, agreed with that goal "to even things out."[13] However, as the school board and the community discovered, the racial balancing process would set off a new round of protests by both white and black parents. However fair any balanced plan might appear in the abstract, significant numbers of affected students and parents would believe they were being treated unfairly.

The Bi-racial Committee's support for a uniform countywide racial balance in the schools brought its members into the middle of Alachua County's reaction to the events of 1970. In the days before caller ID, the anonymous threatening or harassing telephone call was the favorite tactic of those who wanted to intimidate citizens who were trying to make desegregation work. Hebron Self's family became the target of many such calls. "White trash" was the typical epithet. The family stood firm against a faction they saw as trying to divide Gainesville. "All we wanted was fairness," Hazel Self says. Hebe remained on the Bi-racial Committee through its active phase.[14]

By the end of the 1970–71 school year, the school population was 66 percent white and 33 percent black. The county's population was estimated to be 72 percent white and 28 percent black. In some areas of the county, racial balance was tilting more toward either one race or the other. Racial balance was a moving target, complicating the board's capacity to create an equitable desegregation plan.[15]

Superintendent Talbot quickly took his concerns before Gainesville business groups. He warned that these shifts could cause whites to exit the public schools in large numbers. Speaking to the Gainesville Realtors Board in November 1970, he repeated his view that a tipping point would be reached if black student population reached 40 percent. Talbot, like the Bi-racial Committee, saw more busing, not less, as the answer to changing demographics in the county and fairness to all residents. He said that neighborhood schools had failed as a concept because the blacks were not being educated. He added that to educate all students, some classes would be segregated because of widely differing levels of education. "You can't teach first graders to read when some of the kids are pre-kindergarten."[16]

At an October 1970 Lions Club meeting, Talbot rebuked the Gainesville business community for looking the other way while leaving the schools to deal with the problems of integration. He said those problems would not be solved until the business community opened its doors to blacks looking for better jobs, decent housing, better education, and an all-around better life for themselves and their families. He also defended the school board's use of federal funds, but not the federal restrictions that accompanied those funds.[17]

Talbot was not trying to pose as a civil rights leader. He spoke to remind Gainesville's white business interests that they and the entire community benefited from strong public schools. However, Talbot should be credited with the courage to take that message and his recommendations to audiences that needed to hear them. Talbot spoke truth, as he saw it, to power, whether that power was the white establishment or the black leadership. Talbot's message now about the dangers of white flight to the Realtors Board was the same message Charles Chestnut III heard during the Lincoln strike. To the Lions Club, he spoke from his heart. It was one thing to urge businessmen and professionals to support a bond issue for new schools, but quite another to tell them that the black community deserved nondiscriminatory housing and employment policies.

On the same issues, the school board sought help from city and county governments during 1971. The school board and the city commission had a joint meeting in May 1971 to begin the discussions. Eugene Todd asked, "Why should all the pressure of integration fall on the school board? All three governments should be involved. The choice is between permanent cross-busing or integrated housing." The school board pleaded with the city commission to disperse new government-sponsored housing around the city.[18]

Talbot appeared before the North Central Florida Regional Planning Commission in September 1971 to oppose approval of a new housing project in a black neighborhood of southeast Gainesville. Developer Phil Emmer said that the project would replace slum housing and would not add to or subtract from the segregated housing patterns. Talbot countered that the ratio of blacks to whites had increased in that area. "The federal government can finance us into a ghetto, and I think they have in this area." Talbot said that the more unbalanced housing patterns became, the more children would have to be assigned to schools outside their community to achieve racial balance.[19]

Enneking told the Alachua County Commission, "The general tenor of our problem is the way people live in the county has resulted in an inordinate expense." Todd asked if the county had considered the neighborhood around the Santa Fe Junior College site on the northwest side for some integrated housing. Howard Weston, the county administrator, replied, "We presume housing should be available to all races. The fact that something other than that is happening has its roots in economics. I don't think we can use zoning as a tool to promote a better mixture of the races." Pressed, Weston admitted that there was some land zoned R-3 in the northwest area on which apartments could be built, "but I don't think the price of the apartments would even be coming up."[20]

The city commission referred the issue to the city's housing board. Finally, the Gainesville Housing Board agreed to tackle the problem of Gainesville's racially segregated housing patterns. The board members identified problems with the city's ordinances and building codes and other "sacred cows." Member Carl Opp said, "It's going to be done one way or the other or somebody's going to burn down part of the town." The housing board agreed to contact the city and county housing authorities after consulting with some community leaders.[21] The city passed an ordinance outlawing racial discrimination in housing in 1972.[22] But during the early years of school desegregation, segregated housing patterns would continue in Alachua County.

Talbot was, by his own agreement, coming to the end of his service as superintendent. The school board's superintendent search began in March 1971 with the appointment of a seven-person search committee.[23] Although Talbot's term as elected superintendent would not expire until January 1, 1973, the board hoped to appoint a new superintendent in time to take over on July 1, 1972.[24]

The board appointed James W. Longstreth, EdD, to succeed Talbot as superintendent on January 11, 1972. Longstreth was thirty-six and had been school superintendent in Charlotte County since 1968. At that time Charlotte County had about one-fourth the students and teachers as Alachua County. Longstreth had coached football and basketball at Manatee High School in the early 1960s. He had grown up in Manatee County. His salary of $28,000 would increase over his four-year appointment to $32,000. As elected superintendent, Talbot's salary had been limited by statute to $23,000. Talbot, then fifty-three, had known Longstreth since he was a graduate student in 1967 and then as a member of the Florida school superintendents organization. To allow for an early transition, Talbot resigned, effective March 1, 1972. Longstreth said that he wanted to be in office in time to work on the budget for 1973.[25]

Talbot said he felt a weight had been lifted from his shoulders. Eyes watering, he said, "Only in America could someone from Altha, Florida, come to work for Alachua County. There has been no pressure on me, at any time. Jim (Longstreth) and I are not strangers. I would prefer to be a principal at an elementary school next year, but I'll go where he wants me to go."[26] Talbot had been superintendent since January 1965, seven years earlier. Since December 1968, he had declared his willingness to step aside in favor of a superintendent appointed by the board. Desegregation had caused other white and black leaders in the schools to make untimely exits. The time had finally come for Talbot to leave his post.

Talbot did not leave politics. He announced a run for a Gainesville City Commission seat on February 28, 1973, emphasizing law and order.[27] Grateful city voters would elect Talbot to a term on the commission before his early descent into Alzheimer's disease. He was joined on the city commission by Russell Ramsey, by then serving as principal of the Lincoln vocational center. They each defeated candidates who were viewed as more oriented toward the local civil rights movement.

As the school board considered plan after plan to achieve the 70/30 ratio, the board stirred up protest after protest. A further complication was the move from junior highs to middle schools. To achieve equitable racial balance at the elementary, middle, and senior high school levels, there were only bad choices.

The Bi-racial Committee and the school board held a workshop to discuss racial balance on June 8, 1971.[28] Under one proposal, twenty-six white students from Monteocha, a rural community north of Gainesville, would be reassigned to the Alachua district. A mother from Monteocha told the school board, "Some of those children are only nine years [old] and this will be the fourth time they have been reassigned. How can you expect them to have any loyalty for any school?"

Earl Bergadine, a white engineer for the state and member of the Bi-racial Committee, lived on Gainesville's northeast side and was the parent of an Eastside student. He accused the school board of telling a "bald faced lie" when it said it was for a countywide solution. "People in East Gainesville are tired of this double talk, and they don't have to live there. There's a lot of us can afford to move out to West Gainesville if we have to." Arthur Spencer, assistant principal at Mebane, warned that white families in Alachua were disappointed. "They stayed with us because they thought the school board was going to be more aggressive about desegregation in the county [outside Gainesville]."

Board member Todd said, "Why should Eugene Todd always be the one raising questions about segregation when we have an attorney [representing] this board? We've spent thousands of dollars fighting cross-busing. I'm in favor of spending another $1,000 or so to force people out of these private schools set up specifically to escape integration." Enneking answered, "I'm not at all willing to go back to court or to say those people don't have a constitutional right to send their children to whatever private schools they desire." Enneking was correct on the law, given the absence of any governmental connection to the private schools in Alachua County. The three-hour meeting was not intended to produce any formal action, but no consensus emerged between the board and the Bi-racial Committee.[29]

Under another plan, parts of the Gainesville district would be carved off to Archer, Newberry, and Hawthorne to achieve better racial balance in schools in those communities.[30] That plan created new problems. First, the rural schools often did not offer the same courses as the larger schools in Gainesville. To address this issue, Tomlinson said that relief could be granted in individual cases if a student had a legitimate need for a course not offered in his rural school. Second, there was a testing gap between students at the rural high schools and those in the Gainesville schools. That gap could be interpreted by some parents as proof that their children would not be well prepared if they were zoned to a rural school. At Gainesville High in the 1970–71 school year, 42 percent of all seniors (including those transferred from Lincoln and Mebane) scored 300 or better on the senior placement test. A score of 300 or better was required for admission to a four-year state university. At Santa Fe, 26 percent attained that score, and at Newberry and Hawthorne, 10 percent.[31]

Another proposal required busing pupils from High Springs and Alachua between the two towns, which are about seven miles apart. The elementary and middle schools in Alachua had a 50/50 racial balance, and those in High Springs were 65 percent white and 35 percent black. At Mebane Middle School in Alachua, 90 percent of students were reading below grade level, and the average student was two or three years below grade level in mathematics. Many white students from Alachua had enrolled in the private Rolling Green Academy. "Just when we thought busing was settled you come up with this idea. Why is High Springs always at the bottom in this county?" Another parent: "We resent you throwing around statistics about children like you were talking about hogs and cows." John Hill, the group's leader, told the board that changing the racial balance in High Springs would drive more students into private schools. Hill also said that High Springs had desegregated peacefully, with community support. He said that new disruptions in the schools there would harm the town's efforts to attract new business.[32]

The school board decided in December 1971 that it would not try to correct the significant racial imbalance between Eastside and Buchholz for the 1972–73 school year. "If you start moving seniors around you'll end up with a riot that will make the Lincoln riot look like a picnic," said Earl Bergadine, who had resigned from the Bi-racial Committee in November. Board chair Samuels justified a cautious approach because the current school year was proving to be the best of the last several years. Samuels also wanted to avoid major changes until the new superintendent could give his ideas.[33]

The district's Bi-racial Committee had its last recorded meeting on February 15, 1972, with only chair Frances Lunsford, Benny Walker, Hebron Self, and Robert James present. The Rev. Wright arrived later and attended for fifteen minutes. At recent meetings, African American members had complained about the disciplining of black students and assignments to special education classes. Available records do not show any decision by the school board either to continue or discontinue the committee. Gainesville had previously had successful official and unofficial biracial groups, as had the schools during the 1970 desegregation. Biracial committees were operating at individual schools. Like every other aspect of desegregation, the county school biracial committee had no precedent. Perhaps, in the end, its members simply grew weary of having to deal with problems that they could not solve.[34]

Now it was Longstreth's turn to grasp the desegregation nettle. After study, he proposed a plan for 1972–73 that would move the district closer to the target of 70 percent white, 30 percent black in each school. As part of that plan, Duval and Williams, the two elementary schools in the east-side black neighborhood, would house all prekindergartens and kindergartens. The white fifth and sixth graders currently being bused to those schools would return to their neighborhood schools.[35]

The plan was also dead on arrival. When the public hearing on the plan opened in the Gainesville High auditorium on March 3, 1972, "the uproar . . . was nearly as loud as the thunderstorm that raged outside . . ." A capacity audience cheered thirty-five speakers, every one of whom opposed the plan. Both black and white leaders opposed the plan. The Gainesville Women for Equal Rights argued that Duval and Williams were effectively being eliminated as active school centers and that the plan placed even more of a burden for desegregation on black students. The GWER suggested that if the board wanted kindergarten centers, it should use more centrally located schools such as J. J. Finley, on the northwest side; Kirby Smith, in a white neighborhood on the east side; or A. Quinn Jones, located in Gainesville's downtown black neighborhood. Stephan Mickle, the son of African American schoolteachers Andrew and Catherine Mickle, then a law professor, agreed. "We are opposed to the idea of reverting to neighborhood schools by closing black schools in the process. The entire burden of desegregation is being placed on the blacks and it was not the blacks that created the problem." President Bill Clinton would nominate Mickle in 1998 to the US District Court for the Northern District of Florida, the same court that heard *Wright v. Board*. Earl Bergadine, the Eastside parent, accused the board of busing out students from the more affluent black neighborhoods while leaving students from the poor black neighborhoods at Eastside. A teacher at Duval presented a petition from Duval teachers urging the board to consider the quality academic programs that had been developed for fifth and sixth graders at the two schools.[36]

The board, however, had to implement a full middle school plan for 1973–74. An initial version of this plan had Howard Bishop and Westwood Junior Highs becoming middle schools housing grades 6, 7, and 8. A new middle school would be built on Gainesville's west side. The three senior high schools would each take grades 9–12. All elementary schools in 1973–74 would house grades K–5. Kirby Smith Elementary School, on Gainesville's east side, would be converted to an administrative building and replaced by a new elementary school on the west side. Although Duval and Williams would again house grades K–5, racial balance at those schools would be maintained by busing white pupils from adjacent areas. With last-minute adjustments, the racial balance in the high schools was planned to be 40 percent black at Eastside, 29 percent black at Gainesville High, and 19 percent black at Buchholz.[37] Racial balance at Buchholz and Eastside would be achieved by busing ninth graders from the Williams and Duval area to Buchholz, and by a mostly white ninth grade at Eastside. Longstreth rejected the idea that some all-black schools might remain. "Every school should be a desegregated school."[38]

In the midst of these disputes, the school board was faced with the possible loss of members Benford Samuels, DDS, and William Enneking, MD. Their current terms would end in December 1972.

In January 1972, Samuels had thought that his term was over and initially said that he needed to resign to attend to his dental practice.[39] However, he remained on the board and in June 1972 announced that he would run for a second term. "There have been several very important programs started since I came on the board. After doing some thinking I have decided I cannot turn away from those programs until they have been followed through to successful completion." He cited the transition of the superintendent's office to appointive, an incentive pay system for teachers, negotiations with the Alachua County Education Association, and busing.[40]

Enneking also decided to run for a second term. Like Samuels, he wanted to help guide the schools' efforts to provide quality education. He saw many of his original goals as accomplished, including an appointed superintendent and integration. He had worked on the liaison agreement between the Alachua County schools and the University of Florida.

Both candidates drew opponents. Samuels was opposed by former board member T. E. Simmons, of Archer, who had been narrowly defeated by Eugene Todd in 1970, and Ralph Selfridge, a white Republican candidate who was a math professor and director of the University of Florida's computing center. Enneking was opposed by Howard Freeman, a twenty-six-year-old white guidance counselor and director of student activities at Santa Fe Junior College.[41] No one favored busing. Samuels and Freeman supported the current school board's policy that racial distribution in the county's schools should be approximately the same throughout the system. Simmons and Selfridge opposed that policy. Enneking did not take a clear position on the issue.[42]

Enneking won his seat by a 58 percent margin over Freeman in the Democratic primary on September 12, 1972. Samuels won narrowly over Simmons, only after absentee ballots were counted.[43] Samuels defeated Selfridge by a large margin in the November general election.[44] The county had declared itself in favor of the current school board members, if not every one of their policies. In January, the board elected Robert Howe chair for a second term, when Enneking decided not to accept the chair.[45]

Now the board would finally have to decide on racial balancing and zoning for 1973–74. The plan for the coming school year continued to change. As the plan went through several iterations, different features drew opposition from different communities. Cutting the knot of segregated neighborhoods, the plan carved out a number of areas within black neighborhoods and added them to the noncontiguous zones of predominantly white, but distant, elementary schools. In the lingo of desegregation, such noncontiguous areas were referred to as "satellites." Those black students would be bused. The east-side middle school, Howard Bishop, would be able to house only seventh and eighth graders. Sixth graders on the east side of Gainesville would remain in elementary schools and would not receive the benefits of the middle school program. Children in the small rural community of Fairbanks were assigned from Rawlings (which was then 18 percent black) to Duval.[46]

In response, Charles Chestnut III asked when another middle school would be located in east Gainesville. He also questioned whether blacks from east Gainesville might eventually be bused all the way to Newberry (seventeen miles to the west).[47] City Commissioner Neil Butler came to a school board meeting on March 22, 1973, to speak about the plan. On the one hand, Butler said, the plan "cleaned up the mess of cluster schools," but on the other hand, "We have a community that continues to be unconcerned about the quality of life for all of its citizens. You are making the lowest income persons the most transported. Blacks continue to get the shaft." Butler criticized the board's decision to build a new middle school on the northwest side, instead of on the southeast side, where he said it was needed more. Butler said the east-side zoning "was unbelievable and blatant." He said that as a result, all pupils on the east side in the sixth grade were being deprived of a middle school education and specialized teaching that they would get by having different teachers for each subject. School board attorney James Lang advised the board that none of the applicable court orders required the 70/30 target racial distribution. "He reminded the board that the figure was its own creation."[48]

A white Fairbanks parent on April 26 accused the board of violating the spirit of desegregation by busing poor rural children into a poor neighborhood. He asserted that Duval "is located in one of the highest crime rate areas of the city." The board was treating the Fairbanks people "like a bunch of hillbillies whose little kids will never learn to read and write anyway." Enneking: "I resent someone implying that their children are hillbillies. This board spent hours and hours going over zone maps. There's no way we can move one group of people without affecting another."[49] At a later meeting on May 10, the Fairbanks parents accused Longstreth of favoring black residents of a new low-income housing project across the street from Rawlings, who they said had displaced their children from Rawlings. "Those people are transients. We work and pay taxes. That school was built with our taxes. Why don't you bus their children to a black school." Rawlings had served Fairbanks for the last four years. Another parent: "You're gonna need Sheriff Crevasse come September." The school board refused to change the plan. The arguments would have played out as just another parent protest but for Longstreth's stunning statement that the reassignments had nothing to do with racial balance. He denied that he had ever said he wanted to equalize the racial distribution of schools. Chair Howe told the parents that the reassignments arose due to the change to a middle school structure.[50]

The 1973–74 school year would be the tenth year since the first black students were admitted to Alachua County's formerly all-white schools in 1964–65. For five of those years, the county had been under freedom of choice. Almost all remnants of its dual system were to be eliminated in 1970–71 with the completion of the new schools funded by the 1968 bond issue, including Eastside and Buchholz Junior/Senior Highs. In 1969–70, at the insistence of the NAACP Legal Defense Fund, the county had moved at midterm to a unitary system, and in 1970–71, the county as ordered had desegregated Duval and Williams. By spring 1973, despite all of the efforts of the school board, the administration, the teachers, the students, the parents, and the community leaders, desegregation was still a work in process.

On July 5, 1973, the school board filed a motion in *Wright v. Board* to change its elementary school districts as described in the school board's plan for the 1973–74 school year. The motion stated that the projected elementary school enrollments under the new zones would be within 5 percent of the 70/30 racial-balance guideline for each school in the district. The motion gave projected enrollments for the schools whose zone lines were being changed, all of which were in the board's Gainesville community area.[51] The NAACP Legal Defense Fund notified the court that it had no objection.[52] Judge Middlebrooks approved the school board's motion.[53] His order was the last action by the court in *Wright v. Board*, which, as we saw in chapter 15, was finally dismissed in 1978. From the summer of 1973 onward, the school board and the community would resolve their differences over desegregation, or not, without resort to the courts.

CHAPTER 18

NEW LEADERS, NEW CHALLENGES

> Last year it was like a pall over the schools. I hated to go visiting. This time I've seen nothing but spirit and determination and it really was enjoyable.
>
> William S. Talbot, September 5, 1971

> They are just crying out for closer student-teacher relationships.
>
> Dan Boyd, GHS principal, March 4, 1972

> We take 2,000 youngsters and put them in one location from all walks of life. The teacher hasn't taken any courses in how to stop fights. Then, some of the public gets upset with us when we can't keep absolute law and order.
>
> Tommy Tomlinson, May 13, 1973

> We are not addressing ourselves to the major problem of human relations. I can tell you that parents are pulling their children out of school because their children are getting their teeth knocked out and they are afraid to go to the toilet.
>
> James W. Longstreth, February 25, 1973

While the superintendent and the school board struggled with the racial-balance issue, teachers, students, principals, and parents had to keep trying to make desegregation work in the classrooms. But new issues such as student drug use, standardized testing, and collective bargaining for teachers were now crowding in just as the schools were beginning to absorb the changes brought about by desegregation.

As schools opened in September 1971, Alachua County hoped for educational gains. All schools would feature minority education and race-relations education on a more or less formal basis. County teachers had prepared curriculum guides and other materials to bring more uniformity to instruction. There would be more team teaching. There were federal grants to support a program for gifted students, two programs to assist students who were not learning at their potential, and a full-year team of twenty-three interns from the University of Florida who were working on master's degrees.[1]

Superintendent Talbot, who made a practice of visiting the schools, told the press that morale was high. "Last year it was like a pall over the schools. I hated to go visiting. This time I've seen nothing but spirit and determination and it really was enjoyable." Enrollment was up by 750, to 22,248, in contrast to the year before, when the number of new students was less than 150. Teacher turnover from 1970–71 was about 19 percent, roughly the same as followed the fruitbasket turnover in 1969–70. New teachers included 157 women and 63 men.[2] No schools would be on double sessions. The county lost its federal funding for adult bus monitors. Talbot said all the money was going to the state's urban counties, which were beginning their own busing programs. A new state law required every kindergarten and first grader to have a medical exam and to provide proof to the schools.[3]

As classes were shifted among the new schools and double sessions were ended, the system needed fewer teachers. There was no court report in *Wright v. Board* for the 1970–71 school year, but the report filed in November 1971 showed that the number of teachers had fallen from 1,003 in 1969–70 to 914 in 1971–72. There were thirty-four fewer white teachers and thirty-seven fewer black teachers. The proportion of black teachers in the system held relatively steady at 21.5 percent, down from 23.3 percent in 1969–70, and still above the 20 percent mandated by the court.[4]

Dan Boyd, then thirty years old, became the new GHS principal in August 1971. Boyd was the son of a former superintendent of schools in Duval County. While Boyd was growing up, among other business interests, Boyd's extended family had owned the Jacksonville Tars baseball team of the Class A South Atlantic League. Boyd, in common with all other school leaders of that time in Alachua County, had played high school football. He says he chose football because he lacked the athletic skills for basketball or baseball. He describes himself as a "thin, slow lineman [who] got beat up quite a bit. But I stuck with it." His lesson from football: "Just that you've got to stick with it, and you've got to keep working." He played at Jacksonville Landon High School, from which he graduated in 1959.[5]

When Boyd enrolled at the University of Florida, on his father's advice he started as a premed with the idea of being a dentist. But after bogging down in the premed courses, he again sought his dad's advice. The elder Boyd sent his son to see a family friend, G. Ballard Simmons, at the College of Education. With Simmons's help, Boyd became a history major and also took courses in the College of Education. As soon as Boyd graduated in December 1963, again on his dad's advice, Boyd enrolled in the administrative master's degree program at the College of Education. Boyd began teaching full-time in Alachua County in September 1964 but continued in the master's program. He was awarded his degree in August 1968.

In the master's program, Boyd was surrounded by older, more experienced educators, especially during summer sessions. He says the professors gave the students practical problems. He was too young to contribute to the discussions, but he learned by listening to his classmates. "And I was just like a little sponge sitting in those classes, and I could just sit and listen to people." He praises his professors R. L. Johns, who taught finance, and Lee Eggert, who taught curriculum.

Boyd spent only the minimum three years as a teacher before becoming assistant principal at Santa Fe High School under L. B. Lindsey. That job led to a principalship at Chiefland High School in Levy County beginning July 1, 1969. In that year, Boyd had to oversee the complete integration of Chiefland High School. Chiefland is a small town in a farming area. It is famous locally for its annual Watermelon Festival, complete with watermelons donated by local farmers, a seed-spitting contest, and a watermelon queen. Black high school students, who had formerly been bused twenty-six miles to the nearest black high school at Williston, now could attend Chiefland High School. The area has a relatively small proportion of black citizens, much lower than Alachua County.

Boyd: "And it was as smooth as glass. There were hardly any problems whatsoever, other than the kids just kind of feeling each other out and making a good effort to get to know each other. We had one fight between a black and a white student. I paddled both of them, and that was the end of the racial unrest." Boyd believes integration went smoothly there: "I think they knew each other. Chiefland is a farming community. I think many of the black and white boys worked side by side in the watermelon fields, the cantaloupe fields, cropping tobacco together, working on the ranches. And I don't think they were unknown to each other. I didn't stay in Chiefland long enough to learn the mores and the folkways of the community. I did know that being a Jacksonville boy there was a lot I had to learn about rural thinking."[6]

Alachua County had not forgotten about Boyd. Neller and Tomlinson sought Boyd as an associate principal at Gainesville High in spring 1970, but he chose to stay at Chiefland. Then, a month or two later, he received a call from Jim Pritchett, his former boss at Newberry: "Danny, Tiny wants to meet you at Mac's Drive In at five in the morning to talk about you becoming the principal at Howard Bishop Junior High School." On the appointed day Boyd got up at 4:00 a.m., drove to Gainesville, "and met Tiny at five in the morning at Mac's Drive In and had some grits and eggs and bacon with him. And he offered me the principalship of Howard Bishop, and I accepted." Boyd held that position for the 1970–71 school year.

Bishop was not Chiefland. It is located on Gainesville's northeast side, in what was then a white neighborhood having a different demographic, as we have seen, than the better-educated, more prosperous west side. "There was always this black/white resentment still. It was an undercurrent, and you can't deny it. And we had some kids who were not happy that Lincoln had been closed. We had to deal with that. And you had some who weren't happy that the blacks were at Bishop because it had been an all-white school just a few years previous to that. And we had to treat all the kids equally. We had to be absolutely fair. We had to be colorblind completely. And we were able to do that because it was in the best interest of everybody to make sure they felt like Bishop was their school."

To bring his students together, Boyd asked them to plan activities for the school, such as intramural sports and dances. With integration, dances became problematic because of blacks and whites dancing together. For dances, his staff asked the students to decide whether to have a band or a disc jockey, to set the dress code, the behavior code, the hours. He wanted the students involved in planning so they would get to know one another and would develop a commitment to the school because their ideas and plans were being carried out. These organizational strategies may sound obvious, and they had been emphasized in academic works at least since 1954,[7] but applying them with adolescents in a newly integrated environment and making them work was not a talent possessed by every white or black principal.[8]

Boyd says that while at Bishop, he kept in touch with Neller, mainly to learn from him about the problems presented by the tougher, older students at GHS. Boyd says that at some point early in his year at Bishop, he let Talbot know that if the principalship at GHS ever came open, he would like Talbot to consider him for it. He believes Talbot gave a noncommittal "okay," and that was the end of the discussion. Boyd disclaims politicking for the job. He was unaware at the time that other candidates were being considered.[9]

The GHS principal's job became vacant when Neller's resignation was announced July 30, 1971. Bi-racial Committee minutes reflect that John Dukes was asked to move to Gainesville High from Eastside but that he chose to remain at Eastside.[10] Dukes had been Eastside principal since the school opened in February 1970 on the Howard Bishop campus. Talbot on Friday, August 6, named four candidates under consideration for the GHS position, one of whom was Dan Boyd. Of the four, Boyd was by far the youngest and least experienced.[11] The school board approved Boyd's appointment on Thursday, August 12.[12]

As Boyd recalls his appointment, he was visiting his parents in Jacksonville on August 6, 1971, when the phone rang. It was Tiny. "He said, 'You're going to Gainesville High School. Can you be at my house in a couple of hours?' I said, 'Yes, sir.' And Tiny and John Neller were sitting in [Tiny's] living room when I got there. And John handed me a bunch of keys. He said, 'Here are your keys, partner, good luck to you.' I don't think Tiny gave me any directions as to anything he wanted me to do other than follow my own instincts and do the best I could to ensure that all of the kids got a good education, and the teachers are happy and content." Boyd believes Jim Niblack, the GHS football coach, supported his appointment behind the scenes. Boyd got to know Niblack when Boyd was an assistant football coach at Newberry High School in 1966.[13]

Boyd looked barely out of high school. Despite Talbot's support, the school board appeared skeptical. The school board warned Boyd that he would be working without a safety net. "He is not to expect a different kind of position if he does not continue the following year." Talbot said Neller had left the school in good order.[14] Once again, Talbot had gone with his instincts, in this case rejecting the safe choice of a more experienced educator or one with stronger connections in Alachua County.

Anyone around then would be astonished that Boyd would continue as GHS principal for the next twenty-four years, until 1995. He joined the county staff in 1995 as assistant superintendent for curriculum and instruction. After a period with the Florida High School Activities Association, he became Alachua County superintendent of schools in 2004, serving until his retirement in 2013.

Boyd later said he had no reservations about taking over a newly integrated high school. He had worked with blacks at his father's orange grove and contracting business. He already had similar experience at Chiefland and Howard Bishop. "I just treated [African Americans] the way I would want to be treated and never had too many problems about it."[15] He also acknowledges that his predecessors Hudson and Neller had by far the harder job, because they had the students who came from Lincoln as juniors and seniors and who really resented being at GHS, and older white students who were more resentful toward the Lincoln transfer students.[16]

Boyd's leadership style responded to the changed environment that followed desegregation. The principal still had to manage the deans and the faculty, but now he had to lead from the front on student racial issues. Students and teachers recall Boyd's visibility on campus, his ability to communicate, and what on a Florida high school campus in 1971 passed for charisma. Three members of the class of 1973, juniors when Boyd took over, saw an immediate break with past perceptions of the principal's role. Ron Perry does not recall Boyd's exact words at his first assembly, but "his posture was a little like Clint Eastwood. Okay. I'm tired of all this crap. You got a new sheriff in town now."[17] Tim Strauser says of Boyd, "He had such a presence. He was imposing and calming and fair. He worked hard at making everybody feel comfortable, fit in, and be a part of the school."[18] Vince

Deconna, now owner of a local ice cream company, remembers that Boyd did not talk down to students and that students could go into Boyd's office any time to talk.[19] In an observation that could not have been made of any former GHS principal, a female student, remembering Boyd's tight jeans, says all the girls had crushes on him.

John Dukes's son, John Dukes III, graduated from GHS in 1974. He played varsity football. Dukes singled out Boyd for gaining the respect of his students. After school, Boyd was in the athletic area, either running laps around the football practice field or lifting weights with members of the by now well-integrated sports teams. Being close to the school's athletes, who were looked up to by other students, helped Boyd's standing as a leader.[20] His closeness to Niblack also helped.

> Boyd:
>
> But getting as many young men, black and white, involved in the athletic programs and holding them to a high standard of conduct and academic performance had just untold benefits on the rest of the student body because when you're involved in an athletic program, and [Jim Niblack's] programs were winning really well, pride in the school quickly developed. And it was something I could never have done without [Niblack's] great success as a football coach. And I was just so lucky to have had him and Wesley Dicks and the other assistant football coaches, who were also teachers on my faculty.
>
> The athletes were looked up to by the other students, and it helped to show that that segment of the school was happy with the school. They were following the rules and regulations of the school. They were cooperating with not only their coaches, but with their classroom teachers and working towards graduating from high school and were acting the part of young ladies and gentlemen with good conduct. Now all of our athletes didn't exhibit good conduct, and I had to deal with them as well as any other student that was out of line.[21]

Boyd traveled with the football team. In Boyd's first year as principal, the team went 7–4 (the second and last year of the combined GHS and former Lincoln teams), but the next year the team was undefeated. That team scored 451 points to its opponents' 53.[22] Boyd believes that thirteen players on the 1972 team were signed to college football scholarships.

For clubs, student government, and other activities, the late Cela Hendrickson remained in charge. Boyd says that Hendrickson performed a role similar to Niblack's, coming up with ways to bring white and black students together to work on projects. In that way, he says, they were able to develop relationships with each other, "which were positive, so they could get to know each other as genuine human beings, fellow students."[23]

In dealing with students, Boyd and his staff would try to avoid imposing their own solution when problems arose. Sam Haywood, a black educator who later served under Boyd as assistant principal, says of Boyd's success:

> But I think the fact that they were involving the kids and then allowing them to work through crucial situations at times by not necessarily taking sides or supporting one group over the other unless there was a need to and someone got too far off course on expectations of behaviors or something. In other words, they didn't allow blacks to over, you know, to, just because you were black and feel you got to be this, it's got to be done this way, or a white kid to go too far out of line with behavior toward a black or something. Now, that wasn't allowed . . . you know, it just was not something that, I'm not saying it didn't happen from either side at times, but not directly where we could see it or the staff could see it and be a part of it.
>
> All kids . . . always have, in my mind, have been made to feel comfortable, at least from the administration side of it with Dan Boyd and people close to him because he was just that way with kids. I mean, everybody accepted him all the time. I've never seen someone that didn't.[24]

Haywood came to Alachua County as an agriculture teacher in January 1970. Haywood had grown up near Bushnell, Florida, one of fourteen children. In common with many blacks from rural areas, Haywood had worked with white boys doing farm labor. He was in one of the first Upward Bound groups, through which he was able to receive a scholarship to Florida A&M. He was introduced to Talbot during his job interview. Talbot said, "I really want you to come to Alachua County." Haywood was impressed that the superintendent took a personal interest in his employment. By 1974, Haywood had his master's degree in education administration from the University of Florida. He was twenty-seven. Boyd, thirty-two, hired Haywood to replace an older black assistant principal who was retiring.[25]

The teachers were perhaps more reserved in their initial reaction to Boyd, but they came to appreciate his presence and his ability to communicate. As superintendent, Boyd favored dark suits and could easily have passed on Wall Street for an investment banker. To his first faculty meeting, he says he probably wore a pair of red, white, and blue shoes; red double-knit slacks; a wide white belt; a colorful dress shirt—red, white, and blue, with maybe a white tie. "And old Cecil Cox, who was the president of the Gainesville High School Quarterback Club, called me the Mod Squad."[26]

Sandra Sharron, an English teacher, regrets what she views as a decline in academic standards at GHS around the time of desegregation. When Boyd was appointed, her reaction was, he's thirty years old. How does he get to be principal? Sharron says Boyd had a lot of wisdom to gain to have the faculty's total respect. They would have liked him to be a little bit more academically driven. But she agrees that he was the right person for the job at that time, because of his desire to have contact with the students and his rapport with them.[27]

Shelton Boyles agrees that Talbot picked the right man to be GHS principal. He believes the trouble under Hudson and Neller was going to happen, regardless of who was running the school, because of the circumstances of the February 1970 desegregation. But by fall 1971, "enough crap had happened that everybody welcomed [Boyd's] strength. We're not having any of this stuff. We're going to do this. And it's beautiful. I mean, that's a beautiful school, still is."[28]

Peggy Finley uses the word *charisma* to describe Boyd. She also says that he had some innovative ideas, among them having a chair of the teaching faculty, elected by the faculty. The faculty chair took over running the faculty meetings, instead of an assistant principal. That step was part of Boyd's strategy of getting people to work together and take ownership of their projects. Finley was eventually elected faculty chair. She recalls that she did not seek the position, but other faculty members approached her and urged her to accept it.[29]

Boyd acknowledges that it was difficult during his principalship to hire black teachers, but he believes he did his best. "And it is a fact that there aren't as many black teacher candidates as there once were. And it is probably because a lot of those that have the ability to go to college and attain a bachelor's degree are going into fields other than education. . . . I think the quality of the man or woman is what we look for. And it had nothing to do with race."[30]

Boyd was also exceptional in his ability to bring support from the business community to Gainesville High School, a particularly valuable talent in an era of insufficient public resources for the schools. As a member of Rotary, he interacted with many other community leaders.[31]

Gainesville High would eventually (but not yet) find stability on Boyd's watch.

As the schools moved forward, there continued to be sessions with so-called experts on improving race relations, mostly through federal grants. Not all of them worked.

Alachua and Bay Counties, the two Florida counties sued by the NAACP Legal Defense Fund in the cases that ended at the Supreme Court in *Carter*, each received a $40,000 federal grant for race-relations workshops. From Alachua County, forty-eight junior and senior high school teachers and counselors, eighteen black and thirty white, participated in a three-week session that began July 5, 1971. On the weekend of August 6–8, the Alachua County group, augmented by some principals and administrators, met at a resort hotel in St. Augustine for a "group encounter." A *Sun* reporter was invited to attend the weekend session, in keeping with the school administration's policy of open communications with the public.

The meetings were led by a federal contractor from Maine. According to the *Sun*, the meetings produced boredom, tardiness, disrespect for the coordinators, and some mass boycotts. One teacher said, "It's like they're up there – our leaders – and we're out here, their students." Another participant commented that one especially verbose person "sounds like one of our school board members." The closest approach to bonding came when the coordinators withdrew from a session as planned and let the school personnel do their own thing.

> An administrator:
>
> One week a school board member will call and ask the county office to try to get more staff personnel out into the schools assisting teachers with materials and direction. The next week a school board member will call and say too many of the county office staff are out in the classrooms, interfering with the regular teachers' duties.
>
> A principal:
>
> They tell us what we are supposed to do, and we are supposed to tell you.
>
> A black teacher:
>
> Why do the blacks always have to give in to the whites? Why do the whites always put up such a fuss when they have to give up so little sometimes?
>
> Last year one of [my] colleagues asked if [I] could get the black children to teach the white children to dance. She was serious. But I was afraid to do this because of the idea of a jukebox in a school and blacks and whites dancing together.

> Now I'm not afraid, because I have a trust level with my principal.

> A mayor (at that time, Neil Butler):

> [Some] might have gotten too much out of the experience. [They] might think they could conquer the entire world of hate, distrust and prejudice within a month or even one school year. Many good feelings would be challenged by situations in and relating to the classroom, and the teacher or counselor who was on the Cloud Nine of trust, love and understanding should be prepared for some unhappy experiences ahead.[32]

Reading the press account today, the sessions call to mind psychologists helicoptering in to save an infantry company under siege in Vietnam. In hindsight, we can recognize the absence of preparation for desegregation, but we also need to recognize that when desegregation came, no one had a magic tool kit to make everything work.

Mary Koru, the school board's grant manager, declared the August 1971 sessions a victory and went after federal money for more workshops. Charles Chestnut III, then chair of the Bi-racial Committee, said that those who really need the workshops don't go. He urged the staff to be more selective in determining who should attend. The Rev. Wright later echoed Chestnut's view. Both had participated as leaders in local workshops.[33]

During Russell Ramsey's term as principal of the Lincoln vocational center, an assistant superintendent from the county staff required Ramsey and his faculty to participate in a sensitivity training session. "I had the vocational staff, a mixture of reading teachers, math teachers, auto mechanics, carpentry, masonry, roofing, plumbing, welding, you know, the whole spectrum, and obviously these men and women came from diverse backgrounds and they needed basics." Instead, the county staff sent over facilitators for a sensitivity session. "And they got us all in this big room and turned the lights out, pitch-black, and then they said now reach out and find somebody's face and feel their face. And I heard the carpentry teacher say the first guy who feels my face is going down on the floor. And I turned the lights back on. And I said this is not what we came for. And boy did I get roasted over that."[34]

The schools appeared calm in comparison to past years, but discipline issues continued. When pressed for greater leniency toward disruptive students by some school board members, Talbot resisted, saying that 54 percent of his time in September 1971 had been spent on "pupil control." Talbot did not approve of rehabilitation inside the school system for every misbehaving student. As an example, he saw no purpose in Mountain Top School if a student were to knife a teacher.[35]

The extent of violence can't be learned from public sources, since virtually all incidents were dealt with in the schools, and not by police. Mass brawls, some of which closed schools, continued to flare around Florida. Weapons included chain belts, steel hair combs, and in one school, guns.[36] Viewed in that context, the disturbances in Alachua County were minor. But as the contemporary *Sun* accounts make clear, the community above all wanted a safe environment in the schools. As hard as the schools were working on the educational challenges presented by desegregation, those efforts would not find broad community support unless the violence ended.

Black students attacked and beat four white students at Gainesville High during fighting that broke out on March 1, 1972. That incident started when black students returned by bus from vocational classes around noon and some of them began roaming the halls to urge other students to leave class. Several windows were broken. Police were called to stop the fighting, and classes were cancelled for the rest of the day.

Then on March 2, fourteen white students, four boys and ten girls, were beaten. A white girl, Mary Rockwood, was assaulted by several black girls in a restroom, and she was treated and released at the local hospital. Another white student suffered a broken nose. The white student body president was hit over the head with a chair when he tried to quiet a group of students in the cafeteria. He said that a black student came to his assistance and prevented worse injuries. Boyd again called police to clear the campus of about 150 black students who refused to go to their classrooms. The school remained open.

Boyd at the time said black student discontent arose because of the school's enforced policy of makeup work for excessive unexcused absences. Students who refused to do the work were given failing grades. Boyd's attempt to discuss grievances with the black students on March 2 ended in a shouting match, with the blacks resuming their protest. Boyd said, "I don't know what else is bugging them. Until today we have had a very good racial climate. I'm going to listen to their complaints, and if changes are needed, we'll make them, but I don't intend to give in to a list of demands that are not in the best interest of the school." Other issues apparently included an inflammatory "KKK" sign on a wall, deans too strict, blacks suspended for fighting, and racial unrest in the Jacksonville schools. Jacksonville's Ribault High was closed due to fighting that apparently was related to the March 14 statewide referendum on busing.[37] Boyd points out that many of the GHS deans were African American and were no less sparing of breaches of school policy than the white deans.[38]

GHS was quiet on March 3. Boyd kept the school open despite significantly reduced attendance but warned any student to stay away if that student did not want to come to school to learn. He said, "It was a lawless element that committed this violence. This group is street-oriented and runs in gangs." Boyd said that the school's student biracial committee was investigating, and a recurring complaint of both black and white students was that teachers needed to "humanize" their relations with students. Student leaders interviewed by the *Sun* agreed that the violent blacks were a very small minority. The school that year enrolled a total of 1,764 students in grades 9–12, including 505 blacks.[39]

Members of the student biracial committee at Gainesville High who spoke to the press said that student grievances targeted the school's administration and were not racial in nature, but that "outside agitators" took advantage of an opportunity to stir up blacks. Faculty members and students decided to hold a car wash to pay for damage to the school. The students said the school needed a strong coalition of students, faculty, and administrators to fend off any attempts by outsiders to encourage violence. The other need was for teachers to be more available to students as counselors. Boyd said, "They are just crying out for closer student-teacher relationships."[40]

Looking back, Boyd remembers that when he became principal, the main grievance of black students was their lack of an equal voice in student government. Boyd resolved that issue by requiring that the senate be composed of equal numbers of white and black students. He adds that seven or eight years after the fruitbasket turnover, students agreed this proportional representation was no longer needed, and candidates were again elected without reference to race.[41] From today's distance, teachers and administrators see the disturbances as issues of adjustment, not issues of discrimination. Boyd recalls hearing complaints by black students against black teachers. "And I thought that was ironic in some ways, but at least they trusted me to hear what their grievance was and to let me know their dissatisfaction with a teacher of their own race."[42] Mary Lewis, a black dean, took the side of the teachers when black students would complain. "The English teachers were hard, but that was all for the best. I would tell them I don't care where you go, it'll be hard. Some students were not familiar with it and didn't want to learn, they were complaining and carrying on."[43] A white English teacher at GHS saw the outbursts as a way to get out of classroom routines.[44]

Jessie Heard remembers an occasion when some black students at Buchholz wanted to walk out. They gathered in the auditorium. Coach Heard:

> I said, well, what's the problem? "Coach, we want to walk out." I said, what you protesting? "I don't know, they protest at GHS and Eastside and all them places, and we want to walk out too." I said, well, let it roll. Boy said, "No, we

> can't walk out before lunch!" And everybody died. So they walked out up toward the street and one girl fainted. And then they said she got hurt. Some kid went and called home, and here come the cops, and everything else. . . . But other than that, the incidents that they had over there was just boy-boy scrap, boy-girl or girl-girls scrap. So if it was a racial thing, you know, you could read it how you want it. But I was there.[45]

Shelton Boyles, speaking of Gainesville High:

> Why are there so many black adolescents in prison? Because they act out. Why are there so many white young kids in prison? Don't they understand that what they're doing is going to lead there? They act out. They do that. That would be close to what I would explain. . . . And I think a lot of it is that fighting was going on just because we can, you know. There's a lot of stuff going on, and there are a lot of white people here that are afraid of me, afraid of us, and we can get away with it. And we have a lot of white young people said, they're not getting away with that. You know, let's isolate one of them and beat the hell out of him. I think that's what the beating of the dean [Tom Evans] and the coaches was about. It's like, going to show them. I don't think it had anything to do with any causes of any kind. It was like incidental violence.[46]

The 1971–72 school year ended at many schools with poor attendance, lapsing discipline, and student fighting. Beatings of students in restrooms, locker rooms, and behind buildings were reported. The incidents were attributed to teacher preoccupation with final grading during the last two days of class, with no remaining classwork to be done. Many children were kept home by their parents.[47]

Neil Butler was again chosen by Gainesville High students to be their graduation speaker:

> I want to share this part of my life with you. I have never carried a picket sign, never walked in a protest march or participated in a sit-in. But my record of protest will compare favorably with anyone in this community. Your mere presence can [produce] change if you get involved in a constructive way.

> It is with fear that I watch you shrug your shoulders and say, "It's not my bag, man, my old man created it, let him change it." No matter who created it, if you don't change it, you will go over the waterfall with your old man.

It was the last GHS graduating class that resulted from the February 1970 desegregation. The class of 943 included a complete class that transferred from Lincoln to GHS as sophomores. Beginning in 1973, Eastside and Buchholz would each graduate their first seniors.[48]

Accreditation by the Southern Association of Colleges and Schools helped the county system's return to more normal operation. Newberry High School, which had lost accreditation before its new building was constructed with bond issue funds, regained accreditation on December 31, 1971. Hawthorne and the two new high schools, Eastside and Buchholz, were all accredited on December 31, 1972.[49]

An important milestone was reached in September 1972 with the opening of the Lincoln Vocational Center in the former Lincoln High School building. Russell Ramsey was chosen to be its principal. In an agreement with the junior college, the school board gained funding and more control over high school vocational programs. The center initially enrolled eight hundred students in seventeen on-site programs, including high-voltage electrical work, carpentry, masonry, roofing, plumbing, welding, automobile mechanics, and tailoring. The students attended half-day sessions at the center and spent the rest of the school day at their regular high schools. Andrew Mickle, the Lincoln High tailoring teacher, found himself back in his former tailoring lab at the center. Mickle had been chosen Alachua County teacher of the year for 1970–71. Mickle commented that the programs at the center would give students a path to economic independence. "They just plain don't know what's going on outside their classrooms. The result is disillusionment, boredom and long welfare lines."[50] Although the programs offered at the center were available only at that location, enrollment was approximately 70 percent black and 30 percent white, according to Ramsey.[51] One eager African American police science student at the Lincoln center was Tony Jones, who became Gainesville's chief of police in 2009.[52]

Reopening the former Lincoln High building, located in Gainesville's east-side black neighborhood, had an additional benefit to that community. Philoron Wright, a son of the Reverend Thomas A. Wright, taught a course for students who might want to go into parks and recreation jobs. After school hours, the City of Gainesville operated athletic programs in the Lincoln gym, in the weight room, and on the baseball and softball fields and tennis courts. The city hired Philoron Wright to run these programs.

According to Wright, the Lincoln gym would be packed every day until 9:00 p.m. He continued to run that program for the city for some years after Lincoln was converted to a middle school for the 1974–75 school year.[53]

During the 1972–73 school year, fewer incidents of group uprisings were reported, but principals could not let down their guard. At Gainesville High, white students were beaten by roving gangs of blacks on January 12, 1973. That incident was related to an attack by four black students on a white teacher on November 30, 1972, when she held them in a room for questioning. The teacher filed charges against the two students that she could identify. They were both assigned to Mountain Top School. One student cooperated, but the other student walked out. Principal Boyd was firm. "A small group of blacks are trying to get this student reinstated, which is not going to happen as long as I am here. It's a matter of a small group trying to decide whether I have the authority to run this school." Boyd held an assembly on January 13 to counteract rumors, but some fights broke out after the assembly.[54] Despite these continuing incidents, Vince Deconna observed that by 1972–73, his senior year, race relations at GHS were much improved over 1970–71, when he entered GHS as a sophomore.[55]

Roberta Berner, the GHS school paper editor in 1969–70, was now on the *Sun* staff. In an article she wrote in May 1973, school personnel and parents could not agree on the extent of violence on campus. Dan Boyd was not an acknowledged source for the article. It was, probably, a case of some viewing the glass as half-empty and others viewing it as half-full. Administrators and teachers at GHS would naturally want to minimize continuing violent behavior. It was their job to control it.

Classroom doors were locked during the lunch hour and teachers' breaks. Theft was agreed to be a problem. A substitute teacher was candid. She saw students pushing others against walls and talking back to teachers. "It's kind of a shock to me how some of the kids act. They're so much rougher than they used to be. I haven't been around long enough to know the specific problems, but you can sense a hostility. At first when I came here, I thought, 'Oh no,' then I found out this goes on all the time." The article told the stories of several girls who had been injured at GHS, Westwood, and Buchholz. The police department was offering courses in self-defense.

Tommy Tomlinson, who had seen it all, summed up the issues still facing the schools:

> I personally don't think we have an excessive amount of [lawbreaking] going on. The school reflects the community, no more, no less than the general temperature, the general atmosphere you find among people today. It's just a change in people and in the community itself. We take what the

> parents send us to work with. Within the last three years, we have seen a steady decrease in fighting among students.
>
> I think as we graduate each class, we're bringing up groups of children that have been together longer under a fully integrated system. The school atmosphere, I feel, is definitely on the upswing. This is not to say we don't have isolated cases. The schools have every type of person there from A to Z.

***

> We take 2,000 youngsters and put them in one location from all walks of life. The teacher hasn't taken any courses in how to stop fights. Then, some of the public gets upset with us when we can't keep absolute law and order.

Tomlinson encouraged parents to buy school insurance. The district could not afford liability insurance for students injured on school grounds.[56]

Violence in Alachua County's secondary schools, the most significant consequence of the 1970 fruitbasket turnover, dissipated rather quickly as white and black students became accustomed to attending class together. School leaders from the years that immediately followed the fruitbasket turnover agree that the main reason for the decrease in violence was simply the passage of time. Dan Boyd: "I think I would say that time is the great healer. And that's why I said Mr. Hudson and John [Neller] had a much more difficult time than I because after you've had that group who would've graduated from Lincoln that started at [GHS] as tenth graders, we had three years to show them that we would offer them a high-quality education, that we were sensitive to their needs. But at the same time, we had high expectations of academic performance, personal conduct." Sam Haywood recalls that there was a big change in personal relationships between the races from 1972 to 1976. He gives credit to Dan Boyd for hiring good teachers and insisting that his staff be fair to everyone. Haywood also gives credit to the students. He believes that the younger Lincoln transfer students who reached GHS after attending formerly white junior high schools were much less angry than the students who went directly to GHS.[57]

School advisory councils broadly representative of each school's community were favored in a 1973 study prepared by Fred Schultz, a former state legislator. He had been appointed by Governor Askew two years earlier to head a committee to study Florida's public schools. At a conference to review the committee's report, the discussion came back around to school disorders. Alachua County's Longstreth was then serving as president of the Florida Association of District School Superintendents, which had its own legislative program. Longstreth said, "We are not addressing ourselves to the major problem of human relations. I can tell you that parents are pulling their children out of school because their children are getting their teeth knocked out and they are afraid to go to the toilet." A black delegate to the conference from Tallahassee said that persons he called black militants had attacked his own son in high school. Schultz told the conference that the purpose of the school advisory councils was to work out the human relations problem.[58]

The Alachua County Education Association, representing the county's teachers, endorsed the Schultz committee's proposals, including the school advisory councils. The school advisory council provisions were enacted by the legislature and continue in effect. In addition to optional functions, the councils must approve school improvement plans and annual school budgets.[59]

The 1972–73 school year closed peacefully for Alachua County, without the fighting that had erupted the previous year. Alachua County's schools had gained a major milestone on the hard, circuitous path that began with the 1968 bond issue.

Throughout the desegregation years, despite the challenges faced by the schools, community support remained strong. Without community support, desegregation would have been even more disruptive. Groups across the political spectrum, from the Gainesville Women for Equal Rights to the Gainesville Junior Women's Club, pitched in.

Since 1968, University of Florida student volunteers had helped the schools through the SAMSON (Student Action Management for Socio-Economic Opportunities Network) project. The 1971 recruitment meeting drew an estimated four hundred students, who were addressed by Charles Chestnut III, Neil Butler, and the late Father Michael Gannon, then pastor of the Roman Catholic student center at the University of Florida. Chestnut warned the students that they would encounter people who had become discouraged with ineffective organizations. "I've seen a lot of talk but little action. Progress can be made, but it takes a great deal of dedication." SAMSON served an estimated three hundred county students at any one time, through tutoring, recreation, adopt a grandparent, Trenton Juvenile Home (in neighboring Gilchrist County), Sunland Training Center (a state residential institution for intellectually disabled persons), and some other programs.[60]

Moving from advocacy to participation, the Gainesville Women for Equal Rights initiated an enrichment project for third and fourth graders at four previously white schools that now had significant numbers of black students. Their project, called "The Best Day of the Week," used sports, art, drama, games and field trips to help students get along in interracial groups and to improve their self-concepts. The program was funded through a grant from the Department of Health, Education, and Welfare under the Emergency School Assistance Program. It ran for two weeks in the summer of 1971 and for ten Saturdays during the 1971–72 school year.[61] Members of the biracial committees at the participating schools worked with the children.[62]

In 1973, Longstreth and GWER sought to replace the "Best Day of the Week" program with a new grant under the Emergency School Aid Act of 1972. The new GWER program sought to increase involvement of minority parents in the schools.[63] Members of GWER wrote the grant application and initially assisted in running the HANDS (Home and School) program. The program received a $72,000 grant in its first year of operation, which funded a director and five home-school coordinators, one each for five county schools. In 1974, the program expanded to five additional schools. Federal budget cuts ended the program when funding for 1976 was denied.[64]

The Gainesville Junior Women's Club began funding a "Reading Is Fundamental" program in 1973. That program encouraged reading by children by allowing them to pick out a book and take it home to keep.[65]

The examples of community support for the schools described here are not meant to be exclusive.

School biracial committees were functioning by February 1971 in almost every Alachua County school. Those committees created another way for community members to become involved in the schools and issues associated with desegregation. The biracial committee of J. J. Finley Elementary School scheduled an afternoon Family Play Day for its children and their parents. "Because integration of our school has been achieved without busing, we believe Finley has a real opportunity to serve a neighborhood and that parents and children will gain value from friendships that may develop at school and that do not end when class is dismissed," said the cochair of the committee. Other issues dealt with by school biracial committees included protecting students crossing busy streets, student transportation, identifying students needing more parental support, lack of respect for black teachers, recruiting tutors and "parent helpers," creating new channels of communication ("PTA is [a] small, closed, money making group. Our committee meets in homes many times"), and the ever-present issue of discipline ("black parent often tells principal to paddle child harder. We must teach him to behave differently, take him as he is, never mind the background").[66]

The school board was only partially successful in broadening its formal relationship with the University of Florida. The idea was not new. Just after county voters approved the 1968 bond issue, George W. Barnard, MD, president of the countywide PTO, made a series of detailed recommendations for more direct contact between the University and the county schools. He wanted the University and the business community to continue and build on the relationships that produced the successful bond issue referendum. Barnard argued that more relationships between the public schools and the University would also bring more contact between the University and the business community.[67]

The school board and the University appointed a liaison committee in March 1971. But the biggest accomplishment of a liaison committee up to December 1971 had been securing the use of Florida Field, the University's football stadium, for high school football games. Although members of the county staff wanted to continue the committee, Enneking opposed. "We have unlimited potential with the University as a resource, but unless we get more formal response there is no need for the board to attempt it unilaterally." Enneking believed the board should seek a high-level commitment from the University's vice president for academic affairs. It was suggested that the University should hire a full-time chair with an office and a secretary.[68] The University declined.[69] However, the relationship produced other improvements, including the opening of some University courses to registration by Alachua County high school students, and access by University professors to the county schools for research projects.[70]

Besides coping with desegregation, the schools were affected by increases in crime and drug use. An FBI survey in fall 1972 had Gainesville with the highest crime rate of the nineteen selected cities around the country in its 100,000 to 125,000 population bracket. Gainesville led that bracket in murders, rapes, and burglaries. A state survey had Alachua County trailing only Broward, Dade, and Duval Counties. Florida overall had the second highest crime rate in the United States, according to the FBI survey. Local authorities blamed bicycle thefts and rock-throwing incidents for boosting the statistics.[71] Poverty probably played a role. Thirty-five percent of Alachua County's school children qualified for free meals in 1971, well above the national average of 25 percent.[72]

A major drug raid by federal and state authorities in December 1972 included nine persons, six of whom were Eastside students, arrested for allegedly selling drugs to students at that school. Principal John Dukes and several students had requested an investigation. The drugs allegedly being sold at Eastside included marijuana, phenobarbital, and hallucinogens.[73] Gainesville High's new open campus policy had its downside, with some students apparently making drug buys while visiting nearby restaurants.[74] The school had started the open campus to avoid having four different lunch hours in the school's overcrowded cafeteria.[75] Isolated drug arrests of students at Gainesville secondary schools had been reported over the past few years.

Alachua County responded to the December 1972 drug raid by appointing a twelve-member Alachua County Hard Drug Committee.[76] The Hard

Drug Committee recognized that all elements of the community needed to focus on illegal drugs, but did not let the schools escape some responsibility for the problem. The committee wanted all educators to be well enough trained about hard drugs to be able to detect the abuse, identify the drug, and counsel the abuser. The committee wanted both teachers and counselors to undergo intensive hard-drug training courses.[77]

The schools pushed back. On January 8, 1973, nine school district employees and board chair Howe gave their views to the Hard Drug Committee. Their responses reflect both battle fatigue and already overcommitted resources. The educators agreed that the problem was not with the schools, but with the community. Once again, they implied, the schools were being asked to solve a community problem.[78]

Another new challenge that the schools had to face was state-mandated testing of students. The Florida legislature passed the state's first mandatory student testing requirement in June 1971. The law required students in second, third, and fourth grades to be tested on reading, writing, and arithmetic. Superintendent Talbot was dissatisfied that the law did not also hold teacher colleges accountable for turning out teachers qualified for the changing needs of the schools.[79] The first round of tests, taken by second and fourth graders to measure success in reading objectives, showed that Alachua County pupils scored close to state averages in most categories. The test was given to 376 second graders and 400 fourth graders (20 percent of each class) who were randomly selected. After reviewing the final test results, the state Department of Education recommended that Alachua County place more emphasis on reading skills in all areas studied, such as mathematics and social studies, not just in reading classes.[80]

Scores of high school seniors on the state senior placement test had come to be used to measure schools' performance. Some legislators criticized the effectiveness of Florida schools because only a small minority made the 300 score needed for admission to a four-year state university. All seniors had been given the test for many years. Superintendents and principals opposed these comparisons, and someone discovered that there was no legal requirement that the test be given to every senior. The state association of county school superintendents unanimously resolved that the test should be made optional. The state education superintendent, Floyd Christian, agreed with the new policy.[81]

The Department of Health, Education, and Welfare in 1973 threatened to cut off $70 million in financial support to Florida universities because of lagging black admissions to formerly white state universities. The state Board of Regents, which then supervised all Florida four-year institutions, began easing the senior placement test in response to charges that the test was biased against blacks.[82]

Superintendent Longstreth asked the school board to approve a separate standardized testing program for Alachua County for the 1973–74 school year. Students would be given the Otis-Lennon Mental Ability Test and the Metropolitan Achievement Test. Longstreth said the program would allow teachers to compare students' mental abilities on the first test to their actual progress in class, which would be measured by the second test.

Longstreth's proposal led to a contentious two-hour discussion before the school board that refocused the discussion on race. Alachua County was now in the midst of the national debate about standardized testing. Teachers who participated in a pilot project using the tests at a Gainesville elementary school generally praised the tests. One black teacher said that her white and black students had performed about the same. Opponents charged that the tests would discriminate against students from backgrounds other than white and middle class, and that the tests would result in permanent labels being placed on students. Charles Chestnut III argued that most standardized testing is culturally biased and said that the tests had "nothing to do with the education of children." He said, "We're going to end up with a tracking of black students. We're going to end up with blacks in special education classes." A University of Florida educational psychologist said the testing companies were only interested in money, not helping students. He said teachers were afraid to speak out against the testing program because they were afraid of losing their jobs. "Oh, that's crap," one teacher yelled. "No, that's not crap," said another teacher.

Longstreth agreed that the test results could be misused, but he told the board that he would rather deal with improper use than prevent teachers from using the data effectively. The school board voted to approve the program by a 3–2 vote, specifying that the results not be used to classify students into special classes or curricula, and that they not be used to judge teachers' effectiveness. Enneking, Samuels, and Manning voted in favor of the program, and Howe and Todd voted against.[83] The results proved disappointing. In math, only 77 percent of county elementary and middle school students performed at or above expectations, versus an intended rate of 90 percent nationally. The countywide reading rate was 84 percent, versus the same 90 percent national rate. Longstreth said the Alachua County results were consistent with scores around the Southeast, which he said were generally below the national average.[84]

Another new test for the schools was collective bargaining with the teachers. The system had recognized the Alachua County Education Association as the bargaining agent for all employees, although the contract was "open shop," meaning that employees were not required to join the association. The first contract, formally approved August 12, 1971, provided a $700 annual across-the-board salary increase for all teachers, a $1,000 raise in the salary of starting teachers, and a $120,000 pool for "career incentive bonuses" (not "merit pay"). The ACEA contract also addressed other issues that had carried over from the 1968 teacher strike. The school board agreed to consult with ACEA on such issues as recruitment of employees, community support for school programs, budget preparation, curriculum, in-service training, class size, teacher turnover, personnel policies, salaries, working conditions, and other mutually agreed issues.[85]

The school board and the ACEA renewed the 1971 agreement to bargain collectively for another two years on January 10, 1973,[86] but that step did not settle any major issues. Some issues at the top of the teachers' list spilled over from integration. The new agreement required school administrators to make every effort to help teachers handle disruptive students. The school board and the ACEA agreed to appoint a joint committee of teachers and administrators to improve discipline procedures. The school board also agreed on a best-efforts basis not to require reading teachers in the county's remedial reading program to teach nonreaders.[87] The board provisionally approved an across-the-board salary increase but wanted to study the way the proposed salary schedule would affect teachers with different levels of experience. There was no more talk of discretionary payments.[88]

In 1964, Alachua County was not ready for desegregation. By June 1973, Alachua County was desegregated but not yet integrated. And the changing educational world was not going to wait for the schools to catch up. Ready or not, the public schools would have to find their way down still more new paths.

CHAPTER 19
THE TEACHERS

There was not a manual, and there was not anything other than let's try this, and with the overriding principle that these young people should not have to pay too big a price both in terms of their academic learning, in terms of their safety, by going through this process, because they didn't volunteer for it either. And we're all in it in that sense. And that was the beauty of it. I mean, there were so many beautiful moments, but a lot of ugly stuff.

Shelton Boyles, former GHS teacher and Alachua County school board member, interview, 2014

I found a long time ago that the more the kids like you, the harder they'll work for you.

Dan Boyd, former GHS principal, interview, 2014

Let us develop a kind of dangerous unselfishness. One day a man came to Jesus, and he wanted to raise some questions about some vital matters of life. At points he wanted to trick Jesus, and show him that he knew a little more than Jesus knew and throw him off base. . . .

Now that question could have easily ended up in a philosophical and theological debate. But Jesus immediately pulled that question from mid-air, and placed it on a dangerous curve between Jerusalem and Jericho. And he talked about a certain man, who fell among thieves. You remember that a Levite and a priest passed by on the other side. They didn't stop to help him. And finally a man of another race came by. He got down from his beast, decided not to be compassionate by proxy. But he got down with him, administered first aid, and helped the man in need. Jesus ended up saying, this was the good man, this was the great man, because he had the capacity to project the "I" into the "thou," and to be concerned about his brother.

The Reverend Dr. Martin Luther King Jr.
"Mountain Top" speech
Memphis, Tennessee
April 3, 1968

Gainesville High School and Lincoln High School were each justifiably proud of their academic reputations. Each school relative to its peers placed a high proportion of its students in two- and four-year colleges. Both schools devoted significant effort to preparing their college-bound students. For white college-bound students, the midterm 1970 desegregation had little impact on the conduct of classes. Although under freedom of choice many blacks were in college-prep courses, the black enrollment in those courses under freedom of choice did not make up a significant proportion of the students. The fruitbasket turnover did not result in many more blacks being added to those classes.[1] College-bound white and black students were engaged with their school work and would be unlikely to turn disruptive even under serious provocation. The white college-bound students also populated the various extracurricular activities at GHS, which gave them additional incentives to keep the school functioning.

But all high school students, whether or not they planned to go to college, had to complete required courses in subjects such as English, math, social studies, and science. For many white and black students who would not go on to college, the academic courses had little relevance. These white and black students tended then, as now, to have lower socioeconomic status and to perform less well in class. Realistically, most students in the general courses either could not or would not achieve at the same level as their college-bound classmates. They tended to be less involved (and less welcome) in extracurricular activities, especially in the service clubs.[2] It would not be much of an exaggeration to say that even before desegregation, GHS was really two schools, one for the college-bound students and the other for those in the general courses.

Before desegregation, disaffected students in the general courses at GHS and Lincoln had no obvious target on which to vent their alienation. But the fruitbasket turnover brought these two groups of less-invested students into the same space, in class, in the halls, in the cafeteria.

The senior placement test scores described previously[3] offer a proxy for the relative academic situations of the white and black students at GHS in 1970–71. There were low-scoring students of both races. But absorbing 580 students from Lincoln High, large numbers of whom were not performing academically at the level of their new white classmates, and who to the very last day had remained loyal to Lincoln, presented an unprecedented challenge. GHS Assistant Principal Caffey, assessing the school's academic program in June 1970, recognized the gap between black and white students "testwise" and a need to develop a definite program to close the gap.[4] There were deficits across all academic areas. Talbot zeroed in on learning deficits as a root problem linked to both academic and disciplinary issues. Talbot attributed the violence at GHS in the spring of 1970 not to race as such but to learning deficits and to the midterm closing of Lincoln High. He said students of very different educational backgrounds, both black and white, had to be taught in the same setting. Talbot said this environment created friction, black to black and white to white. "We've got to set up a climate for learning."[5] Alachua County's teachers, ready or not, would find themselves on the front lines of this effort.

In desegregated schools, students of both races would be educated in the same setting, using the same curriculum, by a white and black faculty. Not surprisingly, however, desegregation posed different challenges for black and white educators. African American teachers and administrators were expected not only to play their normal instructional roles, but also to help black students accommodate to desegregation. White faculty members had to begin educating their new black students from the point those students had reached in the segregated black schools. There would be no easy solutions to the separate challenges faced by black and white educators.

Looking ahead to desegregation, Alachua County for some years had sought to hire teachers "strictly on the basis of qualifications." At the same time, the county recognized a responsibility to help its current African American teachers meet higher expectations. Talbot in 1965 started what the press described as a crash in-service program to tutor black teachers in their weak areas so they would have a better chance of passing the National Teacher Examination. Talbot said, "It is not our intention to run the Negro teachers out of their jobs, but we can never entertain the idea of transferring unqualified teachers into white schools or vice versa." Gaston Cook, principal at Duval Elementary School, told the *Sun* that it was up to blacks to do something about their teacher training. He believed that black teachers would rise to the challenge. "For the last 25 years no one showed any interest in Negro education. We were isolated. Now we have some support and we are determined to meet the standards of quality."[6]

To maintain its African American teaching staff, Alachua County also had to hire new teachers. Despite best intentions, that effort hit two barriers. Starting teacher salaries remained low because of an oversupply of young white teachers who were graduating from the University of Florida, or who were married to UF students. As more opportunities opened up for black college graduates, fewer of the most qualified black students chose to be teachers. After Alachua County completed hiring for the 1964–65 school year, a pool of 300 unhired white applicants remained, but there were only 11 unhired black applicants.[7] Of the 257 newly hired teachers joining the system for the 1968–69 school year, only 5 were black.[8] The system employed approximately 1,066 teachers at that time, excluding specialists paid through federal programs.[9] Superintendent Talbot explained, "Our trouble is we are not getting any new Negro teachers. . . . Counties that pay the best are getting most of the graduates from the Negro teacher colleges. We may do better if and when the University of Florida begins to graduate more Negro teachers."[10] The percentage of black teachers in Alachua County declined from 32 percent in 1963 to 23 percent in February 1970. See table 5.

Table 5. Summary of Teaching Staff in Reports to Court, Wright v. Board

School, year	Teachers, white	Teachers, black	Teachers, total
Gainesville High, Apr. 1974 (9–12)	72	11	83
Bishop, Apr. 1974 (7–8)	39	10	49
Westwood, Apr. 1974 (6–8)	41	13	54
Fort Clark, Apr. 1974 (6–8)	27	6	33
Eastside, Apr. 1974 (9–12)	33	14	47
Buchholz, Apr. 1974 (9–12)	53	9	62
County system total, Apr. 1974	**782**	**(21%) 208**	**990**
Gainesville High, Nov. 1973 (9–12)	71	11	82
Bishop, Nov. 1973 (7–8)	38	9	48
Westwood, Nov. 1973 (6–8)	41	13	54
Fort Clark, Nov. 1973 (6–8)	27	6	33
Eastside, Nov. 1973 (9–12)	33	14	47
Buchholz, Nov. 1973 (9–12)	48	9	57
County system total, Nov. 1973	**729**	**(22%) 206**	**935***
Gainesville High, Apr. 1973 (10–12)	95	23	118
Bishop, Apr. 1973 (7–10)	43	10	53
Westwood, Apr. 1973 (7–10)	42	10	52
Eastside, Apr. 1973 (7–11)	37	13	51
Buchholz, Apr. 1973 (7–11)	49	9	58
County system total , Apr. 1973	**729**	**(22%) 210**	**940***
County system total, Nov. 1971	**713**	**(22%) 197**	**914***
No report for 1970–71 school year			

School, year	Teachers, white	Teachers, black	Teachers, total
Gainesville High, Feb. 1970 (10–12)	109	23	132
Lincoln, Feb. 1970 (7–12)	0	0	0
Bishop, Feb. 1970 (7–9)	43	9	52
Westwood, Feb. 1970 (7–9)	42	11	53
Eastside, Feb. 1970 (7–9)	28	7	35
Buchholz, Feb. 1970 (7–9)	35	11	46
County system total, Feb. 1970	**769**	**(23%) 234**	**1,003**
Gainesville High, Dec. 1969 (10–12)	109	4	113
Lincoln, Dec. 1969 (7–12)	13	55	68
Bishop, Dec. 1969 (7–9)	69	5	74
Westwood, Dec. 1969 (7–9)	61	4	65
County system total, Dec. 1969	**768**	**(23%) 235**	**1,003**
Gainesville High, Oct. 1968 (10–12)	111	1	112
Lincoln, Oct. 1968 (7–12)	16	67	83
Bishop, Oct. 1968 (7–9)	69	2	71
Westwood, Oct. 1968 (7–9)	62	1	63
County system total, Oct. 1968	**747**	**(25%) 253**	**1,000**
Gainesville High, Oct. 1967 (10–12)	100	1	101
Lincoln, Oct. 1967 (7–12)	16	69	85
Bishop, Oct. 1967 (7–9)	64	2	66
Westwood, Oct. 1967 (7–9)	61	0	61
County system total, Oct. 1967	**693**	**(26%) 240**	**933**
County system total, 1963[11]	**563**	**(32%) 263**	**826**

Note: For some years, teachers were disaggregated by full-time and part-time. For those years only full-time teachers are counted. The reports to the court after February 1970 were in extensive computer printouts, from which it was not possible to extract pertinent data effectively for some school years.

**For November 1971, there were two teachers whose race was given as "Oriental" and two teachers with Hispanic surnames. For April 1973, one teacher's race was given as "Oriental." For November 1973 and April 1974, one teacher's race was given as "Oriental" and one teacher had a Hispanic surname. Those teachers are not counted in either white or black tables.*

The 1966–67 school year began with 13 white teachers at Lincoln High School. The Lincoln faculty had the highest proportion of teachers of the other race of any school in the county.[12] During freedom of choice, transfers of teachers to schools of the opposite race were voluntary. Talbot said that only "the exceptional" black teachers were volunteering to teach in the white schools, which created a danger of stripping the black schools of top teachers.[13]

Presciently, in December 1966, as desegregation of faculties began, Talbot told the *Sun* that white teachers were less successful in communicating with black students than black teachers were in communicating with white students.[14] Looking back in 1972, Andrew Mickle reflected that black teachers were sturdier and more stable than the white teachers at Lincoln and devoted themselves to teaching and did the utmost for it. He said most white teachers in the county were just putting their husband through school and were not really interested in their positions.[15]

When Lincoln High closed, there were 13 white and 55 black instructional personnel serving grades 7–12. Gainesville High began the 1969–70 school year with 106 white and 5 black instructional personnel serving grades 10–12.[16] When GHS reopened on February 6, 1970, with the Lincoln transfer students, 19 teachers were added, all of whom were black, for a total of 23 black teachers (17 percent) in a teaching faculty of 132.[17] In the 1972–73 school year, GHS had 23 black teachers (19 percent) in a faculty of 118.[18] By the 1973–74 school year, when Gainesville High had returned to a normal complement of students after the opening of Eastside and Buchholz Junior/Senior High Schools, there were 11 black teachers (13 percent) and 71 white teachers, for a total of 82.[19]

Acknowledging that faculty segregation had resulted in inferior black teaching and inferior education for blacks, the Fifth Circuit Court of Appeals in 1966 agreed that merit selection of teachers should not be sacrificed for the sake of integrating faculties. But that court also stated that when schools closed, school boards at a minimum should reassign displaced teachers into existing vacancies, rather than filling those vacancies with new merit hires.[20] The process of desegregating faculties was further defined in the Fifth Circuit's December 1, 1969, decision in *Singleton*, which directly applied to Alachua County. The Fifth Circuit ordered schools to move toward a ratio of black to white teachers in each school that was substantially similar to the ratio in the entire system. Any teachers dismissed or demoted were to be selected from among all system teachers on the basis of objective, nonracial criteria. Dismissed or demoted teachers, if qualified, were to be given the opportunity to fill any vacancies prior to new hires.[21] The court in *Wright v. Board* in April 1969 had ordered Alachua County in the 1970–71 school year to integrate teaching staff at all schools in a ratio of approximately four white teachers to one black teacher.[22] To settle the Lincoln strike in December 1969, the school board had agreed "the staff of Lincoln will be reassigned in the county to comparable positions by the Superintendent with the approval of the school board."[23]

Forced to choose between complying with both its prior agreement on Lincoln faculty and the court order, or further winnowing black teachers, the school district chose compliance. School board minutes reflect that in February 1970 virtually every Lincoln teacher was initially placed in a secondary school position, either at GHS, the temporary campuses of Eastside and Buchholz, or one of the junior high schools.[24]

The system also redoubled its efforts to recruit more African American teachers. Catherine Mickle, a respected math and business-education teacher from Lincoln High School and the wife of Andrew Mickle, was transferred to the system personnel office when Lincoln closed. She and Garna Williams, the white head of personnel, made recruiting trips together around the South to historically black colleges. Those efforts, according to Catherine Mickle, did not produce many new black teachers for Alachua County.[25]

Recruiting black teachers was not just an Alachua County problem. The chief teacher recruiter for the State of Florida said that for September 1970 the state would need twelve thousand new teachers, and of these, one-quarter should be African American to meet legal desegregation requirements. But he said there was no way, given the competition for black teachers in other Southern states and other regions of the country, that Florida would be able to meet this quota. A Broward County teacher recruiter who visited black colleges said, "Gov. Kirk has put Florida on the map as a highly segregated state with his emphasis on busing. They don't know anything about Broward County but they know about Gov. Kirk. They see more of Kirk than they do of Maddox or Wallace."[26]

Many black teachers were already teaching in the white schools by February 1970, but for some black teachers new to desegregated faculties, the transition was difficult. The black teachers, like the black students, had been together for many years in the segregated schools and had bonded into a mutually supportive community.[27] Some white former Gainesville High teachers recall that, like many Lincoln students, some of the transferred teachers at first seemed fearful or withdrawn.[28] Pointing out the long-term impact of segregation, a white former teacher commented about some black teachers, "And it really wasn't their fault if they hadn't been able to go to good schools or been properly prepared to teach."[29]

Replying to a complaint about black teachers made at a meeting of the Florida Public School Council in Gainesville, Superintendent Talbot said that principals were told they must accept all teachers as good teachers until they proved differently. He acknowledged the problem: "When we integrated our facilities in the ratio prescribed by the court we ran out of good teachers." Talbot said that the process of eliminating less competent teachers would take time.[30] Teachers on annual contracts could simply not be reappointed, but teachers on continuing contracts could be removed only for cause.

The Rev. Wright recalled an instance when Talbot terminated five black teachers. Wright was then serving on the Bi-racial Committee. Two of those teachers attended the Rev. Wright's church. Wright spoke to Talbot about the firings. "And [Talbot] said, I want you to know that some parents went into those classrooms and they took notes of what they saw happening under these teachers. And they brought their notes to me. And if you could see those notes, you would agree with me that they were some very poor teachers. Well, the school was integrated and [before integration] the black parents didn't know about it and put up with it. Caucasian parents wouldn't stand for it. And so I accepted what Mr. Talbot said. I explained to those teachers that I thought they should forget about it. And so we just accepted what they did."[31]

Former GHS Principal Neller states that when assigning English teachers to different classes, he needed to take their abilities into account. He had to persuade some senior black English teachers to take GHS classes whose demands would not exceed their known abilities. He said that process was traumatic and those black teachers agreed only reluctantly. They were persuaded by Neller's example of potential parent and student dissatisfaction. At the same time, Neller says he would tell parents who complained about black teachers that they could not choose their children's teachers. But each complaint had to be investigated.[32]

Whatever their feelings about desegregation, many African American teachers committed themselves to making desegregation work for the benefit of both black and white students. Many of those teachers drew on mutually respectful relations that they had with whites, even during de jure segregation. Possibly the first black teacher selected by Talbot to teach in the white schools, Bettye Jennings grew up in Hawthorne, oldest of eleven siblings:

> My best friend growing up was a white girl. Her grandfather had a big store. My grandfather had a little store. And we played with dolls. She never came to my house. I didn't know why, but I'd go to her house, and we played dolls and I never knew, I didn't know. . . . I knew black people went to their school and white people went to their school, but I didn't know that we were second-class citizens, I guess. I didn't know that we were treated differently. . . . I just never let things like that bother me. Because my grandmother raised me and she said you are special. And don't let anybody tell you any differently. So I always thought I was special.

Jennings was Little Miss Shell at Shell Elementary and later Miss Shell at Shell High School, and valedictorian of her graduating class. By the time she was in the fifth grade, she was playing piano for her church. Jennings admired Billie Holliday and aspired to a singing career. But after learning about the discrimination Holliday faced, she decided to become a teacher. While at Bethune-Cookman College, she sang in the chorus, which toured to raise money for the college. On one trip, the chorus performed at Carnegie Hall. A friend's mother worked for a Du Pont family in Delaware, and Jennings worked with them and other white families in the summers as a domestic. As a Bethune-Cookman student, Jennings joined lunch counter sit-ins in Daytona Beach.

Jennings began teaching in Alachua County's black schools in 1962. Her first assignment in a white school was as a traveling music teacher, to give music courses in both the white and black schools in Archer. Superintendent Talbot called her into his office. "He says, 'Now you are going over there, and some people might accept you, some might not. Some may be racists and some . . .' I said, 'Well I have a job to do and I'm not worried about racists.' So I went over and didn't have any problems." Jennings continued teaching in Alachua County until her retirement, working as both an elementary school teacher and as a music teacher. She says she never had any problems working with white teachers and principals. "I've just always been a people person."[33]

Cora Roberson grew up in Gainesville, the great-granddaughter of a slave who obtained a farm ("the mule and the forty acres") during Reconstruction. She was the oldest of nine children, whom she helped raise as a girl. Like many young girls, white and black, Roberson played school. She also taught Sunday school at Emanuel Missionary Baptist Church. She graduated from Lincoln High in 1943 and was a contemporary of the Rev. Wright at Florida Memorial College in St. Augustine. She remembers her teacher training at Florida Memorial:

> When you were an intern, the advisor was right on your case all the time, and then your supervising teacher, they would go in to see that you did it right. They did not just turn the class over to you and go out to the lounge somewhere. They wanted you to be the best, and I wanted to be one of the best teachers. . . .[34]

Roberson in 1950 began teaching in Alachua County, third grade students during the day and veterans in night school. "I enjoyed teaching third grade because there was more of a challenge at the third grade level. I was young and vivacious and had a lot of child in me, as I still have, and I like to play with the children."[35] Like Mary Lewis, Roberson was able to engage her students. Her principal, Thelma Jordon, would single her out: "I remember Miz Jordon said, 'You know what? I'm tired of going to meetings and coming back, and my office, I can hardly get in it, so many children in there. Cora Roberson does not send children to the office. Say whatever happens down there to her classroom, she takes care of it herself.'" Roberson says, "The successful teachers are the teachers who could handle problems and could relate to children and understand that children do certain things because they are children and that we once were children, and we didn't always do the right thing either."

Thelma Jordon was from a still earlier generation than Roberson. Jordon graduated in 1926 with the second twelfth-grade class to graduate from Lincoln High School. She then began teaching in one- or two-room schools, called "country schools," in Alachua County. To reach one of her schools, at Jerusalem, she rode the caboose on a freight train, and after being dropped off walked three miles through the woods. She would board with a local family during the week. She later graduated from Florida A&M and obtained her master's degree at New York University. Despite receiving offers to teach outside the South, and despite the low pay and segregation, she returned to Alachua County.

> I felt that I was needed. I could see the boys and girls in Gainesville. I could see the teachers that we had too. I figured that maybe I could make a contribution that would help the boys and girls to get to a point that I was not able to reach in my own education. I'm glad I came back. I believe that my being here did make a difference.[36]

Alachua County slowly eliminated the separate country schools for whites and blacks (over the protests of some constituents) during the 1920s, 1930s, and 1940s.[37]

Teaching at A. Quinn Jones Elementary School, Roberson visited the homes of her students.

> . . . When I was over at A. Quinn Jones we had no choice, and I thought it was what we were supposed to do, because we were always taught about home visiting. You should make these home visits and then when I was at Florida Memorial I had to make home visits. Go and talk with the parents, not just when there was a problem but go and see where the children came from and learn something about the families. So, we used to do that at A. Quinn Jones, we used to go out in Rutledge, Arredondo and what have you in the afternoon. Mrs. Josie Mitchell, Mrs. Eunice Carter, Mrs. Ann McGhee,

> Mrs. Marie Allen, Mrs. Catherine Taylor, all of us used to go out in the afternoon and make those home visits. I remember one time in particular we were way back out in the woods in the Arredondo section and our car got stuck in the mud and a fellow out in the cornfield had to come and pull us out with his tractor. So, these were fun times and those were things we were right on top of. We knew why children acted so weird because we went to the home and visited, we were not afraid to go anyplace.

At school, Roberson had lunch with her children and took recess with them, even if there was also a physical education teacher at recess. Roberson believes that because she used these techniques, her students learned the basics of reading and writing, as well as social skills.[38]

In the early 1950s and again in the early 1960s, Roberson taught other teachers during the summer at the University of Florida College of Education. She was recruited on separate occasions by Professor Joyce Cooper and a Dr. Windsor. Roberson says of her second stint that Dr. Windsor, of the University of Florida College of Education, was looking for a black teacher "with a good background in how to teach and how that person reached the children." However limited that program was, it represents an early recognition by the College that its graduates would eventually need to teach black children. In that program, Roberson emphasized the importance of home visits.

> . . . Sometimes children didn't come to school because they didn't have shoes. Some of them didn't have proper clothing and what have you. And whenever I got a child to come back to school, there were other children that I did not neglect. Maybe I got Miz Jones's and Miz Smith's and Miz Williams's children back in school, too.[39]

The University of Florida was still segregated, and Roberson could not be paid by the University. For that work she continued to be paid by the county school board, and at the University she had the status of "visiting teacher." Much later, she became the only black teacher among several Alachua County team leaders who helped train students in the Teacher Corps program.

Roberson, like Jennings, was one of the first black teachers to be assigned to a white school, Kirby Smith Elementary. Initially she was a classroom teacher who also did home visits for her and other teachers' children, now visiting both black and white children in their homes. She believes that the Kirby Smith PTA improved because of the home visits. At this stage, when faculties were just beginning to be desegregated, Roberson encountered some white teachers who would not speak to her, but a few were friendly. Eventually at Kirby Smith she became the school's coordinator of visiting teachers.

> And I found out one thing over at Kirby Smith I never would've known before. I thought all white children would have been treated about the same way in school. And I found out if they were poor, they were treated much like the black children were treated. They were kind of isolated, put in the back of the classroom in some cases. And they were, sometimes I would really say it was just inhuman treatment. You know, put your hand down, shut up . . .[40]

Roberson received her master's degree from Tuskegee Institute in 1962. Her last assignment was as coordinator of the county's Head Start program. With the encouragement of the Gainesville Women for Equal Rights, Roberson ran for city commission against the late Perry McGriff, a prominent white businessman, in 1968. He defeated her by just nine hundred votes. Roberson retired in 1984.

Jessie Heard went from being a community icon at Lincoln to facing a tough crowd of white professional and business parents at the newly opened Buchholz High School. Charles Chestnut III remembers when Heard started at Buchholz, Heard said, "Oh boy, I don't know how this is going to work. Because I'm going to tell you, these kids, they ain't going to be able to play football off of salads."[41] Heard recalls that at first, he had only two or three black football players at Buchholz. "They had to zone me some kids. They zoned Sugar Hill [a black neighborhood], and I was accused of being behind that. I had nothing to do with that. Tiny and them did that, 'cause I didn't have any black kids."[42] Heard is speaking of the racial balancing exercises that followed the schools' initial integration in 1970.

Heard was raised by his grandmother in rural Tallapoosa County, Alabama, on what he calls a one-horse farm. Like most Southerners, Heard was familiar from childhood with the other race. "I was born and raised with white boys. They was my playmates in Alabama, segregated as that was. We went swimming, we went hunting. We worked together, and we'd go to swimming holes so to speak—didn't have a pool, had a swimming hole. And be in the woods all the time, and on Sunday after church, we'd play football in the pasture. . . . I just respect people and like people. So just liking people, plan to treat them like I want to be treated."[43]

As athletic director and head football coach at newly opened Buchholz, Heard had to build his football program (and the school's other sports teams) from the ground up. He chose and hired all of his coaches. Gunnar

Paulson, then interning at GHS, was Heard's first hire, as defensive coordinator and weight coach. "And I got to talking with him, and I wanted a coach, and I wanted me a white coach that could help me with those kids. A young one, I didn't need an old somebody that was going to be opinionated and all of that."[44] Paulson would go on to coach and teach in the Alachua County public schools for forty years. He has served many years on the Alachua County school board.

Heard molded a diverse group of boys into successful football teams. "The work ethic was so mutual. It was no difference between a black kid and a white kid. I mean, you could be sitting next to a millionaire, whatever, and the kids on that side, some of them was very affluent. And the kids just got in there and worked. And respect—there was a lot of respect, because of the ethic and everything. But in the beginning, it was a little rough over there. Man, they didn't want to mix it up. They didn't want to go in and hardnose it, you know. But once you taught them the skills and they got confidence just like the black kids, and we tried to treat them as the same, so to speak. People try to say it's impossible, but we tried to treat them with respect, all kids. They played that race stuff. . . . I don't recall any incidents on our field." Heard is referring to incidents when fathers of players were criticized outside the school for allowing their sons to play for Heard. He says that the fathers defended him and the way he treated his players.[45] "Maybe I didn't know any better, but the pressure, coaching—I just had fun working with the boys. It got to be real quick no difference from over there to Lincoln and over there, with integration. Maybe I didn't know any better, but I didn't see black or white. I just saw us trying to make it. But people beating our tail because we didn't have a senior class, and I wasn't used to that, man. So we got together and put in the summer, the work, and worked and worked and worked, the kids were responsible, and I had some tremendous parents over there."[46]

The white boys who played for Heard had the same bond with Heard as his former players at Lincoln. Some from his first teams went on to successful careers, including Breck Weingart, the chair and president of Charles Perry Partners Inc., a large regional construction company, and Bill Adams, a business consultant now living in Texas. Adams graduated from Buchholz in 1975 and started for Heard as a lineman. Adams believes Heard brought his approach to football with him from Lincoln, and it emphasized toughness. Adams injured a knee as a junior and had to come back to practice in the summer before his senior year. Adams says he went from 190 pounds at the start of summer practice to 168 or 170 pounds at the end. Buchholz began the 1974 season, according to Adams, ranked number one in the state. Then Leesburg beat Buchholz. After the injury, the summer practice, Adams says that, game over, he just sat on the sideline with his helmet on, "weeping like a baby." Heard got Adams on the bus and sat with him on the long ride back to Gainesville. "And the following Monday, we're back on the field, you know." Sometimes, Heard's players would hear things from the sidelines, like "Why are you playing for that nigger?" Adams says those incidents only made them play harder for Heard, to protect him. Adams and Heard have remained close. Working with diverse groups of employees, Adams draws on his experiences under Heard.[47]

Buchholz graduated its first senior class in June 1973. In that year it included grades 9–12 and enrolled 1,181 white students and 285 black students.[48]

After the fruitbasket turnover, black students found themselves in white-majority schools whose teaching staffs were overwhelmingly white, especially at the high schools. All teachers, deans, assistant principals, and principals of both races worked together to keep order. But when black students were unruly, it would frequently fall to black school personnel to take the front line positions and "calm the waters." Heard and his coaching staff at Buchholz had to be vigilant all the time to keep smaller incidents from spiraling out of control. "If something happened down in the school and we dealt with it down there and could get it solved, good. If it went to the front office, it had to move out. Suspended or something. Didn't cuddle nobody down there, but we did a lot of meeting out of the dean's office and out of the front office. [Dean Tom Carr] had me come down and bring a kid, and we'd sit down and we'd work it out right there."[49]

Heard, despite some successful seasons at Buchholz, was removed as coach in 1976. He remained in the schools, eventually serving as an assistant principal at Eastside. He retired in 1987.

Despite the continued dedication of many exceptional African American teachers, however, it would be white teachers, prepared or not, who would have to deal with the set of issues posed by the newly integrated black students. At Gainesville High in the 1970–71 school year, there were about equal numbers of white and black deans and assistant principals. In the classrooms, however, there appeared to be only a scattering of black teachers.[50] There had been many teacher retirements after the 1969–70 school year, but it is not possible to trace individual retirements or the race of the teachers who retired from available school board records.

Black students who entered the white schools in the early years of freedom of choice have mixed impressions of white teachers' willingness to give them equal treatment. But by the time of full desegregation in 1970, the white teachers who remained in the system, with a few exceptions, had committed themselves to teaching students of both races. Malcolm Privette joined the Gainesville High faculty in the 1969–70 school year as a young science teacher. Privette, a minister's son from rural North Carolina, recalls playing with black children when he was growing up. His sister played the piano for a vacation Bible class at a neighboring black church. His community celebrated the successes of its children of both races. Privette says that despite the lack of long-term preparation, when the fruitbasket turnover occurred, the GHS faculty was united in its desire to make desegregation work. "Our job is teaching, end of story. We teach whoever walks in that door. We teach them if they want to learn."[51] Elizabeth Mallonee, a GHS English teacher, was the young wife of a UF medical student. Mallonee later became a career teacher in Saint Lucie County. "The teachers are the people who always, always somehow say let's get together and make this work. Every time we've had some crisis in education that I've been involved in, the teachers just dig in and do it."[52]

In connection with the SACS accreditation evaluation, the GHS faculty adopted a statement of principle, together with a list of goals and implementation strategies, in February 1971. That statement of principle:

> The philosophy and objectives of Gainesville High School must be flexible to allow for changes in student population and changes in society. The school must encourage new courses and flexibility in present courses consistent with student interests, individual and societal needs, and teacher competencies. Ways must be provided for the exchange of ideas among students, teachers, administrators and community. The staff accepts each student at his level of achievement and provides opportunity and encouragement for continuing growth.[53]

The SACS Visiting Committee found that "Gainesville High School can be characterized as a school in transition. As the school has reassessed its role as a changing institution in a changing society, it has added a dynamic dimension to the process of providing a curriculum for the students which it serves." The committee concluded that the administration and staff were working conscientiously toward meeting the instructional challenges they were facing.[54]

A study by the Florida Department of Education released in 1971 found that poor reading was the major problem area of learning in Florida schools.[55] To succeed in any subject, students needed to read. Alachua County school officials avoided characterizing reading deficits as a racial issue, but the *Sun* reported "a visit to almost any school will reveal a preponderance of economically disadvantaged pupils who need help." The midterm 1970 desegregation brought the problem into focus. Unwilling to apply themselves to learning, some of these students turned to disrupting the schools or disrespecting the teachers.[56] But, according to Mary Lewis, it would be a mistake to attribute the violence at GHS just to students with learning deficits.[57] The school would have to find ways to engage or remove troublemakers of both races across a spectrum of academic abilities.

The Alachua County schools had received federal funds for reading programs under the Elementary and Secondary Education Act, P.L. 89–10, at least since spring 1966,[58] but those programs had not had time to help students who were in high school in 1970. A teacher explained, "It's a new ball game with integration. Like it or not, we've got to teach reading." Teacher colleges were not responding to this need. Only students majoring in elementary education were required to take courses in the teaching of reading. Teachers in secondary schools expected to teach their subjects, such as math, science, and social studies, not reading. And the teacher colleges in the past had been preparing students for traditional lecturing, but not for individualized instruction.[59] Alachua County teachers had to improvise. Different approaches were taken at different schools.

At Gainesville High, the English Department took the lead in working with the three hundred students who were screened into the special reading program, as well as all the other students who could not keep up in the English classes previously offered by the school. When the newly integrated GHS English teachers came together to plan for the midterm 1970 desegregation, they realized that they could not continue teaching English in the same set of courses.[60] The 1970–71 SACS Evaluation Committee had special praise for the GHS English teachers, both for their creativity and for their willingness to "undertake whatever explorations they consider necessary to fulfill their students' expressed interests and needs."[61] Three English teachers (all of whom are white) who taught at GHS at the time of the fruitbasket turnover recalled the challenges they faced.

Peggy Finley was then a young English teacher. She grew up in Valdosta, Georgia. Her father was a school principal. In 1958, she graduated first in her class at Tift College in Forsyth, Georgia. "Growing up in the South, I felt very comfortable around black people." After her marriage, she and her husband moved to Gainesville in connection with his work. Tiny Talbot hired her to teach at GHS in 1959, even though she lacked a teaching certificate. She says that some time before the fruitbasket turnover, black and white English teachers had become acquainted through the Alachua County Teachers of English organization.[62] Finley received her master's degree in education from the University of Florida in 1968.

Shelton Boyles is a sixth-generation Floridian who grew up in Gainesville and graduated from Gainesville High in 1960. His mother was a teacher in the Alachua County system. Boyles graduated from the University of Florida in 1964, with concentrations in English, history, and education. He began teaching English at GHS in 1965. He was introduced to working with African Americans in the army. Unlike many of his fellow teachers, Boyles received hands-on training in racial conflict. From

1967 through 1969, Boyles worked toward his master's degree in education administration at the University of Florida College of Education. One of his professors, recently hired in the general area of change management, also participated in a National Training Lab program dealing with racial conflicts. Boyles attended that program. Black Panthers, among others, were called in to meet the students. Boyles would later be elected to the Alachua County school board from 1974 through 1982.[63]

Sandra Sharron was raised in Graceville, Florida. Her father managed a sawmill there, and he knew all the black men who worked there, and they knew him. Sharron says she learned to respect blacks from her father. In February 1970, Sharron had an undergraduate degree in education from the University of Florida, with minors in speech and journalism.[64]

> Shelton Boyles:
>
> There was not a manual, and there was not anything other than let's try this, and with the overriding principle that these young people should not have to pay too big a price both in terms of their academic learning, in terms of their safety, by going through this process, because they didn't volunteer for it either. And we're all in it in that sense. And that was the beauty of it. I mean, there were so many beautiful moments, but a lot of ugly stuff.[65]

Sandra Sharron remembers that by the 1970 spring term, Gainesville High had increasing numbers of academically needy students, both black and white. Courses were evolving away from literature and grammar to reading for pleasure and similar topics. "And so kids were beginning to understand that you could get through school without having to do very much because expectations had been lowered in trying to accommodate these rapid changes that were taking place. . . . And I run into students now who were there, and I was just embarrassed because I felt they were so cheated out of an educational experience because the focus had become interpersonal relationships and not academic advancement."

Students were required to take a full year of English courses in each of their junior high and high school years. The GHS English teachers created a series of elective courses in a wide range of interest areas. By the 1970 spring term, each student was required to take one semester of a required English course, but for the second semester, students could choose from twenty-one different courses. Student groupings were according to interest and not ability. Ruth Duncan Shelley, a black GHS assistant principal for curriculum, said that no matter what a student's reading ability was within a group, he was still able to participate in some aspect of the discussion.

Putting the problem as diplomatically as possible, she said the school had to reach all students, not just the average students, the academically inclined, or the students who expected to enter the workforce after graduation.[66] The electives were one-semester courses, divided into reading and writing courses. Topics included American Literature, Research Paper, Reading for Pleasure, Mythology of the World, Media, Creative Writing, Poetry, and others. Finley said, "We felt like if the kids could choose that somehow that gave them a sense of comfort. And most of the time the kids [would] choose a place where they think they will be successful . . ."

Boyles taught a class in which students read plays. His classes were notoriously boisterous, but he held the interest of his students. John Neller says that an older teacher whose classroom was near Boyles complained about the noise. Neller said of Boyles's students, "They would rather be somewhere else than there. But we knew where they were second period, and they weren't bothering other people." Neller told the complaining teacher, "We've got thirty-two kids in there that could be in your class and everywhere else and they couldn't handle them. But Shelton can handle them."[67]

Finley adds that despite the faculty's efforts to interest more black students in the harder courses, the Lincoln transfer students tended to group themselves in the less demanding courses. Finley taught one of those courses, English Essentials. In that class all of her students were black. She used Scholastic Magazines as her text. The magazines had stories, plays, grammar or vocabulary, puzzles, and cartoons, and they were geared to interest the student. Finley sometimes taught the poetry of James Weldon Johnson. She learned that her black students loved plays. "Anything but most of all they liked me to tell stories."

Finley used contract grading, in which students would agree in advance to do so much for an A, so much for a B, and so on. "Not all teachers did that. But I felt comfortable doing that. And it was a way, maybe it was a way to take the pressure off of me, so that I didn't have to give failing grades or whatever else. But there were some . . ." She also allowed students to submit projects for extra credit that might be outside the course curriculum. "Because I think sometimes each kid has a different way of expressing a reaction or an idea." On teaching writing: "I don't remember being so worried about writing essays as much as I was wanting them to just write to get their feelings out."

According to Finley, teachers needed to be able to work with any kind of student. "And I think my whole philosophy is, you take a kid where he is, and hopefully a lot of them are in the same boat, but a lot of times it isn't the kid's fault that he doesn't know all these big words or whatever it is. So you take the kid, you don't want to make the kid feel like he can't do it." But she adds that she could not reach some black students, either because they were not interested or because they lacked necessary memory skills.

GHS had two reading specialists, Willa "Momma" Gaines, who was black, and Frances Watkins, who was white. Gaines tested students and also provided help before and after regular classes. For Gaines, that was a long day, because on split sessions classes began around 7:00 a.m. and were not over until after 5:00 p.m. Finley relates that if she ever wanted background on a student, she went to Momma Gaines, who was known for caring about her students. Watkins taught remedial reading classes in the school's language lab. Materials were color coded by reading level to avoid the stigma of attaching a specific number. Ruth Duncan Shelley, a GHS assistant principal for curriculum, said that stigma was a major obstacle at the beginning but that students were fast becoming more receptive.[68]

By the 1970–71 school year, ten GHS teachers were taking remedial reading courses on their own at Santa Fe Junior College as if they were problem readers themselves. By experiencing the courses, these teachers expected to be able to reach students with reading problems at GHS.[69]

The GHS English teachers worked out issues in department meetings. Finley believed some of the meetings the teachers had to attend were overkill. "It was like, you know, we're teachers. Let us go into the classroom and try to get this institution moving again. You know, like a broken-down car. I mean, we can work on it all day, but after a while you've got to put it on the road and see if it will run. I know I'm Southern. And I know there are things growing up that I didn't know any better. But I moved beyond that."[70]

Many meetings focused on academic needs. Sharron takes a more charitable view of those meetings. "I was really excited to be part of this movement." She says that the GHS English department had eighteen to twenty teachers. The department was large enough that consultants retained by the county to help with academics would visit the English teachers. Sharron recalls receiving valuable help from reading specialists, who provided tools such as phonics workbooks. She valued the opportunity to discuss problems with them. She also maintained good relations with her professors at the University of Florida College of Education, who would respond to her questions and even come out to help. Alachua County was part of an eighteen-county region of the National Council of Teachers of English. Sharron headed up that group for a year. The regional meetings were helpful because everyone was struggling with the same problems. "How do we, with this changing culture, how do we get the interest and maintain the interest of the students? Again, because so many of them were there because they had to be there, not because they wanted to be." From those meetings, she learned techniques such as breaking classes into smaller groups to allow students to progress at different rates and encouraging the more advanced students to teach other students. She adds, "I feel as a whole that the GHS faculty put everything they had into this integration and to teaching these students who didn't want to be there."[71]

Following the fruitbasket turnover, across the county, other schools confronted the same reading issues as GHS. In fall 1970, Newberry High School identified sixty-five to seventy students who needed intensive reading help. A teacher, Vicki Welsch, organized two sections of a reading lab to engage those students through slide projectors, tape recorders, and videotapes. Students worked in small groups and helped each other. Welsch commented that it doesn't matter so much what they learned in the lab sessions, but that they were motivated to read. Welsch claimed some success, with a fifteen-year-old seventh grader improved from reading ninety words a minute to three hundred words a minute with 80 percent comprehension. Improved reading skills were expected to lower failure rates in other courses.

Alachua Elementary, which served an economically disadvantaged area, obtained federal funds for its program. Students identified as having reading deficits were placed in smaller groups where they could receive more individual attention, without slowing down the rest of their classmates. Some students scored so low on standardized tests that it was doubtful that they would be able to read, but they were learning to read. "The main difference is that every child has a teacher who cares and who has the time to help them individually."

Williams Elementary, the historically black school now paired with two west-side schools, relied on parent volunteers to work with individual students. The parents reported on regular schedules of two forty-five-minute periods per week, working with a total of about one hundred fifth- and sixth-grade students. The parents also took students on field trips. "The most obvious impact we've observed so far is that children understand reading is important. When they see that someone cares enough to work with them they feel important and try harder," according to Jane Hall, the school's curriculum principal.[72]

Not just English departments were affected. Reeves Byrd, who taught math at Gainesville High for a few years, ending in 1969–70, remembers that prior to the February 1970 desegregation, the math teachers were told they would be receiving many students who would not be at high school level. In fact, according to Byrd and other teachers, there were students who could not add or subtract. With those students, the math department could not use a standard high school math text. The math teachers worked together to devise materials that would allow them to reach students who still needed to master the most basic math skills.

Byrd taught five classes of algebra, geometry, or trigonometry, composed mostly of white students, but he also taught one class of basic math that was equally divided between the races. Never having studied the teaching of basic math, Byrd also got help from some of his fellow math teachers, who explained the techniques they used to bring their students forward. As a recent graduate of the University of Florida College of Education, he had learned the technique of small-group instruction, which he applied in his classes. He also sought help, freely given, from one of his professors at the College of Education for teaching basic material.

In Byrd's basic math class, he made a special effort to get to know his students and to interest them in the subject matter. Instead of the usual rows of desks facing the teacher, Byrd arranged his classroom with the desks in a circle. Before beginning math instruction, Byrd would ask each of his students to tell about his or her background and interests, hobbies, and so on. Not only did he get to know each student better, but the students became more familiar with one another. Byrd found his white students to be more troublesome than the blacks. When necessary, Byrd would meet with these students one-on-one. "They're different from me," the white students would complain. Byrd would press them to explain how the black students were different. He found that if he could get these students to open up, they would become more cooperative in class. Byrd would tell them, "Our Father watches over us, does He really care what color we are?" He also remembers receiving help on race issues from Leslie Cosby, a black fellow math teacher who had been one of the first black teachers at GHS. Byrd says that his teaching experiences during desegregation taught him much that helped him in his later life, both as an instructor at Santa Fe Junior College and as an investment adviser and member of community leadership groups.[73]

Another white teacher who reached out to African American students was Dorothy Reaves, the leader of the Gainesville High School orchestra. Reaves mustered local music students into an award-winning orchestra that played classical music. She fostered the program from the elementary school level through high school, working with students in both the white and black schools. For some students whose parents could not afford to purchase instruments, Reaves worked out a rental program with a local music store. One year, during freedom of choice, a black student received the GHS outstanding orchestra member award. Responding to a questioner, Reaves replied, "I didn't give it to him; he earned it." Reaves retired in April 1970, not because of desegregation, but because her husband, who was in dairy science at the University of Florida Extension, left to accept a State Department assignment in El Salvador. The loss of Reaves and her leadership, however, effectively ended the orchestra program at GHS.[74]

To make the curriculum work for African American students after desegregation, the schools had to do more than just redesign existing courses. The *Sun*'s attentiveness to racial issues in the schools led it to cover a lecture in April 1970 at the University of Florida College of Education by Doris Welcome, a black fourth-grade teacher at Gainesville's Idylwild Elementary School. That lecture was part of the College's Black Lecture Series. She had been invited to speak on "Developing a Positive Self-Concept in the Black Elementary Child." Mrs. Welcome told her audience, "Black has been a symbol of all the bad things for too long. In order for the black child to develop a positive self-concept, he must come in contact with his background, the achievements of his race. The education of the black plays a major role in developing a positive self-concept, because from early childhood he has been in contact with white racism." That, together with the black's not knowing his identity, contributes to a black self-hatred. "The black has always been stereotyped, by whites, even when the whites are unaware that they are doing this. The planning and development of school curriculum has been done without any regard for black children." She called for a curriculum that would be more meaningful and truthful about the black race. During the question-and-answer session after her lecture, Mrs. Welcome was asked "if she agreed with the methods of integration used recently." "Integration like this, now, is not good," she said, but she would not elaborate on the subject.[75]

In the 1970–71 school year, under Principal Neller's leadership, Gainesville High added three new courses: Black Studies, Minority Groups in the United States, and Religions of the United States.[76]

There were teachers who may have been successful before integration but who did not survive it. There is no obvious group of teachers that can be singled out for making the right responses. Some individuals succeeded; others did not.

Sharron believes that most of the experienced teachers adjusted successfully. "My sense is that the younger teachers, the new teachers, couldn't take it. They didn't have the wisdom. They didn't have the training to just come into a complex, mature situation like GHS was. And interns, it was harder to manage interns because they didn't particularly want to go to GHS anymore. They had heard it was really hard. And not only that, if they went to GHS, then their supervisor could be in there two times a week if they wanted to be."[77]

But there also were young teachers, new to the profession, who were unencumbered by tradition and who were committed to teaching students of both races. Elizabeth Mallonee says that although she turned in lesson plans, she was free to innovate. "There is something about that young and dumb, thinking you can change the world." She incorporated the paperback series African American Voices into a unit that she taught. Her classes observed Black History Month. She believes that she held the interest of her black and white students. She says that her students were respectful and that she did not have discipline issues. It probably helped that she and her husband made a point of going to GHS sports contests.[78] Another young teacher was Isabelle Norton Whitfield, who taught social studies and who was then married to a UF law student. Whitfield's father was in the air force, but her mother was from Alabama, where Whitfield spent her summers as a child.

> So I remember when the black kids came into class [in February 1970], they were frightened. They seemed very scared, and the big old football players, but we just went on with class. And then I began to realize, when they were turning their papers in, that a lot of black kids, and, like I said, there were some football players in my class, they could barely put their name on the paper. And they could hardly write a paragraph. I remember thinking, oh dear, these kids are so far behind. And of course, they wanted to play football, they needed them on the football team. So I remember coming up with ways that they could do extra credit work. And the ones that really were trying, you just came up with accommodations and ways to help them pass tests and that sort of thing. . . . I got along well with the football players because I love football. I mean, growing up in Uniontown, Alabama, with Bear Bryant and football, it's just in your blood.[79]

Pat Powers was also a successful young teacher. She was the sponsor of *Scribblers*, the creative writing magazine at GHS. The daughter of a prominent Gainesville CPA, she began teaching at GHS in 1966. She loved teaching contemporary poetry, but she and her students were irked by the traditional rows of desks in her classroom. Powers says that some boys in her class scavenged some discarded mattresses from a fraternity at the University and built frames that turned the mattresses into couches. The girls made window curtains from croker sacks. Her classes met in this configuration for about five years. Shortly after she rearranged the furniture, Powers found herself in a graduate class at the University of Florida with Dan Boyd, then still principal at Howard Bishop. Someone asked Boyd what he would do if one of his own teachers attempted to follow Powers's example. "I'd fire her ass," Boyd replied. When Powers heard that Boyd had been assigned as principal of Gainesville High in August 1971, she said, "Oh, shit." But Boyd became one of her supporters. During the time of the elective English courses, Powers taught the Who's rock opera, "Tommy, Pinball Wizard." In some classes, she had her students write and perform music, which appealed to students of both races.

Mary Ann Coxe Zimmerman, a 1966 graduate of Florida State University, began teaching at Howard Bishop Junior High in October 1970 under Dan Boyd. He brought her over to GHS in fall 1972. She later became the county supervisor for language arts. In the junior high school in another county where Zimmerman first taught, students were not tracked by academic ability. She learned to teach students of diverse abilities in the same classroom. Later, at GHS, Zimmerman discarded workbooks. She believed in getting her students to read literature at some level, regardless of their ability. She would, for example, teach five novels of varying difficulty simultaneously, allowing students to choose the one they wanted to study. Like Reeves Byrd, at the beginning of a term, before beginning to teach from the lesson plan, she would have the desks placed in a circle and ask each student to tell the others something about themselves. "It was very helpful to have the kids get to know each other and to share things about each other." In advanced classes, at GHS, her students read Shakespeare's *Romeo and Juliet*. Her less-talented classes worked on the story and watched the movie. She took chances with such works as *The Catcher in the Rye* and *Jesus Christ Superstar* (parents could have their children opt out, but according to Zimmerman, none did).

Some years after the fruitbasket turnover, the state required all high school juniors to pass a functional literacy test to graduate. Zimmerman says that about 4 percent of the GHS students (about equal numbers of white and black) were unable to pass and were required to take a remedial course in their senior year. Zimmerman was asked to develop the course and to instruct other teachers. In the course, each student first wrote the teacher a letter telling her about how the student felt about being in the class. They then focused on practical skills, such as reading a classified ad or showing where they lived on a map. Zimmerman says her students were attentive and tried hard, because they knew they would have to pass the test. The students who landed in the remedial class were diverse, including a young black father, a majorette who was deaf, and a brain-injured son of prominent parents. Like many white and black teachers before her, Zimmerman would not quit on her students. When the young black father stopped coming to class, Zimmerman went to his parents' house to get him back in class. On another occasion, a fight broke out after class between a black student and a white student. Zimmerman says, "I got right down on the floor in my little dress and high heels and I rolled around with them. I got them apart."[80]

If teaching could ever have been regarded as a comfortable rut for young college graduates wishing to escape engineering or business, it could no longer. Tommy Tomlinson: "The most important asset a teacher can have, in my opinion, is flexibility. Secondly, she should be able to look at each child as a distinct individual, to prescribe and administer for that particular person. The greatest liability, I think, is to consider education an easy job – a retirement village – and to try to get by on that attitude. It can only be a great shock. There is only place for those willing to work long and hard hours and to involve themselves in the trial and error that is necessary to make the job work."[81]

Dan Boyd (who became GHS principal in August 1971): "Some [teachers] when the bell rang were ready to beat the kids out the door, and others were there to stay as long as they needed them. Some of the older [teachers] were set in their ways, and you did the best you could with what you had [and] the new ones that you hired. You tried really to help them understand how important it was to develop positive interpersonal relationships with the kids. I found a long time ago that the more the kids like you, the harder they'll work for you." Boyd made sure that he and his administration led by example to encourage the faculty.[82]

Mae Islar, an African American who was a teacher, principal, and administrator in Alachua County for many years, beginning at Lincoln High in 1963: "Any education, public or private, is only as good as teachers are committed to whatever it is that they're doing. And contrary to a lot of popular notions it is not an easy job and people do not go into it for the money."[83]

Sometimes teachers chose to help their students even if it meant breaking rules. Finley:

> I can remember this one [white] boy and he was suspended. I did not think he was a bad boy. And he came back. And I said, tell me what happened. And he said, well, every day at lunch there was this group of black boys that would egg him on, who would pick at him, that would say something, come on, you afraid to fight us.
>
> And these guys, he said, they kept picking on me. And he said I didn't want to fight them. But he said they just kept on and on, and he said after a while I just hauled off and knocked the [*expletive*] out of one them. And of course he got suspended, he hit the, and he knew that. And he said I just couldn't take it anymore. And he said I went home and told my daddy about it and my daddy was sorry I had hit somebody but he understood. He understood. And we weren't supposed to let the kids make the work up but I did. 'Cause, number one, he wanted to. If he hadn't wanted to, I wouldn't have gone the extra, but he wanted to make the work up and I let him do it. You know, I don't remember anything, I think we were all so busy in our own little, I want to say, territory, trying to give, I didn't really worry about Mr. Neller and Mr., I mean I didn't have any problems with them.[84]

Doug Magann, a later school superintendent, visited Mae Islar at her principal's office at Buchholz High School. When the bell rang for a change of periods, Islar said, "Excuse me, I need to be outside." "So I was outside, and he had to stand out there with me and watch the kids. And one of the little girls, whose name was Peaches, black girl, and Peaches could be good or bad depending on her mood, she walked up to me and she said, oh, I had a terrible time in this class. She said, I need a hug. You weren't supposed to touch kids. So she grabs me, and I hug her and everything. And she said, okay, I'm calm now. I feel better. I said, okay. Mind your behavior, okay? So she went on back to class, and he kind of looked at me, he said, you do that all the time? I said sure."[85]

According to Finley, the teachers who had problems in the new environment were those who said, "'This is what I am going to do, and they better shape up and do it the way I say.' 'This is the way I've taught it all my life and I'm not going to change.' . . . But I don't think there were too many of those." She also recalls a black English teacher who apparently believed that the white English teachers knew it all, and it didn't matter what the black teachers said. "Sometimes it can be one little incident that creates that feeling for you. And she never got beyond that." Finley thinks the give-and-take among the English teachers made her stronger, better able to stand on her own two feet and say what she thought was right. "And mostly, I could say it to the students."[86]

One longtime white English teacher at GHS who retired in June 1970 rather than continue trying to teach black students was Winifred Grand. She was among the teachers singled out by Joel Buchanan as having been especially helpful to him.[87] Shelton Boyles: "She knew British literature so well. She taught British literature, and she had all the British humor magazines on tables in her room, and she taught all periods of British literature, and they did plays and all. People really enjoyed her class. And then we integrated, and a lot of the young black students thought, this lady is a pushover, I mean, what the hell is she talking about?" And it so hurt her that she retired. "And that was a loss. I mean, another year or two if she could've hung on, they would have benefited from knowing someone like that. But that was the cost of the newness of it."[88] Like so many other GHS teachers, she had taught many students who became community leaders. Grand was fifty-nine when she retired, and when interviewed by the *Sun*, she said she had retired for health reasons. "I loved teaching. I valued my experiences with 16-year-olds. I know that today's youth will sustain or destroy this world and I consider the school room a battlefield, a place where I would like to be."[89]

One of Gainesville High's most beloved white teachers, Catherine Murphree, retired in December 1970. She was the wife of Walter E. Murphree, MD, the former Gainesville mayor-commissioner. Murphree had taught in the Alachua County public schools for twenty-five years at the time of her retirement. Her students, in addition to performing standard choral fare, had put on full-dress Broadway musicals.[90] The friction in the GHS music department that followed full desegregation in 1970 is described in chapter 20. Murphree later continued her career at Oak Hall School.

Geraldine Miller, Lincoln High's choral director since 1951 and the wife of Jerry Miller, the band director, was transferred to Buchholz in 1970 when Lincoln closed. Coach Heard characterizes her as the "cream of the crop" from Lincoln. The Millers wrote the words and music for Lincoln's alma mater. Geraldine Miller produced Lincoln's only musical, *Bye Bye Birdie*, in 1969. At Buchholz, she was choral director and an English teacher. But according to Heard, Miller did not like Buchholz ("The pressure, you know"), and transferred to Eastside, where her husband was the band director. She remained at Eastside from 1974 until her retirement in 1981.[91]

Generally, in desegregated schools, the separation of students into ability groups, or tracking, meant that white students in the advanced college-prep track studied with fewer African American students. Tracking, long a feature of the American comprehensive high school, was employed at both Gainesville and Lincoln High Schools.[92] According to the 1966 Coleman Report, academic tracking was practiced at 80 percent of both white and black secondary schools in cities of over fifty thousand in the South.[93]

Pat Powers opposed academic tracking and eventually as department chair succeeded in abolishing it for a time for English classes. "My teaching philosophy is I think students learn more from each other than they do from the teacher, unless it's a hard discipline like maybe some science and math classes. But my approach to literature was, okay, what effect does this story, this boy in this novel, have on my life, what does this have to do with me? So the kid who was raised in a poorer section of town has just as much to offer as someone who lived at the country club." Building on a concept developed by Shelton Boyles at the time of the fruitbasket turnover, Powers for several years taught a class called Expression and Communication, which was open to students of all abilities.[94]

In the 1971–72 school year, Barbara Gallant, Martha Green, and Mary Morgan (the last a black English teacher from Lincoln High) began teaching a three-hour block course for seniors, Man and His Environment. The course satisfied humanities, science, and English requirements. In its first year, the course enrolled 101 students deliberately chosen to include students of varying academic abilities. According to Larry Reynolds (a member of the GHS class of 1972, later a federal administrative law attorney), "The class pulled together students to represent everyone attending GHS: white nerds like me, black students, athletes, klutzes, vocational students, those just getting by. It was a great success. . . . Because of this class, I finally did connect with students from Lincoln High School." The students and teachers attended two four-day sessions, in October and April, at the school district's Camp Crystal, "to make their own society," where they worked on environmental research and also on student-led activities such as yoga and photography.[95]

Despite the disciplinary rules adopted after the March 1970 riots, and the curriculum changes that classroom teachers put in place, there were still too many disruptive students at GHS and the other secondary schools. Policemen in the halls were not going to turn these students into good citizens. The 1970–71 SACS Visiting Committee had no answers for this problem; the committee report surprisingly does not even mention it. The Visiting Committee's seeming blindness to in-school violence may reflect an unstated SACS policy that violence, or lack thereof, was irrelevant to accreditation. An equally likely explanation is that teachers colleges had no knowledge to impart on that subject. Although the schools did not cause this problem, they would have to solve it if there were to be public schools in Alachua County. Russell Ramsey headed up the program to deal with these students beginning in the summer of 1970. "To have some old lady school teacher handle this is ridiculous," he said.[96]

The answer, by no means unique to Alachua County, was to remove the most disruptive students from regular classes, so that the learning process could continue for the rest of the students. Ramsey got himself in trouble with the school board for taking it upon himself to name his new isolation facility. He called it Mountain Top, from the speech by Martin Luther King Jr. Ramsey refused to back down, and the name stuck,[97] although the county's isolation class program came to be called Horizon.

King's Mountain Top speech was his last, given April 3, 1968, the day before his assassination. He was in Memphis to support a strike by thirteen hundred sanitation workers. King made many points that could have been relevant to Alachua County's situation, among them, the need for nonviolence, dedication, and courage. We remember the end of the speech:

> Well, I don't know what will happen now. We've got some difficult days ahead. But it really doesn't matter with me now, because I've been to the mountaintop.
>
> And I don't mind.
>
> Like anybody, I would like to live a long life. Longevity has its place. But I'm not concerned about that now. I just want to do God's will. And He's allowed me to go up to the mountain. And I've looked over. And I've seen the Promised Land. I may not get there with you. But I want you to know tonight, that we, as a people, will get to the promised land!

> And so I'm happy, tonight.
> I'm not worried about anything.
> I'm not fearing any man!
> Mine eyes have seen the glory of the coming of the Lord!![98]

More to the point of the schools, in Alachua County and elsewhere, was King's reference to the parable of the Good Samaritan:

> Let us develop a kind of dangerous unselfishness. One day a man came to Jesus, and he wanted to raise some questions about some vital matters of life. At points he wanted to trick Jesus, and show him that he knew a little more than Jesus knew and throw him off base. . . .
>
> Now that question could have easily ended up in a philosophical and theological debate. But Jesus immediately pulled that question from mid-air, and placed it on a dangerous curve between Jerusalem and Jericho. And he talked about a certain man, who fell among thieves. You remember that a Levite and a priest passed by on the other side. They didn't stop to help him. And finally a man of another race came by. He got down from his beast, decided not to be compassionate by proxy. But he got down with him, administered first aid, and helped the man in need. Jesus ended up saying, this was the good man, this was the great man, because he had the capacity to project the "I" into the "thou," and to be concerned about his brother.[99]

Mountain Top admitted students who could not be returned to regular classes after spending time in social-adjustment classes at their regular schools. Terms of attendance were thirty to sixty days. About one-fourth of Mountain Top students came from the county juvenile shelter, on whose grounds Mountain Top was located. Those students might attend for longer periods, based on the terms of their detention. The school taught both boys and girls.

Although desegregation triggered the creation of Mountain Top, it did not deal exclusively with white and black students who were not adjusting to desegregation. There were, in addition, white students who embraced the counterculture of the time, in some cases leaving their parents' homes to live independently while still in high school. Judy Joiner found those students to be less respectful of teachers than most black students.[100] Ramsey had his own take on the white counterculture: "Plainly put, these children are bored, insufficiently guided, and given too much money or unearned privilege. They take up the rhetoric of the college radicals, dress like hippies, use drugs and indulge in wild sexual escapades, all to the endless beat of hardrock music." Others came from traditional Southern conservative families. "These children steal motorcycles, fight in the hallways of the schools, run away, get drunk or rob small stores. Increasingly they dress like the urban counter-culture and share in its racial tolerance, as well as its social destructiveness." The African American Mountain Top students arrived with a separate set of issues. "Juvenile delinquency among the Negro sector is characterized by fighting, stealing, and a general rejection of the integrated schools, where white middle-class values and textbook achievement add up to an unfriendly, frustrating, even bewildering environment."[101] And, "Individual Negro students feel themselves to be unwanted by the community, or see no point in finishing high school."[102]

The school combined strict discipline and constant encouragement. Ramsey said, "It took me a while to get used to the situation. Those kids lie, fight, draw knives on each other, throw things at you. I had to grow accustomed to dealing with deceit and violence." When students came after Ramsey, "I duck and flatten them out." Students when necessary were forced into "physical four knuckle submission."[103]

Teachers at Mountain Top used unconventional ways to get students to learn. Each week the class took up a different topic, such as the automobile, the soldier, the policeman, or the music of the Southerner. That topic served as the focus for teaching basic academic skills in math, science, and English, as well as social values and their consequences. The school obtained published workbooks on town government, family, and personal behavior and its motivation, intended for use by academic underachievers and students with low socioeconomic backgrounds. Particularly effective, according to Ramsey, was "the teaching of academic subjects as social values and controls, especially in the small group circle, outdoors." Field trips to businesses and government offices connected the students to parts of the community they had never encountered before, except perhaps when breaking windows. Ramsey, whose doctorate from the University of Florida was in Latin American history, had only his common sense and his experience as an army officer to guide him.[104]

"Ramsey said the program is made possible by the kind of people who live in Alachua County. He said both private businesses and public agencies have been most helpful in giving the youngsters a chance to observe and participate in the community's functions."[105]

Without precedent to guide him, Ramsey developed his own "Principles of Social Adjustment." Mountain Top and in-school social-adjustment classes were intended to achieve rapid changes in attitude and group behavior. The district policy, authored by Ramsey, made clear that this program was not intended to take on the broader issues of special education, guidance counseling, routine discipline, or juvenile correction. But while a student was at Mountain Top, or in an isolation class at a regular school, the student's classroom teacher in that setting (perhaps by analogy to a company commander in the army) had responsibility for all aspects of his students' learning and behavior. Ramsey rejected trips to see school counselors, although they were involved when students entered and left the social-adjustment classes. "The counselor in Social Adjustment Education is the classroom teacher who is already there and remains with the student throughout the day." He rejected both "liberal educational theory which holds that students should be allowed to experiment and try things out for themselves" and "the concept of traditional authoritarian teaching methods which have been applied for some years in correctional schools."[106]

Ramsey drew on available external sources when relevant. He distributed New York City's How to Do It plan on public school disruption. He said the plan coincided closely with the schools' own rules for dealing with disruptions from April 1970 but provided less detail. "We can do better." At Ramsey's request, materials on visible indicators of disruptive and violent behavior from the staff psychiatrist of the New York City schools were sent to all Alachua County schools.[107]

One of Ramsey's achievements was a more structured relationship with the juvenile court system for the schooling of its inmates. But Ramsey also wrote, "While personnel of the juvenile court facility have been helpful and even suggest a larger social adjustment program, the official philosophy of the court is out of touch with the youth values of the times. As a result, there are continuous difficulties arising from the need to enforce a specified program of social controls over the Juvenile Shelter inmates when they are mixed together with the other students [at Mountain Top]."[108] By the end of the 1970–71 school year, the court and Mountain Top had developed an effective relationship that served as a model for other counties.[109]

By December 1970, of the 30 students who had entered the program, Ramsey said that 13 were attending regular classes successfully, 6 would return to their regular schools after the holidays, 6 were in state correctional institutions, and 5 were attending Mountain Top only sporadically. For the 1970–71 school year, of the 109 students who entered the program, 76 returned to their regular classrooms and completed the school year. Sixty percent of the Mountain Top students were black.[110]

In September 1971, Mountain Top had two temporary classroom buildings and two instructors, including Russell Ramsey, its leader. In November 1971, the system received a $100,000 federal grant to deal with students who were socially maladjusted. Ramsey hired two more instructors at Mountain Top and used the grant money for eight two-person teams to operate social-adjustment classes at eight regular Alachua County public school campuses. The two-person teams included a teacher and an adult paraprofessional. The children they dealt with were less disruptive than those referred to Mountain Top. Ramsey said that this new staff included vocational teachers, a driver's education instructor, a preacher, and an ex-convict, who "were warm, dedicated loving sort of people." "They made home visits and could straighten out an alcoholic mother for abuse or a father for molesting his daughter. They could sit with a kid while crying, or take off their belts if necessary. And they dealt personally with 405 students."[111]

The community wanted order in the schools. A member of the Gainesville Kiwanis Club said Ramsey's speech on February 2, 1972, drew more applause than had Senator Henry Jackson (D-WA) the week before. According to Ramsey, through the new system of disciplinary controls and Mountain Top, the school district had achieved a no-expulsion policy. The entire system also was at 98 percent attendance. "If the kid didn't become a criminal," the school counted him or her a success. According to Ramsey, about 80 percent of Mountain Top students who returned to regular classes went on to graduate.[112]

Mountain Top at that time was about 50 percent white and 50 percent black. Although the social-adjustment teachers sought to involve the children's parents, actually achieving impacts through parents proved very difficult.[113] The school filled the void by providing adult leadership.[114] By December 1972, from the start of the social-adjustment classes, suspensions in the county had fallen from 510 to 177. The ombudsman program had switched from keeping order and advocating for students to instructional assistance.[115]

Returning Mountain Top students to their regular schools presented special problems. Individual school administrations differed as to responsibility for handling disruptive students, so Mountain Top had to identify the right people at each school to receive information about the student. The student's regular school, not Mountain Top, decided whether the student would be readmitted. When returning to his or her regular school, the Mountain Top student received a letter requesting readmission, summarizing progress in academic and social areas, and recommending specific steps in counseling, classroom assignments, academic and vocational tracking, and, when relevant, social services from outside the schools. Copies of the letter were to be distributed by the regular school to each of the student's teachers and to the student's permanent record. Giving the letter directly to the student was viewed as a way of keeping faith with the student, of "stripping off the mask of paranoia which the average disruptive student carries in regard to the school system." Teachers commented that they learned things about their students from these letters that they otherwise would not have found out.[116]

Ramsey also counseled other teachers. Sandra Sharron:

> Where everybody was maybe struggling to take advantage of some aspect of teacher education, he coordinated it. And he put a lot of strength in the help the teachers were trying to get, put a lot of effort into further educating teachers so that they could deal with these cultural changes. He was the best thing that happened to the faculty when he came in and started explaining why we had been the route we had been and what potential we had to move forward.[117]

University of Florida students visited the Mountain Top classes to observe and learn. "The process was particularly valuable to several dozen students, apparently in the 1970–71 school year, who reported that juvenile delinquents appeared much less easy to teach and manage than they had been led to believe during their various academic programs."[118] The program attracted observers from elsewhere in the United States and from other countries.[119] Ramsey was invited to present at the Southeastern States Conference on Community Involvement in the Problems of Neglected and Delinquent Children, held in March 1971 at Daytona Beach, together with heads of facilities in Hillsborough and Dade Counties that served similar purposes.[120] His work also attracted the attention of the Florida School Desegregation Consulting Center at the University of Miami. That organization sent Ramsey to ten other Florida school districts and three junior colleges to speak on "how to integrate classrooms and make them work."[121]

In his presentations to school personnel, Ramsey did not use the stage-managed dramatics that had become popular among facilitators or what he characterized as "humanistic psychology." Martin Luther King Jr.'s speeches were his favorite source. He combined inspiration with straight-ahead advice on changing behavior, "how to welcome everybody into the classroom. And don't stand there and say, what you people do is talk funny. Think of positive things to say about Mary Bethune instead of inferior black education at college level. Just a whole lot of positive things."[122]

Mountain Top accepted students as young as sixth graders, but it never covered elementary schools.[123] Instead, the county system for the first time in 1972–73 placed counselors in seventeen of twenty elementary schools; they dealt with cooling-off students with aggressive behaviors in addition to other problems.[124]

Given the midterm fruitbasket turnover and the resulting overcrowding at Gainesville High, there were going to be disruptive students. The difficulty of Ramsey's task was compounded not just by those events, but also by the general unpreparedness of regular teachers and administrators. Even assuming that anyone else could have been found to take on Ramsey's job in 1970, the odds were stacked against success. Looking back from today's perspective, Ramsey's approach to social adjustment may appear idiosyncratic. We can't isolate the effect of Ramsey's efforts from other forces that contributed to reduced in-school violence over time. But like so many other Alachua County educators, Ramsey made a difference because of his uniqueness, not because he came to his task with an already-proven methodology.

The period this work covers, 1965–1973, was the most crucial inflection point in Southern public education. Why, then, were administrators and teachers essentially on their own to figure out what to do next? Why were they like an army fighting the last war? They performed heroically, but was it necessary that they be heroes in the first place?

Ramsey, no less outspoken at seventy-nine, says that if there is a villain in all of this, it is the University of Florida College of Education.[125] Mae Islar agrees. While working on her PhD in the 1970s, she obtained an assistantship to supervise interns at the University of Florida College of Education. In one required class the discussions between the professor and a graduate student so irked Islar that she quit the program. Islar says she "got too much ivory tower." "I can't take this. I've got college professors trying to teach me what I know they don't know a thing about and you expect me to sit there and listen to this? I said, this doesn't make sense. I said, so-and-so doesn't have the slightest idea what it's like to be in a classroom. And he's trying to teach me? And I hear these little college kids sitting there buttering him up and I said this is the worst travesty I ever heard. I said I don't want any part of this. I'm out." Islar worked out a compromise according to which she obtained her specialist designation but stopped her PhD program and the assistantship. She believes she "opened their eyes to the fact that if you have been at the college level for so long, you do not have a clue as to what's going on, so you cannot teach an intern how to cope. And so we made some changes there."[126]

The College trained most of the county's teachers, either for undergraduate or graduate degrees, or both. But the College, like the rest of the University, was an exclusively white institution from its inception. Even by the early 1970s, the College had very few black students, let alone working black alumni. The public schools into which the College's graduates went to work had also been segregated until very recently. There had never been a need for the College to address education of African Americans, school violence, race relations in extracurricular activities, and so on and on.

Even the youngest tenured professors at the College in 1972 would have been products of segregated public schools and segregated university classes. Senior professors such as R. L. Johns just a few years earlier had been advising school boards on ways to keep their schools segregated. What the College's professors had learned when they studied for their degrees no doubt served them well in teaching white education students to teach in white schools. But with its existing faculty, the College, like a ship, did not suddenly turn onto a different course. When confronted by Tiny Talbot in 1971 about the need for teachers to teach reading to socially promoted students, Johns shot back, "A good point. Accountability will have to start with teacher education, but if college professors don't know about the problem how in the hell can the teachers teach the children?"[127] This, sixteen years after *Brown*, and five years after Congress enacted the Elementary and Secondary Education Act, P.L. 89–10, in 1965.

The 1966 Coleman Report, which used a very large database, confirms these perceptions. "Future teachers [in all regions of the country] of both races are products of segregated schooling to a large extent, and this pattern of segregation is current in their colleges as well as a part of their public school background; though more severe in the South, it is quite pronounced in the North as well. The pattern of segregation applies to their teachers as well as to their classmates. In a word, the Nation's teachers are interracially inexperienced."[128] Further, the report found that the most academically talented education students preferred to teach high-ability students in academic high schools.[129]

Dan Boyd takes a more charitable view than Ramsey toward the College of Education, but he, too, agrees that the College did not respond quickly to the changed environment. "They have been out of step with the requirements of the teaching profession from a practical standpoint. I don't know that they've ever caught up with what really needs to be done." Boyd says that to obtain a teaching certificate, college graduates had to have an endorsement for English as a second language. According to Boyd, the school districts themselves rather than the College of Education had to provide training for that endorsement.[130]

Black teachers had been educated in black colleges to teach in black schools. In the South, there was no other place for them to study or to teach. Their professors likewise were products of segregation and lacked training to prepare their students for the problems they would confront upon integration. And just as school districts were moving to unitary school systems, the black teacher pipeline was drying up.

Brown had been decided in 1954. But dual school systems persisted until 1970, even later in some districts. Under freedom of choice, black students who chose to attend white schools expected, and were expected, to conform to white educational norms. The institutions training teachers, no more than the teachers and administrators in the schools, had little reason to change their curricula.

One would have hoped that Southern schools of education, after *Brown*, would have prepared their students for the changes that the Supreme Court envisioned in 1954. But it did not happen. That passive choice would have a much greater impact on Southern public schools than the massive resistance and demagoguery that captured the attention of the press and public.

Dr. Marzell Smith led a workshop for Alachua County teachers, principals, deans, counselors, and administrators on August 18, 1973. Some parents and students also participated. Smith was an assistant director of the Florida School Desegregation Consulting Center during the desegregation years and taught at the University of Miami. Smith told the group what they already knew, that issues between teachers and students and between teachers and administrators had to be resolved through better communication. As negative forces in student-teacher communication, students listed a fear of openness; a lack of self-confidence in students and teachers; age, sex, and status differences; and racial differences. An administrator offered, as one solution, that in hiring new teachers, the schools needed to select candidates committed not just to their academic subjects but to students and people. "If you're genuinely interested in people you can get your message across."

> "No, that's a copout," answered one black teacher. "You need more. You need a knowledge of each other. Exposure, experience, empathy."
>
> "Where does a teacher get exposure, experience, empathy, if he's already in a classroom that's half black?" someone asked.
>
> No answer.

Smith gave the group cold comfort, stating that the problems in Alachua County were the same as those in other communities experiencing desegregation, in the North as well as in the South. But "Alachua County in particular is far ahead of many Florida counties in terms of really moving toward successfully integrating its school system." Smith gave credit to "'a dynamic, sensitive, forward-looking' superintendent and staff."[131]

There were some white teachers in Alachua County, such as Shelton Boyles and Sandra Sharron, who either sought out some focused training on integrated education or who were able to find help from the College of Education during integration. Even they confirm, however, that for the most part they were innovating as events unfolded. Likewise, there were some black teachers and administrators who had received graduate degrees from integrated Northern universities. But as long as those teachers remained in the black schools, there would have been little reason for them to address what might happen to their students when those schools became integrated.

Mary Ann Coxe Zimmerman says that by 1972, when she began taking graduate courses at the University of Florida for her master's degree, she found her methods courses in English teaching to be extremely helpful. In an informal comment, she told the author that the other teachers in her UF classes and her professors were sharing relevant and practical ideas for integrated classrooms.

Despite mixed reviews of the system's younger white teachers, some had received training in newer teaching techniques that, if not actually modeled for use in integrated classrooms, could be applied successfully in that setting. Dan Boyd, speaking of his tenure as principal, says that he never believed his young teachers were unprepared for the challenges they faced at Gainesville High. He says they were truly enthusiastic and ready to teach their students. "I think the thing that is difficult is to take a white middle-class man or woman and have them truly understand what it's like to live in a poverty environment. But we worked on that, too." Boyd got help with his faculty from the Florida School Desegregation Consulting Center.

Like soldiers, Southern teachers and administrators would have to pass through their own trials by fire. There would be casualties. Others would adapt to their changed mission and find new solutions to new sets of problems.

CHAPTER 20
THE STUDENTS

The standards were different. The curriculum was different. And the only baseline data they had was what they could retrieve from Lincoln, which really wasn't measured by the standards they were using. But I was just one of the ones, I'm sure there were others, but I didn't have a major problem after I realized what I needed to do, because I was determined to graduate from high school and go to college and do well. And I was focused on that, and I said nobody's going to stop me.

Brenda Wims, GHS class of 1971

We always had a few crazy people who wanted to fight the Civil War in April of every year. When negative situations or little sparks of trouble were about to start, our players would find a way to stop or end the problem in most cases. We might grab one of our teammates if they were involved or get directly involved in stopping fights or arguments in order to keep peace and safety at our school. I think the coaches made us leaders both on and off the field. It was somewhat natural for us to prevent the crazy situations created by a few students from destroying our school and our football season.

Melvin Flournoy, GHS class of 1974

Whether desegregation could or would be managed by the adults, it was the students who would have to travel the distance between the South's historical dual and new unitary school systems. "Adults" included parents, teachers, school administrators, police, clergymen, community leaders, lawyers, judges, and, ultimately, the justices of the United States Supreme Court, in short, everyone having anything to do with desegregation except for its presumed beneficiaries. We should not be surprised that, reflecting back today, those students remember feeling like pawns being played by the powers that be.

It was not possible to interview large numbers of former students from the desegregation years, first, because of constraints in locating and contacting them, and second, because a significant proportion of former students declined to be interviewed. To identify potential interviewees, this author used newspaper articles, yearbooks, and, when accessible, class websites. Given that a student's experiences of desegregation were significantly affected by his or her status within the school, much effort was made to locate and speak not just to former class officers and star athletes, but also to more typical students who either went on to college or who entered the workforce or the military. There was a very broad spectrum of responses. Many students said they had little memory of the events narrated in this book. Others, and it is important to remember this point, recalled that even in the midst of those events, their learning experiences were not disrupted. A smaller number had very thoughtful recollections of the impact desegregation had on their lives as students. Reality for most students was probably closer to Barbara Gallant's view[1] than it was to those who charged that no learning was taking place.

Not one of the thirty-three former students who agreed to be interviewed understood in February 1970 what had caused the end of Alachua County's dual system in February 1970 (that cause was also not understood by the many other former students with whom the author had informal contact). Many blamed the school board. They agreed that there was little warning or preparation either at Lincoln or at Gainesville High. Eight weeks remained between the December 13 response of Justice Black to the NAACP Legal Defense Fund, in which Black conditionally ordered several school systems to integrate student bodies by February 1,[2] and the fruitbasket turnover on February 6. A possibility, raised by Frank Coleman, would have been for the school administration to work with the black students and parents already present at GHS under freedom of choice. What had they done to get through it? Those families had never stopped being part of the larger black community. The black GHS students knew the Lincoln students from their earlier school years. Many had girlfriends or boyfriends at Lincoln. The boys continued to play after-school basketball and other neighborhood games with their Lincoln friends. One initial problem with full desegregation turned out to be a leadership vacuum. Coleman asks, why was there not a committee to discuss potential issues that might arise and to have authority to impose solutions? Cynthia Cook pointed out that there was no orientation ("It was just done, boom! Where are the teachers and administrators in all of this?"). There could have been meetings with the Lincoln students and teachers to brief them on what to expect at their new schools, as far as organizations and processes. Student leaders from both schools could have met together before the desegregation to feel each other out. Without such steps, Cook says, the Lincoln students did not feel welcomed or valued.[3]

The school administration would have had to organize and complete a more robust transition plan at the same time that it was organizing the unanticipated midyear desegregation. As Cook noted, adult school leaders during those years were not accustomed to asking opinions of students (that issue also played out on university campuses). And as we have seen, the school board voted on January 19, 1970, contrary to Talbot's request, not to begin implementing the "September Plan in January" unless the county remained under a court order to do so on January 30, 1970. The school board had been advised by Mississippi attorney John Satterfield that if the board somehow became ready to comply with the existing court order, the board's readiness would weaken its pending case for rehearing at the Supreme Court.[4] By January 1970, the school board had no good options. If the board moved forward with midyear desegregation without Eastside and Buchholz, the two secondary schools then under construction, the board would be blamed for any disruptions. If the board followed Satterfield's advice literally, the board would violate Justice Black's December 15 order to Alachua County to take the necessary steps to desegregate student bodies by February 1.

Even if the schools had more time to prepare for total desegregation, there may have been no greater effort at preparation. To school administrators, the experience with both white and black students under freedom of choice underlay an assumption that the remaining black secondary school students could be moved peacefully into white schools without major disruption. Former Associate Superintendent Tommy Tomlinson agrees: "There was very little preparation. I remember a district meeting when everybody was there. There was an alliance among the adults, teachers helping teachers, a spirit that helped it to work. The lack of preparation was not a big problem. We had freedom of choice before. Freedom of choice was working in our mind."[5]

Alachua County, in common with most other Southern counties, had never had to attempt full desegregation. The black students who entered the white schools under freedom of choice did so without special counseling or preparation. It would not have been clear at the time that moving to a unitary system would have significantly different impacts, especially for black students, than freedom of choice. There were warning signs in the persistent rock throwing and arson incidents in black neighborhoods. But the extent to which current public school students were responsible for those incidents was not known.

Nor could school administrators foresee that black adult community leaders and parents would prove unable to prevent black student violence. Under freedom of choice, black students who attended white schools did so upon the insistence or encouragement of black adults. These students continued to have adult support during their years in the white schools. The Lincoln strike ended through the intercession of black adult leaders. Reflecting in June 1970 on the Lincoln strike, the white Reverend Earle Page of Holy Trinity Episcopal Church, who himself served as an ombudsman at GHS, told the *Sun*,

> "The white establishment is under the illusion that it is in communication with the present black community. But in fact they are not – some past leaders, perhaps, but they're the wrong ones."
>
> Rev. Page says that the black community now appears to be represented by the youth.
>
> Some of what Rev. Page says was apparent during the [Lincoln] walkout when black students, backed by their parents in many cases, expressed ignorance and disbelief of the school board's moves, though, as Rev. Page points out, the board did make an "honest effort" to get first hand opinions from the traditional black leadership.[6]

As it turned out, even the younger black leaders such as Charles Chestnut III were unable to contain the frustration of the small number of former Lincoln students who reacted violently after their transfer to GHS.

Alachua County was caught midway in its transition to a unitary system. We need to remember, however, that under the county's court-approved desegregation plan, all of the remaining Lincoln High School students would have been assigned to other schools at the beginning of the next school year in September 1970. Lincoln students then in grades 11 and 12, expected to graduate in June 1971 and June 1972, would have gone to Gainesville High School. The school administration decided to place those upper grades at GHS because the new junior/senior high schools would not be accredited and would not have established student activities and sports programs ready to accept those transfer students.[7] Under *Green* and *Carter*, leaving those students at Lincoln to complete their high school education was not an option (assuming Lincoln was not to be racially balanced with white students as part of the unitary system). And some former students reflect, in hindsight, that the transition would have been hard even if it had been postponed to September 1970.[8]

Beginning in February 1970, there were 3,194 students in grades 10–12 at Gainesville High School, with grades 11 and 12 meeting in the morning and grade 10 meeting in the afternoon. Total enrollment increased by 698, or 28 percent. The proportion of black students increased from about 11 percent to 30 percent.[9] The size of many classes increased.

The courts had decreed there should no longer be black schools or white schools—just schools.[10] But, throughout the South, if the legal distinction between black and white schools had been erased, there was no erasing the distinctions between black and white students. And despite the idealistic view that schools could no longer be identified to one race or the other, black students, especially at the secondary level, would be entering not "just schools," but schools that had been functioning as separate white schools for decades. The more profound adjustments to desegregation by the students of both races were only beginning.

Lincoln and Gainesville High each contained two disparate student populations: the college bound and the others who were there just to gain a high school diploma, taking courses that many found irrelevant to their future lives. The SACS Evaluation Committee pointed out that GHS was moving "from a strong emphasis upon the academic preparation concept to the broader proposition of serving the comprehensive needs of the diversified student body."[11] However, that transition was still a work in process. The school's business-education programs were among the few areas criticized by the committee.[12] The committee viewed the industrial arts program as not meeting the needs of students.[13] The committee saw great potential in the trade, technical, and industrial program, but cautioned that students in that program should not be stigmatized and that the program should not be used as a dumping ground for "non-academic achievers."[14]

In the 1969–70 school year, an estimated 289 black and 142 white students were enrolled in high school trade and vocational programs offered at a central location through Santa Fe Junior College (some vocational courses were still housed at the high schools).[15] Since the founding of Santa Fe Junior College in 1966, the junior college and the school board had disputed which entity would receive funding and jurisdiction over high school vocational education. In the 1970–71 school year, the junior college, not the county school board, financed and organized vocational programs for both high school and adult students. The Lincoln campus, eventually intended to house many of those programs, had just been vacated.[16] None of the programs then available resembled the professional magnet programs that now serve the needs of high school students entering the workforce after graduation.

For the students, the fruitbasket turnover might be appropriately compared to a shuffling of two separate decks of cards. There were white and black students in both the college-bound deck and in the general-course deck, but each deck remained separate from the other in most classes, and more importantly, in many extracurricular activities. At GHS, the division even extended to after-class hangouts, with white college-prep students mostly going to Jerry's and the general-course students to Frisch's Big Boy.[17] Those demographics could not help but affect the course of desegregation.

Mack Hope helped raise the Confederate flag at GHS on March 26, 1970. In the auditorium, just afterward, Hope says Coach Niblack counseled the white students about respect and making matters worse. But at seventeen, he says, he and his peers were not going to listen. Despite recalling some sincere, good teachers, Hope says, "GHS did nothing for me. I was a hindrance to them. They made you feel like a second-class citizen." Hope was later diagnosed with attention deficit hyperactivity disorder. He came from a disadvantaged single-parent family. In junior high, Hope was sent to the school farm to learn agriculture. In the tenth grade, he refused to go, saying he did not want to be a farmer. During high school, Hope says he worked forty hours per week at a gas station and at the Red Barn restaurant. Hope later earned an architectural-hardware license and operated a successful business. He now says that he totally understands the grievances of the black students. "They should have just divided both schools [Lincoln and GHS] and sent half the students from Lincoln to GHS and half from GHS to Lincoln." "We had a nice school, we all got along, until the Lincoln kids got there." He refuses to blame the students, black or white, for the violence; instead, he blames the administration for not handling the problems.[18]

Many college-bound and other students at GHS came together in athletic teams, cheerleading, band, and majorettes, regardless of the academic or socioeconomic deck in which they found themselves. Although only a tiny minority of students participated in these high-visibility, competitive activities, they were influential beyond their numbers in bringing a measure of racial peace to GHS during the desegregation years.

Whether the 1970 desegregation worked or not is still being argued. However, it worked best in the classrooms and on the athletic fields. It worked less well in student government and in extracurricular activities.

In the Classroom

The concept that blacks would obtain equal educational opportunities after desegregation would now be put to the test at Gainesville High. Defining and measuring equal educational opportunity remain most perplexed topics today. We should not be surprised that participants in desegregation don't agree on how far, or even whether, desegregation moved blacks closer to that goal. But now, as contemplated by *Brown* and *Green*, all students would receive the same lessons from the same teachers in the same classrooms using the same resources.

In the college-prep courses, as best we can know, the concept worked. Black students remember that their new teachers, mostly white, did their best to teach their students of both races.

Brenda Wims was a Lincoln transfer student who graduated from GHS in 1971. She recalls that at Lincoln, being an honor student was easy for her, but at GHS she initially struggled. In her first year at GHS, she remembers "floundering around" while the Lincoln transfer students were tested to see where they might fit in academically. "The standards were different. The curriculum was different. And the only baseline data they had was what they could retrieve from Lincoln, which really wasn't measured by the standards they were using." "But I was just one of the ones, I'm sure there were others, but I didn't have a major problem after I realized what I needed to do, because I was determined to graduate from high school and go to college and do well. And I was focused on that, and I said nobody's going to stop me." By her senior year, Wims believes she was being taught at the same level as her white peers, and she was admitted to the GHS National Honor Society.[19] Donnie Batie, the future medical doctor, moved from Lincoln to GHS as a junior in February 1970; he was in the National Honor Society at Lincoln High School and made National Honor Society at GHS. He also was president of the math honor society at GHS, Mu Alpha Theta. But he says he did not receive much help from GHS counselors about attending college.[20]

Black students who came to the white schools under freedom of choice also remember that their GHS teachers made special efforts to help them with academics. Frank Coleman, a member of the GHS class of 1970, desperately wanted to drop his Algebra III class, being taught by veteran GHS teacher Ruth Wallace. Unknown to Coleman, his teacher mother and Julia Cosby, a black GHS math teacher, conspired with Wallace, who worked one-on-one with Coleman to make sure he completed the class. Coleman believes Wallace was more important to his later success than any of his other teachers. He found his math background key to his later success at Morehouse College, in the military, and at IBM.[21] Alvin Butler says that he was not thinking about attending college when he entered GHS. He credits Mary Beth Hodge, a white English teacher, with encouraging him and helping him prepare for college. "I think that was special because it really wasn't necessary, but that was them going beyond just doing their job."[22]

More fortunate was Melvin Flournoy, who began attending a white elementary school in Gainesville in the fifth grade during the freedom-of-choice years when two small segregated schools in Micanopy were closed. He says that the support he received from his white fifth-grade teacher (described in chapter 6) prepared him to hold his own academically in the white schools. By the time Flournoy arrived at GHS for the eleventh grade in 1972, he was succeeding in his college-prep courses. He says that for the most part, by the time he reached GHS, the GHS faculty was very supportive and very accommodating of African American students. Flournoy graduated from GHS in 1974.[23]

Students in the college-prep classes confirm that although there were not many black students in their classes, teaching and learning were continuing without regard to the racial tensions outside the classrooms.[24] Jeanie Whitehead Shaw, class of 1972, says, "But, yeah, so it was very tumultuous, but you kind of really didn't talk about it. It was just the norm of what was going on at school. I think wow, today you'd become upset if there were riots at school, but it was just kind of the way it was. You just went and hoped it would be a calm day."[25] For Susan Holloway Weinkle, MD, who graduated in 1970, classes and academic work in her senior year proceeded normally.[26] Black students in those classes were not disruptive. Frank Coleman remembers, "The [Lincoln transfer students] that were taking the kind of classes that I was taking, they were pretty much cool. Well, everybody was cool. Now if there was a class that we had, where we had discussions about things, and some classes turned into that even though they may have been an advanced math class, a trig class, or something like that, or a French class or a German class and discussions may have started because of the things that were going on, there may have been some heated discussion. But, of course, that's understood."[27]

The muggings, strong-arm robberies, and riots that followed the 1970 desegregation, although undeniably serious, directly involved comparatively small numbers of students. On the day of the March 26, 1970, riot, Tom Deakin walked home and played chess with his father while they watched the aftermath on TV.[28] Ted Covey walked to his car and drove home.[29] Former white students interviewed encountered incidents such as a thrown biscuit[30] and a couple of unsuccessful attempts to steal lunch money.[31] Covey narrowly avoided being mugged in the band lavatory. As he was using the bathroom, some blacks turned out the lights. Covey, a football player who was six feet two, 190 pounds, believes the muggers decided he was not a good target. Covey says the next boy to use the restroom was mugged.[32] After a student government meeting, Jeanie Whitehead Shaw walked into a disturbance already in progress. She was attacked, and her dress was ripped, but a male student intervened before she could be hurt.[33] An exception, Mary Rockwood was the victim of a serious beating by black girls in March 1972 when she attempted to use a restroom during a disturbance.[34]

The beating was just one more incident in Rockwood's troubled high school years. She found a measure of affirmation in Helen Philpott's art class. Philpott was known for her solicitude toward her students, who had included Joel Buchanan. Rockwood worked on a mosaic sculpture and other projects. Knowing that Rockwood should be in her other classes, Philpott would let Rockwood continue working in the art room. Rockwood graduated from GHS in 1973, eventually earned a PhD in nursing from the University of Florida, and is a clinical associate professor at the University of Florida College of Nursing. Rockwood says the comfort she found in art at GHS directly inspired her founding in 1990 of the Shands Arts in Medicine program at the University's teaching hospital. That program became a model for many other such programs.[35]

The increase in the size of many classes unavoidably affected some students. Barbara Gray, a white student who graduated in 1970, flunked trigonometry in her senior year, the only time that she had ever failed a class. Gray remembers her teacher appearing overwhelmed; when Gray went to her for help, Gray was rebuffed. To get graduation credits, she had to work in the school library. For Gray, the second half of her senior year felt more like going to a job.[36] Nell Page is the daughter of the Reverend Earle Page. Nell recalls writing an essay that she thought was terrible, that she needed help with, but finding her teacher completely exhausted.[37] Ted Covey, who graduated in 1971 and eventually obtained a PhD in agricultural economics, believes that by the time he became a senior, the school's required senior thesis had been eliminated.[38]

The academic disparities between the Lincoln transfer students and their new classmates at GHS meant that most of the former Lincoln students would find themselves in the general or vocational courses. There was no way the academic clock could be stopped for those students to catch up. And in those classes the Lincoln students would be placed in close contact with the less academically inclined, lower socioeconomic white students.

For younger students the county had a number of programs that were considered compensatory education, ranging from Head Start to the crash reading programs described in the previous chapter. The county had planned to operate two intensive compensatory education programs at the formerly black A. Quinn Jones Elementary and at the former Lincoln campus. As we saw, the school board discontinued those programs after the Fifth Circuit Court of Appeals ruled that to prevent resegregation, student assignments to those programs would have to be mandatory.

In *Wright v. Board*, the NAACP Legal Defense Fund opposed compensatory education in principle. The Fund saw such programs as a back door for resegregation. The Fund's expert witnesses in *Wright v. Board* testified that the best way to improve minority learning was classroom contact with middle-class white students, which would raise minority students' educational aspirations. The Fund argued, consistent with the 1966 Coleman Report, that disadvantaged students learned best in heterogeneous ability groupings with one-quarter to one-third minority students. The Fund's expert witnesses testified that compensatory programs such as Head Start had no lasting value.[39] One of those experts, however, did testify that desegregation together with compensatory education was more effective for minority students than either desegregation or compensatory education alone.[40] To the Fund, it was irrelevant whether black students wanted to be in classes with whites. Black students would have to take the medicine.

Nor did the academic sources relied on by the Fund contemplate that white classmates would be less than model students.

To that point, Mary Ann Coxe Zimmerman recalls that during freedom of choice, in another county, one of her white junior high students, Billy, complained, "I ain't going to sit next to no nigger." Zimmerman looked up Billy's records. "F, D, F." She looked up Vicki's records. She told Billy, "Vicki has all As. Did it ever occur to you that she might not want to sit next to you?" Zimmerman worked to get Billy as far as he could go. Finally, Billy got paddled in the principal's office. Zimmerman, who had to witness the paddling, was in tears.[41]

When the Lincoln transfer students first arrived at Gainesville High, many could not connect with their new teachers. Some white teachers continued teaching from their lesson plans; to the Lincoln students, who had been using outdated, hand-me-down textbooks, the white teachers were deliberately speaking past them to the white students. Brenda Wims:

> Well, it didn't go well. Just like I said, when you get [to GHS], and you are an easy honor roll student over here [at Lincoln] making all As, and you have just mastered everything over here, and the teachers here could only teach and use those resources that they had available with no incentives to students [such as connections to the University of Florida, community donations, prizes, and scholarships], which brings about an action or change.
>
> But you go over [to GHS], and what are these people talking about? So then you resent that. You come to class. You don't know what they are talking about. And then some of the teachers try to get you involved in the class, and I think they had good intentions, but you dare to call on me to ask me about something in history that is beyond what I've had, and you're treating me like I should already know this?
>
> I don't have lunch money today, and I don't have supplies today. But I'm embarrassed. I'm ashamed. So what do I do? I act out.[42]

Many black students who did not come from middle-class families had not developed the same study habits as their white peers. Alvin Butler: "Where I lived, right off Fifth Avenue, sort of like what they would call the ghetto, it wasn't really popular to take books home from school. So what I was studying that year, I did at school because I didn't take books home. So my parents didn't really push me to excel, but as long as I made As and Bs they didn't care. So I would read extra books of things that I was interested in, just stimulating myself, but making good grades in school was just not a high priority. I just sort of did it because I could. But I definitely was not a student who took books home to look at." Butler recalls that he scored 425 (of a possible 495) on his senior placement test.[43]

Wayne Mosley carried his anger over the Lincoln closing with him to GHS. He says he boarded a bus at 4:15 a.m. for the morning session at GHS. "Everybody was asleep, even the teachers. . . . So the teachers was afraid of us, and we was mainly afraid of them, and/or, didn't care. So my first two periods, all I did was sleep."[44] Mary Rockwood, GHS class of 1973, recalls that the black students in her geometry class were not prepared to do the work. She remembers it was clear they were not going to college. According to Rockwood, most black geometry students just sat around, not really doing the class, cutting up. They were never mean or hostile and did not heckle the teachers. "It wasn't that we were smarter, it just didn't come naturally to them."[45] Mack Hope, who graduated in 1970, agrees that his classes were orderly. But after the March 26, 1970, riot, according to Hope, for the rest of that school year his teachers were just babysitting their classes.[46] That view confirms what some parents told the school board in May 1970. Ron Perry, a white student who graduated in 1973 and became a lawyer, had some science and English classes that were at least half black. He does not remember those classes being disrupted, but he believes that because of the split sessions and the pervasive tension, a normal learning experience was not happening. He states that learning conditions significantly improved during his junior and senior years.[47]

Tim Strauser also graduated from Gainesville High in 1973. Strauser eventually took some classes at Santa Fe Junior College and had a thirty-eight-year career with AT&T. He was a ninth grader at Howard Bishop Junior High, on Gainesville's northeast side, at the time of the fruitbasket turnover. There he found himself the only white in a drafting class with a dozen blacks. Strauser says that these students had no interest in the class; their classes at Lincoln had been broken up. Strauser dropped the class because he did not feel safe. By the time Strauser entered Gainesville High in the 1970–71 school year, he believes that the black students in his classes were involved in learning. His teachers would not tolerate black students gathering in the back of the class. He perceived the "old school" teachers as hiding their feelings and going along with the new regimen because it was their job. But he says that all of his teachers tried to make the best of a bad situation and create a good learning environment. He especially remembers his African American business teacher, a strong woman who "would not put up with crap from anybody."[48]

Student Government

Gainesville High School and Lincoln High School each had student governments. Before the February 1970 desegregation, it was decided at GHS that the student officers and elected student representatives would serve together for the remainder of the 1969–70 school year. It was not that complicated to have co-presidents, co-vice presidents, and so on through the officer ranks. But the two schools operated their representative assemblies differently.

GHS had a constitution, with a student senate and a house of representatives. The senate included eight members elected at large from each class, plus the student body officers and the speaker of the house. The senate met daily as a class for credit. The house of representatives included one representative from each home room, plus a principal's representative and a representative from a national student government organization. The house met weekly. The senate and house could make recommendations on school rules and policies; review and issue or revoke organizational charters; make rules for assemblies, corridors, social events, and public functions; develop and administer a system of awards; and make recommendations about matters outside its designated responsibilities. Another major function was to coordinate the many fund drives that the various student organizations conducted to finance their activities. The principal held a veto power. Both houses followed parliamentary procedures, with senators receiving grades based on their knowledge of those procedures.[49] This structure was intended in part to teach what used to be called civics. Lincoln's student government had similar responsibilities but was not organized so formally. Parliamentary procedures were not strictly followed.

The combined student governments tested the hypothesis that the students would settle the issues posed by desegregation if the adults would leave them alone. The GHS student body president and other GHS officers had been very supportive of combining the two student governments. After the February desegregation, John King and his Lincoln counterpart, William Murray, each held the gavel in the GHS senate on alternate days. But, according to King, the administration encouraged student leaders to continue "business as usual in the Senate and to keep things on track in the school and the standard agenda that we would use to bring up, make decisions and provide information back to the students on what was acceptable and what wasn't, generally, in terms of club and social activity." King adds that the senate did discuss the campus disturbances and what could be done about them, but it was not student government's major focus. In contrast, the Lincoln student government recently had been mostly involved with issues related to desegregation, especially during the events leading up to the Lincoln strike in November 1969 and after, until the school was closed. The new members from Lincoln did not easily adapt to discussions about GHS student activities. The application of parliamentary procedure at GHS also created friction between the GHS and former Lincoln students, and, according to King, led to less order and less respect.[50] Frank Coleman, a senator, says that after February 1970, "in student government from that point on is chaos. There was nothing to get done anymore, not as we were used to doing it."[51] King says that on one occasion, when the senate was discussing race, "One of the female Senators, very blonde, very white, had started a dialogue on love and caring, and how she loved the black students. That prompted a huge negative reaction from several of the black students, who picked up chairs and smashed them against several individuals sitting in the room. The room turned into a complete free-for-all with people trying to back out the other way. [Cela Hendrickson] couldn't control it."[52]

Coleman understood at the time that there was a difference between freedom of choice, under which blacks chose to accommodate to the white schools, and full desegregation, which would bring in the black students who had chosen not to make that accommodation. Those students had just lost their student-teacher relationships, their clubs, their band, their sports teams, their mascot and colors, and the accompanying camaraderie and community support. They did not then see a way to recover or replace those cultural assets at GHS.

The former Lincoln students argued that because the Lincoln students had to give up their school and all that it stood for, the GHS students should also give up something. First, like so many members of his generation, Coleman believed that Lincoln should have been integrated rather than closed. The school board having rejected that choice, Coleman believed that to unify the Gainesville High and Lincoln students, GHS should have been reinvented as a whole new school.[53] Coleman and others were unable to persuade the GHS student government and faculty that unification should have meant more than just combining the two schools' classes, student governments, and sports teams. Lincoln would soon have its day in court, but as we saw in chapter 15, cultural assets of neither race counted in the constitutional analysis.

Coleman remembers that the senate early in the 1969–70 school year already had some sense that the remaining Lincoln students would be coming to GHS. Coleman says the leaders of the student government "really didn't know what to do about the situation, and they chose to ignore it."

> I think that it was new ground for both sides, and I had my hand in both sides. I had my hand in the Gainesville High side because I knew these guys for three years leading up to [the 1970 desegregation]. But I also knew these guys that

> I grew up with, too, and I knew what was about to happen [at Lincoln]. It was a way of taking away something that had been in our community for way longer than we had been born, we grew up with.
>
> And I tried to get folks to understand on the GHS student council that if you put the shoe on the other foot and realize that you're getting ready to lose something that has meant so much and so dear to you, and something that was so dear to you for all your life because some people's parents went to Lincoln just like GHS. And everything centered around that in the black community, because we didn't have any other high schools, and I don't think GHS did either at the time, so I think if we could just be a little accommodating is what the point I was trying to get over.
>
> But I didn't see where there was any accommodations to be made. I saw Ms. Hendrickson kind of let us handle, I never really saw her take a front seat or a back seat in anything when it came to, she did exactly the same thing that she did all three years, two years prior, she didn't try to force us to look at it a particular way. She wanted us to organize it and us to handle it. . . . I never really saw in the eyes of the officers that I worked with, that they really got it, that they really understood what was happening. As a matter of fact, I felt like they just really didn't care about it.[54]

In Coleman's view, the school board should have had the courage to impose an accommodation, rather than leaving the meaning of unification as a cause for continued friction among the students. The GHS senators, according to Coleman, were not ready to deal with the Lincoln students' issues and did not know how to deal with them.[55]

Wayne Mosley, who had been a student leader at Lincoln and a leader of the Lincoln strike, refused to become part of the GHS student government. "I didn't want nothing to do with them. They didn't want me over there, and I didn't want to be over there."[56]

Some work did get done. Coleman recalls the senate working on a procedure for addressing complaints by students who believed they were unfairly treated in class. The senate did not address simple misbehavior.[57]

At GHS, blacks became a minority. The student body elected a number of black officers in the years after the fruitbasket turnover, but the senate and house, without intervention, would have had white majorities. The administration decided that the senate should have equal numbers of each race. Grade requirements for student government also worked against blacks. According to Brenda Wims, grade standards were realigned after she graduated in 1971 so that more blacks could run for student officer and student government positions.[58] Dan Boyd says that seven or eight years later, the students decided there was enough trust that senators should be elected at large, without regard to race, as before.[59]

As the spring 1970 term proceeded, the administration called on John King frequently to help with ongoing conflicts and with sensitivity sessions. "So for people who might remember this as not really having a big effect on their life or that things generally seemed to just go along and were okay their senior year, I have a totally different view. I literally lost my entire second half of the year as I was preparing for college." As a representative of student government, King was regularly pulled out of class by Cela Hendrickson to meet with groups during sensitivity and training sessions, to take questions related to student government, and sometimes to defend school policies. He found such exercises to be extremely stressful. "I was in the middle of everything. I was blasted from all sides. I was trying to get my bearing. I was trying to do what was right, and it seemed like you never could win. It was extremely unnerving." King came to agree with many blacks that the right answer to desegregation was not to close Lincoln and bring all of the blacks over to the white side of town. He believes it would have been better to bite the bullet and give priority in school management to bringing the black and white communities together. However, he is also quick to point out that in all of his dealings with school administrators and even school board members, everyone he encountered was trying to do the right thing, with no intent to disadvantage blacks.[60]

In retrospect, it is not difficult to understand that the white student leaders (and presumably the administration) would reject changes to Gainesville High School's symbols. The only racial content to those symbols, the purple and white colors and the Hurricane mascot, was what the former Lincoln students chose to give them. No more so than the Lincoln transfer students, the white GHS students had not signed up for the fruitbasket turnover. They did not see that the fruitbasket turnover created a debt that they individually owed to the Lincoln students. They did not understand why those students were not content to make the same accommodations to GHS as the freedom-of-choice blacks had made. Nor was it clear that peace could be bought by changing the school symbols. Cynthia Cook: If whites had been transferred to Lincoln, the Lincoln students would not have wanted to change the Terrier.[61] As the years passed, and Gainesville's African American students were dispersed among Eastside, Buchholz, and Gainesville High, it would become less clear that any single high school should stand for the lost Lincoln.

Student Clubs and Activities

Officially, the Lincoln transfer students were to be welcomed into student activities at Gainesville High. Former Lincoln clubs and other activities were not carried over to GHS. The Lincoln transfer students, like the black students under freedom of choice, were expected to find their way into whichever GHS activities appealed to them. Alvin Butler, a freedom-of-choice black who graduated in 1971, confirms, "We want to be open and invite you, but there wasn't a lot of direct conversation about how to make this thing work."[62]

For the Lincoln transfer students, joining and participating in student activities in a new setting could not help but have racial content. Students were expected to contribute financially to participate in some activities, which was beyond the capability of many former Lincoln students. For some activities, particularly for sports teams, there were minimum grade-point requirements. Many Lincoln students had other commitments, such as jobs, caring for younger siblings, or church activities, that kept them from giving the same time to school activities as their white classmates.[63] Pat Powers, the former English teacher, found that some black parents actively discouraged their children from getting involved in after-class activities.[64] The split morning and afternoon sessions served as another barrier to black participation. Practice for activities such as chorus or sports had to be postponed until after the end of the second session and lasted long after the school buses had left to return students to their home neighborhoods. For many black students whose parents could not pick them up after practice, the trip home was taken on city buses or by bicycle.[65]

When he arrived at GHS from Howard Bishop, the multitude of clubs, events, and other student activities at GHS was new to Frank Coleman.[66] Lincoln High had many student organizations, but they were organized around class subjects such as science, math, band, dramatics, or chorus.[67] Entry was generally open to any interested students.

At Gainesville High, as in many Southern white high schools, Gainesville civic organizations such as Rotary, Kiwanis, YMCA, and YWCA sponsored "service clubs." These clubs were separately organized for boys and girls (Kiwanis sponsored a club for boys called the Key Club and a club for girls called Keyettes). A teacher served as faculty adviser to each club. The clubs controlled their own memberships through a pledge procedure, and for many students gaining entry into the club of their choice was not unlike being accepted into a college fraternity or sorority. But there were enough clubs to accommodate everyone who wanted to join.

The clubs mirrored their adult counterparts, which assisted their high school affiliates. Students learned about opportunities for community service and raised money for charitable projects. The hope was that these clubs would motivate students to continue as adults the strong community-service activities that contributed to Gainesville's civic spirit. But in those days, the sponsoring local adult organizations were white.[68] Despite the interest of those organizations in youth programs, they had never organized high school service clubs at the black schools.

At GHS, the clubs gave their members a ready-made social network and a sense of belonging. The clubs provided relief from the tracking that separated students into academic tiers for classes. Before desegregation, the clubs were a major focus of high school social activities, with each club taking a turn sponsoring a dance after football or basketball games, holding other social events, and raising money for club service projects. The clubs' members were predominantly middle class. Before 1970, a few black students had been admitted to Gainesville High service clubs.

After the March 26, 1970, riot, racial issues at GHS were examined in discussion groups among teachers and students, facilitated by psychologists. A radical transformation of GHS to accommodate its changed demographics was among options then under discussion. Dr. Boyd Ayers, the school board's psychologist, told the school board on April 16 that to completely eliminate racial differences, GHS would have to be rebuilt. "The new GHS will not look like the old one," Ayers said to the board. High priority was to be given to desegregating the service clubs.[69] A black student walkout had resulted when some blacks alleged that they had difficulty getting into service clubs the previous year at Miami's Palmetto High.[70] Alachua County's official report put the issue differently: "Revaluate GHS service clubs as to role and membership limitations."[71]

Ayers correctly saw the service clubs as a way to bring black students into the mainstream of activities at GHS. If the clubs could be integrated, they would provide space outside the classroom for white and black students to work together, to socialize, and to find common ground. But it was one thing to bring blacks into the white school for classes, athletic teams, and band and chorus, and quite another to integrate clubs whose student members decided who would be admitted and that were primarily social. Achieving more than token integration of the service clubs would have been transformational, as Ayers believed.

In retrospect, Ayers's hope was another manifestation of a commonly shared belief among whites that as a consequence of integration, blacks should and would be assimilated into the white culture. After all, went this reasoning, blacks had sought admission to the white schools because those schools were superior to the black schools. Having achieved this goal, the blacks only wanted to be accepted, and the whites only needed to initiate their grateful black classmates into the whites' prelapsarian state of grace. Increasing black involvement in the white culture of the schools would eventually lessen racial differences and create a unified community, within the white community's structure. We whites, who had gone our separate way within that structure our whole lives, could not imagine that what we did so casually and innocently was a "culture," much less that it could be perceived as racial. For whatever reasons, the school administration shied away from placing the service clubs on point for further integration of the student body, as recommended by Dr. Ayers.

Jeanie Whitehead Shaw, who was a tenth grader at GHS in 1969–70 and served as president of the school's Interclub Council in 1971–72, says that the Lincoln transfer students were not especially interested in joining the service clubs. "I don't think it was a matter of turning down anybody. I just don't think it was an issue since there weren't applicants."[72] Nell Page agrees.[73] Reeves Byrd, the math teacher, sponsored the Civitan-affiliated service club. He tried to interest blacks in joining without much success. "It just wasn't their thing," in Byrd's perception.[74] Frank Coleman, who enjoyed greater acceptance than many black students at GHS, recalls that most of his senate colleagues were in service clubs. Coleman did not seek to join. "You can imagine that I knew where to stick my neck and where not to stick my neck. It didn't take a genius to figure that out. Being that the clubs were all white, and being that most of the organizations around there were all white, you had a feel for things like that, and you felt when you're wanted, and you felt when you weren't wanted. Now if you didn't you would find out. It wasn't a time to go testing a lot of ground.[75]

In hindsight, Nell Page, then a member of Alpha Tri-Hi-Y, a YMCA/YWCA affiliate, now sees that unification did not have to be a one-way street. "We're part of this. Now let's find out. Let's do a welcoming. Let's make this a whole school and include and find out the history of what Lincoln was about and what the students there are interested in. What kind of service would they be interested in to integrate this?"[76] But in 1970, that model would not have found support. Much later, service clubs were significantly transformed by their sponsoring organizations to be more oriented toward service and member diversity. Schools also imposed more rules. But the role of such clubs in the integrated Alachua County high schools is no longer what it was in the days of all-white schools. According to Tommy Tomlinson, being in clubs, which had been so important to high school students in the 1960s, eventually just ceased to be a priority.[77] Over the same period there had also been a decline in the role of adult service clubs.

Many African American student leaders at GHS, finding the existing student organizations unresponsive to their concerns, started new organizations. After the March 1970 riot, a biracial group came together as S-T-P, or Students-Teachers-Parents. S-T-P sought to bring students of both races together for events such as a unity walk and an outing to a nearby lake. The group planned to look at reorganizing student government and taking on service projects at the school, such as cleanups. The group also expected to review the school's colors, alma mater, and mascot.[78] Donnie Batie was attracted to S-T-P because it sought to mend race relations. "And so we were somewhat a minority because on both ends, most blacks didn't want to deal with whites, and most whites didn't want to deal with the blacks. And rather than being violent toward each other, we were more conciliatory, and trying to get to understand each other." Batie recalls participating in the first Earth Day through S-T-P.[79] The group did not continue after the early years of desegregation.

By the 1970–71 school year, two additional black-oriented student clubs had become active. Some former student leaders from Lincoln High organized the Black Student Union. There had been a Black Student Union at the University of Florida since 1968. Some of its members had supported the Lincoln strike in fall 1969, so the Lincoln students already had the University group as a possible model for a similar group at GHS. A second group, Interface, was intended to be biracial, but in practice it was mostly African American.

Brenda Wims was an organizer and the first president of the Black Student Union. As secretary of the Lincoln student body in 1970, she served as cosecretary of the GHS student body and a member of that school's senate. Wims came to know Cela Hendrickson, who was in charge of student activities. Wims says that some of her friends from Lincoln wanted to approach the senate to have some activities specifically for black students, but they didn't know how to make the request and were afraid of getting in trouble if they did. Wims says that she took the issue to Hendrickson. One of the proposals, from Wayne Mosely, was for a pep rally on behalf of the Lincoln Terriers, "to let everybody know that we're here, and that we have a voice, too." Hendrickson was not pleased with that idea. Wims said, "Well, we're Hurricanes now, and we can't be two." Hendrickson: "That's a smart, smart idea."[80] But Wims was able to convince Hendrickson to allow the group to organize. It became an official GHS activity and was allocated a small budget by the administration.[81] Twenty-one members were pictured in the 1971 *Hurricane* yearbook.

According to Wims, "The purpose for the Black Student Union, at that time, was for us to form a union and to demonstrate that we, too, could function properly and that we could get things done as black people. And we were not stupid. We were not descendants of apes and all this kind of stuff that they were saying. And to prove to the administrative staff that we were there and we wanted to be a part of the school, if we had to be there, and we didn't want to be separate, we wanted to earn our way. So the next year, when we elected officers, we didn't have to have two of everything."[82] The organization helped black students find their way to GHS activities that they did not know how to join, such as dramatics. Students could report unfair treatment by teachers, which would be reviewed by the administration. The group encouraged black students to run for the senate. The BSU also put on programs for Black History Week and Martin Luther King Jr. Day. They sat together at assemblies. "And it gave some of the students the outlets that would not ordinarily happen, because they didn't have the grades to be part of some of the different things that they had, and they certainly didn't have the finances, or they didn't have anybody to support them in their thing."[83]

John Neller, Mary Lewis, and Dan Boyd each praised the Black Student Union for its members' responsible approach to the issues.[84]

Gainesville High and Lincoln each had student newspapers. For whatever reason, black students did not join the Gainesville High newspaper, the *Hurricane Herald*. Vince Deconna, who was editor in his senior year, 1972–73, remembers that the paper had an all-white staff. As best he remembers, issues related to race, and the sporadic violence, had greatly subsided at GHS by his junior and senior years, making for a much more harmonious educational experience. He does not recall specific race-related issues that the paper would have covered. He says editorials were oriented toward national news issues.[85]

Both Lincoln and GHS had marching and concert bands. As we saw in chapter 9, in Lincoln's last years its band lost some of its former luster. Like so many other aspects of GHS, the band proved to be a challenge for the Lincoln transfer students. Donnie Batie says he was one of a handful of Lincoln band members who earned places in the GHS band.[86] Batie gives Richard Miller credit for doing his best as Lincoln band director, but says the Lincoln band was happy if it received a B grade in the annual contests run by the Florida Association of Band Directors for the black high schools. Batie contrasts Miller with Bardwell Donaldson,[87] the longtime GHS band director who traveled around Florida as a judge in band contests. "So he knew everything that the judges looked for, okay? And so he could prepare his band to make nothing but ones. Mr. Miller never had that opportunity, and so on. I think his effort was more than adequate, and he really tried hard. . . . And I think technically, that was one of the weaknesses in general of the black community back then. We tried hard, but we didn't have the complete playbook to perform well."[88]

Chorus was popular with white students at GHS. Many students had an early start in their churches. The GHS program won awards for solo, ensemble, and choral performances, and included full-dress presentations of Broadway musicals. Until December 1970, the GHS program was led by Catherine Murphree (wife of Walter E. Murphree, MD, the former mayor-commissioner).

Singing was also popular among young African Americans. Private piano and vocal lessons were offered by black music teachers. Chorus was taught at Lincoln High School, and many students also sang at their churches. In their ninth-grade year (1966–67) several black girls auditioned for, and were accepted into, the GHS chorus for the following year.[89] According to Cela Hendrickson, during desegregation, Murphree had gone to Lincoln to interview students with voice potential for the GHS chorus.[90]

The lead girls ensemble at GHS was the Melodettes. The ten Melodettes traditionally performed in white semiformal dresses and sang mainstream American songs, many from Broadway musicals. Their theme song was "Blue Moon." Together with other ensembles, they represented GHS when local groups or charities requested entertainment by high school students. In their tenth-grade year, Lana Jackson and Karen Washington auditioned for the Melodettes but were not accepted, despite having private voice lessons and experience performing in their own community. They were going to sing. Washington, Jackson, Cynthia Cook, Janice Cambridge, Sheila Nealy, and Beverly Stoney formed their own ensemble, the Chordettes. According to Cook, the Chordettes earned superior ratings at district and state competitions from 1968 through 1970, the year the first members graduated. Their competition numbers included "Summertime" from Gershwin's *Porgy and Bess*, and "Deep River," a traditional spiritual. Jackson earned superior ratings with her solo performances.

The black students believed that they were not being treated fairly in the audition process and that Murphree was preventing integration of the Melodettes. The issue also was brought up by a parent at a school board meeting in December 1969 during the Lincoln strike.[91] Cook took the issue to Cela Hendrickson, who held meetings with some of the girls and Murphree to try to work out the problem. Cook says their parents had brought them up to speak out if they believed they were not being fairly treated. She believes that the chorus teacher was not accustomed to being challenged by her students and showed some lack of tolerance.[92]

A former white member of the Melodettes, Patricia Crawford, who also graduated in 1970, is reluctant to depict the choral teacher as prejudiced. Crawford remembers that Murphree welcomed black students who wanted to join the chorus. However, Crawford agrees that Murphree was proprietary toward the Melodettes. The Melodettes' repertoire was selected and arranged by the chorus teacher. Crawford also sang with the Chordettes, who met on their own, set their repertoire, and performed newer music. The situation was further complicated by the presence of a second chorus teacher who had transferred from Lincoln and who was much more open to diverse music than her GHS counterpart.[93]

Ultimately, Jackson was accepted into the Melodettes.[94] However, disputes within the choral program continued into the 1970–71 year. One day, Principal Neller went to find out what the issue was. He asked the teacher to leave and spoke to the students. He said, "This disruption is on me. Nothing will happen to any of you. But we can't continue this, so tell me what happened." Neller agreed with the black students that they should be able to perform a different kind of music one day a week. Afterward, he told the music teachers, "I may have been not doing what you wanted me to do on that given day, but I saved you problems for the rest of the year." Neller says it was hard for him, because Murphree was a very, very dear friend, and he did not want to offend her.[95]

Murphree retired in December 1970. The curtain also came down on the Melodettes. To pay tribute to Murphree, former students rented the downtown Florida Theater for a night in January 1971. Many returned from out of state. They performed numbers from musicals and other songs that she had presented during her years at GHS. For the finale, the entire cast joined in on "There's No Business Like Show Business." A University of Florida scholarship fund for voice was established in Murphree's honor.[96]

A former student recalls that the drama teacher, who had also taught for many years at GHS, would not have reached out to blacks.[97] Like Murphree, the drama teacher required students to audition for school productions, which also met as classes.

The 1970–71 year was the first full school year after the fruitbasket turnover. Three of the thirteen varsity cheerleaders were black, as was one of the majorettes. But a look through the 1971 *Hurricane*, the school yearbook, shows that extracurricular activities remained stunningly white. From the activity pictures, one would never imagine that the student body now was 30 percent African American. The 1971 *Hurricane* reveals the determination of most whites to cling to their vision of what high school should be. Even by 1972 and 1973, few blacks showed up in the extracurricular photos (chorus being the exception). Whether black students would, or could, share the white vision was less important to most white students than keeping it alive.

High School Athletics

The thread of high school sports, and especially football, runs through this history, from Tiny Talbot's 1934 column for the Holmes County *Advertiser*, through the exploits of Eddie McAshan, and through the 1970 desegregation. Through good times and bad, high school football molded generations of Gainesville's white and black citizens. In years past, before the rock throwing and vandalism, many whites attended Lincoln High games to cheer for the Red Terriers in what were probably the only integrated public events in Alachua County.[98] Winning games was only part of the coach's job. Bill Adams says that Jessie Heard "knew that he was creating a generation of young men, and he expected us to be of high value."[99] For young men of both races, high school football was the ultimate rite of passage to manhood. They were going to play. Football would not transform the South into a racial promised land, but desegregated teams and coaching staffs would lead by example not just on the field but in the schools and in their communities.

There were no organized youth football programs for either race in Gainesville in those years. Many boys grew up playing sandlot football in their neighborhoods. Students as disparate as Mack Hope[100] and Melvin Flournoy, living on the edges of racially divided neighborhoods, both played unsupervised pickup football games against teams of the opposite race. Flournoy: "When I was at Micanopy, before integration and desegregation, we used to play sandlot football with white kids. We didn't do shirts or skins." A team of blacks would play a team of whites. Each team could have only as many players as the other team; if more white players showed up than black players, the extra white players would have to wait their turn. "We never had a fight, whether it was in basketball or football. We would bruise or accidentally scratch each other up as we knocked the living daylights out of each other. The grown-ups' hatred messed up things!"[101] Alvin Butler, who lived in the older black neighborhood west of downtown, played sandlot football with black friends, including a young Eddie McAshan. Games there might include adults, teenagers, and kids as young as eleven or twelve.[102]

From its earliest days, Gainesville High was the only white high school serving Gainesville and a large rural section of Alachua County (the University's laboratory school, P. K. Yonge, was much smaller but also sought to include a typical cross section of the white community). There were no private schools. The student body at GHS included offspring of old Gainesville families, some relatively prosperous and others not, children of University professors and administrators, and children of high school graduate parents who worked as farmers, mechanics, policemen, secretaries, small-business owners, and so on. Long before desegregation, football brought together boys who wanted nothing more than to play for the Purple and White, like their fathers, uncles, and brothers before them. In the locker room, on the practice field, on the bus, and under the Friday night lights, it did not matter who your daddy was.

Gainesville High had a Quarterback Club that raised money for special team projects and brought in not just parents of players but many local businesses. Games were broadcast on a local radio station for whoever might not be able to make it to Citizens Field. Tiny Talbot, even as county school superintendent, worked in the broadcast booth as a spotter with Ferrell Asbell, who called the games. Clark Hodge, the son of former school board member Lester Hodge, played for GHS at perhaps an overstated weight of 130 pounds. Members of old GHS teams, some now with walkers or in wheelchairs, still gather faithfully to share lies and camaraderie.

In 1958, the year that Talbot became principal of Gainesville High, the school moved from the Florida High School Activities Association Class A to Class AA, which then covered the state's largest white high schools. That move brought the school greater visibility statewide, and in 1959 it was brought into a new conference, the Sunshine Conference, with schools from Orlando and Daytona. In the same year, Jim Niblack took over as GHS head coach. Niblack was a former standout lineman for GHS from 1946 through 1949 and then for the Florida Gators. Niblack early began to seek out opponents for GHS among state football powers and eventually among out-of-state teams. Beginning in the 1964 season, and off and on through 1970, GHS played one or two opponents in Tennessee and South Carolina. Niblack's teams during those years posted some outstanding records despite the tough schedules.[103] The Quarterback Club remained loyal and generous. When GHS went on split sessions, practice had to be held at night. The local electric utility provided lighting for the GHS practice field. Not coincidentally, during those years GHS continued as the only white high school in Gainesville. The 1970 desegregation brought its enrollment to thirty-two hundred.

Even before African American students began going to school with whites in Gainesville, sports provided a catalyst to bring white and black high school students together. Herbert Wagemaker, MD, became the team doctor for the Gainesville High, P. K. Yonge, and Lincoln High football teams. That association enabled Wagemaker to develop relationships with high school students of both races. In 1965, Wagemaker organized a local chapter of Young Life, a faith-based youth program he had first participated in while a student at Wheaton College in Illinois. According to Wagemaker, Tiny Talbot, then still serving as GHS principal, was wary of Young Life. Wagemaker says Talbot told him, "I don't want you there but I can't keep you out." Wagemaker traveled with the teams and ate lunch at the high schools. Young Life's high school gatherings brought groups of sixty to ninety high school students of both races, boys and girls, together at homes of white adult leaders. They sang Christian songs, listened to brief religious lessons, danced to records, and just hung out. Although each meeting included a faith-based program, there was no pressure on anyone to make an individual religious commitment. Ironically, those events took place without complaint or harassment at the same time that Coach Niblack and Eddie McAshan were receiving death threats. Young Life drew mixed reactions from the mainstream churches. According to Wagemaker, some clergy and members at First Baptist Church were supportive, but other churches were less so. Wagemaker singles out Perry and Noel McGriff, members at First Baptist, for becoming active in the organization and eventually leading a college group at the University of Florida.[104] Where there had been no such space before, Young Life made space in a home setting for black and white high school students to be together. Many of those students were athletes. As the only organization of its kind at the time, Young Life helped develop student leaders who would try to make integrated education and sports teams work.

By spring 1970, just when Gainesville High was experiencing the worst of its troubles after the fruitbasket turnover, Wagemaker estimated that eight hundred students of both races were participating in Young Life programs. By now, those programs also included discussions of students' "problems, hopes, tensions and frustrations." Five of the first group of ombudsmen at Gainesville High were active Young Life members.[105]

With the coming of freedom-of-choice desegregation in 1964, blacks became eligible to play football at Gainesville High. Niblack would have had no choice but to accept black players, but driven as he was to win against the toughest opposition, he soon began recruiting black players. One of his first successes was quarterback Eddie McAshan, who started at quarterback from 1966 through 1968. Niblack and McAshan received death threats, and for a short time both he and McAshan were under FBI protection. Niblack, brandishing a baseball bat, chased off some men who were burning a cross on his lawn.[106] McAshan was recruited by Georgia Tech and became that school's first black quarterback.

Niblack wanted to play out-of-state football powers, but the race issue followed the team to some of those games. Alvin Butler, a sophomore on the 1968 team, remembers that some men tried to keep the team from getting off its bus for the game at Alcoa, Tennessee, because they did not want the black players to play (the Hurricanes won, 52–7).[107] On a trip to Greenville, South Carolina, the team was refused rooms at the Holiday Inn. Niblack loaded the team back on the buses and headed back to Florida. Niblack's bus was stopped by a South Carolina Highway Patrol car after about thirty miles. The Greenville High School coach was with two officers, and they asked the team to return to Greenville because the hotel would accommodate all of the players. The team lost that game, but Niblack called the hotel battle, which he won, "the big one."[108]

By the time of the fruitbasket turnover in 1970, Niblack had already established that black football players were welcome at GHS and that he would play the best players regardless of race. Considering the GHS football tradition before desegregation, it was not such a major step from not caring who your daddy was to not caring what color your skin was. Melvin Flournoy, speaking of the coaches: "So, we trusted our coaches and we all wanted to be successful. They played the best players. They took the bullets for doing things that maybe weren't culturally the norm at the time."[109]

Football attracted some of the toughest young males. Frank Coleman:

> That's a funny situation is, you know, that football field was something in its own. You can, if you think about a lot of the guys that were at Howard Bishop who thought they were like really, really bad boys, and the ones at Gainesville High who really thought they were really, really bad boys would usually join the football team, that would be where they could get their aggression out, so they can show how bad they really were.
>
> Now the way Niblack was, he allowed you that freedom to put it into play. You know, if you could take that whatever it is that you have inside you that's boiling over, if you can focus it and put it where it needs to be, then, okay, so be it. And what you learned is, is that you found that you got a lot of respect from each other by being able to funnel that craziness into something positive, and all of the guys who could do that remained on the football team. The ones that couldn't, because they got beat at it, they left. That's what turned that into a very good football team, I think.
>
> ***
>
> Even if I have to do this or do that, it's got to be legal. So the ones that could handle that, the ones that could actually funnel that into legitimate type work on the football field were successful football players. But the ones that couldn't, they ended up going back and raising the Confederate flag and riding around in trucks, you see.[110]

Moving directly from sandlot to GHS meant that players for the first time had equipment, trainers, and facilities. Alvin Butler, who started as a defensive back for GHS and later for the Florida Gators, says that when he got to the University of Florida, the weight room was about half the size of the weight room at GHS. To Butler, Niblack was the toughest coach he ever played for. "And you know, that was just down my alley, so I loved it." Butler says that in high school, each season, he would go through about three helmets, cracking one after the other. One of Niblack's training devices was the Pit. Butler: "I'm sure it was illegal, but we had a pit that was about three feet deep and probably ten by ten, maybe four feet deep. And we'd get in that sometimes three on three. But he'd have last man in the ring. So you know, you'd be throwing other people out of the ring. This was either with equipment or not with equipment, didn't make any difference. And you know, when it rained, it was muddy. So I'm absolutely certain that had to be illegal, but it was the thing that made us good because there was no fear going into a game."

Tough was not mean. Niblack wanted a good relationship with his players "so he could push you in ways that other people couldn't." Niblack had bread and peanut butter in his office. Butler says, "You could go in any time and get a sandwich from him. I mean, that was pretty different back then for him to do that. You could go in and hang out and talk to him. And he was really gruff on the sidelines and gruff in practice, but he'd put his arm around a player in a minute and tell you what a good person you are. So he had the ability to do both of those things, and I think that's what made him great."[111]

Butler quit the team in his junior year when Niblack told Butler that he would not be starting the team's first home game. According to Butler, Niblack chose to start another player whose parent was "giving a lot of money to the team." Butler says he tried to play for Lincoln that year but was told that he couldn't transfer. Niblack welcomed Butler back at spring practice, and Butler played for Niblack in his senior year, 1970.[112]

Lincoln's entire grades 10, 11, and 12 were all assigned to Gainesville High in February 1970, in part so they could participate in existing sports programs during their remaining years of high school. Similar programs would not be up and running at either Eastside or Buchholz, the two new high schools that opened later in 1970. However, because of the consolidation, there would only be half as many starting positions. A second impact, perhaps not foreseen, was that a number of former Lincoln players failed to earn grade-point averages that would allow them to play team sports. According to Brenda Wims, some Lincoln athletes had been able to meet grade-point standards at Lincoln but were not able to do so at GHS. "So a lot of people weren't able to do what they were doing [at Lincoln]. They weren't able to be on the basketball team and the football team once grades came out." Wims says that Hendrickson and other administrators looked into the grade issue because they really wanted the Lincoln students to be part of GHS activities.[113]

Football players from Lincoln no doubt were just as hurt by the closing of their school as their other classmates. But, according to one white football player, "Those guys wanted to play football. And it may be one thing to boycott other programs, but if you want to play football, if you love to play football, you're still going to show up to play football." The GHS coaching staff was augmented by coaches from Lincoln, including Bob Acosta and Amos Hill.[114] According to Alvin Butler, the team took on about thirty-five former Lincoln players.[115]

Former players recall few incidents of a racial nature on the football team. But despite everyone's efforts to maintain discipline, there would occasionally be a flare-up. Tim Strauser's dad pushed him and his brothers to be involved in football. They enjoyed it. Tim calls himself an "ass back," as in "get your ass back on the sideline." Tim ended up starting at safety in his senior year when Don Dickey, the UF coach's son, got hurt. Tim's older brother John was tough and somewhat prejudiced. He got into fights with other players and quit the team. Coach Niblack called the Strausers' house to convince John to play. At that point, Tim's dad intervened and forced John to rejoin the team.[116]

The GHS football team had enjoyed great success during the Eddie McAshan years, 1966–1968. One might have forecast that bringing the remaining Lincoln athletes to the GHS varsity football team would have produced even more lopsided victories over opponents. However, without McAshan, the Hurricanes went 2–8 in 1969, beginning a rebuilding process. During the seasons in which the fruitbasket turnover classes played, 1970 and 1971, the team compiled respectable 7–4 records against very tough opponents. According to Alvin Butler, after adding the former Lincoln students, the team struggled in part because its players had not previously played together. Even so, Butler says that about ten players from the 1970 team were signed to play for college teams.[117] Flournoy recalls that thirteen players on the 1972 team were recruited by NCAA Division I schools.[118]

Picking leaders was part of the coaches' job. Leaders from the football field became leaders within the school. Flournoy was elected junior-class president and student body president in his senior year. Flournoy remembers that Dan Boyd, the principal, and Niblack were back to back when problems occurred. "We always had a few crazy people who wanted to fight the Civil War in April of every year. When negative situations or little sparks of trouble were about to start, our players would find a way to stop or end the problem in most cases. We might grab one of our teammates if they were involved or get directly involved in stopping fights or arguments in order to keep peace and safety at our school. I think the coaches made us leaders both on and off the field. It was somewhat natural for us to prevent the crazy situations created by a few students from destroying our school and our football season."[119] Butler agrees. "Niblack was a very imposing guy. In Florida, football is sort of king of sports. A lot of your good students are good athletes. So I think, in a roundabout fashion, if they have a whole lot of respect for that head coach, then that head coach gets a lot more clout than he would get in another school. . . . And he would challenge people physically to do what they needed to do. And not many people wanted to go against the man."[120]

John Dukes III began playing football at Westwood Junior High and came to GHS in his sophomore year, 1971. He played on the varsity in 1972 and 1973. "Because of the leadership and fairness of a man like Coach

Niblack it became easier at least for us to find a way to blend in and come together as students and friends. We worked together. Everybody worked hard and the discipline was great. It was just one of those things that where they took the attention away from the differences and brought the focus on the things where we were alike and what could happen when we worked together against the opposition."[121]

White players typically had their own cars. Black players did not, and many lived on Gainesville's east side, three miles and more from GHS. Strauser, who lived in a white neighborhood on the east side, often gave rides to black teammates; some of his white friends called him out for offering that courtesy.[122] Jerry Mauldin, a 1973 classmate of Strauser, played varsity basketball. Like Strauser, Mauldin gave rides home to some of his black teammates. It was Mauldin's first introduction to black living conditions. Mauldin remembers that one player would not let Mauldin drive him all the way to the player's house.[123] At the time of the fruitbasket turnover, Mauldin was a ninth grader at Howard Bishop. One of his new black teammates showed up to play basketball in leather shoes. At Lincoln, a coach probably would have seen to it that all of the players had athletic shoes. At Bishop, there was no similar support system. Mauldin talked his father into buying this player a pair of Converses.[124]

At some point, GHS added an intramural sports program. The school had become much too large for the varsity teams to accommodate all of the boys who wanted to play sports. Ted Covey and some white friends played intramural basketball in Covey's sophomore year. "Twice we set records for giving up the most points, as far as we knew, in the history of intramural basketball. And we were getting killed by the senior teams." The next year, the group recruited some black players, "and quite frankly, the black players were the better basketball players on our team. We played fairly good. But, you know, I never saw any problems. We showed up, played, and then I guess, whatever ways we went."[125] Vince Deconna had similar experiences. He played varsity baseball on well-integrated teams, but his service club, Key Club, competed in an intramural flag football league and at volleyball. He remembers the intramural leagues were run by students and helped build student morale.[126]

Gainesville's two new high schools, Eastside and Buchholz, graduated their first senior classes in 1973. By then, each school had its own football program, coached by Rabbit Smith at Eastside and Jessie Heard at Buchholz. From that point, Gainesville High could no longer draw upon the inflated enrollment that it had enjoyed during the transition to a unitary school system. The days of playing out-of-state teams were over. Niblack, seeking greater challenges, in 1974 became an assistant coach for the Jacksonville Sharks team in the new professional World Football

League, and its successor, the Jacksonville Express, the following year. Eddie McAshan and Alvin Butler joined Niblack for the Jacksonville teams' two-year run. Niblack coached for other professional teams in later life but returned to Gainesville High for the 1979 and 1980 seasons, winning the school's only state football championship in 1980.[127]

Trying to Be Friends

White students who were sympathetic to black classmates after the arrival of the Lincoln transfer students soon discovered that sustaining friendships in that strained atmosphere was not going to be easy. Nell Page found black students guarded and defensive. In an awkward moment, a remark intended to be kind came across as patronizing.[128] Jeanie Whitehead Shaw, who formed a lifelong friendship with a former Lincoln student through their ministry activities, sees that friendship as an exception. "But what is really sad to me is what seemed to be very little effort to involve the average student in really getting to know each other. And to just really welcome each other. And to get along. . . . I think just learning some areas of compassion for each other could have really helped. Could have prevented a lot. But to my knowledge or remembrance there wasn't really any of that. . . . I think there was a desire among the students to be accepting but not knowing how, and not knowing the impact that it had."[129]

Mary Rockwood recalls being warned by a black friend that Rockwood would be in danger because of some impending troubles. Rockwood protested that they were friends. The response was "It doesn't matter. You're white." From that conversation Rockwood learned that her feelings about racial matters would not protect her.[130] Ron Perry befriended a black female student. One spring, during a period of tension between blacks and whites, Perry tried to strike up a conversation with her in the hall between classes. "And she just totally ignored me. And I understood that. She had to posture for her friends . . ."[131]

During 1971, Nell Page's humanities teacher showed the class a film about a young black student and his feeling of isolation. The teacher wanted to open up a dialogue. The class included some black students. When the film was over, there was silence. Finally, Nell said she saw the same thing happening at GHS. "As I was going out, there were two black students that came up to me and said thank you so much for saying that. It confused me that others could not relate to the feeling of isolation I saw in the film."[132]

Susan Holloway Weinkle was homecoming queen and captain of the cheerleaders in 1969–70, her senior year. When the Lincoln students came to GHS in February 1970, the cheerleading squad doubled in size; no cheerleaders from either school would lose that status. Weinkle, who became a dermatologist and surgeon, remembers that getting the cheerleaders to perform their routines was not the major problem. The GHS cheerleaders had been together for years and were personally close. It was common after a game to go to someone's house for refreshments. Now, not all of the cheerleaders' parents would allow the black cheerleaders in their homes. Weinkle does not recall developing close relations with the former Lincoln cheerleaders.[133]

Unification brought into stark focus the resentment of some Lincoln students toward blacks who started going to white schools under freedom of choice. Some Lincoln High transfer students, writing under pseudonyms, distributed an unofficial newspaper called "Black." That newspaper brought current black militancy into the school and into the faces of more traditional teachers and students (there had been no similar publication at Lincoln). White students perceived "Black" as advocating racial hatred. The paper solicited nominations for awards such as "Militant of the Week" and "Oreo of the Week." "Oreos" was the epithet used by some Lincoln transfer students for blacks who had previously entered white schools under freedom of choice. The paper advocated that black students wear African attire to the April 4 junior-senior prom. That call caused some moderate black students to decide not to attend the prom at all.[134]

Law-enforcement officials later blamed radical students from the University of Florida for encouraging defiance of rules and laws by black students at GHS.[135] Russell Ramsey, who became head of the school board's off-campus isolation classes, agreed that some black GHS students were receiving advice from black militants at the University.[136]

Black students who already attended GHS were between two hostile camps. One commented, "[The Lincoln transfer students] don't like the idea that we came over here. They call us traitors." A Lincoln student who arrived at GHS in February said, "I thought they were wrong. The year before Lincoln was to be closed, they left. That was like deserting an army. Being at GHS wasn't helping us any. I still hold that as a grudge." But other students from Lincoln defended the black students who were already at GHS for helping to integrate the school.[137] Frank Coleman was one of those students. According to Coleman, the white students who were trying to provoke fights with blacks after February 1970 did not spare their longtime black classmates. And the former Lincoln students did not spare Coleman either, at first.

> That kind of upset me, because even though my heart was just in trying to make things work, I was looked at as a sell-out, and that was hard for me to take, from all the people I grew up with. But they had not really seen and had relations

> with [me] for about three or four years, like we had in the past, so, of course, I was the enemy. And to a certain extent, that caused some emotion, quite a bit of emotion during that period. . . . That for most of us that were already at Gainesville High School, we were being called Oreos, white on the inside, black on the out. And that was, if you think anything would start a fight that would start one with me, or with most of the guys that were over there, especially us who didn't feel like we deserved it.

Coleman says the blacks already at GHS had to earn the respect of the former Lincoln students while at the same time playing their existing roles as senators or other leaders at GHS: "Damned if we do, damned if we don't." Much later, Coleman was allowed to join a group of former Lincoln students from the class of 1970, the Keepers of the Keys, and says "almost all of us had turned into just people who grew up together."[138]

Summing up, white student Patricia Crawford says:

> My thought about the whole thing, it was really impressive the character of high school students. Except for a handful of renegades, and they were renegades in whatever they did, they weren't affiliated with anything, sports, student government, the performing arts, nothing, the rest of the students, from both Lincoln and GHS, I thought were for their age quite impressive, and I celebrate that. I speak at every reunion, and I celebrate that. . . . The majority of the students individually showed great character, courage, integrity. I can't say enough for them. It was a good time for me to see that in young human beings.[139]

AFTERWORD

> And the LORD said unto Cain, Where *is* Abel thy brother? And he said, I know not: *Am* I my brother's keeper?
> Genesis 4:9

African American leaders concluded in the 1930s and 1940s that the most effective path to equal educational opportunity for Southern African Americans was ending the South's dual school systems. Those leaders succeeded in ending separate black and white schools, but whether blacks in desegregated schools enjoy equal educational opportunity remains a most perplexed issue.[1] In this afterword, we return to examine features of the South's black schools and features adopted during desegregation that remain relevant to educating African American and all other students.

There Has Been Progress

Before concluding this exploration of equal educational opportunity, we need to recognize some statistics that show a positive view of African American progress (no suggestion is made that either desegregation or the more recent standards-based reforms are responsible for that progress).

Objectively, in the years immediately after desegregation, African Americans made significant academic gains, as measured by achievement tests.[2] But modern defenders of desegregation, like those from Alachua County profiled in this chapter, argue not so much for short-term impacts that can be measured by test scores, but for the broader impacts on the life chances of blacks who go to school with members of other races. An important objective of *Brown* and other desegregation cases was to gain blacks equal access to networks and mainstream educational institutions.[3]

Recent census data by race for Alachua County are not available, but the table below shows the percentage of blacks in Florida age twenty-five and above with high school diplomas, and with four-year college degrees, from 1940 through 2000 (including non-Hispanic whites for 1980–2000).[4]

Table 6. Alachua County, Education Level by Race, 1940–2000

Black, age 25 and above	**1940**	**1950**	**1960**	**1970**	**1980**	**1990**	**2000**
High school dipl. or better	4.6	8.4	14.5	24.4	44.6	56.4	67.1
4 yr. college degree or better	0.8	1.7	2.8	4.1	7.3	9.8	12.4
White, age 25 and above	**1940**	**1950**	**1960**	**1970**	**1980**	**1990**	**2000**
High school dipl. or better	34.1	42.5	47.4	56.3	69.5	77.0	82.5
4 yr. college degree or better	6.4	7.6	8.6	11.1	15.8	19.3	23.8

In 2015–16, 66.8 percent of Alachua County's black students graduated from high school, up from 54.8 percent in 2011–12. By way of comparison, the graduation rate for Asians was 92.4 percent; whites, 85.0 percent; mixed-race, 71.8 percent; and Hispanics, 82.1 percent.[5] These graduation rates are measured against the number of students who entered the ninth grade. It is not possible to compare these graduation rates to those at Lincoln High before desegregation, but the available anecdotal information implies that the graduation rate for blacks is substantially higher today.[6]

In 1970, in Alachua County, 15.3 percent of white families lived below the poverty level, but 43.1 percent of black families lived below that level. If 125 percent of the poverty level is used, the earnings of 20.4 percent of white families and 54.3 percent of black families failed to exceed that level.[7] By 2009, 22.3 percent of Alachua County's white non-Hispanic families lived below the poverty threshold, and 25.7 percent of black families were below that threshold.[8] More black families continue to enter higher earning brackets, although black earnings still lag considerably behind the earnings of whites.[9]

In 1970, African Americans accounted for only 4.3 percent of full-time undergraduates in formerly white institutions of higher learning in the South.[10] In 2013, African Americans seeking undergraduate and graduate degrees had almost unanimously chosen to attend integrated colleges and universities. Of African American students enrolled in degree programs nationwide, only 10 percent were enrolled in historically black colleges and universities.[11] These statistics suggest that whatever the pluses and minuses of desegregated educational institutions, blacks are choosing to go to school with, and to be taught by, members of all races, not just their own.

What Has Changed, and What Hasn't? Racial Balancing or Racial Isolation?

Like many other Southern school districts, Alachua County retreated from the district-wide racial balancing described in chapter 17. In 2002, Florida adopted a constitutional amendment limiting public school class sizes and mandating free prekindergarten programs for four-year-olds.[12] The school district had to review its allocation of pupils and classrooms. As Earl Bergadine warned in 1971, whites with school-age children abandoned Gainesville's east-side neighborhoods that originally provided racial balance to Eastside High School. On the west side, the population continued to grow. Many African American students continued to be bused long distances to west-side schools to provide racial balance. West-side schools were overcrowded, with many portable classrooms. Some east-side schools had empty classrooms. According to the Florida Department of Education, Alachua County had adequate capacity for its students in existing schools; the county would receive no funds for new schools to comply with the class size mandate.[13] With much community involvement, the county embarked on school redistricting. In 2003, the school board adopted a rezoning plan that eliminated busing for racial balance and returned the system to neighborhood schools.[14] Under the plan, 2,740 elementary students, 200 middle school students, and 580 high school students were shifted to other schools.[15] The busing of approximately 1,500 students to schools outside their neighborhood zones was eliminated.[16]

When Joel Achenbach in 2007 wrote in the *Washington Post* about being bused to Duval Elementary School, he contacted the Rev. Wright. According to Wright, blacks turned against busing. Wright told Achenbach that when racial balancing was discontinued, there was no real fight from the African American community.[17] Speaking in 2004, Charles Chestnut III questioned whether African American students benefited from desegregation, because of the closing of black schools such as Lincoln High School, and noted that under the new zoning plan, "the onus is on the black community to take more responsibility for the achievement of students."[18] On the other hand, Barbara Gallant charged that the plan accelerated resegregation, and she called attention to emotional objections to the plan by some black parents at a hearing at Lincoln Middle School.[19] Barbara Sharpe, then chair of the school board and an African American, was the sole board member to vote against the plan.[20] She had earlier commented, "I'm not ashamed to say when I looked at the consequences of neighborhood schools, as they stand today, it was not a good idea and can be detrimental to low-income students. What's more compelling than racial balance is socioeconomic status. Any addition to what is already there at that high number [of impoverished students] is not a good thing."[21] There could not help but be an impact on black students who were shifted back to east-side schools. A principal commented that the PTA at her school, Williams Elementary, did well to raise $2,000 per year, but a PTA on the west side was able to raise $20,000.[22] Teachers from west-side schools were also shifted to east-side schools, with the least senior teachers required to move under the system's collective bargaining agreement.[23]

The county's districting plan has resulted in approximately 58 percent of African American students attending racially balanced schools as of the 2015–16 school year. However, there remain nine schools whose enrollment in their nonmagnet programs is 50 percent or more black, attended by approximately thirty-seven hundred black students. The black student bodies in these schools continue to be overwhelmingly poor. Lincoln High was closed and replaced by Eastside to maximize the success of desegregation; the nonmagnet program at Eastside is now almost entirely African American.

In 2007, the Supreme Court ruled that school districts may not use racial balancing to remedy de facto segregation. A plurality of the justices concluded that affirmative racial balancing to correct de facto segregation is itself a violation of the Fourteenth Amendment's Equal Protection Clause. Viewing racial balancing as a zero-sum game, four justices held that favoring one race is to discriminate against the other races. That decision rested on earlier cases that struck down aspects of affirmative action programs.[24] Subsequent guidance from the US Justice Department and Education Department encourages school districts seeking to eliminate racially isolated schools to use nonracial criteria, such as the socioeconomic status of students or neighborhoods.[25]

Ironically, Florida in 2016 enacted a return to a version of freedom of choice. Beginning with the 2017–18 school year, any student may choose to attend any public or charter school, subject to capacity, class size, and competitive program admission restrictions. Students choosing this option must provide their own transportation.[26]

From today's vantage point, the African Americans who experienced desegregation, and who told their stories in this book, have decidedly mixed feelings about desegregation's value.

Bettye Jennings: "But I'm saying the court didn't need to say [Alachua County schools had to be racially balanced]. The court could have said, Lincoln High needs to have this category, GHS needs to have this, they need to have the same things in each school. You can choose. Do you want to stay at Lincoln, that's okay. Do you want to stay at GHS, that's okay. But you have the same equipment at each school."[27]

Charles Chestnut III: "[Desegregation] just destroyed the African American community. [Speaking of relations between black teachers and professors at black colleges] And that was that learning and sharing and the empowerment and betterment of the African American educational system. And that was, we just lost it. I mean, it's gone, you know. It is gone."[28]

Cora Roberson believes that smarter students and more of them came out of the segregated schools. She says the schools don't try hard enough with children who don't want to learn. She recognizes that part of the problem today is that many parents are less involved in their children's education. "During the time I was going [to the black schools], you kept that child in the classroom and you taught him, whether he wanted to learn or not. He had to produce some kind of work or else the teacher would be willing to stay with him after school until a mother came looking for him or you could call or send someone to tell their parents Johnny is here with me because Johnny is going to do his work before he goes home. Now that is unheard of now."[29]

Gertrude E. Jones, who urged her community to support desegregation in 1970, says,

> Well, it might have helped some. I think it helped because the blacks back then, they did have to segregate everything, the books, everything else. And a lot of the teachers, they weren't as educated. They taught what they knew and everything, but they were not as educated. [After desegregation] they got better teachers, better everything, which is the way it is now. We are still segregated, believe it or not. I don't know if you understand what I'm saying.

Jones was unsuccessful in obtaining admission for a grandchild, a straight A student, to the Lyceum program, a middle school program that prepares students for the International Baccalaureate.

> Like I told them, well, she says, all the kids that's making the best grades and doing this and that and have the highest score and all that are getting into [the Lyceum and International Baccalaureate programs]. I said, well, just stop and think about it. Don't you think that the kids that are not making such good grades need the help more than the ones that got the good grades? Or do you think they need the help more? That's the way the state is. That's the way the law is. I gave up really. I gave up because there was nothing I could do, nothing. But it's going on.
>
> And as far as the segregation, there's no, I mean, integration, we are not integrated at all, period. And this is not even only in middle school and high school. It's starting in the elementary schools now.

Jones recognizes that some black parents don't care whether their children take advantage of the educational opportunities available to them. "And I'm ashamed to say, a lot of the parents don't care whether the kids get their homework or not. They don't care, period. And when the parent don't care, the kid don't care. And when they don't care, the teachers don't care. So these kids aren't getting an education. And it's sad."[30]

Wayne Mosley:

> Mr. Dukes would slap you right in front of your parents, or either call and tell your parents, hey, Wayne got out of hand today. And my daddy would tell him, well, what you calling me for? He still around here lipping, why you ain't bust his lips? So that's what I mean about the neighborhood took care of each other. And Mr. Dukes was one of those principals. Now, he would give you the sweater off of his back, but you had to do what he said. And he meant what he said. He'll play with you and joke and everything else, but when he would grab that belt, like this here, the pants and pull up, he was getting serious on you, and you knew that. Everybody knew when he did that, all right, you better look out. And Coach Heard was the same thing. I mean, all the coaches you could go to if you had personal problems or you thought you had personal problems. They, most of the time, would have laughed about, boy, I thought something was wrong. That ain't nothing but you just in love or something of this nature.
>
> But they was there for you, you know. I hear the kids now talking about, man, I ain't got nobody to talk to. They scared to talk to the teachers, I guess, because they feel like it going to be publicized over the school or spreaded around. I have no reason why, don't know why. But then they don't have nobody they can go to and look up for like we did during then.
>
> You know, if you needed a dollar for lunch or you wanted to impress your little girlfriend, you go borrow a dollar from the coach. Most of them knew they wasn't going to never get it back unless you went out there and picked up golf balls for them or washed they car. But they knew what you was trying to do. Everybody is for theyself now.[31]

Mosley, after being identified and watched by Gainesville police as a troublemaker (he was arrested in an arson case but not convicted, and for a time hid out under his parents' house), would have a twenty-year career in the air force, ending as an E-6. He later would be hired by Dan Boyd, who knew his past, to work as a custodian at GHS. His daughter would be homecoming queen at GHS.[32]

Others take the opposite view:

Mary Lewis, the black PE teacher at Santa Fe who became a long-serving dean at Gainesville High: "Because life is full of changes and we're going to be better prepared for changes in our lives. We need to know each other. I'm glad we had integration. We have equal opportunity. Better education and employment. No more old books from GHS. The students got to be more loving and caring. The teachers were already very caring. . . . Under integration we can live together. I don't have to be in your door and you don't have to be in my door. But we know one another. We know one another and can learn. . . . When we were on our own side we would see things we couldn't get. After integration we found out we could get those things. We could get a better education. Things were better at the white schools. We didn't know it until we got there. Now we can go to the University of Florida and FSU, not just FAMU."[33]

Sam Haywood, who served as assistant principal at GHS, disagrees that the separate black schools should have been maintained and made equal. "And the reason I say that is because in society, we have to learn to work and get along. We don't have a black society or a white society as a whole. And when we get out in life, and when we move on to bigger and better things, in which, the way it was set up, there was a limited number of opportunities and experiences and exposure that many of the black kids were getting with the segregated system back then. So by us desegregating schools and the system as a whole, I think it helped society as a whole for the blending and the support and the creation of opportunities and experiences that many of the young black kids had not experienced."[34]

John Dukes Jr., the last Lincoln principal, did not want Lincoln to be closed. But according to his wife and his son, he also believed in full desegregation. Bernice Dukes, responding to the question of whether Dukes believed in desegregation or was it just part of his job: "Probably a combination of the two. Because inevitably, integration was coming. And in order to make it work as well as it could, had to be someone who could bring the two together. And I think they saw in him that he could do that because of the respect he commanded in the black community and in the white community."[35]

Speaking of what he believes were his father's views, John Dukes III says,

> But knowing that times call for there to be a change, that call for there to be an integration and a way for blacks and whites in this society to finally be where we have to be. Because it's not a separate country. We can't. . . . It's unsustainable. And

> it was unsustainable in that present state at that time. It is one of those things that historically you know that as you progress this is coming. You have a nationwide fight going on to become more integrated in American society and then we transfer that to the local, well, what's going to happen there? Can't say, "Well, let it happen over here" but not have it happen in places where we choose to just stay in this particular way. Especially when you have a portion of the society that'd be more than happy to say, "You know what? You guys are right. Let's leave it just the way it is." That is the tough choice, but that is exactly what they would have. . . . I mean if that was an option, we'd still be there, you know? So really that option was a false choice.[36]

Jessie Heard recalls his years as Lincoln's football coach with pride and his ever-present sense of humor but says that integration was "for the better." "They just didn't want their way of life disrupted and gone. Those words—you might say they probably didn't know any better. But this was a good life for us. I mean, it was good to us and for us, because everybody felt comfortable in it, and it was being taken away."[37]

T. B. McPherson coached football at Lincoln High before Jessie Heard. He was loyal to Lincoln and regretted its closing. After desegregation, McPherson continued to serve as an assistant principal until he retired in 1974. After retirement, he became a Methodist minister. When asked in 1984 if he thought the community would ever go back to having a black school again, he replied,

> Never. I just believe right now that we ourselves would be the greatest handicap. So we still get people that object to the unity. Maybe, some of the pride and stuff that we worried about may lead right into us digging to get the things that we needed, which is unity. We have made good progress now. Since we started talking on this thing really. I may be wrong on that. I just started thinking about the number of black kids and things that are getting in the universities and on teams. I saw some of the street last night. Made me feel pretty good to see some of the outstanding things kids are doing now. Color does not enter into it.[38]

Catherine Mickle taught at Lincoln and later, for about twenty years until her retirement in 1996, at Eastside. Mickle agrees that in some ways desegregation has helped both African American students and teachers. She says that her white students were sometimes quick to help black students, who might not have been as aggressive in their learning habits, and that the black students did not resent being helped.

Mickle taught mostly girls in her Cooperative Business Education classes at Eastside, and in her reflections on desegregation, she focused mostly on girls. She believes that while she was at Lincoln High, the girls were more respectful toward their parents and other adults. “In the days of Lincoln High School, teachers could talk to them, teachers could talk with their parents, and I think it made a difference.” Now, according to Mickle, too many parents come to school ready to blame the teacher for any issues with their children. A segment of black citizens lack parenting skills. “And when these children grow up, if they aren’t really learning and correcting now, they’re going to be just like what they see Mama do and what Daddy’s doing. And it just goes on and on unless the parents are educated.”[39] After retiring, Mickle, with some other retired teachers, founded the Saturday Academy at Mount Carmel Baptist Church, the Rev. Wright’s church, where they tutor reading and writing skills and computer skills.

Frank Ford: “But there was things going on that, you know, positive things between people. And people that once was prejudiced, once they realized why they was prejudiced and stopped being, and then you became friends, you know. And most of us are taught from birth that what your parents tell you is the truth. It’s not until you grow up and think for yourself and realize that all of what Mom and Dad said wasn’t true. And a lot of us kids was like that.”[40]

Melvin Flournoy became a coach and administrator in Alachua County and in other school systems. He believes that race relations in Alachua County are much improved, with the outlying communities catching up to the more urban areas, “even though there’s a big backlash right now and rural people are becoming more conservative, anti-Obama or whatever you want to call it. . . . I don’t think there are many better communities to live in than Alachua County. Gainesville, in particular, is a great place to raise a family and grow up as an African American. I don’t think there’s a perfect situation. I think we’ve advanced a great deal in our community. There are so many more benefits that we receive because of the desegregation than there are negatives.”

As a negative, Flournoy agrees with others who have pointed out that young persons in the core black community have lost many of the black role models who helped sustain that community prior to desegregation. One of Flournoy’s positions with the Alachua County schools was staffing specialist. Flournoy believes that it will not be possible to bring a greater proportion of blacks back into the teaching profession. And “many of the black community leaders and potential leaders chose to live outside the black community. They’re not community leaders in the true sense of Lincoln Estates and that area. And even though it’s their/our choice to live out west, you can imagine what we could have given back to the black community is lost. Once you desegregate schools, you really desegregated the communities, too, for the most part.”

As benefits, Flournoy cites the friendships between blacks and whites, and the county's acceptance of black leaders, including the current police chief and black mayors. "We've really worked hard in this county to help everybody assimilate and be able to take a leadership role." Among the other benefits: "I have the opportunity to know people and love people who are different than I am."[41]

Brenda Wims, who also became an educator, agrees that there were pros and cons to desegregation. She believes that desegregation was more beneficial than harmful to the black community. "If I had not had the opportunity to receive the education I did at Gainesville High for that last year, I don't know if I would have been as successful early on as I had been. Like I said, I was focused on academics, and you had to make the grade to go where you were going." Wims graduated from the University of North Florida and then was the first recipient at that school of a Delores Auzenne Fellowship, which allowed her to obtain a master's degree. The State of Florida provides Delores Auzenne scholarships and fellowships at its state universities to competitively selected minority students. The awards are named in memory of the first wife of George R. Auzenne, a longtime administrator at Florida A&M University. "On the other hand, as far as the culture and the cohesiveness that existed in the black community, it does not exist anymore. Not only because of integration, but because of changes in law. That was a fact where I lived. The community raised the child. That was a fact." Wims grew up with her mother in Gardenia Gardens, the first low-income housing project in Gainesville. "But overall, I'm glad [desegregation] did happen, because each culture has something to bring to make it better. And we find ourselves now with all the children. You can't say it's just the black race or just the white race anymore. They have really integrated their forces when it comes to doing things that aren't right."[42]

Philoron Wright is the younger son of the Reverend Thomas A. Wright, who brought the Alachua County desegregation suit. Philoron experienced the struggle for desegregation both as a family member and later as a teacher and administrator in the Alachua County schools. Philoron graduated from Lincoln High in 1965 and from Tennessee State University in 1970. While serving as a substitute teacher at Gainesville High, Philoron was picked by Russell Ramsey to help out at Mountain Top, and he went with Ramsey to the Lincoln vocational center in 1972.

For its efforts, the Wright family was the target of threats and hate calls. An example: in the mid-1970s, the Rev. Wright was asked to exchange pulpits with a minister at the white Parkview Baptist Church. The *Gainesville Sun* had published the exchange in its church section on the preceding Saturday. That night, the Wrights' phone rang. The caller told Rev. Wright that he would be killed if he showed up at Parkview. According to Rev. Wright, his wife insisted that he keep the engagement: "that would be a good way to die." Parkview was informed of the threat. Philoron drove his mother and father to the church. When they arrived, according to Rev. Wright, "they had young men dressed in dark suits on each side of the walk, and as we marched down the walk to go into the church, they said, welcome, Reverend and Mrs. Wright, to Parkview. I went in. An assistant minister conducted the service. I preached. And when I got through preaching at Parkview, I didn't see a dry eye in that church." Philoron parked across Thirteenth Street from the church with his pistol in his lap, watching for anyone who might enter the church during the service.[43]

Philoron Wright later obtained his MEd degree from the University of Florida and his leadership certificate. He took courses toward the EdD, but having a family intervened. His career with the Alachua County schools spanned forty-three years, during which he was a teacher, an assistant principal, a principal, and, eventually, an assistant superintendent. His view:

> If it had not been for integration, there would have been pretty much a stalemate in terms of growth and relationships in the communities. Integration helped. After all the efforts people went through and died for, I think if I said it didn't help, I couldn't live with myself to say all that energy was for nothing. And just by having the races together, there's a plus, a huge plus. I think that a lot of the opportunities that African Americans haven't taken advantage of where they could take advantage in terms of education somewhere along the line. We've got to value the whole process of integration, the whole process of education, take advantage of the things that so many people fought for, so many people died for. My family went through some things that maybe your family didn't go through. But I know what was the stress factor for us in our home. And what my dad's involvement was and what my mother's involvement was. They were on the front line. There were a lot of families that were on the front line, black and white. When you talk about those freedom riders, all over this country people were engaging in the struggle. They had a glimpse of the future, I believe, and what it could be. They wanted to change the direction the country was going in. It couldn't exist divided forever. Nothing is in perpetuity. Things must change in some way. You had some leaders out there, some people out there, who understood, if we want to be the strong nation that we are, we can make it better and stronger together. We're not there, we've got a

> long way to go. I think overall I just believe that somehow it has strong possibilities of getting there.[44]

The college and career choices of black students from the desegregation years reflect their mixed feelings about their high school experiences. Some chose recently desegregated white universities; others chose historically black universities.

Frank Coleman, who seemingly had succeeded in his studies and in his forays into student activities and sports at GHS, went to Morehouse. But he recognizes that his experiences in the white schools, both good and bad, helped prepare him for a successful career. He credits his talent for math, first developed at GHS, for his success in the military and during his career at IBM. From football, he learned to value team participation. "People have almost forgotten what team is all about. It used to be big when I was coming up. It used to be big in corporate America and in IBM as well at one point. It's gotten so competitive now, nobody thinks about team anymore. It's all about self. And that's just something that, I think one of the reasons that I retired when I did." Coleman's experiences in a desegregated environment also taught him to make an extra effort either to listen and not jump to conclusions or to just watch and see what is going to happen. "I think that alone helped more than anything else."[45] His feelings of isolation at times at the white schools led Coleman to work with groups, to try to pull together, instead of competing and trying to get promoted.[46]

Cynthia Cook's parents wanted her to go to the University of Florida. They had her fill out the application forms, and she was accepted. However, after her experiences in the white schools in Gainesville, Cook wanted to go to a college with people who looked like her. Her parents were unaware that Cook had applied to Florida A&M University; she says that she forged their names on her application. When she told them that she was going to FAMU, they questioned her about the way she had been able to file the application without their knowledge. She adds that she needed to get away from home and grow up. At FAMU, Cook graduated magna cum laude. She says that in any term in which a student made a 4.0 average, tuition was refunded. Choosing a teaching career, Cook came back to Alachua County, where she held various positions in the integrated schools for twenty-two years. While there, Cook earned a master's in education from the University of Florida. She also passed the Florida Leadership in Education (FELE) exam and met the required performance standards. She served as an assistant principal in Fulton County, Georgia, for seventeen years before retiring in 2013.[47]

Donnie Batie, who remained at Lincoln until it closed, went to the University of Florida. He was influenced by his experiences at Gainesville High, successfully competing with whites, and by his perception that the

University had opened up to blacks. "I really wanted to go to a white college. I didn't see anything [at the University of Florida] that I couldn't handle." Batie welcomed the anonymity of a large university. "All you had to do was show up and do your work, and you were fine. . . . I wasn't judged on my color, how tall I was, how handsome. But I had gotten to that point academically." He lived at home, had a part-time job, and bicycled to his University classes. Batie's premed adviser encouraged Batie to take his organic chemistry course, and that relationship also helped Batie succeed as an undergraduate. He continued at the University of Florida for his MD.[48]

Oliver Jones is the son of A. Quinn Jones, the longtime Lincoln High principal. Oliver Jones became a teacher and administrator in the public schools of Alachua and other counties, retiring after twenty-eight years. His perception is that desegregation helped some black students but hurt others:

> The desegregation of the schools for the black student who's above average, desegregation probably helped that student. But for the average black student and those a little below average, desegregation didn't help them very much. I think because for the smarter students whether the teacher helps them like the teacher should or not, they're going to learn anyway because of their ability. I think the students did not receive enough attention from the teacher with the desegregation of the schools. But there again, the smarter students would achieve any way. The average and below average, they were good students, too, but they needed that extra encouragement, that extra push. Knowing more about their experiences in the home background, that was lost with desegregation in schools because you teach children in terms of their experiences. If you are not well acquainted with their experiences, the students' experiences, then you are handicapped in doing the best job helping them. . . . Because white teachers was limited in knowing the community in which the children came from and the children's experiences.[49]

Mae Islar believes there were more gains than losses as a result of desegregation. She says that black parents were initially more defensive of their children with white teachers, because the black parents were more comfortable coming to black teachers and talking about their children. Islar says black parents now are better able to talk to white teachers. She perceives that during segregation a higher proportion of blacks succeeded academically and graduated from high school, because their parents pushed them. "And there's nothing like a black person when they make up their mind that they're going to teach, and you're going to learn. . . . I think white teachers were a little more fearful of a kind of behavior that they had not been used to. And yet people like Sandy Sharron who said I don't care what color you are, this is what you're going to do. . . . Yes, we lost some kids, maybe, but I think we won a whole lot more than we lost. And it was worth it, it needed to happen. People needed to see people as people. There were good people no matter what color they are, and they're still that way. I'm a liberal. I believe in it."[50]

Dr. Batie agrees.

> [Desegregation] helped some blacks. It's somewhat of a mixed answer. I think it opened up opportunities to blacks that we did not have before. It opened up a whole community that we were not able to participate in before. But sometimes, the way I try to explain to people is that previously, in the black community, there were low-income, medium-income, and high-income blacks. When desegregation took place, the high income blacks automatically left the black community. They helped integrate the rest of the community. Then most of the medium income blacks also, they struggled, and they also got outside the black community. . . . Before, you could look at the guy next door, or down the street, and as a poor person, you could say, I have to do more with my life. . . . You don't have any references that you can use to motivate, stimulate the people to do more, because they've all left. They've gone to other parts of the community. That is what the black community continues to struggle with. And that's the really unfortunate part of what desegregation really did to the black community.[51]

Denise C. Morgan, a prominent black legal scholar, concluded in 1991 that the continuing controversy over desegregation had overwhelmed the real goal of education litigation, which was adequate education for people of color. She wrote,

> Framing the desegregation question in terms of associational rights (the right to choose the company one keeps) made integration appear to be a chastisement of school boards and communities that were guilty of racism. However, the aim of integration was not to penalize whites for their sins. Fault, blame and punishment are not terms which should be relevant in a discussion of the right of children of color to educationally adequate schooling. Fault is irrelevant because

> "the injury of racial inequality exists irrespective of the decisionmakers' motives" [footnote omitted].[52]

Standards-Based Reforms

As school districts were turning away from busing for racial balance, standards-based reforms became the new path to equity for minority students. Schools had to implement a prescribed curriculum, high-stakes testing and school grading, and, eventually, metrics intended to measure teacher performance. Florida was a leader of this movement beginning in 1971.[53] Nationally, accountability reforms began in 1994 under President Clinton.[54] Those reforms had support from both Democrats and Republicans.

No Child Left Behind was the name given to the 2001 reauthorization of the Elementary and Secondary Education Act during the administration of President George W. Bush. The law's statement of purpose refers specifically to the achievement gap between minority and nonminority students.[55] No Child Left Behind required states to achieve 100 percent proficiency in reading and math by 2014 by all demographic groups (including major racial and ethnic groups).[56]

It turned out that 100 percent proficiency by 2014 was a completely unrealistic target. The Elementary and Secondary Education Act was finally reauthorized in 2015, during the Obama administration, as the Every Student Succeeds Act. According to that law, "the purpose of [Title I] is to provide all children significant opportunity to receive a fair, equitable, and high-quality education, and to close educational achievement gaps."[57] The Every Student Succeeds Act, although retaining the separate reporting of test and graduation results by major racial and ethnic groups,[58] abandoned the requirement of No Child Left Behind that public schools achieve a specific level of student proficiency. The states are now allowed to set their own standards for achievement provided those standards conform to the basic requirements of the Every Student Succeeds Act.[59]

Despite many billions of dollars of investment in standards-based reforms over more than twenty years, however, there remains a significant achievement gap between white and black students in Alachua County, in Florida, and in the United States. Historical data from the National Center for Education Statistics shows a reduction in that achievement gap as measured by the National Assessment of Educational Progress (NAEP) test from 1992 through about 2003, followed by only minimal changes (see table 7).

Table 7. White-Black Achievement Gap on National Assessment of Educational Progress (NAEP)

	Grade 4 math		Grade 4 reading		Grade 8 math		Grade 8 reading		Grade 12 math		Grade 12 reading	
Year	Florida	US	Florida	US	Florida	US	Florida	US	Florida	US	Florida	US
2015	23	24	23	26	27	31	21	26				
2013	23	25	24	26	27	30	20	25	24	29	28	29
2011	23	25	25	25	29	31	22	25				
2009	22	26	22	25	25	32	21	26	23	29	20	27
2007	25	26	24	27	29	31	24	26				
2005	23	26	26	29	35	33	26	26				
2003	28	27	31	30	37	35	29	27				
2002			30	29			25	27				
1998			31	31			28	36				
1996	33	31			42	39						
1994			36	38								
1992	34	35	33	32	36	40						

Values shown are the differences between white and black average scale scores on the NAEP for tests and years stated. If no value is shown, none was available. Source is National Center for Education Statistics, https://nces.ed.gov/nationsreportcard/, accessed December 26, 2016. Differences shown above reflect rounding and may not equal subtracted average scores in table below.

	Grade 4 math		Grade 4 reading		Grade 8 math		Grade 8 reading		Grade 12 math		Grade 12 reading	
Year	Florida	US	Florida	US	Florida	US	Florida	US	Florida	US	Florida	US
2015	251/ 228	248/ 224	235/ 213	232/ 206	285/ 258	291/ 260	272/ 251	273/ 247				
2013	251/ 228	250/ 224	236/ 212	231/ 205	291/ 264	293/ 263	274/ 254	275/ 250	157/ 134	161/ 131	295/ 267	296/ 267
2009	250/ 228	248/ 222	253/ 211	229/ 204	289/ 264	292/ 260	272/ 250	271/ 245	156/ 133	160/ 131	298/ 269	295/ 268
2003	243/ 215	243/ 216	229/ 198	227/ 197	286/ 249	287/ 232	268/ 239	270/ 244				
1992	224/ 189	227/ 192	218/ 185	223/ 191	272/ 236	276/ 236						

Values shown are the average white and black scale scores on the NAEP for tests and years stated. Source is National Center for Education Statistics, https://nces.ed.gov/nationsreportcard/, accessed December 26, 2016.

The current gap on average reading and math scores in Florida is somewhat less than the national average but remains approximately 9 percent in 2015 fourth- and eighth-grade math and reading scores. The gap in 2013 average twelfth-grade math scores (the most recent available) is 15 percent, and for twelfth-grade reading scores, 9.5 percent.

Separate NAEP data are not available for Alachua County, but percentages of students of different racial and ethnic groups scoring at the satisfactory level or above on state assessments and end-of-course exams in English and math in 2014–15 and 2015–16 are shown below:[60]

Table 8. Alachua County Achievement Gap on State Assessments

Percent scoring satisfactory or above	**English language arts**				**Math**			
	White	Black	Hispanic	Asian	White	Black	Hispanic	Asian
Alachua County 2015–16	72%	27%	58%	88%	71%	28%	56%	88%
Florida 2015–16	64%	34%	51%	78%	65%	35%	56%	81%
Alachua County 2014–15	73%	29%	61%	86%	72%	30%	58%	88%
Florida 2014–15	65%	34%	51%	77%	64%	35%	51%	79%

The barriers identified by Alachua County schools to achieving their goals under the Florida Continuous Improvement Model remain essentially the same as the difficulties the schools faced during desegregation. At a high school: "The African American population historically has exhibited lower levels of academic achievement, excessive tardiness, excessive behavioral referrals, as well as out of school suspensions." At a high school: "Lack of foundational literacy skills (reading far below grade level), vocabulary deficiency, lack of academic stamina, confidence and motivation, limited access to technology at home, poor attendance, behavioral issues." At a middle school: "Chronically disciplined students lack social skills to navigate through confrontations with students and teachers," and "There is a disconnect between an ever-changing diverse student population and a primarily white, middle aged teaching force." At another middle school: "Lack of parental involvement." "Loss of instructional time in class due to disciplinary referrals and consequences." With respect to new instructional methods for disadvantaged students: "Inadequate staff training," and "Teachers not familiar with implementation programs." At an elementary school: "Parents, school and community need to learn effective methods to prepare students to develop leadership abilities in themselves." At the district level: "Lack of teacher retention, Challenges of recruiting veteran, highly effective teachers."[61]

What Lessons Should We Learn?

Separate by law could never be equal, according to the US Supreme Court in *Brown*, and so the South's dual-race education system was abolished, not with "deliberate speed," as it turned out, but precipitously after that court's 1968 decision in *Green*. As desegregation cases moved through the courts, courageous judges such as John Minor Wisdom stood fast for the integrationist ideal. In 1968, as African Americans began to divide over the benefits of desegregation, Judge Wisdom gave his own view:

> There is a bridge under construction, resting on the constitution, connecting whites and Negroes and designed to lead the two races, starting with young children, to a harmonious, peaceful, civilized existence. The bridge is a plan for equal educational opportunities for all in integrated, unitary public school systems based on school administrators affirmatively finding ways to make the plan work.
>
> Black nationalists and white racists to the contrary, school integration is relevant. It is an educational objective as well as a constitutional imperative.[62]

That desegregation by itself could not equalize educational opportunities for African American students should be apparent from the history recounted here. Nevertheless, this history should also demonstrate that without individual school leaders, teachers, parents, and students making desegregation work, court orders would have made little difference. We should be proud and forgiving that so many people, not just in Alachua County but throughout the South, devoted themselves to desegregation, as best they could, for the benefit of all citizens.

John Dukes Jr. on Tiny Talbot:

> Tiny and I became very close and a lot of people do not understand Tiny. You know, when you are dealing with a person, if you know their philosophical viewpoints, it really represents what they think. I do not have any problem with

> that. I have problems with the person who had all these different philosophies for different occasions. Tiny made it quite clear to me. He said, "John I am an educator, but I am a damn good politician." By way of comparison, he is better at the latter than he was at the former. By his constantly telling me that – I had him tell me that more than once – I watched him and I learned to really appreciate the man. I do not necessarily expect an educator to act or react the same as a politician. I have my definitions for both and he demonstrated that. There were many times when things were accomplished for the betterment of blacks, but few blacks understood why Tiny did what he did. But my guess is, and I would say this anyway, that for the period that we went through in integration, I have known Jim [Longstreth], I have known [Walter Sickles], I have known Paul Peters, and I have known Doug McGann, but in my opinion the characteristics needed to do the job that he did during that time, none of those men could measure up to Tiny Talbot for that particular period. . . . I know no one who could have done the job better than Tiny Talbot, and I might add that I am not the only one in this county who feels that way either. There are other persons who have expressed similar feelings, but I felt this a long time before I ever heard anyone else say it.[63]

Improving outcomes for black students can be no less a priority for schools now than it was at the time of desegregation. And, as we learned with desegregation, it is not the process and rules of standards-based reforms that will cause this improvement; it is school leaders, teachers, parents, and students overcoming obstacles and making those rules work. This historical analysis can't presume to make specific recommendations, but it can provide a set of timely questions based on that history.

It has been argued that reconstituting the black school model of the 1960s, assuming equal resources, would bring us closer to equal educational opportunities, especially in racially isolated environments. "Nostalgia without memory"[64] may be at work here. We have to ask whether the significant numbers of African Americans who have achieved middle-class status in integrated environments would return to black schools under the type of freedom of choice that Bettye Jennings describes. Students in reconstituted black schools would have only a remnant of that formerly pervasive middle-class student enrollment and parental support. We also have to ask whether a reconstituted black school would be able to recruit and retain the black staff that advocates remember as the sustaining and loving core of the segregated black schools.

The table below shows the demographics of teachers in the Alachua County schools in 2015–16, the most recent available data:[65]

Table 9. Current Alachua County Teacher Demographics

	White	Black	Hispanic	Asian	Nat.	Haw.	2/>	Total
Elementary	619	93	44	6	2		10	774
Secondary	479	56	29	4			4	572
Exceptional	225	30	16	5			3	279
Other	5		2					7
Total	1,328	179	91	15	2		17	1,632
Percent	81.4%	11.0%	5.3%	0.9%			1.0%	

The proportion of black teachers in Alachua County is about one-half what it was in 1970.

Alachua County, like many other districts, has to choose between eliminating some de facto segregation or eliminating neighborhood schools. If the county decides to eliminate some de facto segregation, it will have to resort to busing. Will blacks be disproportionately burdened, as geography and history suggest? Will placing black students in schools with a better statistical racial balance change the racial composition in their classrooms? As in the time of desegregation, there are more whites in programs such as the International Baccalaureate and college-prep courses and more blacks who are not. That problem needs other solutions. Also, redistricting may not employ explicit racial criteria under *Parents Involved.* On the other hand, if neighborhood schools are retained, the question must be asked, Are the resources, from buildings to teachers, at racially isolated schools at least equal to those in integrated and white-majority schools? As we have seen, Nathan Margold and the NAACP decided that it would be impractical to force equalization of resources in the separate black schools. However, unequal resources for African American students are no more justifiable today than they were in the 1930s. Every school system should act affirmatively to evaluate and equalize those resources.

Equalizing resources for African American students is only a first step to equal educational opportunity. Under pressure to keep to a set pace through standards-based curricula, are today's teachers still talking past many of their students, whether black or white? Before any progress can be made in learning, students must be engaged. Unintentionally identifying the problem, a former teacher asked this author, "But what if they don't want to learn?" "The most powerful tool teachers have to encourage engaged learning is their emotional connection with their students."[66] From our historical analysis, we can identify a set of questions about engaging students, but especially African American students. Those questions derive from the best features of the historically black public schools. Do students feel welcome in the school and in the classroom? Are they respected? Do teachers take time to learn about their students and bond with them? Do teachers encourage their students to get to know and interact with one another? Do teachers get to know their students' families, even if they have to do home visits (in a recent informal discussion, Catherine Mickle pointed out that today, visits to some parents might endanger the teachers)? Does the school have strong community ties, through athletics, churches, social clubs, and neighborhood connections? Do teachers and administrators understand the disadvantages of poverty and the other social ills that their students might be experiencing? Can they provide role models of the same race for their students, even if such models aren't on the school staff?

John Dukes III:

> I work with young men now in the schools, and you see so much of it. These are kids who, they're not really having someone in the school or a collective of people in that school embrace them and recognize that they come from situations that, you know, it'd be nice if they came from the same place as some of the other kids in your class, but he doesn't perform as well on these tests, because he has a whole lot of other concerns that that other kid doesn't have. He comes from a home where it's my home. You know, my son, we ask him, "What do you want for breakfast?" This kid come to school *for* breakfast! That's a different child than mine. When he's sitting in your classroom he may be thinking about lunch, not about your lesson. There are so many little things that may be missing in his life, that they look alike sitting side by side and still and quiet and saying nothing, but their lives have different levels of turmoil and for different reasons.
>
> His problems? He has an environment full of them. Trying to navigate his way through that, and then come to school and you want him to be happy to be here. He's hungry. He's frustrated by something that went on in his household. He's seen things that you've only seen on TV or at a movie. He lives it. And you're asking him to come into your classroom and throw all of that out of his mind and fill it up with all this good stuff which you have. Sorry, he just doesn't have room right now. And if you go into his neighborhood

> maybe what you'll find out is that maybe when you come back here what I need to do is kind of readjust my teaching style. Readjust my language and embrace the fact that I need to work with him in his difficult times as well as expecting him to come to me with some comfortable moments as well. You'll get a trade if he finds out you genuinely care about him. Let me tell you right now, if he thinks that all you are is somebody who sits up here or at a board, you're just another period in the day. He just needs to get past you. And that is one of the things we're facing right now and I don't know how we change it, because we've got so much economic segregation. That may be a worse problem than what we had during that time where you knew you were poor, but everybody around you was, so it wasn't a big deal. You didn't realize that you could slide to the other side, you just wanted to be able to find comfort.[67]

The point of this discussion is not to denigrate standards-based reforms. The point is that if students don't somehow make the transition from disengagement (or opposition) to engagement, neither desegregation nor the billions of dollars that have been and continue to be spent on standards-based products will make a difference for them. Some standards-based interventions may reinforce alienation. Those processes divert resources that could be used to enrich the educational experiences of all students. And disengaged students of every race impair education not just for themselves but for their classmates and entire school systems.

However well-intentioned and well-founded these instructional approaches may be, one can't see black students responding more willingly to them than they would to Cora Roberson walking up the steps of their parents' house, to Mae Islar's hug for Peaches, or to John Dukes Jr.'s playing football with Vernon Hayes to find out how to get Hayes to do math. These educators refused to let blacks be victims. Today, white teachers have to make these connections with black students. White teachers may be at a disadvantage, but during desegregation they proved that they could do it. We have the examples of Dan Boyd working out in the GHS weight room, Frances Lastinger pulling Melvin Flournoy out of recess in the fifth grade, Ruth Wallace pushing Frank Coleman in Algebra III, Mary Ann Coxe Zimmerman's Shakespeare lessons, Russell Ramsey (without benefit of counselors) working with his isolation classes, and many more.

Educators in the South's black schools struggled with these issues for generations before desegregation. Under adverse conditions, they took on student engagement as their personal responsibility. Their numbers dwindle, but we still need to learn from them. *Caring* is one term that has been used to set apart effective teachers in the historically black schools and in current mainstream teacher education literature.[68] People care; without caring, processes remain empty gestures, the sounding brass or tinkling cymbal.

ACKNOWLEDGMENTS

This book explores deeply controversial and divisive historical issues. I have told all of my sources that the bulk of any profits and a portion of each sale of this book will be donated by me to the Education Foundation of Alachua County. I believe it would be improper for me to exploit this subject for personal gain. Rather, I see this book as a project in which we are all working to bring understanding, and perhaps reconciliation, to Alachua County, our home.

In that context, I am first of all grateful to everyone who agreed to be interviewed and to have their stories and opinions appear in this book. I hope that my efforts are worthy of the trust they placed in me by agreeing to participate.

I also am grateful to the research assistants who worked with me at various stages of the project: Diana Dombrowski and Sarah Blanc, then of the Samuel Proctor Oral History Project at the University of Florida; Holly Fisher, then of Santa Fe College; Brandon Jett, then doctoral candidate in history at the University of Florida; Bradley Beall of the Florida Law Review; and Jamie Gray, then at the University of West Florida.

I wish to thank especially Professor Sevan Terzian of the University of Florida College of Education for his review of an earlier draft of the manuscript and for his helpful comments. Ansley T. Erickson of the faculty at Teachers College, Columbia University, also had important research recommendations.

The administration of the Alachua County public schools has also been very helpful, especially Jackie Johnson, director of communications and community initiatives.

And, finally, I want to thank all the librarians, too numerous to mention individually, who responded to my questions at the University of Florida Smathers Libraries, the Marston Science Library, the Lawton Chiles Legal Information Center at the University of Florida Law School, the Alachua County Library District, the Matheson History Museum, and at the University of Wisconsin Memorial Library, the Wisconsin Historical

Society Library, and the University of Wisconsin Law School library. In this digital age, their knowledge is even more indispensable. Without their help, this book never would have been completed. I wish each of them future success and recognition.

APPENDIX

Photographs

William S. Talbot
William S. Talbot Jr.

John Dukes Jr. and wife Bernice, 1954. John Dukes Jr. was Lincoln's last principal, Eastside's first. Bernice was among the first black teachers to teach in a white school.

Bernice Dukes

Charles Chestnut III, leader of NAACP Youth Council.

Charles Chestnut III

The Reverend Earle Page, Holy Trinity Episcopal Church

Ann Page

The Reverend Thomas A. Wright Sr., President of Gainesville NAACP chapter.

Mount Carmel Baptist Church, Gainesville, FL

Tommy Tomlinson, Ed.D., Assistant Superintendent focusing on desegregation.

Bruce Tomlinson

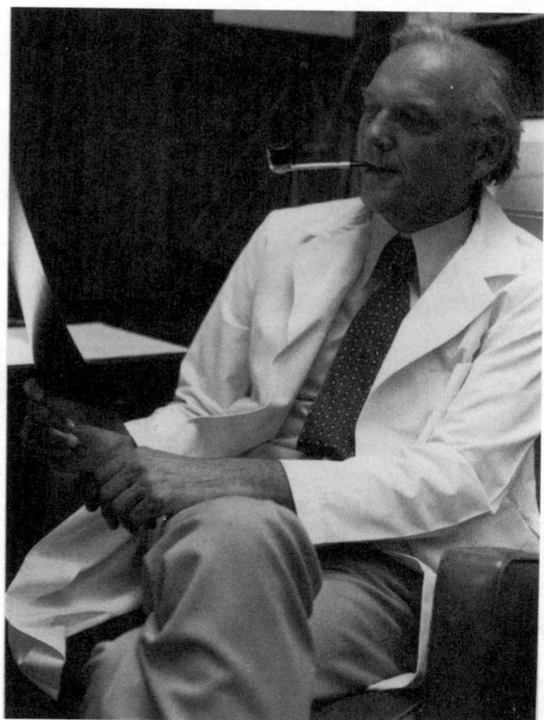

William Enneking, MD, school board member.

University of Florida

Jessie Heard with players Curtis Simmons (L) and Andrew Lovett (R), 1969; Heard's last season at Lincoln.

Jessie Heard

Jim Niblack, head football coach at Gainesville High after winning state championship in 1980.

Richard Niblack

Lincoln High School students march to protest the school's closing, 1969. Wayne Mosley, strike leader, is on truck on the left, facing marchers.
Gainesville Sun

Brenda Wims, student leader at Lincoln High and Gainesville High, as president of GHS Black Student Union, speaking about black history.
Courtesy of the Matheson History Museum

John King, Gainesville High student body president, 1969–70 school year.
John King

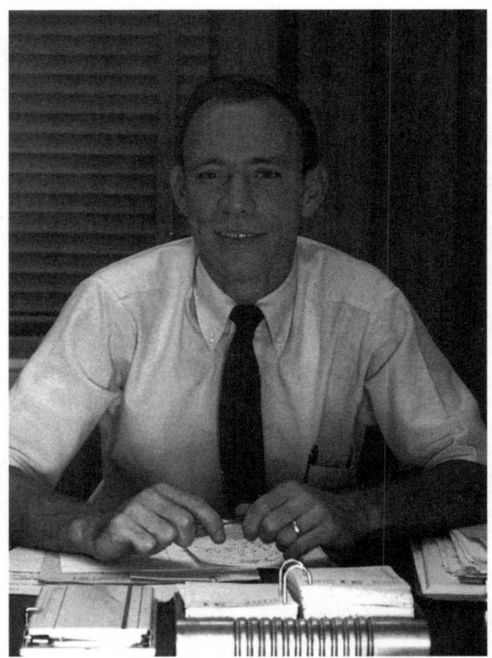

John Neller, GHS principal, 1970–71 school year.
John Neller

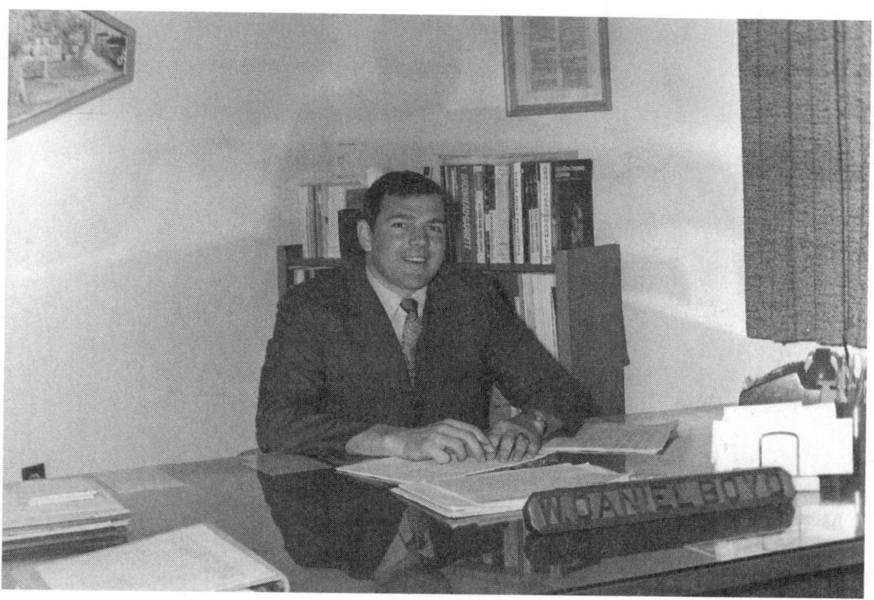

Dan Boyd, GHS principal, 1971–1995

Dan Boyd

Cora Roberson, teacher and administrator.

Cora Roberson

Peggy Finley, Gainesville High English teacher and later president of the faculty.

Peggy Finley

Gainesville High cheerleaders, 1971

Courtesy of the Matheson History Museum, 1971 Hurricane

Gainesville High Chordettes, 1971

Courtesy of the Matheson History Museum, 1971 Hurricane

Clif Cormier, *Gainesville Sun* education editor.

Leslie Samler

Data

Table 2. Impact of Freedom-of-Choice Desegregation on Enrollment, Alachua County

A. Blacks in White Schools, 1964–65 School Year (from letter of Tommy Tomlinson to Judge G. Harrold Carswell, July 5, 1967, *Wright v. Board*): 12

B. Blacks in White Schools, 1965–66 School Year (from Memorandum of W. S. Talbot, May 24, 1965, Alachua County Board of Public Instruction file, and from letter of Tommy Tomlinson to Judge G. Harrold Carswell, July 5, 1967, *Wright v. Board*): 329, or 4.9 percent, of 6,600 black students exercised choice and were assigned to white schools (Memorandum, May 24, 1965). 317 black students attended white schools (Letter, July 5, 1967).

C. Blacks in White Schools, 1966–67 School Year (from letter and report of Tommy Tomlinson to Judge G. Harrold Carswell, July 5, 1967, *Wright v. Board*): 878 Interpolating black total enrollment between 1965–66 and 1967–68, it may be assumed that the black enrollment in 1966–67 was 6,692, of whom 13 percent attended white schools.

D. Blacks in White Schools, 1967–68 School Year (from report of December 13, 1967, *Wright v. Board*):

Grades	B W	B W	B W	B W	B W	B W	Total B	% B	Total W
Gainesville									
W Gainesville K–6							491	19%	6,702
B Gainesville K–6							2,054	81%	1
Grand total							**2,545**	**100%**	**6,703**
W Bishop, 7–9	**77** 418	**63** 426	**69** 416				209	18%	1,260
W Westwood, 7–9	**17** 399	**8** 453	**8** 392				33	3%	1,244
B Lincoln 7–9	**329** -	**307** -	**271** -				907	79%	1
Grand total							**1,149**	**100%**	**2,505**
W GHS, 10–12				**60** 726	**36** 693	**17** 614	113	17%	2,033
B Lincoln, 10–12				**204** -	**180** -	**161** -	545	83%	1
Grand total							**658**	**100%**	**2,034**

Grades	B W	B W	B W	B W	B W	B W	Total B	% B	Total W
County									
W County K–6							116	8%	1,722
B County K–6							1,384	92%	
Grand total							**1,500**	**100%**	**1,722**
W Hawthorne 7–9	**39** 54	**34** 60	**17** 48				90	19%	162
W Newberry 7–9*	**7** 43	**3** 59	**5** 63				15	3%	165
W Santa Fe 7–9	**6** 100	**6** 118	**1** 112				13	3%	330
B Mebane 7–9	**142** -	**101** -	**116** -				359	75%	
Grand total							**477**	**100%**	**657**
W Hawthorne 10–12				**12** 44	**10** 37	**7** 27	29	8%	108
W Newberry 10–12				**1** 46	**2** 45	**2** 52	5	1%	143
W Santa Fe 10–12				**-** 96	**2** 90	**7** 86	9	3%	272
B Mebane 10–12				**146** -	**82** -	**80** -	308	88%	
Grand total							**351**	**100%**	**523**

**The table filed with the court on December 13, 1967, does not contain grade 7–9 enrollment for Newberry High School. The enrollment numbers shown are from a table filed on July 5, 1967, showing the status of enrollment choices for the 1967–68 school year for those grades at Newberry.*

Note: Separate totals by grade are not shown for K-6. Special education students are included only in Gainesville K–6 totals. The school board table showed a total of 173 black and 190 white special education students for 1967–68. Total enrollment was 21,130, of whom 6,785 were black and 14,395 were white. There were 1,123 black students enrolled in white schools, or 17 percent of the non–special education black student population.

E. Blacks in White Schools, 1968–69 School Year (from Report of Alachua County Board of Public Instruction, October 15, 1968, *Wright v. Board*,):

Grades	B W	B W	B W	B W	B W	B W	Total B	% B	Total W
Gainesville									
W Gainesville K–6							641	32%	6,844
B Gainesville K–6							1,372	68%	1
Grand total							**2,013**	**100%**	**6,845**
W Bishop, 7–9	**72** 419	**116** 344	**61** 396				249	22%	1,159
W Westwood, 7–9	**14** 484	**15** 402	**5** 441				34	3%	1,327
B Lincoln 7–9	**316** -	**271** -	**282** -				869	75%	
Grand total							**1,152**	**100%**	**2,486**
W GHS, 10–12				**55** 779	**60** 718	**30** 687	145	20%	2,184
B Lincoln, 10–12				**269** -	**174** -	**154** -	597	80%	
Grand total							**742**	**100%**	**2,184**
County									
W County K–6							161	13%	1,692
B County K–6							1,093	87%	1
Grand total							**1.254**	**100%**	**1,693**
W Hawthorne 7–9	**36** 45	**45** 54	**36** 50				117	23%	149
W Newberry 7–9	**15** 60	**8** 50	**5** 68				28	6%	178
W Santa Fe 7–9	**8** 121	**12** 105	**12** 116				32	6%	342
B Mebane 7–9	**118** -	**115** -	**97** -				330	65%	
Grand total							**507**	**100%**	**669**
W Hawthorne 10–12				**20** 41	**12** 39	**6** 35	38	11%	115
W Newberry 10–12				**8** 72	**5** 42	**6** 45	19	6%	159
W Santa Fe 10–12				**7** 101	**3** 85	**3** 75	13	4%	261
B Mebane 10–12				**89** -	**112** -	**69** -	270	79%	
Grand total							**340**	**100%**	**535**

Note: Separate totals by grade are not shown for K-6. Special education students are included only in Gainesville K–6 totals. The school board table showed a total of 236 black and 167 white special education students for 1967–68. Total enrollment was 21,708, of whom 7,008 were black and

14,700 were white. There were 1,477 black students enrolled in white schools, or 22 percent of the non–special education black student population.

F. Blacks in White Schools, 1969–1970 School Year (from Report of Alachua County Board of Public Instruction, September 26, 1969, *Wright v. Board*,). The 1969–70 school year was the last year in which freedom of choice operated.

Grades	B W	B W	B W	B W	B W	B W	Total B	% B	Total W
Gainesville									
W Gainesville K–6							1,338	54%	6,739
B Gainesville K–6							1,129	46%	78
Grand total							**2,467**	**100%**	**6,817**
W Bishop, 7–9	**130** 412	**100** 399	**94** 384				324	29%	1,195
W Westwood, 7–9	**33** 519	**27** 502	**23** 407				83	7%	1,428
B Lincoln 7–9	**223** -	**233** -	**266** -				722	64%	
Grand total							**1,129**	**100%**	**2,623**
W GHS, 10–12				**114** 795	**88** 745	**62** 607	264	32%	2,147
B Lincoln, 10–12				**228** -	**184** -	**157** -	569	68%	
Grand total							**833**	**100%**	**2,147**
County									
W County K–6							232	15%	1,842
B County K–6							1,270	85%	
Grand total							**1,502**	**100%**	**1,842**
W Hawthorne 7–9	**43** 52	**32** 50	**48** 59				123	22%	161
W Newberry 7–9	**10** 55	**19** 54	**17** 50				46	8%	159
W Santa Fe 7–9	**18** 144	**16** 124	**18** 118				52	10%	386
B Mebane 7–9	**137** -	**109** -	**79** -				325	60%	
Grand total							**546**	**100%**	**706**
W Hawthorne 10–12				**42** 55	**27** 41	**16** 39	85	22%	135
W Newberry 10–12				**7** 62	**16** 69	**5** 36	28	7%	167

Grades	B W	B W	B W	B W	B W	B W	Total B	% B	Total W
W Santa Fe 10–12				**16** 115	**11** 94	**1** 79	28	7%	288
B Mebane 10–12				**74** -	**80** -	**97** -	251	64%	
Grand total							**392**	**100%**	**590**

Note: Separate totals by grade are not shown for K-6. It was not possible to include special education student numbers for any categories except Gainesville K–6. Alachua County reported 270 black special education students and 143 white special education students in all grades in September 1969. There were a total of 14,887 white students and 6,986 black students enrolled in Alachua County in September 1969, for a total enrollment of 21,873.

There were 2,603 black students enrolled in white schools or 39 percent of the non–special education black student population.

NOTES

PREFACE

1 Alfred Dennis Mathewson, *Segregated Proms in 2003,* in Law Touched Our Hearts: A Generation Remembers *Brown v. Board of Education* 19 (Mildred Wigfall Robinson & Richard J. Bonnie eds., 2003).

2 Green v. Cty. School Bd., 391 U.S. 430, 442 (1968); cf. U. S. v. Jefferson Cty. Bd. of Education, 380 F.2d 385, 389 (5th Cir.), *cert. denied,* 389 U.S. 840 (1967).

3 Gary Orfield, *Losing Brown, Fearing Plessy,* in School Resegregation: Must the South Turn Back? 3–9 (John Charles Boger & Gary Orfield eds., 2005).

4 Argument: The Oral Argument Before the Supreme Court in *Brown v. Board of Education of Topeka,* 1952-1955 402 (Leon Friedman ed., 1969).

5 Alexander v. Holmes Cty. Bd. of Education, 396 U.S. 1218, 1220 (1969).

6 Parents Involved in Community Schools v. Seattle School District No. 1, 551 U.S. 701 (2007).

CHAPTER 1

1 Tiny got this nickname from a sergeant when he was serving in the Army Air Corps during World War II. Talbot was not tall, but in later years he achieved some girth.

2 Clif Cormier, *1964-1972, The Talbot years in Alachua County,* Gainesville Sun, Feb. 27, 1972, at 1B.

3 The main sources for the profile of John Dukes, Jr., are: interview by Joel Buchanan with John Dukes, Jr., in Gainesville, Fla. (Aug. 2, 1985), http://ufdc.ufl.edu/UF00005423/00001; Nick Tatro, *"Learning" the Hard Way,* Gainesville Sun, Aug. 26, 1968, at 18; interview with John Dukes III, in Gainesville, Fla. (Mar. 5, 2014) (on file with author); interview with Bernice Dukes, John Dukes III & Carmen Dukes, in Gainesville, Fla. (July 11, 2014) (on file with author).

4 The family background comes from genealogical research by Tiny's brother, James Talbot.

5 Tatro, *"Learning" the Hard Way,* Gainesville Sun, Aug. 26, 1968, at 18.

6 Dukes does not mention that Branford High School, a white school in the Suwannee County system, had operated there for many years and was operating there when Dukes was a boy. That area of Suwannee County has historically had a black population that is a very small percentage of the area's total population.

7 Flossie's two other children also went to college. Tiny's sister, Edna, put herself through three years at Florida State Women's College. Tiny's younger brother, Jim, graduated from the University of Florida in 1950 and earned his master's degree in educational administration in 1957. He lived with Tiny and Reba during his undergraduate years.

8 Talbot's service records are unavailable and were probably destroyed in the fire at the National Personnel Records Center in Saint Louis, Mo., on July 12, 1973.

9 This incident took place in the old Lincoln High building that was built in 1923 and that later became A. Quinn Jones Elementary School after the new Lincoln opened in 1956.

10 The auditorium stage at the 1923 Gainesville High School building also served as the school gymnasium. It served the same purpose after 1955, when that building operated as the white Buchholz Junior High.

11 Dukes's interview appears to be confused as to dates; some events he attributes to 1965 and 1966 actually did not occur until 1969.

12 Interview with Jessie Heard, in Gainesville, Fla., at 17–18 (Feb. 4, 2014) (on file with author).

CHAPTER 2

1 Telephone interview with Brenda Gresham Rainsberger (May 12,2016) (on file with author); Obituary, Peggy Wray Gresham, Gainesville Sun, Oct. 31, 2015, http://www.legacy.com/obituaries/gainesville/obituary.aspx?pid=176290597, accessed Aug.30, 2016.

2 *County Endorses Work of Bi-Racial Board*, Gainesville Sun, July 10, 1963, at 1. For example, the county had no public library accessible to blacks. When Rosa B. Williams as a young woman worked for the family of Delbert Sterrett, a music professor at the University of Florida, Mrs. Sterrett would check out library books for Ms. Williams to read. Mrs. Sterrett later went to the library with Ms. Williams and asked that the library issue Ms. Williams her own card. Ms. Williams states that she was the first black in Gainesville to have a library card. University of Florida Samuel Proctor Oral History Program, interview by Joel Buchanan with Rosa B. Williams, in Gainesville, Fla., at 8 (Feb. 27, 1996).

3 Harold Rummel, *Complete Hospital Integration "Impractical" Say Trustees*, Gainesville Sun, July 17, 1963, at 1; Bill Hager, *Integration Is Working Well in Gainesville*, Gainesville Sun, Nov. 19, 1963, at 1.

4 Earle C. Page, "The Field We Toil," (sermon), May 19, 1963 (on file with author).

5 Doris Grimmage, *Bi-Racial Committee Chairman's Ancestry Here Dates to 1850s*, Gainesville Sun, Oct. 4, 1970, at 3C.

6 Interview with Charles Chestnut III, in Gainesville, Fla., at 1–10 (Sept. 10, 2014) (on file with author); interview by Gayle Yamada with Joel Buchanan, in Gaines-

ville, Fla., at 11 (Feb. 12, 1984), Samuel Proctor Oral History Project, University of Florida Digital Collections, URL: http://ufdc.ufl.edu/UF00005406/00001, accessed Jan. 22, 2017.

7 Rummel, *City Acts on Racial Problem*, Gainesville Sun, June 3, 1970, at 1.

8 *Id.; City Picks Bi-Racial Committee*, Gainesville Sun, June 4, 1963, at 1.

9 Bob Fisher, *Winn Calls for Peaceful Integration*, Gainesville Sun, June 6, 1963, at 1; Hager, *Commissioner Winn Resigns*, Gainesville Sun, Feb. 2, 1965, at 1.

10 Linda Liston, *Church Group Urges Racial Cooperation*, Gainesville Sun, June 14, 1963, at 1.

11 *Local NAACP Leader Vetoes Demonstrations*, Gainesville Sun, June 7, 1963, at 1.

12 Charles Reid, *The Old South Is in His Blood*, Gainesville Sun, Jan. 11, 1965, at 2.

13 Interview with Clif Cormier, in Gainesville, Fla., Nov. 8, 2013 (on file with author).

14 Interview with Attorney John F. Roscow III, in Gainesville, Fla., Oct. 26, 2015 (notes on file with author).

15 Sigsbee L. Scruggs, Letter to the Editor, *$3 Million Bought Negro Malice*, Gainesville Sun, June 13, 1963, at 4. These are only excerpts from this letter. William Pepper, writing in 1996, stated that the actual consideration received by the family for the *Sun* was $2 million, following an evaluation of its books. W. M. (Bill) Pepper III, The History of the Gainesville Sun (Feb. 12, 1996), at 8 (unpublished manuscript at the Matheson Museum library, Gainesville).

16 Jean Marshall, *Pair Fined After Picketing Disorder*, Gainesville Sun, July 31, 1963, at 2; Rummel, *4 More Negroes Jailed Here for Restaurant Sit-In*, Gainesville Sun, July 25, 1963, at 1. Blacks were served at the Humpty Dumpty just after the Civil Rights Act of 1964 took effect. Norm LaCoe, *Racial Barriers Fall Here at 3 Places, One Arrested*, Gainesville Sun, July 6, 1964, at 1.

17 Editorial, *We Wear It Well*, Gainesville Sun, June 15, 1963, at 4.

18 Bill Raulson, *Mayor, Negro Youth Leader Praise City*, Gainesville Sun, June 28, 1963, at 1.

19 *Id.*

20 *Charles Chestnut III, 23, Is Leader of NAACP "Youth Movement" Here*, Gainesville Sun, July 7, 1963, at 2C.

21 Rummel, *500 Klansmen Rally at Ocala, Hear Plea for Massive Membership Drive*, Gainesville Sun, Sept. 9, 1963, at 14.

22 Rummel, *40 Gather for KKK Rally at Lake Butler*, Gainesville Sun, Dec. 2, 1963, at 2.

23 *Obey Rights Law, Bryant Tells Florida*, Gainesville Sun, July 20, 1964, at 1.

24 LaCoe, *Racial Barriers Fall Here at 3 Places, One Arrested*, Gainesville Sun, July 6, 1964, at 1.

25 *Obey Rights Law, Bryant Tells Florida*, Gainesville Sun, July 20, 1964, at 1.

26 LaCoe, *County's Negro Voters Swiftly Growing Force*, Gainesville Sun, Oct. 30, 1964, at 12.

27 Peggy Blanchard, *Durrance Dubs Poverty Here "Strange,"* Gainesville Sun, Oct. 27, 1965, at 25.

28 Neil A. Butler, Letter to the Editor, *City Progresses on Racial Front,* Gainesville Sun, Jan. 24, 1965, at 4A.

29 Gene Roberts, *Militant Civil Rights Tune Dying Out in Dixie,* Gainesville Sun, May 31, 1967, at 22 (New York Times service).

30 Hager, *Police Discrimination Will Bring Violence, City Told,* Gainesville Sun, Dec. 5, 1967, at 1.

31 Hager, *Police Activities Due Grand Jury Inquiry,* Gainesville Sun, Dec. 12, 1967, at 1.

32 Thomas v. Crevasse, 415 F.2d 550, 551 (5th Cir. 1969).

33 LaCoe, *Two Civil Rights Figures Draw Prison Terms Here,* Gainesville Sun, Dec. 28, 1967, at 1.

34 *Denies Bond for Pair in Rights Case,* Gainesville Sun, Dec. 29, 1967, at 1.

35 Dawkins v. State, 205 So.2d 691 (Fla. Dist. Ct. App. 1968) (bail); Dawkins v. State, 208 So.2d 119 (Fla. Dist. Ct. App.) (criminal contempt), *appeal dismissed,* 211 So.2d 209 (Fla.), *cert. denied,* 211 So.2d 211 (Fla. 1968); *cert. denied,* 393 U.S. 854 (1968); Dawkins v. Crevasse, 391 F.2d 921 (5th Cir. 1968); *Dawkins, Thomas Still Jailed; Awaiting Orders from Capital,* Gainesville Sun, Feb.8, 1968, at 1; *Dawkins, Thomas Released on Bond,* Gainesville Sun, Feb. 9, 1968, at 1.

36 Thomas v. Crevasse, *supra* note 32, 415 F.2d at 551.

37 Jack Moro, *3 Arson Cases Investigated Here,* Gainesville Sun, Jan. 5, 1968, at 1.

38 Moro, *Judge Adkins' Home Hit by Fire Bombs,* Gainesville Sun, Jan. 5, 1968, at 1; Moro, *Second Court Official's Home Hit by Firebomb,* Gainesville Sun, Feb. 5, 1968, at 1.

39 Walter Brown Manley II & Canter Brown, Jr., *The Supreme Court of Florida, 1917-1972* 316–20 (2006).

40 Reid, *Curfew Crackdown to Start Monday,* Gainesville Sun, Mar. 20, 1966, at 1.

41 *Racial Calm Asked by NAACP Head,* Gainesville Sun, Apr. 5, 1968, at 1.

42 Eric Filson, *Six Charged in Firebombing,* Gainesville Sun, Mar. 18, 1968, at 1; the other five persons arrested were all age twenty or younger. Dawkins was bound to district court for trial on findings of probable cause on March 28, after one of the other young defendants testified against Dawkins. Moro, *Dawkins May Face Trial for Arson,* Gainesville Sun, Mar. 29, 1968, at 1.

43 Harvey Alper and Hager, *Guards, Riot Squad Placed on Alert Here,* Gainesville Sun, Apr. 7, 1968, at 1; Filson and Hager, *Guardsmen Moved Into City,* Gainesville Sun, Apr. 8, 1968, at 1.

44 *Dawkins to Be Tried in Marion,* Gainesville Sun, May 23, 1968, at 1; Tatro, *Mrs. Thomas Free, Calls for Violence,* Gainesville Sun, Dec. 31, 1968, at 1.

45 Filson and Hager, *Guardsmen Moved into City,* Gainesville Sun, Apr. 8, 1968, at 1. Marshall Jones would later write about his experiences in Gainesville in Berkeley of the South (1970) (unpublished manuscript, University of Florida Smathers Library, Special Collections).

46 Filson and Hager, *Guardsmen Moved into City,* Gainesville Sun, Apr. 8, 1968, at 1. The city rapidly returned to normal, although isolated instances of rock throwing and arson continued. Moro, *City Is Quiet Under Curfew,* Gainesville

Sun, Apr. 9, 1968, at 1; Filson, *City Ends 2-Day Curfew*, Gainesville Sun, Apr. 10, 1968, at 1A.

47 Hager, *Kirk Flies Here, Outlines Goals of Operation Concern*, Gainesville Sun, June 20, 1968, at 1; Hager and Filson, *Slum Fight Gets Vigorous Start*, Gainesville Sun, June 21, 1968, at 1; Diane Devine, *Police Begin Plan in "Problem Areas,"* Gainesville Sun, June 1, 1968, at 1.

48 Tatro, *City Arson Cases Soar – Losses Drop*, Gainesville Sun, May 8, 1969, at 8A.

49 Editorial, *Bring Your Own*, Gainesville Sun, Apr. 16, 1968, at 6.

50 Tatro, *SE Boys' Club Gutted, Looted*, Gainesville Sun, Nov. 20, 1969, at 1; Tatro, *Volunteer Crew Revitalizes Boys Club After Vandalism*, Gainesville Sun, Dec. 6, 1969, at 9.

51 Editorial, *Poetic Justice*, Gainesville Sun, June 11, 1970, at 6. Mosquito fogging was necessary throughout Gainesville to prevent mosquito-borne diseases such as malaria.

52 Cormier, *School Disorders Here Bring Crackdown*, Gainesville Sun, Apr. 30, 1969, at 8D; *Student Expelled, Another Due Hearing in Knifings*, Gainesville Sun, Apr. 11, 1969, at 7.

53 Informal contact, author and Shelton Boyles.

54 Marty Jourard, *Music Everywhere: The Rock and Roll Roots of a Southern Town* (2016).

55 Employment Opportunities Council of Gainesville and Alachua County, A Survey of Employment Opportunities in Gainesville and Alachua County, Florida, October 1969, at 42 [hereinafter *Employment Opportunities Council 1969 Report*].

56 *Id.* at 42.

57 LaCoe, *Low-Income Public Housing Is Planned for Gainesville*, Gainesville Sun, Sept. 12, 1966, at 1; LaCoe, *Works for Better Housing*, Gainesville Sun, Oct. 10, 1966, at 14.

58 *Gainesville's Low Rent Housing Taking Shape*, Gainesville Sun, Dec. 1, 1968, at 1D.

59 *City Warned of "Pie in the Sky" Effort*, Gainesville Sun, Apr. 16, 1968, at 1; Filson and Hager, *Jobs Are Key to Race Relations Here*, Gainesville Sun, Apr. 18, 1968, at 1.

60 *Employment Opportunities Council 1969 Report, supra* note 55, at 60; *Practicing Equality Urged in City Report*, Gainesville Sun, Apr. 2, 1968, at 1.

61 Hager, *Public Support Needed to Provide Negroes Jobs*, Gainesville Sun, Apr. 22, 1968, at 4.

62 Filson, *Job Program Will Get Under Way*, Gainesville Sun, July 17, 1968, at 1.

63 *Skills Matched with the Needs*, Gainesville Sun, July 27, 1969, at 1; Don Grooms, *Summer Jobs Help Teenagers Learn*, Gainesville Sun, July 26, 1969, at 1.

64 *Employment Opportunities Council 1969 Report, supra* note 55, at 5 and 60.

65 *Id.* at 4–5.

66 *Id.* at 30–31.

67 *Id.* at 32–33.

68 *Id.* at 37.

69 *Id.* at 7.

70 *Id.* at 7, 14–15, and 36.

71 *Id.* at 45.

72 *Id.* at 46 and 60–66.

73 *Id.* at 56.

74 *Id.* at 57–59; Ed Pavelka, *Why Do 6,000 County Families Live in Poverty?*, Gainesville Sun, Nov. 7, 1969, at 1.

CHAPTER 3

1 Justice John M. Harlan of Kentucky, appointed in 1877, was the grandfather of Justice John M. Harlan of New York, appointed in 1955.

2 Jane Landers, Black Society in Spanish Florida 7–66, 79–83, and 246–248 (1999); Jane Landers, *Free and Enslaved*, in The History of Florida 179–94 (Michael Gannon ed., 2013), and William Earl Weeks, John Quincy Adams and the American Global Empire 147–75 (1992).

3 Daniel L. Schafer, *U.S. Territory and State*, in The History of Florida 236–39 (Michael Gannon ed., 2013).

4 Act of Apr. 9, 1866, ch. 31, 14 Stat. 27.

5 Act of Mar. 1, 1875, ch. 114, 18 Stat. 335.

6 Act of Mar. 22, 1867, ch. 6, 15 Stat. 2; Act of July 19, 1867, ch. 30, 15 Stat. 14.

7 Eric Foner, Reconstruction: America's Unfinished Revolution, 1863-1877 504–05, 532–34, and 553–556 (2002).

8 Foner, *supra* note 7, at 144–48; Jerrell H. Shofner, Nor Is It Over Yet: Florida in the Age of Reconstruction 72–74 and 150 (1974).

9 Richard Kluger, Simple Justice 618–19 (2004).

10 Thomas Everette Cochran, History of the Public School Education in Florida 28–31 (1921).

11 Fla. Const. of 1868, art. I, § 1; *id.* art. IV, §§ 4–5; *id.* art. VI. The oath required of electors (art. VI § 3) required them to affirm that they had not previously held a federal or state appointment and thereafter engaged in insurrection or rebellion against the United States.

12 Act of Jan. 30, 1869, ch. 1,686, 1869 Fla. Laws 7; Fla. Const. of 1868, art. IX.

13 Shofner, *supra* note 8, at 151.

14 Jeffry L. Charbonnet, The Public School System of Alachua County 1821-1955 83–84 (1991) (unpublished master's thesis, University of Florida) (on file with author).

15 Act of Jan. 25, 1873, ch. 1947, 1873 Fla. Laws 25, § 1.

16 *Id.* § 3. The law also affirmatively required juries to be summoned without regard to race, color, or previous condition of servitude.

17 Shofner, *supra* note 8, at 341, 344.

18 Fla. Const. of 1885, art. XII, § 12.

19 Fla. Stat. § 228.09 (1955); *id.* § 230.23(4)(a).

20 Act of May 31, 1965, ch. 65–239, 1965 Fla. Laws 585.

21 Shofner, *supra* note 8, at 16.

22 Plessy v. Ferguson, 163 U.S. 537, 550–551 (1896). *Plessy* rested in part on a Massachusetts case that upheld the constitutionality of segregated schools. *Id.* at 544–45 (citing Roberts v. City of Boston, 5 Cush. (59 Mass.) 198 (1850)). Massachusetts later abolished school segregation by statute. Act of April 28, 1855, ch. 256, 1855 Mass. Acts 674. *See also* Gladys Tignor Peterson, *The Present Status of the Negro Separate School as Defined by Court Decisions*, 4 J. Negro Educ. 351 (1935). Segregation of the District of Columbia schools was declared unconstitutional in Bolling v. Sharpe, 347 U.S. 497 (1954), under the equal protection clause of the Fifth Amendment to the U.S. Constitution. *Bolling* was a companion case to *Brown v. Board of Education.*

23 House Memorial No. 594, 1955 Fla. Laws 1281; Richard Kluger, Simple Justice 265, 492, 675 (2004); James T. Patterson, *Brown v. Board of Education*: A Civil Rights Milestone and Its Troubled Legacy xviii (2001).

24 *See* William H. Watkins, The White Architects of Black Education: Ideology and Power in America, 1865-1954 (2001); James D. Anderson, The Education of Blacks in the South, 1860-1935 (1988).

25 *See generally* Paul Ortiz, Emancipation Betrayed: The Hidden History of Black Organizing and White Violence in Florida from Reconstruction to the Bloody Election of 1920 (2005).

26 *See infra* ch. 4.

27 Sherman Dorn & Deanna L. Michael, *Education Finance Reform in Florida, in* Education Reform in Florida: Diversity and Equity in Public Policy 56–58 (Kathryn M. Borman & Sherman Dorn eds., 2007).

28 Hesser, Charles, *Florida Is Improving Its Negro Institutions*, Miami Daily News, Jan. 25, 1953, at 3B, University of Florida Special and Area Studies Collections, Education in Florida Subject Files, No. 5, Education History – Negro Schools 1950-1966 [hereinafter *Education History – Negro Schools File*].

29 Beaudoin, Mike, *Florida Makes Big Strides in Education of Negroes*, St. Petersburg Times, July 19, 1952,Education History – Negro Schools File.

30 Editorial, *Will Florida Abolish Its Schools*, Melbourne Times, May 26, 1953, *Education History – Negro Schools File.*

31 Martin A. Dyckman, Floridian of His Century: The Courage of Governor LeRoy Collins 75 (2006).

32 102 Cong. Rec. 4515–16 (1956).

33 House Memorial No. 594, 1955 Fla. Laws 1281.

34 Florida governors were limited to a single term. Following the death in office of Governor Dan McCarty, Collins had been elected to a special term in 1955, defeating Acting Governor Charley Johns. The state Supreme Court confirmed that Collins could run for a full term in 1955.

35 Dyckman, *supra* note 31, at 114–18; *see* Helen L. Jacobstein, The Segregation Factor in the Florida Democratic Gubernatorial Primary of 1956 (1972), http://ufdc.ufl.edu/AM00000079/00001; Deirdre Cobb-Roberts & Barbara Shircliffe, *The*

Legacy of Desegregation in Florida, in Education Reform in Florida: Diversity and Equity in Public Policy 25–26 (Kathryn M. Borman & Sherman Dorn eds., 2007).

36 Dyckman, *supra* note 31, at 120–21.

37 David R. Colburn & Richard K. Scher, *The Aftermath of the* Brown *Decision in Florida: The Politics of Interposition in Florida*, 1 Tequesta no. 37 62, 66 (1977). Collins later served as chair of the 1960 Democratic convention, and he was appointed by President Johnson as the first director of the Community Relations Service under the Civil Rights Act of 1964. Collins would be defeated in his campaign for a U.S. Senate seat in 1968 in large part because of his later outspoken advocacy for racial justice.

38 Jacobstein, *supra* note 35, at 76.

39 S. Con. Res.17–XX, 35th Leg., Extraordinary Sess., 401 (Fla. 1956).

40 H.R. Con. Res. 174, 36th Leg., Reg. Sess. (Fla. 1957); Colburn & Scher, *supra* note 37, app. A.

41 S. Con. Res. 116, 36th Leg., Reg. Sess., 1957 Fla. Laws 1191.

42 Act of July 26, 1956, ch. 31380, 1956 Fla. Laws 30; Act of May 31, 1955, ch. 29746, 1955 Fla. Laws 302; Act of June 19, 1959, ch. 59–428, 1959 Fla. Laws 1455.

43 Act of Oct. 25, 1957, ch. 57–1975, 1957 Fla. Laws (Extraordinary Sess.) 10.

44 H.R. Journal, 1957 Reg. Sess. 2268–69 (Fla. 1957). The House failed to override the governor's veto.

45 A Report of the Special Committee Appointed by the Governor and Cabinet of the State of Florida to Recommend Legislative Action Relating to Public School Education and Other Internal Affairs of Such State Deemed Expedient After Consideration of Recent Decisions of the Supreme Court of the United States 2 (July 16, 1956) [hereinafter *Special Committee 1956 Report*].

46 *Special Committee 1956 Report, supra* note 45, at 20.

47 Act of July 26, 1956, ch. 31380, 1956 Fla. Laws 30 (codified at Fla. Stat. § 230.232 (1957)).

48 Fla. Stat. § 230.232(2) (1957), *amended by* Act of June 19, 1959, ch. 59–428, 1959 Fla. Laws 1455. Sections 2 and 3 of Florida's pupil-assignment law were not repealed until 1980. Act of July 2, 1980, ch. 80–295, 1980 Fla. Laws 1289, § 16.

49 Act of July 26, 1956, ch. 31380, 1956 Fla. Laws 30, § 3(a). A companion law provided for the automatic closing of any school if national guard or other military forces were used at or near that school to prevent acts of violence. Laws of Florida, ch. 57–1975 (1957).

50 Carson v. Warlick, 238 F.2d 724 (4th Cir. 1956).

51 Shuttlesworth v. Birmingham Bd. of Educ., 162 F. Supp. 372 (N.D. Ala.), *aff'd*, 358 U.S. 101 (1958). The NAACP Legal Defense Fund elected not to attack the pupil-assignment laws as invalid on their face, but rather to build a record that would demonstrate that the laws were being used to perpetuate segregation. Jack Greenberg, Crusaders in the Courts, Legal Battles of the Civil Rights Movement 269–70 (Anniversary ed. 2004). Courts after a time found constitutional defects in the applications of these laws. Note, *The Federal Courts and Integration of*

Southern Schools: Troubled Status of the Pupil Placement Acts, 62 Colum. L. Rev. 1448 (1962). Eventually, they were superseded as a practical matter by court-ordered or HEW-approved school district desegregation plans.

52 Report of the Advisory Commission on Race Relations to Governor LeRoy Collins (Mar. 16, 1959), https://archive.org/details/ReportOfTheAdvisoryCommissionOnRaceRelationsToGovernorLeroyCollins [hereinafter *Advisory Commission 1959 Report*].

53 Gibson v. Bd. of Pub. Instruction, 170 F. Supp. 454, 457–58 (S.D. Fla. 1958), *rev'd*, 272 F.2d 763 (5th Cir. 1959). A year later, the Fifth Circuit held that black plaintiffs were not obliged to exhaust their remedies under the Florida pupil-assignment law prior to seeking injunctive relief against de jure segregation. Mannings v. Bd. of Pub. Instruction, 277 F.2d 370 (5th Cir. 1960).

54 *Advisory Commission 1959 Report, supra* note 52, at 18–19.

55 *Gibson, supra* note 53, 272 F.2d at 766.

56 *See* Joseph Aaron Tomberlin, *The Negro and Florida's System of Education: The Aftermath of the Brown Case* (1967) (unpublished Ph.D. dissertation, Florida State University) (on file with author); Jacobstein, *supra* note 35.

CHAPTER 4

1 Vanessa Siddle Walker, Their Highest Potential (1996); James T. Patterson, *Brown v. Board of Education*, A Civil Rights Milestone and Its Troubled Legacy 167–69 (2001); Vivian Gunn Morris & Curtis L. Morris, *Before Brown, After Brown: What Has Changed for African-American Children?*, 16 U. of Fla. J. of Law and Pub. Policy 215 (2005).

2 William W. Watkins, The White Architects of Black Education: Ideology and Power in America, 1865-1954 (2001); James D. Anderson, The Education of Blacks in the South, 1860-1935 (1988).

3 Adams v. Califano, 430 F. Supp. 118, 120 (D.D.C. 1977); Adams v. Richardson, 480 F.2d 1159, 1165–66 (D.C. Cir. 1973). Florida was among five Southern states that had failed to adopt any plan for desegregating its higher education institutions in 1973. Adams v. Richardson, 356 F. Supp. 92, 93 (D.D.C. 1973), *mod.*, Adams v. Richardson, *supra*.

4 Paul Hond, *Justice's Son*, Columbia Magazine, Spring 2013, http://magazine.columbia.edu/features/spring-2013/justices-son?page=0,0 (last visited Sept. 8, 2017).

5 Memorandum of the Committee on Negro Work of the American Fund for Public Service (no date given), quoted in Nathan Margold, Preliminary Report to the Joint Committee Supervising the Expenditures of the 1930 Appropriation of the American Fund for Public Service to the NAACP (1931)[hereinafter *Margold Report*], 3. The version cited here is from the Collections of the Manuscript Division of the Library of Congress.

6 He was recommended to the NAACP for this task by Felix Frankfurter, then a professor at Harvard Law School. Richard Kluger, Simple Justice 133 (Anniversary ed., 2004).

7 Margold Report, *supra* note. 5.

8 Roberts v. City of Boston, 5 Cushing (59 Mass.) 198 (1849); People v. Gallagher, 93 N.Y. 438 (1883), Plessy v. Ferguson, 163 U.S. 537 (1896).

9 Margold Report, *supra* note 5, 15–20.

10 Margold Report, *supra* note 5, 20–28.

11 Memorandum of the Committee on Negro Work, *supra* note5, quoted in Margold Report, 3.

12 Margold Report, *supra* note 5, 29–95.

13 Yick Wo v. Hopkins, 118 U.S. 356 (1886).

14 Margold Report, *supra* note 5, 92–94.

15 Charles H. Thompson, *Court Action the Only Reasonable Alternative to Remedy Immediate Abuses of the Negro Separate School*, 4 J. Negro Educ. 419, 420 (1935); Gladys Tignor Peterson, *The Present Status of the Negro Separate School as Defined by Court Decisions*, 4 J. Negro Educ. 351, 374, citing Gong Lum v. Rice, 275 U.S. 78 (1927).

16 Howard Hale Long, *Some Psychogenic Hazards of Segregated Education of Negroes*, 4 J. Negro Educ. 336 (1935).

17 W. E. Burghardt Du Bois, *Does the Negro Need Separate Schools?*, 4 J. Negro Educ. 328, 328 (1935).

18 *Id.*

19 *Id.* at 328–29; *see also* at 335.

20 *Id.* at 330.

21 *Id.* at 333–35.

22 *Id.* at 330–331.

23 Kluger, *supra* note 6, at 506, quoting from the record of Davis v. County School Board of Prince Edward County, 103 F. Supp. 337 (E D. Va. 1952), *rev'd sub nom.* Brown v. Board of Education of Topeka, 347 U.S. 483 (1954).

24 Kluger, *supra* note 6, at 576.

25 Du Bois, *supra* note 17, at 335.

26 Alain Locke, The Dilemma of Segregation, 4 Journal of Negro Education 406, 406 (1935).

27 *Id.* at 408.

28 *Id.* at 410–11.

29 *Id.* at 407.

30 Thompson, *supra* note 15, at 420–21.

31 *Id.* at 422–26.

32 *Id.* at 425.

33 *Id.* at 426–27.

34 *Id.* at 420.

35 *Id.* at 433.

36 McLaurin v. Oklahoma State Regents for Higher Education, 339 U.S. 647 (1950); Sweatt v. Painter, 339 U.S. 629 (1950); Murray v. Maryland, 182 A. 590 (Md. 1936).

37 Kluger, *supra* note 6, at 293; Mark V. Tushnet, The NAACP's Legal Strategy Against Segregation, 1925-1950, 135–27 (2004, with new Epilogue).

38 Kluger, *supra* note 6, at 293–94.

39 Tushnet, *supra* note 37; the first edition was published in 1987.

40 Robert L. Carter, *The NAACP's Strategy Against Segregated Education*, 86 Mich. L. Rev. 1083, 1088–89 (1988).

41 *Id.*

42 The plaintiffs in the school segregation cases were represented by lawyers employed or contracted to the NAACP Legal Defense and Educational Fund Inc., a separate charitable corporation spun off from the NAACP in 1939 but at that time still closely aligned with the NAACP.

43 Kluger, *supra* note 6, at 3–25.

44 Briggs v. Elliott, 98 F. Supp. 529 (D.S.C. 1951); 103 F. Supp. 920 (D.S.C. 1952); Brown v. Bd. of Educ. of Topeka, 98 F. Supp. 797 (D. Kan. 1951); Davis v. Cty. School Board of Prince Edward Cty., 103 F. Supp. 337 (E.D.Va. 1952), and Belton v. Gebhardt and Bulah v. Gebhardt, 87 A.2d 862 (Del. Ch. 1951); 91 A.2d 137 (1953). A separate case decided at the same time as *Brown* held that in the District of Columbia, a federally administered area, the Fifth Amendment of the U.S. Constitution also made de jure segregation a per se violation of its due process clause. Bolling v. Sharpe, 347 U.S. 497 (1954).

45 U.S. Const., Amend. XIV, § 1.

46 Brown v. Bd. of Educ. of Topeka, 347 U.S. 483, 492–93 and discussion at 489–93 (1954) [hereinafter *Brown I*].

47 *Id.*, 347 U.S. at 495.

48 *Id.*, 347 U.S. at 494 and 494 n.11.

49 *Id.*, 347 U.S. at 485 n.1 and 490–92.

50 Kluger, Simple Justice, *supra* note 6, at 620. The Legal Defense Fund stated that the prior legal actions in *Brown* had cost $58,000 to date.

51 The federal Solicitor General in his *amicus curiae* brief in *Brown* urged, alternatively, that the black plaintiffs be immediately admitted to the white schools because the black schools had been demonstrated to be unequal, or that the court overrule Plessy v. Ferguson. Kluger, Simple Justice, *supra* note 6, at 559–63; Jack Greenberg, Crusaders in the Courts, 71–81 and 89–94 (2004).

52 Brown v. Bd. of Educ. of Topeka, 349 U.S. 294, 301 (1955) [hereinafter *Brown II*].

53 *Id.*, 349 U.S. at 299.

54 Briggs v. Elliott, 132 F. Supp. 776, 777 (D.S.C. 1955) (*per curiam*, by a three-judge panel).

55 Daniel J. Meador, *The Constitution and the Assignment of Pupils to Public Schools*, 45 Va. L. Rev. 517, 525 (1959).

56 Richard W. Brown, "Freedom of Choice in the South: A Constitutional Perspective," 28 La. L. Rev.455, 459 n.27 (1968); Bradley v. School Board of City of Richmond, Va., 345 F.2d 310, 317 (4th Cir.), *vacated on other grounds per curiam*, 382

U.S. 103 (1965); Kelley v. Bd. of Educ. of the City of Nashville, Davidson County, Tenn., 270 F.2d 209, 228–30 (6th Cir.), *cert. denied*, 361 U.S. 924 (1959), and Avery v. Wichita Falls Ind. School Dist., 241 F.2d 230, 233 (5th Cir.), *cert. denied sub nom.* Wichita Falls Ind. School Dist. v. Avery, 353 U.S. 938 (1957). As we will see in chapter 7, the Fifth Circuit eventually overruled its prior cases that relied on *Briggs*.

CHAPTER 5

1 Jeffry L. Charbonnet, The Public School System of Alachua County 1821-1955 247–48 (1991) (unpublished master's thesis, University of Florida) (on file with author).

2 *Id.* at 198–200 and 255.

3 *See Minutes*, Alachua Cty. Bd. Pub. Instruction, vol. 11, at 2562 (Aug., 1960) [the collected minutes are hereinafter *School Board Minutes*].

4 Winston Arnow was appointed a U.S. District Court judge in 1967. He would sit on the controversial desegregation case involving Escambia High School. The U.S. District Courthouse in Pensacola is named in his honor.

5 The North Carolina pupil-assignment law had been held constitutional in Carson v. Warlick, 238 F.2d 724 (4th Cir. 1956). *See supra*, ch.3.

6 *Board Sets "Freeze" on Pupil Transfer*, Gainesville Sun, Aug. 21, 1956, at 1.

7 *See supra*, ch.3, note 55.

8 *School Board Minutes, supra* note 3, Vol. 11 at 2601–04 (Dec. 13, 1960).

9 *Supra*, ch.3, note 48.

10 Fla. Const. of 1885, art. VIII, § 6; *id.* art. XII, § 2B (amended 1964).

11 Cormier, *Talbot Lays Politics to School Board*, Gainesville Sun, Oct. 29, 1963, at 1.

12 *Talbot May Quit as GHS Principal*, Gainesville Sun, Oct. 30, 1963, at 1.

13 Marshall, *Superintendent to Stay Elected*, Gainesville Sun, Nov. 6, 1963, at 1.

14 *Talbot Resignation Letter is Still "On File,"* Gainesville Sun, Nov. 6, 1963, at 8.

15 *Talbot Announces Candidacy*, Gainesville Sun, Jan. 9, 1964, at 1.

16 Cormier, *1964-1972, The Talbot Years in Alachua County*, Gainesville Sun, Feb. 27, 1972, at 1B.

17 Butch graduated from GHS in 1958. Subsequently Butch was away from Gainesville as a college student, dental student, naval officer, and oral surgeon resident. He has little personal knowledge of events in his dad's life during these times.

18 Interview with Tommy Tomlinson, in Gainesville, Fla. (Sept. 10, 2014) (on file with author).

19 Cormier, *Talbot, Williams and Joiner Victors in School Contests*, Gainesville Sun, May 6, 1964, at 1.

20 Interview with John Neller, in Gainesville, Fla. 4–5 (June 9, 2014) (on file with author).

21 Telephone Interview with Tommy Tomlinson 1 (Aug. 27, 2014) (notes on file with author).

22 *Id.*; interview with Tommy Tomlinson, *supra* note 18, at 1–2.

23 Telephone Interview with Tommy Tomlinson, *supra* note 21; interview with Tommy Tomlinson, *supra* note 18, at 1–2.

24 Cormier, *Planning for Integration Pledged,* Gainesville Sun, Apr. 30, 1964, at 1.

25 The school board later asserted that the first attempt by black students to attend white county schools occurred in 1964. Answer by Defendants at 11, Wright v. Bd. of Pub. Instruction, Civ. No. 367 (N.D. Fla. Oct. 21, 1964). [hereinafter *Wright v. Board*].

26 *Id.* at 6; Deposition of Willard E. Williams at 23 (*Wright v. Board,* Mar. 25, 1965).

27 Answer by Defendants, *supra* note 25, at 6; Deposition of Willard E. Williams, *supra* note 26; *see* Cormier, *Assign Schools to County Pupils,* Gainesville Sun, Apr. 19, 1964, at 28.

28 Answer by Defendants, *supra* note 25, at 6.

29 *School Board Minutes, supra* note 3, vol. 12, at 3030 (June 9, 1964). In referring to the pending applications for assignment, the board probably intended the pending-as-of date of "June, 1963" to read, "June, 1964."

30 Cormier, *Planning for Integration Pledged,* Gainesville Sun, Apr. 30, 1964, at 1; Cormier, *School Candidate Claims Misquote,* Gainesville Sun, May 1, 1964, at 17. Incumbent Willard Williams (who won election) deflected the question by stating that the Florida pupil-assignment law does not provide for race to influence the school to which a pupil is assigned, and that he would never advocate anything but peaceful administration of school affairs.

31 Thomas A. Wright, Sr., Courage in Persona 133 (1993); interview with Thomas A. Wright, Sr., in Gainesville, Fla. (Mar. 30, 2012) (on file with author)

32 Cormier, *Three Students . . . July '64,* Gainesville Sun, Jan. 25, 1970 at 9A.

33 Wright, *supra* note 31.

34 Cormier, *Three Students . . . July '64,* Gainesville Sun, Jan. 25, 1970 at 9A.

35 Complaint (*Wright v. Board,* July 2, 1964).

36 Complaint, *supra* note 35, at 8.

37 Attorney Motley had served with the NAACP Legal Defense Fund since her 1946 graduation from Columbia Law School. She withdrew from the Alachua County case in February 1966, following her election as Manhattan borough president. She was the first African American woman to be appointed to the federal bench. Lyndon Johnson appointed her a judge in the U.S. District Court for the Southern District of New York in September 1966.

38 Wright, *supra* note 31, at 101–17.

39 *Id.* at 126, 130.

40 *Id.* at 126; Stephen R. Prescott, *White Robes and Crosses: Father John Conoley, the Ku Klux Klan and the University of Florida,* 71 Florida Historical Quarterly 18 (1992).

41 Wright, *supra* note 31, at 130.

42 *School Board Minutes, supra* note 3, vol. 12, at 3039 (June 9, 1964). Following Cornelia Rawls's appeal of that denial, the school board held the hearing required by the pupil-assignment law. The school board denied her appeal because at Gainesville High Rawls would be placed on the track for students with abilities

considered below average. The school board found that Rawls would be discouraged from participating in music and other activities and would not keep pace with the regular GHS curriculum. *School Board Minutes, supra* note 3, vol. 12, at 3046 (July 23, 1964). Rawls had been voted "Best Actress" in a Lincoln High production at the statewide Florida Intercollegiate Speech and Drama Association conference in April 1964. Maxine Ross & Helen Wilson, *Lincoln in the Sun*, Gainesville Sun, Apr. 14, 1964, at 4.

43 The University of Florida laboratory school, P. K. Yonge, also accepted token black students in 1964.

44 Answer by Defendants, *supra* note 25, at 6.

45 LaCoe, *U.S. Suit Filed Demanding County School Integration*, Gainesville Sun, July 9, 1964, at 1 (quoting court clerk Miss Pixie Hampton). Judge Carswell had been nominated by President Dwight Eisenhower to the Northern District of Florida in 1958, and he served as chief judge of that court from 1958 to 1969. President Richard Nixon nominated Judge Carswell to the Fifth Circuit Court of Appeals, where he was seated on June 20, 1969. Following the U.S. Senate's rejection of Clement Haynsworth to replace Abe Fortas on the Supreme Court, Nixon nominated Carswell for the Supreme Court. The Senate also voted against Carswell's nomination. Justice Harry Blackmun was eventually nominated and confirmed for the Supreme Court vacancy. Carswell resigned from the Fifth Circuit in 1970 to run as a Republican for the U.S. Senate. He was overwhelmingly defeated in the Republican primary by U.S. Rep. William Cramer of St. Petersburg. Lawton Chiles, the Democrat, went on to defeat Cramer in the general election.

46 Motion to Dismiss (*Wright v. Board*, July 27, 1964); Answer by Defendants, *supra* note 25.

47 Answer by Defendants, *supra* note 25, at 3–4, 7–8.

48 Gibson v. Bd. of Pub. Instruction, 272 F.2d 763 (5th Cir. 1959).

49 Motion to Dismiss, *supra* note 46, at 1, ¶ 2.

50 Brief of Appellee at 60–63, Question V, McLaughlin v. Florida, 379 U.S. 184 (Sept. 30, 1964), 1964 WL 81160.

51 McLaughlin v. Florida, *supra* note 50. The Supreme Court held unconstitutional a Florida criminal statute that punished cohabitation by blacks and whites of opposite sexes, but not by members of the same race. The court determined that the classification was based on race, was without sufficient justification, and therefore violated the Equal Protection Clause of the Fourteenth Amendment.

52 For a description of those challenges and responses, see Ferdinand F. Fernandez, *The Constitutionality of the Fourteenth Amendment*, 39 S. Cal. L. Rev. 378 (1966).

53 Answer by Defendants, *supra* note 25, at 11.

54 School Desegregation Plans, 29 Fed. Reg. 16,298 (Dec. 4, 1964), to be codified at 45 C.F.R. Part 80. Those regulations were published under the Civil Rights Act of 1964, Pub. L. No. 88–352, tit. VI, 78 Stat. 241, 252–53 (1964). Formal HEW approval of the plan was then needed under 45 C.F.R. § 80.4(c) because the system was not yet under a court order to desegregate. More complete guidance

for such plans was subsequently given by HEW in U.S. Dept. of Health, Education, and Welfare, Office of Education, General Statement of Policies Under Title VI of the Civil Rights Act of 1964 Respecting Desegregation of Elementary and Secondary Schools, April 1965 [hereinafter *HEW 1965 General Statement*], in Alachua County Board of Public Instruction, Informal Desegregation File 50-55 (undated) [hereinafter *School Board File*]. To comply, school systems were required to adopt plans based either on single geographical attendance areas for all schools, freedom of choice, or a combination of those two methods of compliance. *HEW 1965 General Statement*, § V, *School Board File* 51–55. The HEW 1965 General Statement was subsequently published as 45 C.F.R. Part 180 (later corrected to Part 181) at 30 Fed. Reg. 9981 (Aug. 11, 1965), with renumbered sections.

55 *School Board Minutes, supra* note 3, vol. 13, at 3134–37 (Mar. 2, 1965).

56 *School Board Minutes, supra* note 3, vol. 13, at 3134 (Mar. 2, 1965).

57 *See* Answer by Defendants, *supra* note 25, exhibits B, C, D & E (letters to parents on pupil assignments from 1961 through 1964). HEW guidelines for desegregation plans prohibited the use of pupil-assignment laws "to limit desegregation through restriction of any pupil's right to free choice." *HEW 1965 General Statement, supra* note 54, § V.D.2, at 3.

58 *Id.*

59 Deposition of Willard E. Williams, *supra* note 26, at 24–25; Deposition of William S. Talbot at 4–5 (*Wright v. Board*, Mar. 25, 1965).

60 Board of Public Instruction of Alachua County, Instructions for Registration, 1965-66 School Year, § 8, at 2, *School Board File, supra* note 54, at 31–39 (1965) [hereinafter *School Board 1965 Instructions*].

61 *School Board Minutes, supra* note 3, vol. 13, at 3135 (Mar. 2, 1965).

62 *School Board 1965 Instructions, supra* note 60, at 3.

63 *School Board Minutes, supra* note 3, vol. 13, at 3136 (Mar. 2, 1965). The court in *Wright v. Board* had previously orally ruled that it would not consider any issues related to segregation of school staff at the preliminary injunction phase of the case. A committee of white and black educators and administrators to work on school staffing issues under the plan was approved by HEW on June 14, 1965. *School Board Minutes, supra* note 3, vol. 13, at 3211 (Aug. 12, 1965).

64 *School Board Minutes, supra* note 3, vol. 13, at 3290 (Feb. 10, 1966).

65 *HEW 1965 General Statement, supra* note 54, § V.B.1.a.

66 *Id.* § V.B.1.b.

67 *School Board Minutes, supra* note 3, vol. 13, at 3136–37 (Mar. 2, 1965).

68 *Court Adopts County School Integration Plan*, Gainesville Sun, Apr. 6, 1965, at 1. No transcript of this hearing is part of the record of the case.

69 *Id.*

70 Decree (*Wright v. Board*, Apr. 7, 1965).

71 Department of Health, Education, and Welfare, Policies on Elementary and Secondary School Compliance with Title VI of the Civil Rights Act of 1964, Sec. 4, 33 Fed. Reg. 4955 (Mar. 23, 1968); School Desegregation Plans, 31 Fed. Reg. 5624

(Ap. 9, 1966), codified at 45 C.F.R. §181.6; School Desegregation Plans, 29 Fed. Reg. 16,300 (Dec. 4, 1964), codified at 45 C.F.R. §80.4(c).

72 Plaintiffs' Motion to Supplement Record and Amend Decree (*Wright v. Board*, Apr. 14, 1965).

73 Green v. Cty. Sch. Bd., 391 U.S. 430 (1968).

74 Department of Health, Education, and Welfare, Policies on Elementary and Secondary School Compliance with Title VI of the Civil Rights Act of 1964, Secs. 12(a) and 17, 33 Fed. Reg. 4956 and 4957 (Mar. 23, 1968); School Desegregation Regulations, 31 Fed. Reg. 5624 (Ap. 9, 1966), codified at 45 C.F.R. §181.11 and §§181.41–181.55.

75 Memorandum of W. S. Talbot *in School Board File, supra* note 54, at 56–58. The table accompanying the memorandum showed that of the 329 black students initially granted assignments, 28 withdrew their requests and an additional 12 requested assignment at the second stage of the assignment process, for a net 313 black pupils assigned to white schools in September 1965.

76 *Id.*

77 Letter from W. S. Talbot to James T. Campbell, State Department of Education (June 11, 1965) *in School Board File, supra* note 54, at 60; *School Board Minutes, supra* note 3, vol. 13, at 3186 (June 10, 1965).

78 *School Board Minutes, supra* note 3, vol. 13, at 3262 (Jan. 13, 1966).

79 *Integration Is Working Smoothly in Gainesville*, Gainesville Sun, Nov. 19, 1965, at 1.

80 *School Board Minutes, supra* note 3, vol. 13, at 3341 (May 12, 1966).

81 *Desegregation Institute for Teachers Declined*, Gainesville Sun, May 13, 1966, at 17.

82 *HEW 1965 General Statement, supra* note 54, § V.D.

83 *Id.*, § V.E.

84 *See infra* ch. 6, tbl. 2.

CHAPTER 6

1 Alachua County Board of Public Instruction, Informal Desegregation File 64 (undated) [hereinafter *School Board File*].

2 Interview with Shelton Boyles, in Gainesville, Fla. 2 (June 10, 2014) (on file with author).

3 Because of the tabular presentation to the court, special education students above grade 6 cannot be counted in this statistic. *See* tbl. 2.

4 Plan of the Board of Public Instruction of Alachua County, Florida at 5 and accompanying maps, Attachment to Certificate of Service (*Wright v. Board*, Feb. 28, 1969) and Order, (*Wright v. Board*, Apr. 3, 1969).

5 Plan of the Board of Public Instruction of Alachua County, Florida, Feb. 28, 1969, *supra* note 4, at 9.

6 Arthur O. White, The History of Lincoln High: "The Big Red" 16 (undated), http://ufdc.ufl.edu/AA00008787/00001, (last visited Jan. 28, 2017).

7 *See* Alachua County Bd. of Pub. Instruction, reports to court dated Dec. 13, 1967, Oct. 15, 1968, and Sept. 26, 1969, *Wright v. Board*. The enrollment for

September 1965 is from the report of the Records Committee, Section VIII, Publications at 3, University of Florida Special and Area Studies Collections, Education in Florida Subject Files, Box 13, MS Group 149, File 38/I/7 [hereinafter *EDF 600 File*]. "The Big Red" (*supra* note 5) is a twenty-two-page typed very high level summary of this research prepared by the Vocational Office Education Department at what became the Lincoln vocational center. Much of "The Big Red," especially related to desegregation (as distinguished from the interview excerpts) is inaccurate.

8 Interview by Gayle Yamada with Joel Buchanan, in Gainesville, Fla., at 15–16 (Feb. 12, 1984), University of Florida Digital Collections, http://ufdc.ufl.edu/UF00005406/00001 (last visited Jan. 26, 2017).

9 Interview, Joel Buchanan, *supra* note 8, at 16.

10 Albert White and Kevin McCarthy, Lincoln High School, Its History and Legacy 289 (2011).

11 *EDF 600 File*, *supra* note 7, Field Notes at 13.

12 Interview with Thomas A. Wright, in Gainesville, Fla. 7 (March 26, 2012); Thomas A. Wright, Sr., Courage in Persona 134 (1993).

13 Interview with Joel Buchanan, *supra* note 8, at 16–18.

14 Interview with Joel Buchanan, *supra* note 8, at 18–20.

15 Judy Spiro, *Queen's Florist – Buchanan's Career Blossoms into Success*, Gainesville Sun, Aug. 9, 1970, at 3E.

16 Interview with Joel Buchanan, *supra* note 8, at 19.

17 Interview with Frank Coleman, Janice Cambridge Hagillih, & Cynthia Cook, in Gainesville, Fla. at 1, 3 (May 24, 2016) (on file with author).

18 Telephone Interview with Frank Coleman 3 (Jan. 13, 2016) (on file with author).

19 Interview with John Dukes III, in Gainesville, Fla. 4–5 and 11 (March 5, 2014) (on file with author); interview with Bernice Dukes, Carmen Dukes & John Dukes III, in Gainesville, Fla. 6–7 (July 11, 2014) (on file with author).

20 Interview with John Dukes III, *supra* note 19 at 7–8.

21 Interview with Bernice Dukes, Carmen Dukes & John Dukes III, *supra* note 19, at 7.

22 Interview with John Dukes III, *supra* note 19, at 7.

23 Interview with John Dukes III, *supra* note 19, at 7–8.

24 Interview with John Dukes III, *supra* note 19, at 18.

25 Interview with Melvin Flournoy, in Gainesville, Fla. 2, 10–11 and 16 (Oct. 1, 2015) (on file with author).

26 Interview with Alvin Butler, in Gainesville, Fla. 1–2 (March 11, 2016) (on file with author).

27 Interview with Frank Coleman, *supra* note 18, at 14–15.

28 Interview with Alvin Butler, *supra* note 26, at 4–5.

29 Interview with Frank Coleman, Janice Cambridge Hagillih, & Cynthia Cook, *supra* note 17, at 1.

30 Interview with Frank Coleman, *supra* note 18, at 1 and 13.

31 Interview with Frank Coleman, Janice Cambridge Hagillih, & Cynthia Cook, *supra* note 17, at 3–4.

32 *Id.* at 1.

33 Interview with Melvin Flournoy, *supra* note 25, at 5.

34 Minutes of Bi-racial Committee, Feb. 3, 1971, Attachment #1, at 1 and 5; *School Board File, supra* note 1, at 572 and 576.

35 Interview with Frank Coleman *supra* note 18, at 9.

36 Telephone Interview with Judy Segler Joiner (May 30, 2014) (notes on file with author).

37 Interview with Peggy Finley, in Gainesville, Fla. 5 (April, 2012); interview with Sandra Sharron and Frank Ford, in Gainesville, Fla. 9, 12–13 (Sharron) (Oct. 30, 2014) (on file with author).

38 U.S. Civil Rights Comm'n, 89th Cong., Survey of School Desegregation in the Southern and Border States 1965-66, at 30, 51 (1966) [hereinafter *Civil Rights Commission 1966 Survey*]. *See* ch. 7, *infra.*

39 *Civil Rights Commission 1966 Survey, supra* note 38, at 33–34.

40 *Id.* at 35.

41 *Id.* at 35–42.

42 *Id.* at 51.

43 Telephone Interview with Donnie Batie, M.D. 2–11 (July 28, 2015) (on file with author).

44 Interview with Brenda Wims, in Gainesville, Fla. 1–4, 8–9 and 19–20 (Jan. 28, 2016) (on file with author).

45 Interview with Gertrude E. Jones, in Gainesville, Fla. 16–17 and 20–21 (Sept. 28, 2015) (on file with author).

46 Interview with Alvin Butler, *supra* note 26, at 12.

47 Interview with Sandra Sharron and Frank Ford, *supra* note 37, at 36–37, 39 and 41 (Ford).

48 Interview with Donnie Batie, M.D., *supra* note 43, at 10.

49 Interview with Wayne Mosley, in Gainesville, Fla. 4 (Sept. 11, 2014) (on file with author)

50 Interview with Wayne Mosley, *supra* note 49, at 21.

CHAPTER 7

1 U.S. Civil Rights Comm'n, 89th Cong., Survey of School Desegregation in the Southern and Border States 1965-66, at 30, 51 (1966) [hereinafter *Civil Rights Commission 1966 Survey*]; Jim Leeson, *Desegregation: Faster Pace, Scarcer Records,* S. Educ. Rep., Jan.–Feb. 1966 28, 30.

2 *Civil Rights Commission 1966 Survey, supra* note 1, at 30, 51.

3 *Id.* at 26.

4 *Id.* at 12–17.

5 The Defense Fund's local attorney in *Wright v. Board* had opposed freedom of choice at the 1965 court hearing on Alachua County's first desegregation plan. *Court Adopts County School Integration Plan*, Gainesville Sun, Apr. 6, 1965, at 1.

6 Leeson, *supra* note 1; *see* U.S. v. Jefferson Cty. Bd. of Educ., 372 F.2d 836, 903–05, app. B (5th Cir. 1966), *corrected*, 380 F.2d 385 (5th Cir.) (en banc), *cert. denied*, 389 U.S. 840, *reh'g denied*, 389 U.S. 965 (1967).

7 *Id.*

8 *See supra*, tbl. 3.

9 *Civil Rights Commission 1966 Survey*, *supra* note 1.

10 *Id.* at 30–42.

11 *NAACP Hits Fla. School Integration*, Gainesville Sun, Jan. 26, 1966, at 15; *see* Jack Greenberg, Crusaders in the Courts, Legal Battles of the Civil Rights Movement 409–11 (Anniversary ed. 2004).

12 *NAACP Hits Fla. School Integration*, *supra* note 11.

13 U.S. Department of Health, Education, and Welfare, Office of Education, Revised Statement of Policies for School Desegregation Plans under Title VI of the Civil Rights Act of 1964, March 1966, in Alachua County Board of Public Instruction, Informal Desegregation File 68, 70 (undated) [hereinafter *School Board File*]; subsequently published at 31 Fed. Reg. 5623 (Apr. 9, 1966), and codified at 45 C.F.R. Part 181 (1967) [hereinafter *HEW March 1966 Revised Statement*]. The HEW March 1966 Revised Statement became effective for desegregating schools for the 1966-67 school year.

14 *HEW March 1966 Revised Statement*, *supra* note 13, 45 C.F.R. § 181.11.

15 *HEW March 1966 Revised Statement*, *supra* note 13, 45 C.F.R. §§ 181.11 and 181.54.

16 *HEW March 1966 Revised Statement*, *supra* note 13, 45 C.F.R. § 181.11.

17 There was at this time no separate cabinet Department of Education; the commissioner of Education was the senior education administrator within the Department of Health, Education, and Welfare.

18 *HEW March 1966 Revised Statement*, *supra* note 13, 45 C.F.R. § 181.54. The Alachua County school board's attorney, Winston Arnow, correctly stated that because the Alachua County schools were subject to a desegregation court order, the school board was not technically required to take any new action as a result of the Revised Statement. *Integration Policy Satisfactory Here*, Gainesville Sun, March 11, 1966, at 5; *HEW March 1966 Revised Statement*, *supra* note 13, 45 C.F.R. § 181.6.

19 *Jefferson County*, 372 F.2d at 848 n. 13.

20 *See* Singleton v. Jackson Mun. Separate Sch. Dist., 355 F.2d 865, 869 (5th Cir. 1966); Singleton v. Jackson Mun. Separate Sch. Dist., 348 F.2d 729, 731 (5th Cir. 1965).

21 *Supra* note 6, 372 F.2d 836. The Supreme Court by denying certiorari in *Jefferson County* allowed the decision to take effect immediately. The Supreme Court affirmed another case decided on much the same grounds as Jefferson County. Lee v. Macon Cty. Bd. of Educ., 267 F. Supp. 458 (M.D. Ala.), *aff'd per curiam*

sub nom., Wallace v. U.S., 389 U.S. 215 (1967), thus expressing approval of both decisions. Jack Bass, Unlikely Heroes 306–08 (1990).

22 The author's opinion is reinforced by that of Judge John Minor Wisdom, who regarded it as the most important decision of his career. Bass, *supra* note 21, at 298. Professor Frank Read ranked *Jefferson County* among the four most important school desegregation cases. F. T. Read, *Judicial Evolution of the Law of School Integration Since* Brown v. Board of Education, 39 L. & Contemp. Probs. 7, 23 (1975).

23 The defendant school districts in Alabama and Louisiana were represented by lawyers who had built their careers around defending against desegregation, including John Satterfield of Yazoo City, Mississippi, and Maurice Bishop of Birmingham, Alabama.

24 Bass, *supra* note 21, at 41–55.

25 Thornberry on the Fifth Circuit had a close relationship with another Texan appointed by Johnson, Irving Goldberg, also a defender of civil rights. *Id.* at 303–05.

26 Douglas O. Linder, *Bending Toward Justice: John Doar and the Mississippi Burning Trial*, 72 Miss. L. J. 731 (2002).

27 One author attributes this failure to Judge Wisdom's need to preserve a majority for his decision in the Fifth Circuit's en banc consideration of the opinion that he knew would follow the three-judge panel's decision. Bass, *supra* note 21, at 306.

28 *Jefferson* County, 372 F.2d at 845 (citations omitted).

29 For examples, *see id.* at 845 n.3, 852, 853–54, 895, 895, 895 n.123, and app. B.

30 *Id.* at 847 (emphasis in original).

31 *Id.* at 848.

32 *Id.* at 848–49.

33 *Id.* at 852–53, 853 n.31, 856.

34 *Id.* at 849. The Fifth Circuit had previously held that it would give great weight to the earlier HEW guidelines. *See* Singleton v. Jackson Mun. Separate Sch. Dist., 348 F.2d 729, 730–31 (5th Cir. 1965).

35 *Jefferson County*, 372 F.2d at 849.

36 *Id.* at 850.

37 *Id.* (emphasis in original).

38 *Id.* at 852–59.

39 *Id.* at 854.

40 *Id.* at 859. The court's reference to the guidelines must be taken to include the *HEW March 1966 Revised Statement, supra* note 13, because of the court's specific reference thereto at 851 n.29.

41 *Id.* at 861.

42 *Id.*

43 *See supra* ch. 4; *Jefferson County*, 372 F.2d at 861–73.

44 *Jefferson County*, 372 F.2d at 867–68. Judge Wilson had previously stated this view in Singleton v. Jackson Mun. Separate Sch. Dist., 355 F.2d 865, 869 (5th Cir. 1966) and Singleton v. Jackson Mun. Separate Sch. Dist., 348 F.2d 729, 730 n. 5 (5th Cir. 1965).

45 *Jefferson County*, 372 F.2d at 871–73.
46 *Id.* at 868.
47 For examples, *see id.* at 845 n.3, 852, 853–54, and app. B.
48 *Id.* at 868.
49 *Id.* at 876. The court's discussion relied on jury and voting rights cases, as well as a Fourth Circuit case which agreed that schools could take affirmative action to desegregate in de jure cases, Wanner v. Cty. Sch. Bd., 357 F.2d 452, 454–55 (4th Cir. 1966); *Jefferson County*, 372 F.2d at 876–78. Under recent Supreme Court precedents, in de facto cases, assignment to schools by race is unconstitutional unless narrowly tailored to achieve a compelling government interest—a test that such assignments in de facto cases usually fail. *See* Parents Involved in Cmty. Schs. v. Seattle Sch. Dist. No. 1, 551 U.S. 701, 702–03 (2007); *infra* ch. 15 and afterword.
50 *Jefferson County*, 372 F.2d at 878.
51 Civil Rights Act of 1964, P.L. 88–352, § 401(b), 78 Stat. 246, subsequently codified at 42 U.S.C. § 2000c(b).
52 Civil Rights Act of 1964, P.L. 88–352, § 407(a)(2), 78 Stat. 248, subsequently codified at 42 U.S.C. § 2000c–6(a).
53 *Jefferson County*, 372 F.2d at 878–81.
54 *Id.* at 880.
55 Civil Rights Act of 1964, P.L. 88–352, § 604, 78 Stat. 253, subsequently codified at 42 U.S.C. § 2000d–3.
56 *Jefferson County*, 372 F.2d at 883. For the discussion, see *id.* 882–86.
57 *Id.* at 873–76.
58 Read, *supra* note 22, at 25 n.80.
59 *Jefferson County*, 372 F.2d at 888–902.
60 *Id.* at 891.
61 *HEW March 1966 Revised Statement*, *supra* note 13, §181.13.
62 *Jefferson County*, 372 F.2d at 892 (citation omitted).
63 *Id.* at 893.
64 *Id.* at 891–92.
65 United States v. Jefferson Cty., 380 F.2d 385, 389 (5th Cir. 1967).
66 *Id.* at 389, 389 n.3.
67 The conflicting views of the four Circuit Courts of Appeal having some jurisdiction in the South are discussed in Richard W. Brown, *Freedom of Choice in the South: A Constitutional Perspective*, 28 La. L. Rev. 455, 462–65 (1968).
68 *Jefferson County*, 372 F.2d at 907–09 (Cox, J., dissenting); *Jefferson County*, 380 F.2d at 397–410 (Gewin, J., dissenting); *Id.* at 410–17 (Bell, J., dissenting); *Id.* at 417–20 (Coleman, J., concurring in result); and *Id.* at 420–27 (Godbold, J., dissenting).
69 *Jefferson County*, 380 F.2d at 397 (Gewin, J., dissenting).
70 *Id.* at 411 (Griffin Bell, J., dissenting).
71 *Id.* at 404 (Gewin, J., dissenting).
72 *Id.* at 405–06.

73 *Id.* at 404 (Griffin Bell, J., dissenting), referring to Swann v. Charlotte-Mecklenburg Bd. of Educ., 369 F.2d 29 (4th Cir. 1966) (en banc). The Supreme Court reversed a later Fourth Circuit decision in this litigation, as we will see.

74 Cormier, *County's Schools Must Re-Register*, Gainesville Sun, Apr. 4, 1967, at 1.

75 Calendar – Pupil Assignment for 1967-68 in *School Board File, supra* note 13, at 97; Letter of Superintendent William S. Talbot to Parents, Apr. 17, 1967 in *School Board File, supra*, at 133.

76 Decree (*Wright v. Board*, Apr. 25, 1967). A cover letter from Attorney Arnow to Judge Carswell transmitting the draft decree shows that Arnow based the decree language on similar decrees provided to him by Judge Carswell that covered Escambia and Bay Counties. Letter from Winston Arnow to Judge G. Harrold Carswell, Apr. 24, 1967 *in School Board File, supra* note 13, at 110–11.

77 *Cf.* Initial Provision of Model Decree, United States v. Jefferson Cty. Bd. of Educ., 372 F.2d 836, 896 (5th Cir. 1966).

78 Decree, *supra* note 76, at 1.

79 *Id.* at 7; *Jefferson County*, 372 F.2d at 899–990.

80 Cormier, *Federal Desegregation Ruling Not an Issue Here – Talbot,* Gainesville Sun, Dec. 30, 1966, at 1; Talbot gave a similar reaction to the en banc decision. Cormier, *Talbot: District Court Ruling Not Pointed at Alachua County,* Gainesville Sun, Mar. 30, 1967, at 1.

81 Cormier, *Talbot Takes a 'Year End' Look at School System*, Gainesville Sun, Dec. 27, 1966, at 1.

CHAPTER 8

1 *See supra*, tbl.1.

2 Jeffry L. Charbonnet, The Public School System of Alachua County 1821-1955 253–54 (1991) (unpublished master's thesis, University of Florida) (on file with author). This effort was led by Superintendent Paul Peters, a former principal of Gainesville High School.

3 Defendants' Answers to Interrogatories at 1–3 (*Wright v. Board*, Nov. 26, 1964).

4 *Minutes*, Alachua Cty. Bd. Pub. Instruction, vol. 13, at 3169 (May 13, 1965) [the collected minutes are hereinafter *School Board Minutes*].

5 Deposition of Willard E. Williams at 33–35 (*Wright v. Board*, Mar. 25, 1965).

6 *School Bonds Get Big "Yea,"* Gainesville Sun, June 1, 1966, at 1, and *County Finally "Facing the Music" on Schools*, Gainesville Sun, Apr. 26, 1966, at 1. Schools in Duval County, where Jacksonville was located, had lost accreditation.

7 *School Board Minutes, supra* note 4, vol. 13, at 3216 (Sept. 9, 1965).

8 Howard Covington, *Alachua Schools May Face "Duval" Problems,* Gainesville Sun, Oct. 20, 1965, at 1.

9 *See Door to Make "Fire Trap" Room Safe,* Gainesville Sun, Nov. 17, 1965, at 1 (quoting Superintendent Talbot).

10 *School Board Minutes, supra* note 4, vol. 13, at 3205 (July 29, 1965), and 3282 (Jan. 13, 1966).

11 Sherman Dorn & Deanna L. Michael, *Education Finance Reform in Florida, in* Education Reform in Florida: Diversity and Equity in Public Policy 56–57 (Kathryn M. Borman & Sherman Dorn eds., 2007).

12 *School Millage Vote Nov. 7,* Gainesville Sun, Nov. 2, 1967, at 5.

13 Ad, paid for by W.S. Talbot, Gainesville Sun, Oct. 31, 1965, at 4D. One mill equals one-tenth of a cent.

14 Dollar estimate given by Superintendent Talbot in Cormier and Jim Kelly, *Millage Vote Supported and Countered,* Gainesville Sun, Oct. 27, 1965, at 1. Of the 3 mills, only 2.1 mills ($628,000) were used when the school board budget was completed for 1967. That amount was about 5 percent of the total budget of $11,882,000. *Not All the Allowable Is Being Used,* Gainesville Sun, Aug. 12, 1966, at 5.

15 Dorn and Michael, *supra* note 11 at 58–78.

16 *School Bond Issue Seen as Only Hope,* Gainesville Sun, Jan. 7, 1966, at 1.

17 Cormier, *$13 Million Needed for Schools,* Gainesville Sun, Jan. 14, 1966, at 1.

18 State of Florida, Dep't of Educ., Update of Survey of School Plants, Alachua County (Feb. 1965), Jan. 1966.

19 *Id.* at 22–23.

20 *Id.* at 22–23.

21 Cormier, *$13 Million Needed for Schools,* Gainesville Sun, Jan. 14, 1966, at 1; *4 Schools Lose Top 3 Grades,* Gainesville Sun, Feb. 18, 1966, at 1.

22 Cormier, *Buchholz to Become Junior College,* Gainesville Sun, Jan. 14, 1966, at 1.

23 Cormier, *Protest Heard from High Springs,* Gainesville Sun, March 11, 1966, at 5, and *Aged Man Sheds Tears for a Declining School,* Gainesville Sun, March 20, 1966, at 1.

24 Cormier, *School Bond Issue Backed, but Many Problems Ensue,* Gainesville Sun, Feb. 18, 1966, at 1.

25 *Id.*

26 Cormier, *Aged Man Sheds Tears for a Declining School,* Gainesville Sun, March 20, 1966, at 1. The integrated elementary school in Hawthorne continues to bear Chester Shell's name.

27 *Id.*

28 *School Board Minutes, supra* note 4, vol. 13, at 3326–27 (Apr. 16, 1966); Cormier, *School Bond Plans Unfolded,* Gainesville Sun, Apr. 12, 1966, at 1.

29 *Citizens' Report on Schools Ready,* Gainesville Sun, Apr. 11, 1966, at 1.

30 *Id.*

31 Cormier, Public *Hearing Draws Nigh for Big School Bond Issue,* Gainesville Sun, May 29, 1966, at 1.

32 Cormier, *School Bonds Get Big "Yea,"* Gainesville Sun, June 1, 1966, at 1.

33 *School Board Minutes, supra* note 4, vol. 13, at 3354 (June 9, 1966).

34 *School Bd. Candidates Quizzed,* Gainesville Sun, Apr. 26, 1966, at 8; *County School Board Candidates Air Their Views,* Gainesville Sun, Apr. 27, 1966, at 17.

Just before the primary election, the Democratic winner, incumbent G. Hugh Williams, died. In the runoff, all three candidates supported the bond issue, although one candidate recommended other ways to finance schools. Hager, *A Look at the Candidates as School Vote Nears*, Gainesville Sun, Sept. 11, 1966, at 4A; *School Board Election – Who's Who*, Gainesville Sun, Oct. 2, 1966, at 2D; Hager, *All School Board Members, Candidates Back Bond Issue*, Gainesville Sun, Oct. 2, 1966, at 2D.

35 *Turlington, Lee Co-Chairmen for School Bond Committee*, Gainesville Sun, July 24, 1966, at 1.

36 Georgia Marsh, *Scruggs Backs Bond Issue as His "Debt to Children,"* Gainesville Sun, Sept. 20, 1966, at 1.

37 NAACP Executive Committee, Letter to the Editor, *How Should Negroes Vote*, Gainesville Sun, Oct. 1, 1966, at 4.

38 *School Board Minutes, supra* note 4, vol. 13, at 3437 (October 7, 1966).

39 Hager, *Bond Issue Defeated, Bryant, Ebling in Runoff*, Gainesville Sun, Oct. 5, 1966, at 1; Ron Wiggins, *Why the Rural Vote Killed the Bond Issue*, Gainesville Sun, Oct. 5, 1966, at 2; and precinct returns, at 2.

40 Cormier, *Supt. Talbot: "Maybe Next Year,"* Gainesville Sun, Oct. 9, 1966, at 1; *Bond Issue Called Blow to Industry Here*, Gainesville Sun, Oct. 12, 1966, at 3.

41 E.A. Spencer, Jr., Letter to the Editor, *Dubious Credit Due City Voters*, Gainesville Sun, Oct. 9, 1966, at 4A.

42 *Ebling Scores Upset*, Gainesville Sun, Oct. 19, 1966, at 1.

43 Editorial, *Mr. Wershow's Roar*, Gainesville Sun, Oct. 11, 1966, at 4; Buzz Mixson, *Oppose Tax Levy Exceeding 10 Mills*, Gainesville Sun, Oct. 22, 1965, at 17.

44 Cormier, *School Board May Discuss Bond Vote*, Gainesville Sun, March 9, 1966, at 1; *School Board Minutes, supra* note 4, vol. 13, at 3504 (March 9, 1967).

45 Cormier, *Teacher Reaction to Kirk: "Stealing from Children,"* Gainesville Sun, Ap. 28, 1967, at 1; Stephanie Wysong, *Education "Cutback" Shocks Christian*, Gainesville Sun, May 3, 1967, at 1. The governor's budget proposed some increases in spending for teacher salary increases, but those increases were well below levels supported by the legislature and the Florida Education Association. *Teacher Pay Raise Hiked in Senate*, Gainesville Sun, May 17, 1967, at 1.

46 Cormier, *Repairs on Old Schools Are Costly*, Gainesville Sun, July 26, 1967, at 1.

47 *Form School Citizens Group*, Gainesville Sun, Oct. 1, 1967, at 8B.

48 Cormier, *Interest Replaces Apathy in Alachua*, Gainesville Sun, Oct. 1, 1967, at 1A.

49 Cormier, *Public School Forum Slated*, Gainesville Sun, Oct. 22, 1967, at 1A.

50 *School Millage Supporters Plan Organizational Meet*, Gainesville Sun, Oct. 19, 1967, at 15.

51 *School Crisis Public Forum Tonight*, Gainesville Sun, Oct. 23, 1967, at 1; Cormier, *School Needs, Small Crowd Adds to Woes of Backers*, Gainesville Sun, Oct. 26, 1967, at 1.

52 *School Board Minutes, supra* note 4, vol. 13, at 3612 (Oct. 2, 1967), and 3624 (Nov. 9, 1967).

53 *Talbot Thanks Groups Which Backed Four Mills*, Gainesville Sun, Nov. 8, 1967, at 2.

54 Cormier, *School Bond Vote Sought by C of C,* Gainesville Sun, Nov. 8, 1967, at 1.

55 *School Board Minutes, supra* note 4, vol. 13, at 3624 (Nov. 9, 1967).

56 Cormier, *GHS Accreditation "Honor" Won't Be a Happy Event,* Gainesville Sun, Nov. 14, 1967, at 1; *Newberry High Losing Accreditation,* Gainesville Sun, Nov. 14, 1967, at 2.

57 State of Florida, Dep't of Educ., Update of Survey of School Plants, Alachua County (Feb. 1965), Dec. 1967, at 24 [hereinafter *1967 Update of School Plant Survey*].

58 State of Florida, Dep't of Educ., Update of Survey of School Plants, Alachua County (Feb. 1965), Jan. 1966, at 4.

59 *1967 Update of School Plant Survey, supra* note 57, at 24 and 32. The plant at Lincoln High School was classified C-1 for grades 7–9, meaning that no major alterations were needed for the school to remain in use as a junior high school. The plant at Mebane High School was classified C-2 for grades 7–9, indicating that the facility would continue as a junior high school. Both school plants eventually became integrated middle schools and continue under their former names as part of the Alachua County system.

60 *1967 Update of School Plant Survey, supra* note 57, at 35, Table I.

61 Cormier, *10 More Alachua County Schools Said Needed,* Gainesville Sun, Dec. 16, 1967, at 1.

62 *New County Schools Are Supported,* Gainesville Sun, Dec. 15, 1967, at 1. According to Chick, building new high schools in Newberry and Hawthorne would add $1.8 million to the anticipated $16.5 million new construction costs recommended for all Alachua County schools.

63 Cormier, *Johns Airs School Program Problems,* Gainesville Sun, Dec. 6, 1967, at 2A; *Cormier, School Needs Survey Being Launched,* Gainesville Sun, Dec. 12, 1967, at 1; Cormier, *County School Bond Issue Has Built-in Politics,* Gainesville Sun, Dec. 21, 1967, at 24. Newberry and Hawthorne continue to have their own high schools.

64 *New County Schools Are Supported,* Gainesville Sun, Dec. 15, 1967, at 1.

65 Cormier, *No Good Solution Found for County's School Woes,* Gainesville Sun, Jan. 28, 1968, at 8A.

66 *Id.*

67 Cormier, *High Springs, Alachua Schools: Old and Crowded,* Gainesville Sun, May 23, 1968, at 1.

68 *School Board Minutes, supra* note 4, vol. 14, at 3867 (Feb. 8, 1968).

69 Cormier, *Purchase of 2 Sites Okayed for Future High Schools Here,* Gainesville Sun, Feb. 9, 1968, at 1.

70 U.S. Department of Health, Education and Welfare, Office of Education, Revised Statement of Policies for School Desegregation Plans under Title VI of the Civil Rights Act of 1964 (As Amended for the School Year 1967-68), Dec. 1968, in Alachua County Board of Public Instruction Informal Desegregation File [hereinafter *School Board* File] 82, § 181.15 at 85 (not published in Fed. Reg. or codified) [hereinafter *1967–68 Revised Statement*].

71 *Id.*, § 181.54, *School Board File, supra* note 70, at 89–90. To compare the HEW March 1966 Revised Statement, *see* §§ 181.15 and 181.54(d) thereof.

72 Proposed Decree of Appellants in No. 23116 and Appellant-Intervenors in Nos. 23274, 23331, 23335 & 23365, United States v. Caddo Parish Sch. Bd., No. 23274 and other cases (5th Cir. June 23, 1965), at 21–22. That decree had included the language, "Any school to be newly constructed and any school to be substantially expanded by the construction of additional classrooms shall be planned, located, expanded and operated on a desegregated basis. No construction shall be undertaken which will have the effect of maintaining a dual system or promoting segregation. . . . All newly constructed schools and expansion of existing school plants shall be designed to eliminate the dual school structure . . ."

73 *Jefferson County*, 380 F.2d at 393–94.

74 Decree at 8 (*Wright v. Board*, Apr. 25, 1967).

75 *Christian Praises Board*, Gainesville Sun, Jan. 24, 1969, at 12.

76 See Jeffrey L. Littlejohn and Charles H. Ford, Elusive Equality, Desegregation and Resegregation of Norfolk's Public Schools 144-45 (2012); Beckett v. School Bd. of the City of Norfolk, 308 F.Supp. 1274, 1292–93 (E.D. Va. 1969), rev'd sub nom. Brewer v. School Bd. of the City of Norfolk, 434 F.2d 408, cert. denied sub nom. School Bd. of the City of Norfolk v. Brewer, 399 U.S. 929 (1970).

77 Cormier, *School's Closed: The Great Teacher Walkout of '68*, Gainesville Sun, Feb. 18, 1973, at 14A.

78 *Legislators Wrap Up "Hopeless" Package*, Gainesville Sun, Feb. 16, 1968, at 1. For more detailed accounts of the 1968 Florida teachers' strike, *see* Arthur O. White, Florida's Crisis in Public Education (1975).

79 Hager, *Says Teachers "Morally Right,"* Gainesville Sun, Feb. 28, 1968, at 1A (quoting Howard Bishop, a former county superintendent). The bill became law without Kirk's signature on March 7, 1968.

80 Cormier, *School's Closed: The Great Teacher Walkout of '68*, Gainesville Sun, Feb. 18, 1973, at 14A.

81 Interview by Helen Smith with Thomas F. Tomlinson, University of Florida Oral History Project, Apr. 16, 1982, at 7; Hager, *Parents in Uproar*, Gainesville Sun, Feb. 21, 1968, at 1; Superintendent Talbot stated he had only sixty-four substitutes with college degrees.

82 Hager, *Parents in Uproar*, Gainesville Sun, Feb. 21, 1968, at 1; *Use Qualified Teachers Only, Wilcox Said*, Gainesville Sun, Feb. 22, 1968, at 7.

83 *Close School, Says Women Vote League*, Gainesville Sun, Feb. 22, 1968, at 19.

84 *Urges Visit to Schools*, Gainesville Sun, Feb, 28, 1968, at 3A.

85 *Classroom Visits by Public Held Up*, Gainesville Sun, March 6, 1968, at 1. That action was later labeled "unofficial," and parents vowed to continue visits. *School Ruling Said "Unofficial,"* and Filson, *Parent Group Plans Visits to Schools Despite Ruling*, Gainesville Sun, March 7, 1968, at 1.

86 Filson, *Parent Group Plans Visits to Schools Despite Ruling*, Gainesville Sun, March 7, 1968, at 1.

[87] Hager, *Area Teachers Decide Sunday if They'll Return to Classes*, Gainesville Sun, March 9, 1968, at 1.

[88] *FEA Calls Off Walkout*, Gainesville Sun, March 8, 1968, at 1; Martin Waldron, *Teacher Walkout Appears at End*, Gainesville Sun, March 9, 1968, at 1 (NY Times Service).

[89] Cormier, *Teacher Recruiters Here*, Gainesville Sun, March 7, 1968, at 5.

[90] *School Board Minutes, supra* note. 4, vol. 14, at 3715 (March 14, 1968); *Resignations Are Being Returned*, Gainesville Sun, March 15, 1968, at 5.

[91] Interview by Helen Smith with Thomas F. Tomlinson, *supra* note 81, at 11.

[92] Cormier, *Teacher Pay Raises Approved in County*, Gainesville Sun, May 3, 1968, at 1.

[93] Cormier, *School's Closed: The Great Teacher Walkout of '68*, Gainesville Sun, Feb. 18, 1973, at 14A.

[94] *Half of County Teachers Out*, Gainesville Sun, Feb. 19, 1968, at 1.

[95] Cormier, *School Bond Vote Likely on May 28*, Gainesville Sun, March 15, 1968, at 1.

[96] *School Board Minutes, supra* note 4, vol. 14, at 3716 (April 4, 1968).

[97] Cormier, *Bond Issue Tops the Ballot*, Gainesville Sun, May 26, 1968, at 1.

[98] Cormier, *School Bond Needs Outlined at Forum*, Gainesville Sun, Apr. 10, 1968, at 1A.

[99] Cormier, *High Springs, Alachua Schools: Old and Crowded*, Gainesville Sun, May 23, 1968, at 1.

[100] Cormier, *School Bond Needs Outlined at Forum*, Gainesville Sun, Ap.10, 1968, at 1A.

[101] *School Board Minutes, supra* note 4, vol. 14, at 3724 (Apr. 11, 1968).

[102] *School Board Minutes, supra* note 4, vol. 14, at 3726 (Apr. 11, 1968).

[103] Cormier, *School Bond Needs Outlined at Forum*, Gainesville Sun, Apr.10, 1968, at 1A; Cormier, *GHS Keeps Accreditation, Not So for Mebane High*, Gainesville Sun, Nov. 15, 1968, at 1.

[104] *School Board Minutes, supra* note 4, vol. 14, at 3722–27 (Apr. 11, 1968).

[105] Cormier, *Students Resent Newberry's Outmoded Schools*, Gainesville Sun, May 22, 1968, at 1.

[106] *SFJC, School Board Part Ways*, Gainesville Sun, May 17, 1968, at 2.

[107] Cormier, *Some Sparks Fly in School Board Race*, Gainesville Sun, Apr.16, 1968, at 1; Cormier, *School Choice Plan Attacked at Board Forum*, Gainesville Sun, Apr. 24, 1968, at 1; *Superintendent of Public Instruction*, Gainesville Sun, May 5, 1968, at 3D (Candidate Q&A).

[108] Cormier, *School Choice Plan Attacked at Board Forum*, Gainesville Sun, Apr. 24, 1968, at 1.

[109] www.gainesville.com/news/20050915/september-15-2005 (last visited May 25, 2017).

[110] Telephone Interview with Kayser Enneking, M.D., Jan. 22, 2015 (notes, on file with author).

[111] Telephone Interview with Tommy Tomlinson at 1 and 7 (Aug. 27, 2014) (notes, on file with author).

[112] Interview with Tommy Tomlinson, in Gainesville, Fla., at 13 (Sept. 10, 2014) (on file with author).

[113] *School Board Minutes, supra* note 4, vol. 14, at 3765 (May 29, 1968).

114 *PTA Plans Home Visits on Bond Issue*, Gainesville Sun, May 20, 1968, at 4.

115 Cormier, *School Bond Issue Approved*, Gainesville Sun, May 29, 1968, at 1.

116 Green v. Cty. School Bd., 391 U.S. 430, 437 (1968). The Supreme Court took note of the same Civil Rights Commission report that had been discussed by the Fifth Circuit in *Jefferson County*. 391 U.S. at 440 n.5. The Supreme Court rejected the argument that the Fourteenth Amendment can be used only to strike down discriminatory state action, but not to require affirmative actions to correct such discrimination. In so holding, the court interpreted *Brown II*'s mandate for "a racially nondiscriminatory school system" to mean that every dual system must be converted to a unitary system to remedy its prior unconstitutional deficiencies. 391 U.S. at 437. Judge Wisdom had made the same interpretation in *Jefferson County*.

117 *Id.* at 439–41.

118 *Id.* at 441–42.

CHAPTER 9

1 Lincoln High School Alma Mater, in Albert White & Kevin McCarthy, Lincoln High School, Its History and Legacy 198 (2011).

2 *See infra* ch. 15.

3 Jeffry L. Charbonnet, The Public School System of Alachua County 1821-1955, at 69 (1991) (unpublished master's thesis, University of Florida) (on file with author) (citing an 1866 letter from Barnes and Bent).

4 Murray D. Laurie, *The Union Academy: A Freedmen's Bureau School in Gainesville, Florida*, 65 Fla. Hist. Q. 163, 166–68 (1986).

5 Charbonnet, *supra* note 3, at 78.

6 Laurie, *supra* note 4, at 169–71; Charbonnet, *supra* note 3, at 95.

7 Thomas Everette Cochrane, History of Public-School Education in Florida 73–75, 97–98 (1921); Charbonnet, *supra* note 3, at 139.

8 Cochrane, *supra* note 7, at 99–100; Charbonnet, *supra* note 3, at 138–39.

9 Charbonnet, *supra* note 3, at 140.

10 A. Quinn Jones, Sr., Retrospections, November 1967 48–52 (2003).

11 Charbonnet, *supra* note 3, at 68–70, 74–75, 95, 114–15, 158–59, 199–200, 210, 230; Laurie, *supra* note 4, at 163. A new white high school was also constructed on West University Avenue using the same bond issue.

12 Jones, *supra* note 10, at 20, 59–60, 68, 78–80, 87.

13 Eric Foner, Reconstruction: America's Unfinished Revolution, 1863-1877 535 (2002).

14 Nathan Mayo, State of Fla., The Fifth Census of the State of Florida Taken in the Year 1925, at 16 tbl.2, 78 tbl.19 (1926).

15 *Id.* at 94 tbl.25.

16 Jones, *supra* note 10, at 47–48; White & McCarthy, *supra* note 1, at 28.

17 Charbonnet, *supra* note 3, at 323.

18 White & McCarthy, *supra* note 1, at 49, 57.

19 Arthur O. White, The History of Lincoln High: "The Big Red" 7 (undated), http://ufdc.ufl.edu/AA00008787/00001, (last visited Jan. 28, 2017); Dale A.

Thomas, A Band in Every School: Portraits of Historically Black School Bands in Florida 62, 126 (2008). Lincoln High hosted one of the last northern district band festivals of the black Florida Association of Bandmasters in 1965. Thomas, *supra*, at 116.

20 Ben Childs, *Around Town with Ben Childs*, Gainesville Sun, Oct. 29, 1965, at 5; *Drum Up New GHS Band Outfits*, Gainesville Sun, Nov. 7, 1965, at 6A.

21 Jones, *supra* note 10, at 83–86.

22 Telephone Interview with Catherine Mickle 4 (Oct. 2, 2015) (on file with author).

23 Interview with Charles Chestnut III, in Gainesville, Fla. 30 (Apr. 14, 2014) (on file with author).

24 See *infra* ch. 5.

25 *Lincoln High Fully Accredited 1st Time*, Gainesville Sun, Dec. 3, 1964, at 1.

26 For information on White's background, see White & McCarthy, *supra* note 1, at 207.

27 Sherman Dorn & Deanna L. Michael, *Education Finance Reform in Florida, in* Education Reform in Florida: Diversity and Equity in Public Policy 57 (Kathryn M. Borman & Sherman Dorn eds., 2007).

28 Interview by Joel Buchanan with Cora Roberson, in Gainesville, Florida 13 (Feb. 19, 1986), http://ufdc.ufl.edu/UF00005433/00001; interview with Cora Roberson, in Gainesville, Fla. (Nov. 3, 2014) (on file with author); interview with the Rev. Thomas A. Wright, Sr., in Gainesville, Fla. 10 (March 26, 2012) (on file with author).

29 Interview with Charles Chestnut III, *supra* note 23, at 3–4.

30 *Id.* at 3.

31 *See generally* Diedre Faith Houchon, The Transcendent Pedagogy of Lincoln High School, 1921-1955: The Aims, Pursuits and Professional Development of African American Education During *De Jure* Segregation (2015) (unpublished Ph.D. dissertation, University of Florida) (on file with author).

32 White & McCarthy, *supra* note 1, at 19–20.

33 *Id.* at 83–84.

34 Records Committee Report, § VIII, at 4, *in* University of Florida Smathers Library Special and Area Studies Collections, Box 13, MS Group 149, File 38/I/7 (from student handbook, 1963-64) [hereinafter *EDF 600 File*]. This file contains materials from a 1972 College of Education course taught by Professor Arthur O. White. The Records Committee for the course completed a paper that summarized available records from Lincoln High at that time. The paper states that records prior to 1950 are very incomplete and have information only for a few students. From 1950 through the school's closing in 1969, the records "seem to be very complete." White, *supra* note 19, is a twenty-two-page typed very high level summary of the course's work that was prepared by the Vocational Office Education Department at what became the Lincoln vocational center. Much of this general history, especially related to desegregation (as distinguished from the interview excerpts) is inaccurate.

35 White & McCarthy, *supra* note 1, at 206.

36 Interview with Rev. Thomas A. Wright, *supra* note 28, at 5–6.

37 White & McCarthy, *supra* note 1, at 37. James Weldon Johnson taught and later served as principal at Stanton School in nearby Jacksonville, before migrating to New York. Among his many later achievements, he served as executive secretary of the NAACP and was a leader of the Harlem Renaissance.

38 Interview with Wayne Mosley, in Gainesville, Fla. (Sept. 11, 2014) (on file with author).

39 Interview by Joel Buchanan with John Dukes, Jr., in Gainesville, Fla. (Aug. 2, 1985), http://ufdc.ufl.edu/UF00005423/00001; Joel Achenbach, *The Boy on the Bus*, Wash. Post, July 8, 2007, at B1.

40 Interview with Jessie Heard, in Gainesville, Fla. 11 (Feb. 4, 2014) (on file with author).

41 Interview with the Rev. Thomas A. Wright, *supra* note 28, at 3. Attorney Drew Days III of the NAACP Legal Defense Fund in October 1969 became lead counsel for the plaintiffs in *Wright v. Board*. Notice of Appearance (*Wright v. Board*, Oct. 6, 1969).

42 *Court Adopts County School Integration Plan*, Gainesville Sun, Apr. 6, 1965, at 1. *See supra*, ch. 5.

43 Supplement to Motion for Further Relief (*Wright v. Board*, Sept. 26, 1966).

44 Thomas A. Wright, Sr., Courage in Persona 134 (1993); interview by Joel Buchanan with Reverend Thomas A. Wright, in Gainesville, Fla. (Jan. 23, 1986), http://ufdc.ufl.edu/UF00005427/00001 (last visited Jan. 29, 2017).

45 Interview with Charles Chestnut III, in Gainesville, Fla. 2–5 (Sept. 10, 2014) (on file with author).

46 *Id.* at 2.

47 Cormier, *Integration Plan Disliked*, Gainesville Sun, Mar. 3, 1969, at 1.

48 Interview by Mathletha Fuller with Dr. John C. Rawls, in Gainesville, Fla. (Apr. 13, 2011), Samuel Proctor Oral History Project, audio recording at 1:55:40.

49 Terry Leiva, *Summary of Interview with Andrew Mickle, in EDF 600 File, supra* note 34, at 2. Mickle is referring to teachers who passed the National Teachers Exam; *see infra* at note 70.

50 Field notes, *in EDF 600 File, supra* note 34, at 20.

51 Interview with Bettye & Ed Jennings, in Gainesville, Fla. 7 (Feb. 7, 2013) (on file with author).

52 *Id.* at 8.

53 Interview with Brenda Wims, in Gainesville, Fla. 12 (Jan. 28, 2016).

54 Interview with Charles Chestnut III, *supra* note 23, at 23.

55 See *infra* ch. 6, at notes 38–42.

56 James T. Patterson, A Civil Rights Milestone and Its Troubled Legacy 19–20 (2002).

57 Derrick A. Bell, Jr., *Serving Two Masters: Integration Ideals and Client Interests in School Desegregation Litigation*, 85 Yale L. J. 470, 478 (1976).

58 *Id.* at 470 n.1, 482–83; *see* J. Anthony Lukas, Common Ground: A Turbulent Decade in the Lives of Three American Families (1986).

59 Bell, *supra* note 57, at 476 n. 21.

60 *EDF 600 File, supra* note 34.

61 *See* Interview Report of Sam Taylor, Jr., *in EDF 600 File, supra* note 34.

62 Charles Chestnut III was twenty-three in 1963. He was profiled in the *Sun* as the leader of the 295-member Youth Movement, the junior branch of the NAACP. He is quoted as saying, "I didn't know how inadequate my education had been" until he attended an integrated embalming school in Philadelphia. However, from that article, it appears that Chestnut attended Ocala Howard High School and Bethune-Cookman College. *Charles Chestnut III, Is Leader of NAACP "Youth Movement" Here*, Gainesville Sun, July 7, 1963, at 2C. Neil Butler graduated from Lincoln High in 1947. His 1963 comments on Lincoln are discussed later. Neil Butler, Letter to Editor, *Negro Tells of Humiliation and Hopes*, Gainesville Sun, July 29, 1963, at 4.

63 Interview by Donald Sanchez with Dr. Isaac Jones, in Gainesville, Fla. (June 4, 2010), http://ufdc.ufl.edu/AA00015856/00001 (voice recording); Paper, Interview, Sam Taylor, Jr., 1964 Graduate, in *EDF 600 File, supra* note 34 (some teachers had low expectations); interview with Sandra Sharron & Frank Ford, in Gainesville, Fla. 27 (Oct. 30, 2014) (on file with author) ("We could have used some better teachers at Lincoln. Some of the teachers at Lincoln was really out of date and should have been retired and wasn't. Why? I don't know").

64 Interview with Brenda Wims, *supra* note 53, at 10.

65 Telephone Interview with Donnie Batie, M.D. 8–9 (July 28, 2015) (on file with author).

66 Interview with Alvin Butler, in Gainesville, Fla. 11–12 (March 11, 2016).

67 Cormier, *Negro Teachers Casualties of City Integration?*, Gainesville Sun, July 8, 1965, at 1.

68 *Id.*

69 Cormier, *School Headaches Return Like Migraine*, Gainesville Sun, Aug. 12, 1971, at 1.

70 Records Committee Report, *EDF 600 File, supra* note 34, § IV.

71 U.S. Department of Health, Education, and Welfare, Office of Education, Equality of Educational Opportunity (James S. Coleman *et al.*) 20 (1966). This report was conceived and prepared in response to the Civil Rights Act of 1964, Pub. L. No. 88–352, 78 Stat. 241 (1964).

72 Cormier, *Students Poor Readers*, Gainesville Sun, Dec. 17, 1965, at 1.

73 Cormier, *Lincoln Students Get Meeting with School Board*, Gainesville Sun, Nov. 30, 1969, at 1.

74 Interview by Donald Sanchez with Dr. Isaac Jones, *supra* note 63.

75 Records Committee Report, *EDF 600 File, supra* note 34, § V, Miscellaneous Information About Graduation ¶ 5.

76 White & McCarthy, *supra* note 1, at 201–02.

77 Amicus Curiae Brief of the Attorney General of Florida at 7–11 and 189–190, Brown v. Bd. of Educ., 349 U.S. 294 (1954), no. 1, Oct. Term, 1954, 1954 WL 45715, at 7–9 and 101.

78 *Id.*, app. A, tTable 4, 1954 WL 45715 at 104–5.

79 Field notes, *in EDF 600 File, supra* note 34, at 24.

80 *Id.* at 20–21. Lincoln graduated 144 seniors in 1969, its last full year of operation. White & McCarthy, *supra* note 1, at 272–74.

81 Interview by Joel Buchanan with Andrew Mickle, in Gainesville, Fla. 16–17 (July 31, 1985), http://ufdc.ufl.edu/UF00005422/00001.

82 Records Committee Report, *EDF 600 File, supra* note 34, § III, at 5–6, § VIII, at 2; Field notes, *in EDF 600 File, supra* note 35, at 20 (Mabel Dorsey).

83 Records Committee Report, *EDF 600 File, supra* note 34, § IX.D (Internship During Spring Quarter 1969).

84 Field notes, *in EDF 600 File, supra* note 34, at 20 (Mabel Dorsey).

85 Interview by Joel Buchanan with A. Quinn Jones & his son Oliver & daughter Vera, in Gainesville, Fla. 8–9 (Sept. 7, 1994) (transcript on file with University of Florida Samuel Proctor Oral History Project).

86 *Id.* at 6.

87 Interview by Mathletha Fuller with Dr. John C. Rawls, *supra* note 48, at 1:11.

88 Interview with Charles Chestnut III, *supra* note 23, at 4–5.

89 Interview with Sandra Sharron & Frank Ford, *supra* note 63, at 19.

90 Records Committee Report, *EDF 600 File, supra* note 34, § XI.

91 *Infra* tbl.5.

92 Telephone Interview with Donnie Batie, M.D., *supra* note 65, at 16–17.

93 The 1963–64 school year was the last before the first black students began attending white schools in Alachua County under freedom of choice.

94 At the time Taylor attended Lincoln, the principal was Otha W. Nealy and the school superintendent was E.D. Manning Jr.

95 Paper, Interview, Sam Taylor, Jr., 1964 Graduate, in *EDF 600 File, supra* note 34. The name of the interviewer does not appear in the file. The report contains a number of spelling errors that are not corrected.

96 Summary of Interview with Albert Daniels, in *EDF 600 File, supra* note 34; interview by Joel Buchanan with John Dukes, Jr., *supra* note 40, at 20.

97 Interview by Joel Buchanan with John Dukes, Jr., *supra* note 39, at 24–25.

98 *Id.* at 24.

99 Summary of Interview with Albert Daniels, *supra* note 96, at 2.

100 Interview by Joel Buchanan with John Dukes, Jr., *supra* note 39.

101 Cornelius Norton, a longtime black teacher and principal, states Jones's position was changed so that he ceased to have authority to hire and fire teachers and principals. When schools desegregated, there was no need for a supervisor of black schools. Interview by Joel Buchanan with Dr. Cornelius Norton, in Gainesville, Fla. 9–10 (Apr. 24, 1984), http://ufdc.ufl.edu/UF00005409/00001.

102 Interview by Gayle Yamada with Joel Buchanan, in Gainesville, Fla. 6–7 (Feb. 12, 1984), http://ufdc.ufl.edu/UF00005406/00001; interview by Steve Davis with Rosa Williams, in Gainesville, Fla. (Apr. 28, 2009) (audio record on file with University of Florida Samuel Proctor Oral History Project).

103 CORE is the Congress of Racial Equality, and SNCC was the Student National Coordinating Committee. Both organizations were, at the time, considered more militant, with younger leaderships, than the NAACP.

104 Interview by Douglas Malenfant with Thomas Coward, in Gainesville, Fla. (June 5, 2009), audio record at http://ufdc.ufl.edu/AA00015871/00001; White & McCarthy, *supra* note 1, at 95, 255.

105 Interview with Bernice Dukes, John Dukes III & Carmen Dukes, in Gainesville, Fla. 17–18 (July 11, 2014) (on file with author).

106 White & McCarthy, *supra* note 1, at 153 (Dukes's position on the county staff).

107 Interview by Joel Buchanan with John Dukes, Jr., *supra* note 39, at 15–16.

CHAPTER 10

1 *See supra* tbl.2, ch. 6.

2 Attachment to letter from Alachua County Board of Public Instruction to Honorable G. Harrold Carswell (*Wright v. Board*, July 7, 1967).

3 *See infra*, tbl.5, ch. 17, and Report to Court, Alachua County Board of Public Instruction (*Wright v. Board*, Oct. 15, 1968).

4 Cormier, *County's Pupils Integrating but Faculty Mixing Is Slow*, Gainesville Sun, June 24, 1968, at 1, quoting Tommy Tomlinson.

5 Cormier, *Alachua Co. School Board to Study Educational System*, Gainesville Sun, July 28, 1968, at 6A; *Minutes*, Alachua Cty. Bd. Pub. Instruction, vol. 14, at 3922 (Jan. 9, 1969) [the collected minutes are hereinafter *School Board Minutes*].

6 Plaintiffs' Motion for Further Relief (*Wright v. Board*, Oct. 21, 1968).

7 *School Board Minutes*, *supra* note 5, vol. 13 at 3655 (Dec. 14, 1967).

8 *Desegregation Challenge Stalls Lincoln Expansion*, Gainesville Sun, Jan. 24, 1969, at 12. The court record in *Wright v. Board* is devoid of any mention of Arnow's participation, and there is no transcript of this hearing. Judges are usually disqualified from participating in cases in which they acted as advocates prior to being appointed to the bench.

9 *Desegregation Challenge Stalls Lincoln Expansion*, Gainesville Sun, Jan. 24, 1969, at 12.

10 Order (*Wright v. Board*, Jan. 23, 1969),

11 *Desegregation Challenge Stalls Lincoln Expansion*, Gainesville Sun, Jan. 24, 1969, at 12; Cormier, *County Schools Facing New Crisis in Race Problems*, Gainesville Sun, Dec. 19, 1968, at 1.

12 Cormier, *County Schools Facing New Crisis in Race Problems*, Gainesville Sun, Dec. 19, 1968, at 1.

13 *Desegregation Plan Here Due Airing*, Gainesville Sun, Feb. 26, 1969, at 1.

14 Cormier, *Board Okays School Plan to Integrate*, Gainesville Sun, Feb. 27, 1969, at 1.

15 Certificate of Service accompanying Plan of the Board of Public Instruction of Alachua County, Florida for compliance with Section VI of the Civil Rights Act and the Orders of the United States District Court for the Northern District of Florida (*Wright v. Board* Feb. 28, 1969) [hereinafter *February 1969 Plan*].

16 *February 1969 Plan*, *supra* note 15, at 2–3.

17 *Id.* at 9.

18 *Id.* at 8.

19 Florida School Desegregation Consulting Center, "A Desegregation Plan for Alachua County Public Schools," Apr., 1969, at 13–16, in Alachua County Board of Public Instruction, Informal Desegregation File at 249–52 (undated) [hereinafter *School Board File*].

20 *February 1969 Plan*, *supra* note 15, at 3–9.

21 Cormier, *GHS Keeps Accreditation, Not So for Mebane High*, Gainesville Sun, Nov. 15, 1968, at 1.

22 *Id.*

23 *February 1969 Plan*, *supra* note 15, at 3 and 9.

24 Cormier, *County Schools Facing New Crisis in Race Problems*, Gainesville Sun, Dec. 19, 1968, at 1.

25 Telephone Interview with Tommy Tomlinson, at 7 (Aug. 27, 2014) (on file with author).

26 Cormier, *Integration Plan Disliked*, Gainesville Sun, March 3, 1969, at 1.

27 *See supra*, ch. 8; *New County Schools Are Supported*, Gainesville Sun, Dec. 15, 1967, at 1; Cormier, *County Schools Facing New Crisis in Race Problems*, Gainesville Sun, Dec. 19, 1968, at 1; and *Desegregation Challenge Stalls Lincoln Expansion*, Gainesville Sun, Jan. 24, 1969, at 12.

28 Cormier, *GHS Keeps Accreditation, Not So for Mebane High*, Gainesville Sun, Nov. 15, 1968, at 1.

29 Cormier, *Board Okays School Plan to Integrate*, Gainesville Sun, Feb. 27, 1969, at 1.

30 *Id.*

31 *Id.*

32 Cormier, *Integration Plan Disliked*, Gainesville Sun, Mar. 3, 1969, at 1.

33 Cormier, *You Don't Get the Whole Story at School Board Meetings*, Gainesville Sun, Oct. 20, 1968, at 5B.

34 Cormier, *School Plan Due Appeal by NAACP*, Gainesville Sun, Mar. 5, 1969, at 1.

35 *Id.*

36 The school board court filing for the 1969–70 school year showed that approximately 32 percent of county students were black. Roughly the same ratio applied to grades 10–12. Letter from Tommy Tomlinson to Honorable G. Harrold Carswell (*Wright v. Board*, Sept. 26, 1969).

37 Thomas A. Wright, Sr., Letter to the Editor, Gainesville Sun, Mar. 3, 1969, at 6. *See* ch. 14, *infra*.

38 Plaintiffs' Objections to Defendant Board's Plan of Desegregation for Second Semester 1969-70 and for the Academic Year 1970-71, *Wright v. Board* (March 9, 1970)

39 Plaintiffs' Motion for an Evidentiary Hearing on Defendants' Proposed Plan for the School Year 1969-70, *Wright v. Board* (Feb. 28, 1969).

40 *Judge Carswell Lauds County School Mixing Plan*, Gainesville Sun, Mar. 4, 1969, at 1.

41 *Id.*

42 Cormier, *School Plan Due Appeal by NAACP*, Gainesville Sun, Mar. 5, 1969, at 1.

43 *Id.*

44 *Judge Carswell Lauds County School Mixing Plan*, Gainesville Sun, Mar. 4, 1969, at 1.

45 Order Denying Motion for an Evidentiary Hearing on Defendants' Proposed Plan for the School Year 1969-70, *Wright v. Board* (Mar. 4, 1969).

46 Jack Bass, *Unlikely Heroes* 322, general discussion at 318–23 (1990).

47 Paul R. Baier, *Framing and Reviewing a Desegregation Decree: Of the Chancellor's Foot and Fifth Circuit Control*, 47 La. L. Rev. 123 (1986).

48 U. of D.C., David A. Clarke School of Law, Biography of William L. Robinson, Olie W. Rauh Prof. of Law, www.law.udc.edu/?page=WRobinson, (last visited Sept. 25, 2016); Greenberg, *Crusaders in the Courts* (2004), 406.

49 The Defense Fund also argued that the school board had failed to substantiate the nature of the "confusion and multiple transfers" that would result if freedom of choice were to be abandoned a year before the new schools were ready. The Fund stated that multiple transfers were possible and occurred each year under freedom of choice. The Fund also sought leave to file separate objections at a later time to the portions of the plan to be implemented in the 1970–71 school year. Plaintiffs' Objections to Defendants' Proposed Plan, *Wright v. Board* (Mar. 19, 1969).

50 Defendants' Motion to Strike Plaintiffs' Objections to Proposed Plan and, in the Alternative, Response to Plaintiffs' Objections to Defendants' Proposed Plan, *Wright v. Board* (Mar. 24, 1969).

51 Order, *Wright v. Board* (Apr. 3, 1969).

52 Notice of Appeal, *Wright v. Board* (May 2, 1969).

53 Letter and attached spreadsheets, *supra* note 36. *See also supra*, tbl.2, ch. 6.

54 *Id.*

55 In approving a minor modification to the plan, Judge Carswell had given the school board permission to modify the plan without notice or court approval as long as the modification did not change enrollment at any school by more than 2 percent. Order Granting Motion of Defendants to Amend Plan of Desegregation, (*Wright v. Board*, July 23, 1969).

56 Notice of Appearance, *Wright v. Board* (Oct. 6, 1969); Motion to Withdraw as Counsel, *Wright v. Board* (Oct. 30, 1969); Order, *Wright v. Board* (Nov. 10, 1969).

57 Albert White & Kevin McCarthy, Lincoln High School, Its History and Legacy, at 38 (2011).

58 Yale Law School, Drew S. Days III biography, https://www.law.yale.edu/drew-s-days-iii (last visited Jan. 30, 2017).

59 Department of Health, Education, and Welfare, Office of Civil Rights, Policies on Elementary and Secondary School Compliance with the Civil Rights Act of 1964, 33 Fed Reg. 4955, § 11, at 4956 (Mar. 23, 1968) (not codified in C.F.R.). This guidance superseded the HEW policies issued in Mar., 1966, and amended in Dec., 1966, as 45 C.F.R. Part 181. *Id.*, § 5, at 4955.

60 Green v. Cty. School Bd., 391 U.S. 430, 438–39 (1968).

61 *Nixon Counters Supreme Court Stand on "Freedom of Choice,"* Gainesville Sun, Nov. 16, 1968, at 16.

62 Dean J. Kotlowski, Nixon's Civil Rights, at 27–31 (2001). An insider's account of that period is given by Leon Panetta, then serving as director of HEW's Office of Civil Rights, HEW's enforcement arm. Leon Panetta and Peter Gall, Bring Us Together (1971).

63 Greenberg, *supra* note 48, at 413.

64 Alexander v. Holmes Cty. Bd. of Education, 396 U.S. 1218 (1969).

65 Adams v. Matthews, 403 F.2d 181 (5th Cir. 1968).

66 U.S. v. Hinds Cty. School Bd., 417 F.2d 852, 857–58 (5th Cir. 1969), *cert. denied*, 396 U.S. 1032 (1970).

67 *Id.*, 417 F.2d at 858–59.

68 U.S. Dept. of Justice, Statement by The Honorable Robert H. Finch, Secretary of the Department of Health, Education, and Welfare, and The Honorable John N. Mitchell, Attorney General, July 3, 1969, https://www.justice.gov/sites/default/files/ag/legacy/2011/08/23/07-03-1969.pdf, (last visited Jan. 21, 2017).

69 Greenberg, *supra* note 48, at 413; Kotlowski, *supra* note 62, at 30–31.

70 Memorandum for the United States as Amicus Curiae, Green v. Cty. School Bd. and two other cases, Nos. 695, 740 and 805 (U.S. Supreme Court, Feb. 29, 1968).

71 The history of this litigation is summarized in Alexander v. Holmes Cty. Bd. of Education, *supra* note 64, 396 U.S. 1218.

72 Alexander v. Holmes Cty. Bd. of Education, *supra* note 64, 396 U.S. at 1220. Justice Black served as the circuit justice for the Fifth Circuit, which meant that as an individual justice he received and ruled on any requests for extraordinary relief from decisions of that circuit.

73 This committee was led by many prominent lawyers. The case was argued by Louis F. Oberdorfer, a native of Birmingham, Alabama. Oberdorfer had clerked for Justice Black and at the time was a prominent Washington, DC, attorney. He later became a federal district court judge. He was supported on the brief by, among others, Cyrus Vance.

74 Alexander v. Holmes Cty. Bd. of Education, 396 U.S. 19 (1969); Greenberg, *supra* note 48, at 414–16.

75 U.S. v. Hinds Cty. School Bd., 423 F.2d 1264 (5th Cir. 1969).

76 Greenberg, *supra* note 48, at 416.

77 Memorandum of the United States, Singleton v. Jackson Municipal School Dist., Nos. 26285, 27863, 28045, 28261, 28340, 28342, 28349, 23450, 28361, 28407, 28408, and 28049, at 1 (5th Cir., undated, post-*Alexander*).

78 *Id.* at 73–75 and Brief for Appellants, LaVon Wright v. Board of Public Instruction of Alachua County, Florida, No. 27983 (5th Cir, Aug. 9, 1969). The caseloads of both the Justice Department and the Defense Fund show in these briefs. The Justice Department misunderstood Alachua County's plan, arguing that achievement of a unitary system would be postponed until the 1971–72 school year. Department of Justice Memorandum, 73–76. The Defense Fund, although competently reciting the applicable law, also misunderstood that the three-year phasing of the plan was not intended to preserve black schools, but was instead intended to allow students currently in the tenth and eleventh grades to complete high school at Gainesville High, rather than being transferred first to Gainesville High and then to either of the two new secondary schools. The Defense Fund, casting doubt on Alachua County's credibility, characterized its construction plan as a "grandiose, complex program of school construction that may be completed by September 1970." Brief for Appellants at 7. The National Archive file on this Fifth Circuit case is incomplete, having been damaged in New Orleans during Hurricane Katrina. What remains is currently housed at the National Archives in Fort Worth, Texas.

79 Telephone Interview with Tommy Tomlinson, *supra* note 25, at 5.

80 *South Instant Integration Order Looms*, Gainesville Sun, Nov. 19, 1969, at 1.

81 Singleton v. Jackson Mun. Separate School Dist., 419 F.2d 1211 (5th Cir. 1970), en banc, *vacated in part sub nom.* Carter v. West Feliciana Parish School Bd., 396 U.S. 226 (1969); *rev'd sub nom.* Carter v. West Feliciana Parish School Board, 396 U.S. 290 (1970).

82 *Id.*, 419 F.2d at 1216–17.

83 *Id.*, 419 F.2d at 1217 and n.1.

84 *Id.*, 419 F.2d at 1217–19 and n.2.

85 *Id.*, 419 F.2d at 1222.

86 Carter v. West Feliciana Parish School Board, 396 U.S. 226 (1969). Justice Black issued a similar order in the remaining cases in *Singleton* on December 15, 1969, in Stout v. Jefferson Cty. Bd. of Education, U.S. Supreme Court, Order, Dec. 15, 1969 (unpublished; copy in *School Board File*, at 344–45).

87 Memorandum for the United States, Carter v. West Feliciana Parish School Board, Nos. 944 and 972 (U.S. Supreme Court, Dec. 1969).

88 Carter v. West Feliciana Parish School Board, 396 U.S. 290, 291 (1970). The other Fifth Circuit cases in *Singleton*, including *Wright v. Board*, were also disposed of in this decision.

89 *Id.*, 396 U.S. at 291–293.

90 *Id.*, 396 U.S. at 293.

91 *Id.*, 396 U.S. at 293–4.

92 *Singleton, supra* note 81, 425 F.2d 1211. Judge Carswell, who had been nominated by President Nixon to the Supreme Court on January 19, 1970, was not among the dissenters.

93 Kotlowski, *supra* note 62, at 36–37 and 41–43; Joan Hoff, Nixon Reconsidered, at 83–90 (1994); Tom Wicker, One of Us: Richard Nixon and the American Dream, at 501–507 (1991).

94 P.L. 92–318, tit. VII, 86 Stat. 354 (1972); William Bagley, Emergency School Assistance, Issue Brief No. IB74082, The Library of Congress, Congressional Research Service (1976), http://digitalcollections.library.cmu.edu/awweb/awarchive?type=file&item=401682 (last visited Jan. 21, 2017).

95 *See* Erica Frankenberg and Kendra Taylor, *ESEA and the Civil Rights Act: An Interbranch Approach to Furthering Desegregation*, 1 Russell Sage Foundation J. of the Social Sciences 32, 42–42 (2015).

CHAPTER 11

1 Cormier, *Cool Air – New Clothes – Fading Tans*, Gainesville Sun, Aug. 31, 1969, at 1.

2 *Id.*

3 Cormier, *Teachers Receive Lesson in How the Students Talk*, Gainesville Sun, Aug. 21, 1969, at 1.

4 Alfred L. Awbrey, Jr., 100 Years & More of Gainesville High School Football, 1906-2010, 60 (2011).

5 Jack Hairston, *Niblack, McAshan Got Protection from FBI*, Gainesville Sun, July 23, 1971, at 13.

6 Fla. Stat. § 230.222 (1969).

7 Cormier, *GHS Newcomers Came, Saw and They Cheered*, Gainesville Sun, Aug. 31, 1969, at 13A.

8 Letter from Tommy Tomlinson to Honorable G. Harrold Carswell (*Wright v. Board*, Sept. 26, 1969) (including attached spreadsheets). It is not possible from the report to disaggregate special education students at Lincoln High School by grade. Also, these proportions by class could be affected by different zones and different dropout rates for each school.

9 *Id.*

10 Cormier, *"Believe in Yourselves,"* Gainesville Sun, June 7, 1969, at 3.

11 *Id.*

12 Ed Pavelka, *Coach Heard's Other Wife*, Gainesville Sun, Sept. 3, 1969, at 8A.

13 *Lincoln High Conversion to Be Explained Further*, Gainesville Sun, Sept. 12, 1969, at 18.

14 *LHS Plans Draw New Fire*, Gainesville Sun, Oct. 24, 1969, at 9.

15 Cormier, *New High School Named Lakewood over Protests*, Gainesville Sun, Nov. 21, 1969, at 1; Cormier, *Lincoln Students Get Meeting with School Board*, Gainesville Sun, Nov. 30, 1969, at 1.

16 Green v. Cty. School Bd., 391 U.S. 430, 442 (1968).

17 Cormier, *1964-1972, The Talbot Years in Alachua County*, Gainesville Sun, Feb. 27, 1972, at 1B.

18 Cormier, *New High School Named Lakewood over Protests*, Gainesville Sun, Nov. 21, 1969, at 1.

19 Editorial, *What's in a Name?*, Gainesville Sun, Nov. 25, 1969, at 6.

20 Dave Hunter, *Terriers Need a Hand*, Gainesville Sun, Nov. 21, 1969, at 15.

21 Doug Hawley, *Eastside, Buchholz Heads Have Similar Backgrounds*, Gainesville Sun, Nov. 16, 1971, at 2B; interview with Jessie Heard, in Gainesville, Fla. (Feb. 4, 2014) (on file with author).

22 *Id.*

23 *Id.*

24 Interview with Wayne Mosley, in Gainesville, Fla., at 5–6 (Sept. 11, 2014) (on file with author).

25 Interview with Jessie Heard, *supra* note 21.

26 *Id.*

27 *Id.*

28 Ralph Mueller, *Lincoln's Thomas Makes (Grid) Scene*, Gainesville Sun, Sept. 4, 1968, at 1B; Ad, *Football Jamboree*, Gainesville Sun, Sept. 4, 1968, at 3B; *GHS, Lincoln, Starke Await Jamboree Tests*, Gainesville Sun, Sept. 5, 1968, at 1B; Don Ashley, *Jamboree Provides Excitement*, Gainesville Sun, Sept. 6, 1968, at 13.

29 Interview with Jessie Heard, *supra* note 21.

30 Interview with Bernice Dukes, John Dukes III & Carmen Dukes, in Gainesville, Fla. 14–15 (July 11, 2014) (on file with author).

31 *"Last Roundup" for Lincoln High*, Gainesville Sun, Nov. 22, 1969, at 13.

32 Jim Almand, *Lincoln Has Happy Ending*, Gainesville Sun, Nov. 23, 1969, at D2.

33 Interview with Jessie Heard, *supra* note 21.

34 Interview by author, Bernice Dukes, John Dukes III & Carmen Dukes, *supra* note 30, at 12.

35 Interview with Wayne Mosley, *supra* note 24, at 10.

36 Cormier and Tatro, *Lincoln High Students Protest*, Gainesville Sun, Nov. 25, 1969, at 1.

37 *Id.*; interview with Wayne Mosley, *supra* note 24.

38 Cormier and Tatro, *Lincoln High Students Protest*, Gainesville Sun, Nov.25, 1969, at 1.

39 Cormier, *1964-1972, The Talbot Years in Alachua County*, Gainesville Sun, Feb. 27, 1972, at 1B.

40 Cormier, *Talbot, Students Not in Harmony*, Gainesville Sun, Nov. 26, 1969, at 1.

41 Cormier, *1964-1972, The Talbot Years in Alachua County*, Gainesville Sun, Feb. 27, 1972, at 1B.

42 Editorial, *What's in a Name?*, Gainesville Sun, Nov. 25, 1969, at 6.

43 *School Close Review Asked*, Gainesville Sun, Nov. 17, 1968, at 1B; Bill Griffin, *Move to Halt Closing of Negro School Fails*, Gainesville Sun, Nov. 27, 1968, at 17.

44 Bill Griffin, *Move to Halt Closing of Negro School Fails*, Gainesville Sun, Nov. 27, 1968, at 17.

45 *Biracial School Boycott Ends at Kirk's Urging*, Gainesville Sun, Mar. 24, 1969, at 15 (Apopka); *Boycotting Pupils Are Suspended*, Gainesville Sun, Apr. 2, 1969, at 1A (West Palm Beach); *Black Boycott Leaves Deland School 75% Empty*, Gainesville Sun, Apr. 12, 1969, at 8; *Put Whites in Black Schools, Daytona Boycotters Urge*, Gainesville Sun, Apr. 15, 1969, at 13; *Sarasota Parents Ignore Threats of Fines, Arrest*, Gainesville Sun, May 9, 1969, at 15; Van Gieson, *Will Florida Schools Finally Be Integrated?*, Gainesville Sun, Aug. 9, 1970, at 12A (Ocala Howard).

46 Eric Sharp, *Black Majority Schools Have Problems*, Gainesville Sun, Aug. 31, 1969, at 5A; Sharp, *Florida Schools' "Tail in the Door,"* Gainesville Sun, Sept. 3, 1969, at 4B.

47 Interview with the Rev. Thomas A. Wright, in Gainesville, Fla., 4–5 (Mar. 26, 2012) (on file with author).

48 Sharp, *Florida Schools' "Tail in the Door,"* Gainesville Sun, Sept. 3, 1969, at 4B.

49 *See infra* ch. 15.

50 Sharp, *Black Boycotts Against Florida Schools to Increase*, Gainesville Sun, Apr. 6, 1969, at 3B.

51 Cormier, *Talbot, Students Not in Harmony*, Gainesville Sun, Nov. 26, 1969, at 1; *New March Held Today*, Gainesville Sun, Nov. 26, 1969, at 1.

52 Interview with Janice Cambridge Hagillih, Frank Coleman & Cynthia Cook 3 (May 24, 2016) (notes on file with author)

53 *Lincoln Students, Parents Continue School Boycott*, Gainesville Sun, Dec. 6, 1969, at 5.

54 Interview with Wayne Mosley, *supra* note 24, at 13 and 26–27.

55 Interview with Brenda Wims, in Gainesville, Fla. 7 (Jan. 28, 2016) (on file with author).

56 *See* Interview with Jessie Heard, *supra* note 21, at 26; interview with Sandra Sharron and Frank Ford, in Gainesville, Fla. 43 (Oct. 30, 2014,) (Ford) (on file with author).

57 Interview with Brenda Wims, *supra* note 55 at 7.

58 *Students Recess Protests for Holiday Weekend*, and *Talbot Says Name Could Be Changed*, Gainesville Sun, Nov. 27, 1969, at 1.

59 The area has been cleaned up, and its narrow but paved streets are lined with modest but mostly well-restored homes. It is still predominantly black.

60 Larry Jordan, *Blacks See Many Facets to Lincoln High Issue*, Gainesville Sun, Dec. 18, 1969, at 1.

61 Tatro, *Boycott Continues at Lincoln*, Gainesville Sun, Dec. 1, 1969, at 1.

62 *Minutes*, Alachua Cty. Bd. Pub. Instruction, vol. 14, at 4119 (Dec. 1, 1969).

63 Cormier, *Neither Side Will Yield in Lincoln High Hassle*, Gainesville Sun, Dec. 2, 1969, at 1.

64 *School Board Minutes*, *supra* note 62, at 4119.

65 Cormier, *Neither Side Will Yield in Lincoln High Hassle*, Gainesville Sun, Dec. 2, 1969, at 1.

66 *LHS Students Checked,* Gainesville Sun, Dec. 4, 1969, at 1.

67 *Court Action Possible in Lincoln Rift,* Gainesville Sun, Dec. 5, 1969, at 1.

68 *Id.*

69 Cormier, *Truancy Summons Due in Lincoln High Boycott,* Gainesville Sun, Dec. 8, 1969, at 1.

70 *Lincoln Students, Parents Continue School Boycott,* Gainesville Sun, Dec. 6, 1969, at 5.

71 The State of Florida had recently issued bonds to fund new highway construction.

72 Gainesville Sun, Dec. 6, 1969, at 7. The two letters reproduced here were among five appearing that day. See also more letters, Gainesville Sun, Dec. 10, 1969, at 6A.

73 Interview with Wayne Mosley, *supra* note 24.

74 Florida School Desegregation Consulting Center, A Desegregation Plan for the Alachua County Public Schools, at 18, at 16A (*Wright v. Board,* Jan. 26, 1970).

75 *See* Department of Health, Education, and Welfare, Office of Civil Rights, Policies on Elementary and Secondary School Compliance with Title VI of the Civil Rights Act of 1964, §4, 33 Fed. Reg. 4955 (Mar. 23, 1968).

76 Cormier, *Truancy Summons Due in Lincoln High Boycott,* Gainesville Sun, Dec. 8, 1969, at 1.

77 Tatro, *48 Summonses Issued in Lincoln High Dispute,* Gainesville Sun, Dec. 9, 1969, at 1A.

78 Editorial, *We Still Believe,* Gainesville Sun, Dec. 9, 1969, at 6A.

79 Wilson was referring to the trial of the "Chicago Seven," including Abbie Hoffman, by U.S. District Judge Julius Hoffman, for their actions during protests at the 1968 Democratic convention in Chicago.

80 Tatro, *Dismiss Truancy Case Over Procedural Error,* Gainesville Sun, Dec. 10, 1969, at 1.

81 *Id.*

82 Cormier, *School Integration Changes Outlined,* Gainesville Sun, Dec. 11, 1969, at 1.

83 Cormier, *Lincoln Students Return After Pact,* Gainesville Sun, Dec. 12, 1969, at 1.

84 *Id.*

85 *School Board Minutes, supra* note 62, at 4126–27 (Dec. 11, 1969).

86 *Id.* at 4127.

87 Cormier, *Lincoln Students Return After Pact,* Gainesville Sun, Dec. 12, 1969, at 1.

88 *Court Action Possible in Lincoln Rift,* Gainesville Sun, Dec. 5, 1969, at 1.

89 Wright v. Bd. of Pub. Instruction, 431 F.2d 1200, 1202 (5th Cir. 1970).

90 Decree at 7 (*Wright v. Board,* Apr. 25, 1967).

91 *School Board Minutes, supra* note 62, at 4200 (May 12, 1970). Orange and green were the colors of Florida A&M University and also of the University of Miami.

92 Order (*Wright v. Board,* Apr. 3, 1969).

93 Singleton v. Jackson Mun. Separate Sch. Dist., 419 F.2d 1211 (5th Cir. 1969).

CHAPTER 12

1 Cormier, *School Zoning Is Blamed for Off-Balance of Pupils*, Gainesville Sun, Sept. 4, 1969, at 1.

2 Cormier, *Cool Air – New Clothes – Fading Tans*, Gainesville Sun, Aug. 31, 1969, at 1A; *Pupil Tally 2,000 Under Estimates*, Gainesville Sun, Sept. 2, 1969, at 4.

3 This ratio was the ultimate ratio required by the April 3, 1969, plan. The plan approved for Alachua County following the Supreme Court reversal of *Singleton* would require one black teacher to four white teachers in secondary schools and one to four in elementary schools. Report of the Board of Public Instruction of Alachua County, Florida, on Implementing a Unitary School System Effective February 1, 1970, at 5 (*Wright v. Board*, Feb. 9, 1970).

4 Cormier, *Jan. 1 Integration Possible, but Difficult, Talbot Says*, Gainesville Sun, Nov. 20, 1969, at 1.

5 Cormier, *School Integration Changes Outlined*, Gainesville Sun, Dec. 11, 1969, at 1.

6 Cormier, *Lincoln Students Struggle to Make Up for Lost Time*, Gainesville Sun, Dec. 15, 1969, at 1.

7 Motion for an Injunction Requiring Immediate Implementation of a School Desegregation Plan in Bay County, Florida, and Alachua County, Florida, Pending Certiorari to Review a Judgment of the United States Court of Appeals for the Fifth Circuit, Youngblood v. Bd. of Pub. Instruction, Wright v. Bd. of Pub. Instruction (U.S. Supreme Court, Oct. Term, 1969, Dec. 13, 1969 [hereinafter *Legal Defense Fund Dec. 13 Motion*], in Alachua County Board of Public Instruction, Informal Desegregation File 325–40 [hereinafter *School Board File*].

8 *Legal Defense Fund Dec. 13 Motion*, *supra* note 7, at 7.

9 *Id.* at 8–9.

10 *Id.* at 9–10.

11 Telephone Interview with William L. Robinson, June 15, 2017 (on file with author).

12 396 U.S. 226 (1969).

13 Order, Stout v. Jefferson County Board of Education, (U.S. Dec. 15, 1969) (unpublished; copy in *School Board File*, *supra* note 7, at 344–345; *see also* correspondence, John F. Davis, Clerk, U.S. Supreme Court, to Attorney Harry Duncan, among others, Dec. 15, 1969, *School Board File*, *supra*, at 341–43.

14 Transcript of Proceedings Before the Honorable Charles R. Scott, Gainesville, Florida, at 4–11 and 28–30 (*Wright v. Board*, Dec. 19, 1969); *Rush Integration, Schools Here Told*, Gainesville Sun, Dec. 19, 1969, at 1.

15 Order (*Wright v. Board*, Dec. 22, 1969).

16 Cormier, *Desegregation Ruling Clear: Judge Scott*, Gainesville Sun, Dec. 20, 1969, at 1.

17 Cormier, *New School Mixing Plans Stir Up Debate*, Gainesville Sun, Dec. 23, 1969, at 1.

18 Editorial, *The Whole Picture*, Gainesville Sun, Dec. 28, 1969, at 6A.

19 Desegregation Possibilities to be Aired Monday, Gainesville Sun, Dec. 28, 1969, at 5E.

20 Interview with John Dukes III, in Gainesville, Fla., at 18–19 (Mar. 5, 2014) (on file with author).

21 Telephone Interview with Tommy Tomlinson at 5 (Aug. 27, 2014) (notes) (on file with author).

22 Pavelka, *Parents Protest Fast Integration*, Gainesville Sun, Dec. 30, 1969, at 1.

23 Cormier, *Legal Ground Prepared for Desegregation Battle*, Gainesville Sun, Jan. 7, 1970, at 1A.

24 *Id.*

25 Brief of Respondents, the Board of Public Instruction of Alachua County, Florida, *et al.*, in Response to Petition for Writ of Certiorari to the United States Court of Appeals for the Fifth Circuit, Singleton v. Jackson Mun. Separate School District, No. 972 at 6, 7 (U.S. Dec. 31, 1969). The Gainesville Sun printed portions of the brief, *Here's School Board Petition on Desegregation Issue*, Gainesville Sun, Jan. 3, 1970 at 14. School board attorney Harry Duncan assisted Dell on the brief.

26 *Minutes*, Alachua Cty. Bd. Pub. Instruction, vol. 14, at 4129 (Jan. 6, 1970) [hereinafter *School Board Minutes*].

27 Cormier, *Black-White Ratio in School Mixing Aired*, Gainesville Sun, Jan. 9, 1970, at 1.

28 C. Douglas Weaver, Every Town Needs a Downtown Church: A History of First Baptist Church, Gainesville, Florida 130 (2000).

29 Smith had announced in January 1969, upon assuming the chair of the board, that he would not seek another term. Cormier, *Big Problems Lie Ahead but School Head Confident*, Gainesville Sun, Jan. 8, 1969, at 1.

30 *Ebling Named Chairman*, Gainesville Sun, Jan. 7, 1970, at 1A.

31 *Warn of School Closings if Desegregation Rushed*, Gainesville Sun, Jan. 14, 1970, at 2.

32 Carter v. West Feliciana Parish School Board., 396 U.S. 290 (1970).

33 *17 School Board Counsels Seek to Delay Court Order*, Gainesville Sun, Jan. 16, 1970, at 13.

34 *Planning Lacking, FEA Says*, Gainesville Sun, Jan. 17, 1970, at 5.

35 *NAACP Studies Contempt Charges Against Schools*, Gainesville Sun, Jan. 18, 1970, at 1A; *NAACP Warns of Jail*, Gainesville Sun, Jan. 19, 1970, at 11.

36 White and Harlan had issued a separate concurring opinion in Carter v. West Feliciana Parish School Board, 396 U.S. 290, 291–93, in which they stated their belief that the Supreme Court should have provided procedural guidelines for the lower courts in deciding whether integration plans met the immediacy requirements of *Alexander* and *Carter*. Without directly referring to Alachua County's situation, White and Harlan had determined that "in no event" should more than eight weeks elapse between a finding of noncompliance to "the time of the operative effect of the relief," including judicial review.

37 Cormier, *School Delay – Last Ditch Try*, Gainesville Sun, Jan. 20, 1970, at 1; *School Board Minutes, supra* note 26, vol. 14, at 4138 (Jan. 19, 1970).

38 *School Board Minutes, supra* note 26, vol. 14, at 4138 (Jan. 19, 1970).

39 Cormier, *School Delay – Last Ditch Try*, Gainesville Sun, Jan. 20, 1970, at 1. There is no evidence that Alachua County sought political assistance from its senators or representatives in Congress. The Justice Department had not previously been involved in the Alachua County case at the district court level.

40 Telephone Interview with Tommy Tomlinson, *supra* note 21, at 7.

41 Cormier, *School Vacation Plans Still Being Molded*, Gainesville Sun, Jan. 23, 1970, at 1; *School Calendar Straightened Out Again*, Gainesville Sun, Jan. 28, 1970, at 2D.

42 *Id.*

43 Interview with John King, in Gainesville, Fla. at 8 (Apr. 30, 2016) (on file with author).

44 *Id.*

45 *Injuries Reported in Rock Throwings*, Gainesville Sun, Jan. 25, 1970, at 2A.

46 Cormier, *Three Students . . . July '64*, Gainesville Sun, Jan. 25, 1970, at 9A.

47 *Kirk Calls Wallace a "Flaming Liberal,"* Gainesville Sun, Dec. 8, 1967, at 1.

48 Nick Thimmesch, *Wallace in Position to Harry the President*, Los Angeles Times, June 8, 1970, at B9.

49 *Kirk: I'll Go to Jail*, Gainesville Sun, Jan. 24, 1970, at 1; *Kirk Suits Greeted with Joy?* Gainesville Sun, Jan. 30, 1970, at 15.

50 *Christian Charges Kirk "Careless,"* Gainesville Sun, Jan. 25, 1970, at 1. Christian was a decorated artillery battalion commander in World War II who received the Legion of Merit among other medals. After leaving office in 1973, he was investigated for corruption and served jail time for tax evasion.

51 *State Integration Situation Clouded*, Gainesville Sun, Jan. 25, 1970, at 1.

52 *Social, Legal Hassles as Desegregation Nears*, Gainesville Sun, Jan. 27, 1970, at 13; *Kirk Files to Intervene in 4 More School Cases*, Gainesville Sun, Jan. 28, 1970, at 1D.

53 Cormier, *School Plans Proceed Here*, Gainesville Sun, Jan. 27, 1970, at 1.

54 *Confusion Is the Word in Many Dixie Schools*, Gainesville Sun, Feb. 2, 1970, at 2.

55 Rich Oppel, *Kirk Latches On to a Popular Issue*, Gainesville Sun, Jan. 25, 1970, at 11A.

56 *High Court Denies Desegregation Plea*, Gainesville Sun, Jan. 26, 1970, at 1; Carter v. West Feliciana Parish School Board and Singleton v. Jackson Separate Mun. School District, 396 U.S. 1048 (1970) (Denying motion of the governor of Florida for leave to intervene and to recall judgments).

57 Cormier, *School Plans Proceed Here*, Gainesville Sun, Jan. 27, 1970, at 1.

58 Respondents' Petition for Rehearing with Motion to Expedite Hearing at 6–8, Wright v. Bd. of Pub. Instruction, No. 972 (U.S. Jan. 22, 1970).

59 *Id.* at 8–9.

60 Singleton v. Jackson Separate Municipal School District, 396 U.S. 1053 (1970), denying rehearing petitions of The Board of Public Instruction of Alachua County, Florida, and The Board of Public Instruction of Bay County, Florida, No. 972, Jan. 26, 1970.

61 *Court Rejects Kirk Plea*, Gainesville Sun, Jan. 28, 1970, at 1.

62 Dave Reddick, *Lincoln Closes with Violence*, Gainesville Sun, Jan. 30, 1970, at 1.

63 Reddick, *Police Version Is Given of Tear Gas Use at LHS*, Gainesville Sun, Feb. 4, 1970, at 4A.

64 *School Board Minutes, supra* note 26, Vol. 14, at 4141 (Feb. 12, 1970).

65 *School Board Minutes, supra* note 26, Vol. 14, at 4167 (Mar. 12, 1970).

66 Reddick, *Lincoln Closes with Violence*, Gainesville Sun, Jan. 30, 1970, at 1.

67 Filson, *Operation Concern Progress Fails to Mirror Black Unrest*, Gainesville Sun, Jan. 30, 1970, at 1.

68 *Arrest Made in GHS Row*, Gainesville Sun, Jan. 31, 1970, at 4; *LHS Student Facts Cleared*, Gainesville Sun, Feb. 3, 1970, at 16. The Lincoln student who was arrested in this incident, Frank Ford, states that he was acquitted in the assault at Lincoln. Interview with Sandra Sharron and Frank Ford, in Gainesville, Fla., at 38–39 (Oct. 30, 2014) (Ford) (on file with author).

69 Joe Halberstein, *Era Ends for Lincoln and Mebane*, Gainesville Sun, Jan. 31, 1970, at 13.

70 Duane Bradford, *Kirk Orders 2 Counties to Halt School Transfers*, Gainesville Sun, Jan. 31, 1970, at 1.

71 Letter, Earl Faircloth to Honorable Floyd Christian, Feb. 2, 1970 (*Wright v. Board*, Feb. 6, 1970); *Kirk Threat Merely "Friendly Advice,"* Gainesville Sun, Feb.3, 1970, at 13. Faircloth was a decorated World War II veteran who later ran for governor unsuccessfully.

72 Cormier, *Schools Brace to Reopen as Unitary System,* Gainesville Sun, Feb. 1, 1970, at 10A.

73 Report, Feb. 9, 1970, *supra* note 3, tbl.6. That report provides more details on the system's reorganization to comply with Judge Scott's order of Dec. 22, 1969, in *Wright v. Board.*

74 Certificate of Service accompanying Plan of the Board of Public Instruction of Alachua County, Florida for compliance with Section VI of the Civil Rights Act and the Orders of the United States District Court for the Northern District of Florida, 9 (*Wright v. Board*, Feb. 28, 1969).

75 Report, Feb. 9, 1970, *supra* note 3, tbl.8.

76 *Id.* at 15.

77 Cormier, *Schools Brace to Reopen as Unitary System*, Gainesville Sun, Feb. 1, 1970, at 10A.

78 *We Can Do It*, editorial reprinted in Gainesville Sun, Feb. 1, 1970, at 10A. Berner, won an award from *Photolith* magazine for her work on "Recognition of Changing Times in Student Publications." *GHS Editor Captures National Writing Contest*, Gainesville Sun, Feb. 1, 1970, at 6D.

79 *Schools to Reopen Friday in County*, Gainesville Sun, Feb. 5, 1970, at 1.

80 Willie Morris, Yazoo 16 (Ballantine 1972), quoting from an NBC News program.

81 Cormier, *School Integration Just Like Clockwork*, Gainesville Sun, Feb. 6, 1970, at 1.

82 *County Schools Did the Impossible*, Gainesville Sun, Feb. 12, 1970, at 1.

CHAPTER 13

1 *Bay Schools Close After Violence*, Gainesville Sun, Feb. 12, 1970, at 17.

2 Students Clash In Manatee County, Gainesville Sun, Feb. 5, 1970, p.1; Bay Schools Close After Violence, Gainesville Sun, Feb. 12, 1970, at 17.

3 *Id.*

4 *Desegregation Foments Trouble*, Gainesville Sun, Feb. 13, 1970, at 16.

5 *School Violence Blamed on State Leaders*, Gainesville Sun, Feb. 15, 1970, at 7A; Editorial, *Restless Gethsemane*, Gainesville Sun, Mar. 1, 1970, at 4A.

6 *School Violence Blamed on State Leaders*, Gainesville Sun, Feb. 15, 1970, at 7A.

7 Reddick, *Schools Mixed, but Are the Classes?* Gainesville Sun, Feb. 13, 1970, at 1.

8 Cormier, *Segregated Archer Classes to Be Dissolved This Week*, Gainesville Sun, Feb. 17, 1970, at 11; *Archer Classes Will Be Mixed*, Gainesville Sun, Feb. 20, 1970, at 17.

9 Letter from the County of Alachua Board of Public Instruction to Honorable G. Harrold Carswell (*Wright v. Board*, Sept. 25, 1969) (including attached spreadsheets).

10 Report of the Board of Public Instruction of Alachua County, Florida on Implementing a Unitary School System Effective Feb. 1, 1970, at 9 (*Wright v. Board*, Feb. 9, 1970).

11 *Negroes Boycott Santa Fe High*, Gainesville Sun, Feb. 19, 1970, at 18.

12 *"Rebels" Protest at Santa Fe High*, Gainesville Sun, Feb. 21, 1970, at 2; Cormier, *Why Tension Tightened at Santa Fe High School*, Gainesville Sun, Feb. 26, 1970, at 1.

13 *Id.*

14 Editorial, *Restless Gethsemane*, Gainesville Sun, Mar. 1, 1970, at 4A; Editorial, *Gethsemane Revisited*, Gainesville Sun, Mar. 12, 1970, at 6.

15 *Dick Gonzales Heads SFHS Biracial Group*, Gainesville Sun, Mar. 3, 1970, at 11.

16 *Mascot "Johnny Reb" Voted into Retirement*, Gainesville Sun, Mar. 17, 1970, at 9.

17 *It's the "Raiders" at Santa Fe High*, Gainesville Sun, Apr. 14, 1970, at 11.

18 *See supra* ch. 6.

19 *Jr. High Dances Cut Out*, Gainesville Sun, Sept. 9, 1965, at 3.

20 *See* ch. 17, *infra*.

21 *Principals List Few Riots in School Unrest Survey*, Gainesville Sun, Feb. 25, 1970, at 5A.

22 *Minutes*, Alachua Cty. Bd. Pub. Instruction, vol. 14, at 4143 (Feb. 12, 1970) [the collected minutes are hereinafter *School Board Minutes*].

23 *Id.* at 4154 (Feb. 26, 1970).

24 Telephone interview with Judy Segler Joiner (May 30, 2015) (notes on file with author).

25 Berner, *Gainesville High School Ends Year of Frustration, Heartbreak, Change,* Gainesville Sun, June 16, 1970, at 10.

26 *See infra* ch. 18.

27 Reddick, *Two Racial Beatings at GHS,* Gainesville Sun, Mar. 6, 1970, at 1.

28 *Vandals Hit LHS, Smash 600 Windows,* Gainesville Sun, Mar. 6, 1970, at 2.

29 *School Board Minutes, supra* note 22, vol. 14, at 4156 (Mar. 12, 1970).

30 *Two GHS Students Arrested,* Gainesville Sun, Mar. 12, 1970, at 20.

31 Berner, *Unresolved Racial Tensions Led to GHS Riot,* Gainesville Sun, Mar. 31, 1970, at 8.

32 Cormier, *Communications Gap Fans Race Issue at GHS,* Gainesville Sun, Apr. 2, 1970, at 1A.

33 Interview with Mack Hope, in High Springs, Fla. (Feb. 3, 2016) (notes on file with author).

34 Telephone Interview with Elizabeth Mallonee, at 18–19 (Jan. 26, 2016) (on file with author).

35 Telephone Interview with Ted Covey, at 16 (Feb. 7, 2016) (on file with author); telephone interview with Elizabeth Mallonee, *supra* note 34, at 18–19.

36 Interview with Brenda Wims, in Gainesville, Fla., at 12 (Jan. 28, 2016) (on file with author).

37 Telephone Interview with Frank Coleman at 22–23 (Jan. 13, 2016) (on file with author))

38 Cormier, *School Board Hears Protest by Parents,* Gainesville Sun, Mar.13, 1970), at 1.

39 Telephone Interview with Jeanie Whitehead Shaw at 2–3 (July 11, 2014), (on file with author)

40 Telephone Interview Florence Reaves (Feb. 2016) (notes on file with author).

41 Telephone Interview with Tommy Tomlinson at 7 (Aug. 27, 2014) (notes on file with author).

42 Berner, *Unresolved Racial Tensions Led to GHS Riot,* Gainesville Sun, Mar. 31, 1970, at 8.

43 Interview with Mack Hope, *supra* note 33.

44 Telephone Interview with John King (Apr. 30, 2016) (on file with author).

45 Cormier, *School Board Hears Protest by Parents,* Gainesville Sun, Mar. 13, 1970, at 1.

46 Motion for an Injunction Requiring Immediate Implementation of a School Desegregation Plan in Bay County, Florida and Alachua County, Florida Pending Certiorari to Review a Judgment of the United States Court of Appeals for the Fifth Circuit, Youngblood v. Bd. of Pub. Instruction and Wright v. Bd. of Pub. Instruction, at 8–9 (U.S. Dec. 13, 1969), copy in Alachua County Board of Public Instruction, Informal Desegregation File at 325–40 (undated) [hereinafter *School Board File*].

47 Cormier, *School Board Hears Protest by Parents,* Gainesville Sun, Mar. 13, 1970, at 1.

48 Cormier, *School Racial Conflict Angers Concerned Parents*, Gainesville Sun, Mar. 15, 1970, at 1A.

49 *Id.*; Cormier, *School Board Hears Protest by Parents*, Gainesville Sun, Mar.13, 1970, at 1.

50 Cormier, *School Racial Conflict Angers Concerned Parents*, Gainesville Sun, Mar. 5, 1970, at 1A.

51 Barbara Gallant, Letter to the Editor, *Most Students Are Trying to Make Do*, Gainesville Sun, Mar. 22, 1970, at 6.

52 Interview with Mary Rockwood Lane, Ph.D., in Gainesville, Fla. (May 26, 2015) (on file with author).

53 Interview with John Dukes III, in Gainesville, Fla. at 7–8 (Mar. 5, 2013) (on file with author).

54 Telephone Interview with Frank Coleman, *supra* note 37, at 24–25.

55 Interview with Peggy Finley, in Gainesville, Fla. 10 (Apr. 2013) (on file with author).

56 Interview with Sandra Sharron & Frank Ford, in Gainesville, Fla. 46–48 (Oct. 30, 2014) (on file with author).

57 Cormier, *School Board Hears Protest by Parents*, Gainesville Sun, Mar. 13, 1970, at 1.

58 Cormier, *Eastside School Outlook Bright After Shaky Beginning*, Gainesville Sun, Mar. 23, 1970, at 1.

59 Cormier, *GHS Police Guard Debated by Parents*, Gainesville Sun, Mar. 30, 1970, at 1.

60 Filson, *Call for Calm in GHS Fracas*, Gainesville Sun, Mar. 27, 1970, at 1; Berner, *Unresolved Racial Tensions Led to GHS Riot*, Gainesville Sun, Mar. 31, 1970, at 8; Cormier, *Communication Gap Fans Race Issue at GHS*, Gainesville Sun, Apr. 2, 1970, at 1.

61 *Student Battle Closes GHS*, Gainesville Sun, Mar. 26, 1970, at 1; Cormier, *GHS Police Guard Debated by Parents*, Gainesville Sun, Mar. 30, 1970, at 1; interview with Tommy Tomlinson, in Gainesville, Fla., 8 (Sept. 10, 2014) (on file with author).

62 Cormier, *Communications Gap Fans Race Issue at GHS*, Gainesville Sun, Apr. 2, 1970, at 1.

63 Telephone Interview with Elizabeth Mallonee, *supra* note 34, at 12–14.

64 Interview with Mack Hope, *supra* note 33.

65 *Student Battle Closes GHS*, Gainesville Sun, Mar. 26, 1970, at 1.

66 Filson, *Call for Calm in GHS Fracas*, Gainesville Sun, Mar. 27, 1970, at 1.

67 Robert K. Oglesby, *GHS Parents Discuss Plans to Thwart Future Incidents*, Gainesville Sun, Mar. 28, 1970, at 1.

68 Filson, *Call for Calm in GHS Fracas*, Gainesville Sun, Mar. 27, 1970, at 1.

69 Pavelka, *Blacks to Return to GHS Tuesday*, Gainesville Sun, Mar. 27, 1970, at 1.

70 *Rumor Mill Active After GHS Melee*, Gainesville Sun, Mar. 27, 1970, at 4.

71 Oglesby, *GHS Parents Discuss Plans to Thwart Future Incidents*, Gainesville Sun, Mar. 28, 1970, at 1.

72 Cormier, *GHS Police Guard Debated by Parents*, Gainesville Sun, Mar. 30, 1970, at 1.

73 Oglesby, *GHS Parents Discuss Plans to Thwart Future Incidents*, Gainesville Sun, Mar. 28, 1970, at 1.

74 Gertrude E. Jones, Letter to the Editor, *Black and White Is Beautiful*, Gainesville Sun, Mar. 29, 1970, at 9A.

75 Interview with Gertrude E. Jones, in Gainesville, Fla. 22 (Sept. 28, 2015) (on file with author).

76 *Id.* at 9–13.

77 Telephone Interview with Russell Ramsey, Ph.D., 11–12 (June 6, 2014) (on file with author).

78 *City Commission Seat Is Sought by Ramsey*, Gainesville Sun, Feb. 13, 1973, at 1A; *Russell Ramsey*, Gainesville Sun, Apr. 16, 1973.

79 Cormier, *GHS Police Guard Debated by Parents*, Gainesville Sun, Mar. 30, 1970, at 1; *GHS Probe Continuing*, Gainesville Sun, Mar. 30, 1970, at 4.

80 Filson, *Police at GHS Debated – They'll Just be "Available,"* Gainesville Sun, Mar. 31, 1970, at 1.

81 Interview with Tommy Tomlinson, *supra* note 61, at 10.

82 *GHS Opens, All Is Calm*, Gainesville Sun, Mar. 31, 1970, at 1.

83 Interview with Tommy Tomlinson, *supra* note 61, at 10.

84 *4 Suspended for Inciting GHS "Riot,"* Gainesville Sun, Apr. 1, 1970, at 1D.

85 *Newberry High Tense but Quiet*, Gainesville Sun, Mar. 31, 1970, at 13.

86 *Deputies Get Apology from Bishop Student*, Gainesville Sun, Apr. 5, 1970, at 11A; *2 Seminars on Drugs Underway in Gainesville*, Gainesville Sun, Apr. 2, 1970, at 3B.

87 *Black, White Students Tangle at Howard Bishop Junior High*, Gainesville Sun, Apr. 2, 1970, at 1.

88 Interview with Tim Strauser, in Gainesville, Fla., May 27, 2015 (on file with author).

89 Cormier, *New Disturbances at School Here*, Gainesville Sun, Apr. 3, 1970, at 1.

90 *Id.; Unrest Continues Friday at Bishop-Eastside School*, Gainesville Sun, Apr. 4, 1970, at 1.

91 *GHS Student Gets Broken Jaw in Melee*, Gainesville Sun, Apr. 5, 1970, at 12A.

92 *Shotgun Blast Damages Talbot Home*, Gainesville Sun, Apr. 6, 1970, at 1.

93 Oppel, *Kirk: Put Bus Issue to Supreme Court*, Gainesville Sun, Apr. 7, 1970, at 1; *Manatee School Head "In Control,"* Gainesville Sun, Apr. 7, 1970, at 1.

94 *3 Kirk Aides Ordered Arrested*, Gainesville Sun, Apr. 9, 1970, at 1.

95 *"Superintendent" Kirk on the Job*, Gainesville Sun, Apr. 10, 1970, at 1.

96 *Judge Fines Kirk $10,000 a Day*, Gainesville Sun, Apr. 12, 1970, at 1A.

97 *Manatee Officials Return, Kirk Journeys to Court*, Gainesville Sun, Apr. 13, 1970, at 1.

CHAPTER 14

1 Cormier, *Communication Gap Fans Race Issue at GHS*, Gainesville Sun, Apr. 2, 1970, at 1A.

2 Cormier, *Joe Hudson Steps Off the Firing Line*, Gainesville Sun, June 14, 1970, at 8A.

3 Cormier, *Communications Gap Fans Race Issue at GHS*, Gainesville Sun, Apr. 2, 1970, at 1.

4 Interview with Wayne Mosley, in Gainesville, Fla., at 15 (Sept. 11, 2014).

5 Interview with Bettye & Ed Jennings, in Gainesville, Fla. at 7 (Feb. 7, 2013) (on file with author).

6 Interview with Sam Haywood, in Gainesville, Fla., at 12–13 (July 14, 2014).

7 Cormier, *Parents Renew Protests over School Disruptions*, Gainesville Sun, Apr. 3, 1970, at 1.

8 *School Discipline Recommendations*, Gainesville Sun, Apr. 3, 1970, at 4.

9 *New School Instructions*, Gainesville *Sun*, Apr. 5, 1970, at 1.

10 Cormier, *Talbot Gets Temporary Police Patrol at Schools*, and *Police at 3 Schools*, Gainesville Sun, Apr. 7, 1970, at 1; *County Gives OK to School Patrol*, Gainesville Sun, Apr. 8, 1970, at 4B.

11 *County Gives OK to School Patrol*, Gainesville Sun, Apr. 8, 1970, at 4B.

12 *Burglars Enter Newberry High*, Gainesville Sun, Apr. 8, 1970, at 1D; Cormier, *Can Young Adult "Buffers" Avert New School Crises?*, Gainesville Sun, Apr. 10, 1970, at 1.

13 Cormier, *Can Young Adult "Buffers" Avert New School Crises?*, Gainesville Sun, Apr. 10, 1970, at 1.

14 *Newberry Arrests Follow Shouting, Gun Toting*, Gainesville Sun, Apr. 7, 1970, at 15.

15 *Minutes*, Alachua Cty. Bd. Pub. Instruction, vol. 14, at 4177–78 (Apr. 9, 1970) [the collected minutes are hereinafter *School Board Minutes*].

16 Cormier, *"Progress Report" on GHS Sees Hope for the Future*, Gainesville Sun, Apr. 17, 1970, at 1; Don Yokel, *GHS Group Talks Reduce Hostility*, Gainesville Sun, Apr.17, 1970, at 9; *Burglars Enter Newberry High*, Gainesville Sun, Apr. 8, 1970, at 1D; Cormier, *Talbot Gets Temporary Police Patrol at Schools*, Gainesville Sun, Apr. 7, 1970, at 1. Matola was identified as the leader in Cormier, *Students Say Trouble Over*, Gainesville Sun, Apr. 16, 1970, at 2D.

17 Telephone Interview with Barry Wolfe, Ph.D., Aug. 28, 2015 (on file with author).

18 Telephone Interview with Judy Segler Joiner, May 30, 2015 (on file with author).

19 *School Board Minutes, supra* note 15, vol. 14, at 4178–79 (Apr. 9, 1970).

20 C. Douglas Weaver, Every Town Needs a Downtown Church: A History of First Baptist Church, Gainesville, Florida 130 (2000).

21 Eunice Martin, *G'ville Children Sing New Song*, Gainesville Sun, Aug. 11, 1968, at 3A.

22 Cormier, *Can Young Adult "Buffers" Avert New School Crises?*, Gainesville Sun, Apr. 10, 1970, at 1; *School Board Minutes, supra* note 15, vol. 14, at 4179 (Apr. 9, 1970).

23 Cormier, *Can Young Adult "Buffers" Avert New School Crises?*, Gainesville Sun, Apr. 10, 1970, at 1.

24 *No More Police at Schools Here*, Gainesville Sun, Apr. 14, 1970, at 1.

25 *It'll Be PTA Plus an "S" at GHS Tuesday*, Gainesville Sun, Apr. 13, 1970, at 16; *New GHS PTSA Has Election*, Gainesville Sun, Apr. 15, 1970, at 2D.

26 *New GHS PTSA Has Election*, Gainesville Sun, Apr. 15, 1970, at 2D.

27 Cormier, *Students Say Trouble Over*, Gainesville Sun, Apr. 16, 1970, at 2D; *In the Community*, Gainesville Sun, Apr. 12, 1970, at 3C.

28 Cormier, *Students Say Trouble Over*, Gainesville Sun, Apr. 16, 1970, at 2D.

29 Cormier, *"Progress Report" on GHS Sees Hope for the Future*, Gainesville Sun, Apr. 17, 1970, at 1; Yokel, *GHS Group Talks Reduce Hostility*, Gainesville Sun, Apr. 17, 1970, at 8.

30 Cormier, *GHS Principal Hudson Asks for Reassignment*, Gainesville Sun, Apr. 29, 1970, at 1A.

31 Interview with Tommy Tomlinson, in Gainesville, Fla. (Sept. 10, 2014) (on file with author).

32 Cormier, *Neller Is Favored by GHS Teachers*, Gainesville Sun, May 1, 1970, at 1.

33 *GHS to Have Adult "Go-Betweens,"* Gainesville Sun, May 1, 1970, at 7; *School Board Minutes, supra* note 15, vol. 14, at 4191 (Apr. 30, 1970).

34 Cormier, *Joe Hudson Steps Off the Firing Line*, Gainesville Sun, June 14, 1970, at 8A.

35 Bob Arndorfer, *Retiring Minister Leaves His Mark in Gainesville*, Gainesville Sun, Sept. 9, 1985, at 1A.

36 Yokel, *GHS Group Talks Reduce Hostility*, Gainesville Sun, Apr. 17, 1970, at 8.

37 Doris Grimmage, *Student-Teacher Groups Termed Big Help at GHS*, Gainesville Sun, May 1, 1970, at 7.

38 Telephone Interview with Barry Wolfe, *supra* note 17.

39 Ad, Gainesville Sun, May 7, 1970, at 10A.

40 *GHS Blacks Present Demands to Hudson*, Gainesville Sun, May 8, 1970, at 17.

41 *New Protest by Blacks Stirs GHS*, Gainesville Sun, May 12, 1970, at 1.

42 *School Board Minutes, supra* note 15, vol. 14, at 4192 (May 12, 1970); Cormier, *Neller Named New GHS Principal*, Gainesville Sun, May 13, 1970, at 1.

43 Cormier, *Neller Named New GHS Principal*, Gainesville Sun, May 13, 1970, at 1.

44 Cormier, *Students Need Guidance From Parents, Caffey Says*, Gainesville Sun, May 18, 1970, at 5.

45 Interview with Shelton Boyles, in Gainesville, Fla. at 4 (June 10, 2014) (on file with author).

46 Telephone Interview with Russell Ramsey (June 6, 2014) (on file with author).

47 Telephone Interview with Isabelle Norton Whitfield at 18–22 (Nov. 13, 2015) (on file with author).

48 Cormier, Neller Named New GHS Principal, Gainesville Sun, May 13, 1970, at 1.

49 Cormier, *Three Principals Shifted, New School Building Pushed*, Gainesville Sun, May 15, 1970, at 1.

50 Cormier, *Students Need Guidance From Parents, Caffey Says*, Gainesville Sun, May 18, 1970, at 5.

51 Dave Hunter, *'Canes Planning Trophy Room*, Gainesville Sun, May 20, 1970, at 1D.

52 Suzanne K. Wade, Letter to the Editor, *A Tribute to Principal Tower*, Gainesville Sun, May 22, 1970, at 6.

53 *GHS to Add 10th Grade Class of 500*, Gainesville Sun, May 27, 1970, at 1.

54 *School Board Minutes, supra* note 15, vol. 14, at 4208 (May 28, 1970); Cormier, *Millage Election Is Urged*, Gainesville Sun, May 29, 1970, at 1.

55 Cormier, *Millage Election Is Urged*, Gainesville Sun, May 29, 1970, at 1.

56 Telephone interview with Elizabeth Mallonee, at 23 (Jan. 26, 2016) (on file with author).

57 *868 Seniors in 3 Schools to Share Graduation Day*, Gainesville Sun, June 3, 1970, at 1A; *Blood, Sweat and Tears Bear Fruit for Seniors*, Gainesville Sun, June 7, 1970, at 10A.

58 Bennett, *This Year's GHS Graduates Look Ahead to College*, Gainesville Sun, June 7, 1970, at 1C; Cormier, *"Care for Your Fellow Man," Grads Urged*, Gainesville Sun, June 10, 1970, at 1.

59 Telephone Interview with William L. Robinson (June 15, 2017) (on file with author).

CHAPTER 15

1 Gilbert v. Webster Parish Sch. Bd., 382 F. Supp. 8, 11–12 (W.D. La. 1974). This passage has not been cited or followed in other decisions.

2 The Supreme Court never explicitly endorsed the disproportionate impact principle. In Swann v. Charlotte-Mecklenburg Cty. Bd. of Educ., 402 U.S. 1, 20–21 (1971), the court only held that a pattern of abandoning schools in black neighborhoods and constructing new schools far from those neighborhoods "is a factor of great weight" in determining whether a school authority is moving in good faith away from a segregated system. On remand from the Supreme Court, the district court in *Swann* disallowed reducing enrollment or closing some black schools to which white students could be bused because there was no non-racial basis for the decisions. Swann v. Charlotte-Mecklenburg Cty. Bd. of Educ., 328 F. Supp. 1346, 1347–49 (W.D.N.C 1971), *aff'd*, 433 F.2d 1377 (4th Cir. 1972).

3 Plaintiffs' Objections to Defendant Board's Plan of Desegregation for Second Semester 1969-70 and the Academic Year 1970-71 (*Wright v. Board*, Mar. 9, 1970) [hereinafter *Plaintiffs' Objections to Defendant Board's Plan*].

4 Order (*Wright v. Board*, Apr. 24, 1970).

5 *Plaintiffs' Objections to Defendant Board's Plan, supra* note3, at 3–4.

6 Brice v. Landis, 314 F. Supp. 974, 978 (N.D. Cal. 1969).

7 Opinion of Court, Quarles v. Oxford Mun. Separate Sch. Dist., Civ. No. WC6962-K (N.D. Miss. Jan. 7, 1970), *Plaintiffs' Objections to Defendant Board's Plan, supra* note 3. The Oxford school district was one of the fifteen districts that, together with Alachua County, were part of the *Carter* case at the Supreme

Court and were, in January 1970, under Justice Black's order to take no steps that would interfere with February 1 conversion to a unitary system.

8 Florida School Desegregation Consulting Center, *A Desegregation Plan for the Alachua County Public Schools, January, 1970, Wright v. Board*; transcript at 23–24 (*Wright v. Board*, April 20, 1970).

9 Transcript, *supra* note 8, at 15.

10 *Id.* at 32–33.

11 *Id.* at 43–44.

12 *Id.* at 57–58.

13 *Id.* at 122–34 and Plaintiff's Ex. 1.

14 Apparently referring to 42 U.S.C. §§ 2000e(b) and 2000c-6, sections of the Civil Rights Act of 1964 that forbade any official or court of the United States to issue any order requiring busing to achieve racial balance.

15 Monroe v. Bd. of Comm'rs, 391 U.S. 450, 459 (1968) (*Monroe* was a companion case to *Green* but decided in a separate opinion); *see also* Quarles v. Oxford Mun. Separate Sch. Dist., Civ. No. WC6962-K (N.D. Miss. Jan. 7, 1970).

16 The Fifth Circuit had already decided this issue. United States v. Jefferson Cty. Bd. of Educ., 372 F.2d 836, 886 (5th Cir. 1966). In April 1971, the Supreme Court would reach the same conclusion. Swann v. Charlotte-Mecklenburg Bd. of Educ., 402 U.S. 1, 16–18 (1970).

17 Transcript, *supra* note 8, at 138–40.

18 *See supra* ch. 8.

19 Department of Health, Education, and Welfare, Policies on Elementary and Secondary School Compliance with Title VI of the Civil Rights Act of 1964, 33 Fed. Reg. 4856 (Mar. 23, 1968).

20 Decree at 8 (*Wright v. Board*, Apr. 26, 1967).

21 A Desegregation Plan for the Alachua County Public Schools, *supra* note 8, at 16.

22 Transcript, *supra* note 8, at 143.

23 Order, *supra* note 4, at 6–10.

24 Wright v. Bd. of Pub. Instruction, 431 F.2d 1200, 1202 (5th Cir. 1970).

25 *Id.* at 1201–03. District Judge Middlebrooks issued his own order implementing the Fifth Circuit decision on August 7, 1970, and required the school board to report on August 27, 1970, showing that the Fifth Circuit's requirements had been met. Order, *supra* note 4; Order Extending Time for Filing Report (*Wright v. Board* Aug. 19, 1970).

26 *Cf.* U.S. v. Scotland Neck City Bd. of Educ., 407 U.S. 484, 490–91 (1972); Stout v. Jefferson Cty. Bd. of Educ., 537 F.2d 800, 802 (5th Cir. 1976).

27 *See* Johnson v. Bd. of Educ., 604 F.2d 504, 516–19 (7th Cir. 1979) (Chicago, probably not good law in the context of de facto segregation; *see* Parents Involved in Cmty. Schs. v. Seattle Sch. Dist. No. 1, 551 U.S. 701 (2007).

28 Mae O. Clemons, Florida's Forgotten Legacy: Segregated Black Secondary Schools (2006).

29 Allen v. Bd. of Pub. Instruction, 312 F. Supp. 1127, 1132–33 (S.D. Fla.), *aff'd in part and rev'd in part*, 432 F.2d 362, 366 (5th Cir. 1970).

30 Clemons, *supra* note 28, at 28–29.

31 Drew S. Days III, *The Other Desegregation Story: Eradicating the Dual School System in Hillsborough County, Florida*, 61 Fordham L. Rev. 33, 36 (1992).

32 Middleton High School, http://middleton.mysdhc.org/Home%20Page (last visited Mar. 11, 2015); Barbara J. Shircliffe, The Best of That World: Historically Black High Schools and the Crisis of Desegregation in a Southern Metropolis 121–51, 212–13 (2006); Clemons, *supra* note 28, at 122–23.

33 Manning v. Sch. Bd., 244 F.3d 927 (11th Cir.), *cert. denied*, 524 U.S. 824 (2001); *see* Fla. State Advisory Comm. to the U.S. Comm'n on Civil Rights, Desegregation of Public School Districts in Florida 18, 50 (released 2006).

34 Telephone Interview with Steve Hegarty (Mar. 18, 2015) (notes on file with author); Shircliffe, *supra* note 32, at 212, 216–17.

35 *School Accountability Reports*, Fla. Dep't of Educ., schoolgrades16(3).xls, last visited Feb. 2, 2017, and http://schoolgrades.fldoe.org/reports/index.asp (last visited Mar. 22, 2015).

36 James A. Schnur, *Desegregation of Public Schools in Pinellas County, Florida*, 13 Tampa Bay Hist. 26, n.33 (1991), http://dspace.nelson.usf.edu/xmlui/handle/10806/115 (last visited Mar. 23, 2015).

37 Clemons, *supra* note 28, at 51–54, 62–64, 224–25; Jones High School, http://www.ocps.net/lc/southwest/hjo/Pages/default.aspx (last visited Sept. 7, 2014); Schnur, *supra* note 36.

38 Clemons, *supra* note 28, at 81–84, 121–24, 157–61, 169–74; Booker T. Washington High School, http://www.escambia.k12.fl.us/schscnts/wash/services.htm (last visited Sept. 7, 2014); Dunbar High School, http://dhs.leeschools.net (last visited Sept. 7, 2014); Tallahassee Lincoln, http://www.leonschols.net/lincoln (last visited Feb. 1, 2017).

39 Order of Dismissal, (*Wright v. Board.* May 17, 1971).

40 *See* Plaintiffs' Motion to Alter and Amend Judgment 3 (*Wright v. Board*, May 31, 1971); Notice of Appeal of plaintiffs (*Wright v. Board*, June 24, 1971).

41 Wright v. Bd. of Pub. Instruction, 445 F.2d 1397 (5th Cir. 1971).

42 Order (*Wright v. Board*, June 15, 1977).

43 Response to Show Cause Order (*Wright v. Board*, June 24, 1977).

44 Order (*Wright v. Board*, Aug. 14, 1978).

45 Russell W. Ramsey, *The Lincoln Center for the Human and Mechanical Arts of the Alachua County Public Schools, Pilot Study, School Year 1972-1973*, Postscript, Feb. 1974.

CHAPTER 16

1 Editorial, *Calling the Roll*, Gainesville Sun, Oct. 12, 1970, at 6.

2 *Private School Will Open Here*, Gainesville Sun, July 23, 1969, at 1D; *Private School to Open Sept. 3*, Gainesville Sun, Aug. 24, 1969, at 4B; Cormier, *Private School Possibilities Explored Again*, Gainesville Sun, Dec. 21, 1969, at 1.

3 Cormier, *Private Schools Point Up Woes of School System*, Gainesville Sun, Mar. 14, 1971, at 1A.

4 Cormier, *Private School Possibilities Explored Again*, Gainesville Sun, Dec. 21, 1969, at 1; Cormier, *School Plans Proceed Here*, Gainesville Sun, Jan. 27, 1970, at 1.

5 Cormier, *Helped Out Private School, but Not Principal, Blount Says*, Gainesville Sun, Mar. 12, 1970, at 1; Filson, *County Votes to Get Back Furniture*, Gainesville Sun, Mar. 20, 1970, at 1.

6 Cormier, *Private Schools Point Up Woes of School System*, Gainesville Sun, Mar. 14, 1971, at 1A.

7 Huess, *Rolling Green Academy, A Colorful Past*, Alachua *Post* (2002), http//alachuapost.com/All.1090.html?2800, last visited Mar. 4, 2014; this site is no longer active.

8 Arline Haufler, *Church Opens Junior High, Discipline Is Keystone*, Gainesville Sun, May 23, 1970, at 2; Ad, *Heritage Christian School Offers Junior High Program for '70-'71*, Gainesville Sun, May 24, 1970, at 6C.

9 Cormier, *School Recruiting Draws "Battle Cry,"* Gainesville Sun, June 4, 1970, at 2.

10 *Heritage School Expands Fall Elementary Program*, Gainesville Sun, Sept. 1, 1970, at 12.

11 Cormier, *Private Schools Point Up Woes of School System*, Gainesville Sun, Mar. 14, 1971, at 1A.

12 *Didn't Criticize Public School Teachers, He Says*, Gainesville Sun, Sept. 5, 1970, at 4.

13 Cormier, *Private Schools Point Up Woes of School System*, Gainesville Sun, Mar. 14, 1971, at 1A.

14 Haufler, *New Private School Will Open in Fall*, Gainesville Sun, June 19, 1970, at 9.

15 Some other private elementary schools would be founded later, and some still operate.

16 Cormier, *Private Schools Point Up Woes of School System*, Gainesville Sun, Mar. 14, 1971, at 1A.

17 *See* Mark Newman, Getting Right with God: Southern Baptists and Desegregation, 1945-1995, 178, 209 (2012).

18 Sandra J. Davis, Letter to the Editor, *I Am Free to Choose, Amen*, Gainesville Sun, Oct. 3, 1970, at 6.

19 Cormier, *Legislators Charge Fla. School Officials*, Gainesville Sun, Jan. 24, 1971, at 11A.

20 Wright v. Bd. of Pub. Instruction, 431 F.2d 1200, 1201–2 (5th Cir. 1970).

21 *Minutes*, Alachua Cty. Bd. Pub. Instruction, vol. 15, at 4256–57 (Aug. 18, 1970) [the collected minutes are hereinafter *School Board Minutes*]; Order (*Wright v. Board*, Aug. 19, 1970).

22 Cormier, *New County School Ruling Contains Some Headaches*, Gainesville Sun, Aug. 6, 1970, at 1; Donna McElroy, *Talbot Says City Is Shunning School Responsibilities*, Gainesville Sun, Oct. 14, 1970, at 1A.

23 Cormier, *White Parents Pledge Boycott*, Gainesville Sun, Aug. 18, 1970, at 1. The railroad tracks divided the white neighborhoods on the east side from the black neighborhoods in which Duval and Williams were located.

24 Minutes, Bi-Racial Committee, Aug. 20 and 24, 1970, in Alachua County Bd. of Pub. Instruction, Informal Desegregation File (undated) at 532–35 and 542 [hereinafter *School Board File*]; Memorandum, Recommendations, from Bi-racial Committee to Alachua County School Board, Aug. 20, 1970, *School Board File, supra*, at 540.

25 *1,000 Pupils Miss Opening Day but Most Will Drift In*, Gainesville Sun, Sept. 15, 1970, at 1.

26 Florida School Desegregation Consulting Center, *A Desegregation Plan for the Alachua County Public Schools, January 1970*, at 17–18 (*Wright v. Board*, Jan. 26, 1970).

27 Cormier, *Face Major Shakeup*, Gainesville Sun, Aug. 25, 1970, at 1; *see School Board File* at 543–555 for minutes and reports.

28 Minutes, Bi-racial Committee, Aug. 25, 1970, in *School Board File, supra* note 24, at 548.

29 Cormier, *School Cluster Plan OK'd as Parents Air Objections*, Gainesville Sun, Aug. 26, 1970, at 1.

30 Report of Alachua County School Board Pursuant to Court Order (*Wright v. Board*, Aug. 27, 1970).

31 Cormier, *Williams PTA Opens New Era*, Gainesville Sun, Sept. 3, 1970, at 1.

32 Cormier, *County's School Buses Set for Massive Transport Job*, Gainesville Sun, Sept. 11, 1970, at 1.

33 Cormier, *Busing Puts Brakes on Board Meeting*, Gainesville Sun, Oct. 29, 1970, at 1; Cormier, *Sidewalk Haves and Have Nots*, Gainesville Sun, Nov. 3, 1970, at 1.

34 Margery Johnston, *A Day in the Life of a Paraprofessional*, Gainesville Sun, Feb. 15, 1971, at 7.

35 *1,000 Pupils Miss Opening Day but Most Will Drift In*, Gainesville Sun, Sept. 15, 1970, at 1.

36 Cormier, *Time to "Fish or Cut Bait" on Schools*, Gainesville Sun, Jan. 29, 1971, at 1.

37 Joel Achenbach, *The Boy on the Bus*, Washington Post, July 8, 2007, at B01.

38 Cormier, *Tired Teachers Wrap It Up, Hope Years Ahead Improve*, Gainesville Sun, June 16, 1971, at 1A.

39 Christine Moore, *Children Call Him the Greatest*, Gainesville Sun, May 29, 1971, at 5.

40 Report of Alachua County School Board Pursuant to Court Order, *supra* note 30.

41 Wright v. Bd. of Pub. Instruction, *supra* note 20, 431 F.2d at 1222–23.

42 *Minutes*, Bi-racial Committee, Aug. 20, 1970, at 4, *School Board File*, at 535.

43 *Minutes*, Bi-racial Committee, Aug. 20, 1970, at 5–8, *School Board File*, at 536–39; Memorandum, Bi-racial Committee to Alachua County School Board,

Aug. 20, 1970, *School Board File*, at 540; *Minutes*, Bi-racial Committee, Aug. 24, 1970, *School Board File*, at 541.

44 Cormier, *Reading Program Zeroes In*, Gainesville Sun, Mar. 30, 1969, at 2A.

45 *Health Services Fund Set Up for A. Q. Jones*, Gainesville Sun, Dec. 12, 1969, at 7.

46 Cormier, *No Change in County's Plans*, Gainesville Sun, July 8, 1969, at 1; Minutes, Bi-racial Committee, Aug. 20, 1970, at 4 (Mrs. Koru), *School Board File*, at 535.

47 Order at 10–12 (*Wright v. Board*, Apr. 24, 1970).

48 Cormier, *Face Major Shakeup*, Gainesville Sun, Aug. 25, 1970, at 1. As required by the U.S. District Court, the school board filed its report showing compliance on Aug. 27, 1970. Report of Alachua County School Board Pursuant to Court Order, *supra* note 30.

49 Cormier, *School Cluster Plan OK'd as Parents Air Objections*, Gainesville Sun, Aug. 26, 1970, at 1

50 Wright v. Bd. of Pub. Instruction, *supra* note 20, 431 F.2d 1200.

51 Cormier, *County's School Buses Set for Massive Transportation Job*, Gainesville Sun, Sept. 11, 1970, at 1.

52 *6 in Races for 3 School Board Seats*, Gainesville Sun, Aug. 23, 1970, at 19A.

53 Cormier, *Todd Likely Winner in Close School Board Race*, Gainesville Sun, Sept. 7, 1970, at 1; *Todd Is Winner for School Bd.*, Gainesville Sun, Sept. 10, 1970, at 1; Editorial, *Cast Your Bucket*, Gainesville Sun, Sept. 24, 1970, at 6A; *Manning Is Elected*, Gainesville Sun, Oct. 1, 1970, at 1; *The School Board: A Knowledgeable Education Body*, Gainesville Sun, Sept. 5, 1971, at 3B.

54 Cormier, *Appointive School Head OK'd by Large Margin*, Gainesville Sun, Nov. 4, 1970, at 1; Cormier, *Superintendent Referendum Won by Playing It Cool*, Gainesville Sun, Nov. 8, 1970, at 1A.

55 As a result of the 1968 bond issue, all nine new county schools constructed with those funds would be air-conditioned. Cormier, *Schools Gulp Kilowatts*, Gainesville Sun, Nov. 11, 1971, at 1A.

56 Cormier, *Students, Parents Showing New Spirit at Eastside*, Gainesville Sun, Sept. 4, 1970, at 1.

57 Interview with John Dukes III, in Gainesville, Fla. (Mar. 5, 2014) (on file with author).

58 *What Do Kids Want from School?* Gainesville Sun, Sept. 5, 1971, at 1B.

59 Interviews with Hazel Self, Donna Self Elliott, Dan Self & Dana Self Powers in Gainesville, Fla. (Mar. 1, 2016) (notes on file with author); telephone interview with Hazel Self (Feb. 11, 2016) (notes on file with author); interview with Hazel Self, University of Florida Samuel Proctor Oral History Project, POF 045 (June 8, 2013).

60 Cormier, *Parents Protest 7 a.m. School Bell . . . But to No Avail*, Gainesville Sun, Dec. 18, 1970, at 1.

61 Interview with John Dukes III, *supra* note 57; interview with Tommy Tomlinson, in Gainesville, Fla. (Sept. 10, 2014) (on file with author).

62 Earl Bergadine, Letter to the Editor, *Unjust to Eastside Teachers*, Gainesville Sun, Mar. 3, 1971, at 8A; Cormier, *Talbot Criticized for Shuffling Teachers*, Gainesville

Sun, Feb. 19, 1971, at 1; Doug Hawley, *Eastside, Buchholz Heads Have Similar Backgrounds*, Gainesville Sun, Nov. 16, 1971, at 2B.

63 Cormier, *Education, Just as Students, Is Changing at GHS*, Gainesville Sun, Sept. 11, 1970, at 12.

64 Interview with John Neller, in Gainesville, Fla., at 2 (June 9, 2014) (on file with author)

65 Cormier, *Education, Just as Students, Is Changing at GHS,* Gainesville Sun, Sept. 11, 1970, at 12; Cormier, *School Opens Here Monday*, Gainesville Sun, Sept. 13, 1970, at 1A; Berner, *Everything's New for GHS*, Gainesville Sun, Sept. 13, 1970, at 1C; interview with John Neller, *supra* note 64, at 7–8.

66 Editorial, *Fearing Fear Itself*, Gainesville Sun, Sept. 10, 1970, at 6A.

67 Telephone Interview with Wayne Floyd (Aug. 28, 2015).

68 State of Florida, Dep't of Educ., Update of Survey of School Plants, Alachua County (Feb. 1965), Jan. 1966, tbl.II.

69 *Resurrection for Lincoln High?*, Gainesville Sun, Sept. 25, 1970, at 1; Talbot said such a concept was under review, Cormier, *School Cluster Plan OK'd as Parents Air Objections*, Gainesville Sun, Aug. 26, 1970, at 1.

70 *See* Joshua E. Kimberling, *Black Male Academies: Re-Examining the Strategy of Integration*, 42 Buff. L. Rev. 829 (1994); Drew S. Days III, *Rethinking the Integrative Ideal*, 34 Wm. & Mary L. Rev. 53, 60–62 (1992); Helaine Greenfield, *Some Constitutional Problems with the Resegregation of Public Schools*, 80 Geo. L. J. 363 (1991).

71 *Beating Suspect Back to GHS*, Gainesville Sun, Sept. 11, 1970, at 2.

72 Interview with John Neller, *supra* note 64, at 25–26; Cap Wilson, *Teachers Charge Boy with Assault*, Gainesville *Sun,* Oct. 3, 1970, at 4; *School Board Minutes, supra* note 21, vol. 15, at 4296 (Oct. 8, 1970); *Two Youths Expelled Permanently*, Gainesville Sun, Oct. 9, 1970, at 12; *Former GHS'er Assault Trial Date Set*, Gainesville Sun, Oct. 22, 1970, at 7. The *Sun* accounts state that the teachers signed the affidavits on their own and that Neller asked the police to let the school handle the incident because this type of issue was difficult to prosecute. When interviewed in 2014, Neller reviewed that account and disagreed.

73 *Two Youths Expelled Permanently*, Gainesville Sun, Oct. 9, 1970, at 12; *School Board Minutes, supra* note 21, vol. 15, at 4296 (Oct. 8, 1970).

74 *Youth Admits Assaulting Teacher*, Gainesville Sun, Jan. 19, 1971, at 15.

75 Cormier, *School Discipline Growing Problem*, Gainesville Sun, Nov. 25, 1970, at 1.

76 Interview with Mary Lewis, in Gainesville, Fla. (June 4, 2014) (on file with author).

77 Interview with John Neller, *supra* note 64, at 18; interview with Dan Boyd, in Gainesville, Fla., at 14 (June 10, 2014) (on file with author).

78 Southern Assoc. of Colleges and Schools, Evaluation Report, 1970-1971, Gainesville High School, Gainesville, Florida, at 4 [hereinafter *1971 GHS SACS Report*].

79 *Id.*

80 *1971 GHS SACS Report, supra* note 78, at 77.

81 *Teacher Aide Corps Plan Approved*, Gainesville Sun, Jan. 15, 1971, at 2.

82 Cormier, *Illness in Rural Schools: An Eye-Opener at Mebane*, Gainesville Sun, Jan. 17, 1971, at B1; Eileen Feinberg, *Mebane Students Health Studied*, Gainesville Sun, May 11, 1971, at 2D.

83 *School Dental Program to Operate Here by May*, Gainesville Sun, Jan. 20, 1971, at 2A.

84 Cormier, *Teacher Force Wins Round*, Gainesville Sun, Jan. 27, 1971, at 1A.

85 Cormier, *Teacher Merit Pay to Be Heard Again, Todd Promises*, Gainesville Sun, Feb. 1, 1971, at 16.

86 Cormier, *Teacher Force Wins Round*, Gainesville Sun, Jan. 27, 1971, at 1A.

87 Larry Stein, *A. Quinn Jones Adult School Badly Damaged by Firebomb*, Gainesville Sun, Apr. 21, 1971, at 1A; *Talbot Finds Firebomb in Office*, Gainesville Sun, Apr. 21, 1971, at 4A.

88 Interview with Tommy Tomlinson, in Gainesville, Fla. (Sept. 10, 2014) at 7.

89 *Buchholz Closed After Disturbance*, Gainesville Sun, Mar. 31, 1971, at 1; Reddick, *Buchholz to Reopen Friday; Classes Cancelled Again Today*, Gainesville Sun, Apr. 1, 1971, at 1; *Classes Resume at Buchholz Under Close Supervision*, Gainesville Sun, Apr. 2, 1971, at 1.

90 Bill Griffin, *Santa Fe High School Reported Near Normal*, Gainesville Sun, Apr. 27, 1971, at 15; Griffin, *No More Violence at Santa Fe High*, Gainesville Sun, Apr. 28, 1971, at 1E; *20 Students at Santa Fe Suspended*, Gainesville Sun, June 9, 1971, at 1D.

91 *Freeze on Teacher Hiring*, Gainesville Sun, May 14, 1971, at 7.

92 Cormier, *2 School Board Decisions Nixed*, Gainesville Sun, May 28, 1971, at 1.

93 Cormier, *City Told: Mix Housing to Mix Schools*, Gainesville Sun, May 21, 1971, at 1.

94 School Bd. of Alachua Cty., Report of Expulsions for 1970-71, May 25, 1971, Attachment #5 to Minutes, Bi-Racial Committee, May 24, 1971, *School Board File, supra* note 24, at 655–57.

95 Interview with John Neller, *supra* note 64, at 5.

96 Cormier, *Tired Teachers Wrap It Up, Hope Years Ahead Improve*, Gainesville Sun, June 16, 1971, at 1A.

97 Tommy Lane, *The Kids Are Getting It All Together*, Gainesville Sun, June 20, 1971, at 4B.

98 *Id.*

99 *Neller Resigns at GHS*, Gainesville Sun, July 30, 1971, at 1; *Dan Boyd Appointed New GHS Principal*, Gainesville Sun, Aug. 13, 1971, at 5.

100 Cormier, *Principal Prospects Named*, Gainesville Sun, Aug. 7, 1971, at 1.

101 Interview with John Neller, *supra* note 64.

102 Cormier, Declares Youth Testing Elders, Gainesville Sun, June 16, 1971, at 1A.

CHAPTER 17

1 *Askew: "Is Apartheid What We Want in This Country?,"* Gainesville Sun, Nov. 19, 1971, at 1D.

2 Report of Alachua County School Board Pursuant to Court Order at 2 (*Wright v. Board*, Aug. 27, 1970).

3 Swann v. Charlotte-Mecklenburg Bd. of Educ., 402 U.S. 1 (1971) (companion cases listed at 402 U.S. 5 n.1).

4 *Id.* at 29–31.

5 *Id.* at 24.

6 *Id.* at 22–25.

7 *Id.* at 25–27.

8 *Id.* at 31–32. That proviso assumed that the school authorities had not contributed to the changes in racial composition through, for example, the siting of new schools or abandonment of others. *Id.* at 20–21.

9 *Id.* at 22–23.

10 Cormier, *'72 School Busing Plan "City-to-City,"* Gainesville Sun, June 28, 1971, at 1.

11 United States v. Jefferson Cty., 380 F.2d 385, 394 (5th Cir. 1967).

12 Milliken v. Bradley, 433 U.S. 267, 281–91 (1977) (reviewing a district court order to the Detroit school system).

13 Interview by Stuart Landers with Dr. Sue Legg, in Gainesville, Fla. 20 (Aug. 4, 1992), http://ufdc.ufl.edu/UF00093318/00001; At the time of her interview, Dr. Legg served as associate director, Office of Instructional Resources, for the State of Florida. *Id.* at 33.

14 Interview with Hazel Self, Donna Self Elliott, Dan Self, & Dana Self Powers, in Gainesville, Fla. (Mar. 1, 2016) (notes on file with author).

15 Cormier, School Integration *"Slippage"* May Plague County, Gainesville Sun, June 9, 1971, at 1A.

16 Grimmage, *No GHS Racial Problems, Talbot Tells Realtors Board,* Gainesville Sun, Nov. 21, 1970, at 1.

17 McElroy, *Talbot Says City Is Shunning School Responsibility,* Gainesville Sun, Oct. 14, 1970, at 1.

18 Cormier, *City Told: Mix Housing to Mix Schools,* Gainesville Sun, May 21, 1971, at 1.

19 Reddick, *70-30 Ratio in Housing Projects Called Ridiculous,* Gainesville Sun, Sept. 3, 1971, at 1.

20 Skip Perez, *Problem of Busing, Land Use Debated,* Gainesville Sun, Oct. 1, 1971, at 1A.

21 *See Minority Housing "Balance" in Gainesville,* Gainesville Sun, Feb. 2, 1972, at 8A.

22 Editorial, *To the Mountain,* Gainesville Sun, Jan. 16, 1973, at 4A.

23 Cormier, *Hunt for Superintendent Is On,* Gainesville Sun, Mar. 26, 1971, at 1.

24 Cormier, *School Superintendent Hunt Not Actually in "Sunshine,"* Gainesville Sun, Oct. 8, 1971, at 1A.

25 Cormier, *Charlotte School Head Named Superintendent,* Gainesville Sun, Jan. 12, 1972, at 1A; Cormier, *Quality Schools Is Goal, Says New Superintendent,* Gainesville Sun, Jan. 14, 1972, at 1A.

26 *What's the Future Hold for Talbot?,* Gainesville Sun, Jan. 24, 1972, at 12A.

27 *Talbot Enters Race for City Commission,* Gainesville Sun, Feb. 28, 1973, at 1A.

28 Bi-racial Committee, Minutes (June 8, 1971) in Alachua County Board of Public Instruction, Informal Desegregation File (undated) at 659 [hereinafter *School Board File*].

29 Cormier, *School Integration "Slippage" May Plague County,* Gainesville Sun, June 9, 1971, at 1A.

30 Cormier, *'72 School Busing Plan "City to City,"* Gainesville Sun, June 25, 1971, at 1; Cormier, *School Board Ponders Pupil Shuffle,* Gainesville Sun, Dec. 10, 1971, at 1A.

31 Cormier, *School Headaches Return Like Migraine,* Gainesville Sun, Aug. 12, 1971, at 1.

32 Cormier, *Board Fails to Act on Lincoln Future,* Gainesville Sun, Jan. 26, 1972, at 6C; Cormier, *High Springs Group Protests School Plan,* Gainesville Sun, Jan. 5, 1972, at 1A.

33 *Minutes,* Alachua Cty. Bd. Pub. Instruction, vol. 15, at 4605, 4610 (Dec. 9 & 17, 1971); Cormier, *School Board Adopts Racial Balance Plan,* Gainesville Sun, Dec. 18, 1971, at 1A; Minutes, Bi-racial Committee, *School Board File, supra* note 28, at 696 (Nov. 23, 1971). The zones were to be Gainesville, Waldo-Hawthorne, Alachua-High Springs, and Newberry-Archer.

34 Minutes, Bi-racial Committee, Feb. 15, 1972, *School Board File, supra* note 28, at 709–10; *see generally School Board File,* at 532–711.

35 Cormier, *School Mix Plan Faces Public Thursday,* Gainesville Sun, Mar. 1, 1972, at 1A.

36 Cormier, *School Mix "K-Plan" Protested, May Go,* Gainesville Sun, Mar. 3, 1972, at 1A.

37 Cormier, *School Lines Drawn; Waldo Wins Its Plea,* Gainesville Sun, Mar. 29, 1972, at 1A.

38 *Id.;* Cormier, *School Zone Freeze Asked,* Gainesville Sun, Mar. 25, 1972, at 1A.

39 Cormier, *2 School Board Reformers Have Their Doubts About Running Again,* Gainesville Sun, May 17, 1972, at 1D; *Howe to Head School Board,* Gainesville Sun, Jan. 5, 1972, at 3A.

40 *Samuels Announces Reelection Bid,* Gainesville Sun, June 11, 1972, at 1A; *Alachua County School Board,* Gainesville Sun, Aug. 31, 1972, at 6C.

41 *Alachua County School Board,* Gainesville Sun, Aug. 31, 1972, at 6C–7C; Cormier, *School Board Race Heats Up over Merit Pay,* Gainesville Sun, Sept. 7, 1972, at 1A; Editorial, *Gentle Schoolmen,* Gainesville Sun, Sept. 9, 1972, at 4A; *School Board Election 72,* Gainesville Sun, Sept. 9, 1972, at 8A (responses to League of Women Voters questions); Cormier, *Air Views on Busing,* Gainesville Sun, Sept. 11, 1972, at 1D.

42 *School Board Election 72,* Gainesville Sun, Sept. 9, 1972, at 8A; Cormier, *Air Views on Busing,* Gainesville Sun, Sept. 11, 1972, at 1D; *Commission, School*

Board, Registration Races Get Airing, Gainesville Sun, Nov. 1, 1972, at 1A; Cormier, *It Has Been a Low Key Race*, Gainesville Sun, Nov. 5, 1972, at 1C.

43 Cormier, *Enneking Wins, Other School Board Race Still Undecided*, Gainesville Sun, Sept. 13, 1972, at 1A; Will Cofrin, *Samuels Defeats Simmons*, Gainesville Sun, Sept. 14, 1972, at 1A.

44 Cormier, *Samuels Wins School Board Election by Wide Margin*, Gainesville Sun, Nov. 8, 1972, at 1A.

45 Cormier, *Howe Reelected Chairman Of County School Board*, Gainesville Sun, Jan. 3, 1973, at 1A.

46 Cormier, *Fairbanks Parents Protest New Busing Setup*, Gainesville Sun, Apr. 27, 1973, at 1A; Cormier, *Busing Plan Protests to Bring Revisions*, Gainesville Sun, Mar. 16, 1973, at 1A; Cormier, *Proposed Pupil Housing Plan for 1973-74*, Gainesville Sun, Mar. 14, 1973, at 7A; Cormier, *Sixth Graders Left in Limbo*, Gainesville Sun, Jan. 12, 1973, at 1A.

47 Cormier, *Busing Plan Protests to Bring Revisions*, Gainesville Sun, Mar. 16, 1973, at 1A.

48 Cormier, *Pupil Assignment Plan Passes Amid "Grumbles,"* Gainesville Sun, Mar. 23, 1973, at 1A.

49 Cormier, *Fairbanks Parents Protest New Busing Setup*, Gainesville Sun, Apr. 27, 1973, at 1A.

50 *Id.*; Cormier, *Parents Lose Busing Fight*, Gainesville Sun, May 11, 1973, at 1A.

51 Motion for Approval of School Zone Lines, Alachua County School Board (*Wright v. Board*, July 9, 1973).

52 Response to Motion for Approval of Zone Lines (*Wright v. Board*, Aug. 9, 1973).

53 Order (*Wright v. Board*, Aug. 6, 1973).

CHAPTER 18

1 Berner, *Some New Happenings on Tap for Alachua County Classrooms*, Gainesville Sun, Aug. 29, 1971, at 2B.

2 *New Teachers Meet and Greet During Lunch*, Gainesville Sun, Sept. 2, 1971, at 11; *Pupil Count for County Is 22,248*, Gainesville Sun, Sept. 16, 1971, at 4A.

3 Cormier, *Schools Opening: Spirits Are High*, Gainesville Sun, Sept. 5, 1971, at 1A; *New Teachers Meet and Greet During Lunch*, Gainesville Sun, Sept. 2, 1971, at 11; *Tommy Tomlinson: The Man Who Drew the Lines*, Gainesville Sun, Sept. 5, 1971, at 1B.

4 *See infra*, tbl.5.

5 Interview with Dan Boyd, in Gainesville, Fla., at 1–2 (June 10, 2014) (on file with author). The information that follows about Boyd is taken from that interview.

6 *Id.* at 4–5 and 9.

7 Gordon W. Allport, *The Nature of Prejudice* (1954).

8 Interview with Dan Boyd, *supra* note 5, at 6–9.

9 *Id.* at 8–9.

10 Bi-racial Committee, Minutes (Aug. 23, 1971) *in* Alachua County Board of Public Instruction, Informal Desegregation File (undated) at 672 [hereinafter *School Board File*].

11 Cormier, *Principal Prospects Named*, Gainesville Sun, Aug. 7, 1971, at 1.

12 *Dan Boyd Appointed New GHS Principal*, Gainesville Sun, Aug. 13, 1971, at 5.

13 Interview with Dan Boyd, *supra* note 5, at 8 and 10.

14 *Minutes*, Alachua Cty. Bd. Pub. Instruction, vol. 15, at 4527 (Aug. 12, 1971) [the collected minutes are hereinafter *School Board Minutes*]; Cormier, *Principal Prospects Named*, Gainesville Sun, Aug. 7, 1971, at 1; *Dan Boyd Appointed New GHS Principal*, Gainesville Sun, Aug. 13, 1971, at 5.

15 Katina Prokos, *Alachua County Superintendent to Retire After Almost 50 Years in Education*, WUFT News, Sept. 2, 2013, www.wuft.org/news/2013/09/02/boyd-profile/, (last visited Feb. 10, 2017).

16 Interview with Dan Boyd, *supra* note 5, at 8.

17 Interview with Ron Perry, in Gainesville, Fla., at 2 (June 9, 2014) (on file with author).

18 Interview with Tim Strauser, in Gainesville, Fla., May 27, 2015 (notes on file with author).

19 Telephone Interview with Vince Deconna (Mar. 22, 2016) (notes on file with author).

20 Interview with John Dukes III, in Gainesville, Fla. (Mar. 6, 2014) (on file with author); interview with Dan Boyd, *supra* note 7, at 11; interview with Vince Deconna, *supra* note 19.

21 Interview with Dan Boyd, *supra* note 5, at 10–13.

22 Alfred L. Awbrey, Jr., 100 Years & More of Gainesville High School Football, 1906–2010, 63–64 (2011).

23 Interview with Dan Boyd, *supra* note 5, at 11.

24 Interview with Sam Haywood, in Gainesville, Fla., at 18 (July 14, 2014) (on file with author).

25 Interview with Sam Haywood, *supra* note 24, at 1–5 and 26.

26 Interview with Dan Boyd, *supra* note 5, at 10.

27 Interview with Sandra Sharron and Frank Ford, in Gainesville Fla., at 30–35 (Oct. 30, 2014) (on file with author).

28 Interview with Shelton Boyles, in Gainesville, Fla., at 7 (June 10, 2014) (notes on file with author).

29 Interview with Peggy Finley, in Gainesville, Fla., at 24 (April, 2012) (on file with author).

30 Interview with Dan Boyd, *supra* note 5, at 28.

31 Telephone Interview with Pat Powers (Nov. 13, 2015) (notes on file with author).

32 Perez, *The Teachers Get It Together. . .and Find Understanding*, Gainesville Sun, Aug. 8, 1971, at 1A.

33 Minutes, Bi-racial Committee, *School Board File, supra* note 10 at 684–85 (Sept. 27, 1971); *School Board File* at 695 (Nov. 23, 1971), and *School Board File* at 710 (Feb. 15, 1972).

34 Telephone interview with Russell Ramsey at 21 (June 6, 2014) (on file with author).

35 Cormier, *School Board Sets Age Precedent*, Gainesville Sun, Sept. 24, 1971, at 1A.

36 For example, violent outbreaks were reported in February 1973 in Escambia, Hillsborough, Pinellas, Palm Beach, and Washington Counties. *Seek to Ease Racial Tension*, Gainesville Sun, Feb. 5, 1973, at 1D; *1 School Opens, 1 Closes Following Racial Strife*, Gainesville Sun, Feb. 6, 1973, at 5A; *Boca School Closes in Gun Crackdown*, Gainesville Sun, Feb. 8, 1973, at 1D; *Racial Clashes Disrupt Schools*, Gainesville Sun, Feb. 9, 1973, at 5A.

37 Editorial, *Face in the Drizzle*, Gainesville Sun, Mar. 2, 1972, at 6A.

38 Interview with Dan Boyd, *supra* note 5, at 13.

39 Cormier and Reddick, *New GHS Violence Injures 14 but School Remains Open*, Gainesville Sun, Mar. 2, 1972, at 1A; Reddick, *GHS Principal's Warning: Go to Class or Stay Clear*, and *School Quiet Today*, Gainesville Sun, Mar. 3, 1972, at 1A.

40 Arnold Matyas, *Students Say School Heads, Not Race, Caused Violence*, Gainesville Sun, Mar. 4, 1972, at 1A.

41 Interview with Dan Boyd, *supra* note 5, at 13–14.

42 *Id.* at 14.

43 Interview with Mary Lewis, in Gainesville, Fla. at 4 (June 4,2014) (on file with author).

44 Interview with Peggy Finley, *supra* note 29, at 24.

45 Interview with Jessie Heard, in Gainesville, Fla., at 23–24 (Feb. 4, 2014) (on file with author).

46 Interview with Shelton Boyles, *supra* note 28, at 7–8.

47 Cormier, *Changes Planned in School Windup*, Gainesville Sun, June 12, 1972, at 1A.

48 Cormier, *"Largest" Class Graduates GHS*, Gainesville Sun, June 10, 1972, at 1A.

49 Advance-ED, www.advanc-ed.org/oasis2/u/par/search, (last visited Mar. 29, 2014).

50 Cormier, *Lincoln Vocational Center: The Miracle of SE 11th Street*, Gainesville Sun, Oct. 27, 1972, at 1A; *County, SFJC Combine on Vocational Programs*, Gainesville Sun, Nov. 10, 1972, at 6B; interview with Russell Ramsey, *supra* note 34, at 22.

51 *Id.* at 18.

52 Interview with Philoron Wright, in Gainesville, Fla. (Nov. 1, 2016) (notes on file with author).

53 *Id.*

54 *Police Alert at GHS Following Racial Incident*, Gainesville Sun, Jan. 15, 1973, at 1D.

55 Interview with Vince Deconna, *supra* note 19.

56 Roberta (Berner) Davis, *Rumor and Fact Mirror Current School Atmosphere*, Gainesville Sun, May 13, 1973, at 2E.

57 Interview with Sam Haywood, *supra* note 24, at 10–18; Mary Lewis agrees that by 1972 things started settling down. Interview with Mary Lewis, *supra* note 43, at 3.

58 Cormier, *Education's Structure in Florida Needs Change*, Gainesville Sun, Feb. 25, 1973, at 3A.

59 *See* Fla. Stat. § 1001.452 (2016).

60 Beverly Cheuvront, *Untold Work to Be Done on Equality, Chestnut Says*, Gainesville Sun, Oct. 1, 1971, at 4B; Margery Johnston, *They Volunteer "Volunteers,"* Gainesville Sun, Mar. 11, 1971, at 3C.

61 *Project Gives Boost to Students During First Desegregation Years*, Gainesville Sun, June 1, 1971, at 11.

62 *Minutes*, Bi-racial Committee, at 1–2 and Attachment 1 (Feb. 18, 1971) *School Board File, supra* note 10, at 578–79 & 585–86; *id.*, at 1–2 (March 29, 1971), *School Board File, supra* note 10 at 588–89.

63 *School Board Sets Special Public Meet*, Gainesville Sun, Dec. 15, 1971, at 7A; Cormier, *School Board Seeks More Federal Aid*, Gainesville Sun, Dec. 19, 1972, at 1A; *"Minority" Parents School Activity Increase Sought*, Gainesville Sun, Dec. 21, 1972, at 2D.

64 Interview by Stuart Landers with Dr. Sue Legg, in Gainesville, Fla. 24–25 (Aug. 4, 1992), http://ufdc.ufl.edu/UF00093318/00001; Stuart Landers, The Gainesville Women for Equal Rights, 1963-1978 83–84 (1995) (unpublished master's thesis, University of Florida) (excerpts on file with author).

65 Mary Nell Reeves, *Area Group Funds Reading Program for Children*, Gainesville Sun, Mar. 20, 1973, at 6A.

66 *"Family Play Day" Set at Finley Elementary*, Gainesville Sun, May 15, 1971, at 5B; *Minutes*, Bi-racial Committee (Feb. 2, 1971), *School Board File, supra* note 10 at 571–76; *id.*, (Mar. 29, 1971), *School Board File* at 589; *id.*, (Apr. 26, 1971), *School Board File* at 598–601.

67 George W. Barnard, M.D., President, Alachua County Parent-Teacher Organization, Letter to the Editor, *School Bonds Are Only a Start*, Gainesville Sun, June 3, 1968, at 4.

68 *Coordination Between UF, County System Eyed*, Gainesville Sun, Dec. 10, 1971, at 12A; *School Board Minutes, supra* note 14, vol. 15 at 4409 (March 11, 1971); *id.* at 4455 (May 13, 1971); *id.* at 4593 (Dec. 9, 1971).

69 *School Board Minutes, supra* note 14, Vol. 15 at 4623 (Feb. 25, 1972).

70 *Alachua County School Board, W.F. Enneking*, Gainesville Sun, Aug. 31, 1972, at 7C.

71 Reddick, *Gainesville Heads Crime List*, Gainesville Sun, Sept. 17, 1972, at 1A.

72 Brenda Gevertz, *35% Get Free Lunches in County*, Gainesville Sun, May 14, 1971, at 12.

73 Cowrin & Matyas, *Drug Raid Biggest in County*, Gainesville Sun, Dec. 8, 1972, at 1A; Will Corbin, *Nab 8 for Drug Sale at School*, Gainesville Sun, Dec. 12, 1972, at 1A.

74 Cormier, *Odd-Ball Examples in Truant Report*, Gainesville Sun, Nov. 10, 1972, at 1A.

[75] Wanda Perry, *What's Happening on the (Open) Gainesville High Campus Today,* Gainesville Sun, Dec. 17, 1972, at 4F.

[76] *Hard Drug Committee Findings, Recommendations,* Gainesville Sun, Mar. 16, 1973, at 6A.

[77] *Hard Drug Committee Findings, Recommendations,* Gainesville Sun, Mar. 16, 1973, at 6A.

[78] Matyas, *Drug problem Is with Youths, Not in Schools, Committee Told,* Gainesville Sun, Jan. 9, 1973, at 9A; Cormier, *"It's Not Up to Schools to Solve Drug Problems,"* Gainesville Sun, Feb. 7, 1973, at 1A.

[79] Cormier, *County Schools Got Boost from Legislature, Talbot Says,* Gainesville Sun, June 29, 1971, at 1; Reddick, *School "Accountability" Act Called Path to Excellence,* Gainesville Sun, Sept. 24, 1971, at 11A.

[80] Cormier, *How County's Students Compare,* Gainesville Sun, Dec. 13, 1972, at 9A; Cormier, *Reading Tests Evaluated,* Gainesville Sun, Jan. 19, 1973, at 6A.

[81] *School Chiefs Oppose 12th Grade Testing,* Gainesville Sun, Sept. 23, 1971, at 1A.

[82] Cormier, *Regents Favor Eased 12th Grade Placement Test,* Gainesville Sun, June 6, 1973, at 12A.

[83] Cormier, *School Bd. in Open, Then Closed,* Gainesville Sun, May 25, 1973, at 1A; Cormier, *New School Testing Program OK'd,* Gainesville Sun, June 6, 1973, at 1A.

[84] Cormier, *After County-Wide Testing, Time for Questions,* Gainesville Sun, Dec. 8, 1973, at 1B.

[85] Cormier, *County Schools Got Boost from Legislature, Talbot Says,* Gainesville Sun, June 29, 1971, at 1; Cormier, *'72 School Busing Plan "City to City,"* Gainesville Sun, June 25, 1971, at 1; Bridges, *County Teachers Get $700 Pay Boost, Incentive Bonuses,* Gainesville Sun, July 27, 1971, at 1; *School Board Minutes, supra* note 14, vol. 15, at 4492 (June 24, 1971). The pay raises for teachers went into effect despite the president's wage and price freeze on August 15, 1971, because they predated that action.

[86] *Teachers Retain Bargaining Power,* Gainesville Sun, Jan. 11, 1973, at 18A.

[87] Cormier, *Teachers Approve Accord,* Gainesville Sun, June 9, 1973, at 1A.

[88] Cormier, *County's Teachers Get 10 Per Cent Wage Boost,* Gainesville Sun, June 14, 1973, at 1A.

CHAPTER 19

[1] Telephone Interview with Roberta Berner, at 1 (Mar. 22, 2012) (notes on file with author); telephone interview with author of Jeanie Whitehead Shaw, at 7 (July 11, 2014) (on file with author); interview with Nell Page, in Gainesville, Fla., at 13 and 26 (Dec. 26, 2014) (on file with author); telephone interview with Susan Holloway Weinkle, M.D., (Jan. 15, 2016) (notes on file with author).

[2] Service clubs were student clubs sponsored by organization such as Rotary and Kiwanis. The student members of each club selected new members every year in a process similar to fraternity pledging. *See infra,* ch. 20.

[3] *See supra,* ch. 9 at note 69.

4 Berner, *Majority of GHS's Student Body Works for Harmony*, Gainesville Sun, June 17, 1970, at 11A.

5 Grimmage, *No GHS Racial Problems, Talbot Tells Realtors Board*, Gainesville Sun, Nov. 21, 1970, at 1.

6 Cormier, *Negro Teachers Casualties of City Integration*, Gainesville Sun, July 8, 1965, at 1.

7 *Id.*

8 Cormier, *Schools Open Tuesday on Revised Schedule*, Gainesville Sun, Sept. 2, 1968, at 1.

9 *10 Teachers Are Needed*, Gainesville Sun, Sept. 13, 1968, at 9.

10 Cormier, *Schools Open Tuesday on Revised Schedule*, Gainesville Sun, Sept. 2, 1968, at 1.

11 *Minutes*, Alachua Cty. Bd. Pub. Instruction, vol. 13, at 3134-37 (Mar. 2, 1965) [the collected minutes are hereinafter *School Board Minutes*], Ex. A, Plan for Compliance, Title VI of the Civil Rights Act of 1964 by Alachua County Board of Public Instruction, Gainesville, Florida.

12 Cormier, *A Typical School Start with Typical Problems*, Gainesville Sun, Sept. 2, 1966, at 1.

13 Cormier, *Federal Desegregation Ruling Not an Issue Here – Talbot*, Gainesville Sun, Dec. 30, 1966, at 1.

14 *Id.*

15 Terry Leiva, *Summary of Interview with Andrew Mickle*, in University of Florida Smathers Library Special and Area Studies Collections, Box 13, MS Group 149, File 38/I/7 [hereinafter *EDF 600 File*].

16 Letter from Tommy Tomlinson to Honorable G. Harrold Carswell (including attached table) (*Wright v. Board*, Sept. 26, 1969).

17 Report of the Board of Public Instruction of Alachua County, Florida on Implementing a Unitary School System Effective Feb. 1, 1970 at tbl.6 (*Wright v. Board* Feb. 9, 1970)

18 Report to the Court at exhibit C (*Wright v. Board*, June 25, 1973).

19 Report to the Court at exhibit C (*Wright v. Board*, Apr. 4, 1974); *see* tbl.5.

20 United States v. Jefferson Cty. Bd. of Educ., 372 F.2d 836, 892–93 (5th Cir. 1966); *see supra* ch. 7.

21 Singleton v. Jackson Mun. Separate Sch. Dist., 419 F.2d 1211, 1217–18 (5th Cir. 1969).

22 Certificate of Service and Plan of the Board of Public Instruction, exhibit A at 9 (*Wright v. Board*, Feb. 28, 1969); Order (*Wright v. Board*, Apr. 3, 1969) (approving the plan).

23 *Minutes*, Alachua Cty. Bd. Pub. Instruction, vol. 14, at 4126–27 (Dec. 11, 1969) [the collected minutes are hereinafter *School Board Minutes*]; *see supra*, ch. 11.

24 *School Board Minutes, supra* note 23, vol. 14, at 4147–48 (Feb. 12, 1970).

25 Telephone Interview with Catherine Mickle, at 6–9 (Oct. 2, 2015) (on file with author).

[26] *School Recruiter Seeks More Blacks as Teachers*, Gainesville Sun, June 1, 1970, at 15.

[27] Interview with Frank Coleman, Janice Cambridge Hagillih & Cynthia Cook, in Gainesville, Fla. 1 (May 23, 2016) (notes on file with author).

[28] Telephone Interview with Isabelle Norton Whitfield (Nov. 13, 2015) (on file with author); telephone interview with Judy Segler Joiner (May 30, 2015) (notes on file with author); interview with Peggy Finley, in Gainesville, Fla., Apr. 2012 (on file with author).

[29] Interview with Isabelle Norton Whitfield, *supra* note 28.

[30] Cormier, *Parents Here Point to School Failings*, Gainesville Sun, Mar. 25, 1970, at 1.

[31] Interview with Thomas A. Wright, Sr., in Gainesville, Fla., at 4 (Mar. 26, 2012)

[32] Interview with John Neller, in Gainesville, Fla., at 20–21 (June 9, 2014) (on file with author).

[33] Interview with Bettye & Ed Jennings, in Gainesville, Fla., at 1–5 (Feb. 7, 2013).

[34] Interview by Joel Buchanan with Cora Roberson, in Gainesville, Fla., 13 and 23–24 (Feb. 19, 1986), http://ufdc.ufl.edu/UF00005433/00001.

[35] *Id.*

[36] Interview by Joel Buchanan with Thelma Jordan, in Gainesville, Fla., 8 and 17 (Jan. 24, 1984), http://ufdc.ufle.edu/UF00005405/00001.

[37] Jeffry L. Charbonnet, The Public School System of Alachua County 1821-1955, at 220–233 (1991) (unpublished master's thesis, University of Florida) (on file with author).

[38] *Interview with Cora Roberson, supra note 34, at 13-14 and 23-24.*

[39] Interview with Cora Roberson, in Gainesville, Fla. at 2 (Nov. 3, 2014) (on file with author). Unless otherwise specified, the source of this discussion of Ms. Roberson's career is this interview by author.

[40] *Id.* at 15–16.

[41] Interview with Charles Chestnut III, in Gainesville, Fla., 24 (Apr. 14, 2014) (on file with author).

[42] Interview with Jessie Heard, in Gainesville, Fla., 27 (Feb. 4, 2014) (on file with author).

[43] *Id.* at 29.

[44] *Id.* at 30.

[45] *Id.* at 26–28.

[46] *Id.* at 33.

[47] Telephone interview with William Adams (May 19, 2015) (on file with author).

[48] Tbl.5.

[49] Interview with Jessie Heard, *supra* note 42, at 30–31.

[50] Gainesville High School *Hurricane*, at Faculty section (1971).

[51] Interview with Malcolm Privette, in Gainesville, Florida (Aug. 25, 2015) (notes on file with author).

[52] Telephone Interview with Elizabeth Mallonee 8 (Jan. 26, 2016) (on file with author).

53 Southern Assoc. of Colleges and Schools, Evaluation Report, 1970-1971, Gainesville High School, Gainesville, Florida at 10 [hereinafter *1971 GHS SACS Report*].

54 *Id.* at 12.

55 Cormier, *Student Tests to Test Teaching Quality*, Gainesville Sun, May 20, 1971, at 8A.

56 Cormier, *Dick, Jane and Spot Fast Becoming Has-Beens*, Gainesville Sun, Feb. 21, 1971, at 12A.

57 Interview with Mary Lewis, in Gainesville, Fla., at 4 (June 4, 2014) (on file with author).

58 *School Board Minutes, supra* note 23, vol. 13, at 3315 (Mar. 31, 1966) notes that the system had been unable to hire qualified reading specialists and had to reassign the federal funding for those positions.

59 Cormier, *Dick, Jane and Spot Fast Becoming Has-Beens*, Gainesville Sun, Feb. 21, 1971, at 12A

60 Interview with Peggy Finley, supra note 28.

61 1971 GHS SACS Report, *supra* note 53, at 31.

62 *Id.*

63 Interview with Shelton Boyles, in Gainesville, Fla. (June 10, 2014) (notes on file with author).

64 Interview with Sandra Sharron and Frank Ford, in Gainesville, Fla. (Oct. 30, 2014) (on file with author).

65 Interview with Shelton Boyles, *supra* note 63, at 2.

66 Cormier, *Dick, Jane and Spot Fast Becoming Has-Beens*, Gainesville Sun, Feb. 21, 1971, at 12A.

67 Interview with John Neller in Gainesville, Fla., 23 (June 9, 2014).

68 Cormier, *Dick, Jane and Spot Fast Becoming Has-Beens*, Gainesville Sun, Feb. 21, 1971, at 12A; interview with Peggy Finley, *supra* note 28, at 14.

69 *Id.*

70 Interview with Peggy Finley, *supra* note 28, at 16.

71 Interview with Sandra Sharron and Frank Ford, *supra* note 64, at 14–18 and 27.

72 Cormier, *Dick, Jane and Spot Fast Becoming Has-Beens*, Gainesville Sun, Feb. 21, 1970, at 12A.

73 Interview with Reeves Byrd, in Gainesville, Fla. (Sept. 30, 2015) (notes on file with author); interview by author, Malcolm Privette, *supra* note 51.

74 *School Board Minutes*, supra note 23, at 4188 (Apr. 9, 1970); Letter from Florence Reaves to author, Jan. 30, 2016, and telephone interview (Feb. 2016) (letter and notes on file with author).

75 Grimmage, *Urges Teachers "Beautify" Black*, Gainesville Sun, Apr. 17, 1970, at 9.

76 Gainesville High School *Hurricane, supra* note 50, at 42.

77 Interview with Sandra Sharron and Frank Ford, *supra* note 64, at 35.

78 Interview with Elizabeth Mallonee, *supra* note 52, at 10–12, 15–16 and 21.

79 Telephone Interview with Isabelle Norton Whitfield, at 7 (Nov. 13, 2015) (on file with author).

80 Interview with Mary Anne Coxe Zimmerman, in Gainesville, Fla. (Aug. 31, 2015) (on file with author).

81 Laura Chambless, *Tommy Tomlinson Has an Interest in People,* Gainesville Sun, Nov. 19, 1972, at 12F.

82 Interview with Dan Boyd, in Gainesville, Fla., 25 (June 10, 2014) (on file with author).

83 Interview with Mae Islar, in Gainesville, Fla., at 59:00 (Mar. 1, 2011) (on file with the University of Florida Samuel Proctor Oral History Project, Recording No. AAHP 162).

84 Interview with Peggy Finley, *supra* note 60, at 24.

85 Interview with Mae Islar, in Newberry, Fla. 14 (May 29, 2015).

86 Interview with Peggy Finley, *supra* note 60, at 22.

87 Interview by Gayle Yamada with Joel Buchanan, in Gainesville, Fla. 18 (Feb. 12, 1984), http://ufdc.ufl.edu/UF00005406/00001.

88 Interview with Shelton Boyles, *supra* note 63.

89 Louis Cuayo, *Teacher Retires from Spot She Prefers. . .the Schoolroom,* Gainesville Sun, July 27, 1970 at 8.

90 C. E. Partusch, *"A Night with Catherine Murphree" Covers 25 Years of Musical Teaching,* Gainesville Sun, Jan. 18, 1971, at 8.

91 Interview with Jessie Heard, *supra* note 42, at 32–33; Albert White & Kevin McCarthy, Lincoln High School, Its History and Legacy 132 (2011).

92 David F. Labaree, Someone Has To Fail: The Zero-Sum Game of Public Schooling 98 and 175 (2012); Diedre Faith Houchon, The Transcendental Pedagogy of Lincoln High School, 1921-1955: The Aims, Pursuits and Professional Development of African American Education During De Jure Segregation (2015) (unpublished Ph.D. dissertation, University of Florida) (on file with author).

93 U.S. Dep't of Health, Education, and Welfare, Equality of Educational Opportunity Study, James S. Coleman, principal investigator, at 8 and 14 (1966).

94 Telephone Interview with Pat Powers (Nov. 13, 2015) (on file with author).

95 Block Course at Crystal, 101 Attend 4-Day Session, Hurricane Herald, Oct. 23, 1971, at 1 (on file with author); e-mail response, Apr. 13, 2017, from Larry Reynolds (on file with author).

96 Larry Stein, *Ramsey: Use Mountain Top Concept, Not Reform Schools,* Gainesville Sun, Feb. 3, 1972, at 7A.

97 Telephone Interview with Russell Ramsey 4 (June 6, 2014) (on file with author).

98 Martin Luther King Jr., I've Been to the Mountaintop (Apr. 3, 1968), http://www.americanrhetoric.com/speeches/mlkivebeentothemountaintop.htm.

99 *Id.*

100 Telephone Interview with Judy Segler Joiner, *supra* note 28.

101 Russell W. Ramsey, Social Adjustment Education in the Alachua County, Florida, Public Schools 4 (1972) (unpublished).

102 Ramsey, Annual Report, Pilot Year, Mountain Top Class for Social Adjustment and Public Order Program, 1970–71, at Annex 1, Memorandum of Dec. 17, 1970 (Aug. 15, 1971) (unpublished).

103 Stein, *Ramsey: Use Mountain Top Concept, Not Reform Schools,* Gainesville Sun, Feb. 3, 1972, at 7A.

104 Ramsey, *supra* note 101; Ramsey, *supra* note 102; interview with Russell Ramsey, *supra* note 97, at 4; Dee Esposito, *Mountain Top: Some Kids Get a Second Chance,* Gainesville Sun, Oct. 15, 1972, at 10F; *see also* Stacey Bridges, *Mountain Top School: Teach, House Runaways,* Gainesville Sun, Apr. 9, 1972, at 1A; Stein, *Ramsey: Use Mountain Top Concept, Not Reform Schools,* Gainesville Sun, Feb. 3, 1972, at 7A.

105 Stein, *Ramsey: Use Mountain Top Concept, Not Reform Schools,* Gainesville Sun, Feb. 3, 1972, at 7A.

106 Ramsey, Principles of Social Adjustment, Alachua County Public Schools (undated, unpublished).

107 Ramsey, *supra* note 102, at Annex 1, Memorandum of Aug. 24, 1970).

108 Ramsey, *supra* note 102, at Annex 1, Memorandum of Dec. 17, 1970.

109 Ramsey, *supra* note 102, at 17.

110 Ramsey, *supra* note 102, at 3–4. *See also* Esposito, *Mountain Top: Some Kids Get a Second Chance,* Gainesville Sun, Oct. 15, 1972, at 10F; *"Flower Children" Curbed at Schools,* Gainesville Sun, Dec. 18, 1970, at 7; *1-Room "Mountain Top School" to Work with Suspended Students,* Gainesville Sun, Aug. 21, 1970, at 12.

111 Esposito, *Mountain Top: Some Kids Get a Second Chance,* Gainesville Sun, Oct. 15, 1972, at 10F.

112 Stein, *Ramsey: Use Mountain Top Concept, Not Reform Schools,* Gainesville Sun, Feb. 3, 1972, at 7A.

113 Ramsey, *supra* note 102, at 10–11.

114 *Id.*

115 Cormier, *School Board Seeks More Federal Aid,* Gainesville Sun, Dec. 19, 1972, at 1A.

116 Ramsey, *supra* note 102, at 9–10.

117 Interview with Sandra Sharron and Frank Ford, *supra* note 64, at 28.

118 Ramsey, *supra* note 102, at 16.

119 Interview with Russell Ramsey, *supra* note 103, at 2–3.

120 Alachua Cty. Sch. Bd., Southern States Conference on Community Involvement in the Problems of Neglected and Delinquent Children (Russell W. Ramsey ed., 1971) (unpublished).

121 Interview with Russell Ramsey, *supra* note 97, at 22.

122 *Id.* at 21–23.

123 Cormier, *Transfers Save Jobs for 37 GHS Teachers,* Gainesville Sun, Apr. 23, 1971, at 5.

124 Ramsey, *supra* note 101, at 3; Cormier, *School Drug Problem Called Typical Here,* Gainesville Sun, March 22, 1973, at 1A.

125 Interview with Russell Ramsey, *supra* note 97, at 1.

126 Interview with Mae Islar, *supra* note 85, at 2:16.

127 Cormier, *Legislators Charge Fla. School Officials*, Gainesville Sun, Jan. 24, 1971, at 11A.

128 U.S. Dep't of Health, Education, and Welfare, Equality of Educational Opportunity Study, James S. Coleman, principal investigator, at 364–66 (1966).

129 *Id.* at 356–57.

130 Interview with Dan Boyd, *supra* note 82, at 26.

131 Michelle Kratish, *Teachers, Students, Parents Meet on Differences*, Gainesville Sun, Aug. 19, 1973, at 3A.

CHAPTER 20

1 *See* ch. 13, *supra*, n.51.

2 Carter v. West Feliciana Parish School Board., 396 U.S. 226, 227–28 (1969); the similar order that applied specifically to Alachua County came down two days later, Order, Stout v. Jefferson Cty. Bd. of Education, (U.S. Dec. 15, 1969) (unpublished); copy in Alachua County Board of Public Instruction, Informal Desegregation File 344–45 [hereinafter *School Board File*].

3 Interview with Frank Coleman, Janice Cambridge Hagillih & Cynthia Cook, in Gainesville, Fla. at 4–5 (May 24, 2016) (notes on file with author).

4 *See* ch. 12, *supra*.

5 Telephone Interview with Tommy Tomlinson at 7 (Aug. 27, 2014) (notes on file with author).

6 Dave Osler, *Racial Gains Help But Negroes Still Feel Isolated*, Gainesville Sun, June 16, 1970, at 16.

7 *See* ch. 10, *supra*.

8 Telephone Interview with Donnie Batie, M.D., at 22 (July 28, 2015) (on file with author); telephone interview with Brenda Gresham Rainsberger (May 12, 2016) (notes on file with author).

9 Report of Bd. of Public Instruction of Alachua County, Florida on Implementing a Unitary School System Effective Feb. 1, 1970, at 9 (*Wright v. Board*, Feb. 9, 1970).

10 Green v. Cty. School Bd., 391 U.S. 430, 442 (1968); U.S. v. Jefferson Cty. Bd. of Education, 380 F.2d 385, 389 (5th Cir. 1967).

11 Southern Assoc. of Colleges and Schools, Evaluation Report, 1970-1971, Gainesville High School, Gainesville, Florida at 12 [hereinafter *1971 GHS SACS Report*].

12 *1971 GHS SACS Report*, at 21–29.

13 *1971 GHS SACS Report*, at 42.

14 *1971 GHS SACS Report*, at 61–62.

15 Transcript at 22–23, testimony of Walter Ebling (*Wright v. Board*, Apr. 20, 1970).

16 *Id.* at 33–39.

17 Interview with Mack Hope, in High Springs, Fla. (Feb. 3, 2016) (notes on file with author).

18 *Id.*

19 Interview with Brenda Wims, in Gainesville, Fla. at 10–12 and 22 (Jan. 28, 2016) (on file with author).

20 Interview with Donnie Batie, M.D., *supra* note 8, at 7 and 25.

21 Telephone Interview with Frank Coleman, at 15 (Jan. 13, 2016) (on file with author).

22 Interview with Alvin Butler, in Gainesville, Fla., at 15–16 (Mar. 11, 2016).

23 Interview with Melvin Flournoy, in Gainesville, Fla., at 4, 8, 11 (Oct. 1, 2015).

24 Telephone Interview with Jeanie Whitehead Shaw, 7, 9–10 (July 11, 2014); telephone interview with Ted Covey, Class of 1971, 17 (Feb. 7, 2016); interview with Thomas Deakin, class of 1971, in Gainesville, Fla. (Feb. 21, 2016); interview with Andy Adkins, class of 1972, in Gainesville, Fla., 8 (Feb. 22, 2016) (all on file with author).

25 Interview with Jeanie Whitehead Shaw, *supra* note 24, at 7.

26 Telephone Interview with Susan Holloway Weinkle, M.D. (Jan. 15, 2016) (notes on file with author).

27 Interview with Frank Coleman, *supra* note 21, at 27.

28 Interview with Thomas Deakin, *supra* note 24.

29 Interview with Ted Covey, *supra* note 24, at 19.

30 Interview with Andy Adkins, *supra* note 24, at 5.

31 Interview with Ron Perry, in Gainesville, Fla., 13 (June 9, 2014) (on file with author).

32 Interview with Ted Covey, *supra* note 24.

33 Interview with Jeanie Whitehead Shaw, *supra* note 24, at 3.

34 *See* ch. 19, *infra*.

35 Interview with Mary Rockwood Lane, in Gainesville, Fla. (May 26, 2015) (notes on file with author).

36 Telephone interview with Barbara Gray Brown (Feb. 23, 2016) (notes on file with author).

37 Interview with Nell Page, in Gainesville, Fla. 22 (Dec. 26, 2014).

38 Interview with Ted Covey, *supra* note 24, at 10–11.

39 Transcript at 85–122 (Robert Curran, Ed.D., and Gerald Byron Webster) (*Wright v. Board*, Apr. 20, 1970). *See* U.S. Dep't of Health, Education, and Welfare, Equality of Educational Opportunity Study, James S. Coleman, principal investigator, at 22–23 and 182 (1966).

40 Transcript, *supra* note 39, at 119–21 (Gerald Byron Webster).

41 Interview with Mary Ann Coxe Zimmerman, in Gainesville, Fla. (Aug. 31, 2015) (notes on file with author).

42 Interview with Brenda Wims, *supra* note 19, at 10–11 and 21–22.

43 Interview with Alvin Butler, *supra* note 22, at 16.

44 Interview with Wayne Mosley, in Gainesville, Fla., at 17–18 (Sept. 11, 2014) (on file with author).

45 Interview with Mary Rockwood Lane, *supra* note 35.

46 Interview with Mack Hope, *supra* note 17.

[47] Interview with Ron Perry, *supra* note 31, at 3–9.

[48] Interview with Tim Strauser, in Gainesville, Fla. (May 27, 2015) (notes of file with author).

[49] Student Handbook, 1970–71, Gainesville High School, 20–23; interview with Frank Coleman, *supra* note 21, at 10.

[50] Telephone Interview with John King, 3–4 (Apr. 30, 2016) (on file with author).

[51] Interview with Frank Coleman, *supra* note 21, at 22, 27–28.

[52] Interview with John King, *supra* note 50, at 6–7.

[53] Interview with Frank Coleman, *supra* note 21, at 27–29.

[54] *Id.* at 20–22.

[55] *Id.* at 28.

[56] Interview with Wayne Mosely, *supra* note 44, at 17–18.

[57] Interview with Frank Coleman, *supra* note 21, at 8.

[58] Interview with Brenda Wims, *supra* note 18, at 18.

[59] Interview with Dan Boyd, in Gainesville, Fla. 13–14 (June 10, 2014) (on file with author).

[60] Interview with John King, *supra* note 50, at 2–11 and 13–14.

[61] Interview with Frank Coleman, Janice Cambridge Hagillih & Cynthia Cook, *supra* note 3, at 5.

[62] Interview with Alvin Butler, *supra* note 22, at 14.

[63] Interview with Brenda Wims, *supra* note 18, at 17 and 28.

[64] Telephone Interview with Pat Powers, 16–17 (Nov. 13, 2015) (on file with author).

[65] Interview with Frank Coleman, Janice Cambridge Hagillih & Cynthia Cook, *supra* note 3, at 2.

[66] Interview with Frank Coleman, *supra* note 21, at 6.

[67] Albert White & Kevin McCarthy, Lincoln High School, Its History and Legacy 206 (2011).

[68] The local organizations reflected practices tolerated, if not mandated, by their national organizations. Jeffrey A. Charles, Service Clubs in American Society (1993), 30 and 155; Susan Kerr Chandler, "Almost a Partnership": African-Americans, Segregation and the Young Men's Christian Association, 21 J. of Sociology & Soc. Welfare 97 (2015). The YMCA international organization formally desegregated in 1946.

[69] Cormier, *"Progress Report" on GHS Sees Hope for the Future*, Gainesville Sun, Apr. 17, 1970, at 1.

[70] *Racial Violence Flares at Palmetto High, Miami*, Gainesville Sun, May 7, 1970, at 2D.

[71] Yokel, *GHS Group Talks Reduce Hostility*, Gainesville Sun, Apr. 17, 1970, at 8.

[72] Interview with Jeanie Whitehead Shaw, *supra* note 24, at 7–9.

[73] Interview Nell Page, *supra* note 37, at 19.

[74] Interview with Reeves Byrd, in Gainesville, Fla, (Sept. 30, 2015) (notes on file with author).

75 Interview with Frank Coleman, *supra* note 21, at 10.

76 Interview with Nell Page, *supra* note 37, at 22.

77 Interview with Tommy Tomlinson, in Gainesville, Fla. 16–17 (Sept. 10, 2014) (on file with author).

78 *Gainesville High Students to Walk for Unity Sunday*, Gainesville Sun, Apr. 30, 1970, at 19.

79 Interview with Donnie Batie, M.D., *supra* note 8, at 18–19 and 30–31.

80 Interview with Brenda Wims, *supra* note 18, at 16.

81 *Id.* at 18.

82 *Id.* at 9–10.

83 *Id.* at 17–18.

84 Interview with John Neller, in Gainesville, Fla. 18 (June 9, 2014) (on file with author); interview with Mary Lewis, in Gainesville, Fla., 3 (June 4, 2014) (on file with author); interview with Dan Boyd, *supra* note 59, at 14.

85 Telephone Interview with Vince Deconna (Mar. 22, 2016) (notes on file with author).

86 The 1971 *Hurricane* yearbook shows only a scattering of black band members.

87 Donaldson led the GHS band from 1946 until his retirement in 1976. Alfred L. Awbrey, Jr., 100 Years & More of Gainesville High School Football, 1906-2010 (Vol. II), 44 (2012).

88 Interview with Donnie Batie, M.D., *supra* note 8, at 11–12.

89 Interview with Frank Coleman, Janice Cambridge Hagillih & Cynthia Cook, *supra* note 3, at 1–2.

90 Partusch, *"A Night with Catherine Murphree" Covers 25 Years of Musical Teaching,"* Gainesville Sun, Jan. 18, 1971, at 8.

91 Cormier, *Neither Side Will Yield in Lincoln High Hassle*, Gainesville Sun, Dec. 2, 1969, at 1.

92 Interview with Frank Coleman, Janice Cambridge Hagillih & Cynthia Cook, *supra* note 3 at 1–2.

93 Telephone Interview with Patricia Crawford (May 23, 2016) (notes on file with author).

94 Interview with Frank Coleman, Janice Cambridge Hagillih & Cynthia Cook, *supra* note 3 at 1–2.

95 Interview with John Neller, *supra* note 84, at 9–10.

96 Partusch, *"A Night with Catherine Murphree" Covers 25 Years of Musical Teaching*, Gainesville Sun, Jan. 18, 1971, at 8.

97 Interview with Nell Page, *supra* note 37, at 30.

98 At Florida Field, blacks were allowed to sit in a roped-off section of the south end-zone bleachers for one dollar to watch the all-white Gators. That many did is more evidence of football's universal appeal.

99 Telephone Interview with William Adams at 5 (May 19, 2015) (on file with author).

100 Interview with Mack Hope, *supra* note 17.

101 Interview with Melvin Flournoy, *supra* note 23, at 13.

102 Interview with Alvin Butler, *supra* note 22, at 3–4.

[103] Much of the information about team records and opponents is from Alfred L. Awbrey, Jr., 100 Years & More of Gainesville High School Football, 1906-2010 (2011).

[104] Telephone Interview with Herbert Wagemaker, M.D. (Mar. 5, 2016) (notes on file with author); interview with Frank Coleman, *supra* note 21, at 11–13; *Parent Night on Program*, Gainesville Sun, May 16, 1970, at 2.

[105] *Parent Night on Program*, Gainesville Sun, May 16, 1970, at 2.

[106] John Patton, *Ex-GHS Coach Niblack Dies*, www.gainesville.com/article/20070612/SPORTS/706120334?p=3&TC=pg (last visited 2-8-2017).

[107] Interview with Alvin Butler, *supra* note 22, at 10; Awbrey, *supra* note 103, at 60.

[108] Patton, *Ex-GHS Coach Niblack Dies*, *supra* note 106.

[109] Interview with Melvin Flournoy, *supra* note 23, at 8.

[110] Interview with Frank Coleman, *supra* note 21, at 18.

[111] Interview with Alvin Butler, *supra* note 22, at 8–9.

[112] *Id.* at 9 and 11.

[113] Interview with Brenda Wims, *supra* note 18, at 18.

[114] Interview with Ted Covey, *supra* note 24, at 7–8.

[115] Interview with Alvin Butler, *supra* note 22, at 13.

[116] Interview with Tim Strauser, *supra* note 48.

[117] Interview with Alvin Butler, *supra* note 22, at 13–14.

[118] Patton, *Ex-GHS Coach Niblack Dies*, *supra* note 106.

[119] Interview with Melvin Flournoy, *supra* note 23, at 8–9.

[120] Interview with Alvin Butler, *supra* note 22, at 14.

[121] Interview with John Dukes III, in Gainesville, Florida, 13–14 (Mar. 5 2014) (on file with author).

[122] Interview with Tim Strauser, *supra* note 48.

[123] Interview with Jerry Mauldin, in Gainesville, Fla., at 15 (Feb. 16, 2016) (on file with author).

[124] *Id.* at 16.

[125] Interview with Ted Covey, *supra* note 24, at 15.

[126] Interview with Vince Deconna, *supra* note 85.

[127] Patton, *Ex-GHS Coach Niblack Dies*, *supra* note 106.

[128] Interview with Nell Page, *supra* note 37, at 22.

[129] Interview with Jeanie Whitehead Shaw, *supra* note 24, at 3–4.

[130] Interview with Mary Rockwood Lane, *supra* 35.

[131] Interview with Ron Perry, *supra* note 31, at 14.

[132] Interview with Nell Page, *supra* note 37.

[133] Interview with Susan Holloway Weinkle, M.D., supra note 26.

[134] Roberta Berner, *Unresolved Racial Tensions Led to GHS Riot*, Gainesville Sun, Mar. 31, 1970, at 8.

[135] Cormier, *Communications Gap Fans Race Issue at GHS*, Gainesville Sun, Apr. 2, 1970, at 1A.

[136] Telephone Interview with author, Russell Ramsey at 2 and 14 (June 6, 2014) (on file with author).

137 Berner, *Gainesville High School Ends Year of Frustration, Heartbreak, Change,* Gainesville Sun, June 16, 1970, at 10.

138 Interview with Frank Coleman, *supra* note 21, at 23–25.

139 Interview with Patricia Crawford, *supra* note 93.

AFTERWORD

1 *See, e.g.,* Gloria J. Powell, Black Monday's Children: A Study of the Effects of School Desegregation on Self-Concepts of Southern Children (1973); Eric A. Hanushek, John F. Kain & Steven G. Rivkin, *New Evidence About* Brown v. Board of Education*: The Complex Effects of School Racial Composition on Achievement* (Nat'l Bureau of Econ. Research, Working Paper No. 8741, 2002); Russell W. Rumberger & Gregory J. Palardy, *Does Segregation Still Matter? The Impact of Student Composition on Academic Achievement in High School,* 107 Teachers C. Rec. 1999 (2005) (abbreviated version *in* School Resegregation: Must the South Turn Back? 127 (John C. Boger & Gary Orfield eds., 2005)). Other sources are cited in the bibliography.

2 Amy Stuart Wells et al., Both Sides Now: The Story of School Desegregation's Graduates 18–20 (2009).

3 Amy Stuart Wells, *The "Consequences" of School Desegregation: The Mismatch Between the Research and the Rationale,* 28 Hastings Const. L. Q. 771 (2001); Amy Stuart Wells et al., Both Sides Now: The Story of School Desegregation's Graduates (2009). Other sources available in the bibliography.

4 U.S. Census Bureau, A Half-Century of Learning: Historical Census Statistics on Educational Attainment in the United States, 1940 to 2000: Detailed Tables tbls.11, 12, 7, 8 (last visited Dec. 8, 2016), http://www.census.gov/hhes/socdemo/education/data/census/half-century/tables.html. More recent equivalent data are not available.

5 https://edstats.fldoe.org/SASWebReportStudio/gotoReportSection.do?sectionNumber=2, last visited June 11, 2017.

6 *See supra,* ch. 9.

7 Bureau of the Census, U.S. Dept. of Commerce, 1970 Census of Population, vol. 1, pt. 11, tbls.124, 125 (1972).

8 *Alachua County, Florida,* City-data.com, http://www.city-data.com/county/Alachua_County-FL.html (last visited Feb. 23, 2015).

9 Eugene Robinson, Disintegration: The Splintering of Black America 90–93 (2011).

10 Nat'l Ctr. for Educ. Statistics, The Traditionally Black Institutions of Higher Education 1860 to 1982 ix (1985), https://nces.ed.gov/pubs84/84308.pdf.

11 Nell Porter Brown, *Morehouse Man, Redux,* Harv. Mag., Nov.–Dec. 2013, at 72–75.

12 Fla. Const. art. IX, § 1(a); Act of June 9, 2003, Fla. Laws, ch. 2003–391.

13 *Reality Hits Home,* Gainesville Sun, Mar. 12, 2003, www.Gainesville.com/section/archive (last visited Feb. 13, 2017) [hereinafter *Sun Archive*].

14 Douane C. James, *School Zone*, Gainesville Sun, Dec.3, 2003, *Sun Archive, supra* note 13.

15 James, *Decision Time for School Transfers*, Gainesville Sun, Mar. 8, 2004, *Sun Archive, supra* note 13.

16 James, *Cross-Town Busing Reaches the End of the Road*, Gainesville Sun, May 31, 2004, *Sun Archive, supra* note 13.

17 Achenbach, *The Boy on the Bus*, Wash. Post, July 8, 2007, at B01.

18 James, *Brown v. Board, Panel Revisits Historic Decision*, Gainesville Sun, May 15, 2004, *Sun Archive, supra* note 13.

19 Gallant, Letter to the Editor, *The Resegregation of Gainesville*, Gainesville Sun, Oct. 13, 2003, *Sun Archive, supra* note 13. Gallant was retired from Gainesville High School and had also served on the school board.

20 James, *School Zone*, Gainesville Sun, Dec. 3, 2003, *Sun Archive, supra* note 13.

21 Cathi Carr, *Schools Imbalanced by Population, Race and Economics, Lessons Learned, Past School Boards Failed to Act*, Gainesville Sun, May 11, 2002, *Sun Archive, supra* note 13.

22 Carr, *School Board Considers Rezoning Proposal*, Gainesville Sun, Feb. 9, 2002, *Sun Archive, supra* note 13.

23 James, *County Schools Taking Next Steps (etc.)*, Gainesville Sun, Dec. 8, 2003, *Sun Archive, supra* note 13.

24 Parents Involved in Cmty. Schs. v. Seattle Sch. Dist. No. 1, 551 U.S. 701, (2007); *see* James E. Ryan, *Supreme Court and Voluntary Integration*, 121 Harv. L. Rev. 131 (2007); Martha Minow, *We're All for Equality in U.S. School Reforms: But What Does it Mean?, in* Just Schools, Pursuing Equality in Societies of Difference (Martha Minow, Richard A. Schweder & Hazel Rose Markus eds., 2008). For the story of the black and white parents and students who sued to end the Jefferson County, Kentucky, racial balancing plan, *see* Sarah Garland, Divided We Fail: The Story of an African American Community That Ended the Era of School Desegregation (2013); Tracy E. K'Meyer, From Brown to Meredith: The Long Struggle for School Desegregation in Louisville, Kentucky, 1954-2007 (2013). Jefferson County was a companion case to *Parents Involved*.

25 U.S. Dep't of Justice & U.S. Dep't of Educ., Guidance on the Voluntary Use of Race to Achieve Racial Diversity and Avoid Racial Isolation in Elementary and Secondary Schools, https://www2.ed.gov/about/offices/list/ocr/docs/guidance-ese-201111.html (last visited Dec. 2, 2016).

26 Fla. Stat. § 1002.31 (2016); Act of Apr. 14, 2016, ch. 2623, 2016 Fla. Laws 237, § 5.

27 Interview with Bettye & Ed Jennings, in Gainesville, Fla. 7 (Feb. 7, 2013) (on file with author).

28 Interview with Charles Chestnut III, in Gainesville, Fla. 11 and 28–29 (Apr. 14, 2014) (on file with author).

29 Interview by Joel Buchanan with Cora Roberson, in Gainesville, Fla. 31 (Feb. 19, 1986), http://ufdc.ufl.edu/UF00005433/00001.

30 Interview with Gertrude E. Jones, in Gainesville, Fla. 26–28 (Sept. 28, 2015) (on file with author).

31 Interview with Wayne Mosley, in Gainesville, Fla. 16 (Sept. 11, 2014) (on file with author).

32 *Id.* at 2–3, 14–15 and 25.

33 Interview with Mary Lewis, in Gainesville, Fla. 4–5 (June 4, 2014) (on file with author).

34 Interview with Sam Haywood, in Gainesville, Fla. 25 (July 14, 2014) (on file with author).

35 Interview with Bernice Dukes, John Dukes III & Carmen Dukes, in Gainesville, Fla. 17 (July 11, 2014) (on file with author)

36 Interview with John Dukes III, in Gainesville, Fla. 15 (March 5, 2014) (on file with author).

37 Interview with Jessie Heard, in Gainesville, Fla. 14–15, 22, and 31 (Feb. 4, 2014) (on file with author).

38 Interview by Joel Buchanan with T. B. McPherson, in Gainesville, Fla. 16 (Mar. 7, 1984), http://ufdc.ufl.edu/UF00005407/00001/.

39 Telephone Interview with Catherine Mickle, 15–17 (Oct. 2, 2015) (on file with author).

40 Interview with Sandra Sharron & Frank Ford, in Gainesville, Fla. 51 (Oct. 30, 2014) (on file with author).

41 Interview with Melvin Flournoy, in Gainesville, Fla. 24–27 (Oct. 1, 2015) (on file with author).

42 Interview with Brenda Wims, in Gainesville, Fla., 25–28 (Jan. 28, 2016) (on file with author).

43 Interview with the Rev. Thomas A. Wright, in Gainesville, Fla. 7–8 (Mar. 26, 2012) (on file with author); interview with Philoron Wright, in Gainesville, Fla. (Nov. 1, 2016) (notes on file with author).

44 Interview with Philoron Wright, *supra* note 43.

45 Interview with Frank Coleman, in Gainesville, Fla. 19 (Jan. 13, 2016) (on file with author)

46 Interview with Frank Coleman, Janice Cambridge Hagillih & Cynthia Cook, in Gainesville, Fla. 5 (May 24, 2016).

47 Interview with Frank Coleman, Janice Cambridge Hagillih & Cynthia Cook, *supra* note 46, at 2–3.

48 Telephone Interview with Donnie Batie, M.D., 25–27 (July 28, 2015) (on file with author).

49 Interview by Joel Buchanan with A. Quinn Jones, Oliver Jones & Vera Jones, in Gainesville, Fla. 12–13 (Sept. 7, 1994), Samuel Proctor Oral History Project, University of Florida.

50 Interview with Mae Islar, in Newberry, Fla. 26–27 (May 29, 2015) (on file with author).

51 Interview with Donnie Batie, M.D., *supra* note 48, at 31–32.

52 Denise C. Morgan, *What Is Left to Argue in Desegregation Law?: The Right to Minimally Adequate Education*, 8 Harv. BlackLetter J. 99, 110–111 (1991).

53 The Educational Accountability Act of 1971, ch. 71–197, 1971 Fla. Laws 1148; Deanna L. Michael & Sherman Dorn, *Accountability as a Means of Improvement: A Continuity of Themes, in* Education Reform in Florida: Diversity and Equity in Public Policy 91–95 (Kathryn M. Borman & Sherman Dorn eds., 2007).

54 Improving America's Schools Act of 1994, Pub. L. No. 103–382, § 1001(a), 108 Stat. 3518–22 (1994).

55 No Child Left Behind Act of 2001, Pub. L. No. 107–110, § 1001, 115 Stat. 1439–40 (2002).

56 Pub. L. No. 107–110, §§ 1111(b)(2)(F), 1111(b)(2)(C)(v), 115 Stat. 1446–48.

57 Pub. L. No. 114–95, § 1001, 129 Stat. 1814 (2015).

58 Pub. L. No. 114–94, §§ 1111(b)(2)(B)(xi), 1111(c)(2), 129 Stat. 1827, 1834 (2015).

59 S. Rep. No. 114–231, at 2–6 (2016).

60 For 2015–16 values, *see* Fla. Dept. of Educ., AMO Outcomes, 2015–16 (last visited Jan. 5, 2017), http://schoolgrades.fldoe.org. For 2014–15 values, *see* Fla. Dept. of Educ., AMO Outcomes, 201–15 (last visited Jan. 5, 2017), http://schoolgrades.fldoe.org/reports/index.asp.

61 The examples of current instructional techniques and community involvement are taken from School Improvement Plans filed annually with the Florida Department of Education by school districts and individual schools pursuant Elementary and Secondary Education Act tit. I, 20 U.S.C. § 6311(d)(1) and Fla. Stat. § 1001.42(18) (2016). *See* Continuous Improvement Management System, https://www.floridacims.org/districts. The Alachua County plans were accessed during December 2016 and January 2017.

62 Broussard v. Houston Ind. School District, 395 F.2d 817, 828 (Wisdom, J., dissenting), dismissed for mootness and reh'g en banc denied, 403 F.2d 34 (5th Cir. 1968).

63 Interview by Joel Buchanan with John Dukes, Jr., in Gainesville, Fla. 24 (Aug. 2, 1985), http://ufdc.ufl.edu/UF00005423/00001.

64 The phrase is used by Arjun Appadurai in Modernity at Large: Cultural Dimensions of Globalization 30 (1996).

65 Fla. Dept. of Educ., Staff in Florida's Public Schools, Fall 2015 (last visited Jan. 4, 2017), http://www.fldoe.org/accountability/data-sys/edu-info-accountability-services/pk-12-public-school-data-pubs-reports/staff.stml; ARInstructionalStaff.xls (excel file) ("Staff in Florida's Public Schools, Fall 2015")(last visited Jan. 4, 2017).

66 David F. Labaree, Someone Has to Fail: The Zero-Sum Game of Public Schooling 143 (2010).

67 Interview with John Dukes III, *supra* note 36, at 17.

68 Vivian Gunn Morris & Curtis L. Morris, *Before* Brown, *After* Brown*: What Has Changed for African-American Children?* 16 U. of Fla. J. of Law and Pub. Policy 215, 236 (2005).

BIBLIOGRAPHY

Government Documents

1970 Census of Population. Washington: US Dept. of Commerce, Bureau of the Census: 1972.

Advisory Commission on Race Relations to Governor Leroy Collins, Report. March 16, 1959. https://archive.org/details/ReportOfTheAdvisoryCommissionOnRaceRelationsToGovernorLeroyCollins.

Alachua County Board of Public Instruction, Minutes. All minutes from 1964 through 1973 were reviewed. Selected minutes from dates outside this period were also reviewed.

Bagley, William. *Emergency School Assistance, Issue Brief No. IB74082*. Library of Congress, Congressional Research Service. 1976. http://digitalcollections.library.cmu.edu/awweb/awarchive?type=file&item=401682.

Employment Opportunities Council of Gainesville and Alachua County. *A Survey of Employment Opportunities in Gainesville and Alachua County, Florida*. October 1969.

Florida Department of Education, Race to the Top Executive Summary. December 2015. https://www2.ed.gov/programs/racetothetop/state-reported-sharing/flexsumm.pdf.

Mayo, Nathan. *State of Florida, The Fifth Census of the State of Florida Taken in the Year 1925*. Tallahassee, FL: T.J. Appleyard, 1926.

School Board of Alachua County, Informal File on Desegregation. Undated.

Special Committee Appointed by the Governor and Cabinet of the State of Florida to Recommend Legislative Action Relating to Public School Education and Other Internal Affairs of Such State Deemed Expedient after Consideration of Recent Decisions of the Supreme Court of the United States. Report. July 16, 1956.

State of Florida, Department of Education, *Update of Survey of School Plants, Alachua County (Feb. 1965), Dec. 1967.*

State of Florida, Department of Education, *Update of Survey of School Plants, Alachua County (Feb. 1965), Jan. 1966.*

United States Census Bureau, "A Half-Century of Learning: Historical Census Statistics on Educational Attainment in the United States, 1940 to 2000: Detailed Tables," tables 11, 12, 7, and 8. Last visited Dec. 8, 2016. https://www.census.gov/data/tables/time-series/demo/educational-attainment/educational-attainment-1940-2000.html.

US Civil Rights Commission, 89th Congress. *Survey of School Desegregation in the Southern and Border States 1965-66.* 1966.

United States Commission on Civil Rights, Florida Advisory Committee. *Desegregation in Public School Districts in Florida: 18 Public School Districts Have Unitary Status, 16 Districts Remain Under Court Jurisdiction.* Undated, released 2006.

United States Commission on Civil Rights, Office of the General Counsel. *Closing the Achievement Gap: The Impact of Standards-Based Education Reform on Student Performance, Draft Report for Commissioners' Review.* July 2, 2004.

James S. Coleman, principal investigator. *US Department of Health, Education, and Welfare, Equality of Educational Opportunity Study.* 1966.

US Department of Justice, Civil Rights Division, and US Department of Education, Office for Civil Rights. *Guidance on the Voluntary Use of Race to Achieve Diversity and Avoid Racial Isolation in Elementary and Secondary Schools.* Undated. https://www2.ed.gov/about/offices/list/ocr/docs/guidance-ese-201111.pdf.

US Department of Justice. *Statement by the Honorable Robert H. Finch, Secretary of the Department of Health, Education, and Welfare, and the Honorable John N. Mitchell, Attorney General.* July 3, 1969. https://www.justice.gov/sites/default/files/ag/legacy/2011/08/23/07–03–1969.pdf.

Books

Alexander, Michelle. *The New Jim Crow: Mass Incarceration in the Age of Colorblindness.* New York: The New Press, 2012.

Allport, Gordon W. *The Nature of Prejudice.* New York: Basic Books, 1979.

Anderson, James D. *The Education of Blacks in the South, 1860–1935.* Chapel Hill: University of North Carolina Press, 1988.

Appadurai, Arjun. *Modernity at Large: Cultural Dimensions of Globalization.* Minneapolis: University of Minnesota Press, 1996.

Baker, R. Scott. *Paradoxes of Desegregation.* Columbia: University of South Carolina Press, 2006.

Bass, Jack. *Unlikely Heroes.* Tuscaloosa: University of Alabama Press, 1990.

Bell, Derrick. *Silent Covenants,* Brown v. Board of Education *and the Unfulfilled Hopes for Racial Reform.* Oxford: Oxford University Press, 2004.

Bentley, George R. *A History of Holy Trinity Episcopal Church, Gainesville, Florida.* Gainesville: Holy Trinity Church, 1998.

Boger, John Charles, and Gary Orfield. *School Resegregation: Must the South Turn Back?* Chapel Hill: University of North Carolina Press, 2005.

Borman, Kathryn M., and Sherman Dorn, eds. *Education Reform in Florida: Diversity and Equity in Public Policy*. Albany: State University of New York Press, 2007.

Charles, Jeffrey. *Service Clubs in American Society*. Champaign: University of Illinois Press, 1993.

Clemons, Mae O. *Florida's Forgotten Legacy: Segregated Black Secondary Schools*. Tallahassee: Mae O. Clemons, 2006.

Cochrane, Thomas Everette. *History of Public-School Education in Florida*. Lancaster, PA: New Era, 1921. Public domain reprint.

Dawsey, Darrell. *Living to Tell About It: Young Black Men in America Speak Their Piece*. New York: Anchor Books, 1996.

Dyckman, Martin A. *Floridian of His Century: The Courage of Governor LeRoy Collins*. Gainesville: University Press of Florida, 2006.

Emmons, Caroline. "A State Divided, Implementation of the *Brown* Decision in Florida, 1954–1970." In *With All Deliberate Speed: Implementing* Brown v. Board of Education, edited by Brian Daugherity and Charles Bolton. Fayetteville: University of Arkansas Press, 2008.

Erickson, Ansley T. *Making the Unequal Metropolis: School Desegregation and Its Limits*. Chicago: University of Chicago Press (2016).

Fairclough, Adam. *Teaching Equality: Black Schools in the Age of Jim Crow*. Athens: University of Georgia Press, 2001.

Foner, Eric. *Reconstruction: America's Unfinished Revolution, 1863–1877*. New York: Perennial Classics, HarperCollins, 2002.

Friedman, Leon, ed. *Argument: The Oral Argument Before the Supreme Court in* Brown v. Board of Education *of Topeka, 1952–55*. New York: Chelsea House Publishers, 1969.

Gannon, Michael, ed. *The History of Florida*. Gainesville: University Press of Florida, 2013.

Garland, Sarah. *Divided We Fail: The Story of an African American Community That Ended the Era of School Desegregation*. Boston: Beacon Press, 2013.

Greenberg, Jack. *Crusaders in the Courts: Legal Battles of the Civil Rights Movement*. Anniversary ed. New York: Twelve Tables Press, 2004.

Hale, Grace Elizabeth. *Making Whiteness: The Culture of Segregation in the South, 1890–1940*. New York: Vintage Books, 1998.

Hildreth, Charles H., and Merlin G. Cox. *A History of Gainesville, Florida*. Gainesville: Alachua County Historical Society, 1981.

Hoff, Joan. *Nixon Reconsidered*. New York: Basic Books, 1994.

Jacobstein, Helen L. "The Segregation Factor in the Florida Democratic Gubernatorial Primary of 1956." Gainesville: University of Florida Press, 1972. http://ufdc.ufl.edu/AM00000079/00001/2.

Jones, A. Quinn, Sr. *Retrospections, November 1967*. Gainesville: 1stBooks, 2003.

Jourard, Marty. *Music Everywhere: The Rock and Roll Roots of a Southern Town*. Gainesville: University Press of Florida, 2016.

Klarman, Michael J. *From Jim Crow to Civil Rights: The Supreme Court and the Struggle for Racial Equality*. New York: Oxford University Press, 2004.

Kluger, Richard. *Simple Justice*. New York: Vintage Books, 2004.

K'Meyer, Tracy E. *From Brown to Meredith: The Long Struggle for School Desegregation in Louisville, Kentucky, 1954–2007*. Chapel Hill: University of North Carolina Press, 2013.

Kotlowski, Dean J. *Nixon's Civil Rights*. Cambridge: Harvard University Press, 2001.

Kurlansky, Mark. *1968: The Year That Rocked the World*. New York: Random House, 2005.

Labaree, David F. *Someone Has to Fail: The Zero-Sum Game of Public Schooling*. Cambridge: Harvard University Press, 2012.

Landers, Jane. *Black Society in Spanish Florida*. Urbana: University of Illinois Press, 1999.

LaNier, Carlotta Walls. *A Mighty Long Way: My Journey to Justice and Little Rock Central High School*. With Lisa Frazier Page. New York: One World Trade Paperbacks, 2010.

Littlejohn, Jeffrey L., and Charles H. Ford. *Elusive Equality: Desegregation and Resegregation in Norfolk's Public Schools*. Charlottesville: University of Virginia Press, 2012.

Lukas, J. Anthony. *Common Ground: A Turbulent Decade in the Lives of Three American Families*. New York: Vintage Books, 1986.

Manley, Walter Brown, II, and Canter Brown Jr. *The Supreme Court of Florida, 1917–1972*. University Press of Florida, 2006.

Margold, Nathan R. *Preliminary Report to the Joint Committee Supervising the Expenditure of the 1930 Appropriation by the American Fund for Public Service*. 1931. NAACP Records, Manuscript Division, Library of Congress.

Metz, Mary Haywood. *Classrooms and Corridors: The Crisis of Authority in Desegregated Secondary Schools*. Berkeley: University of California Press, 1978.

Minow, Martha. *In Brown's Wake: Legacies of America's Educational Landmark*. Oxford: Oxford University Press, 2010.

Minow, Martha, Richard A. Schweder, and Hazel Rose Markus, eds. *Just Schools: Pursuing Equality in Societies of Difference*. New York: Russell Sage Foundation, 2008.

Morris, Willie. *Yazoo*. New York: Ballantine Books, 1971.

Motley, Constance Baker. *Equal Justice Under Law*. New York: Farrar, Strauss & Giroux, 1998.

Newman, Mark. *Getting Right with God: Southern Baptists and School Desegregation, 1945–1995*. Tuscaloosa: University of Alabama Press, 2001.

Newton, Michael. *The Invisible Empire: The Ku Klux Klan in Florida*. Gainesville: University Press of Florida, 2001.

Ortiz, Paul. *Emancipation Betrayed: The Hidden History of Black Organizing and White Violence in Florida from Reconstruction to the Bloody Election of 1920*. Berkeley: University of California Press, 2005.

Panetta, Leon, and Peter Gall. *Bring Us Together: The Nixon Team and the Civil Rights Retreat*. Philadelphia: J. B. Lippincott, 1971.

Patchen, Martin. *Black-White Contact in Schools: Its Social and Economic Effects.* West Lafayette, IN: Purdue University Press, 1981.

Patterson, James T. Brown v. Board of Education: *A Civil Rights Milestone and Its Troubled Legacy.* New York: Oxford University Press, 2002.

Patterson, James T. *Grand Expectations: The United States, 1945–1974.* New York: Oxford University Press, 1996.

Perry, Theresa, Claude Steele, and Asa Hilliard III. *Young, Gifted and Black: Promoting High Achievement Among African-American Students.* Boston: Beacon Press, 2003.

Powell, Gloria J. *Black Monday's Children: A Study of the Effects of School Desegregation on Self-Concepts of Southern Children.* New York: Appleton-Century-Crofts, 1973.

Pride, Richard A. *The Political Use of Racial Narratives: School Desegregation in Mobile, Alabama, 1954–97.* Urbana: University of Illinois Press, 2002.

Pride, Richard A., and J. David Woodward. *The Burden of Busing: The Politics of Desegregation in Nashville, Tennessee.* Knoxville: University of Tennessee Press, 1985.

Read, Frank T., and Lucy S. McGough. *Let Them Be Judged: The Judicial Integration of the Deep South.* Metuchen, NJ: The Scarecrow Press, 1978.

Robinson, Eugene. *Disintegration: The Splintering of Black America.* New York: Anchor Books, 2010.

Robinson, Mildred Wigfall, and Richard J. Bonnie. *Law Touched Our Hearts: A Generation Remembers* Brown v. Board of Education. Nashville: Vanderbilt University Press, 2009.

Shircliffe, Barbara J. *The Best of That World: Historically Black High Schools and the Crisis of Desegregation in a Southern Metropolis.* Cresskill, NJ: Hampton Press, 2006.

Shofner, Jerrell H. *Nor Is It Over Yet: Florida in the Age of Reconstruction, 1863–1877.* Gainesville: University Presses of Florida, 1974.

Sizemore, Barbara A. *Walking in Circles: The Black Struggle for School Reform.* Chicago: Third World Press, 2008.

Southern Education Foundation. *Redeeming the American Promise: Report of the Panel on Educational Opportunity and Postsecondary Desegregation.* Atlanta: Southern Education Foundation, 1995.

Thomas, Dale A. *A Band in Every School: Portraits of Historically Black School Bands in Florida.* Tallahassee: Harmonie Publishing, LLC, 2008.

Tushnet, Mark V. *The NAACP's Legal Strategy Against Segregated Education, 1925–1950.* Chapel Hill: University of North Carolina Press, 1987 and 2004.

Walker, Vanessa Siddle. *Their Highest Potential: An African American School Community in the Segregated South.* Chapel Hill: University of North Carolina Press, 1996.

Watkins, William H. *The White Architects of Black Education: Ideology and Power in America, 1865–1954.* New York: Teachers College Press, 2001.

Weaver, C. Douglas. *Every Town Needs a Downtown Church, A History of First Baptist Church of Gainesville, Florida*. Nashville: Southern Baptist Historical Society, 2000.

Webber, Carl. *The Eden of the South: Descriptive of the Orange Groves, Vegetable Farms, Strawberry Fields, Peach Orchards, Soil, Climate, Natural Peculiarities, and the People of Alachua County, Florida, Together with Other Valuable Information for Tourists, Invalids*. New York: Leve & Alden's Publication Department, 1883. Public Domain Reprint.

Weeks, William Earl. *John Quincy Adams and American Global Empire*. Lexington: University Press of Kentucky, 1992.

Wells, Amy Stuart, Jennifer Jellison Holme, Anita Tijerna Revilla, and Awo Korentemaa Atanda. *Both Sides Now: The Story of School Desegregation's Graduates*. Berkeley: University of California Press, 2009.

White, Albert, and Kevin McCarthy. *Lincoln High School, Gainesville Florida: Its History and Legacy*. Gainesville, 2011.

White, Arthur O. *Florida's Crisis in Public Education: Changing Patterns of Leadership*. Gainesville: University Presses of Florida, 1975.

White, Arthur O. *One Hundred Years of State Leadership in Public Education in Florida*. Gainesville: University Presses of Florida, 1979.

Wicker, Tom. *One of Us: Richard Nixon and the American Dream*. New York: Random House, 1991.

Woodward, C. Vann. *The Strange Career of Jim Crow*. Commemorative ed. Oxford: Oxford University Press, 2002.

Wright, Thomas A., Sr. *Courage in Persona*. Ocala: Special Publications Inc., 1993.

Periodicals

Every issue of the *Gainesville Sun* beginning in 1963 and ending in March 1973 was reviewed. Selected issues before and after that period were also reviewed. References to the Holmes County *Advertiser* are specific to issues published between 1931 and 1935.

Achenbach, Joel. "The Boy on the Bus." *Washington Post*, July 8, 2007.

Alston, Jon P., and Melvin J. Knapp. "Black Attitudes Toward Speed of School Integration, 1969." *Journal of Negro Education* 41 (1972): 331.

Baier, Paul R. "Framing and Reviewing a Desegregation Decree: Of the Chancellor's Foot and Fifth Circuit Control." *Louisiana Law Review* 47 (1986): 123.

Beaudoin, Mike. "Florida Makes Big Strides in Education of Negroes." *St. Petersburg Times*, July 19, 1952.

Bell, Derrick A., Jr. "*Brown v. Board of Education* and the Interest-Convergence Dilemma." *Harvard Law Review* 93 (1980): 518.

Bell, Derrick A., Jr. "Serving Two Masters: Integration Ideals and Client Interests in School Desegregation Litigation." *Yale Law Journal* 85 (1976): 470.

Bickel, Alexander M. "The Decade of School Desegregation – Progress and Prospects." *Columbia Law Review* 64 (1964): 193.

Black, Derrick. "Civil Rights, Charter Schools, and Lessons to Be Learned." *Florida Law Review* 64 (2012): 1723.

Bolner, James, and Arnold Vedlitz. "The Affinity of Negro Pupils for Segregated Schools: Obstacle to Desegregation." *Journal of Negro Education* 40 (1971): 313.

Borman, Kathryn M., Tamela McNulty Eitle, Deanna Michael, David Eitle, Reginald Lee, Larry Johnson, Dierdre Cobb-Roberts, Sherman Dorn, and Barbara Shircliffe. "Accountability in a Post-Desegregation Era: The Continuing Significance of Racial Segregation in Florida Schools." *American Education Journal* 41 (2004): 605.

Bradley, Laurence A., and Gifford W. Bradley. "The Academic Achievement of Black Students in Desegregated Schools." *Review of Educational Research* 47 (1977): 399.

Brown, Nell Porter. "Morehouse Man, Redux." *Harvard Magazine*, November–December (2013): 72–75.

Brown, Richard W. "Freedom of Choice in the South: A Constitutional Perspective." *Louisiana Law Review* 28 (1968): 455–459.

Bruno, Anthony Francis. "Is Achieving Equal Educational Opportunity Possible? An Empirical Study of New York State Public Schools." *Journal of Civil Rights and Economic Development* 25 (2011): 225.

Bullock, Charles S., III. "Adjusting to School Desegregation: Perceptions and Correlates of Post-Desegregation Problems." *The Negro Education Review* 29 (1978): 87.

Bullock, Charles S., III. "Interracial Contact and Student Prejudice: The Impact of Southern School Desegregation." *Youth & Society* 7 (1976): 271.

Carter, Robert L. "The NAACP's Legal Strategy Against Segregated Education." *Michigan Law Review* 86 (1988): 1083.

Chandler, Susan Kerr. "'Almost a Partnership': African-Americans, Segregation and the Young Men's Christian Association." *Journal of Sociology & Social Welfare* 21 (2015): 97.

Colburn, David R., and Richard K. Scher. "The Aftermath of the Brown Decision in Florida: The Politics of Interposition in Florida." *Tequesta* 1, no. 37 (1977): 62.

Comment. "Administrative Law – Desegregation – Judicial Adoption of Administrative Agency Guidelines." *Iowa Law Review* 53 (1967): 195.

Days, Drew S., III. "*Brown* Blues: Rethinking the Integrative Ideal." *William and Mary Law Review* 34 (1992): 53.

Days, Drew S., III. "The Other Desegregation Story: Eradicating the Dual School System in Hillsborough County, Florida." *Fordham Law Review* 61 (1992): 33.

Dingus, Jeannine E. "'Doing the Best We Could': African American Teachers' Counterstory on School Desegregation." *Urban Review* 38 (2006): 211.

Du Bois, W. E. Burghardt. "Does the Negro Need Separate Schools?" *Journal of Negro Education* 4 (1935): 328.

Editorial. "Will Florida Abolish Its Schools?" *Melbourne Times*, May 26, 1953.

Egalite, Anna J., Brian Kisida, and Marcus A. Winters. "Representation in the Classroom: The Effect of Own-Race Teachers on Student Achievement." *Economics of Education Review* 45 (2015): 44.

Ethridge, Samuel B. "Impact of the Brown v. Topeka Board of Education Decision on Black Educators." *Negro Education Review* 30 (1979): 217.

Fernandez, Ferdinand F. "The Constitutionality of the Fourteenth Amendment." *Southern California Law Review* 39 (1966): 378.

Fiss, Owen M. "Racial Imbalance in the Public Schools: The Constitutional Concepts." *Harvard Law Review* 78 (1965): 564.

Ford, Richard Thompson. "*Brown*'s Ghost." *Harvard Law Review* 117 (2004): 1305.

Frankenberg, Erica, and Kendra Taylor. "ESEA and the Civil Rights Act: An Interbranch Approach to Furthering Desegregation." *Russell Sage Foundation Journal of the Social Sciences* 1 (2015): 32–42.

Franklin, John Hope. "Behind the *Brown* Decision: A Conversation with John Hope Franklin." *Stetson Law Review* 34 (2005): 433.

Gellhorn, Walter. "A Decade of Desegregation – Retrospect and Prospect." *Utah Law Review* 9 (1964): 3.

Gewirtz, Paul. "Remedies and Resistance." *Yale Law Journal* 92 (1983): 585.

Greenfield, Helaine. "Some Constitutional Problems with the Resegregation of Public Schools." *Georgetown Law Journal* 80 (1991): 363.

Hawley, Willis D. "The New Mythology of School Desegregation." *Law & Contemporary Problems* 42 (1978): 214.

Hesser, Charles. "Florida is Improving Its Negro Institutions." *Miami Daily News*, January 25, 1953.

Hond, Paul. "Justice's Son." *Columbia Magazine*, Spring 2013, http://magazine.columbia.edu/features/spring-2013/justices-son?page=0,0. Accessed Sept. 8, 2017.

Huess. "Rolling Green Academy, A Colorful Past." *Alachua Post*, 2002. http://alachuapost.com/All.1090.html?2800. Accessed March 4, 2014; this site is no longer active.

Hutchinson, Darren. "Social Movements and Judging: An Essay on Institutional Reform Litigation and Desegregation in Dallas, Texas." *Southern Methodist University Law Review* 62 (2009): 1635.

Irvine, Russell W., and Jacqueline Jordan Irvine. "The Impact of the Desegregation Process on the Education of Black Students: Key Variables." *Journal of Negro Education* 52 (1983): 410.

James, Bernard, and Julie M. Hoffman. "*Brown* in State Hands: State Policymaking and Educational Equality After *Freeman v. Pitts*." *Hastings Constitutional Law Quarterly* 20 (1993): 521.

Jeynes, William H. "A Meta-analysis of the Factors that Best Reduce the Achievement Gap." *Education and Urban Society* 47 (2014): 523.

Jones, Nathaniel R., and Derrick A. Bell Jr. "Correspondence, School Desegregation." *Yale Law Journal* 86 (1976): 378.

Kimerling, Joshua E. "Black Male Academies: Re-examining the Strategy of Integration." *Buffalo Law Review* 42 (1994): 829.

Landsberg, Brian K. "Equal Educational Opportunity: The Rehnquist Court Revisits *Green* and *Swann*." *Emory Law Journal* 42 (1993): 821.

Laurie, Murray D. "The Union Academy: A Freedmen's Bureau School in Gainesville, Florida." *Florida Historical Quarterly* 65 (1986): 163.

Leeson, Jim. "Desegregation: Faster Pace, Scarcer Records." *Southern Education Report*, January/February 1966: 28–30.

Linder, Douglas O. "Bending Toward Justice: John Doar and the Mississippi Burning Trial." *Mississippi Law Journal* 72 (2002): 731.

Locke, Alain. "The Dilemma of Segregation." *Journal of Negro Education* 4 (1935): 406.

Long, Howard Hale. "Some Psychogenic Hazards of Segregated Education of Negroes." *Journal of Negro Education* 4 (1935): 336.

Meador, Daniel J. "The Constitution and the Assignment of Pupils to Public Schools." *Virginia Law Review* 45 (1959): 517.

McUsic, Molly. "The Future of *Brown v. Board of Education*: Economic Integration of the Public Schools." *Harvard Law Review* 117 (2004): 1334.

Morgan, Denise C. "What Is Left to Argue in Desegregation Law?: The Right to Minimally Adequate Education." *Harvard BlackLetter Journal* 8 (1991): 99.

Morris, Vivian Gunn, and Curtis L. Morris. "Before *Brown*, After *Brown*: What Has Changed for African-American Children?" *University of Florida Journal of Law and Public Policy* 16 (2005): 215.

Note. "Civil Rights – Desegregation – Freedom-of-Choice Plans Are Not To Be Used When More Effective Means for Desegregation Are Available." *Vanderbilt Law Review* 21 (1968): 1093.

Note. "Civil Rights – Desegregation – School Authorities Have Affirmative Duty to Integrate School System." *Vanderbilt Law Review* 20 (1967): 1336.

Note. "Constitutional Law – Civil Rights – School Desegregation – HEW Guidelines Constitutionally Require School Boards to Affirmatively Abolish the Existing Effects of De Jure Segregation." *Rutgers Law Review* 21 (1967): 753.

Note. "Constitutional Law – Equal Protection of the Laws – The HEW Guidelines are Minimum Standards for a Free Choice School Desegregation Program." *Harvard Law Review* 81 (1967): 474.

Note. "The Federal Courts and Integration of Southern Schools: Troubled Status of the Pupil Placement Acts." *Columbia Law Review* 62 (1962): 1448.

Note. "Integration: A Tool for the Achievement of the Goal of Quality Education." *Howard Law Journal* 14 (1968): 372.

Orfield, Gary. "How to Make Desegregation Work: Adaptation of Schools to Their Newly-Integrated Student Bodies." *Law & Contemporary Problems* 39 (1975): 314.

Parker, Laurence, ed. "Special Issue on The Elementary and Secondary Education Act at 40: Reviews of Research, Policy Implementation, Critical Perspectives, and Reflections." *Review of Research in Education* 29 (2005).

Peterson, Gladys Tignor. "The Present Status of the Negro Separate School as Defined by Court Decisions." *Journal of Negro Education* 4 (1935): 351.

Prescott, Stephen R. "White Robes and Crosses: Father John Conoley, the Ku Klux Klan and the University of Florida." *Florida Historical Quarterly* 71 (1992): 18.

Prokos, Katina. "Alachua County Superintendent to Retire After Almost 50 Years in Education." WUFT News, September 2, 2013. Accessed February 10, 2017. https://www.wuft.org/news/2013/09/02/boyd-profile/.

Read, F. T. "Judicial Evolution of the Law of School Integration Since *Brown v. Board of Education*." *Law & Contemporary Problems* 39 (1975): 7.

Roundtable Discussion. "Knights at the Roundtable: Panel Reflections and Discourse on *Brown I* and *Brown II*." *Stetson Law Review* 34 (2005): 499.

Rumberger, Russell W., and Gregory J. Palardy. "Does Segregation Still Matter? The Impact of Student Composition on Academic Achievement in High School." *Teachers College Record* 107 (2005): 1999.

Russell Sage Foundation. "The Elementary and Secondary Education Act at Fifty and Beyond." *Russell Sage Foundation Journal of the Social Sciences* 1, no. 3 (2015).

Ryan, James E. "The Supreme Court and Voluntary Integration." *Harvard Law Review* 121 (2007): 131.

Schafer, Daniel L. "A Class of People Neither Freemen nor Slaves: From Spanish to American Race Relations in Florida, 1821–61." *Journal of Social History* 26 (1993): 587.

Schnur, James A. "Desegregation of Public Schools in Pinellas County, Florida." *Tampa Bay History* 13 (1991): 26.

Shircliffe, Barbara J. "Desegregation and the Historically Black School: The Establishment of Howard W. Blake in Tampa, Florida." *Urban Review* 34 (2002): 135.

Silverman, Irwin, and Marvin E. Shaw. "Effects of Sudden Mass School Desegregation on Interracial Interaction and Attitudes in One Southern City." *Journal of Social Issues* 29 (1973): 133.

Slavin, Robert E., and Nancy A. Madden. "School Practices That Improve Race Relations." *American Educational Research Journal* 16 (1979): 169.

Spindel, Frederic T. "Constitutional Law – In Order to Eliminate the Effects of Past Segregation Policies, School Boards Are Under an Affirmative Duty to Achieve Substantial Integration in Formerly De Jure Segregated School Systems." Note. *Texas Law Review* 46 (1967): 266.

Stephan, Walter G. "School Desegregation: An Evaluation of Predictions Made in *Brown v. Board of Education*." *Psychological Bulletin* 85 (1978): 217.

Thimmesch, Nick. "Wallace in Position to Harry the President." *Los Angeles Times*, June 8, 1970.

Thompson, Charles H. "Court Action the Only Reasonable Alternative to Remedy Immediate Abuses of the Negro Separate School." *Journal of Negro Education* 4 (1935): 419–420.

Tolsdorf, Peter. "If Separate, Then at Least Equal." *George Washington Law Review* 73 (2005): 668.

Vedlitz, Arnold. "Factors Affecting the Attitudes of Black High School Students Toward 'Freedom of Choice' School Integration." *Negro Education Review* 31 (1975): 37.

Vettel, Quenta. "Social Unrest Through the Alligator's Lens." 2013. (University of Florida College of Journalism and Communications). http://www.humanities.ufl.edu/calendar/20130128-Academic-Freedom.html. Accessed July 8, 2013

Wells, Amy Stuart, and Robert L. Craig. "Perpetuation Theory and the Long-Term Effects of School Desegregation." *Review of Education Research* 64 (1994): 531.

Yergin, Rebecca I. "Rethinking Public Education Litigation Strategy: A Duty-Based Approach to Reform." *Columbia Law Review* 116 (2015): 563.

Theses, Dissertations, and Research Papers

Charbonnet, Jeffry L. "The Public School System of Alachua County 1821–1955." Master's thesis, University of Florida, 1991. On file with author.

Coleman, James S., Sara A. Kelly, and John A. Moore. "Trends in School Desegregation, 1968–1973." The Urban Institute, Washington, DC, 1975. http://www.eric.ed.gov/?id=ED117252.

Hanushek, Eric A., John F. Kain, and Steven G. Rivkin. "New Evidence about *Brown v. Board of Education*: The Complex Effects of School Racial Composition on Achievement." National Bureau of Economic Research, Cambridge, MA, 2002.

Houchon, Diedre Faith. "The Transcendent Pedagogy of Lincoln High School, 1921-1955: The Aims, Pursuits and Professional Development of African American Education During De Jure Segregation." PhD dissertation, University of Florida, 2015. On file with author.

Knapp, Colin A. "The Effects of Unitary Status on Academic Achievement and School Finance: Essays on the End of the Court-Ordered Desegregation Era." PhD thesis, University of Florida, 2010. http://etd.fcla.edu/UF/UFE0042126/knapp_c.pdf

Landers, Stuart. "The Gainesville Women for Equal Rights, 1963-1978." Master's thesis, University of Florida, 1995. Excerpts on file with author.

Martinelli, Amy Camille. "A Moderate Calm? Florida's Struggle Over School Desegregation After *Brown*, 1955–1961." EdM thesis, University of Florida, 2007. http://ufdc.ufl.edu/UFE0020155/0001/9j.

Poppell, Judith Bockel. "The Desegregation of a Historically Black High School in Jacksonville, Florida." (1998), EdD thesis, University of North Florida, 1968. On file with author.

Southern Association of Colleges and Schools. *Evaluation Report, Gainesville High School, Gainesville, Florida, 1970–1971*. 1971.

Tomberlin, Joseph Aaron. "The Negro and Florida's System of Education: The Aftermath of the Brown Case." PhD thesis, Florida State University, 1967. On file with author.

Interviews

William Adams, in discussion with the author, May 19, 2015. On file with author.

Andy Adkins, in discussion with the author, February 22, 2016. On file with author.

Donnie Batie, MD, in discussion with the author, July 28, 2015. On file with author.
Roberta Berner, in discussion with the author, March 22, 2012. Notes on file with author.
Dan Boyd, EdD, in discussion with the author, June 10, 2014. On file with author.
Shelton Boyles, in discussion with the author, June 10, 2014. Notes on file with author.
Joel Buchanan, interview by Gayle Yamada, February 12, 1984. Samuel Proctor Oral History Project, University of Florida Digital Collections. http://ufdc.ufl.edu/UF00005406/00001.
Alvin Butler, in discussion with the author, March 11, 2016. On file with author.
Reeves Byrd, in discussion with the author, September 30, 2015. Audio on file with author.
Janice Cambridge Hagillih, in discussion with the author, May 24, 2016. Notes on file with author.
Jean Chalmers, in discussion with the author, August 28, 2015. On file with author.
Charles Chestnut III, in discussion with the author and Marilyn Tubb, April 14, 2014. On file with author.
Charles Chestnut III, in discussion with the author and Marilyn Tubb, September 10, 2014. On file with author.
Frank Coleman, in discussion with the author, January 13, 2016. On file with author.
Frank Coleman, in discussion with the author, May 24, 2016. Notes on file with author.
Cynthia Cook, in discussion with the author, May 24, 2016. Notes on file with author.
Jay Cooper, in discussion with the author, October 1, 2015. On file with author.
Clif Cormier, in discussion with the author, November 8, 2013. Notes on file with author.
Theodore Covey, PhD, in discussion with the author, February 7, 2016. On file with author.
Thomas Coward, interview by Douglas Malenfant, June 5, 2009. Audio record at http://ufdc.ufl.edu/AA00015871/00001.
Mary Anne Coxe Zimmerman, in discussion with the author, August 31, 2015. Audio on file with author.
Patricia Crawford, in discussion with the author, May 23, 2016. Audio on file with author.
Albert Daniels, 1972. Summary in EDF 600 File.
Orion W. Davis, in discussion with the author, January 18, 2012. Notes on file with author.
Thomas Deakin, in discussion with the author, February 21, 2016. Audio on file with author.
Vince Deconna, in discussion with the author, March 22, 2016. Audio on file with author.
Charles Denny, in discussion with the author, January 18, 2012. Notes on file with author.
Bernice Dukes, in discussion with the author, July 11, 2014. On file with author.

Carmen Dukes, in discussion with the author, July 11, 2014. On file with author.

John Dukes Jr., interview by Joel Buchanan, August 2, 1985. http://ufdc.ufl.edu/UF00005423/00001.

John Dukes III, in discussion with the author, March 5 and July 11, 2014. On file with author.

Miles Eldridge, in discussion with author, February 2013.

Kayser Enneking, MD, in discussion with the author, January 22, 2015. Notes on file with author.

Peggy Finley, in discussion with the author, April 2012. On file with author.

Melvin Flournoy, in discussion with the author, October 1, 2015. On file with author.

Wayne Floyd, in discussion with author, August 25, 2015. Audio on file with author.

Frank Ford, in discussion with the author, October 30, 2014. On file with author.

Barbara Gray Brown, in discussion with the author, February 23, 2016. Audio on file with author.

Brenda Gresham Rainsberger, in discussion with the author, May 12, 2016. Audio on file with author.

Sam Haywood, in discussion with the author, July 14, 2014. On file with author.

Jessie Heard, in discussion with the author, February 4, 2014. On file with author.

Steve Hegarty, in discussion with the author, Hillsborough County School District, March 18, 2015. Notes on file with author.

Susan Holloway Weinkle, MD, in discussion with the author, January 15, 2016. Notes on file with author.

Mack Hope, in discussion with the author, February 3, 2016. Notes on file with author.

Mary Beth Hutchinson, in discussion with the author, May 23, 2015. Notes on file with author.

Mae Islar, March 1, 2011. On file with the University of Florida Samuel Proctor Oral History Project, AAHP 162, audio.

Mae Islar, in discussion with the author, May 29, 2015. On file with author.

Bettye & Ed Jennings, in discussion with the author, February 7, 2013. On file with author.

Gertrude E. Jones, in discussion with the author, September 28, 2015. On file with author.

A. Quinn Jones and his son Oliver and daughter Vera, interview by Joel Buchanan, September 7, 1994. Samuel Proctor Oral History Project.

Dr. Isaac Jones, interview by Donald Sanchez, June 4, 2010. http://ufdc.ufl.edu/AA00015856/00001.

Thelma Jordon, interview by Joel Buchanan, January 24, 1984. http://ufdc.ufle.edu/UF00005405/00001.

John King, in discussion with the author, April 30, 2016. On file with author.

Sue Legg, PhD, interview by Stuart Landers, August 4, 1992. http://ufdc.ufl.edu/UF00093318/00001.

Mary Lewis, in discussion with the author, June 4, 2014. Notes on file with author.

Elizabeth Mallonee, in discussion with the author, January 26, 2016. On file with author.

Jerry Mauldin, in discussion with the author, February 16, 2016. On file with author.

Andrew Mickle, interview by Terry Leiva, 1972. Summary in EDF 600 File.

Catherine Mickle, in discussion with the author, October 2, 2015. On file with author.

T. B. McPherson, interview by Joel Buchanan, March 7, 1984. http://ufdc.ufl.edu/UF00005407/00001/.

Wayne Mosley, in discussion with the author, September 11, 2014. On file with author.

John Neller, in discussion with the author, June 9, 2014. On file with author.

Dr. Cornelius Norton by Joel Buchanan, April 24, 1984. http://ufdc.ufl.edu/UF00005409/00001.

Isabelle Norton Whitfield, in discussion with the author, November 13, 2015. On file with author.

Nell Page, in discussion with the author, December 26, 2014. On file with author.

Ron Perry, in discussion with the author, June 9, 2014. On file with author.

Malcolm Privette, in discussion with the author, August 25, 2015. Audio on file with author.

Pat Powers, in discussion with the author, November 13, 2015. On file with author.

Russell Ramsey, PhD, in discussion with the author, June 6, 2014. On file with author.

Dr. John C. Rawls, interview by Mathletha Fuller, April 13, 2011. Samuel Proctor Oral History Project, AAHP 171, audio.

Florence Reaves, letter to author, January 30, 2016, and telephone interview, February 2016. Letter and notes on file with author.

Lawrence D. Reynolds, in discussion with the author, response by e-mail, April 13, 2017. On file with author.

Cora Roberson, interview by Joel Buchanan, February 19, 1986. http://ufdc.ufl.edu/UF00005433/00001.

Cora Roberson, in discussion with the author, November 3, 2014. On file with author.

Attorney William L. Robinson, in discussion with author, June 15, 2017. On file with author.

Mary Rockwood Lane, PhD, in discussion with the author, May 26, 2015. Audio on file with author.

Attorney John F. Roscow III, in discussion with the author, October 26, 2015. Notes on file with author.

Judy Segler Joiner, in discussion with the author, May 30, 2014. Audio on file with author.

Dan Self, in discussion with the author, March 1, 2016. Notes on file with author.

Dana Self Powers, in discussion with the author, March 1, 2016. Notes on file with author.

Donna Self Elliott, in discussion with the author, March 1, 2016. Notes on file with author.

Hazel Self, June 8, 2013. University of Florida Samuel Proctor Oral History Project, POF 045, audio.

Hazel Self, in discussion with the author, February 17 and March 1, 2016. Notes on file with author.

Sandra Sharron, in discussion with the author, October 30, 2014. On file with author.

Tim Strauser, in discussion with the author, May 27, 2015. Audio on file with author.

Sammie Talbot, in discussion with the author, January 13, 2012. Notes on file with author.

William S. Talbot Jr., DDS, in discussion with the author, November 3, 2011. Audio on file with author.

William S. Talbot IV, PhD, in discussion with the author, December 23, 2011. Notes on file with author.

Sam Taylor Jr., 1972. Interview report in EDF 600 File.

Thomas F. Tomlinson, EdD, in discussion with Helen Smith, April 16, 1982. University of Florida Oral History Project.

Tommy Tomlinson, EdD, in discussion with the author, August 27, 2014. Notes on file with author.

Tommy Tomlinson, EdD, in discussion with the author, September 10, 2014. On file with author.

Herbert Wagemaker, MD, in discussion with the author, March 5, 2016. Notes on file with author.

Jeanie Whitehead Shaw, in discussion with the author, July 11, 2014. On file with author.

Rosa B. Williams, interview by Joel Buchanan, February 27, 1996. University of Florida Samuel Proctor Oral History Project.

Rosa Williams, interview by Steve Davis, April 28, 2009. Audio record on file with University of Florida Samuel Proctor Oral History Project.

Brenda Wims, PhD, in discussion with the author, January 28, 2016. On file with author.

Philoron Wright, in discussion with the author, November 1, 2016. Audio on file with author.

Thomas A. Wright Sr., interview by Joel Buchanan, January 23, 1986. http://ufdc.ufl.edu/UF00005427/00001.

Thomas A. Wright Sr., in discussion with the author, March 30, 2012. On file with author.

Barry Wolfe, PhD, in discussion with the author, August 28, 2015. On file with author.

Cases

Adams v. Califano, 430 F. Supp. 118 (D.D.C. 1977).

Adams v. Matthews, 403 F.2d 181 (5th Cir. 1968).

Adams v. Richardson, 356 F. Supp. 92 (D.D.C.), *mod.*, 480 F.2d 1159 (D.C. Cir. 1973).

Alexander v. Holmes Cty. Bd. of Education, 396 U.S. 1218 (1969).

Alexander v. Holmes Cty. Bd. of Education, 396 U.S. 19 (1969).

Allen v. Bd. of Pub. Instruction, 312 F. Supp. 1127 (S.D. Fla.), *aff'd in part and rev'd in part*, 432 F.2d 362, 366 (5th Cir. 1970).

Avery v. Wichita Falls Ind. School Dist., 241 F.2d 230, 233 (5th Cir.), *cert. denied sub nom.* Wichita Falls Ind. School Dist. v. Avery, 353 U.S. 938 (1957).

Beckett v. School Bd. of the City of Norfolk, 308 F. Supp. 1274, 1292–93 (E.D. Va. 1969), *rev'd sub nom.* Brewer v. School Bd. of the City of Norfolk, 434 F.2d 408, *cert. denied sub nom.* School Bd. of the City of Norfolk v. Brewer, 399 U.S. 929 (1970).

Belton v. Gebhardt and Bulah v. Gebhardt, 87 A.2d 862 (Del. Ch. 1951); 91 A.2d 137 (1953).

Bolling v. Sharpe, 347 U.S. 497 (1954).

Bradley v. School Bd. of City of Richmond, Va., 345 F.2d 310 (4th Cir.), *vacated on other grounds per curiam*, 382 U.S. 103 (1965).

Brice v. Landis, 314 F. Supp. 974 (N.D. Cal. 1969).

Briggs v. Elliott, 98 F. Supp. 529 (D.S.C. 1951); 103 F. Supp. 920 (D.S.C. 1952); 132 F. Supp. 776 (D.S.C. 1955).

Broussard v. Houston Ind. School District, 395 F.2d 817, *dismissed for mootness and reh'g en banc denied*, 403 F.2d 34 (5th Cir. 1968).

Brown v. Bd. of Educ. of Topeka, 98 F. Supp. 797 (D. Kan. 1951).

Brown v. Bd. of Educ. of Topeka, 347 U.S. 483 (1954).

Brown v. Bd. of Educ. of Topeka, 349 U.S. 294, 301 (1955).

Carson v. Warlick, 238 F.2d 724 (4th Cir. 1956).

Carter v. West Feliciana Parish School Bd., see Singleton v. Jackson Mun. Separate School Dist., 419 F.2d 1211.

Davis v. Cty. School Bd. of Prince Edward Cty., 103 F. Supp. 337 (E.D. Va. 1952).

Dawkins v. Crevasse, 391 F.2d 921 (5th Cir. 1968).

Dawkins v. State, 205 So. 2d 691 (Fla. Dist. Ct. App. 1968).

Dawkins v. State, 208 So. 2d 119 (Fla. Dist. Ct. App.), *appeal dismissed*, 211 So. 2d 209 (Fla.), *cert. denied*, 211 So. 2d 211 (Fla.); *cert. denied*, 393 U.S. 854 (1968).

Estes v. Metropolitan Branches of Dallas NAACP, 444 U.S. 437 (1980).

Gibson v. Bd. of Pub. Instruction of Dade Cty., 272 F.2d 763 (5th Cir. 1959).

Gilbert v. Webster Parish Sch. Bd., 382 F. Supp. 8 (W.D. La. 1974).

Green v. Cty. School Board of New Kent Cty., 391 U.S. 430, 442 (1968).

Kelley v. Bd. of Educ. of the City of Nashville, Davidson County., Tenn., 270 F.2d 209 (6th Cir.), *cert. denied*, 361 U.S. 924 (1959).

Kelley v. Metro. Cty. Bd. of Educ., 492 F. Supp. 167 (M.D. Tenn. 1980).

Kelley v. Metro. Cty. Bd. of Educ., 511 F. Supp. 1363 (M.D. Tenn. 1981), *aff'd in part, rev'd in part*, 687 F.2d 814 (6th Cir. 1983), *cert. denied*, 459 U.S. 1183, *on remand*, 572 F. Supp. 312 (M.D. Tenn. 1983).

Johnson v. Bd. of Educ., 604 F.2d 504 (7th Cir. 1979).

Manning v. Sch. Bd., 244 F.3d 927 (11th Cir.), *cert. denied*, 524 U.S. 824 (2001).

Mannings v. Bd. of Pub. Instruction of Hillsborough Cty., 277 F.2d 370 (5th Cir. 1960).

McLaughlin v. Florida, 379 U.S. 184 (1964).

McLaurin v. Oklahoma State Regents for Higher Education, 339 U.S. 647 (1950).

Milliken v. Bradley, 433 U.S. 267 (1977).

Monroe v. Bd. of Comm'rs, 391 U.S. 450, 459 (1968).

Murray v. Maryland, 182 A. 590 (Md. 1936).

Parents Involved in Cmty. Schools. v. Seattle Sch. Dist. No. 1, 551 U.S. 701 (2007).

People v. Gallagher, 93 N.Y. 438 (1883).

Plessy v. Ferguson, 163 U.S. 537 (1896).

Quarles v. Oxford Municipal Separate School District, Civ. Action #WC6962-K (N.D. Miss., Jan. 7, 1970).

Roberts v. City of Boston, 59 Mass. (5 Cushing) See p. 246.

Shuttlesworth v. Birmingham Bd. of Educ., 162 F. Supp. 372 (N.D. Ala.), *aff'd*, 358 U.S. 101 (1958).

Singleton v. Jackson Mun. Separate Sch. Dist., 348 F.2d 729 (5th Cir. 1965).

Singleton v. Jackson Mun. Separate Sch. Dist., 355 F.2d 865 (5th Cir. 1966).

Singleton v. Jackson Mun. Separate School Dist., 419 F.2d 1211 (5th Cir. 1970) (en banc), *vacated in part sub nom.* Carter v. West Feliciana Parish School Bd., 396 U.S. 226 (1969); *reversed sub nom.* Carter v. West Feliciana Parish School Bd., 396 U.S. 290 (1970).

Singleton v. Jackson Separate Mun. School District, 396 U.S. 1048 (1970).

Singleton v. Jackson Separate Mun. School District, 396 U.S. 1053 (1970).

Stout v. Jefferson Cty. Bd. of Educ., 537 F.2d 800 (5th Cir. 1976).

Swann v. Charlotte-Mecklenburg Bd. of Educ., 369 F.2d 29 (4th Cir. 1966) (en banc).

Swann v. Charlotte-Mecklenburg Bd. of Educ., 402 U.S. 1 (1970).

Swann v. Charlotte-Mecklenburg Cty. Bd. of Educ., 328 F. Supp. 1346 (W.D.N.C 1971), *aff'd*, 433 F.2d 1377 (4th Cir. 1972).

Sweatt v. Painter, 339 U.S. 629 (1950).

Tasby v. Wright, 520 F. Supp. 683, 689–90, 711 (N.D. Tex. 1981), *aff'd in part, rev'd in part*, 713 F.2d 90 (5th Cir. 1983).

Tasby v. Wright, 585 F. Supp. 453 (N.D. Tex. 1984), *aff'd*, Tasby v. Black Coalition to Maximize Educ., 771 F.2d 849 (5th Cir. 1985).

Thomas v. Crevasse, 415 F.2d 550, 551 (5th Cir. 1969).

U.S. v. Hinds Cty. School Bd., 417 F.2d 852 (5th Cir. 1969), *cert. denied*, 396 U.S. 1032 (1970).

U.S. v. Hinds Cty. School Bd., 423 F.2d 1264 (5th Cir. 1969).

U.S. v. Jefferson Cty. Bd. of Educ., 372 F.2d 836 (5th Cir. 1966), *corrected*, 380 F.2d 385 (5th Cir. 1967) (en banc), *cert. denied*, 389 U.S. 840 (1967), *reh'g denied*, 389 U.S. 965 (1967).

U.S. v. Scotland Neck City Bd. of Educ., 407 U.S. 484 (1972).

Wanner v. Cty. Sch. Bd. of Arlington Cty., Va., 357 F.2d 452 (4th Cir. 1966).

Wright v. Bd. of Pub. Instruction of Alachua County, Civ. No. 367 (N.D. Fla. July 2, 1964) (record).

Wright v. Bd. of Pub. Instruction, 431 F.2d 1200 (5th Cir. 1970).

Yick Wo v. Hopkins, 118 U.S. 356 (1886).

Other

Advance-ED. Accessed March 29, 2014. http://www.advanc-ed.org/oasis2/u/par/search.

Alachua County Public Schools, Annual Report, Pilot Year, Mountain Top Class for Social Adjustment and Public Order Program, School Year 1970–71. August 15, 1971.

Awbrey, Alfred L., Jr. *100 Years & More of Gainesville High School Football, 1906–2010.* Gainesville: Stormii Publications, 2011.

Booker T. Washington High School. Accessed September 7, 2014. http://www.escambia.k12.fl.us/schscnts/wash/services.htm.

City-data.com. "Alachua County, Florida." Accessed February 23, 2015. http://www.city-data.com/county/Alachua_County-FL.html. http://schoolgrades.fldoe.org/reports/index.asp.

Dunbar High School. Accessed September 7, 2014. http://dhs.leeschools.net.

Florida Department of Education. "School Accountability Reports: schoolgrades16(3).xls." Accessed March 22, 2015. http://schoolgrades.fldoe.org/reports/index.asp.

Florida Department of Education. "Staff in Florida's Public Schools, Fall 2015: ARInstructionalStaff.xls." Accessed January 4, 2017. http://www.fldoe.org/accountability/data-sys/edu-info-accountability-services/pk-12-public-school-data-pubs-reports/staff.stml

Gainesville High School *Hurricane.* Yearbook. 1970, 1971, 1972 and 1973.

Gainesville High School. "Student Handbook, 1970–71."

Jones High School. Accessed September 7, 2014. http://www.ocps.net/lc/southwest/hjo/Pages/default.aspx.

King, Martin Luther, Jr. "I've Been to the Mountaintop." April 3, 1968. Transcript and embedded audio, American Rhetoric. http://www.americanrhetoric.com/speeches/mlkivebeentothemountaintop.htm.

Lincoln High School. Accessed February 1, 2017. http://www.leonschools.net/lincoln.

Middleton High School. Accessed March 11, 2015. http://middleton.mysdhc.org/Home%20Page.

Miracle, Andy. "Social Analysis of a High School Football Program" Unpublished manuscript, 1974. On file with author.

Mountain Top School, Alachua County Schools, University of Florida Practicum 670. Fall Quarter, 1971.

National Center for Education Statistics. "The Nation's Report Card." Accessed December 26, 2016. https://nces.ed.gov/nationsreportcard/.

National Center for Education Statistics. "The Traditionally Black Institutions of Higher Education 1860 to 1982." 1985. https://nces.ed.gov/pubs84/84308.pdf.

Page, Earle C. "The Field We Toil." Sermon. May 19, 1963.

Pepper, W. M. (Bill), III. "The History of the Gainesville Sun." A talk presented to the Matheson Historical Society, Gainesville, FL, February 12, 1996. http://ufdc.ufl.edu/MH00002567/00001.

Ramsey, Russell W. *The Lincoln Center for the Human and Mechanical Arts of the Alachua County Public Schools, Pilot Study, School Year 1972-1973*. 1974.

Ramsey, Russell W. "Principles of Social Adjustment, Alachua County Public Schools." Unpublished manuscript, undated.

Ramsey, Russell W., ed. *School Board of Alachua County and Florida State Department of Education, Office of Federal—State Relations, Report, Southeastern States Conference on Community Involvement in the Problems of Neglected and Delinquent Children, Daytona Beach, Florida*. March 15–17, 1971.

Ramsey, Russell W. "Social Adjustment Education in the Alachua County, Florida, Public Schools." Unpublished manuscript, revised February 1972.

University of Florida Smathers Library Special and Area Studies Collections, Box 13, MS Group 149, File 38/I/7 [referred to as EDF 600 File].

University of the District of Columbia, David A. Clarke School of Law. "Biography of William L. Robinson, Olie W. Rauh Prof. of Law." Accessed September 25, 2016. http://www.law.udc.edu/?page=WRobinson.

US Census Bureau. "A Half-Century of Learning: Historical Census Statistics on Educational Attainment in the United States, 1940 to 2000: Detailed Tables." Accessed December 8, 2016. http://www.census.gov/hhes/socdemo/education/data/census/half-century/tables.html.

White, Arthur O. "The History of Lincoln High: 'The Big Red.'" Accessed January 28, 2017. http://ufdc.ufl.edu/AA00008787/00001.

Yale Law School. "Drew S. Days III biography." Accessed January 30, 2017. https://www.law.yale.edu/drew-s-days-iii.

INDEX

C

D

E

F

G

N

S

T

U

V

W

Y

Z

ABOUT THE AUTHOR

Michael T. Gengler graduated from Gainesville High School in Florida in 1962. He received his AB degree from Columbia College (New York) in 1966, magna cum laude, and was elected to Phi Beta Kappa. He was a member of the managing board of the *Columbia Daily Spectator*. In 1969, he received his JD degree from Harvard Law School. Until 1974, he served as an assistant staff judge advocate in the USAF. For most of his career, he was a corporate lawyer in Boston and Chicago. He also worked for a few years as a full-time volunteer lawyer for Legal Action of Wisconsin, Madison, representing clients who could not afford counsel. He lives in Gainesville and is a vocal advocate for public school education.